FUTURE
English for Results

5

TEACHER'S EDITION
AND LESSON PLANNER

Lynda Terrill

Betsy Lindeman Wong

Series Consultants

Beatriz B. Díaz

Ronna Magy

Federico Salas-Isnardi

PEARSON
Longman

Future 5
English for Results
Teacher's Edition and Lesson Planner

Pearson Education, 10 Bank Street, White Plains, NY 10606

Staff credits: The people who made up the **Future 5** team, representing editorial, production, design, and manufacturing, are Rhea Banker, John Barnes, Maretta Callahan, Elizabeth Carlson, Aerin Csigay, Dave Dickey, Nancy Flaggman, Irene Frankel, Mike Kemper, Katie Keyes, Martha McGaughey, José Antonio Mendez, Linda Moser, Liza Pleva, Joan Poole, and Stella Reilly.

Cover design: Rhea Banker
Cover photo: Kathy Lamm/Getty Images
Text design: Lisa Delgado
Text composition: ElectraGraphics, Inc.
Text font: Minion Pro

ISBN-13: 978-0-13240924-7
ISBN-10: 0-13-240924-0

Printed in the United States of America

3 4 5 6 7 8 9 10—V011—14 13 12

Contents

The instructional design of *Future* has been carefully crafted and draws on tried-and-true methods. In *Future*, current research findings are put into practice. Each of the skill sections reflects sound pedagogy and offers a logical progression from unit to unit within a level as well as from one level to the next throughout the series. The instructional design is tailored to meet the interests and needs of students at their language level and at the same time to fulfill curriculum mandates.

Future has been designed to help students persist in their English studies. The program motivates students to keep coming to class through its situational contexts that reflect students' real lives, its touches of humor, and its community–building group work. If outside factors cause students to miss classes, the strategies and study skills presented in the Student Book, along with the Practice Plus CD-ROM, help students continue their studies until they are able to return to class.

Future also helps students make a successful transition into academic programs. The levels of *Future* progressively introduce academic skills so that students feel empowered to continue their education. By continuing on into academic programs, students improve their chances of entering the job market with all the skills and tools they need to be successful.

Future is truly an integrated-skills course: listening, speaking, reading, and writing are woven together throughout the lessons, just as they are naturally woven together outside the classroom. For example, students practice their listening and speaking skills not just on the Listening and Speaking page, but also in other lessons throughout the unit.

Following are some of the key pedagogical features of the skill sections of *Future 5*.

Vocabulary

- **Multiple encounters with target vocabulary.** Vocabulary related to the unit theme is recycled so that students have numerous exposures to key terms. Current research shows that the more encounters learners have with a target word, the more likely they are to retain that word.[1]
- **Vocabulary in context exercises.** To understand the readings and complete the exercises that follow them, students must use context clues to get the meanings of boldfaced words.
- **Self-directed learning tasks.** Throughout the book, in a section called "Word Work," students are directed to keep a log of words they want to remember from the readings. The Pre-Unit provides specific tips on how to keep these logs and what to do to help learn these new words.
- **Learning strategies and supplemental vocabulary practice in the Workbook.** Each unit of the Workbook includes a vocabulary learning strategy, such as categorizing words and using the key word method.[2] Additional practice exercises focus on developing dictionary skills and building word knowledge, including word families, roots, and idioms.

Listening

- **Multiple genres.** Throughout *Future*, students are exposed to a variety of listening types such as conversations, interviews, radio talk shows, and lectures.
- **Natural language.** Natural discourse is presented in the listening selections throughout *Future* so that students hear authentic language models. The listening selections are recorded at natural speed, reflecting what students will hear outside of class.
- **Multiple exposures to the same listening selection.** Students listen to the same listening material more than once—but for different reasons: for example, first, to take notes and then to get specific information. By hearing the same text many times, students become more comfortable with the content and vocabulary and increase their comprehension.

Speaking

- **Numerous speaking opportunities.** Throughout the book, students have multiple opportunities for discussion. The speaking tasks vary; for example, students may be asked to give their opinion, make comparisons, or explain something. Because they are provided with specific speaking tasks, students will gain confidence and feel more comfortable engaging in different kinds of discourse on a wide range of topics.[3]
- **Communications skills in every unit.** Every unit includes one Communication Skill, such as expressing agreement and disagreement. Students are taught alternate ways of expressing themselves, with particular attention to appropriateness and politeness.[4]
- **Negotiation of meaning.** Many of the exercises in each unit require students to work together to negotiate meaning. Giving students the opportunity to interact and negotiate meaning supports development of their language skills.[5]
- **Problem-solving tasks.** In each unit, students have the opportunity to discuss solutions to a particular problem related to the unit theme. These tasks engage students' critical thinking skills and allow them to focus on fluency.

Pronunciation

- **Systematic pronunciation syllabus.** The Practice Plus CD-ROM includes pronunciation practice based on the texts in the Listening and Speaking lessons in the book. Students are given an opportunity to compare their pronunciation to the pronunciation of a native speaker of English.

[1] Folse, K. (2006). The Effect of Type of Written Exercise on L2 Vocabulary Retention. *TESOL Quarterly,* Vol. 40, No. 2, 273–93.

[2] Teaching Reading to Adult English Language Learners: A Reading Instruction Staff Development Program.

[3] *Practitioner Toolkit: Working with Adult English Language Learners*—Activities to Promote Interaction and Communication (at http://www.cal.org/caela/tools/program_development/elltoolkit/Part2-41Interaction&Communication.pdf

[4] *Second Language Acquisition in Adults: From Research to Practice* at http://www.cal.org/caela/esl_resources/digests/SLA.html

[5] Mackey, A. (1999). Input, interaction, and second language development: An empirical study of question formation in ESL. *Studies in Second Language Acquisition, 21,* 557–587.

- **Focus on stress and intonation.** The pronunciation syllabus focuses on the natural stress, intonation, and rhythm of English. Information about the pronunciation point is provided in a Pronunciation Watch note.

Grammar

- **Grammar input in the listening and reading texts.** Grammar in *Future* is first presented receptively through the text in the Listening and Speaking or Reading lesson so that students first encounter the target language in a meaningful way, in context.
- **Grammar charts display the target.** Grammar charts at the beginning of the grammar lesson explicitly show the target structures. Grammar Watch notes provide explanations, as needed, and the Grammar Reference in the back of the book expands on the grammar when appropriate.
- **Practice with both meaning and form.** Presentations focus on meaning as well as form, enabling learners to incorporate more new structures into their language use.[6]
- **Discovery, then controlled, then productive practice.** Exercises progress from receptive to productive and from controlled to communicative, providing students with ample written and spoken practice in the target structure.
- **Contextualized, content-based activities.** Exercises are contextualized, recycling themes and vocabulary from the unit. In many cases, the grammar exercise also presents new, related content so that students are gaining additional information as well as grammar practice.

Reading

- **High-interest, informative articles.** The reading articles in *Future* present interesting, useful information related to the unit theme. The structures and vocabulary in the texts are often controlled so that students can be successful readers.
- **Pre-reading activities.** As in the Listening and Speaking lessons, the Reading lessons have pre-reading activities to help build students' cultural schema, an important factor in successfully completing a reading task.[7]
- **Recorded reading selections.** The readings in *Future* are recorded so that students can listen as they read along. Research has shown that listening while reading can have a positive effect on reading fluency.[8]
- **Opportunity to apply the information.** A *Show What You Know* activity at the end of many reading lessons allows students to synthesize and apply the information they have just learned through a writing task, a role play, or a speaking activity.

- **Building of reading skills.** Skills such as finding the main idea, comparing and constrasting, and scanning for information are explicitly presented and then practiced.
- **Inclusion of document literacy.** In addition to high-interest articles, *Future* gives students practice reading documents that they are likely to encounter in their everyday lives, such as an OSHA poster or performance review.

Writing

- **Balanced writing syllabus.** The writing curriculum includes both academic writing, such as a descriptive essay, and practical writing, such as a formal e-mail.
- **FYI Boxes and Writing Tips.** FYI sections and Writing Tips provide helpful information about the structure and format of the writing students are about to do.
- **Exercises guide students through the writing process.** Extenseive pre-writing activities activate students' background knowledge and build schema. A model of the writing genre is presented before students do their own writing assignment. Students plan and organize their writing through graphic organizers. After writing, students are given a checklist of questions to help them edit and proofread their work. Students use it to make sure that they have successfully completed the assignment and incorporated the writing skill. Teachers can then ask students to write additional drafts, as well as do peer editing.[9]

Review and Assessment

- **Checkpoints to track progress.** Every unit begins with a list of competencies to be covered. As students complete each lesson, they check off the goal they have completed. At the end of the unit, students are directed to review the goals list to see their progress. Keeping track of goals completed motivates students and reinforces their sense of success and accomplishment.
- **Opportunities for ongoing assessment.** Teachers can use the *Show what you know* activities at the end of most lessons and at the end of every unit to assess their students' progress in particular language skills and competencies. For teachers who want to do a more formal assessment of what their students have learned, the *Tests and Test Prep* book with **Exam**View® *Assessment Suite* provides reproducible unit tests as well as a midterm and final test. Additionally, the **Exam**View® *Assessment Suite* gives teachers the option to create their own customized tests.

---

[6] Ellis, R., Basturkmen, H., & Loewen, S. (2001). Learner uptake in communicative ESL lessons. *Language Learning, 51,* 281–318.

[7] Burt, M., Peyton, J. K., & Adams, R. (2003). *Reading and adult English language learners: A review of the research.* Washington, DC: Center for Applied Linguistics.

[8] Kruidenier, J. (2002). *Research-based principles for adult basic education reading instruction.* Washington, D.C.: National Institute for Literacy, Partnership for Reading.

[9] *CAELA Guide for Adult ESL Trainers*—Teaching Writing to Adult English Language Learners at http://www.cal.org/caela/scb/III_E_TeachingWriting.pdf

Each unit begins with **a list of course components** that can be used in class or assigned for homework.

Teaching ideas for the unit **opener picture** help teachers establish the context of the unit and get students ready for the unit theme.

4

Are You Safe?

Classroom Materials/Extra Practice

CD 1
Tracks 22–29

Workbook
Unit 4

Interactive Practice
Unit 4

Unit Overview

Goals
- See the list of goals on the facing page.

Grammar
- Past modals

Listening and Speaking
- Talk about natural disasters and their survivors
- Talk about how to be safe during a flood
- Talk about keeping latchkey kids safe
- *Communication Skill:* Making Suggestions

Reading
- Learn about tornadoes
- *Reading Skill:* Summarizing
- Learn about workers' rights to a safe workplace
- *Reading Skill:* Monitoring comprehension

Writing
- Write safety instructions
- *Writing Tip:* Imperatives

Life Skills
- Identify home safety measures
- Identify workplace safety measures

Preview
- Welcome students and have them look at page 65.
- Say: *Look at the picture. What's happening? Where is everyone? Have you ever seen anything like this?* (Possible answers: It's a tornado. There's a rainbow. It's the Midwest. The people are hiding because they're afraid.)
- Ask: *What is about to happen?* Elicit guesses from students, offering prompts as needed. (*Where is this? Can you guess? Would you be scared?*)
- Say: *In this unit, we'll talk about natural disasters.* Explain as needed that a natural disaster is an extreme weather condition that destroys property and often kills people.
- Ask: *What would you do to stay safe?* Offer prompts as needed to elicit discussion.
- Say: *In this unit, you'll learn about natural disasters, how to prepare for them, and how to stay safe. You'll explore home and workplace safety. You'll also read about your responsibility to keep children safe at home and your right to safety at work.*

Unit Goals
- Ask students to read the Unit Goals.
- Explain unfamiliar vocabulary as needed. (Examples: *latchkey kids*—children who come home from school and stay by themselves at home; *measures*—actions or steps to take to prevent or fix a situation)
- Tell students to circle the goal that is the most important to them.
- Say: *As we complete this unit, we will look back at this page and reread the goals. We will check each goal as we complete it.*

T-65   UNIT 4

A comprehensive **list of competencies and skills** provides an overview of the unit.

Teaching notes are organized in **a lesson plan**: Getting Started, Presentation, Controlled Practice, Communicative Practice. **Suggested times** for each part of the lesson plan are based on a 60-minute class. This time may vary depending on class size.

Lesson 1 Talk about natural disasters and their survivors

Presentation   10 minutes

- Direct students to the note on sequence.
- Ask a student to read the text aloud.
- Say: *Dates and other time words help you find your way logically through a conversation or written text. Time order words such as these—first, after, and later—not only help you understand what you are listening to or reading, they can also help you organize your own writing.*
- Brainstorm a list of other time order words, for example, *second, third, next, after that, finally.*
- Write the list on the board and give students time to add any new or unfamiliar words to their vocabulary logs.

Teaching Tip

Whenever time permits, write or have students write answers or brainstorm lists on the board, a transparency, or a flipchart. This gives students who may not have gotten the answer correct a chance to fix their own work. Also, write answers or new information on the board. This helps less proficient students to keep up.

Controlled Practice   10 minutes

3 PRACTICE

 The story of the earthquake...

- Ask students to read the directions.
- Say: *Listen again and answer the questions. Listen for clue words that reveal the sequence of events to help you answer.*
- Play Track 22 again.
- Walk around while students are listening and answering to see whether this exercise seems easy or challenging for most students.

Answers: 1. The earthquake struck after people had gone to work or school. 2. Mr. Liu was trapped under the rubble. 3. Mr. Liu was found on Thursday—the third day after the earthquake. 4. She had to go for help. 5. Mr. Liu was rescued by the soldiers.

4 RETELLING A NEWS STORY

STEP 1. Read the news story...

- Ask students to read the directions.
- Say: *Read the news story.*
- Ask: *What's the first important detail in the story?* (the date of the earthquake in China, May 12, 2008)
- Brainstorm the types of key details, such as dates, people's names, or an event students should include. Make sure they understand that they should not write complete sentences.

STEP 2. PAIRS. Close your books...

- Ask students to read the directions.
- Say: *Now use your notes to retell the story. Take turns retelling the events, in order.*
- Students may use their notes if they need to but should try to retell the story without their notes.
- To follow-up, ask: *What did you notice about how you retold the story and how your partner did?* Ask students to give details and examples.

Communicative Practice   15 minutes

5 MAKE IT PERSONAL

GROUPS. Discuss. What personality traits...

- Ask students to read the directions.
- Review examples of *personality traits* (see Unit 1). Explain as needed.
- Ask groups to consider the two questions. Say: *There are no right or wrong answers, but please give reasons for your ideas. We don't know how we would act in a natural disaster, but it's useful to think and talk about these issues in case we are caught in such a situation.*

Teaching Tips give helpful teaching techniques and strategies.

Step-by-step teaching notes help teachers give **clear grammar presentations**. Teachers can also refer students to the **Grammar Reference section** starting on page 223 in the back of the student book.

Language Notes offer insightful and helpful information about English. The notes also offer ideas for **Community Building and Networking** activities in the classroom to help students get to know their classmates.

Lesson 4   Talk about mistakes made during emergencies

Getting Started   5 minutes

- Write on the board: *The U.S. government should have _____. The mayor of New Orleans should have _____.*
- Say: *When we talked about Hurricane Katrina, we talked about mistakes. Today we're going to use the grammatical structure of past modals to talk more about what should have been done in such an emergency.* Point to the examples on the board.

Presentation   15 minutes

Past Modals

- Copy the grammar chart onto the board.
- Point to the modals in the example. Explain that a modal is a helping verb that talks about what is possible, advisable, mandatory, optimal, or regrettable.
- Read each sentence and have the class repeat.
- Ask students to read the Grammar Watch.
- Say: *We use modals in the present or past tense. How is the past modal formed?* (The modal—*should, could, may, might*—+ *have* + the past participle of the verb) Write this on the board.

Active voice

- Review active and passive. See the Language Note.
- Point to the upper part of the grammar chart and read the first example.
- Say: *Use* should have *plus the past participle to express regret about something that happened or didn't happen in the past—that is, feeling sorry that a different decision wasn't made.* Ask: *What was the decision in this example that wasn't made?* (The government did not evacuate people earlier.)
- Read the second and third examples. Say: *Use* could have, might have, *or* may have *plus the past participle to express something that was possible in the past but didn't happen.* Ask: *In these examples, what was possible in the past but didn't happen?* (Pets could have been killed by the flood. People could have used a safe to protect their financial records.)

Language Note

- Help students understand the concept of active and passive voice.
- Write on the board: *1. John is washing the car. 2. The car is being washed right now.*
- Say: *Sentence one is active. The subject is doing the action. Sentence two is passive. The subject is receiving the action.*
- Write more examples on the board, and have students identify active or passive. For example, *Tornadoes cause a lot of damage.* (active) *A lot of damage is caused by tornadoes.* (passive)

Passive voice

- Point to the lower part of the grammar chart and read the examples.
- Ask: *In the first sentence, who is receiving the action?* (we) *Do we know who should have performed the action of evacuating people earlier?* (No—the sentence doesn't say.)

Controlled Practice   15 minutes

1   PRACTICE

Read about the experiences...

- Say: *Choose the sentence that best states what the flood survivors should or might have done differently.*
- Walk around and check students' work, clarifying vocabulary and offering help as needed.
- Call on students to say the answers. After each answer, ask students if the past modal was used to express regret about something that happened or didn't happen in the past or something that was possible in the past but didn't happen. (The modal *should have* was used in all answers to express regret.)

UNIT 4   **T-72**

Lesson 6 Identify home safety measures

Getting Started   5 minutes

1 DISCUSS CHILD SAFETY PRODUCTS

A CLASS. Everyone wants children...

- Say: *In the last lesson, we talked about safety of latchkey kids, children who are home alone after school. What are some ways to help these children be safe at home?* Elicit ideas from students, offering prompts as needed. (For example: *What should children do if a stranger calls? Or if their friends want them to do something that's not allowed?*)
- Say: *Now let's talk about another safety issue with much younger children.*
- Read and discuss the question, offering prompts as needed to elicit answers. (For example: *What about the stairs? Can children have an accident there?*)
- Say: *Today we're going to look at some home safety products designed to prevent small children from having accidents at home. Do you have anything in your home to prevent children from getting hurt accidentally?*

Presentation   15 minutes

B Read the online catalog page...

- Clarify unfamiliar terms as needed. Examples: *doorstop*: something to hold a door open—refer students to the picture; *slammed*: to have something close on you—demonstrate with fingers in the doorway; *pinched*: to have a body part caught in something—demonstrate with fingers next to the hinge of a door; *electric shock*: a shock—and physical pain—you receive if you touch an unprotected wire, for example, or stick your finger in an electrical outlet; *choking*: when you swallow something that is too big to go down your throat; *screws*: as a verb, to fasten a part to something—pantomime screwing a hinge into the wall; *latch*: an extra piece that keeps a door closed. Refer students to the picture and remind them of what they learned in the previous lesson.
- Ask: *Have you seen or purchased any of these items?* Elicit answers from students, encouraging them to say why, if they feel it has been effective.

Culture Connection

In the U.S., the government is responsible for regulating the safety of all consumer products, including children's toys and safety equipment. The agency in charge of this is the U.S. Consumer Product Safety Commission (http://www.cpsc.gov).

Expansion: Speaking Practice for 1B

- Tell students that they will act out possible accidents and say what could have been used to prevent them.
- Write on the board: *What could have been used to prevent accidents?* Ask: *What kind of verb structure is* could have been used? (past modal)
- Review the past modal. Write on the board: *You could have . . .*
- Ask for a volunteer to come to the front of the room and pantomime an accident, such as falling down the stairs.
- Other students guess what the accident is and say, *You could have installed . . .*
- Repeat the exercise with another student.

C PAIRS. Answer the questions...

- Ask students to read the directions.
- Call on a student to read each question aloud.
- Have students form pairs to answer the questions.
- Monitor students as they discuss the questions, offering help when needed.
- Go over the answers as a class.

Answers: 1. cabinet latches; 2. safety gates; 3. window guards—(possible answer) They should buy the window guards first because the most serious danger is a fall from the window.

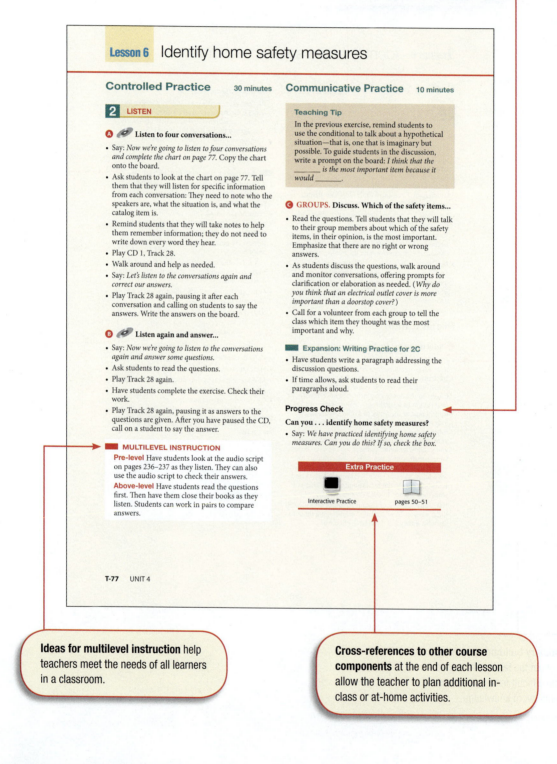

Progress Checks allow students to reflect on their ability to use the competencies presented in the lesson.

Lesson 6 Identify home safety measures

Controlled Practice   30 minutes

2 LISTEN

A Listen to four conversations...

- Say: *Now we're going to listen to four conversations and complete the chart on page 77.* Copy the chart onto the board.
- Ask students to look at the chart on page 77. Tell them that they will listen for specific information from each conversation: They need to note who the speakers are, what the situation is, and what the catalog item is.
- Remind students that they will take notes to help them remember information; they do not need to write down every word they hear.
- Play CD 1, Track 28.
- Walk around and help as needed.
- Say: *Let's listen to the conversations again and correct our answers.*
- Play Track 28 again, pausing it after each conversation and calling on students to say the answers. Write the answers on the board.

B Listen again and answer...

- Say: *Now we're going to listen to the conversations again and answer some questions.*
- Ask students to read the questions.
- Play Track 28 again.
- Have students complete the exercise. Check their work.
- Play Track 28 again, pausing it as answers to the questions are given. After you have paused the CD, call on a student to say the answer.

MULTILEVEL INSTRUCTION

Pre-level Have students look at the audio script on pages 236–237 as they listen. They can also use the audio script to check their answers.
Above-level Have students read the questions first. Then have them close their books as they listen. Students can work in pairs to compare answers.

Communicative Practice   10 minutes

Teaching Tip

In the previous exercise, remind students to use the conditional to talk about a hypothetical situation—that is, one that is imaginary but possible. To guide students in the discussion, write a prompt on the board: *I think that the _____ is the most important item because it would _____.*

C GROUPS. Discuss. Which of the safety items...

- Read the questions. Tell students that they will talk to their group members about which of the safety items, in their opinion, is the most important. Emphasize that there are no right or wrong answers.
- As students discuss the questions, walk around and monitor conversations, offering prompts for clarification or elaboration as needed. (*Why do you think that an electrical outlet cover is more important than a doorstop cover?*)
- Call for a volunteer from each group to tell the class which item they thought was the most important and why.

Expansion: Writing Practice for 2C

- Have students write a paragraph addressing the discussion questions.
- If time allows, ask students to read their paragraphs aloud.

Progress Check

Can you . . . identify home safety measures?

- Say: *We have practiced identifying home safety measures. Can you do this? If so, check the box.*

Extra Practice

Interactive Practice   pages 50–51

Ideas for multilevel instruction help teachers meet the needs of all learners in a classroom.

Cross-references to other course components at the end of each lesson allow the teacher to plan additional in-class or at-home activities.

Review & Expand

Show what you know!

1 REVIEW

For your grammar review, go to page 228.

- Say: *Today we're going to review the skills we have practiced in this unit and apply them to a problem. What are some of the skills we have practiced?* Elicit answers, noting them on the board as students say them. (Possible answers: reading and talking about natural disasters and ways to stay safe during disasters; identifying home and workplace safety measures; discussing workers' rights; writing safety instructions)
- Ask students to complete the grammar review exercise at the bottom of page 228.

2 ACT IT OUT

Teaching Tip

While pairs are performing role plays, use the scoring rubric for speaking on page Txiv to evaluate each student's vocabulary, grammar, fluency, and how well he or she completes the task. You may want to review the completed rubric with the student.

PAIRS. You are discussing...

- Say: *You're going to form groups of three. Student A will look back at Lesson 2 and explain how to stay safe during a tornado. Student B will review Lessons 3 and 4 and describe how to stay safe during a flood. Student C will reread Lessons 7 and 8 and explain some safety measures you can take at work.*
- Remind students to use the imperative to give safety instructions. Elicit an example: *Close the windows and go to the basement.*
- Say: *When you wrote your safety instructions, you used signal words to help readers follow a sequence of directions. What are some signal words that you used?* Elicit words from students and write them on the board. (Examples: *first, next, then, afterwards, finally, last*)
- Tell students to review the lessons before they begin working groups.

3 READ AND REACT

STEP 1. Read about Jean-Pierre.

- Say: *Now we're going to apply our knowledge from this unit to a problem involving a character, Jean-Pierre. Let's read about Jean-Pierre.*
- Have students read the story.
Possible answers: *Problem:* Jean-Pierre has discovered a serious health hazard at work but doesn't want to lose his new job if he reports it. *Solution:* He could speak to OSHA about the problem or try to convince a group of employees to meet with a manager to discuss it.

STEP 2. GROUPS. What is Jean-Pierre's...

- Tell students that they may want to refer to Lesson 7 as they discuss possible solutions.
- Ask volunteers to present the group's ideas to the class.
- After each presentation, encourage feedback. Ask: *What do you think about Group 1's suggestions for Jean-Pierre? Which idea do you like best?*

Teaching Tip

Write sample feedback prompts on the board: *I really like the idea of . . . I disagree with that idea about what Jean-Pierre should do . . . Instead, I think Jean-Pierre should . . . If it doesn't work, what about trying . . . ?*

4 CONNECT

Turn to page 215 for your Community-building Activity. See page Txii for general teaching notes for Community-building activities.

Progress Check

Which goals can you check off? Go back to page 65.
Ask students to turn to page 65 and check off any remaining goals they have reached. Call on them to say which goals they will practice outside of class.

CD-ROM Practice

 Go to the CD-ROM for more practice.

If your students need more practice with the vocabulary, grammar, and competencies in Unit 4, encourage them to review the activities on the CD-ROM.

UNIT 4   **T-84**

Persistence Activities

A **Persistence Activity** for each unit of *Future 5* is in the back of the book. Cross-references at the end of each unit indicate at what point each activity should be completed. Following are some general notes that apply to all of the activities.

Persistence Activities: Community Building, Goal Setting, Developing Study Skills

The Persistence activities are classroom-tested activities that support students in continuing their studies. Recent research has shown that students are more likely to persist when they feel they are part of a learning community and when they are able to set educational goals they believe they can achieve. Programs can also support student persistence by showing students how to study efficiently and how to monitor their learning.

Each Persistence activity in *Future* fits one of these categories: community building, goal setting, or developing study skills. Students fill out a graphic organizer in each activity, as they explore specific topics, such as their expectations for the class, the importance of reading and good reading habits, ways of building vocabulary, using writing strategies and a writing toolbox, becoming a lifelong learner, and moving forward with your goals and dreams.

Step 1: Introduce the activity
- Say the name of the activity. Then explain the objective of the activity. For example, for Unit 1, say: *We're going to explore your expectations about this English class, including your expectations about how the teacher will behave, the kind of work you will do, or what you will learn.*
- Put students in pairs or groups, if necessary, depending on the activity.

Step 2: Get ready
- Read the directions for the first part of the activity and make sure students understand what they need to do.
- Review any language students need for the activity. If students will need to write sentences, write an example sentence on the board.
- Model the activity. If the activity has students working in groups of three, call two on- or above-level students to the front of the room. Model the activity with them, taking one part yourself. If the activity requires students to work independently, write the exercise on the board and call on a few students to give sample responses. Write their responses on the board.

Step 3: Start the activity
- Have students start working in groups or independently, as necessary for the activity. Walk around the room while students are working. Check to make sure they are on task and provide help as needed.
- If the activity has a second part, check to make sure all students have had sufficient time to complete the first part before moving on. When students are ready, repeat Steps 2 and 3 for the second part of the activity.

Step 4: Wrap up
- After students have completed all parts of the activity, call on a few students to share their work with the class.

Speaking and Writing Activities

Future provides students with multiple opportunities to build their speaking and writing skills. Speaking tasks are integrated throughout the course, and each unit culminates with pairs or groups summarizing key points of the unit content. Each unit also contains a writing lesson that teaches students a practical, step-by-step approach to the writing process and culminates in an essay-length writing assignment. Cross-references within the unit indicate at what point each activity should be completed. If you wish to formally assess students' speaking or writing, you may use the rubrics provided on pages Txiv–Txv.

Speaking Activities

The final page of every unit of *Future* contains an Act It Out activity and a problem-solving activity. These activities offer students an opportunity to demonstrate their ability to use the vocabulary, grammar, and competencies from the unit and the course.

If you wish to use this activity for evaluation purposes, use the Speaking Rubric on page Txiv to make notes about each student's performance. For each category listed in the rubric (Vocabulary, Grammar, Fluency, and Task completion), include comments about both *strong points* and *weak points*. You can then use those comments to give each student a rating of 1, 2, or 3 for each category.

The purpose of this kind of evaluation is to give fair and clear feedback to students and to give them specific points to work on so that they can improve their fluency. It is important to use language that a student can understand and to give examples of what the student did or didn't say when possible. For example, you might say, *You used a lot of vocabulary related to the unit theme* or *You need to work on the past perfect. Review the grammar charts in the unit.* Feedback should be given to students in a timely manner in order to be most effective and helpful.

Writing Activities

Each unit of *Future* includes a two-page writing lesson that takes students step by step through the process of writing an essay, letter, or e-mail. First, students are given information about the writing genre and a writing tip about how to organize such writing. Then they brainstorm about the writing topic and read and discuss a model composition that illustrates the genre and writing tip. Before they begin writing, students use a graphic organizer or an outline to organize their ideas in a logical way. After they complete a first draft, they receive guidance on revision, editing, and proofreading. The writing task gives students an opportunity to implement what they have learned about the writing genre and use the writing tip to structure or format their writing. The task also gives them a chance to apply their knowledge of the grammar and vocabulary they have learned in the unit and throughout the course while also allowing them to build their writing skills and develop their writing fluency.

If you wish to evaluate the students' writing formally, use the Writing Rubric on page Txv to make notes. For each category listed in the rubric (Vocabulary, Grammar, Mechanics and Format, and Task completion), include comments about both *strong points* and *weak points*. You can then use those comments to give each student a rating of 1, 2, or 3 for each category.

The purpose of this kind of evaluation is to give fair and clear feedback to students and to give them specific points to work on so that they can improve their writing skills. It is important to use language that a student can understand and to give examples of what the student did or did not do when possible. For example, you might say: *You organized your essay logically but need to edit for repetitions* or *You need to work on punctuation. Remember to capitalize names.* Feedback should be given to students in a timely manner in order to be most effective and helpful.

Speaking Rubric

Name: _____

Class: _____ Date: _____

Activity: _____ Unit: _____ Page: _____

Vocabulary	Score	Comments
Uses a variety of vocabulary words and expressions related to the unit theme	3	
Uses some vocabulary words and expressions related to the unit theme	2	
Uses few vocabulary words or expressions related to the unit theme	1	
Grammar	**Score**	**Comments**
Uses grammar with control and accuracy	3	
Uses grammar with less control and accuracy	2	
Uses grammar with little control or accuracy	1	
Fluency	**Score**	**Comments**
Speech is authentic and fluent; there is authentic communication with partner	3	
Speech is overly rehearsed at points; is not true communication	2	
Speech is not authentic; is not really listening to and communicating with partner	1	
Task completion	**Score**	**Comments**
Student completed the task successfully	3	
Student mostly completed the task; student went off topic at various points	2	
Student was not able to successfully complete the task: see comments	1	

Writing Rubric

Name: _____

Class: _____ Date: _____

Activity: _____ Unit: _____ Page: _____

Vocabulary	Score	Comments
Uses a variety of vocabulary words and expressions appropriate for the task and/or related to the unit theme	3	
Uses some vocabulary words and expressions appropriately but sometimes misuses a word or fails to vary wording	2	
Uses many vocabulary words or expressions inappropriately	1	
Grammar	**Score**	**Comments**
Uses grammar with control and accuracy	3	
Makes some grammatical errors; uses grammar with less control and accuracy	2	
Uses grammar with little or no control or accuracy	1	
Mechanics (Spelling, Punctuation, Capitalization) and Format	**Score**	**Comments**
Makes very few or no mechanical errors; follows format and structure of model	3	
Makes some mechanical errors that do not affect comprehensibility; follows format of model with some errors	2	
Makes many mechanical errors that reduce comprehensibility; does not follow format of model	1	
Task completion	**Score**	**Comments**
Student completed the task successfully; the writing assignment is focused, well-organized, and complete	3	
Student mostly completed the task; the writing assignment is complete, but is sometimes off topic and disorganized	2	
Student was not able to successfully complete the task; the writing assignment is incomplete and lacks focus and organization	1	

Acknowledgments

The author and publisher would like to extend special thanks to our Series Consultants whose insights, experience, and expertise shaped the course and guided us throughout its development.

Beatriz B. Díaz Miami-Dade County Public Schools, Miami, FL
Ronna Magy Los Angeles Unified School District, Los Angeles, CA
Federico Salas-Isnardi Texas LEARNS, Houston, TX

We would also like to express our gratitude to the following individuals. Their kind assistance was indispensable to the creation of this program.

Consultants

Wendy J. Allison Seminole Community College, Sanford, FL
Claudia Carco Westchester Community College, Valhalla, NY
Maria J. Cesnik Ysleta Community Learning Center, El Paso, TX
Edwidge Crevecoeur-Bryant University of Florida, Gainesville, FL
Ann Marie Holzknecht Damrau San Diego Community College, San Diego, CA
Peggy Datz Berkeley Adult School, Berkeley, CA
MaryAnn Florez D.C. Learns, Washington, D.C.
Portia LaFerla Torrance Adult School, Torrance, CA
Eileen McKee Westchester Community College, Valhalla, NY
Julie Meuret Downey Adult School, Downey, CA
Sue Pace Santa Ana College School of Continuing Education, Santa Ana, CA
Howard Pomann Union County College, Elizabeth, NJ
Mary Ray Fairfax County Public Schools, Falls Church, VA
Gema Santos Miami-Dade County Public Schools, Miami, FL
Edith Uber Santa Clara Adult Education, Santa Clara, CA
Theresa Warren East Side Adult Education, San Jose, CA

Piloters

MariCarmen Acosta American High School, Adult ESOL, Hialeah, FL
Resurrección Ángeles Metropolitan Skills Center, Los Angeles, CA
Linda Bolognesi Fairfax County Public Schools, Adult and Community Education, Falls Church, VA
Patricia Boquiren Metropolitan Skills Center, Los Angeles, CA
Paul Buczko Pacoima Skills Center, Pacoima, CA
Matthew Horowitz Metropolitan Skills Center, Los Angeles, CA
Gabriel de la Hoz The English Center, Miami, FL
Cam-Tu Huynh Los Angeles Unified School District, Los Angeles, CA
Jorge Islas Whitewater Unified School District, Adult Education, Whitewater, WI
Lisa Johnson City College of San Francisco, San Francisco, CA
Loreto Kaplan Collier County Public Schools Adult ESOL Program, Naples, FL
Teressa Kitchen Collier County Public Schools Adult ESOL Program, Naples, FL
Anjie Martin Whitewater Unified School District, Adult Education, Whitewater, WI
Elida Matthews College of the Mainland, Texas City, TX
Penny Negron College of the Mainland, Texas City, TX
Manuel Pando Coral Park High School, Miami, FL
Susan Ritter Evans Community Adult School, Los Angeles, CA
Susan Ross Torrance Adult School, Torrance, CA
Beatrice Shields Fairfax County Public Schools, Adult and Community Education, Falls Church, VA
Oscar Solís Coral Park High School, Miami, FL
Wanda W. Weaver Literacy Council of Prince George's County, Hyattsville, MD

Reviewers

Lisa Agao Fresno Adult School, Fresno, CA
Carol Antuñano The English Center, Miami, FL
Euphronia Awakuni Evans Community Adult School, Los Angeles, CA
Jack Bailey Santa Barbara Adult Education, Santa Barbara, CA
Megan Belgarde-Carroll Evans Community Adult School, Los Angeles, CA
Robert Breitbard District School Board of Collier County, Naples, FL
Diane Burke Evans Community Adult School, Los Angeles, CA
José A. Carmona Embry-Riddle Aeronautical University, Daytona Beach, FL
Donna Case Bell Community Adult School, Huntington Park, CA
Veronique Colas Los Angeles Technology Center, Los Angles, CA
Carolyn Corrie Metropolitan Skills Center, Los Angeles, CA
Marti Estrin Santa Rosa Junior College, Sebastopol, CA
Sheila Friedman Metropolitan Skills Center, Los Angeles, CA
José Gonzalez Spanish Education Development Center, Washington, D.C.
Allene G. Grognet Vice President (Emeritus), Center for Applied Linguistics
J. Quinn Harmon-Kelley Venice Community Adult School, Los Angeles, CA
Edwina Hoffman Miami-Dade County Public Schools, Coral Gables, FL
Eduardo Honold Far West Project GREAT, El Paso, TX
Leigh Jacoby Los Angeles Community Adult School, Los Angeles, CA
Fayne Johnson Broward County Public Schools, Ft. Lauderdale, FL
Loreto Kaplan, Collier County Public Schools Adult ESOL Program, Naples, FL
Synthia LaFontaine Collier County Public Schools, Naples, FL
Gretchen Lammers-Ghereben Martinez Adult Education, Martinez, CA
Susan Lanzano Editorial Consultant, Briarcliff Manor, NY
Karen Mauer ESL Express, Euless, TX
Rita McSorley North East Independent School District, San Antonio, TX
Alice-Ann Menjivar Carlos Rosario International Public Charter School, Washington, D.C.
Sue Pace Santa Ana College School of Continuing Education, Santa Ana, CA
Isabel Perez American High School, Hialeah, FL
Howard Pomann Union County College, Elizabeth, NJ
Lesly Prudent Miami-Dade County Public Schools, Miami, FL
Valentina Purtell North Orange County Community College District, Anaheim, CA
Barbara Raifsnider San Diego Community College, San Diego, CA
Mary Ray Fairfax County Adult ESOL, Falls Church, VA
Laurie Shapero Miami-Dade Community College, Miami, FL
Felissa Taylor Nause Austin, TX
Merari Weber Metropolitan Skills Center, Los Angeles, CA
Meintje Westerbeek Baltimore City Community College, Baltimore, MD

Thanks also to **MaryAnn Florez**, D.C. Learns, for the Persistence Activities.

About the Series Consultants and Authors

SERIES CONSULTANTS

Dr. Beatriz B. Díaz has taught ESL for more than three decades in Miami. She has a master's degree in TESOL and a doctorate in education from Nova Southeastern University. She has given trainings and numerous presentations at international, national, state, and local conferences throughout the United States, the Caribbean, and South America. Dr. Díaz is the district supervisor for the Miami-Dade County Public Schools Adult ESOL Program, one of the largest in the United States.

Ronna Magy has worked as an ESL classroom teacher and teacher-trainer for nearly three decades. Most recently, she has worked as the ESL Teacher Adviser in charge of site-based professional development for the Division of Adult and Career Education of the Los Angeles Unified School District. She has trained teachers of adult English language learners in many areas, including lesson planning, learner persistence and goal setting, and cooperative learning. A frequent presenter at local, state and national, and international conferences, Ms. Magy is the author of adult ESL publications on life skills and test preparation, U.S. citizenship, reading and writing, and workplace English. She holds a master's degree in social welfare from the University of California at Berkeley.

Federico Salas-Isnardi has worked for 20 years in the field of adult education as an ESL and GED instructor, professional development specialist, curriculum writer, and program administrator. He has trained teachers of adult English language learners for over 15 years on topics ranging from language acquisition and communicative competence to classroom management and individualized professional development planning. Mr. Salas-Isnardi has been a contributing writer or consultant for a number of ESL publications, and he has co-authored curriculum for site-based workforce ESL and Spanish classes. He holds a master's degree in applied linguistics from the University of Houston and has completed a number of certificates in educational leadership.

AUTHORS

Lynn Bonesteel has been teaching ESL since 1988. She is currently a full-time senior lecturer at Boston University Center for English Language and Orientation Programs (CELOP). Ms. Bonesteel is also the author of *Password 3: A Reading and Vocabulary Text*, and co-author of *Center Stage: Express Yourself in English 2, 3, and 4* (Pearson Longman).

Arlen Gargagliano has been an ESL adult school teacher and program coordinator for over 20 years. Ms. Gargagliano was most recently the coordinator for Westchester Community College's library program and is currently a teacher in that same program. She has written two student textbooks on the topic of writing, as well as the corresponding teacher's books, and regularly facilitates workshops on the subject of teaching writing to adults. She also writes cookbooks, teaches cooking, and is a regular culinary guest on Spanish-language television.

Jeanne Lambert has worked in the field of adult ESL as an instructor, program coordinator, and curriculum developer for over 12 years. She began her career in Adult Education in Tampa. In New York City, she has worked in ESL programs for The City University of New York (CUNY) and the Brooklyn Public Library. She has presented at conferences in the areas of writing, grammar, and civics-based ESL instruction and has developed a curriculum for CUNY with an emphasis on American History. Ms. Lambert holds a master's degree in writing from Brooklyn College of The City University of New York. She currently works as an ESL materials writer and teaches an ESL Practicum for undergraduates at the New School University in New York City.

Scope and Sequence

UNIT	LISTENING AND SPEAKING	GRAMMAR	LIFE SKILLS	
Pre-Unit **Getting Started** *page 2*	• Ask for personal information • Give personal information	• Grammar terms review • Verb tense review		

1
Setting Goals,
Pursuing Dreams
page 5
	• Describe personality traits
	• Listen to several career counseling sessions and take notes
	• Discuss long-term career goals
	• Talk about a career path
	• Talk about SMART goals
	• *Communication Skill:* Using examples
	• *Presentation Skills:*
	  ◦ Make eye contact
	  ◦ Explain and refer to your chart
	  ◦ Ask for suggestions
		• Verbs followed by gerunds and/or infinitives
		• Gerunds following prepositions
			• Talk about job-related interests and abilities
			• Complete an interests survey
			• Analyze skills needed for particular jobs	

2 **Getting a Job** *page 25*	• Talk about interview do's and don'ts • Listen to a career counselor's advice about interviewing • Listen to and critique job applicants' responses to interview questions • Listen to and role-play a job interview • *Communication Skill:* Asking questions	• Present perfect • Present perfect vs. present perfect continuous	• Analyze the content, structure, and language of résumés • Learn the difference between a chronological and a functional résumé • Write a chronological résumé	
3 **Road Trip** *page 45*	• Listen to and take notes as a driving instructor talks about what to do in case of an accident • Talk about driving laws and customs • *Communication Skill:* Taking part in discussions	• Inseparable and separable phrasal verbs • *Grammar Watch:* Gerunds and infinitives in general statements	• Identify car parts and related problems • Understand different types of car insurance, including special insurance terms • Use online traffic information, including a detour map • Interpret Internet maps and directions	
4 **Are You Safe?** *page 65*	• Listen to a story of survival • Retell a news story about an earthquake • Listen to a news report about Hurricane Katrina • Discuss safety and evacuation procedures • Listen to and take part in discussions about child safety • *Communication Skill:* Making suggestions	• Past modals	• Identify safety measures that can prevent accidents at home and work • Use an online catalog page to learn about child safety products • Interpret information about workplace safety measures	
5 **Advancing on the Job** *page 85*	• Listen to a performance review • Talk about how to respond to constructive criticism • Listen to discussions about job-training opportunities • Use a company Intranet site to role-play a conversation about on-the-job training • Talk about factors that influence job promotions • Discuss job-performance evaluations • *Communication Skill:* Clarifying	• Clauses with *although* and *unless*	• Use a course catalog to complete a course schedule	

READING	WRITING	PROBLEM SOLVING	PERSISTENCE
• Learn to use a glossary • Develop vocabulary learning skills	• Take notes		• Community building • Orientation to book

• Read about doing job research
• Read about setting goals and achieving what you want
• Read about overcoming an obstacle
• *Reading Skills:*
  ◦ Highlighting/Underlining key information
  ◦ Previewing
	• Use word webs to gather and organize information
	• Write a descriptive essay about your interests, skills, and goals
	• *Writing Tip:* Topic sentences
		• Suggest ways for someone to achieve a long-term career goal despite obstacles	• *Study Skills:* Exploring Your Expectations

• Read about preparing for a job search
• Read about tricky interview questions and how to answer them
• *Reading Skills:*
  ◦ Using prior knowledge
  ◦ Comparing and contrasting
	• Use a T-chart to list job requirements and those skills and traits that make you a good candidate for a job
	• Write a cover letter for a résumé
	• *Writing Tip:* Using language from a job ad in a cover letter
		• Give advice to someone who is nervous about a job interview	• *Community Building:* Speaking English Well

• Read about what to do if your car breaks down
• Read about what to do if the police stop you
• Read and interpret Internet driving directions
• *Reading Skills:*
  ◦ Paraphrasing
  ◦ Understanding sequence
	• Use a chart to brainstorm and organize an argument
	• Write a letter to the editor about whether people should be allowed to use cell phones while driving
	• *Writing Tip:* Supporting details and examples
		• Suggest ways to improve someone's daily drive to work so that the person can be more punctual	• *Study Skills:* The Importance of Reading

• Read about tornadoes, including safety measures you can take
• Read about workers' rights to a safe workplace
• *Reading Skills:*
  ◦ Summarizing
  ◦ Monitoring comprehension
	• Use a chart to brainstorm and organize instructions
	• Write an essay that gives instructions about how to avoid a common safety hazard
	• *Writing Tip:* Imperatives
		• Advise someone about how to handle a workplace safety issue	• *Community Building:* Sharing Strengths and Challenges

• Read about factors that influence promotion
• Read a job-performance review
• Read about *I* and *You* statements
• Read about sports idioms used in the workplace
• *Reading Skills:*
  ◦ Identifying the main idea
  ◦ Scanning
	• Use an outline to organize a self-evaluation
	• Write a self-evaluation about your performance at work or school
	• *Writing Tip:* Using good examples
		• Give advice to someone who is upset by negative comments on a performance review	• *Study Skills:* Building Your Vocabulary All the Time

Text in red = Civics and American culture

UNIT	LISTENING AND SPEAKING	GRAMMAR	LIFE SKILLS
6 **Health** *page 105*	• Listen to a conversation about a medical problem • Talk about medical specialists and the conditions they treat • Describe medical problems • Listen to a presentation and take notes • Discuss diabetes • Ask and answer questions about health • *Communication Skill:* Giving advice	• Embedded *Wh-* questions • Embedded *Yes/No* questions	• Identify side effects of medications • Identify how to take medications properly
7 **Citizenship** *page 125*	• Discuss how a bill becomes a law • Listen to a lecture on naturalization and take notes • Discuss becoming a U.S. citizen • *Communication Skill:* Exchanging opinions	• *Grammar Watch:* Passive with *get* • The past perfect	• Learn about different kinds of maps • Interpret a historical map of the U.S. • Identify the special features of a map
8 **Knowing the Law** *page 145*	• Listen to a lecture on the rights of people accused of crimes and take notes • Discuss the *Miranda* warning • Listen to a lecture on types of crimes • Talk about one's opinions • *Communication Skill:* Qualifying opinions	• Future real conditional	• Recognize sexual harassment in the workplace • Understand sexual harassment laws
9 **Saving the Planet** *page 165*	• Listen to an interview about a carpooling program • Discuss carpooling • Discuss tips for greening your community • Talk about doing your share for the environment • Listen to a conversation about recycling • *Communication Skill:* Expressing comparison and contrast	• The past subjunctive with *wish* • The past unreal conditional	• Discuss recycling rules • Interpret a recycling calendar • Identify items that are recyclable
10 **Technology** *page 185*	• Listen to a lecture on the history of the Internet and take notes • Talk about the growth of the Internet • Listen to a discussion on how the Internet is affecting communication • Discuss the pros and cons of the Internet • Listen to a conversation about the language of text messaging • Discuss text messaging as a way of communicating • *Communication Skill:* Expressing agreement and disagreement	• Adjective clauses	• Understand how to use an instruction manual

READING	WRITING	PROBLEM SOLVING	PERSISTENCE

• Read about preparing for a doctor appointment
• Identify the main idea
• Read about first aid and emergency procedures
• Read message board posts
• Read about preventive health screenings
• *Reading Skills:*
  ○ Visualizing
  ○ Recognizing cause and effect
	• Use a chart to organize ideas
	• Write a persuasive essay for or against smoking bans in public places
	• *Writing Tip:* Introductory paragraphs
		• Suggest ways a parent can help an inactive, overweight child control diabetes	• *Study Skills:* Studyng in the U.S.

• Read about the beginnings of the United States
• Read about the organization of the U.S. government
• Read about individual rights in the Constitution
• Read about the benefits of U.S. citizenship
• *Reading Skills:*
  ○ Using a T-chart to take notes
  ○ Using text structure and formatting
	• Use a T-chart to brainstorm and organize ideas
	• Write a formal e-mail to an elected official about a problem that concerns you
	• *Writing Tip:* Using a problem/solution structure
		• Give advice about ways the U.S. legal system can be used to improve construction safety measures	• *Study Skills:* Writing Strategies

• Read about the right to vote
• Read about child abuse laws
• Read about sexual harassment
• Read about traffic tickets and traffic court
• Read about the importance of paying fines
• *Reading Skills:*
  ○ Distinguishing fact from opinion
  ○ Making inferences
	• Use a Venn diagram to organize points of comparison and constrast
	• Write an essay comparing and contrasting the legal systems in your home country and the U.S.
	• *Writing Tip:* Showing similarities and differences
		• Suggest a method of dealing with suspected child abuse	• *Study Skills:* Reading Skills/Strategies

• Read about ways to protect the environment and save money
• Read a blog about one student's experience with recycling
• Read about how daily life is changing our world
• Read about the "greening" of Greensburg, Kansas
• *Reading Skills:*
  ○ Understanding the style and structure of blogs (web-logs)
  ○ Using visuals
	• Use a chart to arrange events in a logical order
	• Write a personal narrative about how you have tried to help the environment
	• *Writing Tip:* Using time order
		• Suggest ways an office manager can "green" an office	• *Study Skills:* Becoming a Lifelong Learner

• Read about virtual driving
• Read about computer training
• Read about the history of the Internet
• *Reading Skills:*
  ○ Identifying an author's purpose
  ○ Using a timeline
	• Use a chart to structure an autobiographical essay
	• Write an autobiographical essay about a challenge you faced
	• *Writing Tip:* Using concrete examples and sensory details
		• Give advice to a new employee who is struggling to learn about unfamiliar computer equipment and procedures	• *Goal Setting:* Moving Forward

Text in red = Civics and American culture

Correlations

UNIT	CASAS Reading Basic Skill Content Standards	CASAS Listening Basic Skill Content Standards	
1	**U1:** 1.1; 1.2; 1.3; 1.4; 2.2; 3.2; **L1:** 3.4; **L2:** 2.8; **L4:** 2.7; 3.5; 7.2; **L6:** 6.2; 6.6; **L7:** 4.8; **L8:** 3.3; **SWYK Review and Expand:** 3.3	**U1:** 2.3; **L2:** 3.1; **L3:** 3.1; 4.7; 5.8; 5.9; 6.5; **L6:** 5.8; **L7:** 6.5; **L8:** 5.8; **SWYK Review and Expand:** 5.6	
2	**U2:** 1.1; 1.2; 1.3; 1.4; 2.2; 3.2; **L1:** 3.4; **L2:** 1.6; **L3:** 3.6; **L4:** 3.12; **L5:** 3.4; 7.3; **L6:** 3.9; **L9:** 3.4; 4.8; **SWYK Review and Expand:** 3.3	**U2:** 2.3; **L1:** 5.8; **L4:** 5.8; **L5:** 5.6; **L6:** 3.9; 4.2; **L7:** 4.6; **L8:** 3.9; 4.2; **SWYK Review and Expand:** 5.6	
3	**U3:** 1.1; 1.2; 1.3; 1.4; 2.2; 3.2; **L1:** 3.1; 4.1; 5.1; **L2:** 3.4; 6.4; 7.6; **L5:** 3.4; 3.13; **L6:** 3.3; 7.4; **L7:** 3.4; **L8:** 4.9; **L9:** 3.3; **SWYK Review and Expand:** 3.3	**U3:** 2.3; **L1:** 2.4; 2.9; 4.2; **L2:** 5.5; 6.1; **L4:** 5.5; 5.8; **L5:** 2.9; 4.2; **L6:** 4.7; **SWYK Review and Expand:** 5.6	
4	**U4:** 1.1; 1.2; 1.3; 1.4; 2.2; 3.2; **L1:** 3.5; 7.4; **L2:** 3.5; 7.7; **L3:** 3.3; **L5:** 3.3; **L6:** 3.3; 3.12; **L7:** 3.5; 5.5; **L8:** 3.2; **L9:** 3.4; **SWYK Review and Expand:** 3.3	**U4:** 2.3; **L1:** 4.6; **L2:** 5.6; **L3:** 4.11; 5.8; **L4:** 3.1; **L5:** 4.6; **L6:** 4.2; **L7:** 5.6; **SWYK Review and Expand:** 5.6	
5	**U5:** 1.1; 1.2; 1.3; 1.4; 2.2; 3.2; **L1:** 3.5; 7.2; **L2:** 3.4; 4.1; 6.2; 6.6; **L5:** 3.4; 4.1; 4.3; **L6:** 3.4; 4.2; 4.3; 4.8; **L7:** 3.2; **L8:** 3.4; 3.12; 3.15; **L9:** 3.3; **SWYK Review and Expand:** 3.3	**U5:** 2.3; **L1:** 5.9; 6.1; **L3:** 2.4; 4.6; 5.8; 6.7; **L5:** 4.6; **L7:** 4.3; **L8:** 2.3; **SWYK Review and Expand:** 5.6	
6	**U6:** 1.1; 1.2; 1.3; 1.4; 2.2; 3.2; **L1:** 6.5; 7.2; **L3:** 4.10; 3.5; **L4:** 3.7; **L5:** 3.3; **L7:** 3.5; 6.5; **L9:** 3.3; **SWYK Review and Expand:** 3.3	**U6:** 2.3; **L1:** 5.6; 6.1; **L2:** 2.9; 4.2; **L3:** 6.5; **L4:** 5.6; **L5:** 4.6; **L6:** 3.6; 3.14; **L7:** 5.6; **L8:** 5.8; **SWYK Review and Expand:** 5.6; 6.6	
7	**U7:** 1.1; 1.2; 1.3; 1.4; 2.2; 3.2; **L1:** 3.5; **L2:** 4.1; 4.3; **L3:** 3.5; **L4:** 3.5; **L5:** 2.12; **L6:** 3.5; 4.10; 7.2; **L8:** 4.9; **L9:** 3.4; **SWYK Review and Expand:** 3.3	**U7:** 2.3; **L1:** 4.2; 5.9; 6.2; **L3:** 5.9; **L4:** 5.9; **L5:** 4.11; **L6:** 5.9; 6.1; **L7:** 5.10; **SWYK Review and Expand:** 5.6	
8	**U8:** 1.1; 1.2; 1.3; 1.4; 2.2; 3.2; **L1:** 2.12; 3.2; 5.5; **L2:** 3.4; **L3:** 3.5; 7.10; **L4:** 3.5; **L5:** 3.5; **L6:** 3.5; 7.8; **L7:** 5.5; **L8:** 3.5; **L9:** 3.4; **SWYK Review and Expand:** 3.3	**U8:** 2.3; **L1:** 5.9; **L2:** 3.13; **L3:** 5.8; 6.11; **L5:** 5.8; **L6:** 5.8; 6.10; **L7:** 5.8; 6.10; **L8:** 5.8; **SWYK Review and Expand:** 5.6	
9	**U9:** 1.1; 1.2; 1.3; 1.4; 2.2; 3.2; **L1:** 3.5; **L2:** 3.3; 4.3; 4.8; **L3:** 3.4; **L4:** 3.5; **L5:** 3.5; 4.8; **L8:** 3.5; 3.12; 4.10; **L9:** 3.4; **SWYK Review and Expand:** 3.3	**U9:** 2.3; **L1:** 5.8; **L3:** 5.8; **L4:** 5.8; **L5:** 5.8; **L6:** 4.6; **L7:** 3.13; **L8:** 5.8; **SWYK Review and Expand:** 3.6	
10	**U10:** 1.1; 1.2; 1.3; 1.4; 2.2; 3.2; **L1:** 2.11; 2.12; 3.5; **L2:** 3.7; 4.9; **L4:** 3.5; 7.11; **L5:** 3.9; **L6:** 2.7; **L7:** 3.5; 4.3; **L8:** 3.3; **L9:** 3.4; 4.8; **SWYK Review and Expand:** 3.3	**U10:** 2.3; **L1:** 5.8; **L3:** 5.8; **L4:** 5.8; **L6:** 5.8; **L7:** 5.8; **L8:** 4.6; **SWYK Review and Expand:** 5.6	

CASAS Competencies	LAUSD ESL Low Advanced Competencies	Florida Adult ESOL Course Standards
U1: 0.1.2; 0.1.5; 0.1.7; 0.2.1; 0.2.4; **L1:** 0.2.1; 0.2.4; 4.1.3; 4.1.8; 4.1.9; **L2:** 4.1.9; **L3:** 4.1.9; **L4:** 4.1.7; **L5:** 4.1.9; **L6:** 7.1.1; **L7:** 7.1.1; 7.1.2; **L8:** 7.1.3; **L9:** 0.2.1; 4.1.9; **SWYK Review and Expand:** 4.1.9; 7.1.1	3a; 5; 7	6.03.13; 6.03.14
U2: 0.1.2; 0.1.5; 0.1.7; 0.2.1; 0.2.4; **L1:** 4.1.3; 4.1.5; **L2:** 4.1.2; **L3:** 0.2.2; 4.1.2; **L4:** 4.1.5; 4.1.7; **L5:** 4.1.5; 4.1.7; **L7:** 4.1.5; 4.1.7; **L9:** 4.1.2; 4.1.8; **SWYK Review and Expand:** 4.12; 4.15; 4.17	3a; 25	6.03.01; 6.03.02; 6.03.03; 6.03.04
U3: 0.1.2; 0.1.5; 0.1.7; 0.2.1; 0.2.4; **L1:** 1.9.9; **L2:** 1.9.7; **L3:** 1.9.7; **L4:** 1.9.7; **L5:** 1.9.8; **L6:** 1.9.7; **L7:** 2.2.5; **L8:** 2.2.5; **SWYK Review and Expand:** 1.9.7; 7.3.1; 7.3.2	1	6.06.01; 6.06.02; 6.06.04
U4: 0.1.2; 0.1.5; 0.1.7; 0.2.1; 0.2.4; **L2:** 3.4.8; **L3:** 3.4.8; **L4:** 3.4.8; **L6:** 3.4.2; **L7:** 3.4.2; **L8:** 4.3.2; **SWYK Review and Expand:** 3.4.8; 4.3.2	9; 22; 23	6.03.08; 6.03.09; 6.03.15; 6.07.01
U5: 0.1.2; 0.1.5; 0.1.7; 0.2.1; 0.2.4; **L1:** 4.4.1; 4.4.2; 4.4.7; **L2:** 4.4.3; 4.4.4; **L3:** 0.1.6; 4.6.1; 4.8.2; **L4:** 4.4.2; 4.4.4; 4.6.1; **L5:** 4.4.5; **L6:** 2.8.3; 4.4.5; 4.4.8; 7.1.2; 7.1.3; **SWYK Review and Expand:** 4.4.2; 4.4.4; 7.3.1	3; 5; 8; 24; 25	6.03.10; 6.03.11; 6.03.12; 6.03.13; 6.03.14
U6: 0.1.2; 0.1.5; 0.1.7; 0.2.1; 0.2.4; **L1:** 3.1.3; **L2:** 3.6.4; **L3:** 3.3.1; 3.3.2; **L4:** 3.4.3; **L6:** 3.6.4; **L7:** 0.1.4; 3.5.9; **L8:** 3.6.3; **L9:** 3.4.5; **SWYK Review and Expand:** 3.1.2; 3.3.1; 3.5.9	2; 23	6.05.02; 6.05.03; 6.05.04; 6.05.06
U7: 0.1.2; 0.1.5; 0.1.7; 0.2.1; 0.2.4; **L1:** 5.2.1; **L2:** 5.2.1; **L3:** 5.2.1; 5.2.2; 5.5.2; 5.5.3; 5.5.4; **L4:** 5.2.2; 5.3.2; **L5:** 5.5.2; 5.5.4; **L6:** 5.3.6; **L7:** 0.1.3; 5.3.6; **L8:** 5.2.1; **L9:** 7.3.1; 7.3.2; **SWYK Review and Expand:** 5.2.2; 5.3.6; 5.5.2; 5.5.3; 5.5.4	3f; 20; 21	06.02.01
U8: 0.1.2; 0.1.5; 0.1.7; 0.2.1; 0.2.4; **L1:** 5.3.2; 7.4.5; **L2:** 5.3.2; 5.3.7; **L3:** 5.1.1; 5.6.3; **L4:** 4.2.6; 5.3.8; **L5:** 5.3.8; 5.3.9; **L6:** 5.3.7; **L7:** 5.3.7; 7.4.5; **L8:** 5.3.7; **L9:** 7.2.3; 7.2.6; **SWYK Review and Expand:** 4.2.6; 5.3.2; 5.6.3	3a; 14; 20	6.06.05; 6.07.02
U9: 0.1.2; 0.1.5; 0.1.7; 0.2.1; 0.2.4; **L1:** 5.7.1; **L2:** 5.7.1; **L3:** 5.7.1; 7.2.2; 7.3.3; 7.4.2; **L4:** 5.7.1; **L5:** 5.7.1; 7.2.2; **L7:** 5.7.1; **L8:** 5.7.1; **L9:** 5.7.1; 7.2.6; **SWYK Review and Expand:** 5.7.1	13	6.02.02; 6.02.06
U10: 0.1.2; 0.1.5; 0.1.7; 0.2.1; 0.2.4; **L1:** 7.7.1; 7.7.3; **L2:** 7.7.6; **L3:** 7.7.1; 7.7.3; **L4:** 7.7.1; **L5:** 7.7.1; **L6:** 7.7.3; 7.7.4; 7.7.5; **L7:** 6.7.1; 7.7.1; 7.7.3; **L8:** 7.7.1; **SWYK Review and Expand:** 7.7.1	5, 15	6.03.07

All units of *Future* meet most of the EFF **Content Standards**. For details, as well as for correlations to other state standards, go to www.pearsonlongman.com/future.

To the Teacher

Welcome to *Future*
English for Results

Future is a six-level, four-skills course for adults and young adults correlated to state and national standards. It incorporates research-based teaching strategies, corpus-informed language, and the best of modern technology.

KEY FEATURES

Future provides everything your students need in one integrated program.

In developing the course, we listened to what teachers asked for and we responded, providing six levels, more meaningful content, a thorough treatment of grammar, explicit skills development, abundant practice, multiple options for state-of-the-art assessment, and innovative components.

Future serves students' real-life needs.

We began constructing the instructional syllabus for *Future* by identifying what is most critical to students' success in their personal and family lives, in the workplace, as members of a community, and in their academic pursuits. *Future* provides outstanding coverage of life skills competencies, basing language teaching on actual situations that students are likely to encounter and equipping them with the skills they need to achieve their goals. The grammar and other language elements taught in each lesson grow out of these situations and are thus practiced in realistic contexts, enabling students to use language meaningfully, from the beginning.

Future grows with your students.

Future takes students from absolute beginner level through low-advanced proficiency in English, addressing students' abilities and learning priorities at each level. As the levels progress, the curricular content and unit structure change accordingly, with the upper levels incorporating more academic skills, more advanced content standards, and more content-rich texts.

Level	Description	CASAS Scale Scores
Intro	True Beginning	Below 180
1	Low Beginning	181–190
2	High Beginning	191–200
3	Low Intermediate	201–210
4	High Intermediate	211–220
5	Low Advanced	221–235

Future 5 helps students "transition."

With its emphasis on explicit instruction in reading and writing skills, the material in *Future 5* helps students transition into further education, career training, and career advancement. The reading lessons revolve around interesting and informative articles, and include vocabulary-building activities, as well as explicit presentation and practice of reading skills, such as identifying the main idea, summarizing, and recognizing cause and effect. Writing lessons teach students about various writing genres, such as personal narratives, opinion pieces, and compare-and-contrast essays. They guide students through the writing process and present skills that help students write more fluently and accurately.

Future puts the best of 21st-century technology in the hands of students and teachers.

In addition to its expertly developed print materials and audio components, *Future* goes a step further.

- Every **Student Book comes with a Practice Plus CD-ROM** for use at home, in the lab, or wherever students have access to a computer. The Practice Plus CD-ROM can be used both by students who wish to extend their practice beyond the classroom and by those who need to "make up" what they missed in class.
- The **CD-ROM** also includes the entire class audio program as MP3 files so that students can get extra listening practice at their convenience.
- The **Tests and Test Prep** book comes with an **Exam***View®* *Assessment Suite*, enabling teachers to print ready-made tests, customize these tests, or create their own tests for life skills, grammar, vocabulary, listening, and reading.
- The **Teacher Training DVD** provides demo lessons of real teachers using *Future* with their classes. Teachers can select from the menu and watch a specific type of lesson, such as a grammar presentation, or a specific type of activity, such as an information gap, at their own convenience.
- The **Companion Website** provides a variety of teaching support, including a pdf of the Teacher's Edition and Lesson Planner notes for each unit in the Student Book.

Future provides all the assessment tools you need.

- The **Placement Test** evaluates students' proficiency in all skill areas, allowing teachers and program administrators to easily assign students to the right classes.
- The **Tests and Test Prep book** for each level provides:
  - **Printed unit tests** with accompanying audio CD. These unit tests use standardized testing formats, giving students practice "bubbling-in" responses as required for CASAS and other standardized tests. In addition, reproducible test prep worksheets and practice tests provide invaluable help to students unfamiliar with such test formats.

o The *Future* **Exam***View®* *Assessment Suite* is a powerful program that allows teachers to create their own unique tests or to print or customize already prepared tests.

- **Performance-based assessment:** Lessons in the Student Book end with discussions, role plays, or presentations, allowing students to apply what they have learned from the lesson. Each unit culminates with two speaking activities: the first lets students review and synthesize the information in the unit, and then asks them to discuss it or explain it; the second presents a problem that students need to solve in small groups. Both speaking activities require students to demonstrate their oral competence in a holistic way. The **Teacher's Edition and Lesson Planner** provides speaking and writing rubrics to make it easy for teachers to evaluate students' oral and written proficiency.

- **Self-assessment:** For optimal learning to take place, students need to be involved in setting goals and in monitoring their own progress. *Future* has addressed this in numerous ways. In the Student Book, checkboxes at the end of lessons invite students to evaluate their mastery of the material. End-of-unit reviews allow students to see their progress in grammar. And after completing each unit, students go back to the goals for the unit and reflect on their achievement. In addition, the CD-ROM provides students with continuous feedback (and opportunities for self-correction) as they work through each lesson, and the Workbook contains the answer keys, so students can check their own work outside of class.

Future addresses multilevel classes and diverse learning styles.

Using research-based teaching strategies, *Future* provides teachers with creative solutions for all stages of lesson planning and implementation, allowing them to meet the needs of all their students.

- The **Teacher's Edition and Lesson Planner** offers pre-level and above-level variations for every lesson plan as well as numerous optional and extension activities designed to reach students at all levels.
- The **Practice Plus CD-ROM** included with the Student Book is an extraordinary tool for individualizing instruction. It allows students to direct their own learning, working on precisely what they need and practicing what they choose to work on as many times as they like. In addition, the CD-ROM provides all the audio files for the book, enabling students to listen as they wish to any of the material that accompanies the text.
- The **Workbook**, similarly, allows students to devote their time to the lessons and specific skill areas that they need to work on most.

- The **Tests and Test Prep** book, as noted on page xii, includes *Future* **Exam***View®* *Assessment Suite*, which allows teachers to customize existing tests or create their own tests using the databank.

Future's persistence curriculum motivates students to continue their education.

Recent research about persistence has given us insights into how to keep students coming to class and how to keep them learning when they can't attend. Recognizing that there are many forces operating in students' lives—family, jobs, childcare, health—that may make it difficult for them to come to class, programs need to help students:

- Identify their educational goals
- Believe that they can successfully achieve them
- Develop a commitment to their own education
- Identify forces that can interfere with school attendance
- Develop strategies that will help them try to stay in school in spite of obstacles
- Find ways to continue learning even during "stopping out" periods

Future addresses all of these areas with its persistence curriculum. Activities found throughout the book and specific persistence activities in the back of the book help students build community, set goals, develop better study skills, and feel a sense of achievement. In addition, the Practice Plus CD-ROM is unique in its ability to ensure that even those students unable to attend class are able to make up what they missed and thus persist in their studies.

Future supports busy teachers by providing all the materials teachers need, plus the teacher support.

The **Student Book** and **Workbook** were designed to provide teachers with everything they need in the way of ready-to-use classroom materials so they can concentrate on responding to their students' needs. The **Future Teacher Training DVD** gives teachers tips and models for conducting various activity types in their classroom.

Future provides ample practice, with flexible options to best fit the needs of each class.

The Student Book provides 60–100 hours of instruction. It can be supplemented in class by using:

- Teacher's Edition and Lesson Planner expansion ideas
- Workbook exercises
- Tests
- CD-ROM activities
- Activities on the Companion Website (longmanusa.com/Future)

TEACHING MULTILEVEL CLASSES

Teaching tips for pair and group work

Using pair and group work in an ESL classroom has many proven benefits. It creates an atmosphere of liveliness, builds community, and allows students to practice speaking in a low-risk environment. Many of the activities in *Future* are pair and small-group activities. Here are some tips for managing these activities:

- Limit small groups to three or four students per group (unless an activity specifically calls for larger groups). This maximizes student participation.
- Change partners for different activities. This gives students a chance to work with many others in the class and keeps them from feeling "stuck."
- If possible, give students a place to put their coats when they enter the classroom. This allows them to move around freely without worrying about returning to their own seats.
- Move around the classroom as students are working to make sure they are on task and to monitor their work.
- As you walk around, try to remain unobtrusive, so students continue to participate actively, without feeling they are being evaluated.
- Keep track of language points students are having difficulty with. After the activity, teach a mini-lesson to the entire class addressing those issues. This helps students who are having trouble without singling them out.

Pairs and groups in the multilevel classroom

Adult education ESL classrooms are by nature multilevel. This is true even if students have been given a placement test. Many factors—including a student's age, educational background, and literacy level—contribute to his or her ability level. Also, the same student may be at level in one skill, but pre-level or above-level in another.

When grouping students for a task, keep the following points in mind:

- *Like-ability* groups (in which students have the same ability level) help ensure that all students participate equally, without one student dominating the activity.
- *Cross-ability* groups (in which students have different ability levels) are beneficial to pre-level students who need the support of their at- or above-level classmates. The higher-level students benefit from "teaching" their lower-level classmates.

For example, when the activity is a group discussion, like-ability pairings are helpful. The discussion questions can be tailored to different ability levels, and all students can participate equally. When the activity is more complex, such as a brainstorming activity in which students need to come up with new ideas, cross-ability pairings are helpful. The higher-level students can support and give ideas to the lower-level student and help with any new vocabulary.

The *Future* Teacher's Edition and Lesson Planner provides specific suggestions for when to put students in like-ability versus cross-ability groups and how to tailor activities to different ability levels.

Unit Tour

Unit Opener

Each unit starts with a full-page photo that introduces the themes of the unit.

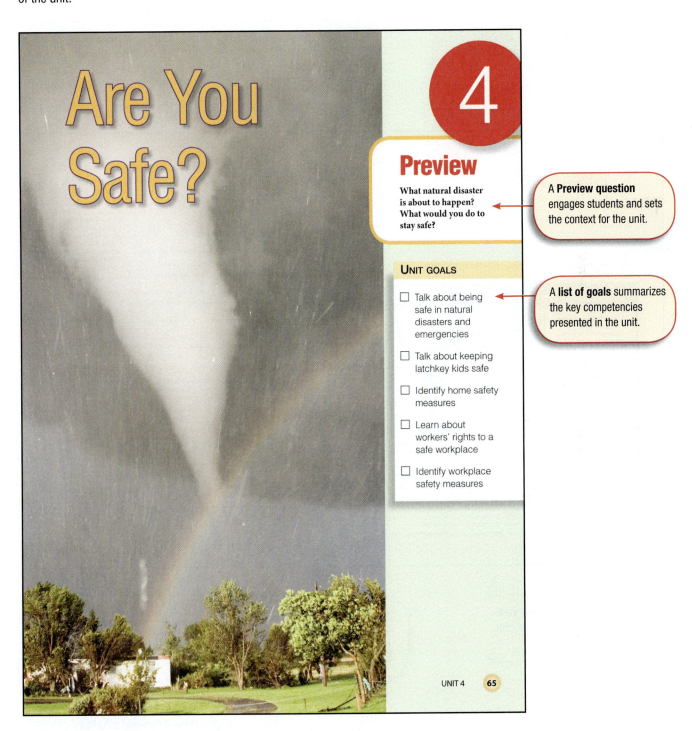

Are You Safe?

4

Preview

What natural disaster is about to happen? What would you do to stay safe?

A **Preview question** engages students and sets the context for the unit.

UNIT GOALS

- ☐ Talk about being safe in natural disasters and emergencies
- ☐ Talk about keeping latchkey kids safe
- ☐ Identify home safety measures
- ☐ Learn about workers' rights to a safe workplace
- ☐ Identify workplace safety measures

A **list of goals** summarizes the key competencies presented in the unit.

UNIT 4   65

Reading

High-interest articles introduce students to cultural concepts and useful, topical information with a focus on preparing students for academic and other real-life reading tasks.

Before You Read exercises activate students' background knowledge and build other **pre-reading skills**.

Comprehension questions check understanding of the article and build reading skills.

Essential **reading skills**, such as summarizing, visualizing, and identifying the main idea, are explicitly taught and practiced.

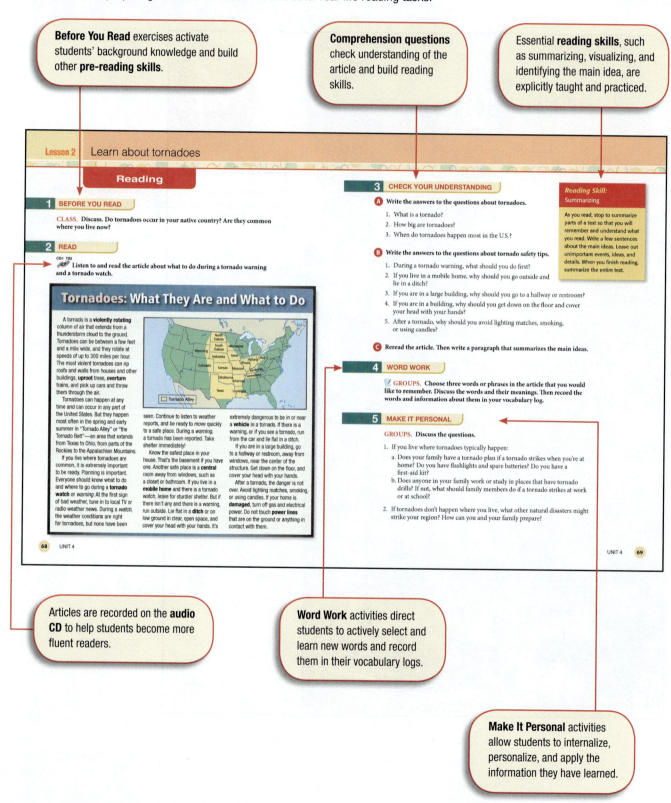

Articles are recorded on the **audio CD** to help students become more fluent readers.

Word Work activities direct students to actively select and learn new words and record them in their vocabulary logs.

Make It Personal activities allow students to internalize, personalize, and apply the information they have learned.

Grammar

Each unit presents one or two grammar points in a logical, systematic grammar syllabus.

Grammar charts clearly present the target grammar.

Grammar Watch notes call attention to specific aspects of the grammar point.

Contextualized grammar practice progresses from controlled to open-ended exercises.

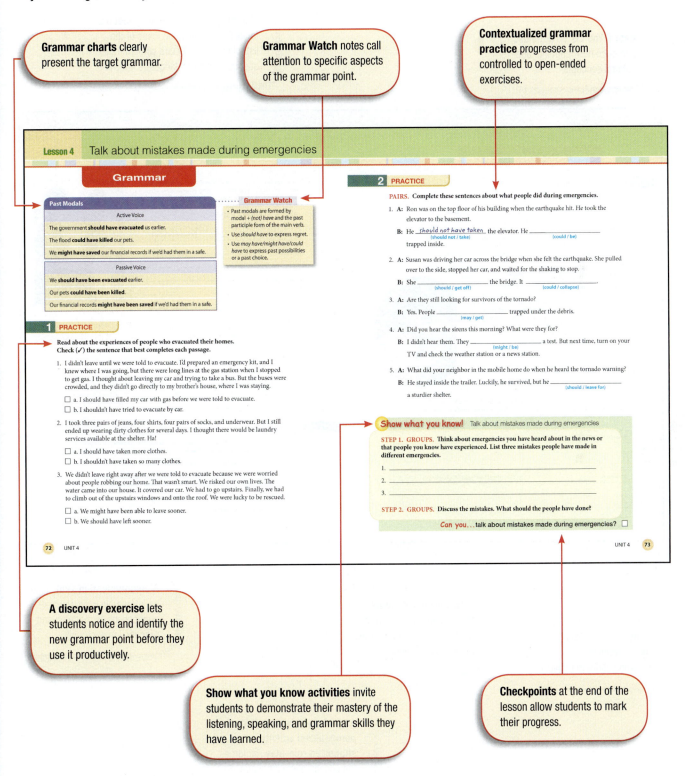

Lesson 4 Talk about mistakes made during emergencies

Grammar

Past Modals

Active Voice
The government **should have evacuated** us earlier.
The flood **could have killed** our pets.
We **might have saved** our financial records if we'd had them in a safe.

Passive Voice
We **should have been evacuated** earlier.
Our pets **could have been killed**.
Our financial records **might have been saved** if we'd had them in a safe.

Grammar Watch

- Past modals are formed by modal + (not) have and the past participle form of the main verb.
- Use *should have* to express regret.
- Use *may have/might have/could have* to express past possibilities or a past choice.

1 PRACTICE

Read about the experiences of people who evacuated their homes. Check (✓) the sentence that best completes each passage.

1. I didn't leave until we were told to evacuate. I'd prepared an emergency kit, and I knew where I was going, but there were long lines at the gas station when I stopped to get gas. I thought about leaving my car and trying to take a bus. But the buses were crowded, and they didn't go directly to my brother's house, where I was staying.

    ☐ a. I should have filled my car with gas before we were told to evacuate.
    ☐ b. I shouldn't have tried to evacuate by car.

2. I took three pairs of jeans, four shirts, four pairs of socks, and underwear. But I still ended up wearing dirty clothes for several days. I thought there would be laundry services available at the shelter. Ha!

    ☐ a. I should have taken more clothes.
    ☐ b. I shouldn't have taken so many clothes.

3. We didn't leave right away after we were told to evacuate because we were worried about people robbing our home. That wasn't smart. We risked our own lives. The water came into our house. It covered our car. We had to go upstairs. Finally, we had to climb out of the upstairs windows and onto the roof. We were lucky to be rescued.

    ☐ a. We might have been able to leave sooner.
    ☐ b. We should have left sooner.

2 PRACTICE

PAIRS. Complete these sentences about what people did during emergencies.

1. **A:** Ron was on the top floor of his building when the earthquake hit. He took the elevator to the basement.
    B: He _should not have taken_ the elevator. He _____ (should not / take) _____ (could / be) trapped inside.

2. **A:** Susan was driving her car across the bridge when she felt the earthquake. She pulled over to the side, stopped her car, and waited for the shaking to stop.
    B: She _____ (should / get off) the bridge. It _____ (could / collapse)

3. **A:** Are they still looking for survivors of the tornado?
    B: Yes. People _____ (may / get) trapped under the debris.

4. **A:** Did you hear the sirens this morning? What were they for?
    B: I didn't hear them. They _____ (might / be) a test. But next time, turn on your TV and check the weather station or a news station.

5. **A:** What did your neighbor in the mobile home do when he heard the tornado warning?
    B: He stayed inside the trailer. Luckily, he survived, but he _____ (should / leave for) a sturdier shelter.

Show what you know! Talk about mistakes made during emergencies

STEP 1. GROUPS. Think about emergencies you have heard about in the news or that people you know have experienced. List three mistakes people have made in different emergencies.

1. _____
2. _____
3. _____

STEP 2. GROUPS. Discuss the mistakes. What should the people have done?

Can you... talk about mistakes made during emergencies? ☐

72   UNIT 4

UNIT 4   73

A discovery exercise lets students notice and identify the new grammar point before they use it productively.

Show what you know activities invite students to demonstrate their mastery of the listening, speaking, and grammar skills they have learned.

Checkpoints at the end of the lesson allow students to mark their progress.

Listening and Speaking

Listening lessons present topical information and the key vocabulary and competencies of the unit.

Before You Listen activities introduce new language and cultural concepts.

Listening comprehension questions focus first on the main ideas of the listening and culminate with inference questions and oral language activities.

Lesson 5 Talk about keeping latchkey kids safe

Listening and Speaking

1 BEFORE YOU LISTEN

A CLASS. Discuss the questions.

1. In your home country, is it common for children to spend time alone, without their parents or others looking after them?
2. At what age do you think a child can be responsible for taking care of himself or herself? At what age do you think a child can be responsible for taking care of younger siblings? Explain.
3. If you have children, where do they go after school?

B Read the information about latchkey children.

"Latchkey children" or "latchkey kids" refers to children who spend time home alone without parents or others to supervise them. Some people believe that the term became widely used during World War II, when many fathers were away fighting the war and many mothers went to work in the factories. Today, there are still many latchkey children, and their numbers are rising. In some cases, children want to go home after school, and they feel they are too old to have a baby-sitter. Older children may pressure parents to allow them to go home after school, even when child care or after-school programs are available. However, many parents of latchkey children do not have a choice: They simply can't afford to pay for child care and have no other options.

C GROUPS. Latchkey children can get into different kinds of trouble when they are home alone. Look at the categories in the chart. Can you think of examples? Write at least one example for each category.

Pressure from Friends to Break Rules	Accidents and Emergencies
Strangers	Emotional and Psychological Issues

74 UNIT 4

2 LISTEN

A CD1 T27 Tania is a single mother who doesn't get home until after 6:00. Her 12-year-old son, Greg, is home alone after school. Listen to her talk with her neighbor Nick about the things she is worried about. Write the problems and the solutions her neighbor suggests.

Possible Problems	Possible Solutions
1. What if strangers call?	
2.	
3.	
4.	
5.	

B CD1 T27 Read the information in the Communication Skill box. Then listen again. Write the phrase Nick uses to offer each suggestion.

Suggestion 1: _Why don't you_

Suggestion 2: _____

Suggestion 3: _____

Suggestion 4: _____

Suggestion 5: _____

Communication Skill:
Making Suggestions

You can begin a suggestion with these phrases:

Why don't you (+ verb)?
Have you thought about (+ gerund)?
Maybe you could (+ verb).
If I were you, I'd (+ verb).
Could you (+ verb)?

3 CONVERSATION

ROLE PLAY. PAIRS. Work with a partner who was not in your group in Exercise 1C. Student A is the parent and Student B is the neighbor.

STEP 1. Select a problem to work on from the chart in Exercise 1C.

STEP 2. Create a conversation like the one between Tania and her neighbor. Use expressions from the Communication Skill box. Write the conversation down.

STEP 3. Practice the conversation. Use gestures and appropriate emotion.

STEP 4. Perform the role play in front of the class.

UNIT 4 75

Students apply **critical thinking skills** in discussions about the topic.

Corpus-informed **model conversations** use target grammar and competencies to model spoken language.

A **problem-solving activity, personalized activity,** or **supported role-play** reinforces the concepts and language learned in the lesson.

A **communication skill**, such as alternative ways to make suggestions, is modeled and practiced in each unit.

Life Skills

Life Skills lessons in each unit focus on functional language, practical skills, and authentic printed materials, such as websites, schedules, maps, catalogs, labels, and signs.

> **Civics, life skills,** and **cultural information** related to life in the U.S. are introduced in context.

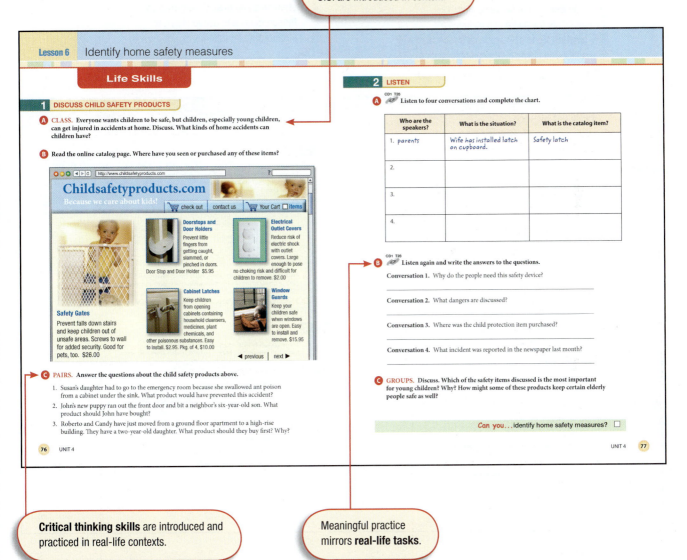

Lesson 6   Identify home safety measures

Life Skills

1 DISCUSS CHILD SAFETY PRODUCTS

A CLASS. Everyone wants children to be safe, but children, especially young children, can get injured in accidents at home. Discuss. What kinds of home accidents can children have?

B Read the online catalog page. Where have you seen or purchased any of these items?

Childsafetyproducts.com
Because we care about kids!

check out   contact us   Your Cart ☐ items

Doorstops and Door Holders
Prevent little fingers from getting caught, slammed, or pinched in doors. Door Stop and Door Holder $5.95

Electrical Outlet Covers
Reduce risk of electric shock with outlet covers. Large enough to pose no choking risk and difficult for children to remove. $2.00

Safety Gates
Prevent falls down stairs and keep children out of unsafe areas. Screws to wall for added security. Good for pets, too. $26.00

Cabinet Latches
Keep children from opening cabinets containing household cleansers, medicines, plant chemicals, and other poisonous substances. Easy to install. $2.95. Pkg. of 4, $10.00

Window Guards
Keep your children safe when windows are open. Easy to install and remove. $15.95

◄ previous   next ►

C PAIRS. Answer the questions about the child safety products above.

1. Susan's daughter had to go to the emergency room because she swallowed ant poison from a cabinet under the sink. What product would have prevented this accident?
2. John's new puppy ran out the front door and bit a neighbor's six-year-old son. What product should John have bought?
3. Roberto and Candy have just moved from a ground floor apartment to a high-rise building. They have a two-year-old daughter. What product should they buy first? Why?

76   UNIT 4

2 LISTEN

CD1 T28
A Listen to four conversations and complete the chart.

Who are the speakers?	What is the situation?	What is the catalog item?
1. parents	Wife has installed latch on cupboard.	Safety latch
2.		
3.		
4.		

CD1 T29
B Listen again and write the answers to the questions.

Conversation 1. Why do the people need this safety device?
_____

Conversation 2. What dangers are discussed?
_____

Conversation 3. Where was the child protection item purchased?
_____

Conversation 4. What incident was reported in the newspaper last month?
_____

C GROUPS. Discuss. Which of the safety items discussed is the most important for young children? Why? How might some of these products keep certain elderly people safe as well?

*Can you...*identify home safety measures? ☐

UNIT 4   77

> **Critical thinking skills** are introduced and practiced in real-life contexts.

> **Meaningful practice** mirrors **real-life tasks**.

Writing

Writing instruction is process-based, leading students to write well-organized short essays or letters about familiar topics. Each unit focuses on key features of a specific genre, such as instructions, letters to the editor, or autobiographical essays.

The **Before You Write** section presents the genre and includes a **writing tip** to help students structure, unify, and clarify their academic writing.

Think on Paper presents writing strategies and **graphic organizers** that students can use to plan and structure their writing.

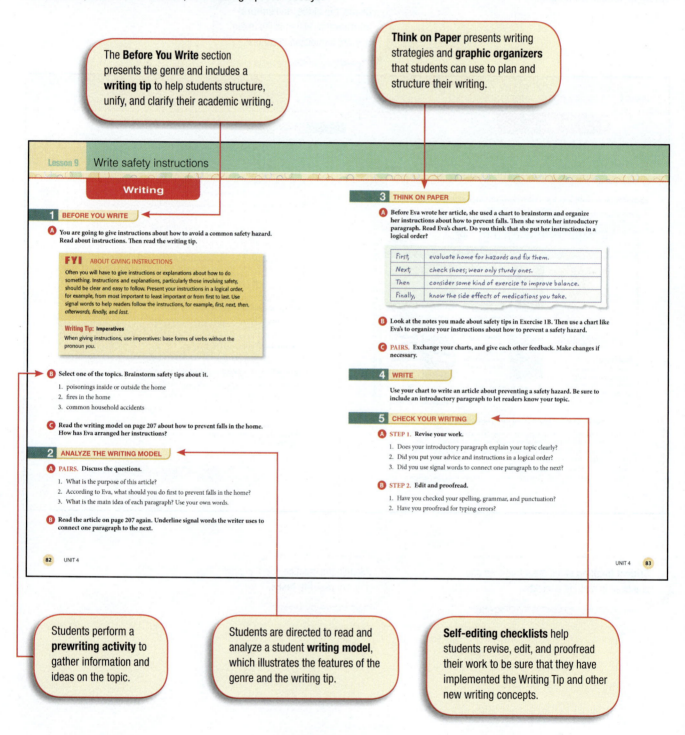

Lesson 9 Write safety instructions

Writing

1 BEFORE YOU WRITE

A You are going to give instructions about how to avoid a common safety hazard. Read about instructions. Then read the writing tip.

FYI ABOUT GIVING INSTRUCTIONS

Often you will have to give instructions or explanations about how to do something. Instructions and explanations, particularly those involving safety, should be clear and easy to follow. Present your instructions in a logical order, for example, from most important to least important or from first to last. Use signal words to help readers follow the instructions, for example, *first, next, then, afterwards, finally,* and *last.*

Writing Tip: **Imperatives**
When giving instructions, use imperatives: base forms of verbs without the pronoun *you.*

B Select one of the topics. Brainstorm safety tips about it.

1. poisonings inside or outside the home
2. fires in the home
3. common household accidents

C Read the writing model on page 207 about how to prevent falls in the home. How has Eva arranged her instructions?

2 ANALYZE THE WRITING MODEL

A PAIRS. Discuss the questions.

1. What is the purpose of this article?
2. According to Eva, what should you do first to prevent falls in the home?
3. What is the main idea of each paragraph? Use your own words.

B Read the article on page 207 again. Underline signal words the writer uses to connect one paragraph to the next.

82 UNIT 4

3 THINK ON PAPER

A Before Eva wrote her article, she used a chart to brainstorm and organize her instructions about how to prevent falls. Then she wrote her introductory paragraph. Read Eva's chart. Do you think that she put her instructions in a logical order?

First,	evaluate home for hazards and fix them.
Next,	check shoes; wear only sturdy ones.
Then	consider some kind of exercise to improve balance.
Finally,	know the side effects of medications you take.

B Look at the notes you made about safety tips in Exercise 1B. Then use a chart like Eva's to organize your instructions about how to prevent a safety hazard.

C PAIRS. Exchange your charts, and give each other feedback. Make changes if necessary.

4 WRITE

Use your chart to write an article about preventing a safety hazard. Be sure to include an introductory paragraph to let readers know your topic.

5 CHECK YOUR WRITING

A STEP 1. Revise your work.

1. Does your introductory paragraph explain your topic clearly?
2. Did you put your advice and instructions in a logical order?
3. Did you use signal words to connect one paragraph to the next?

B STEP 2. Edit and proofread.

1. Have you checked your spelling, grammar, and punctuation?
2. Have you proofread for typing errors?

UNIT 4 83

Students perform a **prewriting activity** to gather information and ideas on the topic.

Students are directed to read and analyze a student **writing model**, which illustrates the features of the genre and the writing tip.

Self-editing checklists help students revise, edit, and proofread their work to be sure that they have implemented the Writing Tip and other new writing concepts.

Review & Expand

The final page of the unit allows students to review and expand on the language, themes, and competencies they have worked with throughout the unit.

Act It Out activities assign different sections of the unit to students to review and present to a partner or group.

Problem-solving tasks encourage critical thinking and allow students to demonstrate understanding of topics in real-life situations.

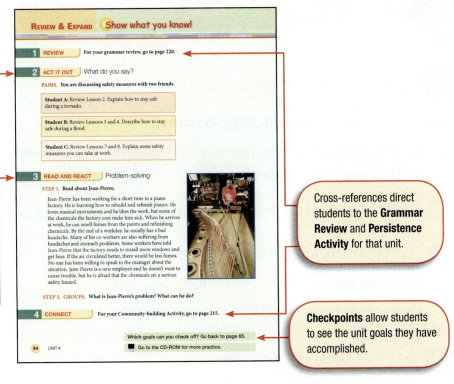

REVIEW & EXPAND Show what you know!

1 REVIEW For your grammar review, go to page 228.

2 ACT IT OUT What do you say?

PAIRS. You are discussing safety measures with two friends.

Student A: Review Lesson 2. Explain how to stay safe during a tornado.

Student B: Review Lessons 3 and 4. Describe how to stay safe during a flood.

Student C: Review Lessons 7 and 8. Explain some safety measures you can take at work.

3 READ AND REACT Problem-solving

STEP 1. Read about Jean-Pierre.

Jean-Pierre has been working for a short time in a piano factory. He is learning how to rebuild and refinish pianos. He loves musical instruments and he likes the work, but some of the chemicals the factory uses make him sick. When he arrives at work, he can smell fumes from the paints and refinishing chemicals. By the end of a workday, he usually has a bad headache. Many of his co-workers are also suffering from headaches and stomach problems. Some workers have told Jean-Pierre that the factory needs to install more windows and get fans. If the air circulated better, there would be less fumes. No one has been willing to speak to the manager about the situation. Jean-Pierre is a new employee and he doesn't want to cause trouble, but he is afraid that the chemicals are a serious safety hazard.

STEP 2. GROUPS. What is Jean-Pierre's problem? What can he do?

4 CONNECT For your Community-building Activity, go to page 215.

Which goals can you check off? Go back to page 65.

■ Go to the CD-ROM for more practice.

84 UNIT 4

Cross-references direct students to the **Grammar Review** and **Persistence Activity** for that unit.

Checkpoints allow students to see the unit goals they have accomplished.

Grammar Review

Grammar Review allows students to check their mastery of the unit grammar.

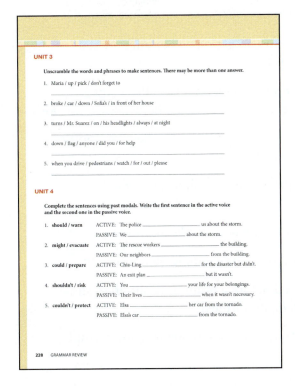

UNIT 3

Unscramble the words and phrases to make sentences. There may be more than one answer.

1. Maria / up / pick / don't forget to

_____

2. broke / car / down / Sofia's / in front of her house

_____

3. turns / Mr. Suarez / on / his headlights / always / at night

_____

4. down / flag / anyone / did you / for help

_____

5. when you drive / pedestrians / watch / for / out / please

_____

UNIT 4

Complete the sentences using past modals. Write the first sentence in the active voice and the second one in the passive voice.

1. **should / warn** ACTIVE: The police _____ us about the storm.
   PASSIVE: We _____ about the storm.

2. **might / evacuate** ACTIVE: The rescue workers _____ the building.
   PASSIVE: Our neighbors _____ from the building.

3. **could / prepare** ACTIVE: Chia-Ling _____ for the disaster but didn't.
   PASSIVE: An exit plan _____ but it wasn't.

4. **shouldn't / risk** ACTIVE: You _____ your life for your belongings.
   PASSIVE: Their lives _____ when it wasn't necessary.

5. **couldn't / protect** ACTIVE: Elsa _____ her car from the tornado.
   PASSIVE: Elsa's car _____ from the tornado.

228 GRAMMAR REVIEW

Persistence Activities

Persistence activities build community in the classroom, help students set personal and language learning goals, and encourage students to develop good study skills and habits.

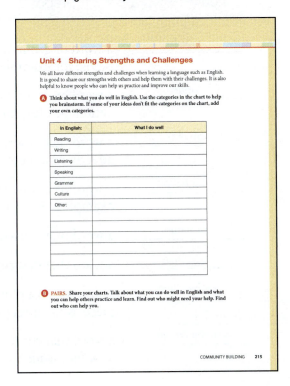

Unit 4 Sharing Strengths and Challenges

We all have different strengths and challenges when learning a language such as English. It is good to share our strengths with others and help them with their challenges. It is also helpful to know people who can help us practice and improve our skills.

A Think about what you do well in English. Use the categories in the chart to help you brainstorm. If some of your ideas don't fit the categories on the chart, add your own categories.

In English:	What I do well
Reading	
Writing	
Listening	
Speaking	
Grammar	
Culture	
Other:	

B PAIRS. Share your charts. Talk about what you can do well in English and what you can help others practice and learn. Find out who might need your help. Find out who can help you.

COMMUNITY BUILDING 215

Getting Started

Welcome to Class

1 LEARN ABOUT YOUR BOOK

A **CLASS.** Turn to page iii. Write the answers to the questions.

1. What information is on this page?
2. How many units are in this book?
3. Which unit is about health?
4. Which two units are about work?

B **CLASS.** Where is the Practice Plus CD-ROM? What kind of practice does it provide?

C **PAIRS.** Where will you find the following? Locate each section. Write the page number.

Grammar Review __226__   Persistence Activities __212__   Glossary __245__

Grammar Reference __223__   Audio Script __232__   Index __248__

2 REVIEW GRAMMAR TERMS

A English grammar has eight parts of speech. Read the definitions. Fill in the blanks with the correct part of speech from the box.

adjective	adverb	conjunction	interjection
noun	preposition	pronoun	verb

_____**verb**_____   a word or group of words that describes an action, experience, or state of being; for example: *work, is feeling, was*

_____**noun**_____   a word or group of words that represents a person, place, thing, quality, action, or idea; for example: *John, teacher, school, book, happiness, study skills*

_____**adverb**_____   a word that describes or adds to the meaning of a verb, adjective, another adverb, or a sentence; for example: *slowly, very*

_____**interjection**_____   a word or phrase that is used to express surprise, shock, or pain; for example, *Ouch! Wow!*

_____**pronoun**_____   a word that is used instead of a noun; for example: *she, us, mine*

_____**adjective**_____   a word that describes a noun or pronoun; for example: *new, easy, our*

_____**preposition**_____   a word or group of words that is used before a noun or pronoun to show place, time, direction; for example, *in, at, through*

_____**conjunction**_____   a word that connects parts of sentences, phrases, or clauses; for example, *and, but, while*

Getting Started

Welcome to Class

Presentation   10 minutes

1 LEARN ABOUT YOUR BOOK

Ⓐ CLASS. Turn to page iii. Write the answers...

- Read Question 1. Instruct students to notice that the page is divided into three sections. Have them scan the page. Ask: *What kind of information is in each section?* Elicit: *The first section ("front matter") has introductory or prefatory information for both the teacher and the student. The middle section consists of the lessons themselves. The last section ("back matter") has extra activities and reference pages.*
- Have students answer the questions and compare them with a partner.
  Answers: 1. The Table of Contents; 2. There are 10 units. 3. Unit 6; 4. Units 2 and 5
- Call on volunteers to say the answers.
- Answer any additional questions students may have about the contents of the book.
- *Optional:* Assign the Unit Tour for homework.

Controlled Practice   20 minutes

Ⓑ CLASS. Where is the Practice Plus CD-ROM?...

- Read the two questions. Invite students to look for the answers.
  Answers: It's in the back of the book, in an envelope. It provides practice activities for Listening, Speaking, Grammar, Reading, Writing, and Life Skills.

Ⓒ PAIRS. Where will you find the following?....

- Have students scan page iii to find the answers. Call on volunteers to say the page numbers aloud.
- Define terms as needed. (For example, *persistence*: the quality of continuing steadily despite problems or difficulties. Persistence activities are designed to encourage students to keep coming to class.)
- Have students turn to the pages and look them over. Ask: *What kinds of activities do you find on each page? In what ways do you think this section will be useful for you?*

2 REVIEW GRAMMAR TERMS

Ⓐ English grammar has eight parts of speech....

- Read the directions. Then read the parts of speech and have students repeat.
- Read the example aloud.
- Pair students. Use one of the following techniques or a technique that you prefer: 1. Two students seated next to each other can form pairs. 2. Students in front turn around and pair up with the students behind them. 3. Random pairing.
- Have students complete the remaining items.
- Call on volunteers to say the answers aloud.
- On the board, write a sentence containing several of the parts of speech. For example: *An old man was sitting alone on a bench in the park.* Have students identify the parts of speech of each word in the sentence.
- *Optional:* Pair students. Challenge them to write a sentence containing all the parts of speech. Give a time limit. Have students write their sentences on the board, and have the class identify the part of speech of each word.

3   LEARN ABOUT THE GLOSSARY

A   Look at the article on the bottom of...

- Define *glossary* if needed (an alphabetical list of terms used in a book and their definitions).
- Have students look at page 16. Then have them use the table of contents and go to the back of the book in order to fill in the missing page numbers.

B   GROUPS. Look at the example below...

- Form groups using one of the following techniques or any other that you prefer: 1. If your class has 25 students or fewer, have them count off by fours or fives. All students with the same number form a group. 2. Form groups consisting of students who are sitting near each other. 3. Form groups consisting of people who speak different languages.
- Have students answer the questions. While students are working, walk around and provide help as needed.
- Call on volunteers to say the answers aloud.

Answers: 1. the part of speech and the meaning 2. A dictionary gives all possible meanings of a word. A glossary gives only the meaning of the word as it is used in the book. 3. noun

Communicative Practice   30 minutes

4   LEARN ABOUT WORD WORK

A   GROUPS. Discuss. Current research on language...

- Elaborate on the phrase *come into contact*. Ask: *What are different ways that someone may encounter a word?* (For example, by listening to people in a line at the supermarket; on the radio or TV; by reading)
- Form groups. If possible, use a different grouping technique than the one you used in Exercise 3B.

- Instruct students to support their answers with examples. Have them share at least one word they have learned recently and explain how they were able to remember it.
- Give a time limit for discussion.
- Bring the whole class back together. Call on volunteers to share their examples.
- *Optional:* Extend the discussion by asking students about techniques they use to help them remember new words.

B   GROUPS. Look at the Word Work activity....

- Have students look at page 35. Explain that a "log" is a record of something, in this case words.
- Read Item 1. If possible, show real examples of different ways that students can keep track of new words, including a vocabulary notebook, index cards, or a computer file.
- Read Item 2. Ask: *What other information would you include?* (For example, phonetic spelling or pronunciation)
- Read Item 3. Ask: *How do you review your new words?* Call on volunteers to answer. Extend by offering suggestions for review. For example, if students are using index cards, encourage them to put new cards in the front or on top and review once a day. Once they feel they know a word, they should move the card to the back or bottom of the pile. They should review all their cards once a week.

3 LEARN ABOUT THE GLOSSARY

A Look at the article on the bottom of page 16. Find the words in bold. The words are in bold because they are in the glossary in the back of the book. Find the glossary. Write the page number it starts on and the one it ends on: ___245___ - ___247___

B GROUPS. Look at the example below of the word *occupation* from the glossary. Compare it to the dictionary entry for the same word from the *Longman Dictionary of American English*. Discuss the questions.

Glossary

occupation n. job or profession

Dictionary

oc·cu·pa·tion /ˌɑkyəˈpeiʃən/ n. **1** [C] *formal* a job or profession [➡ **employment, work**]: *the occupations available to women* **2** [U] the act of entering a place and getting control of it, especially by military force [➡ **occupy**]: *the German occupation of France in the war* **3** [U] *formal* a way of spending your time

1. What information about *occupation* does the glossary provide?
2. Why are there three definitions for *occupation* in the dictionary, but only one definition in the glossary?
3. What does *n.* mean?

4 LEARN ABOUT WORD WORK

A GROUPS. Discuss. Current research on language learning shows that the more times you come into contact with a new word, the more likely you are to remember that word. Do you agree? Is this true for you?

B GROUPS. Look at the Word Work activity on page 35. The directions tell you to write words you want to remember in your notebook. Select the words that interest you. Here are some specific suggestions:

1. Use a separate notebook, a section of your notebook, or a computer file for your vocabulary log.
2. For each word you want to learn, include the following information:
   - new word
   - the place where you saw or heard it
   - the sentence the word was in
   - the definition or translation of the word

Example:

Word	Place I saw or read it	Sentence
environment	Future 5, page 6	I need to have a quiet work environment.

Definition: the situations, people, etc., that influence the way in which people live and work

3. Every week, review the words you want to remember.

5 LEARN ABOUT YOUR CLASSMATES

STEP 1. PAIRS. Introduce yourselves.

STEP 2. PAIRS. Take turns. Interview your partner. Take notes. Answers will vary.

Where did you grow up? _____

What was your hometown like? _____

When did you come to the U.S.? _____

Did you come here alone or with your family? _____

What do you like to do on the weekend? _____

What kinds of food do you like? _____

Do you have any special talents? _____

Have you studied English before? _____

How long have you been a student in this school? _____

Why are you studying English now? _____

Are you taking any other classes? _____

What will you do when you finish this class? _____

Do you work? What do you do? _____

Are you going to change careers in the next five years? _____

STEP 3. CLASS. Introduce your partner to the class. Give your partner's name and say one or two things you learned about him or her.

This is Nidia Alfonso. She's a medical receptionist now. She wants to be an X-ray technician.

6 REVIEW VERB TENSES

GROUPS. Look at the questions in the interview above. Find one example of each of the following verb tenses and write the question on the line. Answers will vary for some items.

Simple present	*What do you like to do on the weekend?*
Simple past	Where did you grow up?
Future	What will you do when you finish this class?
Present perfect	Have you studied English before?
Present continuous	Why are you studying English now?

5 LEARN ABOUT YOUR CLASSMATES

STEP 1. PAIRS. Introduce yourselves.

- Instruct students to say their name and two more facts about themselves, such as their country of origin and how long they've been in the U.S.
- Provide a model by introducing yourself to the class.
- Pair students who are sitting near each other. Alternately, have students stand up and walk around. When you clap your hands or ring a bell, students should stop and introduce themselves to the nearest person. Repeat several times.
- Instruct students to sit with their (last) partner for the next activity.

STEP 2. PAIRS. Take turns. Interview your...

- Explain *take notes*: Students should write key words or short answers only. They shouldn't write complete sentences.
- With a student, demonstrate interviewing and taking notes. Ask two or three of the questions in the list; write the answers on the board.
- Pair students. Give a time limit for the interviews. While students are talking, walk around and provide help as needed.

STEP 3. CLASS. Introduce your partner to...

- Model the activity using information from your interview in Step 2.
- The amount of information that students provide about their partners depends on the size of your class and the amount of time you have. With a small class and plenty of time, students may speak about their partners for up to a minute.
- As a follow-up (and to demonstrate that repetition aids memory, as stated in Exercise 4A), go around the room, point to each student, and have the class repeat the student's name.

6 REVIEW VERB TENSES

GROUPS. Look at the questions in the interview...

- If necessary, explain *verb* and *tense*: Verbs can express an action (such as *walk, eat, write*) or a state (such as *be, become, seem*). *Tense* refers to the various forms of verbs that express different times (for example, past, present, future).
- Form small groups and have students do the exercise. While students are working, walk around and provide help as needed.
- To check answers, make a five-column chart on the board, one column for each tense. Then, for each tense, ask students to state which verbs they wrote.
- As a follow-up, have students make up their own sentences using each tense.

Setting Goals, Pursuing Dreams

Classroom Materials/Extra Practice

CD 1
Tracks 2–8

Workbook
Unit 1

Interactive Practice
Unit 1

Unit Overview

Goals

- See the list of goals on the facing page.

Grammar

- Verbs followed by gerunds and/or infinitives
- Gerunds following prepositions

Listening and Speaking

- Describe personality traits
- *Communication Skill:* Using Examples
- Talk about long-term career goals

Reading

- Read an article about how to find job information
- *Reading Skill:* Highlighting or Underlining Key Information
- Read an article about getting what you want
- *Reading Skill:* Previewing
- Read an article about overcoming an obstacle

Writing

- Write a descriptive essay about your interests, skills, and goals
- *Writing Tip:* Topic sentences

Life Skills

- Talk about job-related interests and abilities

Preview

- Welcome students and have them look at page 5.
- Set the context of the unit by asking questions about setting goals. (For example, *What goals do you have for the immediate future?*) Provide sample answers if needed. (For example, *Our goal here is to improve our English.*)
- Hold up page 5. Ask students how they go about setting goals for themselves. Ask what it means to pursue a dream.
- Say: *Look at the picture. What's happening?* (A man is paragliding—free flying in a foot-launched, recreational aircraft.) *What would your dream job be? What steps would you take to reach that goal?* Ask the Preview questions; offer prompts if necessary. (For example, *Are there subjects in school or sports that you are especially good at? How can identifying those talents help you figure out the right job for you?*) Write responses on the board.
- Say: *In this unit, you'll learn more about career planning. You'll talk about your interests, skills, and goals, and you will learn how to find job information.*

Unit Goals

- Ask students to read the Unit Goals silently.
- Explain unfamiliar vocabulary as needed. (For example: *personality traits*—a person's characteristics.)
- Tell students to circle the goal that is the most important to them.
- Take a poll by reading the goals aloud, with students raising their hand for the goal they circled.
- On the board, write the goal that the greatest number of students circled.
- Say: *As we complete this unit, we will look back at this page and reread the goals. We will check each goal as we complete it.*

Setting Goals, Pursuing Dreams

Preview

What would your dream job be? What steps would you take to reach that goal?

UNIT GOALS

- [ ] Identify and talk about job-related interests and abilities
- [ ] Describe personality traits
- [ ] Discuss how to find job information
- [ ] Talk about abilities and plans
- [ ] Talk about long-term career goals
- [ ] Overcome obstacles to achieving your goals

Life Skills

1   TAKE A SURVEY

A   **CLASS.**   Discuss. What kinds of things do you enjoy doing in your free time? What kinds of things do you enjoy doing at work or in class?

B   Read the statements from a survey. Are they true for you? Check (✓) *yes* or *no*.

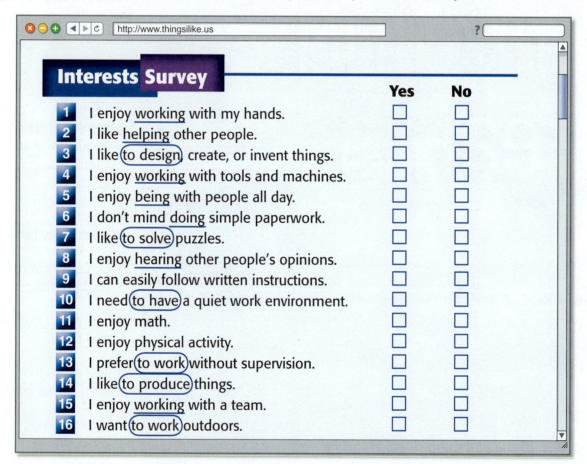

http://www.thingsilike.us

Interests Survey

		Yes	No
1	I enjoy working with my hands.	☐	☐
2	I like helping other people.	☐	☐
3	I like to design, create, or invent things.	☐	☐
4	I enjoy working with tools and machines.	☐	☐
5	I enjoy being with people all day.	☐	☐
6	I don't mind doing simple paperwork.	☐	☐
7	I like to solve puzzles.	☐	☐
8	I enjoy hearing other people's opinions.	☐	☐
9	I can easily follow written instructions.	☐	☐
10	I need to have a quiet work environment.	☐	☐
11	I enjoy math.	☐	☐
12	I enjoy physical activity.	☐	☐
13	I prefer to work without supervision.	☐	☐
14	I like to produce things.	☐	☐
15	I enjoy working with a team.	☐	☐
16	I want to work outdoors.	☐	☐

C   **PAIRS.**   Compare your responses.

2   PRACTICE

A   Read the job descriptions on page 7. Select a job for each person, based on his or her *yes* responses to the Interests Survey.

Ramiro: Questions 1, 4, 9, 12, 14   Job: ___*cabinetmaker*___

Mary: Questions 3, 7, 8, 11, 15   Job: ___graphic designer___

Soon-Young: Questions 2, 5, 6, 12, 13   Job: ___LPN___

Getting Started 5 minutes

1 TAKE A SURVEY

A CLASS. Discuss. What kinds of things do you enjoy...

- Say: *Let's talk about free time. What do you do in your free time?*
- Discuss the question, offering prompts as needed. (*Do you play sports or work out at the gym? Go to parties or movies with your friends? Cook for your family or friends?*)
- Say: *Now, let's talk about work. What kinds of things do you enjoy doing at work?*
- Discuss the question, offering prompts as needed. (*Do you like to meet new people? Use a computer?*)
- Ask: *What do you like about school?*
- Discuss the question, offering prompts as needed. (*Do you like to talk to other people and work in a group? Learn new expressions in English?*)
- Say: *Today we're going to talk about things that you enjoy doing. Then we're going to see how your interests and talents translate into job skills.*

Presentation 10 minutes

B Read the statements from a survey...

- Ask students to read the directions silently.
- Read the survey questions aloud.
- Ask students if there are any words or phrases they don't understand. Clarify unfamiliar terms as needed.
- Ask some vocabulary questions to check students' comprehension. Examples: *What does it mean to do simple paperwork?* (filling out information on forms such as timesheets or inventory lists) *What does it mean to work without supervision?* (starting work on tasks yourself and completing them without a manager guiding or helping you)
- Have students reread the survey items and check *yes* or *no* for each question.
- Walk around the class and help as needed.

C PAIRS. Compare your responses.

- Say: *Now, you're going to find a partner and compare answers.*
- Model the exercise with an above-level student. Have the student ask you: *Do you enjoy working with your hands?* (You answer the question and ask: *How about you?*)
- Repeat for number 2, *I like helping other people.*

Controlled Practice 15 minutes

2 PRACTICE

A Read the job descriptions on page 7....

- Say: *Now we're going to look at how the questions you answered in the survey correspond to jobs.*
- Ask students to read the job descriptions on page 7 silently.
- Ask students if there are any words or phrases they don't understand. Clarify unfamiliar terms as needed. (Examples: *blueprints*—technical drawings that show how to construct something; *compassionate*—the quality of understanding how others feel and acting sympathetically toward them; *work under pressure*—the ability to complete projects that are demanding because of lack of time or difficult personalities involved)
- Turn back to the survey. Say: *Now, you're going to select a job for three people based on their survey answers. Let's start with Ramiro.*
- Have a student read aloud the questions that Ramiro answered with *yes* (items 1, 4, 9, 12, and 14).
- Ask: *Why would the cabinetmaker job be good for Ramiro?* (Possible answers: He can read instructions, work with tools and machines, and likes to produce things.)
- Have students pick jobs for Mary and Soon-Young.
- Ask the class which jobs they chose and why.

Answers will vary but may include: Mary would make a good graphic designer because she likes to design and create things, solve puzzles, and work on a team; Soon-Young would be a good LPN because she likes helping people, enjoys being physically active, and doesn't mind paperwork.

Talk about job-related interests and abilities

Presentation   5 minutes

B PAIRS. Which of the jobs above...

- Say: *Now, you're going to turn to the person next to you and discuss which job you would enjoy the most—and why.*
- Give students a time limit for this activity in advance.
- Circulate as students talk, helping as necessary.

Language Note

Remind students to use the modal *would* to talk about a hypothetical situation—that is, one that is not real at this time. To guide students, write a prompt on the board. (*I would like the _____ job because I enjoy _____.*)

Controlled Practice   10 minutes

C GROUPS. Discuss. Look at the types of skills...

- Say: *When we talk about job skills, we talk about many different types of skills—for example, computer or language skills. Let's look at some other job skills.*
- Ask students to read the skills and examples silently. Check students' understanding by going over the skills.
- Place students in small groups. Say: *You're going to discuss which skills are the most important for each of the three jobs.* Model the activity by reading the sample conversation at the end of the exercise.
- Walk around the room and monitor conversations.
- Call on groups to share the skills that they thought were important for each job—and why.

Possible answers: LPN—Communication and interpersonal skills; nurses need to communicate with families, record information, and be patient.
Graphic designer—Problem-solving and lifelong learning skills; designers need to find solutions to customers' needs, solve problems, and use technology in new ways.

Community Building

Have students count off 1-2-3-4 and regroup accordingly. (Say: *All the 2s, go to the table over there.*) Other ways to create groups are to have students form small groups according to

- which of the four seasons is their favorite
- what time they woke up in the morning
- what kind of pet they'd like to have

You may want to use a more calculated grouping strategy for certain types of activities. You may want to form groups so that a variety of native languages are represented in each one—compelling students to communicate in English. When completing a particularly challenging writing or grammar task, you may want to make sure an above-level student is in each group.

Communicative Practice   15 minutes

D GROUPS. Discuss the questions.

- Read the discussion questions aloud and tell students that they will talk to their group members about the job they would like to have.
- Walk around and monitor conversations, offering prompts for clarification or elaboration as needed. (For example, *How will lifelong learning skills help you as a small business owner?*)
- Have a volunteer from each group tell the class which jobs the group members chose and why.

Progress Check

Can you . . . talk about job-related interests and abilities?

- Say: *We have discussed your job-related interests and abilities. Can you do this? If so, check the box.*

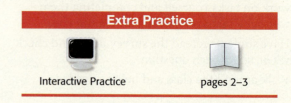

Extra Practice

Interactive Practice   pages 2–3

Cabinetmaker	**LPN (Licensed Practitioner Nurse)**	**Graphic Designer**
Responsibilities: Read blueprints and instructions to make and install cabinets. Use hand tools, power tools, and other machines. Measure cabinet parts. Instruct lower-level personnel. **Qualifications:** High school diploma or GED. Three years' experience.	**Job description:** Assist nurses and physicians with patients' personal care, daily activities, and emotional support. Communicate with patients' families. Complete forms, reports, records. Should be compassionate and patient. **Requirements:** LPN license and minimum 6 months' experience. Must have ability to set priorities, make judgments, and work independently without supervision.	**Responsibilities:** Creative, artistic person able to come up with design proposals for print advertisements with team of designers. Present ideas to customers and be able to revise designs to fit customer needs. Must be able to work under pressure and meet deadlines. **Requirements:** Bachelor's or associate degree in related field. Experience with design software, interest in technology, strong communication and problem-solving skills.

B PAIRS. **Which of the jobs above would you enjoy the most? Why?**

C GROUPS. **Discuss. Look at the types of skills and the examples. Which skills are most important for each job listed in Exercise A? Why?**

Skills	Examples
Communication skills	Write messages, understand spoken and written instructions, listen well, speak clearly
Interpersonal skills	Get along with others; cooperate with, guide, or teach others; resolve conflicts; negotiate
Problem-solving skills	Plan (for example, budget, schedule), solve technical or practical problems, use math
Lifelong learning skills	Take responsibility for learning new skills, use communication and information technology

A: *Which types of skills are important for the cabinetmaker?*
B: *Interpersonal skills are important because the cabinetmaker has to teach others.*
C: *I think problem-solving skills are also important because the cabinetmaker needs to measure and fix things that aren't working correctly.*

D GROUPS. **Discuss the questions.**

1. If you could have any job you wanted, what would it be?
2. How is this job a good match for your interests?
3. How will good communication, interpersonal, problem-solving, and lifelong learning skills help you in this job?

Can you...talk about job-related interests and abilities? ☐

Grammar

Verbs Followed by Gerunds and/or Infinitives

Verb + Gerund	Verb + Infinitive
I **enjoy working** with my hands.	I **need to have** a quiet work environment.
I **don't mind doing** simple paperwork.	I **want to work** outdoors.
Verb + Gerund or Infinitive	
I **like solving** puzzles.	I **like to solve** puzzles.
I **prefer working** without supervision.	I **prefer to work** without supervision.

Grammar Watch

- A gerund is the *-ing* form of a verb and is used as a noun.
- An infinitive is *to* + the base form of a verb.
- Some verbs are followed only by a gerund or only by an infinitive.
- Some verbs are followed by either a gerund or an infinitive.

For a list of verbs followed only by a gerund, only by an infinitive, or by either, see page 223.

1 PRACTICE

A Look at the Interests Survey on page 6. Underline the gerunds and circle the infinitives.

B Complete the sentences with a gerund or an infinitive. Some sentences have two correct answers. Use the list on page 223 to help you.

1. I enjoy ____listening____ to music while I work.
   (listen)

2. I plan ___to continue___ learning about new technology.
   (continue)

3. Angela doesn't like ___to write/writing___ in her second language because it's so difficult.
   (write)

4. Phuong plans ___to take___ some classes at the community college.
   (take)

5. Do you mind ___working___ with sick people?
   (work)

6. I don't have good communication skills, so I hate ___to negotiate/negotiating___.
   (negotiate)

7. Ibrahim has good problem-solving skills, so he agreed ___to create___ a schedule.
   (create)

8. I don't mind ___receiving___ criticism from my supervisor.
   (receive)

Getting Started   5 minutes

- Say: *Today we're going to talk more about our job-related wants, needs, and capabilities. To do so, we'll practice two grammatical structures: verbs followed by gerunds and verbs followed by infinitives.*
- Ask students to look at the survey on page 6 and compare numbers 2 and 3.
- Point out that *like* is sometimes followed by an infinitive and sometimes by a gerund. Say: *We will study verbs that are always followed by a gerund, verbs that are always followed by an infinitive, and verbs that can be followed by either.*

Presentation   10 minutes

Verbs Followed by Gerunds and/or Infinitives

- Copy the grammar chart onto the board.
- To help students understand the difference between infinitives and gerunds, write several examples on the board in random order (*to eat/working/to learn/talking/to produce*) and ask students to say which is which.
- Have students read the Grammar Watch silently.
- Point to the left side of the grammar chart and read the two examples aloud. Ask students which verbs are used as gerunds (*working, doing*) and which verbs they follow (*enjoy, mind*).
- Point to the right side of the grammar chart and read the two examples aloud. Ask students which verbs are used as infinitives (*have, work*) and which verbs they follow (*need, want*).
- Point to the second row of the grammar chart (Verb + Gerund or Infinitive). Read the examples aloud.

Teaching Tip

- Some students may need additional support to understand the concept of a gerund. Say: *Sometimes verbs can be used as nouns. They function as subjects or objects.*
- Write on the board: *He is swimming right now.* Ask: *Is* swimming *a noun or a verb in this sentence?* (A verb; combined with *is*, it tells of an action taking place right now.)
- Write, *I like swimming.* Ask: *Is* swimming *a noun or a verb in this sentence?* (A noun; it is the object of the sentence and talks about "a thing"—not an action.)

Controlled Practice   30 minutes

1   PRACTICE

Ⓐ Look at the Interests Survey on page 6....

- Ask students to read the directions silently. Write sentence 1 on the board: *I enjoy working with my hands.* Ask: *Is there a gerund or infinitive in this sentence?* (a gerund) Underline *working*.
- Write sentence 3 on the board: *I like to design, create, or invent things.* Ask: *Are there gerunds or infinitives in this sentence?* (infinitives) Circle *design*, *create*, and *invent*.
- Have students complete the exercise.
- Ask: *In the survey, which verbs are used with gerunds only?* Write *enjoy* and *mind* on the board. Have a student read aloud the sentences with these verbs.
- Ask: *Which are used with infinitives only?* Write *need* and *want* on the board. Have a student read aloud the sentences with these verbs.
- Ask: *Which are used with both?* Write *like* on the board. Elicit examples of *like* used as a gerund (*I like helping other people.*) and as an infinitive (*I like to solve puzzles.*).

▬ MULTILEVEL INSTRUCTION for 1A

Pre-level Sit with students in a group and offer prompts to help them. (*Let's look for verbs that end with* -ing. *Does the verb come after* to?)

Above-level After they finish the exercise, students can write additional sentences with the verbs they circled and underlined.

Ⓑ Complete the sentences with a gerund...

- Read the directions aloud, noting that some sentences may take a gerund **or** an infinitive.
- Have students complete the exercise.
- Have students turn to page 223 of the Grammar Reference and read the list of verbs followed by a gerund, an infinitive, or both.
- Ask: *Which verbs in this exercise can take either the gerund **or** the infinitive?* (like, hate)

2 PRACTICE

Complete the conversation with the gerund...

- Read the directions, noting that some sentences may take a gerund **or** infinitive.
- Have students complete the exercise. Walk around and help students as they work, referring them to the lists of verbs on page 223.
- Call on students to read sentences and say answers.
- Ask: *Which verbs in this exercise can take either the gerund **or** the infinitive?* (do, use, make)

Teaching Tip

As students complete the previous exercise, tell them to cross out verbs from the box as they use them in sentences. Point out that this technique is very useful when taking tests because it saves time.

■ Expansion: Speaking Practice for 2.

- Write on the board: *like, enjoy, want, prefer, don't mind, need.*
- Tell students that they'll play a game to practice using gerunds and infinitives.
- Divide the class into two teams, A and B.
- Write a T-chart on the board with the teams' names.
- A member of Team A starts a sentence with a verb on the board (*I like . . .*), and a member from Team B has to complete the sentence in a way that is true for him/her. (*I like to go to the park on Saturdays.*)
- If it is a complex sentence (*I like to talk to my friends after class, so I never go home right away.*), it's worth 2 points. If it is a simple sentence (*I like to study English.*), it's worth 1 point.
- Teams take turns giving sentence prompts. Each student has only one turn to complete a sentence.
- Write points for each team on the T-chart.
- At the end, the team with more points wins.

Community Building

- Tell students that talking about one another's work is a good way to start a conversation.
- Have students practice this by walking around and talking to as many different classmates as possible in a short period of time.
    Example:
    A: *So, what do you do?*
    B: *I'm a landscaper.*
    A: *How do you like your job?*
    B: *I like staying outdoors, so this is perfect for me. What about you? What do you do?*

Communicative Practice   15 minutes

🟡 Show what you know!

PAIRS. Check (✓) *Like, Don't mind,* **or...**

- Ask a confident, above-level student to read the directions and sample prompts aloud.
- Ask: *Does* like *take an infinitive or a gerund?* (Explain that it can take either.) Ask: *What about* don't mind?
- Have students form pairs and complete the exercise. Walk around and monitor conversations.
- *Optional:* Have student volunteers present their partner to the class. (*This is Genet. She likes using computers and solving problems. She doesn't mind . . .*)

Progress Check

Can you . . . identify job-related interests and abilities?

- Say: *We have practiced identifying your job-related interests and abilities. Can you do this? If so, check the box.*

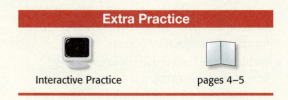

Extra Practice
Interactive Practice   pages 4–5

Complete the conversation with the gerund or infinitive form of the words in the box. There may be more than one correct answer.

be	find	live	meet	use
do	have	make	move	work

A: I've decided I want ___to be___ a dental technician.
1.

B: Really? What does a dental technician do?

A: Basically, a dental technician makes false teeth.

B: And you really think you'd like ___to do/doing___ that?
2.

A: Absolutely. I enjoy ___working___ with my hands. And I like ___to use/using___ tools
3. **4.**
and ___to make/making___ things.
5.

B: Do you need ___to have___ a degree or certification?
6.

A: I'm not sure. I need ___to meet___ with our career counselor. I have an appointment
7.
next week. I'll find out then. What about you? Any plans?

B: Well, I'm considering ___moving___ to Fairbanks. My only brother lives there. I want
8.
___to be/to live___ near my family. But I'll need ___to find___ work before I move.
9. **10.**

Show what you know!   Identify job-related interests and abilities

PAIRS. Check (✓) *Like, Don't mind,* or *Don't like* in the chart. Then talk about each activity.

A: *I like using computers because it's easy for me. I use my computer every day at home. How about you?*
B: *Actually, I don't mind using computers, but it's difficult for me. I want to improve my skills, so I go to the computer lab every day.*

Activity	Like	Don't mind	Don't like
Use computers			
Teach others			
Solve problems			
Talk on the phone			
Work with tools and machines			

Can you... identify job-related interests and abilities? ☐

Listening and Speaking

1 BEFORE YOU LISTEN

A **CLASS.** When you look for a job, you need to consider your interests and abilities. What else do you need to think about?

B **PAIRS.** Match the adjectives that describe personality traits with the correct definitions.

_c_	1. cooperative	a. does not lie, cheat, or steal; sincere
_a_	2. honest	b. outgoing and friendly
_b_	3. extroverted	c. willing to work with others; helpful
_e_	4. intuitive	d. usually positive about things
_d_	5. optimistic	e. able to make judgments and decisions based on feelings rather than facts

C **GROUPS.** Compare your answers. Discuss. What kind of person do you think most employers want to hire? Explain.

2 LISTEN

A **PAIRS.** Look at the picture of Ruben talking to his career counselor. Predict: What questions will the counselor ask? Take notes.

B CD1 T2 Listen. Were your predictions correct?

C CD1 T2 Listen again. Answer the questions.

1. What job does Ruben have now?

   He's a waiter at a hotel restaurant.

2. What job does he think he's interested in?

   Being a chef.

3. Why is he considering this job?

   He wants more money.

4. What are some things he is good at?

   He's good at math, working with coworkers, and dealing with customers.

Lesson 3   Describe personality traits

Getting Started   5 minutes

Say: *Now that you've identified some of your skills and interests, it is also important to know how to talk about them.*

Culture Connection

Tell students that in the U.S., people are expected to be able to talk about skills, interests, and goals. Ask students to compare their own countries and the U.S. Say: *In the United States, one of the first things a person might ask someone at a party is,* What do you do? *or* Where do you work? *Do people behave in the same way in your culture? When is it appropriate to talk about work?*

Presentation   15 minutes

1   BEFORE YOU LISTEN

Ⓐ CLASS. **When you look for a job...**

* Ask students to read the questions silently.
* Repeat the question and solicit responses. Say: *When you look for a job, what* are (emphasize) *the things you need to think about?* If needed, offer examples such as transportation, location, working hours, pay, benefits, childcare issues.
* Make a list of student responses on the board.

Ⓑ PAIRS. **Match the adjectives...**

* Ask students to read the directions silently. Ask: *What is a personality trait? Can you give some examples?* Offer examples as needed, such as conscientious, outspoken, quiet, and talkative. (For example, *A conscientious person is careful and responsible—careful and responsible are two more traits.*)
* Mention that there are both positive and negative personality traits and that, of course, the traits people emphasize when they are looking for jobs are the positive traits.
* Tell the pairs to match the answers they know first and then to make their best guesses on other items.

Ⓒ GROUPS. **Compare your answers...**

* Set up groups.
* Ask students to read and follow the directions.
* Say: *When you talk with your group, discuss other personality traits you think are important.*
* Say: *When you discuss this, it might help to think about what kind of person you want to work with.*

Controlled Practice   15 minutes

2   LISTEN

Ⓐ PAIRS. **Look at the picture of Ruben...**

* Ask students to read the directions silently.
* Tell students to look at the picture of Ruben and his career counselor.
* Ask: *What does a career counselor do?* Offer an example if needed: *A career counselor gives advice to people about jobs that might be good for them.*
* Ask: *What questions do you think the counselor will ask Ruben?*
* Write short versions of student responses on board (such as *interests? job experience? skills?*).

Ⓑ 　 **Listen. Were your predictions correct?**

* Ask students to read the directions; make sure they understand what to write.
* Play CD 1, Track 2.
* Say: *Were your predictions correct? What questions did the counselor ask Ruben?* (Refer back to the list on the board.) *Were you surprised by any of the questions? Which ones?*

Ⓒ 　 **Listen again. Answer the questions.**

* Play Track 2 again.
* Tell students to answer the questions.
* Ask students to share answers with the class. If there are any discrepancies in the answers, let students discuss them to come up with a final answer.

Controlled Practice — 10 minutes

3 PRACTICE

A In the next part of the conversation...

- Ask students to read the directions silently.
- Check to make sure students know they are to complete the descriptions for Ruben, not themselves.
- Write on the board: *I'm (a/an) _____.* Ask: *Can someone explain why after the* I'm *in the phrase on the board, there is a choice of either* a *or* an?
- Say: *In English, you can use an indefinite article—a or an—before a description. You need to use* a *before a word that begins with a consonant (or an* h *that isn't pronounced) and* an *before a word that begins with a vowel sound. So you say,* a *cooperative person but* an *intuitive person or* an *honest man.*
- Explain that they will have to add both types of words (beginning with a vowel or consonant) and that they will have to choose *a/an* according to the word they add in each case.

B **Listen and check your answers.**

- Play CD 1, Track 3.
- Say: *Were there any surprises in the listening?* If there were, clarify misunderstandings.
- Ask for volunteers to give examples or definitions for each of the five adjectives.

Networking

- Say: *The best way to start to feel comfortable speaking and understanding spoken English is to use it outside of class. That's where you can start to feel more comfortable with the many ways that Americans speak English.*
- With students, brainstorm a list of places and situations where students can use English outside of class. (For example: at work, on the bus, at the store, when volunteering, at children's school and sports functions) Keep the list to refer to throughout the quarter or session.
- Ask students to set individual short-term goals for learning English outside of class. (For example: reading a newspaper article in English and bringing it to class to explain what it is about; watching or listening to the news in English as least once a week and coming to class prepared to report on something they heard)

Communicative Practice — 15 minutes

4 MAKE IT PERSONAL

STEP 1. Use the personality traits web...

- Have students fill in the personality traits web with adjectives and examples that describe themselves.

STEP 2. Use your personality traits web...

- Set up groups and ask students to read the directions and examples silently.
- Model the activity with two students who are confident and comfortable about being asked. Use real information about yourself to encourage students to do the same.
- Say: *Talking together is one of the most important things we do in class; we do this so that you can learn to speak English more naturally. Please ask questions and answer questions respectfully. Share as much as you feel comfortable sharing.*

Expansion: Writing Practice

- Ask students to write several sentences about themselves—similar to the sentences about Ruben in Exercise 3A. (For example, *I'm a cooperative person. For example, I always help my roommate to make dinner and wash the dishes.*)

Communication Skill: Using Examples

- Direct students to the Communication Skill box.
- Ask a student to read the text aloud.
- Say: *Giving examples helps you explain or show what you mean. For example, when I say* I talk to everyone I sit next to on the bus *this helps to explain that I'm extroverted.*
- Walk around the room listening to the conversations and joining in, especially with groups who may be slow to interact.

Extra Practice

Interactive Practice

3 PRACTICE

A In the next part of the conversation, Ruben uses the adjectives from Exercise 1B to describe himself. Before you listen, complete the descriptions with the correct adjective.

1. I'm (a/**an**) _____ *honest* _____ person. For example, sometimes customers leave things in the restaurant—like purses or wallets or cell phones. I always try to find the owner.

2. I'm (**a**/an) _____ cooperative _____ person. If another waiter is busy and I'm not, I pour water and coffee for his customers.

3. I'm (a/an) _____ an extroverted/a friendly _____ person. I'm always friendly with new staff. I try to teach them everything they need to know.

4. I'm (a/**an**) _____ optimistic _____ person. I don't know what career I want, but I believe it's waiting for me. And I believe I'll find it.

5. I'm (a/**an**) _____ intuitive _____ person. When I find the job that's right for me, I'll just know.

CD1 T3

B 💿 Listen and check your answers.

4 MAKE IT PERSONAL

STEP 1. Use the personality traits web to describe the kind of person you are. Fill in adjectives and examples.

STEP 2. GROUPS. Use your personality traits web and the adjectives in Exercise 1B to ask and answer questions about the kind of person you are. Be sure to give examples to support your answers.

A: *What kind of person are you? Are you extroverted?*
B: *I think so. I like being with other people and I make new friends easily.*
C: *No. I'm pretty shy. I'm nervous when I meet people, and I like to spend time alone.*

> **Communication Skill:**
> Using Examples
>
> Using examples when you speak can help you get your meaning across to the listener. When you listen, examples can help you understand a speaker's main points.

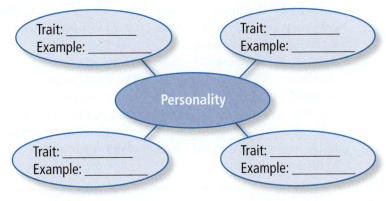

Trait: _____
Example: _____

Trait: _____
Example: _____

Personality

Trait: _____
Example: _____

Trait: _____
Example: _____

Reading

1 BEFORE YOU READ

CLASS. What jobs would you like to know more about? What are some ways that you could find information about them?

The U.S. Department of Labor is a federal organization that publishes a resource called the *Occupational Outlook Handbook (OOH)*. This is available online and describes hundreds of jobs and gives the *outlook*, or *prediction*, about the future for those jobs. It provides information about whether an occupation will grow or become less important in the future (*projections*). It also gives information on salaries and job requirements.

2 READ

CD1 T4

Ali Sheronick is a career counselor. Listen to and read his career advice newsletter.

Ali Sheronick, Career Advisor

Sheronick's Career Advice

Some people decide on the job they want at a young age. I would never **discourage** people from following their dreams. But millions of people don't really know what they want to do. If you are in this **category**, my advice is to find out what **occupations** are going to be **in demand**—and then learn which ones might be good matches for your abilities and interests.

The U.S. Department of Labor website is a great place to find information about jobs. On the homepage, look under *Top 20 Items*. If you click on *Occupational Outlook Handbook*, you can search for a specific occupation, such as "nurse." You will see information about training and education requirements, how much the job pays, what workers do, **working conditions**, and the demand for the job in the next few years. This information is available for hundreds of jobs! Back on the homepage, look under "agencies" and then *Bureau of Labor* **Statistics** *(BLS)* to see information on jobs that are expected to grow the most in the near future. The *Occupational Outlook Handbook* is also available in most public libraries.

To find out about jobs that match your abilities and interests, talk with a career counselor. A counselor can probably help by arranging personality or **aptitude tests** to match you to specific jobs. A counselor may also help you get informational interviews. These are not job interviews. They simply give you a chance to talk with someone who has the job you are interested in or with someone who supervises people with such jobs. These interviews are a great way to learn about working conditions and job duties. Many informational interviews are done by phone, but in some cases you can actually go to the workplace.

Always remember to prepare for any phone interviews or meetings by thinking of questions to ask. And always remember to send a thank-you note to anyone who meets or talks with you. Good luck!

Getting Started   10 minutes

- Say: *So far, we've been talking about our interests, skills, and personality traits. Now the next step is to find information about jobs that will fit well with those interests, skills, and personality traits.*

1 BEFORE YOU READ

A CLASS. **What jobs would you like...**

- Have students read the directions and respond to the two questions. Either jot the answers on the board yourself or ask a student to do so. Save these for later reference in the unit.
- Allow enough time for this activity so that your more reticent students have an opportunity to respond.
- Ask students to silently read the note about the Department of Labor. Go over the note and identify any vocabulary issues. Clarify vocabulary as needed.
- You may want to give students more information about the U.S. Department of Labor. For example, it is one of the 15 cabinet-level divisions of the executive branch that come under the jurisdiction of the president.

Teaching Tip

Always follow up on information you ask students to share so that they continue to do so. Using information they give (such as what jobs they are interested in) can also help you tailor the class to students' needs.

Expansion: Reading Practice for 1

- If the Internet is available, show the handbook online (at www.bls.gov/OCO/) or make transparencies of several copied pages.
- Set up pairs at computers or with a page from the *OCO*. Ask students to review the material and develop a short list of information about a particular job to share with the class.
- Ask students whether they find it easier or harder to read texts online than on paper. Encourage them to practice reading texts online because they will need to be able to read English in many formats.

Presentation   15 minutes

2 READ

Ali Sheronick is a career counselor....

- Ask students to read the directions silently.
- Say: *The writer of this newsletter is a career counselor. Will someone explain what a career counselor does?* Accept any student responses, giving more information as needed (such as that there are many types of counselors—in schools, mental health, and the workplace).
- Say: *As you read, pay particular attention to the advice Ali Sheronick gives.*
- Point out that the words and phrases in boldface (*discourage, category, occupations, in demand, working conditions, statistics, aptitude tests*) are in the glossary on page 245. Encourage students to read the entire article first, before going to the glossary.
- Say: *Listen as you read the article.*
- Play CD 1, Track 4. Students listen and read along.
- Walk around the room; observe whether any students seem to have difficulty reading this passage or keeping the listening and the reading in sync.

Teaching Tip

- Doing timed readings after students have read and listened to each text, can help them improve their reading fluency.
- Set up pairs. Have students take turns reading a paragraph from the reading for 1 minute.
- Ask students to count and record the total number of words they've read. Then have them practice saying difficult words.
- Ask students to read the paragraph three more times and record their speeds.
- Have students record their progress on a chart.

Expansion: Vocabulary Practice for 2

- Divide the class into small groups.
- Ask students to make a list of the boldfaced words in the reading and to discuss the meaning of each. Encourage students to guess the meaning if they are not sure.
- Tell students to look up the words in the glossary on page 245 and to compare the definitions there with what they wrote.

Discuss how to find job information

Controlled Practice — 15 minutes

Reading Skill: **Highlighting or Underlining Key Information**

- Refer students to the Reading Skill box.
- Ask: *How many of you underline or highlight when you read a text? Do you find this useful? Why or why not?*
- Say: *Let's go back to the newsletter on career advice. Which words or phrases would you highlight or underline in the first paragraph?* Accept all answers, but remind students that it makes no sense to underline/highlight too much. Good candidates for underlining/highlighting could be "millions of people don't really know what they want to do" and "occupations . . . in demand."
- Say: *Here's a word of caution: Of course, you shouldn't underline in library, school-owned, or borrowed books. In those cases, you can write short sticky notes with the page number on each note.*

3 CHECK YOUR UNDERSTANDING

A **PAIRS. Read the newsletter again. Find...**

- Set up pairs.
- Tell students to highlight or underline the important information in the second paragraph. Ask for volunteers to share what they've underlined/highlighted. Repeat the process with the third paragraph.
- Students should not have trouble answering these questions, so don't come back together as a whole group to go over the answers. Instead, ask only: *Any questions?*

Answers:
- the U.S. Department of Labor website
- *Top 20 Items, Occupational Outlook Handbook, agencies, Bureau of Labor Statistics*
- aptitude tests, informational interviews

B **Write the answers...**

- Tell students to write the answers to the three questions in their notebooks. In the whole group, ask students to share their answers.

4 WORD WORK

GROUPS. Choose three words...

- Ask students to read the directions silently.
- Set up groups.
- Say: *Remember that when you write in your vocabulary logs, you can always write more than three words or phrases. You can also use the vocabulary log for words you read or hear outside of class.*

Communicative Practice — 20 minutes

Show what you know!

GROUPS. Discuss the questions.

- Ask for volunteers—each to read one of the questions aloud.
- Set up groups of five—one student for each question. Model the activity with four students.
- Say: *I will ask the first question and the rest of the group will take turns answering.* Ask a question and have students respond. Say: *[Student name] will ask us the second question. [Another student] will ask the third question* (and so on; this should be obvious after the first example or two).
- Encourage students to go deeper into the topic or to compare how people find job information in different countries.
- Come back together as a whole group to make a class list of what jobs the class is interested in.
- Write the list on the board, an overhead, or a flipchart to refer to in later lessons.

Progress Check

Can you . . . discuss how to find job information?

- Say: *We have practiced discussing how to find job information. Now look at the question at the bottom of the page. Can you talk about finding job information? If so, check the box.*

Extra Practice

Interactive Practice   pages 6–7

CHECK YOUR UNDERSTANDING

A **PAIRS.** **Read the newsletter again. Find the information below and highlight or underline it in the newsletter. Then check your answers with a partner.**

- the website the writer refers you to
- key words you can use when you look for information on the website
- two things a career counselor might be able to help you with

> **Reading Skill:**
> Highlighting or Underlining Key Information
>
> As you read, highlight or underline main points or information that is especially useful for you. Generally, you should not highlight more than 10 percent of a text.

B **Write the answers to the questions.**

1. Where can you find the *Occupational Outlook Handbook*?

   on the U.S. Department of Labor website or in the public library

2. What information does the *Occupational Outlook Handbook* give about specific jobs?
   training and education requirements, how much the job pays, what workers do, working conditions, and demand for the job in the next few years

3. Where can you look to find out which jobs are expected to grow in the future?

   in the *Occupational Outlook Handbook* under "Bureau of Labor Statistics (BLS)"

4 **WORD WORK**

📝 **GROUPS.** **Choose three words or phrases in the newsletter that you would like to remember. Discuss the words and their meanings. Then record the words and information about them in your vocabulary log.**

Show what you know! Discuss how to find job information

GROUPS. **Discuss the questions.**

1. What are some jobs you think will be in demand over the next ten years?
2. Why do you think they will be in demand?
3. Are you interested in any of them? If yes, which ones?
4. What jobs would you like to read about in the *Occupational Outlook Handbook*?
5. What information would you want to know about these jobs?

Can you ... discuss how to find job information? ☐

Grammar

Gerunds Following Prepositions

A counselor can help **by arranging** personality or aptitude tests.

Prepare **by thinking** of questions to ask.

Grammar Watch

- A gerund is the only form of a verb that can follow a preposition.
- Sample prepositions are *about, at, by, for, in,* and *of.*

1 PRACTICE

A Read the career advice article on page 12 again. Find two more examples of prepositions followed by gerunds and underline them.

B Complete the paragraphs about Andrea with the correct prepositions below and the gerund form of the verbs. Some prepositions may be used more than once.

> about   at   for   in

ONE-STOP
CAREER CENTER

Andrea is looking for a job. She met with a counselor at the One-Stop Career Center in her county and took a series of aptitude tests to find out what skills she is strong or weak in.

Andrea's tests showed that she is good ___at solving___ problems.
 (solve)
She's great at math. Andrea is good ___at working___ with people. She's interested
 (work)
___in learning___ about new technology. Surprisingly, she did not do well in
 (learn)
communication skills, but this may simply be because she needs improvement
___in writing___.
 (write)
Andrea likes variety, and she likes to be free to move around. She wouldn't be
interested ___in sitting___ at a desk all day.
 (sit)
After Andrea got her test results, she had some informational interviews. After each
interview, she wrote notes thanking the interviewers ___for talking___ with her. Now
 (talk)
Andrea is thinking ___about being___ an engineer.
 (be)

Getting Started   5 minutes

- Say: *In the last lesson, we talked about finding job information. What are some ways to do this?* (*OOH, career counselor*)
- Say: *Today we're going to focus on the next step in the job search process—talking about our abilities and plans. To do so, we'll practice the grammatical structure of gerunds that follow prepositions.*

Teaching Tip

- For students who need to review the concept of prepositions, ask: *What is a preposition?* (a small word that can describe location or time)
- Elicit prepositions from students and note them on the board (*in, on, at, by, from, about*).
- Explain that prepositions can also be used with nouns or verbs to provide more information. (*She's good at sports; at* introduces a noun that tells you more details about the student's abilities.)

Presentation   15 minutes

Gerunds Following Prepositions

- Copy the grammar chart onto the board.
- Ask: *Who remembers what a gerund is?* (A verb used as a noun. Gerunds end in *-ing.*) *What are some verbs that take gerunds?* (*like, enjoy, mind*)
- Say: *We know that we can use a gerund after a verb; we can also use it after a preposition.*
- Ask two confident, above-level students to read each point of the Grammar Watch note aloud.
- Write on the board: *I'm good at cooking/swimming.* Ask students to say something they are good at.
- Write on the board: *I'm bad at driving/fixing things.* Ask students to say something they are bad at.

Controlled Practice   15 minutes

 PRACTICE

Ⓐ **Read the career advice article on page 12...**

- Ask students to read the directions. Then have them reread page 12 and complete the exercise.

- Help students, offering prompts as needed. (*Can you find a verb that ends in -ing? Is it used as a noun?*)
- Call on students to say the answers.
- Note: If any students ask, tell them that *working conditions* is not an example of a gerund; *working* in *working conditions* is a participial adjective.

Ⓑ **Complete the paragraphs about Andrea...**

- Ask students to read the directions and the first paragraph of the exercise silently.
- Read the first sentence of the second paragraph aloud. Tell students that when we talk about the way somebody does something, we say *good at/not very good at* plus the gerund.
- Have students complete the exercise and say answers.

Language Note

Clarify for students that when we want to show that someone is considering an idea or future plan, we can say *thinking about* or *thinking of* (*Andrea is thinking about/Andrea is thinking of being an engineer* means that Andrea may do this in the future). However, we can also use *thinking about* in the present continuous to describe what someone has in his/her mind at a particular moment. (*You look worried. What are you thinking about?*)

Multilevel Instruction for 1B

Pre-level Give students a copy of the chart of words below that take prepositions before a gerund. Have students refer to it as they complete the exercise. Tell them to add more words to the chart throughout the lesson.

Above-level Give students a copy of the chart with only the preposition headings. Have students fill in the blank chart as they complete the exercise and add any more words they know that take the four prepositions before the gerund.

At	In	For	About
Good at	Interested in	Thank ___ for	Think about
	Improvement in		

Lesson 5 Talk about abilities and plans

Controlled Practice — 15 minutes

2 PRACTICE

Read about what five people plan...

- Ask students to read the characters' future plans.
- Read the example in item 1 aloud. Explain that we can use the preposition *by* + a gerund to show how someone will execute a future plan.
- Walk around and offer prompts as needed. (*How can I learn Spanish? By getting a tutor.*)

Possible answers: 2. Todd is going to improve his image at work by wearing better clothes. 3. Khenan is going to learn Spanish by getting a tutor. 4. Ilya is going to learn more about working as a physician's assistant by going on an informational interview. 5. Mei-Feng is going to find out more about employment resources by meeting with the librarian at the public library.

Expansion: Writing Practice for 2

- Explain that on or around January 1 each year, it is customary for people to make New Year's resolutions—things they will change or improve in the new year.
- Say: *Now you will make your own New Year's resolutions.*
- Write on the board: *I want to improve _____ by _____. I plan to learn _____ by _____.*
- Say a few examples: *In the New Year, I want to improve my health by exercising 30 minutes a day; I plan to learn more about Excel® by taking a community education course.*
- Have students write and discuss their New Year's resolutions with a partner. Then ask them to share their resolutions with the class.

Communicative Practice — 10 minutes

Show what you know!

STEP 1. Use a gerund and information about...

- Read the directions aloud and elicit an example for item 1. (*I'm good at problem solving.*)
- Have students complete the exercise and share their sentences.

STEP 2. GROUPS. Discuss your answers...

- Set up groups. Ask students to think about jobs they would like to have.
- Say: *Take turns naming the job and giving suggestions on how to find information about it.*
- Make sure groups are on task. Offer suggestions as needed: *What about talking to someone who has that job? What about checking job websites on the Internet?*

Community Building

- Write a chart on the board with these column headings: *Name, Good at, Not good at, Improve English by, Thinking of.* Have students copy it.
- Tell students that they are to stand up, walk around the room, and survey as many classmates as possible in 5 minutes, writing only a few words in each box.
- Model the activity by asking an above-level student: *What is your name? What are you good at? What are you not good at? How are you going to improve your English? What are you thinking of doing in the future?*
- Afterwards, have students tell about a classmate. (*Ana is thinking of volunteering.*)

Progress Check

Can you . . . talk about abilities and plans?

- Say: *We have practiced talking about abilities and plans. Can you do this? If so, check the box.*

Extra Practice

Interactive Practice — pages 8–9

2 PRACTICE

Read about what five people plan to do to get jobs or better jobs. Then write sentences about them, using *by* and a gerund.

Gina is going to improve her math skills by taking classes at the community college.

I want to improve my math skills. I'm going to take classes at the community college.

1 Gina

I want to improve my image at work. I'm going to wear better clothes.

2 Todd

I want to learn Spanish. I plan to get a tutor.

3 Khenan

I want to learn more about work as a physician's assistant. I plan to go on an informational interview.

4 Ilya

I want to find out about employment resources. I'm going to meet with the librarian at the public library.

5 Mei-Feng

Show what you know! Talk about abilities and plans

STEP 1. Use a gerund and information about yourself to complete each sentence.

1. I'm good at _____.

2. I'm not good at _____.

3. As a child, I was interested in _____.

4. I've never been interested in _____.

5. I'm going to improve my English by _____.

6. I'd like to be better at _____.

STEP 2. GROUPS. Discuss your answers. Then talk about the kinds of jobs you might be interested in and how you might find out more about them.

Can you... talk about abilities and plans? ☐

Reading

1 BEFORE YOU READ

CLASS. Discuss. What do you want in the future? Talk about what you want to *be*, to *have*, and to *do*.

2 READ

CD1 T5

Preview the article. Check (✓) the statement that best describes it. Then listen to and read the article more thoroughly.

- [✓] 1. The article discusses the importance of having clear goals.
- [ ] 2. The article presents arguments for choosing goals that serve others.
- [ ] 3. The article discusses the difficulties of achieving goals in the film industry.

> **Reading Skill:**
> Previewing
>
> Good readers preview a text before reading it: They look at photos, illustrations, graphs, or charts. They look over the text quickly to get the main idea, paying special attention to the title and subtitles, and the first and last sentence in each paragraph.

Getting What You Want

What do you want? **Financial security**? Your own home? A successful career? Whatever it is, without a clear goal, you probably won't get it. A goal is a **commitment** to getting what you want. There are two parts to setting a goal. First, visualize the **outcome** you desire —see it clearly in your **imagination**. Then write the outcome you will achieve and the date by which you will achieve it. Make your goal **measurable**. "To get in shape" is not a measurable goal. "To lose 20 pounds by next April" is. You can stand on a scale in April and know if you have succeeded.

A Clear Vision

Many people have discovered the power of goal setting. Bruce Lee was one such person. As a child, Bruce

Lee wasn't strong or healthy, and as a young man, he struggled against **numerous obstacles** in the U.S. film industry, including **racial prejudice**. But Lee went on to achieve great

success in **martial arts** and action movies. It is reported that Lee wrote himself a letter in 1970. He wrote that, by 1980, he would be the best-known Asian movie star in the U.S. and that he would earn $10 million. Lee tirelessly pursued his goal. Sadly, he died before the 1973 release of Enter the Dragon, which finally made him a superstar. But Lee achieved his goal seven years early.

Turn *Your* Dreams into Goals

Not all of us have $10 million goals, but we can all learn from Bruce Lee's example. Like Lee, we can write our goals down on paper. Like Lee, we can make our goals measurable. We can work hard, keeping our goals clearly in mind. And hopefully, like Lee, we'll succeed.

Learn about setting goals

Getting Started 15 minutes

- Say: *We've been working on identifying skills, interests, and personality traits and where and how to get job information and advice. The next step is to understand how to set realistic goals.*
- Write the word *goals* on the board and draw a T-chart. On the horizontal line, write *realistic* and *unrealistic* on each side of the vertical line.
- Ask students to give examples of realistic and unrealistic goals.
- If needed, give a personal example of each. (For example, *I want to take a beginning Spanish conversation class* = realistic vs. *I want to learn to speak Spanish with a perfect accent* = unrealistic.)
- Say: *Keep these ideas of* realistic *and* unrealistic *in mind as we talk about goal setting.*

1 BEFORE YOU READ

CLASS. Discuss. What do you want...

- Ask students to read the directions silently.
- In a column on the board, write *I want to be _____. I want to have _____. I want to (do) _____.* Ask students to complete the sentences. (For example, *I want to be a teacher/nurse. I want to have a good job. I want to do some traveling abroad.*) Point out that a noun or adjective follows *be*, a noun follows *have*, and the verb *do* implies an action or goal. Then ask students use these phrases in their answers.

Reading Skill: **Previewing**

- Direct students to the Reading Skill box.
- Read the text aloud.
- Say: *Look at the parts of the word* preview. *What are the two parts of the word?*
- Ask: *What does the prefix* pre- *mean?* (before) *What does the base word* view *mean?* (look at)
- Say: *When you look carefully at different parts of a word, it can help you understand the word more fully. What you are going to do now is view something before you read it.*
- Say: *When you preview a reading, you look at all the information that can help you—the titles and subtitles, photos, graphics, and the first sentence in each paragraph.*
- Say: *Now we are going to preview the article.*

Presentation 15 minutes

2 READ

Preview the article....

- Ask students to read the directions silently.
- Tell students to read the title. Ask: *Based on the title alone, what do you think the article is about?*
- Provide step-by-step guidance on reading the first paragraph up to *achieve it*, and ask students if those sentences can give them an idea of the topic.
- Have students do the same with the rest of the article.
- After students preview the article—give them just a minute or two—ask for the statement that best describes the article.
- Say: *Now it's time to read the article.*
- Point out that the words and phrases in boldface (*financial security, commitment, outcome, imagination, measurable, numerous obstacles, racial prejudice,* and *martial arts*) appear in the glossary on page 245. Encourage students to read the entire article first, before going to the glossary.
- Play CD 1, Track 5. Ask students to listen and read along.
- After students listen and read, asked if they have any questions about the content, vocabulary, or pronunciation. Answer questions, but also encourage other students to answer questions.

Expansion: Vocabulary Practice for 2

- Divide the class into small groups.
- Ask students to make a list of the boldfaced words in the reading and to discuss the meaning of each. Encourage students to guess the meaning if they are not sure.
- Tell students to look for the words in the glossary and to compare the definitions there with what they wrote.
- Assign one or two words or phrases to each group and have them write one sentence with their assigned word or phrase.
- Ask groups to read their sentences to the class.
- After each group reads a sentence, ask if anyone has any questions about the word or phrase.

Controlled Practice   15 minutes

3   CHECK YOUR UNDERSTANDING

Write the answers...

- Tell students to write the answers to the questions in their notebooks.
- Go over the questions as a class and verify that everyone understood the two parts of goal setting.
Possible answers: 1. making sure that the goal is measurable; 2. Yes, because he had specific goals—that by 1980 he would be the best-known Asian movie star in the U.S. and that he would earn $10 million.

4   WORD WORK

Ⓐ Find these words...

- Have students read the directions silently.
- Ask for volunteers to give answers.

> **Teaching Tip**
>
> In all cases, offer extra help to individuals in a low-key manner. Note that more advanced learners may be acutely aware of lost status or be frustrated that as erudite and well-spoken as they are in their first (or second) language, they have not yet attained English proficiency.

Communicative Practice   15 minutes

Ⓑ GROUPS. Choose three words or phrases...

- Divide the class into small groups.
- Ask students to read the directions.
- Give suggestions about what the groups could discuss (for example: cognates in their own languages, pronunciation, parts of speech).
- Have each group choose one or two words or phrases and ask them to write one sentence for each assigned word or phrase.
- Ask groups to read their sentences to the class.
- Say: *Remember when you write in your vocabulary logs, you can always write more than three words or phrases. You can also use the vocabulary log for words you read or hear outside of class.*

Networking

- Have students find out about a place in the community where they can obtain information about getting jobs and job training.
- With students, brainstorm a list of what they want to know about work, work issues, training assistance, and other related topics.
- Brainstorm another list of places and people where students might find the information.
- Combine the two lists by saying: *Where do you think you can find information about . . . ?* (for example: *career counseling*) *You can find it at . . .* (for example: *the library*).

Show what you know!

STEP 1. Write three more things...

- Copy the chart onto the board.
- Ask students to read the directions. Encourage them to think about areas in their lives where they would like to make a change, not to limit this exercise to work-related issues. Provide examples if needed: *get in better shape, save more money . . .*
- Fill in the first row. Ask a volunteer to supply responses for the next row; write them on the board.
- Tell students to complete a similar chart in their notebooks. Have them check the one item that is most important to them in each column. Say: *Save these charts for later use.*

STEP 2. Write a clear and measurable goal...

- Have students write a goal based on the information they entered in the chart.

Progress Check

Can you . . . learn about setting goals?

Say: *We have practiced talking about setting goals. Now look at the question at the bottom of the page. Can you talk about setting goals? If so, check the box.*

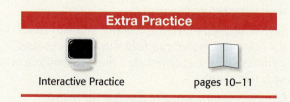

Extra Practice

Interactive Practice   pages 10–11

CHECK YOUR UNDERSTANDING

Write the answers to the questions.

1. Visualizing is an important part of goal setting. What is another important part?
2. Were Bruce Lee's goals measurable? Explain.

4 WORD WORK

A **Find these words in the article. Then use them to complete the sentences.**

> commitment   financial security   obstacles   outcome

1. I don't need to be rich, but ___financial security___ is important to me.
2. Achieving your goals isn't easy. You will always face ___obstacles___.
3. I've made a(n) ___commitment___ to come to class every day.
4. When you are involved in a disagreement with someone, try to think of a(n)
   ___outcome___ that would make both of you happy.

B **GROUPS. Choose three words or phrases in the article that you would like to remember. Discuss the words and their meanings. Then record the words and information about them in your vocabuary log.**

Show what you know!   Learn about setting goals

STEP 1. Write three more things in each column in the chart. Then check (✓) one thing you want most.

	TO BE	TO HAVE	TO DO
1.	an engineer	a house	speak three languages
2.			
3.			
4.			

STEP 2. Write a clear and measurable goal for your choice.

Can you... learn about setting goals? ☐

Listening and Speaking

1 BEFORE YOU LISTEN

GROUPS. Talk about your long-term career goals. What do you want to be doing 10 or 15 years from now? What steps will you have to take to achieve your goals? (If you are retired, or if you don't plan to work, talk about other personal goals.)

2 LISTEN

CD1 T6

A Ruben is talking to his career counselor again. Listen to the first part of the conversation. Write the four things he has done so far.

1. looked online for job descriptions

2. met with his manager to talk about careers at hotel

3. informational interview with catering manager at hotel

4. went to the library and got contact information about starting small business

CD1 T7

B Listen to the rest of the conversation and complete the flowchart for one possible career path for Ruben.

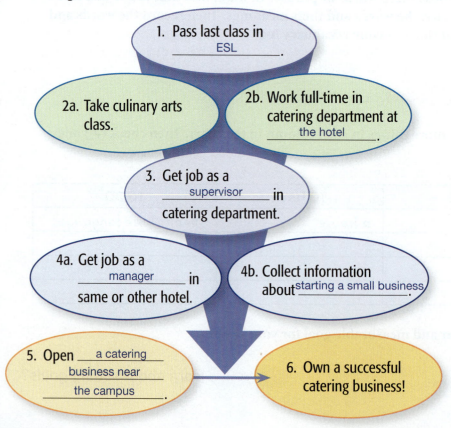

1. Pass last class in ___ESL___.

2a. Take culinary arts class.

2b. Work full-time in catering department at ___the hotel___.

3. Get job as a ___supervisor___ in catering department.

4a. Get job as a ___manager___ in same or other hotel.

4b. Collect information about ___starting a small business___.

5. Open ___a catering business near the campus___.

6. Own a successful catering business!

Talk about long-term career goals

Getting Started 5 minutes

- Say: *People sometimes have different kinds of goals. One might be,* I want to read one complete magazine in English every month. *That's a short-term goal. A long-term goal is a larger goal that may take several years or more to achieve. For example:* I was a mechanic in my country, so I want to become a certified master mechanic in this country. *We are going to listen and share ideas about long-term goals.*
- Write *short-term goals* and *long-term goals* on the board. Ask students to give more examples of each.
- Have students give ideas about how long "short-term" and "long-term" are.

Expansion: Writing Expansion

- Say: *When you thought about coming to the U.S., you probably had both short-term goals, like figuring out how to get from the airport to where you were staying with a relative, and long-term goals, like learning English well enough to get a good job.*
- Ask students to write at least two sentences each about their short-term and long-term goals in coming to the U.S. Tell students just to write the sentences in their notebooks for now.
- Walk around as students write; offer assistance with vocabulary, spelling, and grammar as needed.
- Say: *We will come back to these later in the lesson.*

Presentation 10 minutes

1 BEFORE YOU LISTEN

GROUPS. Talk about your long-term...

- Ask students to read the directions silently; make sure they understand that the task involves discussing steps.
- Set up groups.
- Help students add examples of breaking down goals into steps.

Controlled Practice 15 minutes

2 LISTEN

A **Ruben is talking to his career counselor...**

- Ask students to read the directions silently.
- Confirm they understand what they need to write.
- Play CD 1, Track 6.
- Ask students for the four things; write the answers on the board.

B **Listen to the rest of the conversation...**

- Ask students to read the directions silently.
- Say: *Now we are going to listen to the rest of the conversation with Ruben and his career counselor. Then we are going to complete a flowchart for him.*
- Tell students that the purpose of graphics and charts is to obtain information quickly. Therefore, they must include only the text that is necessary.
- Say: *Look at the flowchart on the page. A flowchart is like a map of a process. Notice how events are written in the order in which they've happened.*
- Play CD 1, Track 7.
- Go over answers with the whole class.

Expansion: Grammar Practice for 2B

- Briefly review the grammar point in Lesson 2; refer students to the grammar chart on page 8.
- Ask students to listen again and write down some of the instances of verb + gerund and verb + infinitive that they hear. (See examples below.)
- Say: *Just write down the phrase, not the whole sentence.* Give the first example.
  - I don't want to discourage you . . .
  - You'll have to spend time . . .
  - I need to pass . . .
  - I'll probably keep working . . .
  - Do you want to stay . . .
  - You're going to take . . .
  - You're going to continue working . . .
  - I suggest talking . . .
  - could be to become . . .
  - would be to open . . .
- As a class, decide, in each case, whether the phrase takes a gerund or an infinitive, or if either one could be used.

Talk about long-term career goals

Controlled Practice   15 minutes

3   PRACTICE

A **Goals that are most likely to be achieved...**

- Ask students to read the directions silently.
- Have them read the SMART goals chart.
- Give an example to help students get familiar with the chart, such as *I want to find a hotel job and become the manager of the hotel within one year.* Ask the class if this goal is specific (yes), measurable (yes), achievable (probably not), etc.

B **PAIRS. Which of these goals is a SMART goal?**

- Ask students to read the directions silently.
- Set up pairs and ask them to discuss the goals.

Possible answers: 1. not SMART because it is not specific, measurable, or time bound; 2. SMART because it is specific, measurable, achievable, and time bound

C **SAME PAIRS. Discuss. How can Ruben...**

- Keep the same pairs.
- Ask students to read the directions silently.
- Rephrase the directions. Say: *Work with your partner to make Ruben's long-term goal specific, measurable, achievable, relevant, and time bound.*

Communicative Practice   15 minutes

4   MAKE IT PERSONAL.

STEP 1. Write a SMART 10-year career goal...

- Give an example on the board or in a handout of Ruben's SMART ten-year goals.
- Ask students to write a long-term goal. Direct them to item 2 in Exercise 3B for an example.
- If a student writes a goal that does not qualify, ask the student questions that will help him or her identify the problem with the goal. (For example: *Do you think it's measurable . . . ?*)

Teaching Tip

- If the Writing Expansion for Getting Started was completed, ask students to review the short-term and long-term goals they wrote.
- Say: *Look back at one of the long-term goals you wrote. If one of those goals is a 10-year goal, revise it to make sure it is a SMART goal. Or, if your long-term career goals have changed or if you are not planning on a career, write another long-term SMART goal.*

STEP 2. PAIRS. Read your goal...

- Ask students to read the directions silently.
- Set up pairs.
- Model this activity with one student. Read a long-term goal that you wrote and discuss it briefly.

STEP 3. Create a flowchart...

- Refer back to the flowchart on page 18. Remind students that there are many types of flowcharts. Say: *There are many ways to create a flowchart, but they all show a process over time.*
- If time permits, work as a whole group to develop a flowchart based on an outgoing and confident student's long-term goal.
- Walk around the class to make sure students write only the information that is needed and that the information appears in chronological order.

STEP 4. GROUPS. Present your SMART goal...

- Set up groups.
- Ask for three volunteers to read each bullet of the Presentation Skills box.
- Say: *These three points are important. Remember that making eye contact is important in this culture, even if it may be difficult at first. I know from personal experience that talking in front of groups gets easier the more you practice.*

Extra Practice

Interactive Practice

A Goals that are most likely to be achieved are called SMART goals. Read the chart below.

SMART goals are:	
Specific	It is easy to see exactly what job the person wants, where he or she wants it, and the salary he or she expects.
Measurable	There is a way to see that the goal has been reached. For example, the person could show pay stubs. These would indicate what the job is, where it is, and what the salary is.
Achievable	It's achievable if it's possible for the goal-setter.
Relevant	It's relevant if it meets the needs of the goal-setter. If the person is a good match for the job, the goal is relevant.
Time bound	There is a specific date tied to the goal.

B PAIRS. Which of these goals is a SMART goal? Why?

1. I'll have a good job in the future.
2. I will have a job as an X-ray technician, with an income of over $50,000 per year, in the Houston area, by 2012.

C SAME PAIRS. Discuss. How can Ruben revise his long-term goal, of owning a catering business, to make it a SMART goal?

4 MAKE IT PERSONAL

STEP 1. Write a SMART ten-year career goal in your notebook.

STEP 2. PAIRS. Read your goal to your partner. Discuss how you will achieve your goal.

STEP 3. Create a flowchart for your career path. Use the flowchart for Ruben's career path as a model.

STEP 4. GROUPS. Present your SMART goal and career path to your group. Follow the steps in the presentation skills box.

Presentation Skills

- Make eye contact, hold up your flowchart, point to your final goal, and read it. Explain how it is a SMART goal.

- Explain your flowchart, step by step. Refer to your chart, but don't read from it. Look at other group members as much as possible.

- Ask if there are any questions or suggestions for improving your flowchart for your career path.

Reading

1   BEFORE YOU READ

GROUPS. Discuss the questions.

1. Why is mastering English a first step toward achieving a career goal for many students?
2. Why do students need to persist, or not give up, in order to succeed?
3. How can students find ways to study even when it's impossible to come to class?
4. How can students return to class after taking time off and complete a program?

2   READ

CD1 T8

Listen to and read the essay about how one student overcame an obstacle to her studies.

A Solution to My Problem   by Alicia Lopez

I am really happy to be back in class. Last term, I dropped out because I had **transportation** problems. Our class was from 7:00 to 9:00 P.M. The last bus from our school was at 9:00. I don't have a car or a driver's license. I tried to leave class early, but sometimes I missed the bus, and that was a big problem. Twice, I had to call my cousin to come pick me up, and he doesn't live near either my house or the school. And when I left in time to catch the bus, I always missed the end of class and our homework assignment. I became discouraged, and I stopped coming to school.

But I really wanted to come back. One day a friend suggested that I ask one of my classmates for a ride. I told her that this was a good idea, but actually I wasn't **comfortable** with it. Then I started to think of other ways to solve my problem. I put up some signs in our school, saying that I was looking for someone to share a ride with. I included my phone number and the nights I had class.

I also realized that if transportation was a problem for me, it was probably also a problem for other students. So I talked with our school counselor and we came up with a plan. I wrote an article for our school newspaper, **informing** students that a new Ride **Referral** Program was starting. Students who needed rides could sign up on a list in the counselor's office. Students who were willing to give rides **in exchange** for part of the cost of gas could put their names on another list. The students from the two lists could contact each other to work out **arrangements**. I was lucky. A student in my neighborhood contacted me. Now she gives me a ride to class, and I help pay for gas.

Getting Started   5 minutes

- Encourage students to think about a common situation in which reaching a personal goal is difficult. If students don't come up with their own suggestions, use this example: *Think about diets. Thousands or maybe millions of people in this country go on diets, but many fail. What are some of the obstacles that people face when they try to stay on a diet?* Accept student responses. Possible examples are *time, logistics—such as having to buy specific ingredients, prepare special meals—people may get bored, other family members don't follow it . . .*
- Ask: *What's some good advice for staying on a diet?* Accept all responses.
- Say: *In this unit, we've been working on identifying our own interests, skills, and personality traits and connecting them to goals. I think we all know that reaching goals isn't easy. There usually seem to be some challenges to reaching goals. Now we will be talking and reading about how to overcome—or conquer—these challenges.*

1 BEFORE YOU READ

GROUPS. Discuss the questions.

- Ask the students to read the questions.
- Set up groups of four.
- Say: *Each group member should read one question and lead the discussion on it. Remember, there is no single correct answer to the questions, but it is important to think about learning, particularly your own learning experiences.*

Presentation   15 minutes

2 READ

 Listen to and read the essay...

- Ask student to read the directions silently.
- Point out that the words and phrases in boldface (*transportation, comfortable, informing, referral, in exchange, arrangements*) are in the glossary on page 245. Encourage students to read the entire article first, before going to the glossary.

- Play CD 1, Track 8 as students listen and read along.
- As you walk around the room, observe whether any students seem to have difficulty reading the essay or keeping the listening and the reading in sync.

▉ Expansion: Vocabulary for 2

- Make sure that everyone understands *overcome/overcame* and *obstacles*.
- Say: *Overcome is an important word in Alicia's story and also when we talk about goals. Can you give some examples of what* overcome *means?* If students don't offer examples, ask questions such as: *What were some of the challenges you had to overcome when you moved to the U.S.? Was difficulty speaking English hard to overcome?*
- Direct students' attention to the irregular past tense in this compound word (overcame). Compare *overcome/overcame* with *overwork/overworked, overlook/overlooked*.
- For *obstacles*, you can describe an obstacle course or a steeplechase horse race where the horse and rider must jump over fences, streams, and other challenges.
- Suggest that students add these words to their vocabulary logs.

▉ Expansion: Vocabulary Practice for 2

- Divide the class into small groups.
- Ask students to make a list of the boldfaced words in the reading and to write the meaning of each. Encourage students to guess the meaning if they are not sure.
- Tell students to look for the words in the glossary and to compare the definitions there with what they wrote.
- Assign one or two words or phrases to each group and have them write one sentence for each of their assigned word(s) or phrase(s).
- Ask groups to read their sentences to the class.
- After each group reads the sentence, ask if anyone has any questions about the word or phrase.

Controlled Practice   15 minutes

3   CHECK YOUR UNDERSTANDING

CLASS. Write the answers...

- Ask students to read the questions silently.
- Read each question and solicit students' responses. For Question 1, ask: *Do you think this is a typical problem?*

Possible answers: 1. no transportation to school; missed end of class and assignments; overcame problem with Ride Referral Program—students share rides; 2. Yes, Alicia's response was a good solution. She could also have tried to convince the bus company to extend the time of the bus service, or asked the school to change the hours of the class to match the bus schedule.

Community Building

If there are transportation issues similar to Alicia's where you teach (with your program administration's prior agreement), encourage student leaders to work with the school administration and students from other classes to set up a Ride Referral Program for the school.

4   WORD WORK

GROUPS. Choose three words or phrases...

- Ask students to read the directions silently.
- Set up groups.
- Say: *Remember that when you write in your vocabulary logs, you can always write more than three words or phrases. You can also use the log for words you read or hear outside of class.*

Communicative Practice   25 minutes

Show what you know!

STEP 1. Think about obstacles to your own...

- Ask students to read and follow the directions.
- Make sure students understand *rank* and how to do it. If an example is necessary, say: *For example, I could rank my favorite foods in a scale of 1 to 5. Chocolate would be number 1. Mango would be 2 . . .*

- Say: *There is no right or wrong in this list of obstacles—the list just gives you a chance to think about your own challenges.*

STEP 2. GROUPS. Compare your answers...

- Keep the same groups as in Exercise 4.
- Say: *It's not easy to come up with solutions—answers to problems or obstacles—but trying gives you an opportunity to think about possible answers.*

STEP 3. Think of a goal...

- Say: *Before you talk with your group again, write notes to refer to as you work toward your goal.*

STEP 4. GROUPS. Talk about your goals...

- Keep the same groups.
- Ask each person in the group to share goals, possible obstacles, and possible solutions.

Teaching Tip

- For various reasons, some students may not want to discuss their goals or obstacles.
- Closely observe all students so that you know how to group emotionally sensitive students. Remember that in some situations, a student may only be able to listen.

Progress Check

Can you . . . overcome obstacles to achieving your goals?

- Say: *We have practiced talking about overcoming obstacles to achieve your goals. Now look at the question at the bottom of the page. Can you talk about overcoming obstacles to achieve your goals? If so, check the box.*

3 **CHECK YOUR UNDERSTANDING**

Write the answers to the questions.

1. What was Alicia's obstacle, and how did she overcome it?

2. Do you think Alicia's response to her obstacle was a good one? Can you think of any other way she could have solved her problem?

4 **WORD WORK**

 **GROUPS.** Choose three words or phrases in the essay that you would like to remember. Discuss the words and their meanings. Then record the words and information about them in your vocabulary log.

Show what you know! Overcome obstacles to achieving your goals

STEP 1. Think about obstacles to your own persistence. Rank the obstacles below from 1 to 6 (1 = most difficult; 6 = least difficult).

_____ work schedule / lack of time

_____ transportation problems

_____ lack of support from family members or friends

_____ no child care available when you need to come to class

_____ lack of money

_____ lack of confidence or feeling of being discouraged

STEP 2. GROUPS. Compare your answers in Step 1. Discuss these and other obstacles and offer one another possible solutions.

STEP 3. Think of a goal that you are trying to achieve right now or that you will try to achieve in the future. Think about possible obstacles.

STEP 4. GROUPS. Talk about your goals and possible obstacles. Present two suggestions for overcoming each obstacle.

Can you... overcome obstacles to achieving your goals? ☐

Writing

1 BEFORE YOU WRITE

A You are going to write a descriptive essay about your interests, skills, and goals. Read about descriptive essays. Then read the writing tip.

> **FYI**   ABOUT DESCRIPTIVE ESSAYS
>
> A descriptive essay includes specific details to help readers picture a person, place, or thing. Like other types of essays, it usually contains an introduction, one or more body paragraphs, and a conclusion.
>
> **Writing Tip:** Topic Sentences
>
> In an academic essay, each paragraph should have a topic sentence. A topic sentence gives the main idea about the topic of the paragraph. All the other sentences in the paragraph support the topic sentence—they give more information about it. The topic sentence is usually the first sentence in a paragraph, but not always; sometimes it occurs in other places.

B Ask yourself these questions. Record your responses.

1. What things interest me the most? Give examples.
2. What skills do I have? Describe them in detail.
3. What is my SMART career goal?
4. What am I doing now (what studies or work)?
5. How do I plan to achieve my goal?

C Read the writing model on page 205. What things does Andrea like to do?

2 ANALYZE THE WRITING MODEL

A PAIRS. Discuss the questions.

1. What are Andrea's main interests?
2. What are two adjectives she uses to describe herself?
3. What is her career goal?

B Read the writing model on page 205 again. Underline the topic sentence in each paragraph.

Lesson 9 · Describe your interests, skills, and goals

Getting Started · 5 minutes

- Say: *We have been talking about our personal and career interests, skills, and goals. We have practiced vocabulary and grammatical structures to describe our abilities and plans, and we have read about ways to find job information, set SMART goals for ourselves, and overcome obstacles. Today we are going to apply all of this knowledge as we write a descriptive essay about our interests, skills, and goals.*

Presentation · 15 minutes

1 BEFORE YOU WRITE

A You are going to write...

- Read the directions aloud. Ask: *What is an essay?* (a short composition that explains, describes, or presents something or someone)
- Say: *Today we're going to write an essay that describes something—so it's called a descriptive essay.*
- Ask students to read the FYI note and Writing Tip.

B Ask yourself these questions. Record...

- Ask students to read the directions and questions silently.
- If students completed the Writing Expansion for Lesson 7, encourage them to review what they wrote about their goals.
- Have students write answers to the questions. Walk around and check students' work, offering prompts as needed. (*What are some of your interpersonal skills? Are you good at resolving conflicts?*)

Teaching Tip

Have students write notes for each question on a separate index card instead of writing full answers on a sheet of paper so that they learn to list and organize ideas before writing complete sentences.

C Read the writing model on page 205...

- Tell students that they will now read a descriptive essay that a student wrote about her interests, skills, and goals. Have students turn to page 205 and read the essay.
- Clarify vocabulary as needed.
- Ask: *What types of things does Andrea like to do?*
  Answer: work outdoors, especially gardening

Controlled Practice · 10 minutes

2 ANALYZE THE WRITING MODEL

A PAIRS. Discuss the questions.

- Say: *Now you are going to analyze Andrea's interests, personality traits, and goals.*
- Ask students to read the directions silently.
- Have students form pairs and answer the questions.
  Answers: 1. main interests—science and nature; 2. *outgoing* and *patient*; 3. to be a tree climber and pruner

B Reread the writing model on page 205 again....

- Say: *Read Andrea's essay a second time and look for the topic sentences. What is a topic sentence?* (a sentence that gives the paragraph's main idea)
- Have students complete the exercise and discuss their answers.
  Answers: 1. I have a wide variety of interests, but my main interests are science and nature. 2. I have many skills. 3. I want to work at something that combines my interests and skills.

Teaching Tip

Help students understand the concept of a topic sentence and the idea that the other sentences in a paragraph should relate to it. Say: *A topic sentence is something like an umbrella, under which everything in the paragraph must fall. All of the sentences under the umbrella should be logically related to the topic sentence.* Have students work in pairs to add a sentence to each of the paragraphs in the model essay—it can be one related or unrelated to the topic sentence. Then they read the sentence to the class. Each pair should be ready to explain why it is or it isn't a good sentence for that paragraph.

Communicative Practice · 30 minutes

3 THINK ON PAPER

A Read the word webs Andrea made...

- Ask students to read the directions silently and look at the word webs.
- Ask: *What is a word web?* Explain as needed that a word web is a diagram used to organize ideas.
- Say: *A word web can be very helpful because it allows you to see, in graphic form, how your ideas are related to one another. It can also help you to see which details and examples are **not** related to your main ideas.*
- Point out that in the word webs, the circles have the main ideas, expressed as single words or short phrases. These main ideas will go into the topic sentences.
- Ask: *What else do you see in the word webs?* (lines coming out from the main ideas, or *callouts*, attached to words or phrases)
- Say: *These callouts show supporting details and examples that relate to the main idea in the middle of the circle. These details and examples will form the middle of each paragraph—the sentences between the topic sentence and the conclusion.*

B Review the notes you made...

- On the board, draw three large circles, with blank lines coming out from each one.
- Say: *Now you are going to use the notes that you made earlier to organize ideas for an essay that describes your interests, skills, and goals. You'll make three circles like the ones you see on the board, and you'll write a main idea in each circle. Then you'll draw lines coming out from the circles to label the supporting details.*
- Ask students to read the directions silently and complete the exercise.
- *Optional:* Students form pairs and exchange word webs. Then they discuss with their partner how well the supporting details relate to the main ideas.

4 WRITE

Use your word webs to write...

- Read the directions aloud. Then have students write the first draft of a descriptive essay.

- Say: *When you finish writing, you're going to read your paper and revise it. What does* revise *mean?* (changing your work—adding, deleting, or rewriting details)

5 CHECK YOUR WRITING

A STEP 1. Revise your work.

- Say: *Read over your essay a first time and answer the questions; if any answers are* no, *revise your work.*
- *Optional:* Have students form pairs, exchange descriptive essays, and give each other feedback.

B STEP 2. Edit and proofread.

- Say: *Now you'll read over your essay a second time and edit and proofread your work.* Direct students to check their essays for grammar, spelling, punctuation, and typos.
- As students revise and edit, walk around and check and/or correct their work, answering questions as needed.
- *Optional:* Have students complete a "clean" second draft of their essay at home, incorporating corrections from the revision and editing steps.

Teaching Tip

You may want to collect student papers and provide feedback. Use the scoring rubric for writing on page Txv to evaluate vocabulary, grammar, mechanics, and how well students complete the task. You may want to review the completed rubric with students.

MULTILEVEL INSTRUCTION for 5A and 5B

Above-level Have students who finish writing and self-editing read and edit a peer's paper using the criteria in Exercises 5A and 5B. Then ask them to discuss the paper with the writer.

Pre-level Have students create and complete a checklist with the revising and editing criteria from Exercises 5A and 5B, checking off a box for each question and making any changes.

Extra Practice

Interactive Practice   pages 14–15

3 THINK ON PAPER

A Read the word webs Andrea made before she wrote her descriptive essay.

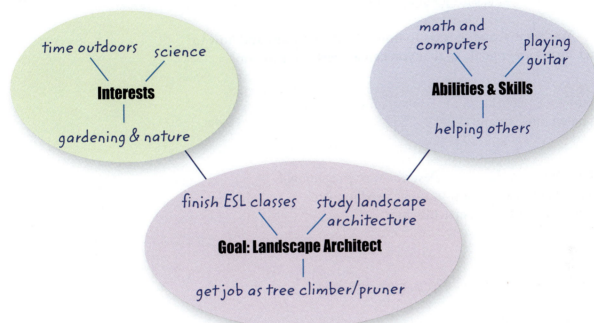

time outdoors science
Interests
gardening & nature

math and computers playing guitar
Abilities & Skills
helping others

finish ESL classes study landscape architecture
Goal: Landscape Architect
get job as tree climber/pruner

B Review the notes you made about your interests, skills, and goals in Exercise 1B. Then use word webs like Andrea's to brainstorm and organize ideas for your essay.

4 WRITE

Use your word webs to write a descriptive essay about your interests, skills, and goals. Be sure to include a topic sentence for each paragraph.

5 CHECK YOUR WRITING

A STEP 1. Revise your work.

1. Have you written three paragraphs—one for each circle in your word web?
2. Does each paragraph have a topic sentence?
3. Have you used specific details to describe yourself and your goals?

B STEP 2. Edit and proofread.

1. Have you checked your grammar, spelling, and punctuation?
2. Have you proofread for typing errors?

1 REVIEW

For your grammar review, go to page 226.

2 ACT IT OUT   What do you say?

PAIRS. You are discussing ways to find the job you want and how to set long-term career goals so that you can achieve your dreams.

Student A: Review Lesson 1. Explain how to identify job-related interests and skills.

Student B: Review Lesson 4. Describe the *Occupational Outlook Handbook* and how it can be used to match someone's interests to a particular job.

3 READ AND REACT   Problem-solving

STEP 1. Read about Lydia.

Lydia has two children and a secure job at a health-care agency, but she doesn't really enjoy the work she's doing. She likes math and is very good with computers. She longs to go to college and get a degree in computer technology. When she told her husband about her desire to go back to school and change jobs, he discouraged her. He said that changing careers would be too risky financially. He reminded her that they have two children to support. Lydia can understand his fears, but she wants a job that is satisfying. She would really like to work in the Information Technology (IT) department of a big company some day.

STEP 2. GROUPS. What is Lydia's problem? What can she do?

4 CONNECT

For your Study Skills Activity, go to page 212.

Which goals can you check off? Go back to page 5.

 Go to the CD-ROM for more practice.

Show what you know!

1 REVIEW

For your grammar review, go to page 226.

- Say: *Today we're going to review the skills that we have practiced in this unit and apply them to a problem. What are some of the skills we have practiced?* Elicit answers, noting them on the board (identifying job interests; describing personality traits; finding job information; talking about career abilities, plans, and goals).

- Ask students to complete the grammar review exercises on page 226.

2 ACT IT OUT

PAIRS. You are discussing ways to find...

- Ask students to read the directions silently. Explain that they will help each other review the skills they practiced in this unit. Student A will look back at Lesson 1 and explain how to identify job-related interests and skills. Student B will look back at Lesson 4 and describe how the *Occupational Outlook Handbook* can be used to match someone's interests to a job.

- *Optional:* Write a prompt on the board to help students get started:

  If you want to . . . the first step is to . . .

- Give students time to review the materials; then have them complete the exercise.

- Walk around the room and monitor conversations.

3 READ AND REACT

STEP 1. Read about Lydia.

- Say: *Now we're going to apply our knowledge from this unit to a problem involving a character, Lydia. Let's read about Lydia.*

- Have students read the story.

STEP 2. GROUPS. What is Lydia's problem?

- Ask students to read the directions silently and then form small groups.

- Give each group a sheet of flipchart paper and markers, or ask them to make notes on a sheet of paper. Tell them that they will write a brief description of Lydia's problem and list at least three possible solutions.

- Ask groups to choose a representative to present the group's ideas to the class.

- Elicit from students language to use for making suggestions (*First, she should . . .*).

- Have students discuss the questions. Walk around the room and monitor conversations.

- *Optional:* Set a discussion time limit and announce when there are 5 minutes left.

- A representative from each group presents the group's ideas.

- After each presentation, encourage feedback, prompting students as needed (*What do you think about Group 1's suggestions for Lydia? Which idea do you like best?*).

Possible answers: *Problem:* Lydia wants to change careers but is worried about the effect it would have on her family financially. *Solution:* She should make a SMART goal; go to school part-time while continuing to work; take classes at night, starting with just one class and building on that.

> **Teaching Tip**
>
> Review gerund and infinitive structures that students can use to give feedback. (*I really like the idea of _____. I disagree with _____ because Lydia needs to _____.*)

4 CONNECT

Turn to page 212 for the Study Skills Activity. See page Txii for general teaching notes for Study Skills activities.

Progress Check

Which goals can you check off? Go back to page 5.
Ask students to turn to page 5 and check off any remaining goals they have reached. Call on them to say which goals they will practice outside of class.

CD-ROM Practice

 Go to the CD-ROM for more practice.

If your students need more practice with the vocabulary, grammar, and competencies in Unit 1, encourage them to review the activities on the CD-ROM.

2 Getting a Job

Unit Overview

Goals
- See the list of goals on the facing page.

Grammar
- Present perfect: Statements and questions; *for* and *since*
- Present perfect vs. present perfect continuous

Listening and Speaking
- Talk about interview do's and don'ts
- *Communication Skill:* Asking Questions

Reading
- Read an article on preparing for a job search
- *Reading Skill:* Using Prior Knowledge
- Read a résumé
- Read an article about commonly asked interview questions
- *Reading Skill:* Comparing and Contrasting
- Read a series of interview questions and answers

Writing
- Write an effective cover letter for a résumé
- *Writing Tip:* Using language from the job ad in the cover letter

Life Skills
- Analyze résumés
- Write and revise a chronological résumé
- Write a T-chart

Preview
- Set the context for the unit by greeting students as they walk into class. Say: *Hi, everyone, now that we've talked about interests, skills, and goals, we are going to starting working on how to get a job.*
- Direct students to the Preview section on page 25.
- Say: *We've talked about previewing as a reading strategy. In this preview, the questions can help us start thinking about how to get a job.*
- Read the first question aloud.
- Rephrase (for example, *How do people look for jobs in Mexico?*) and ask for comments.
- Read the second question aloud unless students have already brought up differences.
- Ask students to comment. Say: *If you think job hunting is different here than in your home country, explain <u>how</u> it is different. Or now with globalization and the Internet and all, is job hunting similar everywhere?*
- Say: *In our first lesson, we will read about how to prepare for a job search in the U.S.*

Unit Goals
- Ask students to read the Unit Goals.
- Repeat each goal and elaborate. (For example: *prepare for a job search—knowing how to go about looking for a job can help you save time and lessen your frustration.*)
- Say: *This is not a long list of goals, but each one is very important when you are trying to get a job.*
- Ask students to look at the list and circle a goal that is very important to them. Ask for volunteers to say what goal they circled and why it is important to them.
- Say: *As we complete this unit, we will look back at this page and reread the goals. We will check each goal as we complete it.*

Getting a Job

Preview

How do people usually find jobs in your home country? Is job-hunting different in your home country from the way it is in the U.S.? Explain.

UNIT GOALS

- [ ] Prepare for a job search

- [ ] Analyze and write a chronological résumé

- [ ] Talk about interview do's and don'ts

- [ ] Prepare for a job interview

- [ ] Talk about your education and work experience

Reading

1   BEFORE YOU READ

CLASS. Discuss. When you search for a job, how do you prepare? Talk about your personal experiences of looking for work.

2   READ

CD1 T9

Listen to and read the online article. How did your prior knowledge help you read the article?

Reading Skill:
Using Prior Knowledge

Before you read a text, ask yourself, "What do I already know about this topic?" Connecting the text to your prior knowledge will help you understand and remember what you read. Also, identifying what you already know may help you realize what you *don't* know. This prepares you to look for new information as you read.

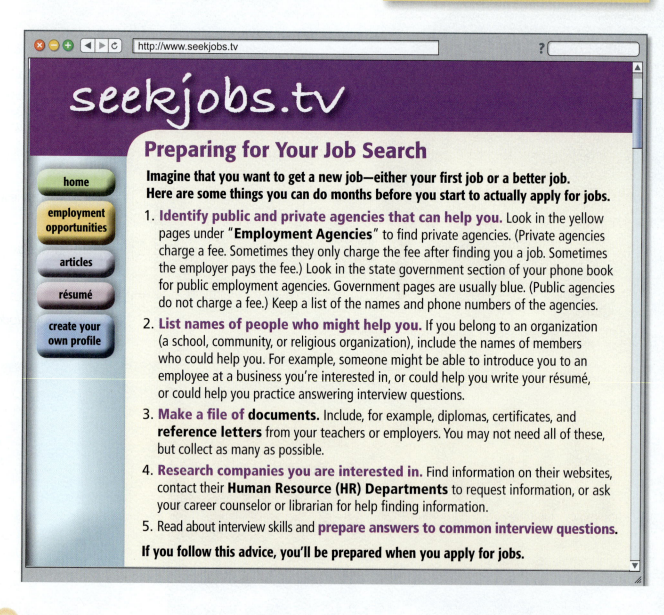

http://www.seekjobs.tv

seekjobs.tv

- home
- employment opportunities
- articles
- résumé
- create your own profile

Preparing for Your Job Search

Imagine that you want to get a new job—either your first job or a better job. Here are some things you can do months before you start to actually apply for jobs.

1. **Identify public and private agencies that can help you.** Look in the yellow pages under "**Employment Agencies**" to find private agencies. (Private agencies charge a fee. Sometimes they only charge the fee after finding you a job. Sometimes the employer pays the fee.) Look in the state government section of your phone book for public employment agencies. Government pages are usually blue. (Public agencies do not charge a fee.) Keep a list of the names and phone numbers of the agencies.

2. **List names of people who might help you.** If you belong to an organization (a school, community, or religious organization), include the names of members who could help you. For example, someone might be able to introduce you to an employee at a business you're interested in, or could help you write your résumé, or could help you practice answering interview questions.

3. **Make a file of** documents. Include, for example, diplomas, certificates, and **reference letters** from your teachers or employers. You may not need all of these, but collect as many as possible.

4. **Research companies you are interested in.** Find information on their websites, contact their **Human Resource (HR) Departments** to request information, or ask your career counselor or librarian for help finding information.

5. Read about interview skills and **prepare answers to common interview questions**.

If you follow this advice, you'll be prepared when you apply for jobs.

Getting Started   10 minutes

- Say: *We've talked about interests, skills, personality traits, and goals, especially career goals. The next step is thinking about how to find a job. Knowing where to look for assistance should make the task easier.*

Teaching Tip

At the beginning of each lesson, explain to students what the class has covered and what's coming next. This validates the idea that the students are adult learners who want and need to know what they are learning and why. It also reinforces vocabulary, grammar, and life skills topics previously presented.

1 BEFORE YOU READ

CLASS. Discuss. When you search for a job...

- Ask students to read the directions. Activate the discussion by offering a short personal example of your own.
- Say: *If you haven't looked for jobs in the U.S., tell us how you looked for a job in your home country.*
- List student responses on the board, an overhead, or a flipchart; keep this record to refer to throughout the unit.

Presentation   20 minutes

Reading Skill: Using Prior Knowledge

- Direct students to the Reading Skill box.
- Ask: *Does anyone know what the word* prior *means?* If students respond correctly, agree with their definitions; if students don't respond or give an incorrect definition, provide examples and explain what *prior* means. (For example, *I can't meet today because I have a prior commitment. My prior job was in construction.*) If needed, tell students *prior* is close in meaning to *earlier* or *previous.*
- Go over any other potentially difficult words or concepts in the skill box such as *text*—since some students may be more familiar with the term *reading, piece of writing, story, paragraph, essay,* or some other word.

2 READ

Listen to and read the online article...

- Ask students to read the directions. Point out that the words and phrases in boldface—*employment agencies, documents, reference letters, Human Resource (HR) Departments*—appear in the glossary on page 245. Encourage students to read the entire article first, before going to the glossary.
- Say: *We'll talk more about the vocabulary after you listen and read.*
- Play CD 1, Track 9 while students read and listen.
- Ask: *What did you think of the article?* Also ask if there were any vocabulary or pronunciation issues and answer as needed.
- Repeat the question from the direction: *How did your prior knowledge help you read the article?* Have students discuss examples of their prior experience with job searches and how this knowledge helped them understand the article.

Expansion: Vocabulary Practice for 2

- Divide the class into small groups.
- Ask students to make a list of the boldfaced words in the reading and to discuss the meaning of each. Have them guess the meaning if they are not sure.
- Tell students to look for the words in the glossary and to compare the definitions there with what they wrote in their lists.
- Have each group write one sentence with each word or phrase.
- Ask groups to read their sentences to the class.

Expansion: Reading Practice for 2

- If you have access to several computers or a computer lab, divide the class into groups of 3 or 4 around the computers.
- Give each group the URL (web address) of a bona fide job search site (such as www.monster.com) and a simple form (name of site, who runs the site, whether or not it is useful for a job search and why) for each group to fill out.
- After the group reviews the website and discusses its content, ask a spokesperson for each group to share the information with the whole group.
- Gather the forms and copy the information to give out during the next class.

Controlled Practice   10 minutes

3 CHECK YOUR UNDERSTANDING

Complete the sentences. Look back...

- Ask students to read and follow the directions.
- Before students begin, ask: *Does anyone have any questions about what to do?*
- If any students are struggling with the activity, sit down with them and try to figure out the source of the difficulty.

4 WORD WORK

GROUPS. Choose three words...

- Ask students to read the directions.
- Set up groups.
- Say: *Remember that when you write in your vocabulary logs, you can always write more than three words or phrases. You can also use the log for words you read or hear outside of class.*

Teaching Tip

- Effective grouping strategies vary not only from class to class, but also over time in the same class. Some classes might be happy and productive with the same grouping; other classes may need to change groups often.
- Also, if you see that one or two people almost always do the talking and others are quiet, change the groups for the next group activity. If students don't want to change groups, say: *It's important to learn how to talk comfortably with as many people as possible.*

Communicative Practice   20 minutes

Show what you know!

PAIRS. Discuss the questions.

- Read the four discussion questions.
- Emphasize that the follow-up questions (*Why? Which ones?*) are very important.
- As pairs talk, walk around the room to listen and give assistance as needed, but mostly let students talk with each other.
- After pairs have finished discussing the questions, say: *Do you have some good ideas about preparing for a job search? What are they?*
- Write responses on the board, an overhead, or a flipchart.
- Refer to the list generated at the beginning of the lesson, and ask students to compare the initial list with the new list.
- Say: *What is the same? What is different? Let's combine the list into one list of good advice.* Do that by adding new information to the original list.

Progress Check

Can you . . . prepare for a job search?

Say: *We have practiced talking about preparing for a job search. Now look at the question at the bottom of the page. Can you prepare for a job search? If so, check the box.*

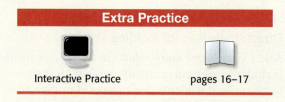

Extra Practice

Interactive Practice   pages 16–17

CHECK YOUR UNDERSTANDING

Complete the sentences. Look back at the article on page 26 to find the information.

1. There are private and public employment ___agencies___ to help you find jobs.

2. If you are a member of a community ___organization___, there may be another member who could help you find a job.

3. You should keep ___documents___, such as diplomas and training certificates, to show to employers.

4. One way to find information about a company is to go to its ___website___ on the Internet.

4 WORD WORK

☑ **GROUPS.** **Choose three words or phrases in the article that you would like to remember. Discuss the words and their meanings. Then record the words and information about them in your vocabulary log.**

Show what you know! Prepare for a job search

PAIRS. Discuss the questions.

1. What advice in the article would be easy for you to follow? Why?
2. What advice in the article would be difficult for you to follow? Why?
3. Have you already done any of the things in the article? If so, which ones?
4. Are there any suggestions in the article that you could follow at this time? If so, which ones?

Can you...prepare for a job search? ☐

Lesson 2 Analyze résumés

Life Skills

1 ANALYZE RÉSUMÉS

CLASS. Look at the résumé on page 29. Discuss the questions. Answers will vary.

1. Do jobs in your home country require résumés? If so, what kinds of jobs?
2. Do you need a résumé for the kind of job you have or are interested in getting in the U.S.?
3. Where can you get help with writing a résumé?

2 PRACTICE

A Read the model résumé on page 29. What kinds of information about yourself should you include in a résumé? Check (✓) the items.

- ✓ 1. work experience
- ✓ 2. job desired
- ☐ 3. age
- ☐ 4. height, weight, and hair color
- ✓ 5. job skills
- ☐ 6. names of references
- ✓ 7. contact information
- ✓ 8. educational background

B PAIRS. Compare answers.

C Notice that in a résumé you don't need to write complete sentences. Compare these sentences to the information in the résumé on page 29. Cross out the words that do not appear in the résumé.

1. ~~I am~~ seeking a full-time, entry-level accounting position.
2. ~~I attended~~ Hillsborough Community College.
3. ~~I took~~ ESL, academic, ~~and~~ computing ~~classes~~.
4. ~~I am~~ responsible for balancing cash registers and for recording sales.
5. ~~I~~ close ~~the~~ store two nights a week.
6. ~~I~~ shelved items in ~~the~~ deli.
7. ~~I~~ assisted with ordering and receiving.
8. ~~I can~~ type 70 words per minute.

28 UNIT 2

Getting Started   10 minutes

  1 ANALYZE RÉSUMÉS

CLASS. Look at the résumé on page 29....

- Say: *Today, we're going to learn about an important step in the job search process—preparing a résumé. What is a résumé?* Elicit answers from students, explaining as needed that a résumé is a summary of your education, experience, and job skills.

- Ask students to preview the résumé on page 29.

- Say: *Have you ever written a résumé? Was it similar to or different from this one? In what ways?*

- Read and discuss Question 1.

- Read and discuss Question 2, explaining that some jobs require you to fill out a job application in print or online, but that you don't always need to submit a résumé with it.

- Read and discuss Question 3, explaining as needed that employment agencies may offer individual help with résumés or group workshops.

Presentation   10 minutes

2 PRACTICE

A **Read the model résumé on page 29....**

- Ask students to read the résumé on page 29.

- Say: *Now you will consider what types of information to include in a résumé.*

- Ask students to check the kinds of items that they should include, using the résumé on page 29.

B **PAIRS. Compare answers.**

- Say: *Now find a partner and compare answers.*

- Model the exercise by asking an above-level student: *Should you include information about your work experience in a résumé?* The above-level student answers the question and asks about the next item: *What about the job desired?*

- Have students discuss whether to include the items in a résumé.

- Read through the items aloud, asking students whether they checked each item.

- Say: *You should not include personal information—age, height, weight, and hair color—on a résumé.*

Culture Connection

Say: *In the U.S., it is considered unprofessional to include personal information—or a photo—on a résumé. Do not list marital status, the number of children that you have, or your religion, because it is considered unlawful discrimination to make hiring decisions based on these items. However, it is acceptable—and often desirable—to list hobbies and leisure activities, particularly sports. These activities often demonstrate that you have special skills or are a team player.*

Controlled Practice   15 minutes

C **Notice that in a résumé you don't...**

- Ask students to read the directions.

- Write the complete item 1 on the board.

- Direct students to the "Position Desired" line at the top of the résumé on page 29.

- Ask: *How was this shortened from the complete sentence?* Cross off *I am* and *a* from the sentence on the board, noting that the résumé phrases do not include the subject (*I*), the helping verb (*am*), or articles (*a*).

- Say: *Now you're going to change these sentences to the way they appear on the résumé on page 29.*

- Have students complete the exercise.

- Call on students to say the answers. As they do so, note the revised phrases on the board.

Multilevel Instruction for 2C

Pre-level Sit with students in a group and help them find the Exercise 2C items in the résumé on page 29. (*Let's look for* ESL, academic, and computing classes. *Where do you see these words in the résumé? Which word with a colon introduces this list of classes?*)

Above-level After they finish the exercise, students can find additional examples of sentences that are shortened in the résumé and share these with the class.

Controlled Practice   15 minutes

D **Read about types of résumés. Which...**

- Ask students to read the information in the exercise.
- Clarify that reverse chronological order means putting the most recent event first.
- Ask: *Which type of résumé did Iris write?* (a chronological résumé) *How do you know that?* (She listed her education and employment experiences in reverse chronological order and grouped all of her skills together at the end.)
- Have students discuss differences between Iris's résumé and the functional résumé on page 222.
- Reinforce the concept of reverse chronological order. Ask which job Iris had first—the assistant manager job or the stockperson job (the stockperson job). Ask: *Did she list this job first?* (No—she listed it last.)
- Then ask which job Iris listed first on her résumé (the last job that she had—the assistant manager job). Reiterate that the first job listed on the résumé is the most recent position—often one that the résumé writer still has.

■ Expansion: Reading Practice for 2D

- Tell students that they will practice scanning (reading a document for specific information).
- Have students scan Iris's résumé to find answers to the following questions:

   How long has Iris been an assistant manager? (since 2008)

   What did she do as a stockperson? (She balanced cash registers, recorded sales, assisted manager with other tasks, helped at cash registers and at food counter, and closed the store two nights a week.)

   What college-level classes has she taken? (She's taken classes in clerical skills, computing, human relations, technical math, and accounting.)

   Is she looking for an entry-level or managerial position? (entry-level) *Note:* Clarify that an entry-level position is a starting-level position.

   Is she looking for a full- or part-time position? (full-time)

   Does she provide references with her résumé? (She will provide them upon request.)

Networking

- Ask students if they know what a reference is. Explain that when people apply for jobs, they may be asked to provide references—names and contact information for professional acquaintances who will answer questions about them. Sometimes these references will be asked to verify employment dates; other times, they may be asked questions about the job applicant, such as what that person's strengths and weaknesses are and why that person left a job. Explain that when you list someone as a reference, you generally give the person's name, position, and contact information, and notify the person in advance.

Communicative Practice   10 minutes

3 **MAKE IT PERSONAL**

GROUPS. Discuss. Which kind...

- Read the discussion questions and tell students that they will talk about them in small groups. Say: *There are no right or wrong answers.*
- Have students form groups and discuss the questions. Offer prompts for clarification or elaboration as needed. (For example, *Why do you think that a chronological résumé would be best for you?*)
- Ask for volunteers to share which type of résumé they prefer to write and why.

Teaching Tip

Students will compose a résumé in the next lesson, so ask them to bring in information about their employment history such as the names of employers, dates of employment, and lists of educational courses and degrees.

Progress Check

Can you . . . analyze résumés?

- Say: *We have practiced analyzing résumés. Can you do this? If so, check the box.*

Extra Practice

pages 18–19

D Read about types of résumés. Which type of résumé did Iris write? (See page 222 for an example of the other type of résumé.)

A **chronological résumé** emphasizes your work history. It lists information about your work experience and education in reverse chronological (time) order.

A **functional résumé** focuses on your skills, not specific jobs. It lists similar skills and abilities together and explains how you used them in previous jobs. People without any previous employment in the field for which they are interviewing should consider using a functional résumé. So should people with gaps in their work history.

Iris Martinez
115 Hammond Avenue, Largo, Florida 33773
Home phone: (727) 555-3296, Cell phone: (727) 555-4860, E-mail: irism@umail.com

Position Desired	Seeking full-time, entry-level accounting position	
Education	2008–present	**Hillsborough Community College, Tampa** One-year course in Accounting Operations Classes: clerical skills, computing, human relations, technical math, accounting
	2007–2008	**Kingly Adult High School, Largo** Classes: ESL, academic, computing
	2007	**Technical bachelor's degree, El Salvador** (equivalent to technical high school degree in U.S.)
Experience	2008–present	**Robertson's Supermarket, Largo** Assistant Manager Responsible for balancing cash registers and for recording sales. Assist manager with other tasks. Help at cash registers and at food counter. Close store two nights a week.
	2007–2008	**Publix, Seminole** Stockperson Shelved items in deli. Assisted with ordering and receiving.
Skills	Type 70 words per minute. Experience with Excel, Word, Access, and QuickBooks. Bilingual in Spanish and English. Excellent interpersonal skills.	
References	Provided upon request	
Transcripts	Provided upon request	

3 MAKE IT PERSONAL

GROUPS. Discuss. Which kind of résumé would be best for you to write? Why?

Can you...analyze résumés? ☐

Life Skills

1 PREPARE TO WRITE A RÉSUMÉ

CLASS. Read the information on résumé tips. Is any information surprising to you? Explain.

Résumé Tips:

• Be brief and clear. Try not to write more than one page.

• Never lie or misrepresent yourself in your résumé. Many employers check the information.

• If you don't know the address of a previous employer, you can check the yellow pages or look online, or you can call and ask for it. If you don't remember your employment dates, you can call your previous employer's Human Resources (HR) Department and ask.

• There shouldn't be any mistakes in your résumé. Check your spelling, grammar, and punctuation. Always have someone proofread your work. People usually have to write several drafts.

• Use high-quality paper. The paper should be white or off-white.

2 PRACTICE

STEP 1. Complete the form on page 31 to organize your information.

STEP 2. PAIRS. Exchange your completed forms. Ask each other questions to clarify details or to provide more information for your résumés.

STEP 3. Write or type your résumé. (All résumés must be typed, but if you are working in class and do not have access to a computer, you can write the first draft by hand.) Use your form and Iris's résumé on page 29 to help you.

STEP 4. PAIRS. Read your partner's résumé. Ask questions or make suggestions to improve the résumé.

STEP 5. Revise your résumé. See how much you can improve it. Then have your partner look at your revisions.

Write a chronological résumé

Getting Started 5 minutes

- Say: *In the last lesson, we talked about creating résumés—what to include and how to organize the information.*
- Ask: *What is some information that should **not** be included on a résumé?* (personal information)
- Ask: *What are two ways of organizing a résumé?* (by date—a chronological résumé; by sets of skills—a functional résumé)

Presentation 10 minutes

1 PREPARE TO WRITE A RÉSUMÉ

A CLASS. Read the information on résumé...

- Ask students to read the directions and the Résumé Tips box.
- Clarify vocabulary as needed. (For example: *off-white* is a light-beige or cream color that is close to white; *crumpled* describes a piece of paper that has been crushed.)
- Ask: *Is any information in the Résumé Tips box surprising to you? Why?*
- Discuss the question, offering prompts as needed to elicit answers. (For example, *Did you know that résumés should always be on white or off-white paper?*)

Controlled Practice 30 minutes

2 PRACTICE

STEP 1. Complete the form on page 31...

- Say: *Today, you're going to write a résumé. First, you're going to organize your information.*
- Ask students to fill out the form on page 31.

STEP 2. PAIRS. Exchange your completed forms....

- Say: *Find a partner and compare your forms. Ask each other questions to clarify details or to provide more information.*
- Model the exercise by looking at an above-level student's form and asking a clarification question. (For example, *Can you tell me more about your duties at the copy shop? How did you help customers?*)

- As students compare forms, walk around the room and ask for elaboration as needed. (For example, *Do you play any sports? Have you ever volunteered?*)

STEP 3. Write or type your résumé....

- Ask students to read the directions.
- Have students look at the sample résumé on page 29. Ask: *How does Iris list her name and contact information?* (in boldface, at the top of the page)
- Note that the headings on the left-hand side are in boldface and that there is a tab space between the left-hand heading, the dates, and the job descriptions.

Communicative Practice 15 minutes

STEP 4. PAIRS. Read your partner's résumé....

- Say: *Now find a partner and compare résumés. Ask each other questions or make suggestions to improve the résumé.*
- Model the exercise by looking at an above-level student's résumé and making a suggestion. (For example, *I like how you included all the details on your résumé, but you might want to use a larger typeface.*)
- Have students form pairs and read and discuss résumés.

Teaching Tip

Note some phrases on the board for students to use in giving feedback: *I like how you . . . You might want to try . . . The résumé would be even stronger if you . . .*

STEP 5. Revise your résumé. See how much...

- Say: *Revise your résumé, incorporating the suggestions that your partner made. Then you'll have your partner read your résumé again.*
- Have students revise their résumés and show them to their Step 4 partner for review.

Community Building

In Step 5, ask students to give positive feedback about the finished products. (*I really like how you . . .*)

NOTES FOR RÉSUMÉ FORM

Personal information

- Remind students to list their full name as it appears on official documents; they may cite a nickname in parentheses and quotation marks, for example: Mai-Lin Xiao Huang ("Amy").

Work history

- Emphasize that students should include employment in their home country as well as employment in the U.S.
- Remind students that they may list volunteer experience as work experience or under its own heading. Have them refer to Nina Sanchez's résumé on page 222. Say: *Nina put her volunteer work under the heading "Community Service."*

Educational information

- Tell students to list their English classes, as this will show employers that they are taking the initiative to improve their language skills.
- Remind students to list any degrees or certificates from their home country, giving the location where the degree or certificate was earned and describing in English what the degree and coursework entailed, for example: bachelor's degree, Universidad de Santa Cruz, Bolivia (bachelor's degree in chemistry, including courses in mathematics and physical science).

Teaching Tip

If students do not have all of the information needed for the form, ask them to highlight what is missing and add it to the form at home.

Additional information

- Tell students that it is very important to list any particular skills or hobbies, as they show employers that one has a wide range of abilities and experiences.
- Note that participating in team sports or community activities shows an employer that you are a team player and have the interpersonal skills needed to participate in a group activity.

Progress Check

Can you . . . write a chronological résumé?

Say: *We have practiced writing a chronological résumé. Can you do this? If so, check the box.*

Extra Practice

Interactive Practice

Personal information

Full name: _____

Address: _____

Phone number(s): _____

E-mail address (if you have one): _____

Work history

Employer 1

Name and city or town of Employer 1 (current or most recent): _____

_____

Year you started employment: _____ Position: _____

Responsibilities: _____

_____

Year employment ended if you're not still working: _____

Employer 2

Name and city and town of Employer 2: _____

_____

Year you started employment: _____ Position: _____

Responsibilities: _____

_____

Year employment ended: _____

Educational information

Name and city or town of current or most recent school or program: _____

_____

Degrees, certificates, types of courses: _____

_____

Additional information

Skills, interests, activities, and volunteer work: _____

_____

_____

Can you...write a chronological résumé? ☐

Listening and Speaking

1 BEFORE YOU LISTEN

GROUPS. Someone you know is going for a job interview. What advice would you give him or her? Suggest at least one idea for each category. Take notes. Answers will vary but could include:

1. Physical appearance

   You should dress appropriately for the job you are interviewing for.

2. Body language

   You should make eye contact with the interviewer.

3. Voice

   Be sure you can be heard.

4. Proper way to address interviewer

   Use *Mr.* or *Ms.*

5. Other

   Be punctual.

2 LISTEN

CD1 T10

A An employment counselor is giving a talk about job interviewing. Listen. What are some of the do's and don'ts he talks about? Take notes. Answers will vary but could include:

1. Physical appearance

   Dress appropriately for the job you want.

2. Body language

   Sit and stand up straight. Use a firm handshake. Smile. Make eye contact.

3. Voice

   Speak clearly and at a normal pace.

4. Proper way to address interviewer

   Use *Mr.* and *Ms.* Say *please* and *thank you*.

B GROUPS. Compare your ideas in Exercise 1 with the employment counselor's ideas. Which ones were the same?

C GROUPS. Discuss the questions.

1. Were any of the tips in the counselor's talk new to you? Which ones?

2. Which tips do you think will be easy for you to remember or follow? Which tips do you think will be difficult?

Talk about interview do's and don'ts

Getting Started   15 minutes

- Say: *We've talked about how to prepare for a job search and how to write an effective résumé. We also read about the interview process and how to prepare answers to common interview questions. A successful job interview is often a deciding factor in whether a person gets a job. So today we are going talk about the do's and don'ts of interviewing.*

- Ask students to share their own experiences looking for jobs, including job interviews.

- Explain the terms *do's* and *don'ts*. Say: *In informal English,* do's *means things we should do and* don'ts *means things we should not do.*

1 BEFORE YOU LISTEN

GROUPS. Someone you know is going for...

- Ask students to read the directions.

- Explain that giving advice can be helpful, but it is important to be respectful and careful in the language you use. Say: *In groups, we will be talking about tips for interviewing, but if you want to give advice to a friend in real life, make your advice sound positive. For example, you shouldn't say, "The clothes you wear are always too casual." You need to say, "Make sure you dress up for the interview."*

- Go through the list of categories and give a quick description or example of what each means. Probably the only categories that might need further description are "body language" and "other." For "other," give one suggestion, such as being several minutes early or making sure you know how to find where you are going.

- Set up groups and give an estimate of how long the groups should expect to work on this activity.

- After groups have finished, solicit the advice for each category and write it on the board.

- Ask the whole class to discuss which ideas are most useful and why.

Culture Connection

- Not only is body language germane to the interview, but it is also an interesting cultural topic because body language is not universal.

- Confirm that body language differs throughout the world. While Americans usually expect a person to make eye contact during a conversation, people from other backgrounds may find this jarring. In many cultures, it is polite to talk to an older person or a person of higher status with lowered eyes.

- Ask: *In your culture, what gesture means* yes, no, I approve, *or that's good?*

- Return to the interview process. Say: *Is this related to having a good interview? How?*

Presentation   10 minutes

2 LISTEN

 A **An employment counselor is giving a talk...**

- Ask students to read the directions.

- Restate the question. Say: *Listen for the do's and don'ts the employment counselor mentions.*

- Play CD 1, Track 10.

Controlled Practice   20 minutes

B GROUPS. Compare your ideas in Exercise 1...

- Keep the same groups as in Exercise 1.

- Ask students to read the directions and complete the exercise.

- Point out to students that they should follow the interviewer's lead in terms of tone and manner of address. For example, if the interviewer speaks in a casual manner, using *ma'am* or *sir* would not be necessary or appropriate.

C GROUPS. Discuss the questions...

- Keep the same groups as in Exercise 2B.

- Debrief with the whole class by asking which tips were new to them.

- Preview the next activity. Say: *Now you'll have a chance to listen to four people answer interview questions. Let's see if they are practicing the interview do's or the don'ts correctly.*

Expansion: Vocabulary Practice for 2D

- *Mistake* is a strong word. Before students complete the following exercises, help them identify some other milder, less direct words and phrases so that they have tactful ways to discuss mistakes.

- Confirm that everyone understands what *mistake* means. Give an example of a common mistake, such as dialing the wrong phone number.

- Say: Making a mistake *is a phrase that could be used in English for everything from dialing the wrong phone number to a driver hitting a pedestrian or a doctor prescribing the wrong medicine. Since not every mistake is terrible, there are some milder, more specific words we can use.*

- Give examples of related words or phrases that might be used instead of *mistake*. Write them on the board, and explain as needed. (For example, *You might have misunderstood the . . . You might have been confused about . . . You might have had the wrong idea about . . .*)

- Ask students to write any new words or phrases in their vocabulary logs.

D ⊘ Now listen to four job applicants...

- Ask students to read the directions.
- Repeat the question. (*What mistakes did . . .?*)
- Play CD 1, Track 11.
- Ask students to identify the mistakes each person made.
- Suggest that students read the audio script on page 233 if they have any trouble identifying the mistakes.

3 **PRACTICE**

PAIRS. Look at the pictures of Fabio and Gosia...

- Model the pronunciation of Fabio and Gosia. Say: *You are going to work in pairs to talk about the two people in the pictures: Fabio and Gosia.*

- Set up pairs. Because the class worked in the same group for several parts of the lesson, change the dynamic by setting up totally different pairs.

- Say: *Now that you are settled with your partners, read the directions, look carefully at the pictures, and answer the questions together.*

- Debrief with the whole group. Ask: *Did you decide that Fabio was correct in his appearance and body language? Why or Why not?* Repeat the same questions and follow up about Gosia.

- Note: It's easier to find "mistakes" in Gosia's appearance and body language. There may be a difference of opinion about whether or not Fabio made any "mistakes," but the discussion will be useful for students as they think about jobs they might want to apply for.

Answers: Fabio—Correct: right suit; smiling; shaking hands. Incorrect: Legs crossed, newspaper on lap; sitting sideways; didn't shave. Gosia—Correct: suit; haircut. Incorrect: blouse is too colorful; not sitting up straight; searching in purse because she didn't turn off cell phone before interview; too much jewelry.

Communicative Practice   15 minutes

4 **MAKE IT PERSONAL**

GROUPS. Talk about experiences you've had...

- Say: *Let's talk about experiences you had at job interviews or other types of interviews, such as school interviews or interviews with the U.S. Citizenship and Immigration Services (USCIS).*

- Set up groups. If the size of your class allows for it, set up different groups than earlier in the lesson. For example, if earlier you used ad hoc groups composed of students sitting together at tables, form the new groups by writing the names in each group on the board or by counting off 1-2-3-4 so that each person in the group will have one question to answer. In that case, say: *Who are the 1s?* (students raise hands) Repeat for the other numbers. Say: *In your group, read that numbered question and lead the discussion for it.*

- Make a list on the board, a transparency, or a flipchart of advice on how to make a good impression. Keep the list up for the rest of the unit and refer to it.

- Tell students that if *make an impression* is a new idiom for them, to write it in their vocabulary logs.

Extra Practice

Interactive Practice

D Now listen to four job applicants answer interview questions. What mistake does each person make? Answers will vary but could include:

1. Beatriz: She speaks too softly and mumbles her words.

2. Said: He uses the interviewer's first name.

3. Bruno: He uses "uh" and "um" a lot when he speaks.

4. Shin-Hae: She's too informal and uses informal language.

3 PRACTICE

PAIRS. Look at the pictures of Fabio and Gosia at their job interviews. Consider the jobs that they are interviewing for. What did they do correctly? What mistakes did they make?

Fabio: Computer Technician | Gosia: Office Assistant

4 MAKE IT PERSONAL

GROUPS. Talk about experiences you've had at job interviews. Discuss the questions.

1. Did you make any mistakes?

2. Are you worried about making mistakes in future interviews?

3. What can you do to avoid such mistakes?

4. A "first impression" is someone's first judgment or idea about another person. What do you do to make a good first impression when you meet people?

Reading

1 BEFORE YOU READ

A **CLASS.** Interviewers often ask applicants general questions. Look at the three questions in the article. Why do you think interviewers ask these kinds of questions?

B Read the article. Which tip do you find most helpful?

Three Commonly Asked Interview Questions

QUESTION 1. Can you tell me a little about yourself?

TIP: The interviewer wants to know… your skills and qualifications, not about your personal life or your problems. If you have not worked before, describe classes you have taken or are taking and how they have prepared you for the job.

QUESTION 2. What is your greatest strength?

TIP: The interviewer wants to know… a strength that will be useful in the job you're applying for. If possible, give an example of how this strength has been useful in another job.

QUESTION 3. What is your greatest weakness?

TIP: The interviewer wants to know … that you are aware of your weaknesses and that you are addressing them. You should mention a work-related weakness that *used to be* a problem and describe the steps you've taken to correct it.

---

2 READ

CD1 T12

Listen to and read the interview questions and answers. How are Eva's and Nabil's responses different?

Reading Skill: Comparing and Contrasting

Making comparisons and contrasts helps you understand a text better. When you compare, you notice how things are similar. When you contrast, you look at how they are different.

Interviewer: Can you tell me a little about yourself?

Eva: I'd really like to stay in school, but I need to work full-time. My husband works, but he doesn't make enough to pay our rent and other bills, and we need to buy a car. Our children need clothes and **supplies** for school. I really need this job, and I'll work very hard if I get it.

Nabil: I've worked in a department store for two years. I started as a part-time employee because I was in school. A few months ago my supervisor offered me a full-time position. But I was still taking classes, so I couldn't take the job. Now I've completed my program in **retail** management, and I'm ready for the full-time responsibilities of an assistant manager.

Getting Started   10 minutes

- Say: *We've talked about how to prepare for a job search, we've learned about résumés and how to write them, and we worked on preparing for a job interview. Now, we will be doing some reading and listening about actual interview questions.*

1 BEFORE YOU READ

Ⓐ CLASS. Interviewers often ask applicants general...

- Ask students to read the directions.
- Say: *Just skim the three questions; we'll read the complete article in a few minutes.*
- Say: *Why do you think interviewers ask these kinds of questions?* Accept all responses.
- Encourage students to try to use specific examples, not just generalities. For example, if a student responds to Question 1 with *The interviewer wants to know what you think is important about yourself,* say: *Can you give me an example?*
- If students can't come up with an example, say: *When answering Question 1, you shouldn't talk about what TV shows or music you like. You should talk about work experience and the classes you took, and why these experiences make you the right person for the job. If you're asked Questions 2 or 3, you should always try to stress the positive, even when you talk about your weaknesses.*

Presentation   15 minutes

Teaching Tip

- Remind students that looking at all the clues surrounding a text will help them understand what is important in it.
- Say: *Looking at the photos, pictures, headlines, numbered lists, or other elements will help you figure out the meaning more quickly and easily.*

Ⓑ Read the article...

- Ask students to read the article.
- Ask: *Did you find these tips helpful?* If a student says *no,* ask: *Why not?*
- Ask individual students: *What tip did you find most helpful? Why?*

Expansion: Vocabulary Practice for 1B

- Tell students that although these questions are typical, they may be phrased differently.
- Ask students to give alternative phrases for *greatest strength* and *greatest weakness.*
- If needed, give examples: *What are some of your strong points? What do you excel in? What do you think your greatest challenge is?*
- Compare *weaknesses* and *challenges.* Say: *Challenges is a more positive word, and many interviewers might use it to make the person looking for a job feel more at ease. However, other interviewers might use* weaknesses *to see how the person is able to handle the direct and strong word.*

Reading Skill: Comparing and Contrasting

- Direct students' attention to the Reading Skill box. Have them read the text.
- Tell students that compare-and-contrast essays show the similarities and differences between two or more people or things. The interview they are about to read contrasts two people's responses to the same set of questions. Tell students that as they read each section/question in the interview, they should look for differences among the responses.

2 READ

 Listen to and read the interview...

- Ask students to read the directions.
- Point out that the words and phrases in boldface—*supplies, retail, impact, customer, ambitious, impression,* and *crash*—appear in the glossary on page 245. Encourage students to read the entire interview first, before going to the glossary to check the meaning of a boldfaced word.
- Play CD 1, Track 12 while students read the article and listen.
- As a class, discuss how Eva's and Nabil's responses differ.

Answers: Eva talks about needing money; Nabil talks about wanting more responsibility. For *greatest strength,* Eva uses an example from work. Nabil uses a personal example. For *greatest weakness,* Eva turns a weakness (too much ambition) into a positive thing (helping co-workers). Nabil reveals that he has a bad temper (he shouldn't) but doesn't turn this into a positive thing (which would be hard to do).

Controlled Practice   15 minutes

3   CHECK YOUR UNDERSTANDING

GROUPS. Discuss. Who do you think...

- Set up groups. Ask students to read the directions.
- Ask the class to vote on the best response for each of the three questions. Say: *How many thought Eva gave the best answer to Question 1? How many thought Nabil gave the best answer to Question 2? How many thought Eva gave the best answer to Question 3?* Write the results on the board and discuss them.
- Tell students that an important rule is never to use the need for money as a reason for why they need a job. Say: *Employers want to find out whether the person they are talking to will be hardworking, intelligent, and honest.*

Possible answers: 1. Nabil; 2. Eva (more relevant to work); 3. Eva (Nabil's answer too negative)

4   WORD WORK

GROUPS. Choose three words...

- Keep the same groups as for Exercise 3.
- Ask students to read the directions.
- Say: *Remember that when you write in your vocabulary logs, you can always write more than three words or phrases. You can also use the log for words you read or hear outside of class.*

Communicative Practice   20 minutes

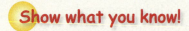 **Show what you know!**

STEP 1. Think of a job you would like to have...

- Ask students to read the directions.
- Review the three questions. Ask: *What are the three common questions interviewers ask?*
- Repeat the question: *How would you answer . . . ?*
- Have students write their answers.

STEP 2. ROLE PLAY. PAIRS. Role-play part...

- Set up pairs.
- Ask students to read the directions.
- Say: *Now that you've answered the three questions, we are going to role-play a job interview.*
- Explain that role-playing is like acting: You pretend you are somebody else.
- Ask students to provide "interviewer" language. (Most should be taken from the three questions, but also allow other language, such as greeting, closing, and small talk.) Write this language on the board.
- Call on an above-level student to give answers to the three questions; write the answers on the board.
- Model the activity with the same above-level student—with you as the interviewer. Include greeting, closing, and other language the student adds.
- Review directions for the activity. Say: *Remember to switch roles, so each of you gets a chance to be the interviewer and the person looking for a job.*

Teaching Tip

While pairs are performing role plays, use the scoring rubric for speaking on page Txiv to evaluate each student's vocabulary, grammar, fluency, and how well he or she completes the task. You may want to review the completed rubric with the students.

Progress Check

Can you . . . respond to interview questions?

- Say: *We have practiced talking about responding to interview questions. Now, look at the question at the bottom of the page. Can you respond to interview questions? If so, check the box.*

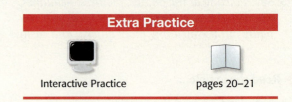

Extra Practice

Interactive Practice   pages 20–21

Interviewer: What is your greatest strength?

Eva: My greatest strength is my commitment to service. For example, in my job, I understand that all of my behavior and actions have an **impact** on the **customer**. If I see something on the floor, I pick it up. If a co-worker needs help, I help. And, of course, I'm polite to customers.

Nabil: Well, I'm optimistic. I don't get discouraged when bad things happen. For example, my father has been ill for many months, but I encourage him and try to be cheerful.

Interviewer: What is your greatest weakness?

Eva: Well, I'm so focused on doing good work that I might seem too **ambitious**. Some people in my department had that **impression**. I realized that I needed to do more to contribute to the success of my co-workers. Since then, I've constantly looked for ways to help them.

Nabil: My greatest weakness is my temper. Sometimes I get angry when computers **crash**. And sometimes I lose my temper if people pressure me when I already have a lot of stress.

---

3 CHECK YOUR UNDERSTANDING

GROUPS. Discuss. Who do you think gave the best answer for each interview question? What's wrong with the other answer for each question?

4 WORD WORK

🖉 **GROUPS.** Choose three words or phrases in the interview that you would like to remember. Discuss the words and their meanings. Then record the words and information about them in your vocabulary log.

Show what you know! Respond to interview questions

STEP 1. Think of a job you would like to have. How would you answer the three interview questions if you were interviewed for this job? Write a short answer for each question.

STEP 2. ROLE PLAY. PAIRS. Role-play part of a job interview. Use the responses you wrote in Step 1 and answer your partner's questions. Then switch roles.

Can you... respond to interview questions? ☐

Grammar

Present Perfect

I**'ve completed** my program in retail management.

My father **has been** ill *for* many months.

Since then, I**'ve looked** for ways to help them.

Grammar Watch

Use the present perfect:
- to talk about an indefinite time in the past.
- to talk about things that happen during a time period that isn't finished.
- with *for* or *since* to talk about things that began in the past and continue to the present. We use *for* with periods of time, for example, *for three weeks, for two months, for over an hour*. We use *since* with specific times in the past, for example, *since last May, since I started this job*.

1 PRACTICE

A **Read the example sentences in the chart and answer the questions.**

1. Which sentence or sentences talk about an indefinite time in the past?
2. Which sentence or sentences talk about things that began in the past and continue to the present?

B **Read about Iris. Underline the verbs in the present perfect.**

Iris <u>has</u> carefully <u>prepared</u> for her interview. She <u>has researched</u> the company, and she <u>has prepared</u> answers to common interview questions. She <u>has written</u> a résumé and cover letter, and she <u>has made</u> copies of both. Iris <u>has never had</u> an interview at a big company before, but she feels confident.

C **Complete the paragraph about Iris. Write the present perfect form of the verbs in parentheses.**

As for her qualifications, Iris is in good shape. She __hasn't/has not completed__ her **(not / complete)** program yet, but she will very soon. She __has finished__ **(finish)** most of her classes, and she __has done__ **(do)** well on her tests. Iris __has worked__ **(work)** part-time for quite a while, and her supervisor will give her a great reference. So Iris has a good chance of getting the job she wants.

Getting Started   5 minutes

- Say: *In the last lesson, we practiced responding to job interview questions. What are some questions that you are likely to be asked in a job interview?* (Possible answers: Can you tell me a little about yourself? What is your greatest strength/weakness?)

- Say: *Today we're going to prepare for a job interview and talk about things we did at some point in the past. To do so, we'll practice the present perfect.*

Presentation   15 minutes

Present Perfect

- Copy the grammar chart onto the board.
- Ask students to read the Grammar Watch.
- Point to the grammar chart. Say: *These sentences are in the present perfect.* Read the sentences aloud.
- Ask students how to form the present perfect (*have* or *has* + past participle). Write this on the board.

> **Language Note**
>
> Remind students that the past participle of regular verbs is the same as the past tense (infinitive + *-ed*). However, many verbs have irregular past participles—for a list, see page 225.

- Write the heading *Indefinite time in the past* on the board. Say: *Use the present perfect for an indefinite time in the past—for something that started and stopped, but it's not clear when. Also use it to talk about an action repeated many times.*

- Write the following sentences under the heading: *I have finished my homework. I have visited Los Angeles many times.* Ask: *Does the sentence tell when you finished your homework?* (no) *Does the sentence say when you visited Los Angeles?* (no)

- Say: *These are indefinite times, not specific times, so use the present perfect. Use the simple past for specific times at which something took place; for example,* I went to Los Angeles last weekend. *In this sentence, it is known when the action started and stopped.*

- Write the heading *Started in the past but not yet finished* on the board.

- Say: *Also use the present perfect to talk about something that has started but not yet finished.*

- Write the following sentences under the heading: *She has been a nurse for two years. They have lived in their house for fifteen years.* Ask: *Did she become a nurse in the past?* (yes) *Is she still a nurse?* (yes) *Did they begin living in their house in the past?* (yes) *Do they continue to live in their house?* (yes)

- Say: *These are actions that began in the past but have not yet finished—so use the present perfect. The present perfect indicates that these conditions are still true.*

- Say: *Likewise, if an action is expected to take place but has not occurred up until now, use the present perfect with* yet. Write an example on the board (*I haven't had breakfast yet.*). Say: *The speaker knows that she will have breakfast at some point in the near future, but the action has not occurred up until now.*

Controlled Practice   15 minutes

1   **PRACTICE**

A   **Read the example sentences in the chart...**

- Ask students to read the directions and answer the questions individually.

- Point to the grammar chart on the board and ask Question 1. (Answer: *I've completed my program in retail management.*) Say: *Do you know when the person completed the program?* (no) *So it's an indefinite time in the past.*

- Point to the grammar chart on the board and ask Question 2. (Answers: *My father has been ill for many months./Since then, I've looked for ways to help them.*) Say: *Did these things begin in the past?* (yes) *Have they continued to the present?* (yes) *Therefore, use the present perfect—not the simple past.*

B   **Read about Iris. Underline the verbs...**

- Ask students to read the directions and complete the exercise.

C   **Complete the paragraph about...**

- Ask students to read the directions.

- Do an example together (changing *complete* in the second sentence to *hasn't completed*), noting that *yet* is used with the negative form of the present perfect to describe an action that has not been completed.

- Have students complete the exercise.

Controlled Practice   10 minutes

2   PRACTICE

A STEP 1. Write *Have you . . . ? questions...*

- Write on the board: *Have you talked with a career counselor? Did you talk with a career counselor before you started your job search?*

- Ask: *Why is the present perfect used with the first question but not with the second? Say: Use the present perfect with questions that ask about an unspecified time in the past. If a question addresses a specific time in the past, use the simple past.*

- Have students complete the exercise.

Expansion: Grammar Practice for 2A

- Give students more practice with the formation of the present perfect. A line dialogue activity based on the questions from Exercise A is particularly helpful for those with a tactile learning style.

- Write the prompts from Step 1 (**not** the completed questions) in large print on sheets of paper, one question per sheet. *Note:* If you have more than fourteen students, make additional prompts; you need one question for every two students.

- Have students with prompt sheets (Group A) form a line in the hallway; they should hold up their prompt sheet so that the students opposite them can see it.

- Have the other students (Group B) line up in the hallway facing the students with the prompt sheets. Group B students move through the line, one by one, saying a question from the phrase on the prompt. For example: Group A sheet says *talk with a career counselor*; Group B says: *Have you talked with a career counselor?* Group A student says, *Yes, I have* or *No, I haven't.* Group B students then move down one.

- When students in Group B complete the activity, have them trade places with Group A and repeat the activity.

B STEP 2. CLASS. **Walk around the class. Ask...**

- Ask students to read the directions and the example.

- Have all students stand up with their books and pens.

- Say: *Now you will walk around and ask your classmates these questions until someone says* yes. *You'll write that person's name in the box to the right of the question.*

- Model the activity by going to an above-level student and asking one of the questions. (*Have you ever written a résumé?*) If the student says *yes,* write the student's name in the book; if the student says *no,* ask another student the same question.

- Have students complete the exercise.

Communicative Practice   15 minutes

Show what you know!

STEP 1. GROUPS. **Discuss. What has your experience...**

- Ask students to read the directions.

- Have students form small groups and discuss their experience with job interviews in the U.S.

- Monitor conversations, offering prompts as needed. (For example, *How many job interviews has he had?*)

STEP 2. **Report to the class about...**

- Ask a representative from each group to tell the class about group members' job interview experiences (how many have had interviews, what jobs they were for, etc.).

Progress Check

Can you . . . prepare for a job interview?

- Say: *We have practiced preparing for a job interview. Can you do this? If so, check the box.*

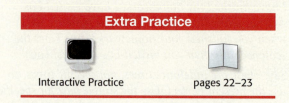

Extra Practice	
Interactive Practice	pages 22–23

A STEP 1. Write *Have you . . . ?* questions using the words below.

1. talk with a career counselor

   Have you talked with a career counselor?

2. write a résumé

   Have you written a résumé?

3. go on any job interviews since you came to the U.S.

   Have you gone on any job interviews since you came to the U.S.?

4. use the Internet to look for employment ads or postings

   Have you used the Internet to look for employment ads or postings?

5. experience any obstacles to reaching your career goals

   Have you experienced any obstacles to reaching your career goals?

6. talk with others who have the kind of job you want

   Have you talked with others who have the kind of job you want?

7. change jobs in the last five years

   Have you changed jobs in the last five years?

B STEP 2. CLASS. Walk around the class. Ask and answer the questions you wrote in Step 1. When you answer, offer some additional information. When someone answers *yes*, write his or her name in the box at the right of the question in Step 1.

A: *Have you ever talked with a career counselor?*
B: *Yes, I have. I talked with Mr. Goodman. He was very helpful.*
                    OR
   No, I haven't. I should do that soon.

Show what you know! Prepare for a job interview

STEP 1. GROUPS. Discuss. What has your experience been with job interviews in the U.S.? Who has had the most experience?

STEP 2. CLASS. Report to the class about your group's job interview experience.

Can you... prepare for a job interview? ☐

Listening and Speaking

1 BEFORE YOU LISTEN

CLASS. What is the correct etiquette, or rules for polite behavior, at a job interview?

1. At an interview, when do you take a seat?
2. Should you accept an offer of coffee or tea?
3. If the interviewer asks if you have any questions, what questions, if any, should you ask?
4. What should you say at the end of the interview?

2 LISTEN

CD1 T13

A Iris went on a job interview. Listen and answer the questions.

1. Did Iris take a seat?
2. Did she accept an offer of coffee or tea?
3. What did she say when the interviewer asked if she had any questions?
4. What did she say at the end of the interview?

B **PAIRS.** Compare answers. Did Iris do the right things?

CD1 T14

C Liam went on a job interview. Listen. What are at least four things that Liam did wrong? Take notes.

3 CONVERSATION

ROLE PLAY. PAIRS. Student A, you are Liam. Student B, you are the interviewer. Review the audio script of Liam's interview on page 234. Then redo Liam's interview so that he makes a better impression. Ask open-ended questions.

Communication Skill:
Asking Questions

A job interview is a two-way conversation. Asking questions helps you find out information and carry on a lively conversation. Ask open-ended questions that begin with the words *Who, What, Where, When, Why,* and *How*. This way you will receive more than a *yes/no* response. For example, you might ask: *What would my typical workday be like in this job?*

Talk about more interview do's and don'ts

Getting Started 5 minutes

- Say: *Because the interview is such an important part of the job search, we are going to learn more about interview etiquette.*
- Ask: *What does* etiquette *mean?* Accept student responses—if correct, repeat what the student said; if not exactly right, change it to make it correct. If no students respond, give your own definition and example. (For example, *According to the dictionary,* etiquette *means the formal rules for polite behavior in society or in a particular group.*)

Presentation 5 minutes

1 BEFORE YOU LISTEN

CLASS. What is the correct etiquette,...

- Ask students to read the directions.
- Students will probably answer Questions 1 and 2 easily. (Question 1: Sit down when the interviewer offers a seat. Question 2: Accept an offer of tea or coffee unless it is against your religion or bad for your health—then ask for a glass of water.)
- For Question 3, say: *Interviewers want a person looking for a job to ask questions related to the work. If a person doesn't, the interviewer will think he or she isn't interested in the job.* Ask students to brainstorm a list of possible questions they should ask.
- For Question 4, students should understand that job applicants need to thank the interviewer and say something like "I hope to hear from you soon."
- See the answers in Exercise 2A for some possible responses to the questions in Exercise 1.

Controlled Practice 15 minutes

2 LISTEN

A **Iris went on a job interview....**

- Ask students to read the directions. Play CD 1, Track 13.

Answers: 1. yes; 2. no; 3. *When will a hiring decision be made?* 4. *Thank you.*

B **PAIRS. Compare answers. Did Iris...**

- Ask students to read the directions; set up pairs.

Communication Skill: Asking Questions

- Direct students to the Communication Skill box.
- Have a student read the text. Say: *Asking* Who, What, Where, *and the other* Wh- *questions is a good strategy in many situations, not just in a job interview. If you ask* Do you know what time the bus comes?, *a person could answer just yes or no. If you ask* When does the bus come?, *you have a better chance of getting the information you need.*

C **Liam went on a job interview....**

- Ask students to read the directions and take notes.
- Play CD 1, Track 14. Ask students to share what they thought Liam did wrong in the interview.

Answers: 1. called the interviewer by his first name instead of "Mr. Samson"; 2. *no problem* is disrespectful and overly familiar; 3. wasn't polite—didn't say *Yes, please*, requested decaf; 4. said something bad about his current boss; 5. gave a bad example about how to cope with work; 6. wasn't prepared to offer a reference; 7. said *uh* and *um* and hesitated too much; 8. didn't have any questions about the company, which revealed that he hadn't researched the job in advance

Communicative Practice 15 minutes

3 CONVERSATION

ROLE PLAY. PAIRS. Student A, you are...

- Ask students to read the directions. Review what Liam's mistakes were.
- Model the role play with an above-level student. Then set up pairs.
- Review directions for the activity. Say: *Remember to switch roles so that each of you gets a chance to be the interviewer and the person looking for a job.*

Possible answers: say *Pleased to meet you, Mr. Samson*; instead of *no problem*, say *That's perfectly understandable, it was no problem at all.*; say *Yes, please* for the coffee or tea; say that he has learned a lot at Quality Exterior Home Repair but that he wants to learn new skills; say *I handle stress by talking with my co-workers and by volunteering as a coach for . . .* ; *I have a list of references with their contact information; please feel free to contact anyone on the list.*; *I do have a couple of questions—What are typical work schedules like?, I read on the company website about some jobs the company has done in other states—how big is the company overall?*

Controlled Practice   10 minutes

 PRACTICE

PAIRS. Here are a few more tips...

- Ask students to read the directions. Say: *Please write the correct letter of the question on the line before its matching tip. Look at the example, number 1.*
- Tell students that this exercise does not show direct questions and answers. It shows questions and tips.
- Say: *Do you understand what we are matching now—a typical interview question and a related tip?*
- Have students complete the exercise.

Communicative Practice   10 minutes

 MAKE IT PERSONAL

STEP 1. How confident are you...

- Ask students to read the directions.
- On the board, draw a long horizontal line. On one end write *1* with *very confident* below it; on the other end of the line write *5* and *not at all confident* below it.
- Write *2, 3, 4* on the remaining space on the line.
- Say: *What shall we put for number 2?* If no one responds, say: *How about* confident *for number 2? What about number 3? Does* mostly confident *sound OK? What about* not very confident *for number 4?* If students disagree, try other wording.
- Say: *Now that we have the scale, think for a minute about how you rate yourself. Try to be realistic— think of your strong points and your challenges.*

STEP 2. GROUPS. Discuss reasons for your...

- Read the directions aloud; emphasize the purpose of this activity.
- As you walk around the class, listen to make sure that each person in each group does some talking. Also make sure suggestions are polite and respectful.
- Debrief with the whole class. Say: *What are some of the suggestions you talked about?*
- Invite students to the board, an overhead, or a flipchart to write the suggestions down.
- Review the suggestions briefly. If any are clearly bad suggestions, explain why they won't work.
- If possible, keep the list posted to refer to at other times, since getting jobs and gaining confidence are ongoing issues.

Community Building

- Set up mock interviews where students can demonstrate their understanding of information and advice about job interviews.
- Set up two large groups—the interviewers and the job applicants. Have each group review Lessons 4, 5, 6, and 7 and (if time permits) research more about job interviewing protocol, questions, and answers—the interviewers concentrate on what an interviewer does; the job applicants concentrate on what a job applicant should say and do.
- In the groups, participants practice their roles and give and receive advice. The interviewer group should develop a list of questions; the job applicant group should develop a list of possible answers.

Extra Practice

Interactive Practice

PAIRS. Here are a few more tips and example responses for questions in a job interview. Match the questions with the tips. Write the correct letter on the line before the tip.

Questions

a. Can you describe how you handled a difficult situation at work?

b. May we contact your references?

c. How do you handle stress on the job?

d. What do you know about our company?

e. Why are you leaving your current employer?

f. How do you respond to criticism?

Tips

__d__ 1. Always have an answer to this question. Research the company before your interview.

__e__ 2. Never say anything negative about your current or past employer. Say something positive, such as "I'm ready to take on more responsibilities, but there are no opportunities for advancement right now."

__c__ 3. You should not lie, but make your answer as positive as you can. "I try to relax outside of work by doing things with my family or listening to music."

__f__ 4. The interviewer wants to hear that you can handle criticism and learn from it. You can honestly say, "I listen to it carefully and I ask what I can do to improve."

__b__ 5. The answer must always be "yes."

__a__ 6. You should prepare an answer for this kind of question and be able to describe the situation.

STEP 1. How confident are you that you could answer questions at a job interview? Rate yourself from 1 to 5 (1 = very confident; 5 = not at all confident).

STEP 2. GROUPS. Discuss reasons for your rating with your group. How could you gain confidence? Give each other suggestions.

Grammar

Present Perfect vs. Present Perfect Continuous

Present Perfect	Present Perfect Continuous
Iris **has done** a lot of research.	Iris **has been doing** a lot of research.
I**'ve taken** courses at Hillsborough Community College.	I**'ve been taking** courses at Hillsborough Community College.
Iris **has worked** evenings as an assistant manager for a year.	Iris **has been working** evenings as an assistant manager for a year.
I**'ve made** an effort to greet everyone at the beginning of my shift since I realized this.	I**'ve been making** an effort to greet everyone at the beginning of my shift since I realized this.

Grammar Watch

- The present perfect focuses on the completion of an action. It describes an action that is finished.
- The present perfect continuous emphasizes the continuation of an action into the present and possibly the future. It focuses on an action in progress.

1 PRACTICE

CD1 T15

Listen to and complete the sentences. Then check (✓) *Continuing Action* or *Completed Action*.

	Continuing Action	Completed Action
1. I've __been working on__ my résumé.	✓	☐
2. I've __been attending__ night classes.	✓	☐
3. My friend has __proofread__ my résumé.	☐	✓
4. I've __been applying__ for full-time jobs.	✓	☐
5. Miriam has __taken__ classes in landscape design.	☐	✓
6. Sheena has __finished__ all of her classes for her degree.	☐	✓
7. We've __been studying__ all day for our math exam.	✓	☐
8. She's finally __completed__ her applications for college.	☐	✓

Getting Started   5 minutes

- Say: *In Lesson 6, we practiced the present perfect:* have *or* has *+ past participle*
- Write examples on the board: *Have you ever used a cash register? I have taken many computer classes. He has worked as an assistant manager since 2005.*
- Ask: *When is the present perfect used, and when is the simple past used?* (Possible answer: The present perfect is used to describe something that happened at an unspecified time or started in the past but is still true—or something that is expected to happen at some point but has not occurred up to now; the simple past is used to describe something that started and stopped at a specific time in the past.)
- Say: *Today we're going to talk about our education and work experience. We'll practice the present perfect and the present perfect continuous.*

Presentation   10 minutes

Present Perfect vs. Present Perfect Continuous

- Copy the grammar chart onto the board.
- Ask students to read the Grammar Watch.
- Point to the grammar chart. Say: *Use the present perfect to talk about an action that started and stopped at an unspecified time in the past **or** an action that started in the past and has continued to the present.*
- Say: *To emphasize that an action started and is still in progress, use the present perfect continuous.*
- Read the first example (both columns) in the grammar chart.
- Say: *If I say that Iris has done a lot of research, I imply that she has completed the research. If I say that she has been doing a lot of research, I imply that she is continuing her research and hasn't yet finished.*
- Read the other examples in the chart.
- Ask students how to form the present perfect continuous (*have* or *has* + *been* + *-ing* form of verb). Write this on the board.

- Write more examples on the board and have students identify them: *I have taken many English classes.* (present perfect) *He has been studying English since 2006.* (present perfect continuous) *She has been working on her homework since eight o'clock.* (present perfect continuous) *We've gone out to eat a lot this month.* (present perfect)

Teaching Tip

- If students are having trouble with the present perfect and the present perfect continuous, write on the board:

    It has rained a lot this summer.

    It has been raining since three o'clock.

- Ask: *Which sentence talks about something that occurred at an unspecified time—or many times—in the past?* (the first sentence) Say: *For that, use the present perfect.*
- Ask: *Which sentence talks about an action that is still taking place right now?* (the second sentence) Say: *For that, use the present perfect continuous.*

Controlled Practice   10 minutes

1 **PRACTICE**

  Listen to and complete the sentences...

- Ask students to read the directions.
- Ask: *How will you know if the speaker is talking about a continuing action?* (You'll hear the present perfect continuous—*has been* or *have been* plus the verb ending in *-ing.*)
- Play CD 1, Track 15.
- Play Track 15 again, pausing after each sentence to elicit the correct answer from students and write it on the board.
- *Optional:* If students are having difficulty grasping the difference between the two verb forms, ask: *Did you hear a verb ending in* -ing? Explain that, if so, this shows that the action was a continuing one.

Controlled Practice   15 minutes

2 PRACTICE

A First, use the words in the chart...

- Ask students to read the directions and write questions in their notebooks with the present perfect continuous using the words in the chart.
- Show an example on the board. Write *Have you*, then write *learn*, and finally add *-ing* to the end of *learn*. Ask students to complete the question.
- Review the questions before students walk around.
- Say: *Walk around and ask your classmates these questions until someone says* yes. *Write that person's name in the chart.*
- Model the activity with an above-level student. If the student says *yes*, write the student's name; if the student says *no*, ask another student the same question.

Answers: Have you been learning new work skills this year? Have you been using English outside of class as much as possible? Have you been working for a temp agency? Have you been learning a new computer skill? Have you been looking for a new job? Have you been trying to correct a work-related weakness?

B PAIRS. Talk about two things...

- Ask students to read the directions and example.
- Elicit an example from a student, offering prompts. (*Have you been exercising? Practicing English?*)
- Have students form pairs and complete the exercise.

Expansion: Writing Practice for 2B

- Have students write an e-mail to a friend in their home country about things they have been doing. They should use the present perfect continuous and write six to eight sentences. Use the following example, clarifying vocabulary as needed.

Hi, Maria, what have you been up to?

Things have been very busy for me! I've been studying English every night and preparing for the TOEFL exam. I've also been taking an exercise class at the gym—you should try it! I've been trying to get a friend to take the class with me! ☺

Hope all is well and that you've been having fun! I've been thinking about everyone back home a lot. Wish you were here—I miss you! Izzy

Communicative Practice   20 minutes

Show what you know!

STEP 1. ROLE PLAY. PAIRS. Describe a job...

- Ask students to read the directions. Set up pairs.
- Say: *First, take a few minutes to talk about the job that you're interested in.* Have students describe the job, referring to the Position Desired or Objective section of their résumés.
- Say: *Before you practice your role play, make a list of questions for the job interview.* Elicit sample questions (*Tell me about your experience. Have you ever used a computer? Tell me about your greatest strength.*). Have students write questions together.
- Remind students to look at the résumés they wrote in Lesson 3 as they plan the role play.

STEP 2. PAIRS. Practice, and then perform your...

- Tell students that they will practice their job interviews and then present them to the class.
- Elicit feedback after each performance. *Did the interviewee make eye contact with the interviewer? Did he speak clearly? Did she sell herself well?*

> **Teaching Tip**
>
> While pairs are performing role plays, use the scoring rubric for speaking on page Txiv to evaluate each student's vocabulary, grammar, fluency, and how well he or she completes the task. You may want to review the completed rubric with students.

Progress Check

Can you . . . talk about your education and work experience?

- Say: *We have practiced talking about your education and work experience. Can you do this? If so, check the box.*

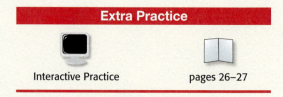

Extra Practice

Interactive Practice   pages 26–27

A First, use the words in the chart to write questions in the present perfect continuous. Then walk around and ask your classmates the questions. Write the name of a classmate who answers *yes*.

Have you . . . ?	Name
learn new work skills this year	
use English outside of class as much as possible	
work for a temp agency	
learn a new computer skill	
look for a new job	
try to correct a work-related weakness	

B PAIRS. Talk about two things you have done this year. Use the present perfect continuous. Ask and answer questions about them.

A: *I've been learning a new computer skill.*
B: *Really? What?*
A: *I've been learning how to download and send photos. I want to exchange pictures with my family back in Ecuador.*

Show what you know!   Talk about your education and work experience

STEP 1. ROLE PLAY. PAIRS. Describe a job you're interested in, and then plan a role play of a job interview. Use the résumés you wrote on page 30.

Interviewee: Sell yourself—eagerly tell about the things you have done and have been doing that will make you a good employee. Use the correct body language, speak clearly and in a positive tone of voice, and maintain good posture and eye contact.

Interviewer: Remember to ask about strengths and weaknesses.

STEP 2. PAIRS. Practice, and then perform your role play for the class.

Can you...talk about your education and work experience? ☐

Write an effective cover letter

Writing

1 BEFORE YOU WRITE

A You are going to write a cover letter for a résumé to a potential employer. Read about cover letters. Then read the writing tip.

> **FYI** ABOUT COVER LETTERS
>
> A cover letter briefly highlights the key points of your résumé. It describes your qualifications for a job, your interest in the position, and your positive personality traits. Like all formal letters, cover letters should be typed, follow a standard format, and be polite in tone. Employers receive many applications and résumés for a single position. The purpose of a cover letter is to attract the attention and interest of the person who has to skim material from potential applicants.
>
> **Writing Tip:** Using language from the job ad in the cover letter
>
> You want your cover letter to show that you are the match the employer is looking for. So read the job ad carefully and use some of the same language in your cover letter.

B Look at the résumé you wrote on page 30 again. Underline key points about your job qualifications and personality traits that you might want to highlight in a cover letter.

C Read the job ad and the writing model for a cover letter on pages 205–206. How does Iris show that she would be a good match for the job?

2 ANALYZE THE WRITING MODEL

A PAIRS. Discuss the questions.

1. What aspects of Iris's educational background does she highlight?
2. What personality traits does she mention?

B Read the writing model on page 206 again. Underline language in the cover letter that matches the requirements in the job ad.

Write an effective cover letter

Getting Started · 5 minutes

- Say: *We have been talking about the job search. We have practiced vocabulary and grammatical structures for talking about our work experience and skills, and we have written résumés. Today we are going to write a cover letter to accompany a résumé. Has anyone ever written a cover letter? What information did you include in it?*

Presentation · 5 minutes

1 BEFORE YOU WRITE

A You are going to write a cover letter...

- Read the directions aloud. Ask students to read the FYI note and Writing Tip.
- *Optional:* Ask students to close their books. Say: *What do you remember from what you just read about cover letters? What can you tell me about them?* (Possible answers: They should be typed, polite, follow a standard format, introduce the job applicant and attract attention, and use some of the same language as the job ad.)

Controlled Practice · 15 minutes

B Look at the résumé you wrote on page 30...

- Say: *Today, you will use information from the résumé that you wrote in Lesson 3 as the basis for a cover letter.*
- Ask students to read the directions.
- Have students complete the exercise. Walk around and check students' work, offering prompts as needed. (*Do any of your responsibilities from your last job match qualifications for a job you might want?*)
- *Optional:* Ask for volunteers to share which job qualifications or personality traits they underlined in their résumé. After each does so, ask: *Why would you include these things in a cover letter? What would that show employers?*

C Read the job ad and the writing model...

- Have students read the directions.
- Ask students to look at pages 205–206 and read the job ad and cover letter.

- Ask: *What qualifications are needed for this job?* (Possible answers: accounting degree or certificate, computer skills, interpersonal and problem-solving skills, someone who is hardworking and dependable)
- Say: *As you read the cover letter, pay attention to how the writer shows that she would be a good match for the job.*
- Clarify vocabulary as needed.
- Have students complete the exercise. Walk around and check students' work.
- Call on students to say answers, and write them on the board.

Possible answer: Iris uses language from the job ad to show that she is a good match for the position; for example, she says that she has excellent problem-solving and communication skills.

2 ANALYZE THE WRITING MODEL

A PAIRS. Discuss the questions.

- Ask students to form pairs and discuss the questions. Walk around and help students as needed.
- Call on students to read the questions and say answers.

Answers: 1. She's finishing an AA degree in accounting. 2. She's dependable, hardworking, and responsible.

- Ask: *Do you feel that Iris's letter is satisfactory? Why or why not?* Offer prompts as needed. (*Did Iris show that she can work in a team environment? Does the letter make her sound like a hardworking, dependable employee?*)

B Read the writing model on page 206 again....

- Say: *Now you're going to read the cover letter a second time and look for language that matches the requirements in the job ad. When you see language that matches the job ad, underline it.*
- Have students complete the exercise. Walk around and check students' work.
- Elicit answers from students and write them on the board, emphasizing that Iris showed that she had the very qualities the company asked for in the ad.

Possible answers: entry-level accountant; AA degree; use all Microsoft® Office programs, as well as QuickBooks™; perform basic bookkeeping and accounting duties; dependable, hardworking and responsible; excellent problem-solving and communication skills

Write an effective cover letter

Communicative Practice   35 minutes

3   THINK ON PAPER

A Read the T-chart Iris made...

- Say: *In the last unit, we used a word web to organize our ideas before writing. Today, we're going to use a different kind of diagram, called a T-chart, to organize our ideas. Then we'll use this T-chart to write a cover letter.*
- Ask students to read the directions and look at the T-chart in the book. Write the T-chart on the board.
- Read the T-chart, noting how the job requirements listed in the left-hand column match the skills/traits/experiences listed in the right-hand column.

B Think about a job that you would...

- Say: *Now you are going to use the T-chart to organize ideas for your cover letter.*
- Ask students to read the directions.
- Say: *Remember that you'll list the skills/traits/experiences from your résumé, but you may imagine the requirements for your job.*
- Have students complete the exercise.

Teaching Tip

Before you have students write cover letters, make sure that they understand the format and language of a business letter. Have students look at the model letter. Ask:

- *Where did the writer put her return address?* (on the left-hand side, at the top, leaving about an inch of space)
- *Where did she put the date?* (2 lines down from the bottom of the return address)
- *Where did she put the company's address?* (2 lines down from the date, on the left-hand side)
- *What did she call the employer?* (Mr. Samson) *What would she call the employer if he were a woman?* (Ms. Samson)
- *Did the writer indent the paragraphs of the business letter?* (yes—by about 5 spaces)
- *How did the writer end the letter?* (by thanking the employer and showing eagerness for further contact)

- *What did the writer use for a closing?* (Sincerely)
- *Where did she put her name?* (She left about 3 spaces between *Sincerely* and her typed name and then signed her name in the space above the typed name.)

4   WRITE

Use your T-chart to write...

- Read the directions aloud, emphasizing that students should follow the format of the model.
- Have students write the first draft of a cover letter.

5   CHECK YOUR WRITING

A STEP 1. **Revise your work.**

- Say: *Read over your cover letter a first time and answer the questions in Step 1. If any answers are no, revise your work.*
- *Optional:* Have students form pairs, exchange letters, and give each other feedback and suggestions.

B STEP 2. **Edit and proofread.**

- Say: *Read over your cover letter a second time to correct grammar, spelling, punctuation, and typos.*
- *Optional:* Have students complete a "clean" second draft of their cover letter at home, incorporating revisions and corrections from the revision and editing steps.

Teaching Tip

You may want to collect student papers and provide feedback. Use the scoring rubric for writing on page Txv to evaluate vocabulary, grammar, mechanics, and how well students complete the task. You may want to review the completed rubric with students.

Extra Practice

Interactive Practice

page 28

3 THINK ON PAPER

A Read the T-chart Iris Martinez made before she wrote her cover letter. In the first column, she listed requirements for the entry-level accounting job at Megametro Media. In the second column, she listed those skills and traits that make her a good candidate for the job.

Entry-Level Accountant: Job Requirements	My Skills/Traits/ Experience
Degree or certificate in accounting	Getting accounting certificate in a month
Knowledge of accounting software and related experience	Know Microsoft Office and QuickBooks; have performed basic bookkeeping/ accounting duties
Team environment	Am a team player
Responsible, dependable, hardworking candidates	Possess all these traits

B Think about a job that you would like to apply for, one that is a good match for your experience and personality traits. What would the job requirements be? If you don't know, make them up. Review the job qualifications and character traits you highlighted on your résumé in Exercise 1B. Then use a T-chart like Iris's to brainstorm and organize ideas for a cover letter.

4 WRITE

Use your T-chart to write a three-paragraph cover letter for a specific job. Follow the same letter format as the writing model on page 206.

5 CHECK YOUR WRITING

A STEP 1. Revise your work.

1. Does your letter match the job's requirements?
2. Have you presented skills and traits that make you an ideal candidate for the job?
3. Have you used the correct letter format?

B STEP 2. Edit and proofread.

1. Have you checked your grammar, spelling, and punctuation?
2. Have you proofread for typing errors?

1 REVIEW

For your grammar review, go to page 227.

2 ACT IT OUT — What do you say?

PAIRS. You are discussing ways to conduct an effective job search and create a good impression during a job interview.

> **Student A:** Review Lessons 1–3. Explain how to prepare for a job search and write an effective résumé.

> **Student B:** Review Lessons 4–7. Describe ways to prepare for a successful job interview, including interview do's and don'ts.

3 READ AND REACT — Problem-solving

STEP 1. Read about José.

José has been searching for a sales job for several months. He answered a job ad for a junior sales position in the inventory department of an electronics store. The human resources manager called him to come in for an interview. José is very excited but also very nervous about how he will act during the job interview. He's afraid that he might forget to follow the correct etiquette. He's also worried about remembering exact details about his previous job experience.

STEP 2. GROUPS. What is José's problem? What can he do?

4 CONNECT

For your Community-building Activity, go to page 213.

Which goals can you check off? Go back to page 25.

 Go to the CD-ROM for more practice.

Road Trip

Preview

Do you have a car? Do you drive to work or school? Do you take driving vacations?

UNIT GOALS

☐ Identify car parts and related problems

☐ Talk about highway safety do's and don'ts

☐ Decide which insurance is best for you

☐ Identify what to do if the police stop you

☐ Describe traffic problems

☐ Use the Internet to get maps and directions

Life Skills

1   IDENTIFY CAR PARTS

A   **GROUPS.**   Discuss. What parts of your car should you check before you start driving?

B   **PAIRS.**   Identify the parts of a car. Write the correct number of the word next to the line pointing to the car part in each picture.

1. ~~accelerator/gas pedal~~	6. emergency brake	11. ignition	16. taillights
2. battery	7. ~~engine~~	12. rear-view mirror	17. tire
3. brake	8. headlight	13. seat belt	18. trunk
4. bumper	9. hood	14. side-view mirror	19. windshield
5. dashboard	10. horn	15. steering wheel	20. windshield wipers

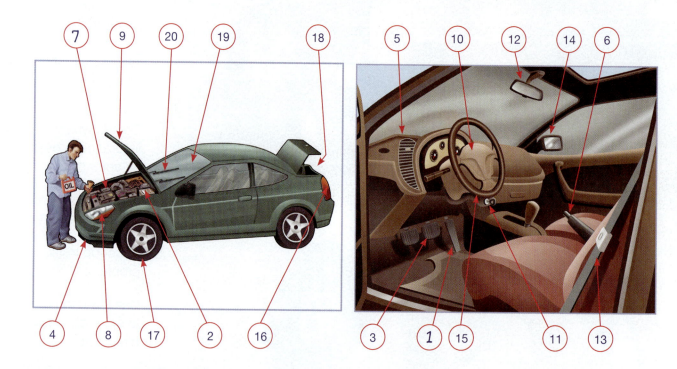

C   What are the different fluids used in cars? Match the fluids with their purpose.

   _d_   1. wiper fluid   a. powers the engine

   _c_   2. oil   b. keeps the engine cool

   _a_   3. gas   c. lubricates, or greases, the moving part of an engine

   _b_   4. engine coolant   d. washes the windshield

Getting Started · 10 minutes

Community Building

Set the stage for this lesson and help students visualize the topic by taping to the board pictures of vehicles from magazine ads. Say: *Today we're going to talk about cars. Which of these cars or trucks would you like to drive? Why?* Have students walk around and discuss with classmates which vehicle they would choose.

1 IDENTIFY CAR PARTS

A GROUPS. Discuss. What parts of your car...

- Have students form small groups. Ask them to read and discuss the question and note answers on a sheet of flipchart or notebook paper.
- Say: *If you don't remember the word for a car part, look at the vocabulary chart in Exercise 1B and see if you can find it there.*
- *Optional:* To guide students, write some discussion prompts on the board:

    You should check the _____ because _____.

    You should check to see if _____.

- Have students complete the exercise.
- Have each group choose a representative to present its ideas to the full group. Ask clarification questions as needed (*What could happen if you didn't have enough air in your tires?*).

Teaching Tip

Be sure that each group includes at least one student who said in the Preview that he or she has a car, since that person may be more familiar with vocabulary relating to car parts.

Presentation · 20 minutes

B PAIRS. Identify the parts...

- Say: *Now, we have talked about some parts of the car that we should always check before a long trip and about some of the problems that we can have with these parts. Let's look at the vocabulary for car parts.*
- Read the vocabulary from the box aloud, eliciting students' help to clarify unfamiliar terms as needed.

- Check students' understanding by asking them to differentiate between pairs of similar items. (For example: *Where are the headlights? Taillights? When I want to stop the car, do I use the gas pedal or the brake? How is the rear-view mirror different from the side-view mirror? If I hear a strange sound in my engine and want to check it, should I open up the trunk or the hood?*)
- Say: *Now you are going to look at the pictures in Exercise 1B and label the parts of the car that you see, using the numbers of the words in the list.*
- Have students complete the exercise. Offer help as needed. (For example, *Is the rear-view or the side-view mirror on the side of the car?*)
- Call on students to say the answers.

Language Note

Ask students to look at the picture on the right. Say: *The floor area of this car has two brakes. Does anyone know why?* (One is the emergency brake.) *What is the emergency brake used for?* (Possible answers: to make sure the car doesn't roll backward when parked on a hill; for extra safety with a standard car)

C What are the different fluids...

- Ask students to read the directions.
- Clarify vocabulary as needed. (For example: A *fluid* is a liquid. To *lubricate* means to use something to reduce the friction between different parts that are in motion.)
- Have students complete the exercise. Walk around and check their work.
- Call on students to say the answers.

Language Note

Direct students attention to the unlabeled clutch (next to the brake) in the diagram on the right. Ask students if they know the difference between an automatic and standard (or *stick-shift*) car. If needed, explain that an automatic car changes gears automatically. With a standard car, you must use both a *clutch* and a gas pedal to change gears and make the car go faster or slower. Ask students how many know how to drive a standard car and whether they prefer to drive this or an automatic car—and why. Offer prompts. (*Which car do you think is more fuel efficient? Better for driving in the city?*)

Controlled Practice   15 minutes

2   PRACTICE

Write the name of the correct...

- Ask students to read the directions.
- Have students complete the exercise.
- Call on students to say the answers.

3   LISTEN

A **Listen to each conversation...**

- Tell students that they will now practice listening to conversations about car problems.
- Ask students to read the directions and the questions about the three conversations.
- Say: *In one of these conversations, you will hear the term* jump-started. *What does that mean?* Elicit a definition from students, providing clarification as needed (*You need to use jumper cables connected to another person's car battery to jump-start your dead car battery.*).
- Play CD 1, Track 16. Have students listen to the conversations and complete the exercise.
- Tell students that they may listen to the conversations again and see if they hear anything that they may have missed the first time.
- Play Track 16 again.

B **PAIRS.** **Listen to the excerpts and try...**

- Ask students to read the directions.
- Say: *You'll listen to parts of three conversations. Try to guess the meaning of the words in items 1–3.*
- Play the excerpts from CD 1, Track 17. Have students listen and complete the exercise.
- *Optional:* Tell students that they'll now listen to the complete conversations and will check their answers. Say: *You'll listen to the complete conversations again. You'll see if knowing the context—that is, the full situation—helps you to understand the meanings of the words.* Play Track 17 again.
- *Optional:* Ask: *Did you change any of your answers after hearing the complete conversations again? If so, what helped you to understand the meaning of the word or words the second time around?*

Culture Connection

Say: *For many people, driving is an important part of life in the U.S. The age when one can legally drive differs from state to state, but in many states a teenager can receive a provisional driver's license—called a* learner's (or learning) permit—*slightly before or at the age of 16. Depending on the state, a person with a learner's permit can drive as long as there is an adult with a driver's license in the car. To receive a driver's license, one must pass a multiple-choice written test with questions about driving rules, as well as a road test to demonstrate to an instructor the ability to drive and/or park in a specified area.*

Communicative Practice   15 minutes

4   MAKE IT PERSONAL

GROUPS. Discuss the questions.

- Set up groups.
- Ask students to read the directions.
- Ask a student to read each question aloud. Model the answers with real information about yourself.
- Ask students to discuss the questions, encouraging them to share their experiences with car repairs.

Progress Check

Can you . . . identify car parts and related problems?

- Say: *We have practiced identifying car parts and related problems. Can you do this? If so, check the box.*

Extra Practice

Interactive Practice

Write the name of the correct car part next to each verb. Some items have more than one correct answer. Answers will vary but could include:

1. change a _____tire_____
2. turn on/off the __engine/headlights__
3. honk the _____horn_____
4. put the key in the _____ignition_____

5. step on/let up on the accelerator/gas pedal
6. open/close the _____hood/trunk_____
7. lift or raise/lower the _____hood/trunk_____
8. fasten your _____seat belt_____

CD1 T16

A Listen to each conversation about car problems. Then listen to the questions and possible answers that follow each conversation. Circle the letter of the correct answer.

Conversation 1
1. What is the situation?   a   (b)   c
2. What does the woman have changed or replaced?   (a)   b   c

Conversation 2
1. What seems to be the problem?   a   b   (c)
2. If the car is jump-started, how long should it be driven afterward?   a   (b)   c

Conversation 3
1. What does the man want the woman to do?   a   (b)   c
2. What does the woman remember?   a   b   (c)

CD1 T17

B **PAIRS.** Listen to the excerpts and try to figure out the meanings of the words. Circle the letter of the correct answer.

1. **top off**
   (a.) add more fluid until it's at the correct level   b. remove and replace fluid

2. **run**
   (a.) turn on a machine and keep it going for a while   b. accelerate or increase speed

3. **tune-up**
   (a.) adjustments made to help a car run well   b. change stereo or audio system

GROUPS. Discuss the questions.

1. Can you do any kind of car maintenance or repairs? If so, what can you do?
2. Which car problems would be hardest for you to fix? Why?

Can you... identify car parts and related problems? ☐

Reading

1 BEFORE YOU READ

CLASS. Discuss the kinds of car trouble you can have on the highway or freeway.

2 READ

CD1 T18

Listen to and read the article about car trouble.

What to Do If Your Car Breaks Down on the Highway

What should you do if your car breaks down on the highway? The National Safety Council has some suggestions.

If you're experiencing a problem with your car—such as the engine not working correctly, a strange noise, or a flat tire—act quickly. At the first sign of car trouble, gently let up on the accelerator. Carefully pull over to the **shoulder** of the road. On an **interstate**, you should try to reach an exit. Signal to drivers behind you, using either your turn signal or your **emergency flashers** (hazard lights). If you have to change lanes, watch your mirrors closely.

Once you are off the road, make sure your car is visible. If you have reflecting triangles, put them behind your vehicle to alert other drivers; keep your emergency flashers on. If it's dark, turn on the car's **interior** light.

If you have a flat tire, be sure that you know how to replace it, that you have the necessary **equipment**, and that you can do it safely.

If you can't get the car running, get **professional** help. Contact the **highway patrol** or roadside assistance. Don't try to **flag down** other vehicles. Raise your hood and hang a white cloth out a window so that the police or **tow truck operators** can find you. If the car is in the roadway, stand away from it and wait for help to arrive.

If your car is safely out of traffic, wait inside with the doors locked. Use your cell phone to call for help. If you don't have a phone, put a sign in your window that reads, "Please call the highway patrol." If someone stops and offers to help, open the window a little and ask him or her to call the police. Watch for a **uniformed** police officer or other emergency **personnel**.

It is not a good idea to walk along the side of an interstate. However, if you have to, be sure to take the key from the ignition. Lock the doors. Walk on the shoulder, facing traffic, and keep as far away from traffic as possible. Safety is your **priority**!

Getting Started   10 minutes

- Say: *In Lesson 1, we talked about car parts and typical problems cars can have. In this lesson, we are going to read and talk about a specific, dangerous problem: what to do if your car breaks down on the highway.*

Expansion: Vocabulary Practice

- Tell students that there are many different English words for roads, based on both the size of the road and geography. (For example: *Drivers in California probably say* freeway *to describe large limited-access roads, but people in Michigan often say* expressway *for the same type of road.*)
- Say: *There are many types of roads. Learn the vocabulary we use around here first. Then, if you travel out of state, find out what kinds of roads you will be on—and the names used for them.*
- Brainstorm road types with students (such as *freeway, highway,* or *interstate*), specific important roads in your area, and local travel issues (such as drawbridges or toll roads).
- Before class, develop a simple grid with these or other categories, possibly including amounts of fees and other relevant information.
- Pass out the grids at the beginning of the brainstorm so that as you write your own information and that of students on the board, students can easily record this information.

Presentation   15 minutes

1 BEFORE YOU READ

CLASS. Discuss the kinds of car trouble...

- Ask students to read the directions.
- Give a personal example of car trouble you've had or use an example from "a friend." Say: *Once my car stopped working at night on a two-lane highway in the mountains—40 miles from nowhere . . .*
- List problems students mention and add others from Lesson 1 and your own knowledge.
- Say: *Now we are going to listen to and read what the experts say a person should do if his or her car breaks down on the highway.*

2 READ

Listen to and read the article...

- Ask students to read the directions.
- Remind students to look at all the clues—the title, photo, and initial question—to help them understand the reading.
- Point out that the words and phrases in boldface—*shoulder, interstate, emergency flashers, interior, equipment, professional, highway patrol, flag down, tow truck operators, uniformed, personnel,* and *priority*—appear in the glossary on page 245. Encourage students to read the entire article first, before going to the glossary.
- Play CD 1, Track 18 while students read the article and listen.
- After students listen and read, ask if they have any questions about the content, vocabulary, or pronunciation. Answer questions, but also encourage other students to answer questions.

Culture Connection

- Discuss what to do if students come across "road rage" on the highway.
- Say: *One important issue to watch out for in the U.S. is road rage.* Ask: *Can anyone give me an example or definition of* road rage? (For example, threatening angry behavior from other drivers)
- Tell students that if they see someone in a road rage, to try to keep away, by dropping back or taking the next exit off the road. Advise them not to respond to another driver's anger by becoming angry themselves.
- Say: *If you have a cell phone, call the Highway Patrol or state troopers.* Give the local number to students. *If you think you are in danger, call 911. Try to tell the operator where you are* (For example: *a mile or two after Exit 71.*).

Controlled Practice   15 minutes

3   CHECK YOUR UNDERSTANDING

A **Write the answers to the questions.**

- Ask students to read and answer the questions by going back to the article.
- Walk around the room as students write. Observe whether anyone is having trouble finding the answers in the article; provide help if needed.
- Ask a different volunteer to answer each of the four questions. Check with the whole class to see if they agree. If there is any disagreement, ask students to go back to the article for the answer.

Reading Skill: **Paraphrasing**

- Direct students to the Reading Skill box.
- Ask a student to read the text.
- If some students seem unsure of the content, ask the same student or another student to reread it.
- Ask students to state the three reasons that being able to paraphrase is a useful skill. (It helps you identify areas you don't understand, enables you to practice writing about the topic, and helps you remember information.)

B **Read this paraphrase...**

- Ask students to read the directions.
- Review the meaning of *skim* if necessary.
- Ask students to read the paraphrase. Ask: *Counting from the top, what paragraph (1, 2, etc.) does this text paraphrase?* (paragraph 5)

C **GROUPS. Each student should...**

- Ask students to read the directions.
- Restate or repeat directions as needed. Say: *Because there are five paragraphs in the article—not counting the one we already worked on and the introduction—we'll have five people in each group.*
- Set up groups by directing students to count (1-2-3-4-5). Say: *Make your own groups, but make sure each group has a 1, 2, 3, 4, and 5.*
- Ask group members to give one another feedback on their paraphrases.

4   WORD WORK

GROUPS. Choose three words...

- Set up groups of three.
- Ask students to read the directions.
- Say: *Remember when you write in your vocabulary logs, you can always write more than three words or phrases. You can also use the vocabulary log for words you read or hear outside of class.*

Communicative Practice   20 minutes

5   MAKE IT PERSONAL

GROUPS. Discuss. Have you experienced...

- Keep the same groups as above.
- Walk around the room as students talk. If someone in a group is sharing an amusing or exciting story, ask that person to share it with the class.

Teaching Tip

- Explain to students that they have been working hard and that you think they need a change of pace. Most students will probably welcome a change, but confirm that you will continue the work shortly.
- This change could be anything from explaining a common yoga stretch, to chanting prepositions of place—still an issue for higher-level students—with descriptive hand movements, to taking a walk around the school to identify the vocabulary of less common objects (such as *podium* or *lectern*).

Extra Practice

Interactive Practice   pages 32–33

3 CHECK YOUR UNDERSTANDING

A **Write the answers to the questions.** Answers will vary but could include:

1. What is the first thing you should do if you realize you are having car trouble?

   let up on the accelerator

2. How can you make sure other drivers see your car when it is sitting on the shoulder?

   use reflecting triangles and flashers

3. How else can you alert others to your need for help?

   turn on the car's interior light

4. If you are inside your car and someone stops to offer assistance, what should you do?

   open the window a little and ask them to call the police

B **Read this paraphrase of one of the paragraphs of the article on page 48. Then skim the article. Identify and circle the original paragraph.**

> If you can't fix your car yourself, call the highway patrol or a roadside assistance service, or wait for a highway patrol car to come by. Don't try to stop other cars to ask for help. Lift your hood and tie some white cloth to the car or hang it out the window. Don't stand near your car if your car is still in the road.

C **GROUPS. Each student should choose a different paragraph from the article to paraphrase. Share your paraphrased paragraphs.**

Reading Skill:
Paraphrasing

When you read, it's helpful to pause occasionally and try to repeat information in your own words. This will help you recognize places where you have trouble understanding the text. It will also give you an opportunity to practice producing language about the topic and help you to remember information from the text.

4 WORD WORK

GROUPS. Choose three words or phrases in the article that you would like to remember. Discuss the words and their meanings. Then record the words and information about them in your vocabulary log.

5 MAKE IT PERSONAL

GROUPS. Discuss. Have you experienced a car breakdown on the highway? Were you a driver or a passenger? What happened? What did you do?

Grammar

Inseparable Phrasal Verbs
Make sure your car is visible so that other drivers don't **run into** it.
Watch out for traffic if you need to walk to get help.

Separable Phrasal Verbs
Don't try to **flag down** other vehicles.
Don't try to **flag** other vehicles **down**.
Don't try to **flag** them **down**.

Grammar Watch

- **A phrasal verb is made up of a verb + a particle.** Particles are words such as *up, down, on, off, after, by, in, into,* and *out.*
- For **inseparable phrasal verbs**, the verb and the particle must stay together.
- For **separable phrasal verbs**, the verb and the particle can stay together or be separated.
- Many phrasal verbs are **transitive**; this means they can take **objects** (nouns or pronouns). When the object of a separable phrasal verb is a noun, the object can come before or after the particle. When the object is a pronoun, the object must come before the particle.
- Some phrasal verbs are **intransitive**; they **don't take objects** and are **always inseparable**.
- Inseparable phrasal verbs sometimes have two particles, for example, *get along with.*

For lists of separable and inseparable phrasal verbs and their meanings, go to page 224.

1   PRACTICE

There are seven phrasal verbs in the paragraph. Underline six more phrasal verbs. Which ones do you think are separable? Check the lists on page 224 to see if you are right.

You wouldn't believe the problems Sylvia had on her way to work this morning. She'd forgotten that road construction workers were putting in a new lane, and traffic was moving very slowly behind the construction crew. An impatient driver tried to pass Sylvia on the right shoulder, and he ran into the rear of her car and broke her taillight. It took the police over half an hour to arrive. After the police came, Sylvia turned on the ignition and the engine light came on. She was very worried that her car was going to break down. Thankfully, later, after the police officer was finished, her car started again. Everything turned out all right. But Sylvia is definitely going to figure out another route to take to work tomorrow!

Getting Started   5 minutes

- Say: *In Lesson 2, we talked about what to do if your car breaks down on the highway. Today we're going to talk more about highway safety. To do so, we'll practice the grammatical structure of phrasal verbs.*

Presentation   20 minutes

Inseparable Phrasal Verbs

- Copy the grammar chart onto the board. Discuss Column 1: Inseparable Phrasal Verbs.
- Say: *Phrasal verbs have two parts: a verb and a particle.* Have a volunteer read the first two sentences in the Grammar Watch aloud. Have another volunteer circle the verb in the first sentence on the chart (*run*) and underline the particle (*into*).
- Ask students for more examples of particles and write them on the board: *through, around, across,* and so on.
- Explain that particles look like prepositions, but when combined with a verb, they act as a unit and can have a different meaning than the verb alone. Use *run* and *run into* to show the difference in meaning between a verb and a phrasal verb: *I often* run *at night. Did you* run into *your sister on the way here?*
- Say: *In an inseparable phrasal verb, the verb and the particle must stay together.* Write on the board: *He ran into a car.* Have volunteers underline the verb, circle the particle, and draw a box around the object.
- Say: *When the phrasal verb takes an object pronoun, the verb and particle also stay together.* Write on the board: *He ran into it.* Draw a box around the object pronoun *it.*
- Have a volunteer read the rest of the Grammar Watch. Remind students that some phrasal verbs have two particles, such as *follow through with, take off with.* These are always inseparable.

Separable Phrasal Verbs

- Direct students' attention to the right-hand section of the grammar chart: Separable Phrasal Verbs.
- Read each sentence aloud. Ask volunteers to underline the verb and circle the particle in each sentence.
- Explain that in separable phrasal verbs, the verb and the particle do **not** have to stay together. In fact, if you use a pronoun, the particle must always come after the pronoun. Point to Sentence 3 in the grammar chart. (Don't try to flag them down.) Draw a box around the pronoun *them.*

Teaching Tip

- To help students with transitive and intransitive phrasal verbs, write the following chart on the board.

Transitive	Intransitive
She handed in her essay.	The noise died down.
He called off the meeting.	She grew up quickly.

- Say: *Transitive verbs always take objects, and intransitive verbs never take objects.*
- Ask students to copy the sentences into their notebooks and circle the phrasal verbs and draw a box around any objects. Give help as needed.
- Explain that most transitive phrasal verbs are separable and that intransitive phrasal verbs are always inseparable.

Controlled Practice   5 minutes

 PRACTICE

There are seven phrasal verbs...

- Ask students to read the directions and complete the exercise.
- Call on students to say the phrasal verbs. After each one, ask: *Is that separable?*

Controlled Practice   15 minutes

2   PRACTICE

Ⓐ PAIRS. Complete the sentences with...

- Say: *Now you will practice using phrasal verbs in sentences.* Ask students to read the directions.
- Have students form pairs to complete the exercise.
- *Optional:* Ask students which sentences had separable phrasal verbs (items 2 and 6). Write them on the board. Then ask students to rewrite them so that the object appears between the verb and the particle. (*2. Never pick a hitchhiker up on the highway. 6. Always drive slowly in construction zones when workers are repairing roads or putting new ones in.*)

Ⓑ Circle the object in each...

- Ask students to read the directions. Remind them that with separable phrasal verbs, the object pronoun always goes between the verb and the particle; with inseparable phrasal verbs, the pronoun goes after the particle.
- Have students complete the exercise.
- Point out that all the verbs in this exercise were separable, so the object pronouns were all placed between the verb and particle. (1. . . . turn it on; 2. . . . flag them down; 3. . . . hang it out; 4. . . . put them up)

▬ Expansion: Writing Practice for 2A and 2B

To help familiarize students with phrasal verbs, have them generate language themselves:

- Have students form pairs and look at the list of separable phrasal verbs on page 224.
- Each partner writes 10 sentences, with a different phrasal verb in each sentence—omitting the particle. (The partner leaves a blank for the particle.)
- Have partners swap papers and, with books closed, guess what particle completes the phrasal verb.
- Repeat the exercise with the list of inseparable phrasal verbs on page 224.

Communicative Practice   15 minutes

Show what you know!

GROUPS. Discuss. What can drivers do...

- Before the discussion, call students' attention to the Communication Skill box, *Taking Part in Discussions.* Ask a student to read it aloud.
- Read the discussion question, and tell students that they will talk with their group members about it. Encourage students to use the phrasal verbs from the grammar chart and word box to frame their discussion.
- Remind students to use the expressions in the Communication Skill box while they are talking.
- Have students form groups and complete the exercise.
- Walk around the room and monitor conversations.
- Call on groups to share their responses.
- *Optional:* As groups present their ideas, make a chart on the board of dangerous situations and ways to deal with them.

Teaching Tip

To help students get into the habit of organizing and presenting notes, have them make notes that they can use to answer the discussion question. Suggest that they look over the phrasal verbs on pages 50–51, choose at least five, write them in a list, and think about their meanings. Then have them add words to the phrasal verbs that relate to highway safety. For example, if a student writes *watch out*, he or she might add *for fast drivers.* They can then use these words to help them answer the discussion question.

Progress Check

Can you . . . talk about highway safety do's and don'ts?

- Say: *We have practiced talking about highway safety do's and don'ts. Can you do this? If so, check the box.*

Extra Practice

Interactive Practice   pages 34–35

A **PAIRS.** Complete the sentences with the correct form of the phrasal verbs from the box. Compare your answers.

> blow out   break down   come on   cut in   pick up   put in

1. If your car <u>breaks down</u> on the highway, call for help. Don't accept a ride from a stranger.

2. Never <u>pick up</u> a hitchhiker on the highway. If you see a person walking and you think he or she needs help, call the highway patrol.

3. If traffic is moving slowly, don't try to <u>cut in</u> ahead of other drivers. It can cause an accident.

4. If your engine or oil light <u>comes on</u> while you are on the highway, slowly drive to the nearest exit and call roadside assistance.

5. You should check your tires regularly. When they get old and worn, they can <u>blow out</u> while you are driving, causing a very dangerous situation.

6. Always drive slowly in construction zones when workers are repairing roads or <u>putting in</u> new ones.

B Circle the object in each sentence. Then rewrite the sentences using object pronouns (*it*, *them*, *her*, or *him*).

1. If it's dark outside, turn on (the interior light).

2. Never try to flag down (other vehicles).

3. Hang out (a white cloth) so that the highway patrol can find you.

4. Put up (reflecting triangles) so that other drivers can see you.

Communication Skill:
Taking Part in Discussions

During group discussions, state your ideas clearly and listen carefully to other people's ideas. To enter or participate in a group discussion, you can use phrases such as these:

First of all, I think that . . .
I agree/disagree with that because . . .
I have a different view of . . .
I'd like to add . . .

Show what you know!   Talk about highway safety do's and don'ts

GROUPS. Discuss. What can drivers do to avoid dangerous situations on the highway? Use phrasal verbs in your discussion.

Can you... talk about highway safety do's and don'ts?   ☐

Listening and Speaking

1 BEFORE YOU LISTEN

CLASS. Look at the photo. What has happened? What should the drivers do?

2 LISTEN

CD1 T19

A Listen to a driving instructor talk about what to do if you are in a car accident with another vehicle. Take simple notes by writing the objects of the verbs below.

If you have a car accident . . .
1. stop *your vehicle.*
2. move out of traffic
3. turn off the ignition
4. make necessary phone calls
5. mark the scene of the accident
6. collect the names of witnesses
7. take notes
8. exchange licenses and insurance cards
9. don't talk about who caused the accident
10. get a copy of the report

B **STEP 1. GROUPS.** Compare your simple notes.

CD1 T19

STEP 2. Add more details about each item above. Then listen again to check your work.

STEP 3. GROUPS. Discuss. Were any of these instructions new to you? If so, which ones?

Getting Started   10 minutes

- Say: *Unfortunately, we can't talk about cars without talking about car accidents. Some accidents are terrible—with passengers getting injured or killed—but luckily many accidents are minor. In this lesson, we will be focusing on what to do in case of minor accidents.*

- Make sure that all students understand what *minor* means (most speakers of Romance languages will understand, but speakers of Arabic or African or Asian languages may not). Contrast with *major*—a minor accident vs. a major accident.

- Ask students to share experiences they've had with minor accidents. Say: *Have any of you had a minor accident?* If students indicate *yes*, say: *Would anyone like to share his or her experience with the class?*

1   BEFORE YOU LISTEN

CLASS. Look at the photo. What has...

- Ask students to read the directions.
- Accept all responses, but if any responses seem unreasonable, ask the class: *Does this seem like a reasonable (or good) idea?* Encourage students who want to describe their own experiences to do so.

Presentation   10 minutes

2   LISTEN

 Listen to a driving instructor...

- Ask students to read the directions. Confirm that all students know what a driving instructor is.

- Reiterate that students are supposed to take simple notes. Go over the example to make sure that students understand what the directions mean by "objects of the verbs." If some are not sure, provide examples ("close *the door*," "make *dinner*," "kick *the ball*," "watch *TV*"). Say: *The object answers the question "What?" after the verb.*

- Play CD 1, Track 19.

- Walk around the room as students listen; observe whether any students are having difficulty writing the objects of the verbs.

- After students listen, ask: *How was that listening—easy, medium, or difficult?* Note the general response or ask for a show of hands. It's useful to get a general idea of whether the listening is the correct level of difficulty for students. If it is too difficult, add more support before the listening; if it is too easy, consider bringing related authentic audio clips from the radio. Asking for—and acting on—adult student input validates your respect for students and their control over their own learning.

Teaching Tip

- You may occasionally have students whose proficiency is on-level, but who may not have a formal background in grammar; they may know how to appropriately use objects in sentences, but they may not know grammar terms, such as *object*, *direct object*, or *transitive verb*.

- If you have one or two students in this situation, work with them explicitly on basic grammar and grammar vocabulary at regular times when the rest of the class is working on group activities. Give them grammar sheets for self-study at home.

Controlled Practice   15 minutes

B STEP 1. GROUPS. Compare your simple notes.

- Ask students to read the directions.
- Set up informal groups. Say: *Work with two or three people sitting near you.*

STEP 2. Add more details...

- Say: *As you listen again, check and add to your notes.*
- Play Track 19 again.

STEP 3. GROUPS. Discuss. Were any of...

- Keep the same groups. Ask students to read the directions and respond to the questions.
- Ask the class whether all the instructions make sense to them. Accept all comments, but encourage students to explain their opinions or ideas.

Controlled Practice   10 minutes

- Have students read the Grammar Watch.
- Briefly review gerunds. Say: *Just like nouns, gerunds often act as subjects. You can think of a gerund as a verbal noun—an* -ing *verb acting as a noun.* Mention that the structure shown in the note is very common.
- Write on the board: *It's + adjective + infinitive.* Underneath, write: *It's nice to see you again.* Ask students to complete sentences like *It's dangerous to . . .* (drive too fast) *It's illegal to . . .* (stop at an intersection). Then ask them to say one or two more sentences with, for example, *easy* and *difficult.* Review the infinitive as *to* + base form of the verb.
- Say: *Americans use this form often; start listening for it outside of class and see how often you hear it.*

 3   PRACTICE

PAIRS. Take turns reading and explaining...

- Ask students to read the directions.
- Model with an above-level volunteer, using the dialogue as an example. Point out that Student B can say more than just *Why.* (For example: *If it's just a minor accident, what does it matter?*)
- Set up pairs and have students do the exercise.
- Answer any questions or comments related to the practice itself or the topic of what to do when there is an accident.

Communicative Practice   15 minutes

 4   MAKE IT PERSONAL

GROUPS. Discuss. What new facts...

- Ask students to read the directions.
- Say: *Now we are going to work in small groups to talk about laws and customs in the U.S. related to driving. We are also going to compare these customs with those in your home countries. How are these driving customs similar to or different from those in your home countries? After you talk together, we will come together to see what we've learned.*

- Set up groups. Have students discuss the questions.
- Bring the class back together. Say: *What was one interesting piece of information you heard from your group?* Take a response from at least two or three groups; if time allows, take a comment from every group. Continue: *Basically, do you think driving rules—specifically, rules involving traffic accidents— are more similar or different around the world?* Accept all comments.

Teaching Tip

- Not all topics will be of interest to all students. This may be true in this case, especially if some students don't drive and/or didn't drive in their home countries.
- Since a main point of group work is for students to communicate in authentic ways, it is OK if students veer off topic, such as comparing countries on other aspects than car or accident customs or talking about how they travel to work.

■ Expansion: Writing Practice for 4

- Ask students to freewrite a description of one of the following topics: traffic in my hometown; a minor car accident I was involved in; how to get from class to my home.
- Suggest that students share their writing with a partner and offer each other feedback.
- *Optional:* You may want to collect paragraphs either at the end of this class or at the beginning of the next class. Read the paragraphs and give one overall positive comment, one substantive comment on structure, one comment on usage, and one comment on mechanics. Thank students when you return the papers.

Extra Practice

Interactive Practice

Gerunds and Infinitives in General Statements

You can often begin a statement by using a gerund. A gerund is a noun formed with the base form of the verb + *ing*:

Speeding *on the highway is dangerous.*

You can also make general statements using *It is/isn't* + adjective + infinitive. Form the infinitive with *to* + the base form of the verb:

It's *dangerous* **to speed** *on the highway.*
It isn't *safe* **to speed** *on the highway.*

3 PRACTICE

PAIRS. Take turns reading and explaining these statements.

1. Leaving the scene of an accident is illegal in most states but wrong in any state.
2. It's important to give the location of the accident right away if you call 911.
3. Getting the names and phone numbers of witnesses is important.
4. It's a good idea to take a picture or draw a diagram of the accident.
5. It isn't a good idea to talk about whose fault the accident is.

Example:
A: *Leaving the scene of an accident is illegal.*
B: *Why?*
A: *Because someone could be hurt or there could be damage to the other vehicle. You should stop and make sure no one is hurt, and you should wait for the police to come and write a report.*

4 MAKE IT PERSONAL

GROUPS. Discuss. What new facts about driving laws and customs have you learned in this unit? Compare and contrast these driving laws and customs with those in your home country. How are they similar? How are they different?

Life Skills

1   UNDERSTAND CAR INSURANCE

A   **CLASS.**   Car owners in the U.S. are required by law to have car insurance. Why do you think that it's illegal to drive without having insurance? Do you agree with the U.S. law?

B   Read about important terms used in car insurance.

Different Types of Auto Insurance Coverage

Bodily Injury: This pays for the treatment of injuries that you cause to other people.

Personal Injury Protection: This pays for treatment of injuries you cause to yourself and your passengers. Sometimes this protection also covers lost wages or funeral costs.

Property Damage Liability: This pays for damage that you cause to another person's car or other property.

Collision: This pays for damage to your car in an accident involving another vehicle. You may have to pay a deductible (the amount of money that you have to pay before the insurance company pays anything).

Comprehensive: This pays for damage to your car caused by something other than a collision with another vehicle, such as vandalism, an accident involving an animal, or fire.

Uninsured and Underinsured Motorist Coverage: This will cover you if you are hit by a hit-and-run driver or by a driver who doesn't have insurance or enough insurance.

C   Write the answers to the questions based on the information in the article.

1. Which types of coverage pay for injuries or damage you do to others?
2. Which types of coverage pay for your own injuries or damage to your car?

2   PRACTICE

PAIRS.   Read the situations. Discuss. Which coverage would help each car owner?

1. Glen's car was damaged by a car that ran a red light.
2. Sandra damaged the side of another car when she tried to merge onto a highway.
3. Someone broke into Mr. Chen's car last night. The person broke a window.
4. Janet had to go to the hospital after her car crashed into a fallen tree at night.
5. Tony hit a car that stopped suddenly in front of him, injuring the other driver.

Getting Started 5 minutes

1 UNDERSTAND CAR INSURANCE

 CLASS. Car owners in the U.S....

- Say: *When you're in a minor car accident, you usually report the accident to your insurance company. Today we'll learn more about car insurance. Do people in your home countries have auto insurance?*

- Say: *In the U.S., car owners are required by law to have car insurance. Why do you think that is?* Offer additional prompts as needed. *(What happens if there's a car accident and one driver doesn't have insurance? If neither driver has insurance?)*

- Read and discuss the second question.

Presentation 15 minutes

B **Read about important terms...**

- Say: *Now we'll look at some important terms used in car insurance.* Ask students to read the information about different types of auto insurance coverage.

> **Language Note**
>
> Explain that the verb *cover* means to protect something or someone by putting something physically over it (*He covered me from the rain with his umbrella.*) or to take the place of someone if that person can't do something. (*I asked her to cover for me at work tomorrow night because I have to go to my son's school.*) *Cover* can also refer to being insured and thus protected from liability. (*My car insurance covers me for collisions.*) The noun *coverage* refers to the possession of insurance and what it protects us from. (*I have bodily injury coverage with my insurance policy.*)

- Clarify other vocabulary as needed. (For example: *bodily*—of or relating to the body; *lost wages*—money that you would have earned if you had been able to work; *vandalism*—the destruction of property; *hit-and-run driver*—someone who causes a car accident, such as hitting another car, but does not stop to leave information with the victim.)

- Check students' understanding of *deductible*. Ask: *If you have a $500 deductible, how much do you have to pay before the insurance company pays anything?* ($500)

C **Write the answers...**

- Have students read the directions and complete the exercise.
Answers: 1. bodily injury, personal injury protection, property damage liability; 2. personal injury protection, collision, comprehensive, uninsured and underinsured motorist coverage

Controlled Practice 15 minutes

2 PRACTICE

PAIRS. Read the situations....

- Ask students to read the directions and the items in Exercise 2.

- Say: *Now you're going to discuss with a partner which types of coverage would be the most helpful in each situation.*

- Have students complete the exercise.
Possible answers:
1. collision (His car was damaged by another vehicle; Glen didn't cause the accident.)
2. property damage liability (She damaged another car, and it was her fault.)
3. comprehensive (Mr. Chen's car wasn't damaged by a collision.)
4. personal injury protection (She injured herself.)
5. bodily injury (He caused an injury to another person.)

▬ MULTILEVEL INSTRUCTION for 2

Cross-ability Group students in cross-ability pairs for Exercise 2 so that the above-level partner can help the pre-level partner find the information.

Controlled Practice   15 minutes

3   UNDERSTAND CAR INSURANCE TERMS

PAIRS. Underline the correct word or words...

- Say: *Now look at the vocabulary in italics. You'll hear this vocabulary used in the next exercise.*
- Have students read the directions, form pairs, and complete the exercise.

Expansion: Reading Practice for 3

If students have computers, have them use the Internet for a critical thinking exercise in shopping around for auto insurance. Elicit ideas for ways to find out insurance rates on the Internet. Have students look up information about—and possibly quotes for—different types of insurance coverage (collision, bodily injury, etc.).

4   PRACTICE

A   **Read the questions. Listen to...**

- Ask students to read the directions.
- Say: *We'll listen to the conversation two times. The second time, you'll check to see if your answers were correct—and you'll fill in any missing information.*
- Play CD 1, Track 20. Have students listen and complete the exercise.
- Play Track 20 again so that students can check their answers.

Answers:

1. Yes. (Possible answers may include: She works in a hospital and knows that if you're in an accident, you're responsible for very expensive medical care costs. She thinks that insurance is so important that she recommends buying more than the minimum to cover health care and car repair costs.)

2. The state has laws about whether you must have car insurance—and if so, what type and how much.

3. bodily injury and property damage

4. For each occupant in a vehicle who is injured, the insurance will pay up to $15,000 to cover medical expenses; if more than one person is injured, it covers up to $30,000 total.

5. property damage in a car accident

6. Yes, because it's required by state law.

Expansion: Speaking Practice for 4A

Have students role-play a telephone call to a car insurance company to report an accident and file a claim. In small groups, students brainstorm questions that the insurance agent might ask. (Examples: *When did the accident occur? What was the location of the accident? Please describe what happened. Who was at fault? What type of coverage do you have? What is your insurance policy number?*)

Communicative Practice   10 minutes

Teaching Tip

Discuss deductibles and how they may affect the cost of monthly or annual insurance premiums. Ask: *If you needed to buy insurance, would you buy a policy with a high or a low deductible? How do you think this would affect your premiums?* Explain that generally, with any type of insurance, the higher the deductible, the lower the premium—and vice versa. Discuss the implications with students. (*You'll pay less each month or year, but when you have an accident, you'll pay more up front.*)

B **GROUPS. Discuss the questions.**

- Have students discuss the questions.

Teaching Tip

Remind students to use the conditional to talk about a hypothetical situation—that is, what kind of auto insurance they would buy. (*I would choose a policy with comprehensive coverage because it would _____.*)

Progress Check

Can you . . . decide which insurance is best for you?

- Say: *We have practiced talking about how to choose which auto insurance is best for you. Can you do this? If so, check the box.*

Extra Practice

Interactive Practice   pages 36–37

UNDERSTAND CAR INSURANCE TERMS

PAIRS. Underline the correct word or words to complete the definitions.

1. *Minimum coverage* is the **smallest** / **largest** amount you have to have.

2. An *occupant* is someone **inside** / **outside** a place.

3. To *wreck* something is to **dent it a little** / **destroy it completely**.

4. To *shop around* is to **look at different options** / **check online** before you buy something.

PRACTICE

CD1 T20

A Read the questions. Listen to two friends talking about insurance. Notice the vocabulary they use to talk about car insurance. Then write the answers to the questions.

1. Does Hua-Ling think it's important to have insurance if you own a car? How do you know?

2. How does the state you live in affect your insurance?

3. What two kinds of insurance does California require?

4. What does *15/30* mean in terms of California's insurance requirements?

5. What does $5,000 cover in California?

6. Do all California drivers buy minimum coverage for property damage? Why or why not?

B GROUPS. Discuss the questions.

1. Have you ever had car insurance?

2. If you have, how did you decide what kind of insurance to buy and what company to buy it from?

3. If you have not had car insurance, how would you make those decisions?

Can you... decide which insurance is best for you? ☐

Reading

1 BEFORE YOU READ

A Do you know what to do if the police stop you? Take the quiz. Check (✓) *True* or *False*. (The answers are at the bottom of the quiz.)

If You're Stopped by the Police, . . .

	True	False
1. You should always pull over to the left.	☐	☑
2. After you pull over, you should get out of your car.	☐	☑
3. You should keep your hands on the steering wheel when the officer talks to you.	☐	☑
4. The officer will probably ask for your driver's license and registration.	☑	☐
5. You should address the police officer as "Officer."	☑	☐
6. You shouldn't try to convince the police officer that he or she is wrong.	☑	☐
7. You need to pay the police officer immediately if you're given a ticket.	☐	☑

Answers: 1. False, 2. False, 3. True, 4. True, 5. True, 6. True, 7. False

B **PAIRS.** Compare answers.

2 READ

CD1 T21

Listen to and read the story on page 57. Notice the sequence in which the events occur. Underline the clue words that help you figure out the order of events.

Reading Skill:
Understanding Sequence

Knowing the sequence, or order, of events in a text will help you understand and remember what you read. Look for clue words such as, *first*, *next*, *before*, *later*, and *finally*. Also look for dates, days of the week, and times of day.

Lesson 6 Identify what to do if the police stop you

Getting Started   10 minutes

- Say: *We've been talking, reading, and writing about cars—car parts, accidents, safety, insurance—almost everything about cars. We also need to talk about what to do if the police stop you. The police or state troopers (or Highway Patrol—use the local name of the law enforcement officers who patrol the highways in your state) can stop you if you're driving too fast or breaking another law. They can stop you for other reasons, too, even if you are not breaking any traffic rules. In this lesson, we going to talk about how to talk to the police.*

- Ask for a quick hand count of how many people in class have a driver's license.

- Ask if anyone wants to talk about an experience he or she has had being stopped by the police. Students may or may not want to share, so don't press the issue.

- Say: *Before we go any further on this topic, you're going to take a quick true/false quiz to see what you think you should do if you're stopped by the police.*

Presentation   25 minutes

 BEFORE YOU READ

A Do you know what to do...

- Students read the directions and complete the quiz.

B PAIRS. Compare answers.

- Say: *Now compare your answers with the answers of someone sitting next to you.* Because this is a simple exercise and the correct answers are already evident, you don't need to ask students to read the directions or to set up formal pairs.

- Say: *In a few minutes, we will read a story about a person who was stopped by the police.*

Teaching Tip

For important, real-life topics such as how to interact with the police or the justice system, bring in local information to make sure you are giving students the correct information. For example, call up the local police department or local office of the state police to see whether they have a written list of what drivers should do if pulled over.

Culture Connection

- Talk about perceptions of police in the U.S. and in other countries.

- Say: *Young children in the U.S. are taught that police officers are friends who will help them if they are lost, scared, or in trouble. What do you think about that idea? Is that how you think about the police?*

- Ask students to compare the police in their home countries with the police in the U.S.

Reading Skill: Understanding Sequence

- Have students read the Reading Skill box.

- Elicit an example of *sequence* and *clue.*

- Ask students to give examples of other sequence words. Write them on the board and add less familiar words or phrases (such as *previously, afterwards, at last*) to a running list. Suggest that students add unfamiliar words to their vocabulary logs.

 READ

Listen to and read...

- *Note:* Before this exercise, find out whether using a cell phone while driving is illegal in your jurisdiction. If it is not illegal, mention that after the reading, but also stress that, legal or not, it is dangerous to use a cell phone while driving.

- Ask students to read the directions.

- Point out that the words and phrases in boldface—*display, distracted, approached,* and *registration*—appear in the glossary on page 245. Encourage students to read the entire story first, before going to the glossary.

- Play CD 1, Track 21. Ask students to listen and read.

- Ask: *Did you notice the sequence words? Did the sequence words help you understand the order in which events occurred?*

Controlled Practice   15 minutes

3 **CHECK YOUR UNDERSTANDING**

Write the answers to the questions.

- Tell students to write the answers to the questions in their notebooks.
- After students finish writing their answers, read or paraphrase each question and ask for one or two students to answer. Ask: *Do you think this story is realistic—is this what you think would happen here in [your community]? Why or why not?* Accept all answers, but ask students to use examples and details to prove their points.

Possible answers: 1. Miriam knew it was against the law. 2. She thought it was an emergency. 3. It was Mr. Mitchell, vice principal of her son Daniel's school. He told her Daniel had broken the school's rule and answered his cell phone in class. 4. a warning; 5. She probably wasn't right to answer the phone: it's dangerous and it's against the law.

Communicative Practice   10 minutes

4 **WORD WORK**

GROUPS. Choose three words...

- Set up groups and ask students to read the directions.
- If time permits, offer and explain other relevant police-related vocabulary to add to the discussion and word lists. (For example: *sir, ma'am, squad car, intoxicated, drunk driving, DUI—driving under the influence, DWI—driving while intoxicated*)
- Say: *Remember when you write in your vocabulary logs, you can always write more than three words or phrases. You can also use the vocabulary log for words you read or hear outside of class.*

Networking

- If possible, invite a police officer (perhaps a police information officer) or state trooper to come to class (or the whole program, since this is an important topic for everyone) to discuss what to do when stopped by police and related topics.
- *Note:* Local officials and other people active in the community (such as firefighters, representatives from the League of Women Voters, and community health care workers) often want to come to adult ESL programs so that they can explain important information. If students understand rules and procedures, it makes the officials' jobs easier.
- Set up the visit a month or two in advance. Several days before the visit, brainstorm with students a list of questions to ask the officer. Most of the questions should be related to the specific topic— what to do when stopped by a police officer—but also allow other, more general police-related questions because this may be the only time that students will have the opportunity to ask questions in a comfortable and anonymous setting.
- Write the questions on the board, an overhead, or a flipchart; later, copy and pass out the questions in advance to the students. Draw lines after every question so that students can take notes.
- Provide the officer with the list of questions in advance, but say that other questions will come up. Explain in advance to the officer that he or she may want to repeat comments, ask for clarification, use only limited idiomatic speech, etc., to maximize students' comprehension.
- Review general greeting and expressing gratitude protocol; ask for volunteers to ask each question.
- After the officer leaves, ask students what they thought of the presentation, what they learned, and what they still would like to know more about. (For example: *What was the most important thing you learned?*)
- Brainstorm with students the language for a short thank-you to the police officer. Send the note.

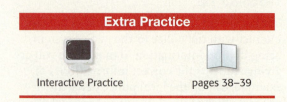

Extra Practice

Interactive Practice   pages 38–39

A Close Call

On Thursday morning, Miriam dropped Daniel off at school and continued on her way to work. She was in heavy traffic when her cell phone rang. She knew it was against the law to use a hand-held phone in the car, so she let it ring until it stopped.

But a few moments later, the phone rang again. Miriam took it from her purse and looked at the number on the **display**. It was Daniel's school. Had he been hurt? Was he sick? She decided to answer.

Soon a voice said, "This is Mr. Mitchell, the vice principal," but Miriam didn't hear more. She was **distracted** by lights flashing in her side mirror. A police car!

Without thinking, Miriam pressed *end call,* dropped her phone on the passenger seat, and stopped along the side of the road. The officer **approached**. "Good morning," he said. "May I see your license and—"

The phone started to ring again. "I'm very sorry, Officer," said Miriam, "but this call is from my son's school. Something could be wrong. May I please take it?"

"All right," said the officer.

Miriam spoke with Mr. Mitchell. "I understand," she said. "I'll talk with him when I pick him up after school. Thank you. Good-bye."

Miriam turned back to the police officer. "I'm sorry. Here's my license, my **registration**, and my insurance card."

The officer took the items Miriam handed him and walked to his car. A few minutes later, he came back, and asked, "Do you know why I stopped you?"

"For talking on my cell phone? I'm so sorry. I thought there was an emergency."

"Well, I'm just going to give you a warning," said the officer. "But next time, you'll get a ticket. So get a headset or turn off your phone when you drive."

"Yes, I will, Officer," said Miriam. "Thank you."

Miriam was glad the police officer hadn't asked questions about the call from Daniel's school. Daniel had broken the same school rule for the third time this week—he had answered his cell phone during class.

3 CHECK YOUR UNDERSTANDING

Write the answers to the questions.

1. Why didn't Miriam answer the phone the first time it rang?

2. Why did she answer it the second time?

3. Who was the caller? What did he tell Miriam?

4. Did the police officer give Miriam a ticket or a warning?

5. Do you think Miriam was right to answer the phone? Why or why not?

4 WORD WORK

GROUPS. Choose three words or phrases in the story that you would like to remember. Discuss the words and their meanings. Then record the words and information about them in your vocabulary log.

Life Skills

1 CHECK ONLINE DETOUR INFORMATION

A   **CLASS.**   Do you ever listen to the radio, watch TV, or look online to check traffic or road conditions? What stations or websites do you check?

B   Look at the map. What does it show?

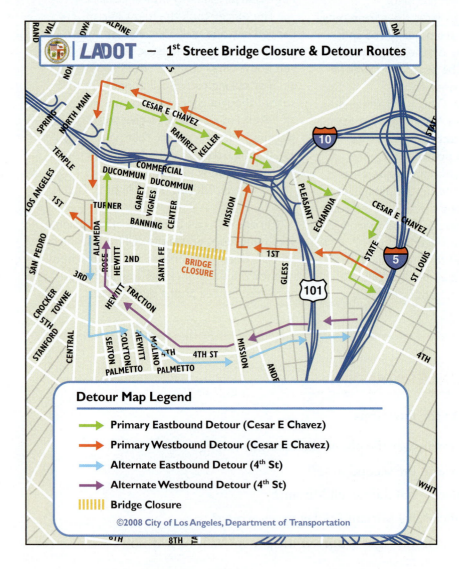

C   **GROUPS.**   Discuss the following words from the map. Use the map to explain or show the meaning of each word.

alternate   closure   detour   legend   primary   route

Describe traffic problems

Getting Started   5 minutes

1 CHECK ONLINE DETOUR INFORMATION

A CLASS. Do you ever listen...

- Say: *In the last lesson, we talked about what to do if the police stop you. Let's see what you remember. What are some things that you should—and shouldn't—do?* Elicit answers from students, offering prompts as needed. (*Should you get out of your car? Try to make the police officer understand that he was wrong? Pay the police officer?*)

- Say: *Now we're going to talk about another problem that you may have on the road: traffic. Have any of you ever been stuck in traffic?*

- Ask: *What do you do when you're stuck in traffic?* (Possible answers: listen to music or the news, try to relax)

- Ask the questions in the directions. Note radio and TV stations and websites on the board that students may use to check traffic or road conditions. (Be sure to write station numbers and URLs and have students copy them for future use.)

Presentation   20 minutes

B Look at the map. What does...

- Tell students that there are websites that show traffic and road conditions. Ask: *How can this help you?* (If you know before you leave the house that a road is closed or that there is a lot of traffic, you can take a different route.)

- Say: *Look at the map. What does it show?* (Possible answers: downtown Los Angeles area, roads and highways in downtown Los Angeles, road closures and alternate routes in downtown Los Angeles)

- Ask some basic questions to help students focus on the map. Examples:

  Major streets are known as main thoroughfares. *What are some of the main thoroughfares in downtown Los Angeles?* (Possible answers: 4th St., Cesar E Chavez, Mission, Alameda)

  What is the blue line with the number 101? (a highway)

  What are the blue lines with the numbers 10 and 5? (freeways)

  Do you see a bridge on the map? (yes) *Where?* (in the middle)

Language Note

Explain that the terms *freeway* and *highway* designate large roads. A *freeway* (or *expressway*) has more lanes than a highway and is meant for high-speed travel. It generally has few intersections and no stops for tolls. You can also mention that these terms vary from region to region: In the Eastern United States, for example, people don't use the term *freeways*.

C GROUPS. Discuss the following words...

- Say: *Now you're going to look at the map more closely and try to guess the meaning of some words used to talk about roads and traffic conditions.*

- Ask students to read the directions. Emphasize that they should use the map to give examples of the words.

- Model the exercise by holding up the map. Say: Closure. *This means that a road is not open. For example, if you look at [name a street], you'll see a road closure, so drivers must take a different route.*

- Have students form small groups and complete the exercise. Walk around and monitor conversations, offering help as needed.

- Call on students to say answers. As they do so, remind them as needed to give an example from the map.

Possible answers: *alternate*—a different way to get somewhere; *closure*—the act of closing something; *detour*—a way you must travel when a road is closed; *legend*—a box that explains symbols and abbreviations in the map (see Teaching Tip below); *primary*—main; *route*—a particular road that something follows to get from one place to another

Teaching Tip

To ensure that students understand the concept of a legend, draw students' attention to the map legend and ask some comprehension questions. Examples:

Why are some roads green, red, blue, or purple? (They are detours.)

What freeway is roughly parallel to Cesar E Chavez? (10)

What is the problem with the bridge? (It's closed.)

Controlled Practice   20 minutes

2 PRACTICE

Ⓐ Read the notes that the...

- Say: *Now we're going to read the notes from the Los Angeles Department of Transportation about the bridge closure.* Ask students to read the notes.
- Clarify unfamiliar terms as needed. (Examples: *weather permitting*—as long as the weather allows something to happen; *emergency responders*—fire trucks and ambulances; *pedestrian*—a walker)
- Check students' comprehension with a few basic questions. Examples: *How long will the First Street Bridge be closed?* (for approximately 1 month, weather permitting); *Will the bridge be open during certain hours?* (no—closed 24 hours/day except for emergency responders); *Will pedestrians be allowed to use the bridge?* (yes—on the south side of the bridge)

Ⓑ PAIRS. Use the map on page 58...

- Ask students to read the questions, form pairs, and complete the exercise.
- Have students say the answers. (*Note:* For Question 1, a student should point to Mission Road on the map and the yellow marks showing the closure.)

Possible answers: 2. N/B—northbound, or going northward (show by pointing up); W/B—westbound, or going westward (show by pointing to the left); S/B—southbound, or going southward (show by pointing down); E/B—eastbound, or going eastward (show by pointing to the right). 3. Emergency responders (fire trucks and ambulances) will be allowed on the bridge. 4. Pedestrian access will be allowed on the south side of the bridge.

Communicative Practice   15 minutes

Ⓒ GROUPS. Discuss the questions.

- Have students form small groups and complete the exercise.
- *Optional:* Have students note their responses in list form for Questions 1–3 on flipchart paper so that they may present them in the class discussion.
- Call on groups to share their responses. For Questions 2 and 3, note responses on the board to make sure that all students are aware of them.

- As students discuss Question 4, react with sample phrases students can emulate to demonstrate empathy. (*What a terrible experience—you must have felt so upset!*)

Teaching Tip

For the discussion, remind students to use the infinitive with the verb *advise* and a gerund with the preposition *of*. Using *would* with the expression makes it more polite. To guide students, write on the board: *I would advise people to avoid Hollywood Boulevard because of filming in the streets. I would advise people to _____ because of _____.*

▨ Expansion: Writing Practice for 2C

- Have students write a paragraph addressing Question 4. Encourage them to include details about how they felt when the incident happened and what they could have done differently. To show regret or missed possibility, explain that students will use a grammatical structure—the past modal—that they will practice in the next unit. Write some examples on the board: *I could have taken an alternate route. I should have called my boss to let her know that I'd be late.* When students finish, ask for volunteers to read their paragraphs aloud if time allows.

Culture Connection

Say: *In some parts of the U.S., being stuck in traffic is a part of everyday life. However, arriving promptly to work or to an appointment is also an expectation in this country.*

Progress Check

Can you . . . describe traffic problems?

- Say: *We have practiced describing traffic problems. Can you do this? If so, check the box.*

Extra Practice

Interactive Practice

A Read the notes that the Los Angeles Department of Transportation posted in 2008 about a bridge closure.

> Beginning on Jan. 27, 2008, the 1st St bridge will be closed from Mission Rd to Vignes St on a 24-hour basis for approximately 1 month, weather permitting.

> *Primary Detour Routes:*
> - W/B traffic on 1st St will be detoured N/B on Mission Rd, to W/B Cesar Chavez, to S/B Alameda, and back to 1st St.
> - E/B traffic on 1st St will be detoured N/B on Alameda, to E/B Cesar Chavez Av, to S/B State St, and back to 1st St.
>
> *Details:*
> - No vehicles allowed on the 1st St bridge, except for emergency responders.
> - Crews will be working during daytime, evening and weekend hours.
> - Pedestrian access will be maintained on the south side of the bridge.

B PAIRS. Use the map on page 58 and the notes in Exercise 2A to locate information.

1. Locate the bridge. Locate Mission Rd. and the yellow marks showing the bridge closure.
2. Look at the legend. Use it, along with the map, to figure out what N/B, W/B, S/B, and E/B mean.
3. Locate information in the notes to find out whether fire trucks and ambulances can get across the bridge.
4. Use the notes to find out whether people can walk across the bridge.

C GROUPS. Discuss the questions.

1. What are the biggest reasons for detours or traffic delays where you live?
2. Do you know about any road work or construction going on in your town or city right now that requires drivers to take a detour? Explain.
3. Are there roads you would advise people to avoid because of construction or slow traffic or frequent accidents? If so, what roads could they take instead?
4. Have you ever been late for work or school because of a road- or traffic-related problem? Could you have done anything to avoid it? Explain.

Can you...describe traffic problems? ☐

Lesson 8   Use the Internet to get maps and directions

Life Skills

1   INTERPRET INTERNET MAPS AND DIRECTIONS

A   **PAIRS.** How good are you at following directions and reading maps? Have you ever used the Internet to get driving directions? Explain.

B   **GROUPS.** Two students are planning to go to a baseball game at Dodger Stadium in Los Angeles. Using the Internet, they find a map and directions from their school to the ballpark. Read the map and directions on page 61 and answer the questions.

1. What do the letters *A* and *B* in the green bubbles indicate?
2. What do the letters *N, S, E,* and *W* mean?
3. What words do the abbreviations *Blvd., Ave.,* and *Fwy.* stand for?
4. What do the black arrows to the left of the driving directions indicate?
5. What color is used to mark the route from W. Olympic Blvd. to Dodger Stadium?

2   PRACTICE

A   **PAIRS.** Reread the map and directions. Then write the answers to the questions.

1. How many miles is the drive?
2. About how long should the drive take?
3. Which road on the route crosses the Hollywood Freeway?
4. If the students have to pick up a friend at the University of Southern California before they head to the stadium, how would the directions change? Explain.

B   **PAIRS.** Use the map on page 61 to give directions.

STEP 1. Student A, give directions from Wilshire Country Club to Silver Lake Reservoir. Student B, mark the route in a color on the map.

STEP 2. Student B, give directions from Exposition Park to Los Angeles City College. Student A, mark the route in a different color.

STEP 3. Check each other's routes.

Can you...use the Internet to get maps and directions? ☐

73

Getting Started   5 minutes

1 INTERPRET INTERNET MAPS AND DIRECTIONS

Ⓐ PAIRS. How good are you at following...

- Say: *We've talked about traffic problems and practiced checking a map for road closures and other traffic conditions. Today we're going to practice reading a map and following directions.*

- Have students form pairs and answer the questions. Afterwards, ask students what Internet sites they have used for driving directions. Write them on the board.

Community Building

Have students ask one another about their favorite places in the community and how to get there. For a starting point, use your school. (For example: *What's your favorite coffee shop? How do I get there from here?*)

Presentation   15 minutes

Ⓑ GROUPS. Two students are planning to...

- Ask: *Have any of you ever been to a baseball stadium? How did you know how to get there?*

- Say: *We're going to use directions from the Internet to find our way to the ballpark.*

- Ask students to read the directions; then have them look at the map on page 61.

- Have students answer the questions.

- *Note:* If students ask about the terms *fork, head, merge, ramp,* or *up to,* explain that they will discuss their meanings in Exercise 2B.

Answers: 1. starting and ending addresses; 2. *N*—north, *S*—south, *E*—east, *W*—west; 3. *Blvd.*—Boulevard, *Ave.*—Avenue; *Fwy.*—Freeway; 4. turn left or right; 5. purple

Controlled Practice   15 minutes

MULTILEVEL INSTRUCTION for 2A

Cross-ability Group students in cross-ability pairs for the following exercise so that the above-level partner can show the pre-level partner where to find information.

2 PRACTICE

Ⓐ PAIRS. Reread the map...

- Have students read the directions and the questions.

- Say: *Let's make sure that we're familiar with all of the abbreviations used in the directions.* Write these abbreviations on the board and elicit the complete terms: *mi* (miles); *min* (minutes).

- Have students form pairs and complete the exercise.

Answers: 1. 6.4 mi.; 2. about 19 min.; 3. N. Alvarado St.; 4. (Possible answer) They could take W. Olympic Blvd. to S. Alvarado St., then head south to S. Hoover St. until they reached the university. Then they would take S. Hoover St. north to S. Alvarado St. and follow it to W. Sunset Blvd. and Elysian Park Ave.

Communicative Practice   25 minutes

Ⓑ PAIRS. Use the map on page 61...

- Tell students to form pairs.

- Explain that Student A gives directions, and Student B traces the route on the map. Then they change roles and repeat.

- Have the pairs check each others' routes.

Teaching Tip

If students have computers, ask them to use a website to find directions to get to a certain point (for example, from their home address to the school). Then have them explore options with the web tool, such as a route that avoids highways.

Progress Check

Can you . . . use the Internet to get maps and directions?

- Say: *We have practiced using the Internet to get maps and directions. Can you do this? If so, check the box.*

NOTES FOR MAP OF LOS ANGELES

Use the map for a speaking activity:

- Set up pairs.
- Have Student A pick out a starting point and a destination on the map and tell Student B the starting point but not the destination.
- Ask Student A to give directions: *You're at the University of Southern California. Take S. Vermont Ave. north until you cross Melrose Ave. Where are you?* (Answer: Los Angeles City College)
- Reverse roles and repeat
- Possible starting and ending points:
  Hollywood Forever Cemetery
  Los Angeles City College
  Wilshire Country Club
  Elysian Park
  Rancho Cienega Recreation Center
  Exposition Park

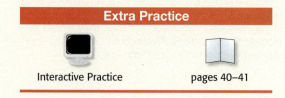

Extra Practice

Interactive Practice   pages 40–41

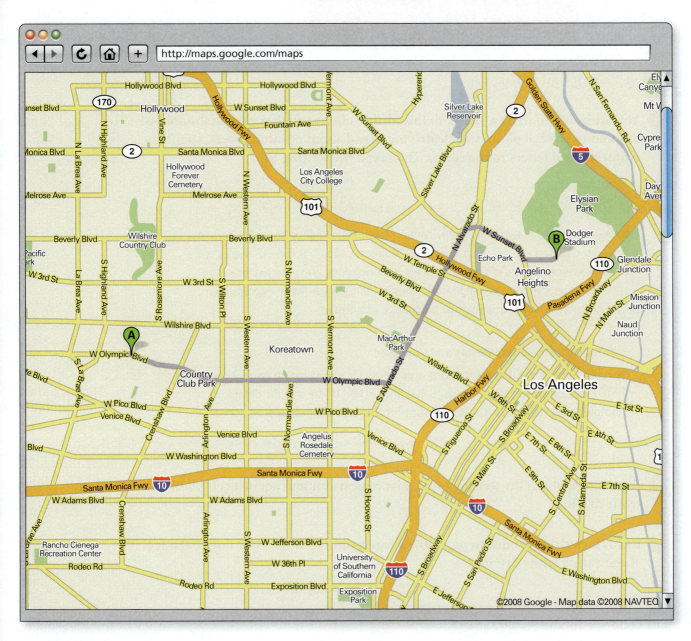

http://maps.google.com/maps

Driving directions to 1000 Elysian Park Ave, Los Angeles, CA 90012
6.4 mi – about 19 mins

(A) **4650 W Olympic Blvd**
Los Angeles, CA 90019

1. Head **east** on **W Olympic Blvd** About 8 mins	go 3.1 mi	total 3.1 mi
↰ 2. Turn **left** at **S Alvarado St** About 7 mins	go 2.0 mi	total 5.1 mi
↱ 3. Turn **right** at **W Sunset Blvd** About 2 mins	go 0.9 mi	total 6.0 mi
↰ 4. Turn **left** at **Elysian Park Ave** About 2 mins	go 0.4 mi	total 6.4 mi

(B) **1000 Elysian Park Ave**
Los Angeles, CA 90012

These directions are for planning purposes only. You may find that construction projects, traffic, weather, or other events may cause conditions to differ from the map results, and you should plan your route accordingly. You must obey all signs or notices regarding your route.

Map data ©2008 NAVTEQ

Writing

1 BEFORE YOU WRITE

A You are going to write a "letter to the editor" about whether people should be allowed to use cell phones while driving. Read about opinion pieces, such as editorials and letters to the editor. Then read the writing tip.

FYI ABOUT EDITORIALS AND LETTERS TO THE EDITOR

Newspapers and magazines usually contain sections for editorials and letters to the editor. Editorial pages, also known as "opinion pages," or "op-ed" pages, are used by editors and publishers to express their opinions about a specific issue. Letters to the editor are also opinion pieces in which readers can express their own point of view about a topic or article in a publication.

Writing Tip: Supporting details and examples

Opinion pieces should present strong arguments for or against an issue. They should include clearly stated reasons that are backed up by specific details or examples. Any sentences that do not support the argument should be deleted.

B Brainstorm about the writing topic. List reasons for and against cell phone use while driving.

C Read the writing model on page 207 about a similar topic. How does Fazil feel about eating while driving?

2 ANALYZE THE WRITING MODEL

PAIRS. Discuss the questions.

1. What argument does Fazil present in paragraph 1?
2. What are the two reasons he gives in support of his argument?
3. In paragraph 2, what details and examples does Fazil use to support his reason?
4. What does Fazil suggest instead of driving while eating?
5. What do you think is the best reason he gives to support his argument? Explain.

State your opinion about cell phone use

Getting Started — 5 minutes

- Say: *We have been talking about driving in the U.S. We have practiced vocabulary and grammatical structures to talk about traffic problems, responses to accidents, and highway safety do's and don'ts. Today we are going to apply all of this knowledge as we write about another safety issue: cell phone use while driving.*

Presentation — 10 minutes

1 BEFORE YOU WRITE

A **You are going to write...**

- Read the directions. Ask: *What is a letter to the editor?* (a letter that someone writes to a newspaper or other publication to express an opinion) Say: *Today we're going to write a letter to the editor about cell phone use while driving.*
- Ask students to read the FYI note and Writing Tip.
- Clarify vocabulary as needed. (Examples: *editorial pages*—pages in a newspaper or magazine that have columns and letters expressing opinions; *backed up*—supported with information and examples)

Language Note

Explain that the term *op-ed page* refers to the page opposite the editorial page. Newspapers frequently have a left-hand page with editorial columns stating the newspaper's opinion on important issues and letters written by readers; the right-hand page has opinion columns written about a variety of issues by professional journalists or guest columnists. Bring in examples of editorial and op-ed pages from different newspapers, such as the *New York Times*, a local paper, or *USA Today*.

B **Brainstorm about the writing topic....**

- Say: *Today you're going to write a letter to the editor stating your opinion about whether people should be allowed to use cell phones while driving. To organize your thoughts, make a list of reasons for and against cell phone use while driving.*
- Write the following chart on the board and have students use it to make their list.

Reasons for	Reasons against
1.	1.
2.	2.
3.	3.

Teaching Tip

If students are using computers in class, have them use the "Table" feature in Microsoft Word to compose their list.

C **Read the writing model on page 207....**

- Ask: *What are some other possibly dangerous things people do while driving?* (listen to the radio, fall asleep, put on makeup)
- If no one mentions eating, tell the class that they will now read a letter to the editor about eating while driving.
- Have students turn to page 207 and read the letter.
- Clarify vocabulary as needed. (Examples: *banned*—officially not allowed; *coordination*—the way parts of the body work together; *distracted*—anxious and not able to think clearly; *have a bite*—to have a quick meal)

Controlled Practice — 10 minutes

2 ANALYZE THE WRITING MODEL

PAIRS. Discuss the questions.

- Tell students that they will work together to find answers to the questions.
- Have students work in pairs to answer the questions. Ask students to share their responses to Question 5 with the class.

Answers: 1. Eating while driving is not safe and should be banned. 2. forces driver to take hands off wheel and lose control; can spill on car or driver and distract driver. 3. Eating requires coordination, for example, unwrapping a burger or taking out a French fry involves taking a hand off steering wheel. 4. Eat at home before driving. 5. Possible answer: The danger of food dropping on the driver or car parts is Fazil's most convincing argument.

State your opinion about cell phone use

Communicative Practice   35 minutes

3   THINK ON PAPER

A **Before Fazil wrote his letter...**

- Say: *Now let's look at how Fazil organized his letter.*
- Ask students to read the directions and the chart.
- Ask: *What information does Fazil give to support his argument that eating while driving is dangerous?*
- Say: *We've talked about the information and examples that Fazil included in his letter. Do you feel that he gave enough reasons to support his argument? Why or why not?* Offer prompts as needed to elicit discussion. (*Did you find that you agreed with him after you read his examples? Which example convinced you the most of his argument?*)

B **Look at the list you wrote...**

- Say: *Now you're going to prepare to write your letter to the editor. First, you need to decide whether you're for or against cell phone use while driving.*
- Ask students to look at the chart in Exercise 3A.
- Say: *Before you write, use a chart like Fazil's to organize your ideas. List your reasons; under each reason, note supporting details and examples.*
- Ask students to create their organizational charts.

Teaching Tip

If students are on computers with a word-processing program, they may cut and paste notes from Exercise 1B into their organizational charts. Then they may cut or copy these notes and paste them into the body of their letters.

4   WRITE

Use your chart to write your...

- Read the directions, and have students write the first draft of their letter to the editor.
- Say: *When you finish writing, you're going to read your letter and revise it.*

5   CHECK YOUR WRITING

A **STEP 1. Revise your work.**

- Say: *You'll read over your letter a first time and answer the questions; if any answers are* no, *revise your work.*
- *Optional:* Have students form pairs, exchange letters, and give each other feedback, noting whether they found their partner's argument convincing and why.

B **STEP 2. Edit and proofread.**

- Say: *Now you'll read over your letter a second time and edit and proofread your work.* Direct students to check their letters for grammar, spelling, punctuation, and typos.
- *Optional:* Have students complete a "clean" second draft of their letter at home, incorporating revisions and corrections from the revision and editing steps.

Teaching Tip

You may want to collect student papers and provide feedback. Use the scoring rubric for writing on page Txv to evaluate vocabulary, grammar, mechanics and how well students complete the task. You may want to review the completed rubric with students.

MULTILEVEL INSTRUCTION for 5A and 5B

Above-level Have students who finish writing and self-editing read and edit a peer's letter using the criteria in Exercises 5A and 5B. Then ask them to discuss the letter with the writer.

Pre-level Have students complete a checklist with the revising and editing criteria from Exercises 5A and 5B, checking off a box for each question and making any changes.

Extra Practice

Interactive Practice   page 42

THINK ON PAPER

A Before Fazil wrote his letter to the editor, he used a chart to brainstorm and organize his argument. Do you think he included enough reasons to support his argument? Why?

> *ARGUMENT: Eating while driving is dangerous and should be banned.*

Reason 1
Eating while driving means taking hand(s) off wheel.

Reason 2
Spilling or dropping food distracts driver and is dangerous.

Details/Examples
Driving requires coordination; unwrapping burger forces driver to take hand off steering wheel and lose control.

Details/Examples
Sandwich leaks sauce; driver worries about clothes, not driving; roll slips onto brake or gas pedal, causing accident; greasy food gets on steering wheel, causing loss of control.

B Look at the list you wrote about cell phone use while driving in Exercise 1B. Decide whether you will write a letter to the editor for or against cell phone use while driving. Use a chart like the one above to brainstorm and organize your argument.

4 **WRITE**

Use your chart to write your letter to the editor. Be sure to give reasons for your opinions and give details and examples to support them.

5 **CHECK YOUR WRITING**

A STEP 1. Revise your work.

1. Is your argument about the topic clearly stated in your first paragraph?
2. Do you give reasons for your point of view?
3. Do you support your reasons with enough details and examples?

B STEP 2. Edit and proofread.

1. Have you checked your grammar, spelling, and punctuation?
2. Have you proofread for typing errors?

1   **REVIEW**   For your grammar review, go to page 228.

2   **ACT IT OUT**   What do you say?

PAIRS. You are discussing car problems, highway do's and don'ts, and car accidents with a friend.

Student A: Review Lessons 1 and 2. Describe some things that can go wrong with a car. Then explain what to do if your car breaks down on the highway.

Student B: Review Lessons 3 and 4. Describe what to do in the event of a car accident, for example, if someone hits your car on the highway.

3   **READ AND REACT**   Problem-solving

STEP 1. Read about Elena.

Elena recently moved to Los Angeles from Chile. She works as a receptionist at Shriners Hospital for Children. The hospital is a 45-minute drive from her home in light traffic. Elena usually allows 45 minutes to get to work, but she is often late for various reasons. First of all, her car is ten years old and breaks down frequently. Last week Elena had a flat tire on the freeway and showed up at work two hours late. Second, she is not used to the layout of the city. To avoid getting lost, she always takes the same route to work. But there is a lot of traffic on her route, especially during morning rush hour. Getting stuck in traffic is a major reason why she is late to work. Elena's boss just spoke harshly to her about her frequent tardiness. She said that Elena will be put on warning if she can't get to work on time. Elena can't afford to lose her job.

STEP 2. GROUPS. What is Elena's problem? What can she do?

4   **CONNECT**   For your Study Skills Activity, go to page 214.

Which goals can you check off? Go back to page 45.

 Go to the CD-ROM for more practice.

Show what you know!

1 REVIEW

For your grammar review, go to page 228.

- Say: *Today we're going to review the skills that we have practiced in this unit and apply them to a problem. What are some of the skills we have practiced?* Elicit answers, noting them on the board. (identifying car parts and problems, talking about highway safety do's and don'ts, making decisions about auto insurance, identifying what to do if the police stop you, describing traffic problems, using the Internet to get directions)
- Ask students to complete the grammar review exercise at the top of page 228.

2 ACT IT OUT

PAIRS. You are discussing car problems...

- Ask students to read the directions. Explain that they will help each other review the skills they practiced in this unit. Say: *Student A will look back at Lessons 1 and 2, describe some things that can go wrong with a car, and explain what to do if your car breaks down on the highway; Student B will look back at Lessons 3 and 4 and describe what to do in case of a car accident—for example, if someone hits your car on the highway.*
- *Optional:* Write prompts on the board to help students get started. Examples:

  If your car breaks down on the highway/If you have a car accident, the first step is to . . .

  Next, you should . . .

  It's also a good idea to . . .

  Be sure to . . .

  Your last step is to . . .

- Have students complete the exercise.

3 READ AND REACT

STEP 1. Read about Elena.

- Say: *Now we're going to apply our knowledge from this unit to a problem involving a character, Elena. Let's read about Elena.*
- Have students read the story. Clarify unfamiliar vocabulary as needed. Examples: *layout*—the way things are arranged; *harshly*—strictly; *put on warning*—given notice that something will occur (such as losing a job) if a condition is not met

STEP 2. GROUPS. What is Elena's...

- Ask students to form small groups.
- Say: *In your group, you will discuss what Elena's problem is and what she can do about it.*
- Give each group a sheet of flipchart paper and markers, or ask them to make notes on a sheet of paper. Tell them that they will write a brief description of Elena's problem and a list of at least three possible solutions.
- Ask groups to choose a representative to present the group's ideas to the class.
- Have students discuss the questions.
- After each presentation, encourage feedback, prompting students as needed (*What do you think about Group 1's suggestions for Elena? Which idea do you like best?*)

Possible answers: *Problem:* Elena's problem is transportation to work. *Solution:* She should leave the house earlier, find another route to work, carpool with a colleague who knows the city better, take the bus.

> **Teaching Tip**
>
> Write sample feedback prompts on the board:
> *I really like the idea of . . .*
> *I don't think Elena should . . . Instead, I think she should . . .*
> *I like the idea for Elena to . . . , but it might not work because . . . What about trying . . . ?*

4 CONNECT

Turn to page 214 for the Study Skills Activity. See page Txii for general teaching notes for Study Skills activities.

Progress Check

Which goals can you check off? Go back to page 45.

Ask students to turn to page 45 and check off any remaining goals they have reached. Call on them to say which goals they will practice outside of class.

CD-ROM Practice

 Go to the CD-ROM for more practice.

If your students need more practice with the vocabulary, grammar, and competencies in Unit 3, encourage them to review the activities on the CD-ROM.

4 Are You Safe?

Classroom Materials/Extra Practice

CD 1
Tracks 22–29

Workbook
Unit 4

Interactive Practice
Unit 4

Unit Overview

Goals
- See the list of goals on the facing page.

Grammar
- Past modals

Listening and Speaking
- Talk about natural disasters and their survivors
- Talk about how to be safe during a flood
- Talk about keeping latchkey kids safe
- *Communication Skill:* Making Suggestions

Reading
- Learn about tornadoes
- *Reading Skill:* Summarizing
- Learn about workers' rights to a safe workplace
- *Reading Skill:* Monitoring comprehension

Writing
- Write safety instructions
- *Writing Tip:* Imperatives

Life Skills
- Identify home safety measures
- Identify workplace safety measures

Preview
- Welcome students and have them look at page 65.
- Say: *Look at the picture. What's happening? Where is everyone? Have you ever seen anything like this?* (Possible answers: It's a tornado. There's a rainbow. It's the Midwest. The people are hiding because they're afraid.)
- Ask: *What is about to happen?* Elicit guesses from students, offering prompts as needed. (*Where is this? Can you guess? Would you be scared?*)
- Say: *In this unit, we'll talk about natural disasters.* Explain as needed that a natural disaster is an extreme weather condition that destroys property and often kills people.
- Ask: *What would you do to stay safe?* Offer prompts as needed to elicit discussion.
- Say: *In this unit, you'll learn about natural disasters, how to prepare for them, and how to stay safe. You'll explore home and workplace safety. You'll also read about your responsibility to keep children safe at home and your right to safety at work.*

Unit Goals
- Ask students to read the Unit Goals.
- Explain unfamiliar vocabulary as needed. (Examples: *latchkey kids*—children who come home from school and stay by themselves at home; *measures*—actions or steps to take to prevent or fix a situation)
- Tell students to circle the goal that is the most important to them.
- Say: *As we complete this unit, we will look back at this page and reread the goals. We will check each goal as we complete it.*

Are You Safe?

Preview

What natural disaster is about to happen? What would you do to stay safe?

UNIT GOALS

☐ Talk about being safe in natural disasters and emergencies

☐ Talk about keeping latchkey kids safe

☐ Identify home safety measures

☐ Learn about workers' rights to a safe workplace

☐ Identify workplace safety measures

Listening and Speaking

1 BEFORE YOU LISTEN

A CLASS. Discuss. What is happening in each picture? Have you or has anyone you know ever experienced one of these events? Describe what happened.

B PAIRS. Discuss the meaning of each word below.

rescuers people who save others from harm or danger

rubble broken stone, bricks, and other objects from a building, wall, or other structure that has been destroyed

survivors people who continue to live after a terrible event, such as a natural disaster, accident, or illness

2 LISTEN

CD1 T22

Listen to one man's story of survival. Write the answers to the questions.

1. How many people were killed in the earthquake?
2. Where did Mr. Liu live?
3. Where was Mr. Liu when the earthquake struck?
4. How long was he trapped under the rubble?
5. Who found him?
6. Who rescued him?

Getting Started   5 minutes

- Say: *In this unit, we are going to explore how to keep safe; how to prepare and deal with natural disasters, how to keep children safe, how to prevent accidents at home, and how to be safe in the workplace.*
- Make sure that students know what a *disaster* is. Accept all student responses; if needed, give examples (hurricanes, floods, etc.).
- Confirm that students understand what *survivors* are. If needed, help out by writing the base verb *survive* on the board.

Presentation   10 minutes

1 BEFORE YOU LISTEN

A CLASS. Discuss. What is happening...

- Pronounce (in a different order) the words for the three kinds of disasters in the pictures: *earthquake, hurricane, tsunami.*
- Say: *Take a minute to label the three disasters.* Confirm that students label them correctly.
Answers (in order): hurricane, tsunami, earthquake

B PAIRS. Discuss the meaning...

- Say: *Work with someone sitting next to you. Take a minute or two to read the vocabulary words and their definitions. If you have any questions about the words or definitions, see if your partner has some ideas.*
- Walk around and listen to the pairs. Answer questions as needed.

Expansion: Vocabulary Practice for 1B

- Offer students more words and phrases related to disasters, for example: *monsoon, tremor, tidal wave* (as a synonym for *tsunami*), *aftershock, Richter scale, Category 5 storm, emergency broadcast system, National Weather Service, emergency workers, siren, evacuation route.*
- Review the definitions for the list. Give real examples when possible.

Controlled Practice   10 minutes

2 LISTEN

 Listen to one man's story...

- Say: *Now we are going to listen to a story about a survivor of a recent natural disaster.*
- Clarify that students should write the answers to the questions in their notebooks as they listen.
- Play CD 1, Track 22.
- Walk around the room as students listen. Help students having difficulty listening and answering at the same time.
- Say: *First, before we go over your answers, what are your reactions to the story you just heard?* Accept all student responses.
- Ask for volunteers to read questions and their answers.
- Play Track 22 again so that students can confirm the correct answers.
- If students need more support, play Track 22 and stop after the information given for each answer. Discuss any questions students may have.

Answers: 1. 50,000; 2. in a small town in China; 3. at the factory where he worked; 4. for 100 hours; 5. his daughter and other family members; 6. soldiers

Presentation   10 minutes

- Direct students to the note on sequence.
- Ask a student to read the text aloud.
- Say: *Dates and other time words help you find your way logically through a conversation or written text. Time order words such as these—first, after, and later—not only help you understand what you are listening to or reading, they can also help you organize your own writing.*
- Brainstorm a list of other time order words, for example, *second, third, next, after that, finally.*
- Write the list on the board and give students time to add any new or unfamiliar words to their vocabulary logs.

Teaching Tip

Whenever time permits, write or have students write answers or brainstorm lists on the board, a transparency, or a flipchart. This gives students who may not have gotten the answer correct a chance to fix their own work. Also, write answers or new information on the board. This helps less proficient students to keep up.

Controlled Practice   10 minutes

3   PRACTICE

 The story of the earthquake...

- Ask students to read the directions.
- Say: *Listen again and answer the questions. Listen for clue words that reveal the sequence of events to help you answer.*
- Play Track 22 again.
- Walk around while students are listening and answering to see whether this exercise seems easy or challenging for most students.

Answers: 1. The earthquake struck after people had gone to work or school. 2. Mr. Liu was trapped under the rubble. 3. Mr. Liu was found on Thursday—the third day after the earthquake. 4. She had to go for help. 5. Mr. Liu was rescued by the soldiers.

4   RETELLING A NEWS STORY

STEP 1. **Read the news story...**

- Ask students to read the directions.
- Say: *Read the news story.*
- Ask: *What's the first important detail in the story?* (the date of the earthquake in China, May 12, 2008)
- Brainstorm the types of key details, such as dates, people's names, or an event students should include. Make sure they understand that they should not write complete sentences.

STEP 2. PAIRS. **Close your books...**

- Ask students to read the directions.
- Say: *Now use your notes to retell the story. Take turns retelling the events, in order.*
- Students may use their notes if they need to but should try to retell the story without their notes.
- To follow-up, ask: *What did you notice about how you retold the story and how your partner did?* Ask students to give details and examples.

Communicative Practice   15 minutes

5   MAKE IT PERSONAL

GROUPS. **Discuss. What personality traits...**

- Ask students to read the directions.
- Review examples of *personality traits* (see Unit 1). Explain as needed.
- Ask groups to consider the two questions. Say: *There are no right or wrong answers, but please give reasons for your ideas. We don't know how we would act in a natural disaster, but it's useful to think and talk about these issues in case we are caught in such a situation.*

3 PRACTICE

CD1 T22

The story of the earthquake is organized in chronological (time) order. Listen again and answer the questions.

1. What happened first on Monday morning?
2. What happened after that?
3. When was Mr. Liu found?
4. What did his daughter do after he answered her?
5. What happened about 12 hours later?

> To determine the sequence of events in a story, note clue words, such as dates, months of the year, and days of the week. Also note words that signal time order, such as *first*, *after*, and *later*.

4 RETELLING A NEWS STORY

STEP 1. Read the news story about an earthquake in China.

One of China's worst earthquakes in recent times occurred on May 12, 2008. Nearly 70,000 people died in the earthquake, and approximately, 5 million people lost their homes. The earthquake affected towns in the eastern part of China's Sichuan province, including the city of Pengzhou. Newspapers reported the amazing story of a retired woman in Pengzhou who had survived by drinking rainwater after being trapped for 195 hours. When the quake first hit, the 60-year-old woman, later identified as Wang Youqun, was knocked unconscious by a steel beam. When Wang became conscious again, she was able to move, but an aftershock later trapped her between two large stones. After more than eight days of being trapped in rubble, Wang Youqun was rescued alive. The rescuers were amazed that after all Wang had been through, she had only a broken hip and bruises on her face.

STEP 2. PAIRS. Close your books, and retell the story. Use words that signal time order. Help each other remember all the details.

5 MAKE IT PERSONAL

GROUPS. Discuss. What personality traits help someone survive a terrible natural disaster like the one described above? How do you think you would do during a natural disaster? Explain your thoughts.

Reading

1   BEFORE YOU READ

CLASS.   Discuss. Do tornadoes occur in your native country? Are they common where you live now?

2   READ

CD1 T23

Listen to and read the article about what to do during a tornado warning and a tornado watch.

Tornadoes: What They Are and What to Do

Tornado Alley

A tornado is a **violently rotating** column of air that extends from a thunderstorm cloud to the ground. Tornadoes can be between a few feet and a mile wide, and they rotate at speeds of up to 300 miles per hour. The most violent tornadoes can rip roofs and walls from houses and other buildings, **uproot** trees, **overturn** trains, and pick up cars and throw them through the air.

Tornadoes can happen at any time and can occur in any part of the United States. But they happen most often in the spring and early summer in "Tornado Alley" or "the Tornado Belt"—an area that extends from Texas to Ohio, from parts of the Rockies to the Appalachian Mountains.

If you live where tornadoes are common, it is extremely important to be ready. Planning is important. Everyone should know what to do and where to go during a **tornado watch** or *warning*. At the first sign of bad weather, tune in to local TV or radio weather news. During a *watch*, the weather conditions are right for tornadoes, but none have been seen. Continue to listen to weather reports, and be ready to move quickly to a safe place. During a *warning*, a tornado has been reported. Take shelter immediately!

Know the safest place in your house. That's the basement if you have one. Another safe place is a **central** room away from windows, such as a closet or bathroom. If you live in a **mobile home** and there is a tornado watch, leave for sturdier shelter. But if there isn't any and there is a warning, run outside. Lie flat in a **ditch** or on low ground in clear, open space, and cover your head with your hands. It's extremely dangerous to be in or near a **vehicle** in a tornado. If there is a warning, or if you see a tornado, run from the car and lie flat in a ditch.

If you are in a large building, go to a hallway or restroom, away from windows, near the center of the structure. Get down on the floor, and cover your head with your hands.

After a tornado, the danger is not over. Avoid lighting matches, smoking, or using candles. If your home is **damaged**, turn off gas and electrical power. Do not touch **power lines** that are on the ground or anything in contact with them.

Learn about tornadoes

Getting Started 10 minutes

- Say: *In this lesson, we are going to listen and read about one type of natural disaster: tornadoes.* Direct students' attention to page 65 and remind them of the discussion about the photograph. Say: *Can someone explain what a tornado is?*
- *Note:* If you live in an area where tornadoes occur, say, for example: *Here in _____, we usually get tornadoes every year, so it's very important that you learn how to prepare.*
- If students want to share experiences related to tornadoes or other extreme weather events, encourage them to do so.

Language Note

Use *tornado/tornadoes* as an opportunity to review *-s* vs. *-es* rules in nouns that end in *o*:

If the final letter o is preceded by a vowel, only *-s* is added; for example, *radio/radios, portfolio/portfolios.*

If the final letter o is preceded by a consonant, *-es* is added; for example, *potato/potatoes, tomato/tomatoes.*

Presentation 15 minutes

1 BEFORE YOU READ

CLASS. Discuss. Do tornadoes occur...

- Rephrase the first question. Say: *Are there tornadoes in [Mexico]? If so, can you tell us about what they are like?* If needed, give an example either from your own experience or from the news.
- For the second question (*Are they common where you live now?*), refer to the earlier discussion in Getting Started. Say, for example: *We mentioned a few minutes ago that we have (or don't have) tornadoes in _____ [name of state] every year.* Encourage students to share information they have about tornadoes in your area.

2 READ

🔘 Listen to and read the article...

- Ask students to read the directions.
- Say: *Remember to look for clues to meaning anywhere you can find them—in the title, the map, or the first sentence of each paragraph.*
- Point out that the words and phrases in boldface (*violently, rotating, uproot, overturn, tornado watch, central, mobile home, ditch, vehicle, damaged, power lines*) appear in the glossary on page 245. Encourage students to read the entire article first before going to the glossary.
- Play CD 1, Track 23 while students listen and read along.
- After students listen and read, ask if they have any other questions about the content, vocabulary, or pronunciation. Answer questions.

Expansion: Vocabulary Practice for 2

- Divide the class into small groups.
- Assign one or two of the boldfaced words or phrases to each group and have them write a sentence for each word or phrase.
- Ask groups to write their sentences on the board. Make any necessary corrections.

Community Building

If computers are available, ask students to work in pairs to find out more information about tornadoes or other natural disasters.

Encourage students to search for helpful information for their neighborhood.

Some helpful websites:

www.fema.gov/hazard/index.shtm
www.bt.cdc.gov/disasters/tornadoes
www.nws.noaa.gov.

Controlled Practice   20 minutes

3   CHECK YOUR UNDERSTANDING

A Write the answers to the questions...

- Read the three questions aloud and say: *Write a short answer to each question in your notebook. Take just a couple of minutes on this; then we will go over the answers.*

- Ask for answers and correct any errors by modeling the correct answer. If it seems useful, go into more detail with the explanation so that all students understand.

Answers: 1. a violently rotating column of air that extends from a thunderstorm cloud to the ground; 2. from a few feet wide to a mile wide; 3. They can happen anytime, but they occur most often in the spring and early summer.

B Write the answers to the questions...

- Say: *Look for tornado safety tips.*

- Go over the answers with the whole class. Confirm that students know the difference between a *tornado watch* and a *tornado warning.*

Answers: 1. Take shelter immediately. 2. Mobile homes are not sturdy enough to withstand a tornado, and it's extremely dangerous to be in or near a vehicle during a tornado. 3. You need to be away from the windows and near the center of the structure. 4. You need to avoid falling objects (debris) that could harm your head (brain); 5. There may be gas fumes or live electrical wires that could cause an explosion or fire.

Reading Skill: Summarizing

- Direct students to the Reading Skill box.

- Ask students how they find the main point of a text. Say: *Do you write notes about the main idea? How do you distinguish details from main ideas?*

C Reread the article. Then...

- Say: *As you reread the article, stop and actively think about what you are reading. As you read, jot down a few sentences about the main points of the article. When you are finished, write a short paragraph.*

- Walk around and answer questions and offer assistance as needed.

Teaching Tip

You may want to collect student paragraphs and provide feedback. Use the scoring rubric for writing on page Txv to evaluate vocabulary, grammar, mechanics and how well students complete the task. You may want to review the completed rubric with students.

4   WORD WORK

GROUPS. Choose three words...

- Set up groups.

- Ask students to read the directions.

- Walk around and provide help as necessary.

- Say: *Remember when you write in your vocabulary log, you can always write more than three words or phrases. You can also use the vocabulary log for words you read or hear outside of class.*

Communicative Practice   15 minutes

5   MAKE IT PERSONAL

GROUPS. Discuss the questions.

- Set up groups. Say: *Work in groups of 4 or 5. Take turns answering the questions.*

- Walk around and provide help as necessary.

- To finish, review class answers to question 2. Write new vocabulary on the board.

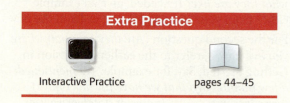

Extra Practice

Interactive Practice   pages 44–45

3 CHECK YOUR UNDERSTANDING

A Write the answers to the questions about tornadoes.

1. What is a tornado?
2. How big are tornadoes?
3. When do tornadoes happen most in the U.S.?

B Write the answers to the questions about tornado safety tips.

1. During a tornado warning, what should you do first?
2. If you live in a mobile home, why should you go outside and lie in a ditch?
3. If you are in a large building, why should you go to a hallway or restroom?
4. If you are in a building, why should you get down on the floor and cover your head with your hands?
5. After a tornado, why should you avoid lighting matches, smoking, or using candles?

C Reread the article. Then write a paragraph that summarizes the main ideas.

Reading Skill:
Summarizing

As you read, stop to summarize parts of a text so that you will remember and understand what you read. Write a few sentences about the main ideas. Leave out unimportant events, ideas, and details. When you finish reading, summarize the entire text.

4 WORD WORK

GROUPS. Choose three words or phrases in the article that you would like to remember. Discuss the words and their meanings. Then record the words and information about them in your vocabulary log.

5 MAKE IT PERSONAL

GROUPS. Discuss the questions.

1. If you live where tornadoes typically happen:
   a. Does your family have a tornado plan if a tornado strikes when you're at home? Do you have flashlights and spare batteries? Do you have a first-aid kit?
   b. Does anyone in your family work or study in places that have tornado drills? If not, what should family members do if a tornado strikes at work or at school?

2. If tornadoes don't happen where you live, what other natural disasters might strike your region? How can you and your family prepare?

Listening and Speaking

1 BEFORE YOU LISTEN

A **CLASS.** Look at the picture. Discuss. Do you live in an area where a flood like this could happen? Have you or has anyone you know ever experienced a flood?

B Read about Hurricane Katrina. What else do you know about this hurricane and the flooding it caused in New Orleans?

In 2005, Americans experienced one of the deadliest hurricanes in their history: Katrina. Hurricane Katrina hit parts of Mississippi and Alabama, but the city of New Orleans, Louisiana, was affected the most. The levees around New Orleans burst and 80 percent of the city was flooded.

2 LISTEN

CD1 T24

A Listen to the first part of a news report about Hurricane Katrina. Write the answers to the questions.

1. When did Hurricane Katrina hit New Orleans?
2. Were there any plans to evacuate people who were sick or old?
3. What is the Superdome? Who was sent there?
4. What happened to the medical supplies?
5. What were people told to do with their pets when they evacuated?

CD1 T25

B Listen to the second part of the news report. What could or should have been done? Complete the sentences.

1. There should have been plans to evacuate hospitals and nursing homes .

2. Public buses could have been used to evacuate people without cars .

3. There should have been police there to keep them safe .

4. People should not have been told to leave pets at home .

Getting Started
10 minutes

- Say: *We've talked about natural disasters and survivors of natural disasters and about tornadoes and how to prepare for them. Now we are going to talk about floods, specifically about the flooding that came with Hurricane Katrina in 2005, one of the worst disasters in U.S. history.*

Presentation
10 minutes

1 BEFORE YOU LISTEN

Ⓐ CLASS. Look at the picture...

- Ask students to look at the picture and describe it.
- Ask: *Have you or has anyone you know ever experienced a flood?* Help students with any vocabulary they need to talk about their experience.
- Write any unfamiliar vocabulary and place names on the board. If you have a world map and/or a U.S. map, ask students to point out where the floods they are talking about occurred.
- Remind students of the expression *to be in* for natural disasters or accidents. (For example, *I've never been in an earthquake.*)

Ⓑ Read about Hurricane Katrina...

- Find a photo or graphic of a levee—in New Orleans. Bring in other news photos to show.
- If possible, show coastal Alabama, Mississippi, and Louisiana on a map.
- Check comprehension of vocabulary in the text.

Culture Connection

Present a short history of Louisiana and New Orleans. Include, for example, information such as how and when the U.S. acquired the Louisiana territory* from France (called the Louisiana Purchase); the settlement of part of the area by Acadians from Canada who were the descendants of the Cajuns; slavery; and New Orleans as an important center for music.

Controlled Practice
10 minutes

2 LISTEN

Ⓐ Listen to the first part...

- Tell students they will listen to the first part of a news report now.
- Clarify that students are to write the answers to the questions in their notebooks as they listen.
- Play CD 1, Track 24.
- Ask for volunteers to read the questions and their answers. Have the class help make any necessary corrections.

Answers: 1. August 29, 2005; 2. no; 3. a football stadium, people without transportation; 4. They were available but not distributed. 5. to leave their pets at home

Ⓑ Listen to the second part...

- Say: *When you listen to this second part, listen for information about what could or should have been done that might have made the disaster less terrible.*
- As you listen, complete each of the sentences.
- Play CD 1, Track 25.
- To review, have students read their completed sentences. Make any necessary corrections.

---

* You may want to refer students to the map on page 140 to show them the extent of the Louisiana territory.

Presentation   10 minutes

 3   PRACTICE

GROUPS. How much do you know...

- Emphasize that the left box is for what to do to be ready to evacuate in a crisis, and that the right box is what you need to do if local officials tell you to evacuate.
- Walk around the room as groups work; answer questions and provide assistance as needed.
- When students are finished, tell them to put the chart aside for now.
- See the answers in Exercise 4A for some possible responses to the chart.

Controlled Practice   10 minutes

4   LISTEN

A **Make another chart...**

- Review the directions step by step; use an example (on notebook paper) to show what the chart should look like.
- Play CD 1, Track 26.

Possible answers:

To be ready to evacuate:
know where you can stay, decide on a meeting place, contact children's school about an emergency plan, learn different routes from home and workplace to a safe place, plan for pets, make sure all family members have contact info, prepare an emergency kit, keep half a tank of gas in car at all times, bring in outdoor items, open basement windows

If asked to evacuate:
go immediately, take emergency kit and important documents, unplug electronic equipment and appliances (but not fridge), shut off gas and water, lock doors, leave a note on property or in mailbox saying when you left and how to reach you, check TV and radio for routes, don't take shortcuts, don't drive through water

B **PAIRS. Compare and revise your notes...**

- Play Track 26 again. Have students check their information.
- Ask volunteers to tell what they have listed in each part of the chart. Write responses on the board.
- Remind students to write any new and relevant vocabulary words in their vocabulary logs.

MULTILEVEL INSTRUCTION for 4B

Cross-ability Assign above-level students to work with pre-level students to make sure they have correct information and to help with vocabulary.

Communicative Practice   10 minutes

5   MAKE IT PERSONAL

GROUPS. Discuss the questions.

- Ask students to take notes in their notebooks about any new information they learn.
- Walk around and listen to the discussions; answer questions and assist as needed.
- Review information for each question and write answers on the board.
- Give the name, address, phone number, and website for the government departments in charge of emergencies in your area.

Networking

- If possible, invite an emergency preparedness official or someone from the local Red Cross to come to class to discuss what to do to prepare for an emergency and what services are available to people who live in your community.
- To prepare for the visit, see the Networking notes on page 57.
- As an alternative to the classroom visit, assign pairs or small groups to find the answers to Make It Personal questions 2, 4, and 7 that are appropriate for your area. After students find the information, ask them to collate it, revise it (with your help), and then present you with the final version to print for the class.

Extra Practice

Interactive Practice

GROUPS. How much do you know about what to do in an evacuation?
Complete the chart with ideas about what you should do.

To be ready for an evacuation...	If you are asked to evacuate...
have a battery-operated radio.	

4 LISTEN

CD1 T26

A Make another chart in your notebook like the one in Exercise 3.
Use a whole page. Write the headings at the top. Then listen to an expert
give advice about flood safety. Take notes in your chart. Write as much
information as you can.

CD1 T26

B PAIRS. Compare and revise your notes. Then listen again to
check your information.

5 MAKE IT PERSONAL

GROUPS. Discuss the questions.

1. Do you have a friend or family member you could stay with if you had to
   evacuate? Explain.

2. Do you know about evacuation routes and plans in your area? If not, do you
   know where to get this information? Explain.

3. Do you know how to turn off utilities at your home? Explain.

4. If you have pets, what is your emergency plan for them?

5. What important items would you want to take with you if you had to evacuate?
   Would they be ready if you had to evacuate your home today?

6. Why should you have spare batteries and a battery-operated radio?

7. Where in your community can you find information about emergency shelter?

8. If you had time to do something before a flood, what might you bring indoors or
   move to the highest levels of your home?

Grammar

Past Modals

Active Voice

The government **should have evacuated** us earlier.

The flood **could have killed** our pets.

We **might have saved** our financial records if we'd had them in a safe.

Passive Voice

We **should have been evacuated** earlier.

Our pets **could have been killed**.

Our financial records **might have been saved** if we'd had them in a safe.

Grammar Watch

- Past modals are formed by modal + *(not) have* and the past participle form of the main verb.
- Use *should have* to express regret.
- Use *may have/might have/could have* to express past possibilities or a past choice.

1 PRACTICE

Read about the experiences of people who evacuated their homes. Check (✓) the sentence that best completes each passage.

1. I didn't leave until we were told to evacuate. I'd prepared an emergency kit, and I knew where I was going, but there were long lines at the gas station when I stopped to get gas. I thought about leaving my car and trying to take a bus. But the buses were crowded, and they didn't go directly to my brother's house, where I was staying.

    ☑ a. I should have filled my car with gas before we were told to evacuate.

    ☐ b. I shouldn't have tried to evacuate by car.

2. I took three pairs of jeans, four shirts, four pairs of socks, and underwear. But I still ended up wearing dirty clothes for several days. I thought there would be laundry services available at the shelter. Ha!

    ☑ a. I should have taken more clothes.

    ☐ b. I shouldn't have taken so many clothes.

3. We didn't leave right away after we were told to evacuate because we were worried about people robbing our home. That wasn't smart. We risked our own lives. The water came into our house. It covered our car. We had to go upstairs. Finally, we had to climb out of the upstairs windows and onto the roof. We were lucky to be rescued.

    ☐ a. We might have been able to leave sooner.

    ☑ b. We should have left sooner.

Getting Started   5 minutes

- Write on the board: *The U.S. government should have _____. The mayor of New Orleans should have _____.*
- Say: *When we talked about Hurricane Katrina, we talked about mistakes. Today we're going to use the grammatical structure of past modals to talk more about what should have been done in such an emergency.* Point to the examples on the board.

Presentation   15 minutes

Past Modals

- Copy the grammar chart onto the board.
- Point to the modals in the example. Explain that a modal is a helping verb that talks about what is possible, advisable, mandatory, optimal, or regrettable.
- Read each sentence and have the class repeat.
- Ask students to read the Grammar Watch.
- Say: *We use modals in the present or past tense. How is the past modal formed?* (The modal—*should, could, may, might*—+ *have* + the past participle of the verb) Write this on the board.

Active voice

- Review active and passive. See the Language Note.
- Point to the upper part of the grammar chart and read the first example.
- Say: *Use* should have *plus the past participle to express regret about something that happened or didn't happen in the past—that is, feeling sorry that a different decision wasn't made.* Ask: *What was the decision in this example that wasn't made?* (The government did not evacuate people earlier.)
- Read the second and third examples. Say: *Use* could have, might have, *or* may have *plus the past participle to express something that was possible in the past but didn't happen.* Ask: *In these examples, what was possible in the past but didn't happen?* (Pets could have been killed by the flood. People could have used a safe to protect their financial records.)

Language Note

- Help students understand the concept of active and passive voice.
- Write on the board: *1. John is washing the car. 2. The car is being washed right now.*
- Say: *Sentence one is active. The subject is doing the action. Sentence two is passive. The subject is receiving the action.*
- Write more examples on the board, and have students identify active or passive. For example, *Tornadoes cause a lot of damage.* (active) *A lot of damage is caused by tornadoes.* (passive)

Passive voice

- Point to the lower part of the grammar chart and read the examples.
- Ask: *In the first sentence, who is receiving the action?* (we) *Do we know who should have performed the action of evacuating people earlier?* (No—the sentence doesn't say.)

Controlled Practice   15 minutes

 1 PRACTICE

Read about the experiences...

- Say: *Choose the sentence that best states what the flood survivors should or might have done differently.*
- Walk around and check students' work, clarifying vocabulary and offering help as needed.
- Call on students to say the answers. After each answer, ask students if the past modal was used to express regret about something that happened or didn't happen in the past or something that was possible in the past but didn't happen. (The modal *should have* was used in all answers to express regret.)

Controlled Practice   15 minutes

2   **PRACTICE**

PAIRS. Complete these sentences...

- Read the directions and do Item 1 with the class.
- Have students complete the exercise. Walk around and offer help as needed. (For example, ask: *Do you need the infinitive or the past participle?*)
- Call on students to read the sentences aloud. Write the answers on the board.
- Ask students which answers were in the passive voice. (*He could have been trapped inside. People may have gotten trapped under the debris.*)

Language Note

When people use past modals in informal speaking situations, they often drop the *have*. For example, *could have* is pronounced as *coulda*. *Should have* is pronounced as *shoulda*. *Would have* is pronounced as *woulda*.

▬ Multilevel Instruction for 2

Pre-level Elicit past participles (*taken, been, gotten, collapsed*) needed in the exercise. Write the following model, and have students refer to it while completing the exercise:

should ⎫
could ⎬ + have + past participle
might ⎪   (*taken, been, gotten, collapsed, left*)
may   ⎭

Above-level After they finish the exercise, have students compare answers with a partner and help each other as needed.

Communicative Practice   10 minutes

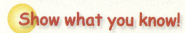 **Show what you know!**

STEP 1. GROUPS. Think about emergencies...

- Ask students to read the directions. Have them form groups and complete the exercise.

STEP 2. GROUPS. Discuss the mistakes....

- Say: *Now you'll talk about the mistakes you listed in your group. As you read each mistake, offer your advice and discuss what the people could or should have done differently.*
- Write the following discussion prompts on the board: *He could have . . . They should have . . .*
- Walk around and ask for clarification or elaboration as needed. (*Is there anything else that she should have done when she heard about the hurricane coming?*)
- Ask for volunteers to share their list of mistakes and their advice for avoiding them.
- After each group presents its ideas, ask for elaboration with the following prompt: *Is there anything else that could have been done to prevent this mistake?*

Community Building

In pairs, have students share a mistake that they made when they first came to this country. For example: getting a "boot" on one's car for not paying parking tickets or mistakenly thinking that something was free. Encourage the partners to offer sympathy and advice. For example: *What a shame! You should have paid the parking tickets right away. You should have called the phone number on them.*

Progress Check

Can you . . . talk about mistakes made during emergencies?

- Say: *We have practiced talking about mistakes made during emergencies. Can you do this? If so, check the box.*

Extra Practice

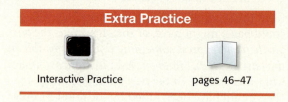

Interactive Practice   pages 46–47

PAIRS. **Complete these sentences about what people did during emergencies.**

1. **A:** Ron was on the top floor of his building when the earthquake hit. He took the elevator to the basement.

   B: He ___should not have taken___ the elevator. He ___could have been___

   (should not / take)   (could / be)

   trapped inside.

2. **A:** Susan was driving her car across the bridge when she felt the earthquake. She pulled over to the side, stopped her car, and waited for the shaking to stop.

   B: She ___should have gotten off___ the bridge. It ___could have collapsed___.

   (should / get off)   (could / collapse)

3. **A:** Are they still looking for survivors of the tornado?

   B: Yes. People ___may have gotten___ trapped under the debris.

   (may / get)

4. **A:** Did you hear the sirens this morning? What were they for?

   B: I didn't hear them. They ___might have been___ a test. But next time, turn on your

   (might / be)

   TV and check the weather station or a news station.

5. **A:** What did your neighbor in the mobile home do when he heard the tornado warning?

   B: He stayed inside the trailer. Luckily, he survived, but he ___should have left for___

   (should / leave for)

   a sturdier shelter.

Show what you know!   Talk about mistakes made during emergencies

STEP 1. GROUPS. Think about emergencies you have heard about in the news or that people you know have experienced. List three mistakes people have made in different emergencies.

1. _____

2. _____

3. _____

STEP 2. GROUPS. Discuss the mistakes. What should the people have done?

Can you... talk about mistakes made during emergencies? ☐

Listening and Speaking

1   BEFORE YOU LISTEN

A   **CLASS.** Discuss the questions.

1. In your home country, is it common for children to spend time alone, without their parents or others looking after them?

2. At what age do you think a child can be responsible for taking care of himself or herself? At what age do you think a child can be responsible for taking care of younger siblings? Explain.

3. If you have children, where do they go after school?

B   Read the information about latchkey children.

"Latchkey children" or "latchkey kids" refers to children who spend time home alone without parents or others to supervise them. Some people believe that the term became widely used during World War II, when many fathers were away fighting the war and many mothers went to work in the factories. Today, there are still many latchkey children, and their numbers are rising. In some cases, children want to go home after school, and they feel they are too old to have a baby-sitter. Older children may pressure parents to allow them to go home after school, even when child care or after-school programs are available. However, many parents of latchkey children do not have a choice: They simply can't afford to pay for child care and have no other options.

C   **GROUPS.** Latchkey children can get into different kinds of trouble when they are home alone. Look at the categories in the chart. Can you think of examples? Write at least one example for each category.

Pressure from Friends to Break Rules	Accidents and Emergencies
Strangers	Emotional and Psychological Issues

Talk about keeping latchkey kids safe

Getting Started   5 minutes

- Say: *Today we are going to speak and listen about another safety issue: keeping latchkey kids safe.*
- Ask students if they know what *latchkey kids* are. Accept student responses
- Point out that *latchkey* is a compound word; *latch* is an older term for a door fastening or lock, and a *latchkey* is the key that opens it.
- Explain that the term *latchkey kid* probably originated during World War II, when it was used to describe a child who spent time alone because one parent was in the armed services and the other had to work.

Presentation   15 minutes

1 BEFORE YOU LISTEN

A CLASS. Discuss the questions.

- Ask for a volunteer to read each question. If needed, clarify and give examples: *In your home country, are children usually with their parents or other relatives, or do they stay home when the adults go to work or to the market?*
- For question 2, write the ages students suggest on the board. Say: *Keep this in mind while we read and listen to information about latchkey children.*
- Students may disagree with each other as well as existing practice in the U.S. Encourage students to respect one another's answers.

Teaching Tip

Adjust the timing of a discussion based on the demographics of your class. For example, if a class is mostly composed of single young people, there will probably be less discussion than in a class made up mostly of parents.

B Read the information about latchkey...

- Ask students to read the directions.
- Have them read the paragraph. Say: *We'll go over any questions you have after you read.*
- Answer any questions about content, vocabulary, or grammar.
- Give students a chance to write any new words in their vocabulary logs.

C GROUPS. Latchkey children can get...

- Confirm that students understand the idiomatic phrase *get into . . . trouble.*
- Give students a series of prompts, such as the following:

  What can happen when a child is home alone and his or her friends call or come over?

  What might happen if a child is alone and a stranger calls or comes to the door?

- First, have students write at least one example in each category before working in groups.
- Clarify what groups need to do. Say: *First, take turns reading what you wrote for each category. Then write one list of all the examples for each category. When you're finished, we'll talk about your examples as a class.*
- Walk around and listen to groups; answer questions and assist as needed.
- Ask one person from each group to write the group's list on the board or a flipchart.
- Tell students to compare the examples. Say: *Which examples are similar? Which are different? Which seem most realistic?*
- Brainstorm a final list of possible dangers that the class agrees with, for example, by a show of hands. Give students time to write the list in their notebooks.

MULTILEVEL INSTRUCTION for 1C

Cross-ability Plan groups of four in advance so that an above-level student will be in every group to help other students who may not be familiar with the idiomatic and culturally based categories, such as *pressure from friends to break rules.*

Controlled Practice   20 minutes

2 LISTEN

 A   **Tania is a single mother...**

- Clarify that students are to write the possible problems and solutions that they hear.
- Say: *It's easy for parents to worry about their children, so sometimes they look for advice or suggestions about what to do.*
- Play CD 1, Track 27.
- Ask volunteers to read the questions and their answers. Let students discuss whether they agree that the "possible problems" are real problems and whether the "possible solutions" are good ones.

Communication Skill: **Making Suggestions**

- Direct students to the Communication Skill box.
- Ask an above-level student to read the text.
- Review these two structures for making suggestions and give examples: *Why don't you <u>practice</u> English outside of class? Maybe you could <u>rent</u> a car for the weekend. Have you thought about <u>practicing</u> English outside of class?*
- Point out that the punctuation varies according to whether or not the suggestion is a question or a statement.
- Say: *Notice that when making suggestions, we often use modals like* could *and* might *and indirect words like* maybe *to soften the suggestion and be more respectful.*

B **Read the information...**

- Ask students to read the directions.
- Say: *Now listen specifically for the phrases Tania's neighbor used when he was making suggestions. The first suggestion is filled in for you. Listen and write the other suggestions as well as you can.*
- Play Track 27 again.
- Walk around the room as students listen. Help as needed.
- To review, ask students to read their suggestions. Make any necessary corrections.

Communicative Practice   20 minutes

Teaching Tip

While pairs are performing role plays, use the scoring rubric for speaking on page Txiv to evaluate each student's vocabulary, grammar, fluency, and how well he or she completes the task. You may want to review the completed rubric with the student.

3 CONVERSATION

ROLE PLAY. PAIRS. **Work with a partner...**

- Ask students to read all of the directions.
- Point out that students need to work with a partner who was not in their group in Exercise 1C.
- Say: *Now we are going to role-play a conversation similar to the conversation between Tania and Nick.*

STEP 1. **Select a problem to work on...**

- Tell pairs that they can choose who will be the parent and who will be the neighbor, etc.

STEP 2. **Create a conversation...**

- Say: *Choose one problem from the chart that we worked on earlier. Write a rough draft of the conversation first. Then add some of the phrases from the Communication Skill box.*

STEP 3. **Practice the conversation...**

- Say: *Practice your conversation several times until you feel comfortable with it. Add gestures and emotions to make your role play realistic.*
- At the front of the room, model the activity with an above-level student. Include a greeting and a closing.

STEP 4. **Perform the role play...**

- Ask pairs to perform in front of the class. Discuss similarities and differences in the role plays.

Extra Practice

Interactive Practice

CD1 T27

A  Tania is a single mother who doesn't get home until after 6:00. Her 12-year-old son, Greg, is home alone after school. Listen to her talk with her neighbor Nick about the things she is worried about. Write the problems and the solutions her neighbor suggests. Answers will vary but could include:

Possible Problems	Possible Solutions
1. *What if strangers call?*	He should say his mom is busy.
2. What if someone comes to the door?	Answer only if he knows the person well.
3. What if his friends come over?	Make a rule—no friends over when an adult isn't home.
4. What if she can't answer the phone because she's working?	He can send a text message.
5. What if there's a fire or other emergency?	Write a fire safety plan./Call 911.

CD1 T27

B Read the information in the Communication Skill box. Then listen again. Write the phrase Nick uses to offer each suggestion.

Suggestion 1: _Why don't you_

Suggestion 2: _If I were you, I'd_

Suggestion 3: _Could you_

Suggestion 4: _Maybe you could_

Suggestion 5: _Have you thought about_

Communication Skill:
Making Suggestions

You can begin a suggestion with these phrases:

Why don't you (+ verb)?
Have you thought about (+ gerund)?
Maybe you could (+ verb).
If I were you, I'd (+ verb).
Could you (+ verb)?

ROLE PLAY. PAIRS. Work with a partner who was not in your group in Exercise 1C. Student A is the parent and Student B is the neighbor.

STEP 1. Select a problem to work on from the chart in Exercise 1C.

STEP 2. Create a conversation like the one between Tania and her neighbor. Use expressions from the Communication Skill box. Write the conversation down.

STEP 3. Practice the conversation. Use gestures and appropriate emotion.

STEP 4. Perform the role play in front of the class.

Life Skills

1 DISCUSS CHILD SAFETY PRODUCTS

A **CLASS.** Everyone wants children to be safe, but children, especially young children, can get injured in accidents at home. Discuss. What kinds of home accidents can children have?

B Read the online catalog page. Where have you seen or purchased any of these items?

http://www.childsafetyproducts.com

Childsafetyproducts.com
Because we care about kids!

🛒 check out   contact us   🛒 Your Cart ☐items

Safety Gates
Prevent falls down stairs and keep children out of unsafe areas. Screws to wall for added security. Good for pets, too. $26.00

Doorstops and Door Holders
Prevent little fingers from getting caught, slammed, or pinched in doors.
Door Stop and Door Holder $5.95

Electrical Outlet Covers
Reduce risk of electric shock with outlet covers. Large enough to pose no choking risk and difficult for children to remove. $2.00

Cabinet Latches
Keep children from opening cabinets containing household cleansers, medicines, plant chemicals, and other poisonous substances. Easy to install. $2.95. Pkg. of 4, $10.00

Window Guards
Keep your children safe when windows are open. Easy to install and remove. $15.95

◀ previous | next ▶

C **PAIRS.** Answer the questions about the child safety products above.

1. Susan's daughter had to go to the emergency room because she swallowed ant poison from a cabinet under the sink. What product would have prevented this accident?

2. John's new puppy ran out the front door and bit a neighbor's six-year-old son. What product should John have bought?

3. Roberto and Candy have just moved from a ground floor apartment to a high-rise building. They have a two-year-old daughter. What product should they buy first? Why?

Getting Started   5 minutes

1 **DISCUSS CHILD SAFETY PRODUCTS**

A **CLASS. Everyone wants children...**

- Say: *In the last lesson, we talked about safety of latchkey kids, children who are home alone after school. What are some ways to help these children be safe at home?* Elicit ideas from students, offering prompts as needed. (For example: *What should children do if a stranger calls? Or if their friends want them to do something that's not allowed?*)

- Say: *Now let's talk about another safety issue with much younger children.*

- Read and discuss the question, offering prompts as needed to elicit answers. (For example: *What about the stairs? Can children have an accident there?*)

- Say: *Today we're going to look at some home safety products designed to prevent small children from having accidents at home. Do you have anything in your home to prevent children from getting hurt accidentally?*

Presentation   15 minutes

B **Read the online catalog page...**

- Clarify unfamiliar terms as needed. Examples: *doorstop*: something to hold a door open—refer students to the picture; *slammed*: to have something close on you—demonstrate with fingers in the doorway; *pinched*: to have a body part caught in something—demonstrate with fingers next to the hinge of a door; *electric shock*: a shock—and physical pain—you receive if you touch an unprotected wire, for example, or stick your finger in an electrical outlet; *choking*: when you swallow something that is too big to go down your throat; *screws*: as a verb, to fasten a part to something—pantomime screwing a hinge into the wall; *latch*: an extra piece that keeps a door closed. Refer students to the picture and remind them of what they learned in the previous lesson.

- Ask: *Have you seen or purchased any of these items?* Elicit answers from students, encouraging them to say why, if they feel it has been effective.

Culture Connection

In the U.S., the government is responsible for regulating the safety of all consumer products, including children's toys and safety equipment. The agency in charge of this is the U.S. Consumer Product Safety Commission (http://www.cpsc.gov).

Expansion: Speaking Practice for 1B

- Tell students that they will act out possible accidents and say what could have been used to prevent them.

- Write on the board: *What could have been used to prevent accidents?* Ask: *What kind of verb structure is* could have been used? (past modal)

- Review the past modal. Write on the board: *You could have . . .*

- Ask for a volunteer to come to the front of the room and pantomime an accident, such as falling down the stairs.

- Other students guess what the accident is and say, *You could have installed . . .*

- Repeat the exercise with another student.

C **PAIRS. Answer the questions...**

- Ask students to read the directions.
- Call on a student to read each question aloud.
- Have students form pairs to answer the questions.
- Monitor students as they discuss the questions, offering help when needed.
- Go over the answers as a class.

Answers: 1. cabinet latches; 2. safety gates; 3. window guards—(possible answer) They should buy the window guards first because the most serious danger is a fall from the window.

Controlled Practice   30 minutes

2 LISTEN

A 🔘 **Listen to four conversations...**

- Say: *Now we're going to listen to four conversations and complete the chart on page 77.* Copy the chart onto the board.
- Ask students to look at the chart on page 77. Tell them that they will listen for specific information from each conversation: They need to note who the speakers are, what the situation is, and what the catalog item is.
- Remind students that they will take notes to help them remember information; they do not need to write down every word they hear.
- Play CD 1, Track 28.
- Walk around and help as needed.
- Say: *Let's listen to the conversations again and correct our answers.*
- Play Track 28 again, pausing it after each conversation and calling on students to say the answers. Write the answers on the board.

B 🔘 **Listen again and answer...**

- Say: *Now we're going to listen to the conversations again and answer some questions.*
- Ask students to read the questions.
- Play Track 28 again.
- Have students complete the exercise. Check their work.
- Play Track 28 again, pausing it as answers to the questions are given. After you have paused the CD, call on a student to say the answer.

▮ MULTILEVEL INSTRUCTION

Pre-level Have students look at the audio script on pages 236–237 as they listen. They can also use the audio script to check their answers.

Above-level Have students read the questions first. Then have them close their books as they listen. Students can work in pairs to compare answers.

Communicative Practice   10 minutes

Teaching Tip

In the previous exercise, remind students to use the conditional to talk about a hypothetical situation—that is, one that is imaginary but possible. To guide students in the discussion, write a prompt on the board: *I think that the _____ is the most important item because it would _____.*

C **GROUPS. Discuss. Which of the safety items...**

- Read the questions. Tell students that they will talk to their group members about which of the safety items, in their opinion, is the most important. Emphasize that there are no right or wrong answers.
- As students discuss the questions, walk around and monitor conversations, offering prompts for clarification or elaboration as needed. (*Why do you think that an electrical outlet cover is more important than a doorstop cover?*)
- Call for a volunteer from each group to tell the class which item they thought was the most important and why.

▮ Expansion: Writing Practice for 2C

- Have students write a paragraph addressing the discussion questions.
- If time allows, ask students to read their paragraphs aloud.

Progress Check

Can you . . . identify home safety measures?

- Say: *We have practiced identifying home safety measures. Can you do this? If so, check the box.*

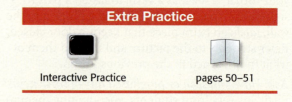

Extra Practice	
Interactive Practice	pages 50–51

CD1 T28

 A **Listen to four conversations and complete the chart.** Answers will vary but could include:

Who are the speakers?	What is the situation?	What is the catalog item?
1. parents	Wife has installed latch on cupboard.	Safety latch
2. customer and salesperson	Woman is concerned about her nephew's safety in her home.	safety gate
3. friends	One friend's child had hurt her fingers in a door.	doorstops and door holders
4. parent and day care worker	Day care worker is showing parent how safe her facility is.	window guards

CD1 T28

B **Listen again and write the answers to the questions.** Answers will vary but could include:

Conversation 1. Why do the people need this safety device?

to keep children away from dangerous household products

Conversation 2. What dangers are discussed?

a young child falling down the stairs

Conversation 3. Where was the child protection item purchased?

at the drugstore

Conversation 4. What incident was reported in the newspaper last month?

a child almost fell from a window

C **GROUPS. Discuss. Which of the safety items discussed is the most important for young children? Why? How might some of these products keep certain elderly people safe as well?**

Can you... identify home safety measures? ☐

Reading

1 BEFORE YOU READ

CLASS. Discuss. Why do workers need protection? What kind of safety information is available for employees at your workplace?

2 READ

CD1 T29

Listen to and read the poster about worker's rights on page 79. Monitor your comprehension as you read.

3 CHECK YOUR UNDERSTANDING

Read the statements. Write *T* (*true*) or *F* (*false*).

___T___ 1. OSHA is a division of the U.S. Department of Labor.

___T___ 2. You can keep your name confidential if you contact OSHA to report unsafe work conditions.

___T___ 3. You can ask OSHA representatives to come to your workplace to inspect for safety hazards.

___F___ 4. Your boss can fire you or reduce your hours if you call OSHA to report a safety problem.

___F___ 5. OSHA can make recommendations, but your employer does not have to follow them if the company or organization cannot afford it.

> **Reading Skill:**
> Monitoring Comprehension
>
> Monitoring your comprehension will help you understand difficult texts, such as government documents. Reread such texts slowly and carefully. List any difficult words. Try to figure out their meanings from clues in the surrounding words and sentences. If you can't figure out a word, look it up in a dictionary. Then try to restate the information in your own words.

4 WORD WORK

GROUPS. Choose three words or phrases in the poster that you would like to remember. Discuss the words and their meanings. Then record the words and information about them in your vocabulary log.

5 MAKE IT PERSONAL

GROUPS. Discuss the questions.

1. What are some reasons people might not want to complain about unsafe working conditions? What advice would you give them?

2. Are there any unsafe or unhealthy conditions at your workplace or school? What could you do, or who could you talk to, to correct them?

Getting Started · 10 minutes

- Say: *We've talked about natural disasters, keeping latchkey children safe, and what should or could have been done during disasters. Now we are going to talk about keeping safe in another environment: the workplace. In this lesson, we will listen to and read about safety rules and safety information available to workers.*

1 BEFORE YOU READ

CLASS. Discuss. Why do workers...

- Ask for a volunteer to read the discussion questions.
- Accept student responses; make a list on the board, an overhead, or a flipchart. (For example: Heimlich maneuver signs and "Employees must wash hands before returning to work" signs)

Presentation · 15 minutes

Reading Skill: **Monitoring Comprehension**

- Direct students to the Reading Skill box.
- Read the text aloud.
- Ask if a student can explain or give an example of what *monitor* means. If needed, give examples: as a noun—a person who assures that things run smoothly, a piece of equipment that receives and shows information inside someone's body, or the part of a computer that shows the information; as a verb—to carefully watch, listen to, or examine something over time.

- Confirm that students understand what *comprehension* means.
- Say: *When you read difficult texts, you need to monitor—or carefully watch—what you are reading and how well you understand. Sometimes you might need to read the text several times. It's a good idea to list any words you can't understand, then look them up in a dictionary.*
- Say: *When you finish a difficult article, try to summarize the point of the article to make sure you understand what you have read.*

2 READ

 Listen to and read the poster...

- Ask students to read the directions.
- Confirm that students know what a *poster* is. Ask them where they have seen informational and governmental posters (for example: at the Department of Motor Vehicles, in hospitals, in buses and subways, at work, in a restaurant).
- Point out that the words and phrases in boldface (*notify, hazards, confidential, retaliation, discrimination, exercising your rights, citations, alleged violation, toxic, substances, comply,* and *furnish*) appear in the glossary on page 245.
- Encourage students to read the entire article first, instead of going to the glossary every time they encounter a boldfaced word.
- Play CD 1, Track 29 while students listen and read along.
- After students listen and read, ask if they have any other questions about the content, vocabulary, or pronunciation; answer questions.

Controlled Practice   20 minutes

 3   CHECK YOUR UNDERSTANDING

Read the statements....

- Review the example with the class.
- Ask for a volunteer to read each statement and tell whether it is true or false. Encourage student to find the information in the poster that supports their answer.

 4   WORD WORK

GROUPS. Choose three words...

- Tell students to choose their three words first, then discuss with their group.
- Give suggestions about what the groups could discuss, such as cognates in their own languages, pronunciation, or parts of speech.
- Walk around the room and offer help as needed in meaning, context, intonation, and pronunciation.
- Say: *Remember when you write in your vocabulary log, you can always write more than three words or phrases. You could also use the vocabulary log for words you read or hear outside of class.*

Communicative Practice   15 minutes

5   MAKE IT PERSONAL

GROUPS. Discuss the questions.

- Ask students to keep the same groups.
- Tell them to have two different people in their group lead the discussion on questions 1 and 2. Also tell the groups to assign one person to write notes from the conversation and one person to be prepared to report the group's ideas to the class.
- Ask the designated reporter from each group to share the group's ideas.

Expansion: Reading Practice for 2

- Say: *Because this government document is quite difficult, let's go over it again slowly and carefully.*
- Set up pairs.
- Say: *Work with your partner to go over each section of the poster, bullet by bullet. Discuss each section. Ask about any information you don't understand.*
- Have a large dictionary available for students to use.
- Walk around to listen, answer questions, and offer assistance as needed.

Expansion: Vocabulary Practice for 4

- Identify (from listening to the groups and by asking) which important vocabulary words need further explanation.
- Take as long as needed to expand on words such as *confidential, retaliation,* and *discrimination.*
- Ask students to give examples of health and safety rules from their current or former jobs. If needed, give examples (wash hands after using the restroom, wear hard hats in a construction zone, wear a seat belt).
- Ask students to share any other work-related health and safety words they know or have questions about. Explain and write the words on the board, a transparency, or a flipchart.

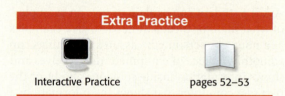

Extra Practice

Interactive Practice   pages 52–53

Job Safety and Health
It's the law!

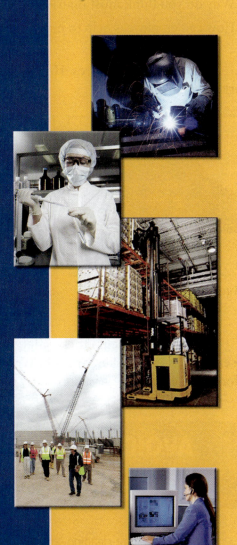

OSHA
Occupational Safety
and Health Administration
U.S. Department of Labor

EMPLOYEES:

- You have the right to **notify** your employer or OSHA about workplace **hazards**. You may ask OSHA to keep your name **confidential**.

- You have the right to request an OSHA inspection if you believe that there are unsafe and unhealthful conditions in your workplace. You or your representative may participate in that inspection.

- You can file a complaint with OSHA within 30 days of **retaliation** or **discrimination** by your employer for making safety and health complaints or for **exercising your rights** under the *OSH Act*.

- You have a right to see OSHA **citations** issued to your employer. Your employer must post the citations at or near the place of the **alleged violation**.

- Your employer must correct workplace hazards by the date indicated on the citation and must certify that these hazards have been reduced or eliminated.

- You have the right to copies of your medical records or records of your exposure to **toxic** and harmful **substances** or conditions.

- Your employer must post this notice in your workplace.

- You must **comply** with all occupational safety and health standards issued under the *OSH Act* that apply to your own actions and conduct on the job.

EMPLOYERS:

- You must **furnish** your employees a place of employment free from recognized hazards.

- You must comply with the occupational safety and health standards issued under the *OSH Act*.

*This free poster available from OSHA -
The Best Resource for Safety and Health*

Free assistance in identifying and correcting hazards or complying with standards is available to employers, without citation or penalty, through OSHA-supported consultation programs in each state.

1-800-321-OSHA
www.osha.gov
OSHA 3165-12-06R

Life Skills

1 TALK ABOUT WORKPLACE SAFETY

A CLASS. Discuss the questions.

1. Why do you think most injuries at work occur?
2. How can employees help to make their workplaces safer?

B PAIRS. Look at the pictures. How can these products help make a workplace safe?

Skid-resistant shoes

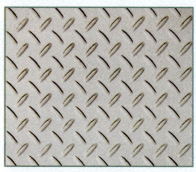

Skid-resistant flooring

Worker safety equipment

C PAIRS. Read and discuss these safety guidelines. Then decide if they are for the employer, the worker, or both. Write *E* (*Employer*), *W* (*Worker*), or *B* (*Both*) before each guideline. Answers will vary but could include:

AVOID SLIPS, TRIPS, AND FALLS

E   Establish a floor-cleaning schedule.

E   Install non-slip flooring, if possible.

E   Consider non-slip rubber or fabric mats.

W   Clean up spills as soon as they happen.

W   Wear close-toe, skid-resistant shoes and keep shoelaces tied.

W   Make sure uniform pant legs don't drag on the floor.

B   See that electric cords don't run across aisles.

E   Make sure there is enough light.

D GROUPS. Compare answers with another pair.

Getting Started   5 minutes

1 TALK ABOUT WORKPLACE SAFETY

A CLASS. **Discuss the questions.**

- Say: *In the last lesson, we talked about workers' rights to a safe workplace. We also learned about OSHA. What is OSHA?* (an agency of the U.S. Department of Labor that regulates workplace safety)*What are some rights that workers have that are guaranteed by OSHA regulations?* (Possible answers: the right to a safe workplace, the right to notify an employer if conditions are unsafe, the right to file a complaint with OSHA)

- Read and discuss the first question, offering prompts as needed to elicit answers. (*Have you ever seen an accident at work? Why did it happen?*)

- Read and discuss the second question, noting students' answers on the board. Offer discussion prompts as needed. (*Does anyone work in a restaurant? What are some ways you can make things safer for the people who work in the kitchen?*)

- Say: *Today we're going to talk about workplace safety, and we'll explore some ways to make your jobs safer.*

Presentation   10 minutes

B PAIRS. **Look at the pictures. How...**

- Say: *Let's look at the pictures.* Ask students what they see in each picture (shoes with rubber soles, a floor with grids, safety helmet, ear protectors, goggles, gloves).

- Have students form pairs and complete the exercise. Walk around and monitor conversations, offering prompts as needed. (*Is the surface of the floor smooth or bumpy? How can a bumpy surface make things safer?*)

Possible answers:

Shoes—Rubber-soled shoes stick to the ground and prevent slipping.

Floor—The bumpy surface of the floor prevents slipping.

Ear protectors, helmet, goggles, gloves: Ear protectors stop hearing loss from loud noises; a helmet protects the head; goggles prevent chemicals or sharp materials from falling into eyes; gloves protect hands, especially during heavy lifting.

Controlled Practice   15 minutes

C PAIRS. **Read and discuss these safety...**

- Say: *Now we'll look at some workplace safety guidelines.* Ask students to read the guidelines.

- Clarify unfamiliar terms as needed: *slip*—occurs when the floor is very smooth, causing one to glide and possibly fall (demonstrate this for students); *slip-resistant*—a surface that prevents one from slipping; *mats*—small rugs; *closed-toe*—shoes that cover your toes (unlike sandals)

- Ask students to read the directions, form pairs, and complete the exercise.

- Walk around and help as needed.

D GROUPS. **Compare answers...**

- Say: *Now you're going to find another pair of students and discuss whether each safety guideline in the last exercise is for the employer or worker—or both.*

- Have students discuss and compare answers. Walk around and offer prompts as needed. (*Who is responsible for providing adequate lighting—the employer or the worker?*)

- To review, read through the guidelines one by one, asking students to whom they apply and why.

Teaching Tip

As a group exercise, rewrite the safety guidelines so that they are questions about one's workplace. (*Is there a floor-cleaning schedule? Are spills cleaned up as soon as they happen?*) Then have students survey each other as to how many of the guidelines for avoiding slips, trips, and falls are followed at their jobs. Note results on the board and tabulate which safety guidelines are followed the most and the least.

Communicative Practice   30 minutes

2   PRACTICE

A **GROUPS. Look at these...**

- Say: *We've talked about safety tips for avoiding slips, trips, and falls. Now we're going to think about other areas in which workplace safety guidelines are needed.*
- Copy the chart onto the board.
- Tell students that they will write at least two safety tips for each category in the chart.
- Check students' comprehension of the safety categories by asking them what *cuts, burns,* and *lifting injuries* are.
- Have students form groups and complete the exercise. As students discuss the questions, walk around and offer prompts as needed. (*Are you more likely to cut yourself if you're tired? What can you do to avoid that? Is that the worker's or the employer's responsibility?*)
- Have a representative from each group present the group's safety tips.
- Model sample feedback for a presentation and encourage others to give it. (*I think that's a very practical idea because it wouldn't cost much and could prevent many injuries*)

Expansion: Speaking Practice for 2A

- To review the past modal structure, have groups look at the safety tips in their chart. Using these tips, have students role-play conversations between an employee and manager to report an accident. The manager notes what safety procedure should have been followed. Example:

  Employee: *I left work early yesterday to go to the emergency room. I hurt my back lifting the roof beams onto the back of the truck.*

  Manager: *You should have worn a back brace.*

  Employee: *I'll follow the procedure next time.*

B **STEP 1. GROUPS. Discuss safety...**

- Have students stay in the same groups.
- Ask students to read the directions for Step 1.
- Say: *Make a list of at least three safety tips for each job represented by a member of your group.* Emphasize that if students don't have a job now, they can make one up and write safety tips for it.

- Have students complete the exercise. Walk around and check their work, offering prompts as needed. (*What kind of accident could a waiter have? How could this be prevented?*)

STEP 2. GROUPS. Discuss each of...

- Ask students to stay in their groups and read the directions and options for Step 2.
- Clarify unfamiliar terms as needed. Examples:

  Safety committee—a representative group that explores issues and makes recommendations to employees and management

  HR (Human Resources)—the division of a company responsible for hiring employees, providing benefits, and administering company policies and procedures

- Tell students that they will first identify which safety tips are not followed at their workplace; then they will talk to their group members about which of the options listed—or which of their own ideas—is the best way to remedy the situation.
- Have students complete the exercise. Walk around and offer prompts for clarification or elaboration as needed. (For example, *If you followed the safety tip by yourself, and others didn't follow it, could that affect you? How?*)
- Call on a volunteer from each group to share the group's advice with the class.

Progress Check

Can you . . . identify workplace safety measures?

- Say: *We have practiced identifying workplace safety measures. Can you do this? If so, check the box.*

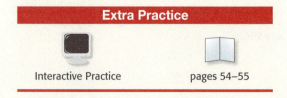

Extra Practice	
Interactive Practice	pages 54–55

A GROUPS. Look at these other safety categories for workers in the food preparation industry. Write at least two safety tips for each category.

SAFETY TIPS

To Avoid Cuts	
Workers	Employers

To Avoid Burns	
Workers	Employers

To Avoid Injury While Lifting	
Workers	Employers

B STEP 1. GROUPS. Discuss safety tips for your own jobs (or for a job you would like). Think of as many tips as possible. Write a list of workplace safety tips for each member of your group.

STEP 2. GROUPS. Discuss each of your lists. Are there safety tips that are not followed at your workplace? For each tip that is not followed, what would be the best advice? Discuss these (or other) options.

1. Follow the safety tip by yourself.
2. Talk to your co-workers about following the safety tip.
3. Ask your boss to provide safety materials, equipment, or procedures.
4. Talk with your co-workers and/or your boss about forming a safety committee.
5. Talk with your Human Resources (HR) department.
6. Notify OSHA.
7. Do nothing.

Can you...identify workplace safety measures? ☐

Writing

1 BEFORE YOU WRITE

A You are going to give instructions about how to avoid a common safety hazard. Read about instructions. Then read the writing tip.

> **FYI**   ABOUT GIVING INSTRUCTIONS
>
> Often you will have to give instructions or explanations about how to do something. Instructions and explanations, particularly those involving safety, should be clear and easy to follow. Present your instructions in a logical order, for example, from most important to least important or from first to last. Use signal words to help readers follow the instructions, for example, *first, next, then, afterwards, finally,* and *last*.
>
> **Writing Tip: Imperatives**
>
> When giving instructions, use imperatives: base forms of verbs without the pronoun *you*.

B Select one of the topics. Brainstorm safety tips about it.

1. poisonings inside or outside the home
2. fires in the home
3. common household accidents

C Read the writing model on page 207 about how to prevent falls in the home. How has Eva arranged her instructions?

2 ANALYZE THE WRITING MODEL

A PAIRS. Discuss the questions.

1. What is the purpose of this article?
2. According to Eva, what should you do first to prevent falls in the home?
3. What is the main idea of each paragraph? Use your own words.

B Read the article on page 207 again. Underline signal words the writer uses to connect one paragraph to the next.

Write safety instructions

Getting Started   5 minutes

- Say: *We have been talking about natural disasters and emergencies, as well as home and workplace safety. We have practiced vocabulary and grammatical structures to talk about what should or could have been done to respond to or prevent emergencies. Today we are going to apply all of this knowledge as we write an essay about how to avoid a common safety hazard.*

Presentation   10 minutes

1 BEFORE YOU WRITE

 You are going to give...

- Say: *In Lesson 4, we made suggestions about what people should have done in past emergencies to avoid mistakes. Today we're going to write advice about how to avoid a safety hazard—that is, something that could cause a dangerous situation.*
- Ask students to read the FYI note and Writing Tip.
- Check students' comprehension by asking what verb forms they should use to give instructions or advice. (the imperative or a modal such as *should*)
- Say: *When explaining a process, use sequence words to signal a new step or idea.* Elicit examples (*first, next, then, afterwards, finally, last*). Say: *These words also help to connect one idea to the next.*

Language Note

Review that the imperative is used to give commands or instructions. It is the same as the infinitive, or base form of the verb—but without *to* or the pronoun *you*, which is understood. Write examples on the board:

Stay in the car.
Turn off the engine.
Don't get out of the car.
Call for help.

Controlled Practice   15 minutes

B Select one of the topics. Brainstorm...

- Ask students to read the directions and topics.
- Tell them that they will choose one item and freewrite about it.
- Set a time limit for the freewriting.
- Remind students that when they freewrite, they shouldn't worry about complete sentences, grammar, or spelling.
- Elicit examples for item 3, noting them on the board. (Examples: *falling down the stairs, slipping in the tub, tripping over an object.*)

C Read the writing model on page 207...

- Tell students that they will now read an article about how to prevent falls in the home.
- Have students turn to page 207 and read the safety instructions. Clarify vocabulary as needed.
- Ask students: *How has the writer arranged her instructions?* (First, she discusses ways to identify possible causes of accidents; then she discusses ways to prevent them.)
- Ask: *What grammatical structure does Eva use for her instructions?* (imperatives)

2 ANALYZE THE WRITING MODEL

A PAIRS. Discuss the questions.

- Ask students to form pairs and discuss the questions.

Possible answers: 1. to explain to readers how to prevent falls at home; 2. identify potential hazards; 3. Falling is a serious problem that could be prevented with a few steps; identify hazards in your home; look at the shoes that you wear and make sure they are not going to cause falls; use exercise to improve your balance and coordination; make sure that you are not taking medications with side effects that may cause you to fall.

B Read the article on page 207...

- Say: *Read Eva's essay a second time and look for signal words that the writer uses to connect one paragraph to the next. What are some signal words?*

Answers: first, next, then, finally

- Walk around and check students' work.
- Elicit signal words from students and write them on the board.

Write safety instructions

Communicative Practice 30 minutes

3 THINK ON PAPER

Ⓐ Before Eva wrote her article...

- Ask: *What is on the left-hand side of the chart?* (words that signal time order) *Why do you think that the writer put them there?* (to help her organize her instructions and signal a progression from one to the next)

- Ask: *Do you think that Eva put her instructions in a logical order? Why or why not?* (Possible answer: Yes—she started with more general advice and then gave specific advice step by step, in logical order.)

Ⓑ Look at the notes you made...

- Have students complete the exercise. Walk around and check students' work, offering prompts as needed. (*Is that a main idea or a detail that supports a main idea?*)

Ⓒ PAIRS. Exchange your charts...

- Review ways to give constructive feedback by modeling sample prompts. (*I like the ideas that you list, but you might want to organize them a little differently. What about rearranging the order of . . . ?*)

4 WRITE

Use your chart to write...

- Read the directions, reminding students to include an introductory paragraph that describes what the safety hazard is.

- Have students write the first draft of an article about preventing a safety hazard.

- Say: *When you finish writing, you're going to read your paper and revise it. Revise means changing your work—adding, deleting, or rewriting details.*

5 CHECK YOUR WRITING

Ⓐ STEP 1. Revise your work.

- Say: *You'll read over your paper a first time and answer the questions in Step 1; if any answers are* no, *revise your work.*

- *Optional:* Have students form pairs, exchange articles, and give each other feedback and suggestions.

Ⓑ STEP 2. Edit and proofread.

- Say: *Now you'll read over your article a second time and edit and proofread your work.* Read the directions and direct students to check their articles for grammar, spelling, punctuation, and typos.

- *Optional:* Have students complete a "clean" second draft of their article at home, incorporating revisions and corrections from the revision and editing steps.

> **Teaching Tip**
>
> You may want to collect student papers and provide feedback. Use the scoring rubric for writing on page Txv to evaluate vocabulary, grammar, mechanics, and how well students complete the task. You may want to review the completed rubric with students.

MULTILEVEL INSTRUCTION for 5A and 5B

Above-level Have students who finish writing and self-editing read and edit a peer's paper using the criteria in Exercises 5A and 5B. Then ask them to discuss the article with the writer.

Pre-level Students complete a checklist with the revising and editing criteria from Exercises 5A and 5B, checking off a box for each question and making any changes.

Extra Practice

Interactive Practice

page 56

3 THINK ON PAPER

A Before Eva wrote her article, she used a chart to brainstorm and organize her instructions about how to prevent falls. Then she wrote her introductory paragraph. Read Eva's chart. Do you think that she put her instructions in a logical order?

First,	evaluate home for hazards and fix them.
Next,	check shoes; wear only sturdy ones.
Then	consider some kind of exercise to improve balance.
Finally,	know the side effects of medications you take.

B Look at the notes you made about safety tips in Exercise 1B. Then use a chart like Eva's to organize your instructions about how to prevent a safety hazard.

C PAIRS. Exchange your charts, and give each other feedback. Make changes if necessary.

4 WRITE

Use your chart to write an article about preventing a safety hazard. Be sure to include an introductory paragraph to let readers know your topic.

5 CHECK YOUR WRITING

A STEP 1. Revise your work.

1. Does your introductory paragraph explain your topic clearly?
2. Did you put your advice and instructions in a logical order?
3. Did you use signal words to connect one paragraph to the next?

B STEP 2. Edit and proofread.

1. Have you checked your spelling, grammar, and punctuation?
2. Have you proofread for typing errors?

1 | **REVIEW**   For your grammar review, go to page 228.

2 | **ACT IT OUT**   What do you say?

PAIRS. You are discussing safety measures with two friends.

> **Student A:** Review Lesson 2. Explain how to stay safe during a tornado.

> **Student B:** Review Lessons 3 and 4. Describe how to stay safe during a flood.

> **Student C:** Review Lessons 7 and 8. Explain some safety measures you can take at work.

3 | **READ AND REACT**   Problem-solving

STEP 1. Read about Jean-Pierre.

Jean-Pierre has been working for a short time in a piano factory. He is learning how to rebuild and refinish pianos. He loves musical instruments and he likes the work, but some of the chemicals the factory uses make him sick. When he arrives at work, he can smell fumes from the paints and refinishing chemicals. By the end of a workday, he usually has a bad headache. Many of his co-workers are also suffering from headaches and stomach problems. Some workers have told Jean-Pierre that the factory needs to install more windows and get fans. If the air circulated better, there would be less fumes. No one has been willing to speak to the manager about the situation. Jean-Pierre is a new employee and he doesn't want to cause trouble, but he is afraid that the chemicals are a serious safety hazard.

STEP 2. GROUPS. What is Jean-Pierre's problem? What can he do?

4 | **CONNECT**   For your Community-building Activity, go to page 215.

Which goals can you check off? Go back to page 65.

 Go to the CD-ROM for more practice.

1 REVIEW

For your grammar review, go to page 228.

- Say: *Today we're going to review the skills we have practiced in this unit and apply them to a problem. What are some of the skills we have practiced?* Elicit answers, noting them on the board as students say them. (Possible answers: reading and talking about natural disasters and ways to stay safe during disasters; identifying home and workplace safety measures; discussing workers' rights; writing safety instructions)

- Ask students to complete the grammar review exercise at the bottom of page 228.

2 ACT IT OUT

Teaching Tip

While pairs are performing role plays, use the scoring rubric for speaking on page Txiv to evaluate each student's vocabulary, grammar, fluency, and how well he or she completes the task. You may want to review the completed rubric with the student.

PAIRS. You are discussing...

- Say: *You're going to form groups of three. Student A will look back at Lesson 2 and explain how to stay safe during a tornado. Student B will review Lessons 3 and 4 and describe how to stay safe during a flood. Student C will reread Lessons 7 and 8 and explain some safety measures you can take at work.*

- Remind students to use the imperative to give safety instructions. Elicit an example: *Close the windows and go to the basement.*

- Say: *When you wrote your safety instructions, you used signal words to help readers follow a sequence of directions. What are some signal words that you used?* Elicit words from students and write them on the board. (Examples: *first, next, then, afterwards, finally, last*)

- Tell students to review the lessons before they begin working groups.

3 READ AND REACT

STEP 1. Read about Jean-Pierre.

- Say: *Now we're going to apply our knowledge from this unit to a problem involving a character, Jean-Pierre. Let's read about Jean-Pierre.*

- Have students read the story.

Possible answers: *Problem:* Jean-Pierre has discovered a serious health hazard at work but doesn't want to lose his new job if he reports it. *Solution:* He could speak to OSHA about the problem or try to convince a group of employees to meet with a manager to discuss it.

STEP 2. GROUPS. What is Jean-Pierre's...

- Tell students that they may want to refer to Lesson 7 as they discuss possible solutions.

- Ask volunteers to present the group's ideas to the class.

- After each presentation, encourage feedback. Ask: *What do you think about Group 1's suggestions for Jean-Pierre? Which idea do you like best?*

Teaching Tip

Write sample feedback prompts on the board: *I really like the idea of . . . I disagree with that idea about what Jean-Pierre should do . . . Instead, I think Jean-Pierre should . . . If it doesn't work, what about trying . . . ?*

4 CONNECT

Turn to page 215 for your Community-building Activity. See page Txii for general teaching notes for Community-building activities.

Progress Check

Which goals can you check off? Go back to page 65.

Ask students to turn to page 65 and check off any remaining goals they have reached. Call on them to say which goals they will practice outside of class.

CD-ROM Practice

 Go to the CD-ROM for more practice.

If your students need more practice with the vocabulary, grammar, and competencies in Unit 4, encourage them to review the activities on the CD-ROM.

5

Advancing on the Job

Classroom Materials/Extra Practice

CD 2
Tracks 2–8

Workbook
Unit 5

Interactive Practice
Unit 5

Unit Overview

Goals

- See the list of goals on the facing page.

Grammar

- Clauses with *although* and *unless*

Listening and Speaking

- Talk about how to respond to constructive criticism
- *Communication Skill:* Clarifying
- Discuss job-training opportunities

Reading

- Read an article about factors that influence promotion
- *Reading Skill:* Identifying the Main Idea
- Read a performance review
- *Reading Skill:* Scanning
- Read a chart of *I* statements and *You* statements
- Read a quiz about workplace sports idioms

Writing

- Write a self-evaluation
- *Writing Tip:* Using good examples

Life Skills

- Use a course catalog

Preview

- Welcome students and have them look at page 85.
- Say: *Look at the picture. Where are the people? What's happening?* (Possible answers: The men are at work/in a warehouse.)
- Ask a volunteer to read the Preview section. Have students discuss how the man might have become a manager.
- Say: *There are many ways to move from an entry-level job to a more challenging one. How many of you have ever gotten a promotion at work?* Have students raise their hands.
- Say: *For those of you who answered yes to the last question, what did you do before you were promoted?* Offer prompts to elicit answers. (*Did you gain experience working for the company? For how long? Did you learn new skills through job training or taking classes?*)
- Say: *In this unit, you'll learn more about ways to advance on the job—that is, to move to a higher-level position, perhaps a managerial one. You'll learn about workplace procedures, techniques, and resources that can help you. You'll also explore opportunities outside of the workplace for continuing your education, which can help you to get ahead at work.*

Unit Goals

- Ask students to read the Unit Goals.
- Tell students to circle the goal that is the most important to them.
- Take a poll by reading the goals aloud, with students raising their hand for the goal they checked.
- Write the goal on the board that most students checked.
- Say: *As we complete this unit, we will look back at this page and reread the goals. We will check each goal as we complete it.*

Advancing on the Job

Preview

This man is a manager. How do you think he got this job?

UNIT GOALS

- ☐ Identify factors that influence promotion
- ☐ Understand performance reviews
- ☐ Talk about how to respond to constructive criticism
- ☐ Discuss job-training opportunities
- ☐ Use a course catalog

Reading

CD2 T2

1 BEFORE YOU READ

CLASS. Discuss. How and why do people get promoted at work?

2 READ

CD2 T2

Listen to and read the newsletter. Identify the main idea.

Reading Skill:
Identifying the Main Idea

Identifying the main idea in a reading helps you understand a writer's key point about the topic. To identify the main idea, look at the title. Ask yourself: "What is the topic of this text?" As you read each paragraph, look for the author's main idea about the topic. Sometimes a writer states the main idea in a sentence. Other times you will have to put the main idea into your own words.

Factors That Influence Promotion

If you come to work on time, do a good job, and stay out of trouble, you will eventually be promoted, right? Not necessarily! Employers expect this of all employees. If you want a **promotion**, you should know the **factors** employers consider when they choose people to promote. Here are a few.

Length of time with the employer

It usually takes months, or even years, to be promoted. There are good reasons for this. First, an employee has to work long enough to **master** the skills required for his or her current job. Second, the employer needs a chance to see how the employee might respond in a variety of situations—especially situations that might come up in the employee's next position.

Relationships with other employees

Some employees have a very strong **work ethic** and are excellent at what they do, but they don't get promoted. Anyone who wants to be a leader or supervisor has to put the success of the team or the company ahead of personal success. It's important to acknowledge co-workers for their work, **share credit** for ideas, and encourage and **mentor** others. Managers want to know that the people they promote are "**team players**."

Flexibility and willingness to learn new things

Employers want to promote people who will **adapt** to new responsibilities easily. They need people who can be **flexible** during times of change and who can help others **adjust** to changes in the workplace. They select people who are eager to learn more about the organization, to improve the skills necessary for their current job, and to develop the skills that may be needed in the future.

Communication skills

Employers value employees who can read and write well. A leader or supervisor needs to be able to choose the right approach and the right words to explain, to offer criticism, to inspire or motivate, and to persuade. Good listening skills are important, too. A supervisor may have to communicate—effectively!—with people from **diverse** backgrounds and in various positions. Whether dealing with customers, co-workers, or bosses, communication skills are important.

Initiative in solving problems

In almost any workplace, you can find people who avoid dealing with problems. They may think, "That's not my job." Or they may be afraid of becoming involved or making a mistake—so they wait for someone else to solve the problem. Employees who **take the initiative** to solve problems stand out. These people are more likely to be considered for promotion than colleagues who don't take action when problems arise.

Getting Started   10 minutes

- Say: *Getting a job is an important step on the employment ladder. Another important step is getting promotions—moving upward on that ladder. Getting a promotion can mean more responsibility, more self-esteem, and, of course, more money, a better schedule, and more benefits. So in this unit, we are going to learn about advancing on the job.*

Culture Connection

- Be sensitive to adult immigrants who may have had more prestigious and higher-paying jobs in their home countries than they do in the U.S.; they are sometimes sensitive or depressed about what they may see as a lowering of economic and social status.
- Ask students to make a simple time line of their lives that can include family, education, work, life experiences (like being in a war or being a refugee)—whatever they wish—in their notebooks.
- On a transparency or flipchart, make a timeline that includes basic information about yourself. (*I was born on May 15, 19_____ in _____. I got married in 19_____.*) Also include information about your previous jobs. (For example, *My first job was as a salad maker in 19_____ in a restaurant. After I finished college in 19_____, I taught English in _____.*)
- After students finish their timelines, encourage them to talk with at least three other classmates about their work experience.
- *Note:* This strategy respects the students' past lives, while allowing each student to control how much he or she talks about his or her past experiences, family, and employment.

1 BEFORE YOU READ

CLASS. Discuss. How and why...

- Have students discuss situations in which they or someone they know has been promoted at work.

Reading Skill: Identifying the Main Idea

- Direct students to the Reading Skill box.
- Ask an above-level student to read the text aloud.
- Say: *We've talked before about how to identify the main idea. Look at the obvious clues, like the title and introductory sentence or paragraph.*
- Ask: *Does anyone have any questions, comments, or suggestions about identifying the main idea?* Accept all student comments.
- Say: *Now as you listen to and read the newsletter, look for the main idea.*

Presentation   15 minutes

2 READ

 Listen to and read the newsletter...

- Ask students to read the directions.
- Say: *When you read this newsletter, compare the factors that influence a promotion here in the U.S. with the factors that typically influence a promotion in your home country.*
- Point out that the words and phrases in boldface (*promotion, factors, master, work ethic, share credit, mentor, team players, adapt, flexible, adjust, diverse, take the initiative*) appear in the glossary on page 245. Encourage students to read the entire article before consulting the glossary.
- Play CD 2, Track 2. Ask students to listen to and read the article.
- After students listen and read, ask them to write the main idea in their notebooks.
- Ask students to discuss similarities and differences between getting a promotion in the U.S. and in their home countries. Then summarize what students say. (For example, *It looks as if factors that help a person get promoted are similar/somewhat different in the U.S. than they are in _____.*)

Controlled Practice   15 minutes

3 CHECK YOUR UNDERSTANDING

A Check (✓) the statement that best describes...

- Ask students to read the directions.
- Ask: *Which statement best describes the main idea?* (item 3)

B Write the answers to the questions.

- Ask students to read the directions. Explain that they only need to write short answers to the questions.

Possible answers:

1. A worker needs to work long enough to master the skill required for his or her current job, and the employer needs a chance to see how the employee might respond in a variety of situations, especially those that might come up in the employee's next position. 2. the success of the team or the company; 3. because they want to promote people who will adapt to new responsibilities easily and help others adjust to change; 4. They need to be able to choose the right words to explain, to offer criticism, to inspire or motivate, and to persuade. They need to have good listening skills and be able to communicate effectively with people from diverse backgrounds and in various positions. 5. because they are more likely to try to solve problems

C PAIRS. Compare answers.

- Say: *Now compare your answers with a partner; the words you use don't need to be the same, but check that you had the same ideas. Don't worry if you disagree on any answers; we will talk about them together in a few minutes.*
- Set up pairs.
- Review only questions pairs don't agree about.
- Ask students if they have any questions, comments, or opinions about the factors themselves.
- Explain that in the American workplace it's important to be a team player and a problem solver. It is also important to be flexible. Ask students if they have any experience related to performance ratings they wish to share.
- Call on a few volunteers to share their experience with performance ratings.

Teaching Tip

- If a student brings up a work problem (unfair performance rating, discrimination, sexual harassment, not being paid), set up groups to discuss possible solutions.
- Provide information about local, state, and federal sources of information and possible assistance (for example, the U.S. Department of Labor compliance assistance website at www.dol.gov/compliance/guide/).

4 WORD WORK

GROUPS. Choose three words...

- Set up groups and have students read the directions.
- Say: *Remember when you write in your vocabulary logs, you can always write more than three words or phrases or use the log for other words.*

Communicative Practice   20 minutes

5 MAKE IT PERSONAL

STEP 1. Rate yourself for each category...

- Ask students to read the directions.
- Explain that *rate* means to judge or to grade. Remind students to skip item 1 if they are not working. Explain that they can rate themselves in items 2 to 4 as students and based on their personal characteristics.

STEP 2. GROUPS. Explain your ratings...

- Ask students to read the directions.
- Tell them to stay in the same groups. Reassure students that they need explain only what they can comfortably share with the class. Encourage them to give specific examples when they talk about their strengths and weaknesses.

Extra Practice

Interactive Practice   pages 58–59

3 CHECK YOUR UNDERSTANDING

A Check (✓) the statement that best describes the main idea.

☐ 1. Promotion depends on getting to work on time and staying out of trouble.

☐ 2. Promotion depends largely on five main factors.

☑ 3. Promotion depends on many factors, none more important than the others.

B Write the answers to the questions.

1. Why can it take time to get a promotion? Give two reasons.
2. What does an employee have to put ahead of personal success in order to be a leader?
3. Why is flexibility important to employers?
4. What are two examples of ways leaders or supervisors need to use communication skills?
5. Why do you think employers like employees who take the initiative?

C PAIRS. Compare answers.

4 WORD WORK

GROUPS. Choose three words or phrases in the newsletter that you would like to remember. Discuss the words and their meanings. Then record the words and information about them in your vocabulary log.

5 MAKE IT PERSONAL

STEP 1. Rate yourself for each category (1 = excellent; 5 = poor). If you don't have a job, skip number 1 and give yourself a general rating in the other areas.

1. Length of time with your employer	1	2	3	4	5
2. Relationships with other employees (or students)	1	2	3	4	5
3. Flexibility and willingness to learn new things	1	2	3	4	5
4. Communication skills	1	2	3	4	5
5. Initiative in solving problems	1	2	3	4	5

STEP 2. GROUPS. Explain your ratings to one another. What are your strengths? What are your weaknesses?

Reading

1 BEFORE YOU READ

CLASS. Eva Rivera works at a manufacturing plant. Look at her performance review on page 89. Discuss. Why do you think many employers have performance reviews?

2 READ

Scan the yellow-tinted part of Eva's performance review. What eight categories are reviewed? Underline them.

Reading Skill:
Scanning

Scanning helps readers find specific information and key words in a text. Scan to answer a specific question or to decide whether a text contains information you need.

3 CHECK YOUR UNDERSTANDING

A **PAIRS.** Read the yellow-tinted part of the performance review more thoroughly. Discuss. Which category do you think is most important? Why?

B Look at the ratings section on the right side of the performance review. Write the answers to the questions.

1. In which category did Eva get the highest rating from her supervisor? interpersonal relationships
2. In which category did Eva give herself the lowest rating? attention to safety
3. Which categories did Eva and her supervisor agree on? quality of work + time management

C Read the comments section at the bottom of the performance review. Write the answers to the questions.

1. What does Eva's supervisor say she needs to work on?
2. How will Eva work on this skill?

4 WORD WORK

GROUPS. Choose three words or phrases in the performance review that you would like to remember. Discuss the words and their meanings. Then record the words and information about them in your vocabulary log.

5 MAKE IT PERSONAL

STEP 1. Read the performance review again. If you have a job (or if you had a job in the past), give yourself a rating for each category.

STEP 2. GROUPS. Discuss your self-ratings. If you don't have a job, talk about areas that you think you might be strong or weak in.

Understand performance reviews

Getting Started   5 minutes

- Say: *In the last lesson, we talked about factors that influence promotion. The factors that influence promotion are often noted in a performance review. Does anyone know what that is?* (A performance review is an evaluation of the way an employee does his or her job, usually covering a 12-month period.)
- *Today we're going to focus on performance reviews.*

Presentation   15 minutes

1 BEFORE YOU READ

CLASS. Eva Rivera works...

- Ask students to read the directions.
- After they preview page 89, discuss the question. Offer prompts as needed to elicit comments.

2 READ

Reading Skill: **Scanning**

- Direct students' attention to the Reading Skill box. Ask a student to read it aloud. Clarify that when we scan, we do not worry about understanding or even reading every word.

Scan the yellow-tinted part....

- Explain what a category is. Say: *A category is a section or a group of similar items, in this case a section of a performance review, like* Quality of work.
- Say: *Scan the performance review and underline the eight categories. Don't read through the entire review; just look quickly for the eight categories.* (The eight categories are boldfaced.)

3 CHECK YOUR UNDERSTANDING

 PAIRS. Read the yellow-tinted part...

- Say: *Now read the performance review.*
- Clarify unfamiliar vocabulary as needed. (For example, *exceed expectations*—do better than expected; *meet expectations*—do as well as expected; *prioritize*—judge which tasks are the most important and complete them first)

- Ask students to form pairs and discuss the question.
- Have students complete the exercise and share their answers with the class.

Controlled Practice   20 minutes

B Look at the ratings section...

- Have students read the directions and complete the exercise.

C Read the comments section...

- Read the directions. Ask students to look at the comments section at the bottom of Eva's review, and have them complete the exercise.

Answers: 1. her English; 2. by continuing to take English classes at night and meeting with a volunteer language tutor once a week for eight weeks

4 WORD WORK

GROUPS. Choose three words...

- Set up groups. Ask students to read the directions.
- Say: *Remember when you write in your vocabulary logs, you can always write more than three words or phrases. You can also use the vocabulary log for words you read or hear outside of class.*

Communicative Practice   20 minutes

5 MAKE IT PERSONAL

STEP 1. Read the performance review again....

- Ask students to read the directions. Clarify that they will first reread Eva's review and then write one for themselves.

STEP 2. GROUPS. Discuss your self-ratings....

- Form groups. Have students discuss their reviews.

Extra Practice

Interactive Practice   pages 60–61

■ **Expansion: Vocabulary Practice for page 89**

Discuss the following concepts with the class:

Time management

- Completing assignments on time is important; however, it's also important to be able to judge which task is the one that needs attention right away (and should be completed first).

Interpersonal relationships

- It's important to interact well with your customers and supervisor. It's considered equally important to serve as part of a team and interact well with your co-workers and share responsibilities on joint projects.

Initiative and problem solving

- In addition to completing your work, you should take opportunities to find other ways to serve the company. For example, you can identify ways to improve processes or procedures, or help out with other projects when you have spare time.

Attendance / Punctuality

- In most companies, you need to request for a leave of absence well in advance, unless it's an emergency or a sick day. Often you must make a formal request in writing if you want to take off for more than a day.

Goals / Objectives / Special Assignments

- Eva and her boss have made a plan with specific steps to take to improve the skill (spoken English) that received the lowest rating.

■ **Expansion: Speaking Practice for page 89**

- Ask students to form small groups.
- Tell them to imagine that they are supervisors at a large company. What qualities would they want in their employees? How would they judge whether their employees were performing well?
- Have each group make a list of the factors that they would use to judge their employees.
- Then each group should present its list to the class and explain why those factors were judged important.

PERFORMANCE REVIEW RATINGS

Name: _Eva Rivera_   Date: _May 6, 2010_

1—exceeded expectations 2—met expectations 3—improvement needed 4—failed to meet expectations	Employee Rating	Supervisor Rating
Knowledge of work: Understands key job duties; uses appropriate equipment, materials, and procedures.	1	2
Quality of work: Work is complete, accurate, and neat.	2	2
Time management: Prioritizes and plans work; meets deadlines; adjusts to unexpected changes to finish tasks on time; can handle multiple assignments.	2	2
Interpersonal relationships: Has a positive attitude; relates well to customers, co-workers, and supervisors; cooperates when working as part of a team.	2	1
Communication: Listens carefully to others and asks questions to understand; speech is clear, brief, appropriate; contributes ideas in team or group situations; understands telephone language and etiquette; can read, write, and type well enough to perform job duties.	2	3
Initiative and problem solving: Performs duties with minimal supervision; requests extra responsibilities when time allows; suggests improvements; continues to develop own skills and to take advantage of training opportunities; identifies problems and finds ways to solve them.	1	2
Attendance / Punctuality: Dependable; comes to work regularly and on time; returns promptly from breaks; absences are requested, in advance if possible; when sick, calls in to report absence at the beginning of shift.	1	2
Attention to safety: Follows safety procedures; uses safety equipment; reports accidents; attends safety training.	3	2

Employee comments:
Sometimes I have trouble taking telephone messages. And sometimes I can't follow everything or think of the right words fast enough to contribute when I'm talking with my whole team or group. But I do good work and I'm always on time. I take classes at night to improve my English, and I think my communication skills are improving.

Supervisor comments:
Eva is very good at what she does, and she does more work than anyone else on my staff. She has good attendance, is punctual, and follows safety procedures. She uses time well and often asks for additional responsibilities or offers to help co-workers. Everyone loves to work with her. However, Eva still needs to work on her English.

Goals / Objectives / Special Assignments
1. Eva will continue taking English classes at night this term.
2. Eva and a volunteer language tutor will meet once a week for eight weeks to work on Eva's English.

Eva Rivera   _5/06/10_
Employee signature   Date

Elena White   _5/06/10_
Supervisor signature   Date

Listening and Speaking

1 BEFORE YOU LISTEN

GROUPS. Discuss the questions.

1. What is "constructive criticism"?
2. What are some reasons supervisors offer constructive criticism?

2 LISTEN

CD2 T3

A Eva and her supervisor, Elena, are talking about Eva's performance review. Listen and answer the questions.

1. Why did Eva get a 3 in communication?
2. Why didn't she get a 1 in initiative?
3. Did Eva get a 1 in attendance/punctuality? How do you know?

CD2 T3

B Listen to the conversation again. Take notes in the chart.

Elena's constructive criticism	Eva's response
Writing needs improvement.	I need to continue to work on my English. What can I do to improve?
Need to participate more in group discussions.	I'll work on improving participation in group discussions.

C **PAIRS.** Discuss. Do you think Eva responded well? Why or why not?

Getting Started   5 minutes

1 BEFORE YOU LISTEN

GROUPS. Discuss the questions.

- Ask students to read the directions and questions.
- Ask for a volunteer to explain or describe *constructive criticism*. Give examples such as this one: *When I was a cashier—my first job—my boss had to tell me how to put all the dollar bills facing the right way. I was embarrassed because I was trying so hard to do everything right, but I accepted his criticism and became a very efficient cashier.*
- Discuss question two.
- Say: *Now we are going to listen to a conversation between a worker and her supervisor.*

> **Teaching Tip**
>
> Allow students to discuss what seems like "unconstructive" criticism from supervisors, but encourage them to try to look at the issue from different perspectives. If time permits, ask students to role-play the problem a student describes and solutions for the problem.

Presentation   10 minutes

2 LISTEN

  Eva and her supervisor...

- Ask students to read the directions silently.
- Play CD 2, Track 3.
- Have students read and answer each question.

Answers:
1. Her written reports aren't clear and thorough. 2. She doesn't offer suggestions in group discussions. 3. No, because the supervisor doesn't give anyone a 1 in attendance/punctuality—everyone is expected to be at work on time.

Controlled Practice   10 minutes

B   **Listen to the conversation again...**

- Ask students to read the directions. Say: *As you listen, concentrate on Eva's response to Elena's criticism.*

C **PAIRS. Discuss. Do you think...**

- Ask students to read the directions, and set up pairs. Say: *Talk about whether you think Eva responded well to her supervisor's feedback. Explain your answer.*

■ **Expansion: Speaking Practice for 2C**

- Give pairs more examples of criticism and response to discuss. Before class, create a chart that includes a supervisor's criticism and an employee's response. The chart could look like this:

Supervisor	Employee
Construction foreman, Joe: Ramon, you are a very hard worker and you get along well with the rest of the crew, but at least once a week you are late.	**Ramon:** Joe, on Wednesdays I need to drop off my brother-in-law at the subway before work. I don't like to be late, but I have to be.
(write your own dialogue here)	

- Pass out one chart to each pair. Have pairs decide whether the supervisor's comment seems constructive and whether the employee's response is positive.
- Ask students to write their own scenario and ask another pair to comment.

Controlled Practice   15 minutes

3   PRACTICE

A **PAIRS. Listen to two people...**

- Ask students to read the directions.
- Play CD 2, Track 4.
- Set up pairs so that each pair has at least one person who is (or was) employed.

B **The sentences and expressions below...**

- Tell partners to take turns reading the sentences aloud.
- Assist as needed with intonation and pronunciation.
- Say: *Now listen again and check the expressions you hear.*
- Play Track 4 again.
- Ask for a volunteer to tell which sentences were used in the listening.

Expansion: Speaking Practice for 3

- Brainstorm a list of responses to criticism that are **not** appropriate. This will help students understand what is considered counterproductive or rude.
- Write some of the responses on the board. If students are having difficulty coming up with examples, use these: *You didn't tell me I was supposed to _____. _____ doesn't punch in on time, either. I hope you marked him down, too.*
- Discuss why each phrase isn't appropriate in American work culture.

4   MAKE IT PERSONAL

Communication Skill: Clarifying

- Have students read the Communication Skill box.
- Say: *It's important for the employee to understand a supervisor's constructive criticism because if the worker doesn't understand what the issue is, he or she might continue to make the same error.*
- Repeat the clarifying phrases as native English speakers say them—more as a single entity than word by word.
- Remind students of other key communication tips such as looking directly at the supervisor and being respectful.

Communicative Practice   20 minutes

ROLE PLAY. PAIRS. **Assign roles...**

- Pair students and have them read the directions.
- Say: *Now you're going to role-play the supervisor and employee during a performance review. Student A will be the supervisor; Student B will be an employee.*
- *Decide what the workplace is and what job the employee does. You can also make up some other details, such as how long the worker has been on the job and how well he or she performs his or her job.*

STEP 1. **Choose a category...**

- Say: *Now choose a category from the performance review form on page 89.*

STEP 2. **The supervisor offers...**

- Have students read Step 2.
- Say: *Student A should, like the supervisors on the CD, give a specific positive comment to the employee before offering constructive criticism. For example, You are a very hard worker, Inga, and you learn quickly.*
- Say: *Student B should respond to the criticism using ideas and language from Exercise 3B and from the communication skill box. However, feel free to use your ideas as well.*

STEP 3. **Practice your role play...**

- Have students read Step 3.
- Model the role play with an above-level student if needed.
- Have volunteer pairs perform their role plays.

Teaching Tip

While pairs are performing role plays, use the scoring rubric for speaking on page Txiv to evaluate each student's vocabulary, grammar, fluency, and how well he or she completes the task. You may want to review the completed rubric with students.

Extra Practice

Interactive Practice

CD2 T4

A 🔘 **PAIRS.** Listen to two people responding to criticism from supervisors and co-workers. Discuss. How well did they respond to criticism?

CD2 T4

B 🔘 The sentences and expressions below are useful for responding to constructive criticism. Read through them. Then listen again to the conversations from Exercise A and check (✓) the expressions you hear.

☐ 1. What can I do to improve?

☐ 2. Thanks for the feedback. I'll work on that.

☐ 3. You have a point. It's true I . . .

☑ 4. Can you give me some examples?

☑ 5. What should I do differently in the future?

☐ 6. Do you have any suggestions for improvement?

☑ 7. I didn't realize this was a problem. I'll work on it from now on.

☑ 8. Thanks. You're right.

4 MAKE IT PERSONAL

ROLE PLAY. PAIRS. Assign roles. Student A is a supervisor. Student B is an employee.

STEP 1. Choose a category in the performance review on page 89.

STEP 2. The supervisor offers constructive criticism about a category in the performance review on page 89. The employee responds to it, using ideas and expressions from Exercise 3B and the Communication Skill box.

STEP 3. Practice your role play and then perform it for the class.

> **Communication Skill:**
> Clarifying
>
> If you need to clarify a supervisor's constructive criticisms, do so tactfully. Use phrases such as these:
>
> *Are you saying that…?*
> *Sorry, but I'm not sure I follow you.*
> *Could you explain what you just said in more detail?*
> *What did you mean when you said…?*

Grammar

Clauses with *Although* and *Unless*

Although **you can do your work**, your writing needs improvement.

I can't give anyone a 2 in communication *unless* **their reports are well written**.

Grammar Watch

- Clauses with *although* and *unless* are dependent clauses. These clauses can come at the beginning or the end of a sentence. When they come at the beginning of a sentence, they are followed by a comma.

- Use *although* to show contrast or an unexpected outcome.

- *Unless* means *if . . . not.*

I'm going to look for another job ***unless*** *I get a promotion this year.*	=	*I'm going to look for another job* ***if*** *I do* ***not*** *get a promotion this year.*

1 PRACTICE

Read the first sentence. Check (✓) the sentence that has the same meaning.

1. He knows he won't get a promotion unless he works on his interpersonal skills.
    - ✓ a. If he doesn't work on his interpersonal skills, he won't get a promotion.
    - ☐ b. If he gets a promotion, he won't work on his interpersonal skills.

2. I didn't get the promotion although I was qualified for it.
    - ☐ a. I didn't get the promotion because I wasn't qualified for it.
    - ✓ b. I was qualified for the promotion, but I didn't get it.

3. Although her communication skills improved, she still didn't get a better rating.
    - ✓ a. The rating didn't improve, but her communication skills did.
    - ☐ b. Because her communications skills improved, she can get a better rating.

4. Unless you ask for a raise or promotion, you probably won't get one.
    - ✓ a. You probably won't get a raise or a promotion if you don't ask for one.
    - ☐ b. If you ask for a raise or a promotion, you probably won't get one.

5. She hasn't been promoted yet although she has worked here for three years.
    - ☐ a. She hasn't been promoted because she hasn't worked here for three years yet.
    - ✓ b. She has worked here for three years but hasn't been promoted.

Getting Started   5 minutes

- Say: *In the last lesson, we talked about how to respond to constructive criticism. Today we're going to talk more about constructive criticism. To do so, we'll practice the grammatical structure of clauses with* although *and* unless.

Presentation   15 minutes

Teaching Tip

- Point out that a dependent clause cannot stand alone; it depends on the main clause to make its meaning clear.
- Write on the board: *I'm doing well at my job although I did not have any prior work experience.*
- Ask: *Which is the main clause?* (I'm doing well at my job) *Which is the dependent clause?* (although I did not have any prior work experience.)

Clauses with *Although* and *Unless*

- Copy the grammar chart onto the board.
- Ask students to read the Grammar Watch.
- Read the first example. Say: Although *is used to introduce an idea. What idea does* although *introduce?* (that you can do your work) *What is the other idea in this sentence?* (that your writing needs improvement)
- Point out that *although* introduces a contrast or an unexpected outcome.
- *Optional:* Say a few clauses beginning with *although* and have students complete them.
- Read the first two Grammar Watch points. Remind students that when *although* introduces a clause at the beginning of a sentence, it is followed by a comma.
- Say: Although *shows a contrast or something that is unexpected.* Unless *means if not.*
- Read the last point in the Grammar Watch.

- Point to the second example in the grammar chart. Explain that *unless their reports are well written* means the same as *if their reports are not well written.*
- Say: Unless *is often used to describe a condition that is not currently true but must become true in order for another action to take place.* Write the following sentence on the board: *I cannot accept the position unless my manager allows me to telecommute.*
- Ask: *Are you allowed to telecommute now?* (no) *If you were allowed to telecommute, what would happen?* (You would accept the position.)

Language Note

- Clarify that *unless* expresses a negative condition. For example, *if I **do not get** a raise* has the same meaning as *unless I **get** a raise.* Write the following prompt on the board: *I'll have to quit the job if they don't offer me more hours.*
- Ask: *How would I change this sentence to include a clause with* unless? (*I'll have to quit the job unless they offer me more hours.*) On the board, cross out *if* and *don't,* and write in *unless.*

Controlled Practice   20 minutes

 PRACTICE

Read the first sentence. Check...

- Ask students to read the directions.
- Ask a volunteer to read the first item out loud. Write it on the board.
- Circle *unless* and remind students that it means the same as *if . . . not.* Erase *unless he works* and replace it with *if he doesn't work.*
- Remind students that *although* is used to show a contrast or unexpected outcome.
- Have students complete the exercise. Walk around and check students' work, offering prompts as needed. (*Did her communication skills improve? Did she get a better rating on her performance review?*)
- Call on students to say the answers out loud.

2 PRACTICE

A Complete the sentences. Use...

- Read the directions, noting that students should write *although* or *unless* **and** a phrase from the box.
- Ask a student volunteer to read the first item. Ask: *Why does this clause take* unless? Explain as needed that *unless* introduces a condition that is not currently true but must happen in order for another action to take place.
- Have students complete the exercise. Offer prompts as needed. (For example, *Does this sentence need a clause that shows a contrast or one that shows something that must happen in order for another action to take place?*)

B Write a sentence that has the same...

- Read the directions, and ask a student volunteer to read the first item. Say: Although *takes the place of two words in the original sentence. What words does it replace?* (even though)
- Ask students to look at item 3. Remind them that *unless*—a subordinating conjunction—expresses a negative idea, so we don't use it with *not*. Ask: *Which is correct:* unless you can't accept criticism *or* unless you can accept criticism?
- Have students complete the exercise. Offer prompts as needed. (For example, *Does this sentence need a clause that shows a contrast or one that shows something that must happen in order for another action to take place?*)

Alternative answers:
2. He isn't really a team player although he seems friendly.
3. It is very hard to be a leader unless you can accept criticism.
4. He's not very flexible although he's smart.
5. How can you improve unless you know your areas of weakness?

Communicative Practice   20 minutes

Show what you know!

STEP 1. Complete the sentences about yourself.

- Have students read the directions. Give them additional practice using *although* and *unless*.
- Write Sentences 1 to 4 on the board.
- Tell students that they will complete the sentences with information about themselves. Model a few sentences. (For example, *Although my computer skills are not perfect, I can use Microsoft® Office with ease. My plan is to change jobs unless I receive a promotion at this job.*)
- Have students complete the exercise. Offer prompts as needed. (For example, *What's something that you'd like to improve? What's your plan for that?*)
- Ask students to stand up, walk around the room, and say one of their sentences to a classmate. The classmate completes the same sentence, finds another student, and shares a different sentence.
- Model the activity with an above-level student. For example:

    A: *Although I'm skilled in industrial engineering, I'm working right now as an auto mechanic. How about you?*

    B: *Although I'm a doctor, I can't work as one until I complete medical school here.*

STEP 2. GROUPS. Discuss your answers.

- Have students share what they learned about one another in their groups.

Progress Check

Can you . . . discuss job performance and promotions?

- Say: *We have practiced discussing job performance and promotions. Now, look at the question at the bottom of the page. Can you discuss job performance and promotions? If so, check the box.*

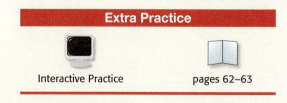

Extra Practice

Interactive Practice   pages 62–63

PRACTICE

A **Complete the sentences. Use *although* or *unless* and an item from the box.**

> your writing needs some work
> you manage your time better
> your attendance this month is good
> you have good problem-solving skills
> you can speak clearly
> I'd like a promotion

1. _Unless you can speak clearly_ , you won't be able to handle phone calls.

2. Your communication skills are generally good _although your writing needs some work_ .

3. _Although your attendance this month is good_ , last month you missed three days.

4. You can't be in charge of difficult situations _unless you have good problem-solving skills_ .

5. You won't be able to complete all your work _unless you manage your time better_ .

6. _Although I'd like a promotion_ , my boss doesn't think I'm ready yet.

B **Write a sentence that has the same meaning as the sentence provided.**
Use *although* or *unless*. Placement of clauses will vary. See T93 for alternative answers.

1. He's very quiet all the time even though he has great language skills.

   Although he has great language skills, he's very quiet all the time.

2. He seems friendly, but he isn't really a team player.
   Although he seems friendly, he isn't really a team player.

3. It is very hard to be a leader if you can't accept criticism.
   Unless you can accept criticism, it is very hard to be a leader.

4. He's smart, but he's not very flexible.
   Although he's smart, he's not very flexible.

5. How can you improve if you don't know your areas of weakness?
   Unless you know your areas of weakness, how can you improve?

Show what you know! Discuss job performance and promotions

STEP 1. Complete the sentences about yourself.

1. Unless I _____, I won't be able to _____.

2. Although my _____ skills are not perfect, _____.

3. My plan is to _____ unless _____.

4. Although I'm skilled in _____, _____.

STEP 2. GROUPS. **Discuss your answers.**

Can you...discuss job performance and promotions? ☐

Listening and Speaking

1   BEFORE YOU LISTEN

A   **CLASS.**   Have you ever taken a career training course? What was the experience like? Would you like to take such a course? Which one?

B   **GROUPS.**   Read the advertisement. How can you get more information about the courses at Eastchester Community College? For which jobs can you get career training there?

Thinking about changing jobs?
Looking to improve your skills?

Eastchester Community College
School of Continuing Education
Credit and Non-Credit Courses

Accounting and Bookkeeping	Electronics	Hotel and Tourism
Aircraft Maintenance	General Business	Landscaping and Horticulture
Automotive Technology	Graphics Design	Nursing
Computer Applications	Health Care	Restaurant and Food Service

Check out our course offerings at www.eastchester.edu.
Make an appointment with a career counselor. Call 555-5000 for more information.

2   LISTEN

A   CD2 T5   André and Claudia are talking about getting job training. Read each statement. Then listen to their conversation. Write *T* (*True*) or *F* (*False*). Correct the false statements.

  T   1. Claudia's supervisor is pleased with her job performance.

  F   2. Claudia asked her supervisor if she is qualified to work as a sales rep.

  T   3. Claudia's supervisor thinks she might be qualified to become an administrative assistant.

  F   4. Claudia's supervisor would like Claudia to develop her skill in speaking English.

  F   5. Claudia's supervisor suggests that she look into online courses.

B   **CLASS.**   What suggestions would you give Claudia? What other places offer job training?

Discuss job-training opportunities

Getting Started 15 minutes

- Say: *We've been studying various aspects of advancing on the job—what factors might lead to a promotion and how to understand and respond to performance reviews and constructive criticism. Another important part of getting ahead on the job is to improve your skills. One way of doing this is to take a career training course.*

1 BEFORE YOU LISTEN

🅐 **CLASS. Have you ever taken...**

- Ask students to read the directions.
- Make sure that students understand *career training*.
- Ask for a volunteer to explain or give an example of career training. Explain further, if needed. For example, say: *Career training is a type of course that is focused specifically on a particular type of job or job skill. In some cases, even if a person has already worked at a job, he or she needs to take career training courses and get certification so he or she can legally work at that job in this country.*
- Ask: *Have any of you taken a training course recently, either through your workplace, at a community college, or somewhere else?*
- Ask students who have taken courses recently: *What was the experience like?* Ask other questions as needed: *Did you think the course was a good investment in time and money? Why or why not?*
- Ask other students: *Would you like to take such a course? Which one? Why?* Accept all responses.

Expansion: Vocabulary Practice for 1A

- Explain that *like* is used in many ways in English. Everyone knows it as a verb, but it can also be a noun, adjective, preposition, or conjunction.
- Explain the use of *like* in the direction line *What was the experience like?* Say: *In this question* like *is used as a preposition. It means the same as* or *similar. The question is asking for the responder to explain what the career training course was similar to or different from.* Explain that this type of question is also a subtle request for a positive or negative review.
- Give other typical examples of this use of *like*. (*I see you work two jobs. What's it like?*)

- Brainstorm a list of similar questions and their meanings.
- Have students write several examples and their meanings in their vocabulary logs.
- Set up pairs as you pass out advanced learner's dictionaries.
- Have pairs review all the entries for *like*, including idioms (such as *like it or lump it*).
- Tell pairs to choose one or two meanings or idioms to add to their vocabulary logs.

Presentation 10 minutes

🅑 **GROUPS. Read the advertisement...**

- Have students read the directions.
- Set up groups and have students complete the exercise.
- Ask volunteers to answer the questions. Answer any questions about content or pronunciation.

Controlled Practice 15 minutes

2 LISTEN

🅐 💿 **André and Claudia are talking...**

- Ask students to read the directions.
- Say: *First, listen to the conversation, then read each statement. Then listen again and decide which statements are true and which are false.*
- Play CD 2, Track 5, and have students do the exercise.
- Play Track 5 again.
- Ask volunteers to read each statement and say whether it is true or false.

🅑 **CLASS. What suggestions would you give...**

- Ask students to read the questions.
- Ask students to offer suggestions to Claudia. Accept all responses, but if any are not appropriate, ask for a show of hands. (For example, *Who thinks Jorge's suggestion that Claudia should ask the supervisor for paid time off to attend classes during the day is a good idea?*) Write appropriate suggestions on the board.
- Ask: *If Claudia lived around here, where could she go for job training?*

3 **LISTEN**

 Mei and Marco are discussing...

- Ask students to read the directions.
- Say: Opportunities for growth *means opportunities for a job promotion or taking on more responsibilities. People don't always want to say things like* I want a promotion *or* I want to make more money and have better benefits; I work hard and deserve them. *So, they typically say something like* opportunities for growth *or* take on new challenges *or some other indirect statement.*
- Tell students to listen and answer the questions.
- Play CD 2, Track 6.
- Ask students to write their answers in their notebooks.

Answers: 1. manufacturing; fixing and maintaining office equipment; He's always had a knack for fixing things. 2. go to a training session, look at bulletin board in kitchen, check out company Intranet site for job postings

Communicative Practice   20 minutes

4 **MAKE IT PERSONAL**

ROLE PLAY. PAIRS. Look at the information...

- Ask students to read the directions.
- Set up pairs. Tell students to work with a partner they have not worked with recently. Facilitate setting up the pairs as needed.
- Say: *It's important to know how to talk to anyone you might meet. At work it's important to be able to work with different co-workers. That's why it's important to get practice in class talking and working with many different people.*
- Restate the directions and confirm that students know what an Intranet is.
- Say: *Read the information about on-the-job-training to yourselves. Then each partner chooses a role—your name, your current job, the job you want—related to the information you read.*
- Tell students to draft a dialogue between the two characters, then try it out, revise, and role-play again.
- After pairs have rehearsed, have pairs perform their role plays for other pairs.

- Walk around; assist pairs as needed with advice on content, dialogue, pronunciation, and delivery.
- Talk to students about role plays. Ask: *Why do you think I ask you to work on role plays in class?*
- Accept all student responses; confirm the reasons why you ask students to role-play (to approximate real-life situations and real-life language; to give students the chance to work independently).
- Draw a T-chart on the board with *Pro* on one side and *Con* on the other side. Ask students about the pros and cons of working on and performing role plays. Record student responses on the chart.
- Say: *I will keep your ideas in mind as I plan for the rest of the class. Thank you for your ideas.*
- Summarize the discussion by saying that researchers studying second language acquisition (SLA) think that students working together on activities that are related to real life is an effective way for students to learn a new language.

Teaching Tip

While pairs are performing role plays, use the scoring rubric for speaking on page Txiv to evaluate each student's vocabulary, grammar, fluency, and how well he or she completes the task. You may want to review the completed rubric with students.

Networking

- If several students in your class are interested in career training courses or are starting to look toward community college and post-secondary education, ask students to research and bring in information about training and education opportunities in your area.
- Suggest going to the public library and asking a reference librarian for help.
- Ask students to bring in materials such as catalogs, information about local organizations that help students, and information about English language testing. Say: *Let's start a resource collection and add to it as we can.*

Extra Practice

Interactive Practice

3 LISTEN

CD2 T6

Mei and Marco are discussing their jobs and opportunities for growth in their company. Listen to their conversation. Then answer the questions.

1. What section of the company is Marco currently working in? What kind of work would he like to do? Why?

2. How can Marco prepare for a different position at the company where he currently works?

4 MAKE IT PERSONAL

ROLE PLAY. PAIRS. Look at the information about on-the-job training on a company Intranet site. Role-play a conversation between two employees about getting on-the-job training.

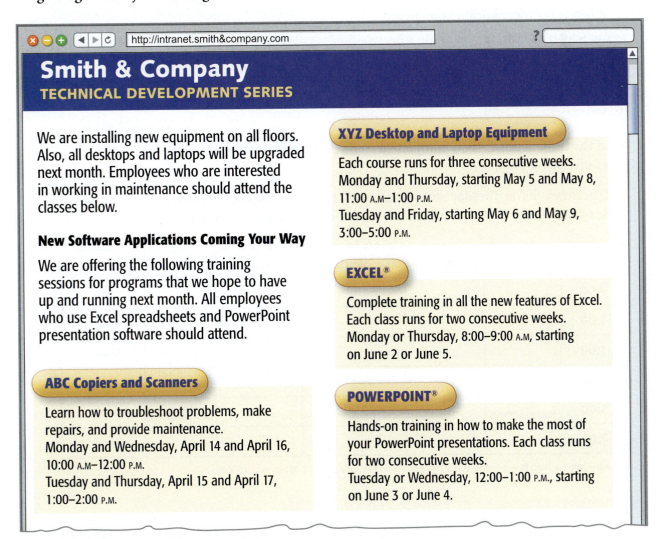

http://intranet.smith&company.com

Smith & Company
TECHNICAL DEVELOPMENT SERIES

We are installing new equipment on all floors. Also, all desktops and laptops will be upgraded next month. Employees who are interested in working in maintenance should attend the classes below.

New Software Applications Coming Your Way

We are offering the following training sessions for programs that we hope to have up and running next month. All employees who use Excel spreadsheets and PowerPoint presentation software should attend.

ABC Copiers and Scanners

Learn how to troubleshoot problems, make repairs, and provide maintenance.
Monday and Wednesday, April 14 and April 16, 10:00 A.M–12:00 P.M.
Tuesday and Thursday, April 15 and April 17, 1:00–2:00 P.M.

XYZ Desktop and Laptop Equipment

Each course runs for three consecutive weeks.
Monday and Thursday, starting May 5 and May 8, 11:00 A.M–1:00 P.M.
Tuesday and Friday, starting May 6 and May 9, 3:00–5:00 P.M.

EXCEL®

Complete training in all the new features of Excel. Each class runs for two consecutive weeks.
Monday or Thursday, 8:00–9:00 A.M, starting on June 2 or June 5.

POWERPOINT®

Hands-on training in how to make the most of your PowerPoint presentations. Each class runs for two consecutive weeks.
Tuesday or Wednesday, 12:00–1:00 P.M., starting on June 3 or June 4.

Life Skills

1 READ COURSE CATALOGS

A Read the course descriptions on page 97. Discuss. Which course or courses should each of these people take?

1. Marta is the administrative assistant in the accounting department. She wants to improve her skill in working with numbers.
2. Linda works in customer support. She receives many phone calls from customers.
3. Carlos wants to improve his writing skills and expand his vocabulary.

B Read the schedule on page 97. Write answers to the questions.

1. What are the abbreviations for Monday–Saturday in the course schedule?
2. When is Business Vocabulary offered?
3. On which days do the classes in Effective Business Writing meet?
4. Which courses can be taken in the evenings? Which ones meet on Saturdays?

2 PRACTICE

Read the information. Then complete a course schedule for Roberto. Use the schedule form below.

Roberto works on Tuesday and Thursday afternoons and all day Saturday. He wants to take Business Vocabulary and Effective Business Writing.

	Mon.	Tues.	Wed.	Thurs.	Fri.	Sat.
9:00						Work
11:00						Work
1:00		Work		Work		Work
3:00	*Business Vocabulary	Work	Business Vocabulary	Work		Work
5:00	Effective Business Writing	Work	Effective Business Writing	Work	Effective Business Writing	Work
7:00						Work

*Roberto could also take Business Vocabulary on Tuesdays and Thursdays from 9:00 A.M. to 11:00 A.M.

Can you... use a course catalog? ☐

Getting Started
5 minutes

- Say: *Let's say you want to receive training. If your workplace does not offer training in the area that interests you, where can you find training?*

- Say: *Many community colleges and adult or community education programs offer classes and vocational training. Today we'll practice reading course descriptions and schedules in order to find the classes that you need at a school or college.*

- Read the discussion question and elicit answers from students, offering prompts as needed.

Presentation
15 minutes

1 READ COURSE CATALOGS

 Read the course descriptions on page 97.

- Say: *Now we're going to look at a set of course descriptions for four college classes.* Ask: *What is a course description?* (a summary of the course's goals)

- Ask students to look at page 97 and read the course descriptions.

- Clarify vocabulary as needed. For example:

  business setting—workplace environment, often but not always an office

  reference materials—dictionaries and other books that provide relevant information

  fraction—part of a whole number in math such as ½ or ⅔

  decimals—a numeric quantity that is less than 1; it follows a period (*0.5 equals half; read as* point five)

  percentages—a numeric quantity that tells how many out of 100 (*Fifty out of 100 people is 50 percent, or point five, or half of 100.*)

- Ask students to read the directions and note which course they think each student should take.

- Ask for student volunteers to read each item aloud and say the answer. Ask other students if they agree with the choice—and if so, why. (*How would the Conversational Business English class help Linda?*)

Possible answers: 1. Marta—Business Math; 2. Linda—Conversational Business English; 3. Carlos—Effective Business Writing and Business Vocabulary

Controlled Practice
20 minutes

B **Read the schedule on page 97....**

- Ask students to look at the schedule on page 97, noting that the classes in the schedule are the same ones listed in the course descriptions.

- Have students read the directions and complete the exercise. Walk around and check students' work.

Answers: 1. M, T, W, Th, F, Sa; 2. Monday and Wednesday 3–5 P.M.; Tuesday and Thursday 9–11 A.M.; 3. Monday, Tuesday, Wednesday, Thursday, Friday, Saturday; 4. Evenings: Effective Business Writing, Business Math; Saturdays: Conversational Business English, Effective Business Writing, Business Math

Communicative Practice
20 minutes

2 PRACTICE

Read the information. Then complete...

- Say: *Now practice making a course schedule.* Ask students to look at the blank course schedule. Say: *Use this chart to make a schedule for Roberto.*

- Have students read the directions.

- Students complete the exercise.

- Ask for student volunteers to share their schedules.

Progress Check

Can you . . . use a course catalog?

- Say: *We have practiced using a course catalog. Now look at the question at the bottom of the page. Can you use a course catalog? If so, check the box.*

NOTES FOR THE CHART

Ref. No.

- Have students look at the first column on the left. Ask: *What do you think* Ref. No. *is?*
- Explain that the reference number is the code number for the class section and is used for recordkeeping.
- Say: *If the same course is offered at different times, the reference number makes it clear which section of the class is offered at a particular time.*
- Give an example: *Conversational Business English is offered at two different times. When is the class with reference number 52173 offered?* (Mondays, Wednesdays, and Fridays from 9 to 11 A.M.) *When is the class with reference number 52174 offered?* (Tuesdays, Thursdays, and Saturdays, from 1 to 3 P.M.)

Credits

- Explain that credits are the number of hours that each course represents; a college degree or certificate requires a set number of credits.
- Ask: *How many credits is Conversational Business English?* (3 credits) *How many is Business Math?* (2 credits)
- Say: *Sometimes courses do not have college credits. They are just for personal enrichment or for learning a new skill. They do not usually have prerequisites and do not require as much work as credit courses. If you're interested in a course but don't need college credit, you should look into the Continuing Education division of your college or university or your local adult or community education program.*

Culture Connection

Say: *In the United States, course descriptions sometimes list prerequisites. Prerequisites are courses that you must have completed before enrolling in a specific course. Sometimes you can enroll without the prerequisites provided you get the permission of the instructor. Let's look at an example.* Write the following on the board:

51204. Calculus 2.

Learn advanced mathematical principles related to calculus.

Preq.: Calculus 1 or permission of instructor.

Ask students: *What is the prerequisite?* (Calculus 1 or permission of instructor)

▉ Expansion: Reading Practice for 2

To give students further practice in reading course descriptions and schedules, bring in course catalogs from community colleges, colleges, and adult or community education programs. Have them work in pairs and look for classes in the catalog that interest them. Have them answer the following questions with their partner:

What courses are you interested in?

When is it offered?

Does it fit into your schedule?

How many credits is it?

Is there a prerequisite for it?

How much is the tuition?

Is there a book fee? How much is it?

What are the goals of the class?

Why do you want to take this class?

When students finish, call on volunteers to present to the class information about the courses they chose.

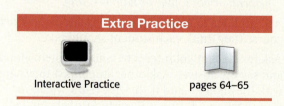

Extra Practice

Interactive Practice   pages 64–65

52173, 52174. Conversational Business English

Focuses on listening and speaking skills needed in a business setting. Students will develop both language and interpersonal skills that they need to communicate clearly and effectively with supervisors, co-workers, and customers.

52363, 52364. Effective Business Writing

Development of skills needed to write effective business letters and other documents. Review of business vocabulary and rules of grammar, punctuation, and capitalization. Use of office reference materials.

52625, 52626. Business Vocabulary

Strategies for expanding general vocabulary useful in business as well as specific business terms. Emphasis will be on correct usage of vocabulary in written and spoken communication.

52629, 52630. Business Math

Review of basic arithmetic—including fractions, decimals, and percentages—and its application to common situations in business and commerce.

Ref. No.	Course Title	Credits	Meeting Days	Time
52173	Conversational Business English	3	M, W, F	9:00 A.M.–11:00 A.M.
52174	Conversational Business English	3	T, Th, Sa	1:00 P.M.–3:00 P.M.
52363	Effective Business Writing	3	M, W, F	5:00 P.M.–7:00 P.M.
52364	Effective Business Writing	3	T, Th, Sa	11:00 A.M.–1:00 P.M.
52625	Business Vocabulary	2	M, W	3:00 P.M.–5:00 P.M.
52626	Business Vocabulary	2	T, Th	9:00 A.M.–11:00 A.M.
52629	Business Math	2	M, W	7:00 P.M.–9:00 P.M.
52630	Business Math	2	Th, Sa	11:00 A.M.–1:00 P.M.

Reading

1 **BEFORE YOU READ**

CLASS. Are there people who do things that annoy you at work, at home, or in your neighborhood? If so, do you say anything to them?

2 **READ**

CD2 T7

Listen to and read the chart of *I* statements and *You* statements. Which kind of statements do you make most often? Which would you rather receive?

I Statements—A Path to Better Communication

I statements simply tell about yourself and your feelings and needs. They are about you rather than the person you are speaking to.

You statements blame the other person. They can make the person feel defensive.

I Statements	*You* Statements
I need to **concentrate** on this right now.	*You*'re bothering me.
I'm allergic to perfume.	*You* wear too much perfume.
I can't take my **break** when you don't get back from yours on time.	*You* always get back from break late.
When you don't come in on time, *I* have trouble getting things ready by myself.	*You* need to come to work on time.
I could hurt my back if I do this without a safety belt.	*You* need to give me a safety belt.
I need more training to **operate** that equipment.	*You* don't give us any training.
I'd like to know how I'm doing.	*You* never give me any feedback.
I waste time when I have to look for equipment.	*You* never put things away.
I think there's a problem.	*You* made a mistake.

Getting Started   10 minutes

- Say: *We've been talking about how to advance on the job and how to understand, talk about, and respond to constructive criticism. We also discussed job-training opportunities and how to use a course catalog. Now we are going to focus on a particularly useful communication strategy—using* I *statements instead of* You *statements. This strategy can be useful in the workplace as well as with families and with friends, at the store, or at medical appointments—just about everywhere.*

- Ask if anyone has heard of *I* and *You* statements or can give examples for each. Accept all student responses.

- Say: *In a few minutes we are going to listen to and read about* I *and* You *statements.*

1 BEFORE YOU READ

CLASS. Are there people...

- Ask students to read the directions.

- Ask a volunteer to explain or give an example of what *annoy* means. If needed, give your own example. (*A nurse at my doctor's office talks to me like I am a not-too-bright child. I can say* She annoys me *or* She is annoying.)

- Explain that being annoying isn't terrible. Say: *Annoy means to make someone feel slightly angry or unhappy about something. TV ads can be annoying, waiting in traffic is annoying, listening to someone explain his or her idea about what kind of car you should buy can be annoying, but none of these situations are terrible.*

- Reassure students that you are not asking them to share personal problems about work or home—just something somewhat superficial about work, home, or neighborhood, such as a bus that is five minutes late.

Teaching Tip

Adapt your lessons to students' knowledge, experiences, and sensibilities so that they learn English at the level and context they need. For example, if students already understand the importance of *I* statements and how to frame them, work with them on other communication strategies, such as how to deflect aggressive language.

Presentation   15 minutes

2 READ

 Listen to and read the chart of...

- Ask students to read the directions.

- Say: *When you listen and read, think about these questions: Which kind of statements do you make most often? Which would you rather receive?*

- Point out that the words and phrases in boldface (*concentrate, break, operate*) appear in the glossary on page 245. Encourage students to read the entire article first, before turning to the glossary.

- Play CD 2, Track 7, while students listen and read along.

- After students listen and read, ask if they have any other questions about the content, vocabulary, or pronunciation. Answer any questions.

Expansion: Vocabulary Practice for 2

- Divide the class into small groups.

- Ask students to make a list of the boldfaced words in the reading and to discuss the meaning of each. Encourage students to guess the meaning if they are not sure.

- Tell students to look for the words in the glossary and to compare the definitions there with what they discussed.

- Assign one or two words or phrases to each group and give them one minute to write one (or two) sentence(s) with their assigned word(s) or phrase(s).

- Ask groups to read their sentences to the class. After each group reads the sentence, ask if anyone has any questions about the word or phrase.

Controlled Practice   15 minutes

3 CHECK YOUR UNDERSTANDING

Change these statements to *I* statements.

- Ask students to read the directions, and go through the example with them.
- Reassure students that there is more than one way to write the *I* statement. Say: *For example, instead of saying,* I feel uncomfortable when you tell jokes, *a person could say,* I feel unhappy whenever you start telling your jokes. *That would mean the same thing.*
- Ask students to share their statements with students sitting close to them.
- Go over only the sentences that students have questions or disagreements about.

4 WORD WORK

GROUPS. Choose three words...

- Set up groups, and ask students to read the directions.
- Say: *Remember when you write in your vocabulary logs, you can always write more than three words or phrases. You can also use the vocabulary log for words you read or hear outside of class.*

Communicative Practice   20 minutes

Show what you know!

STEP 1. Think of things people do...

- Ask students to read the directions.
- Review and give an example.

Who does it?	What do they do?	I Statement
My supervisor	She never asks or tells me before she accepts new work for me.	I feel taken for granted when you accept new work for me without talking to me first.

- Ask students to fill in at least two rows.

STEP 2. ROLE PLAYS. PAIRS. Discuss your...

- Have students read the directions and pair up.
- Say: *First, you are going to talk about what you wrote, and then you are going to do informal role plays.*
- Ask pairs to take turns reading from their charts. Say: *After both of you have shared the information from your charts, choose two or three issues and role-play the statements. The person who writes the I statement should express the statement, and another student should respond. This is just a role play, but it is important to get an idea of how to say I statements and how it feels to be on the receiving end.*
- Tell students not to read from their papers; they should learn each by heart and maintain eye contact with the partner while they talk.
- Answer any questions about the process.

Teaching Tip

While pairs are performing role plays, use the scoring rubric for speaking on page Txiv to evaluate each student's vocabulary, grammar, fluency, and how well he or she completes the task. You may want to review the completed rubric with students.

■ MULTILEVEL INSTRUCTION

Cross-ability Set up pairs so that at least one student is above-level, fluent, and outgoing and can help the other student with the informal role play.

CHECK YOUR UNDERSTANDING

Change these statements to *I* statements. Answers will vary but could include:

1. Your jokes are inappropriate.

   I feel uncomfortable when you tell jokes.

2. You don't explain things clearly.

   I need clearer explanations to understand what you say.

3. You should get better headphones. Your music is too loud.

   I have a hard time concentrating when the music is so loud.

4. You need to do your share of the work or I'll fall behind.

   I'll fall behind in my work if you don't do your share.

5. You didn't return my pen.

   I'd like you to return the pen you borrowed.

6. You talk too much.

   I need some quiet.

4 **WORD WORK**

☑ **GROUPS. Choose three words or phrases in the chart that you would like to remember. Discuss the words and their meanings. Then record the words and information about them in your vocabulary log.**

Show what you know! Use *I* statements

STEP 1. Think of things people do that cause you problems at work or other areas of your life. Complete the chart.

Who does it?	What do they do?	*I* Statement

STEP 2. ROLE PLAY. PAIRS. Discuss your *I* statements and specific requests. Role-play a conversation for each situation.

Reading

1 BEFORE YOU READ

A **GROUPS.** Look at the pictures. Discuss. Which of these sports have you played? Which of these sports do you watch? Do you know the rules for these sports?

B **CLASS.** What do you think the idiom "curveball" means?

> An *idiom* is a group of words that has a special meaning that is very different from the ordinary meaning of the separate words. In English, there are many sports idioms. For example, you can say, *"He really threw me a curveball!,"* which comes from baseball.

2 READ

CD2 T8

Listen to and read the quiz about idioms.

Calling the Shots—
English Sports Idioms

Many English idioms that are used in the workplace come from the world of sports. Take this quiz. Do you know which sports have given us these expressions?

1 **call the shots:** When you call the shots, you have control and make the decisions. For example, *It's too bad, but we really have nothing to say about the solution to this problem. The manager calls all the shots around here.*

2 **carry the ball:** When you carry the ball, you are in charge. For example, *Jerry, this is a very important contract. I want you to carry the ball in the negotiations.*

3 **have two strikes against you:** When you have two strikes against you, you have two or more things that make it very difficult for you to succeed. For example, *Maria isn't likely to get a promotion. After all of the complaints from co-workers and customers, she has two strikes against her.*

4 **kick off:** When you kick something off, you get it started. For example, *The advertising people just kicked off their new campaign.*

Getting Started   10 minutes

- Say: *We've been talking about different aspects of advancing or getting promoted on the job. We've studied factors that influence promotion, performance reviews, how to respond to constructive criticism, how to discuss job-training opportunities, using a course catalog, and using I statements as a strategy for positive communication. Now we are going to talk about common workplace idioms that Americans use all the time—at work and elsewhere.*

- Explain to students that the main point of this lesson is not to talk about sports but to understand the popular phrases that are frequently used in workplaces. Reassure students that it is fine if they don't know or care much about sports in general or American sports in particular.

1 BEFORE YOU READ

A GROUPS. Look at the pictures...

- Ask students to read the directions.
- Set up groups of four or five students.
- Tell students that each person should say whether he or she is a sports player or fan and, if so, what sports he or she plays or follows.
- Say: *Look at the pictures and identify what sport each picture shows. Then discuss which of these sports you have played or watched.*
- Say: *If you know the rules to these games, please describe them to the others in your group.*
- Ask each group to report one interesting piece of information or idea they discussed. (For example: *Everyone in the group likes basketball. American football is boring to watch compared to soccer.*)
- Check that everyone knows what sports the pictures show.
- Now direct students to the note about idioms.
- Ask a student to read the text aloud.
- Reiterate that there are many sports idioms that are used often in the workplace. But there are also many other idioms that come from history, literature, industry, agriculture, and other sources (for example, *barking up the wrong tree*—hunting; *strike while the iron is hot*—blacksmithing).
- Say: *In a little while, we'll be making a list of idioms. Here's the first one:* He really threw me a curveball.

B CLASS. What do you think the idiom...

- Ask: *What do you think the idiom* threw a curveball *means?*
- Accept all student responses. If necessary, explain: *A curveball that a pitcher throws in baseball is hard to hit, so throwing a curveball means to surprise someone with an unexpected question or problem that is difficult to deal with.*

Presentation   15 minutes

2 READ

 Listen to and read the quiz...

- Have students read the directions. Say: *When you read the quiz, think about sports idioms in your home country. Are they at all similar to idioms used in the U.S.?*
- Play CD 2, Track 8 while students listen and read along.
- Afterwards, ask if they have any other questions about the idioms or any other vocabulary, content, or pronunciation. Answer any questions.
- Write the seven sports idioms (including *threw a curveball*) on a flipchart paper. Tell students that the class will make a running list of idioms. Ask them to bring in idioms they read or hear.
- Reiterate that idioms are an important part of both speaking and popular writing, such as newspapers, magazines, and popular books.

Expansion: Vocabulary Practice for 2

- Divide the class into groups of three.
- Have students use the Internet or an idiom book to research idioms about a specific sport.
- Assign each group a particular sport (for example, fishing, tennis, hunting, football, baseball).
- Ask groups to review the idioms related to their sport and choose three to copy onto a flipchart sheet. Collect all flipchart sheets and post them.
- Encourage students to copy the idioms in their notebooks or vocabulary logs.

Controlled Practice   15 minutes

3   CHECK YOUR UNDERSTANDING

PAIRS. Read the sentences...

- Ask students to read the directions. Set up pairs. Explain that they will review the quiz and look for the best idioms to replace the underlined phrases.
- Explain that students may need to adjust the idiom to make it fit correctly in the sentence. Have a volunteer read sentence 1, and ask students to find the appropriate idiom and decide on the correct form (*calling the shots*). If needed, make up another sentence and show how the form of the idiom may need to change.
- Ask volunteers to read the sentences.
  Answers: 1. carry the ball or call the shots; 2. kicking off; 3. calling the shots or carrying the ball; 4. a long shot; 5. two strikes against me; 6. a slam dunk

▬ MULTILEVEL INSTRUCTION for 3

Cross-ability Set up pairs so that one partner who is more comfortable with English grammar and sentence structure can help the other student, who may not know how to adjust the idioms.

4   WORD WORK

GROUPS. Choose three words...

- Set up groups.
- Ask students to read the directions.
- Encourage students to write other idioms (from the class list created in Exercise 2) in their logs.
- Say: *Remember when you write in your vocabulary logs, you can always write more than three words or phrases. You can also use the vocabulary log for words you read or hear outside of class.*

Communicative Practice   20 minutes

Show what you know!

GROUPS. Discuss the questions.

- Ask students to read the directions and questions. Tell them to stay in the same groups.
- Explain that the purpose of this discussion is to summarize what they've discussed about sports idioms.
- Tell each group to list new idioms they talk about.
- Collect any new idioms and add them to the running class list. After class, type up and copy the list and pass it out to students. Leave blank spaces on the list so that students can continue to add to it.

▬ Expansion: Speaking Practice

- Ask students to compare sports idioms in their home countries with those in the U.S.
- Ask: *Does your native language have similar sports idioms? What kinds of idioms are common in your native language—especially in the workplace? Do you think learning idioms is important? Why or why not?*

Progress Check

Can you . . . talk about common workplace idioms from sports?

- Say: *We have talked about common workplace idioms from sports. Now, look at the question at the bottom of the page. Can you talk about common workplace idioms from sports? If so, check the box.*

long shot: When something is a long shot, it's very unlikely to happen. For example, *I'd love to get the job, but it's a long shot—300 people applied for it!*

 slam dunk: When something is a slam dunk, it's sure to happen. For example, *Will you pass the course? It's a slam dunk—you've been studying for weeks!*

Answers: 1. billiards, 2. football, 3. baseball, 4. football, 5. horse racing, 6. basketball

3 CHECK YOUR UNDERSTANDING

PAIRS. Read the sentences. Replace the underlined words with the correct form of one of the idioms in the quiz.

1. Harry is on vacation this week and he asked Kate to <u>be in charge</u> while he's away.

2. Are you going to that meeting on Wednesday? I heard they are <u>starting</u> a new project and they want to tell us all about it.

3. I don't think more staff should be hired right now, and I'm the one <u>making the decisions</u>.

4. Ivan wanted to take a couple of days off, but I told him it's <u>not likely to happen</u> since I asked him to finish that big project.

5. I made a big mistake on my report last week, and today I got a speeding ticket in the company car. With <u>two things against me,</u> it's going to be very hard for me to get a promotion.

6. Alicia will be moving to a nicer office. It's <u>sure to happen</u> now that she got that big raise.

4 WORD WORK

GROUPS. Choose three words or phrases in the quiz that you would like to remember. Discuss the words and their meanings. Then record the words and information about them in your vocabulary log.

Show what you know! Talk about common workplace idioms from sports

GROUPS. Discuss the questions.

1. Which of the idioms in this lesson have you heard before? In what contexts?

2. Which of the idioms in this lesson do you already use?

3. Which of the idioms in this lesson are new to you?

4. What other sports idioms have you heard?

Can you... talk about common workplace idioms from sports? ☐

Writing

1 BEFORE YOU WRITE

A CLASS. You are going to write a self-evaluation about your performance at your current job or a job you had in the past. If you have never had a job, you can write a self-evaluation of your performance at school. Read about self-evaluations. Then read the writing tip.

> **FYI** ABOUT SELF-EVALUATIONS
>
> Many companies ask employees to write self-evaluations, usually during an annual performance review. This allows employees to participate in the review process. In a self-evaluation, you analyze your work performance. You assess your performance and support your judgment with descriptions of your accomplishments, strengths, weaknesses, objectives for the coming year, and long-term career goals. You should present yourself in a positive way. Even weaknesses should be presented as opportunities for growth and learning. A self-evaluation should be organized logically and supported with relevant details, examples, and evidence.
>
> **Writing Tip: Using Good Examples**
>
> When you describe and evaluate your performance, give concrete examples to support your assessment of yourself. Select specific examples that will help your employer picture exactly what you accomplished.

B List your strengths and weaknesses on the job or at school.

C Read the writing model on page 208. Do you think that Pham has done a good job of describing her strengths and weaknesses?

2 ANALYZE THE WRITING MODEL

PAIRS. Discuss the questions.

1. What does Pham feel her greatest strengths are?
2. Why does she give herself a "superior" rating? What examples does she give to support this rating?
3. What weaknesses does Pham mention? How does she present these areas positively?
4. What is she planning to do to improve as a CNA?
5. What is her long-term career goal?

Write a self-evaluation

Getting Started   5 minutes

- Say: *We have learned about factors that affect promotions at work, such as performance reviews. We've also practiced vocabulary and grammatical structures for giving and responding to constructive criticism. Today we are going to apply all of this knowledge as we write a self-evaluation.*

Presentation   5 minutes

1 BEFORE YOU WRITE

 A CLASS. You are going to write...

- Read the directions aloud. Ask: *What is a self-evaluation?* (a process in which an employee rates his or her own job performance, including his or her strengths and weaknesses) *Have you ever had to evaluate yourself?* If a student answers *yes*, say: *Describe the process. How did you do it?*

- Ask students to read the FYI note. Clarify vocabulary as needed (for example: *assess*—to judge or evaluate).

- Ask: *When you write a self-evaluation, do you include a description of your weaknesses?* (yes) *How can you do so in a positive way?* (by presenting a weakness as an opportunity for growth)

- Ask students to read the Writing Tip. Say: *When you write a self-evaluation, include relevant details, evidence, and examples. What kind of examples should you include?* (concrete examples that will help your manager get a good picture of your accomplishments)

B List your strengths...

- Tell students that they will now do some free writing and make a list of their strengths and weaknesses at work or, if they are not working, at school.

- Have students complete their lists.

Teaching Tip

If students are on computers, have them use the "Table" feature to create a two-column chart and organize their list of strengths and weaknesses. They may want to add examples to their charts, cut or copy these notes, and paste them into their outline and the body of their self-evaluation.

Controlled Practice   20 minutes

C Read the writing model...

- Tell students that they will now read a self-evaluation that a student wrote. Say: *As you read the model, think about how the writer described her strengths and weaknesses.*

- Have students read Pham's self-evaluation on page 208. Clarify vocabulary as needed (for example, *compassion*—sympathy for someone who is suffering; *shift*—a period when workers are at work; *geriatric*—relating to the medical treatment and care of elderly people).

- Ask students: *Do you think the writer has done a good job of describing her strengths and weaknesses?* Offer prompts as needed. (*Did she give examples of her strengths? Did she present her weaknesses as opportunities for growth?*)

2 ANALYZE THE WRITING MODEL

Discuss the questions.

- Tell students that they will read Pham's self-evaluation a second time and discuss the questions.

- Ask students to complete the exercise.

- For Question 3, point out that Pham describes her weaknesses as areas in which she would like to learn more in order to take on additional responsibilities. For example, she would like to learn more about how to use complicated medical equipment so that she could help others with the various types of equipment.

Answers:
1. her compassion and attention to detail
2. was named CNA of the month; was praised by lead nurses during her three-month review for the accuracy of her patient records; has never missed a shift
3. has had to depend on more experienced CNAs to help with complicated types of medical equipment and does not know as much as she'd like about the elderly population; presented as areas for growth
4. take a series of workshops to learn more about medical equipment and take a special nursing course to learn more about typical medical problems of the elderly
5. to become a Registered Geriatric Nurse

Communicative Practice   30 minutes

3   THINK ON PAPER

A **Before Pham began writing, she...**

- Ask students what an outline is. Explain as needed that an outline is a list of related items about a topic organized into main ideas (signaled by roman numerals) and supporting details (identified by capital letters under the main ideas).
- *Optional:* Write a template for an outline on the board for students to analyze and use. You can use the one on page 103 as a guide.
- Read the directions. Elicit answers from students, offering prompts as needed. (*Does each outline number correspond to the topic of a paragraph? Do the letters underneath each number list the supporting details given in the paragraph?*)

B **Use the notes...**

- Say: *Now you are going to use the notes that you made earlier to create an outline that organizes ideas for your self-evaluation.*

4   WRITE

Use your outline to write...

- Read the directions aloud, emphasizing that students should present themselves—even their weaknesses—positively, by presenting them as opportunities to learn and grow.
- Have students write the first draft of their self-evaluation.
- Remind students that the concluding paragraph should describe their future goals, both short and long term.
- Say: *When you finish writing, you're going to read your self-evaluation and revise it.*

5   CHECK YOUR WRITING

A STEP 1. **Revise your work.**

- Say: *Read over your self-evaluation a first time and answer the questions in Step 1. If any answers are no, revise your work.*
- *Optional:* Have students form pairs, exchange their self-evaluations, and give each other feedback and suggestions.

B STEP 2. **Edit and proofread.**

- Say: *Read over your self-evaluation a second time and edit and proofread your work.* Direct students to check their papers for grammar, spelling, punctuation, and typos.
- As students write, walk around and check and/or correct their work, answering questions as needed.
- *Optional:* Have students complete a "clean" second draft of their self-evaluation at home, incorporating revisions and corrections from the revision and editing steps.

Teaching Tip

You may want to collect student papers and positive feedback. Use the scoring rubric for writing on page Txv to evaluate vocabulary, grammar, mechanics, and how well students complete the task. You may want to review the completed rubric with students.

▬ **MULTILEVEL INSTRUCTION for 5A and 5B**

Above-level Have students who finish writing and self-editing read and edit a peer's paper using the criteria in Exercises 5A and 5B. Then ask them to discuss their feedback with the writer.

Pre-level Have students complete a checklist with the revising and editing criteria from Exercises 5A and 5B, checking off a box for each question and making the necessary changes.

Extra Practice

Interactive Practice   page 68

3 THINK ON PAPER

A Before Pham began writing, she used a simple outline to organize her self-evaluation. Compare her outline to her self-evaluation. How are they similar?

> I.   Introduction—General Self-Assessment
>   A. Work as a CNA
>   B. Take care of elderly patients
>   C. Strengths: compassion and attention to detail
>
> II. Accomplishments That Show My Strengths
>   A. Named "CNA of the Month" because of praise from patients' relatives
>   B. Praised by lead nurses during three-month review for accuracy
>   C. Never missed a shift
>
> III. Opportunities for Improvement
>   A. Would like to learn more about complicated medical equipment
>   B. Want to learn more about medical problems seniors face
>
> IV. Conclusion—Future Goals and Long-Term Career Goal
>   A. To take a series of workshops about medical equipment
>   B. To take a special nursing course on elder care
>   C. To eventually become a Registered Geriatric Nurse

B Use the notes you made about your strengths and weaknesses in Exercise 1B to create an outline for your self-evaluation.

4 WRITE

Use your outline to write your self-evaluation. You can use Pham's outline as a guide. Be sure to present yourself—even your weaknesses—positively.

5 CHECK YOUR WRITING

A STEP 1. Revise your work.

1. Does your first paragraph give a general evaluation of your performance?
2. Did you describe your strengths, weaknesses, and accomplishments?
3. Did you include concrete examples to support your claims about yourself?

B STEP 2. Edit and proofread.

1. Have you checked your grammar, spelling, and punctuation?
2. Have you proofread for typing errors?

1 REVIEW

For your grammar review, go to page 229.

2 ACT IT OUT — What do you say?

PAIRS. You are discussing promotions and performance reviews with two co-workers.

Student A: Review Lessons 1 and 4. Explain five factors that influence job promotions.	**Student B:** Review Lessons 2 and 4. Describe the purpose and content of a performance review.

3 READ AND REACT — Problem-solving

STEP 1. Read about Diem.

Diem has been working for two years as a receptionist at a fabric design company. She is proud of the work she does, and she thinks that she is good at her job. On her self-evaluation, she included among her strengths her willingness to learn new systems, her helpfulness to co-workers, and her communication skills, particularly with clients. Diem is always on time and rarely takes a sick day. She just received her yearly performance review from her manager, and she is very disappointed by some of the ratings. Her manager wrote on the review that Diem met expectations in five categories: knowledge of work, quality of work, communications skills, punctuality, and attention to safety. But he also noted that Diem needs improvement in time management, initiative, and problem solving. Diem is upset with her manager and feels that he is being overly critical of her. She feels angry and unsure of herself now but she has to meet with him in a week to discuss her review.

STEP 2. GROUPS. What is Diem's problem? What can she do?

4 CONNECT

For your Study Skills Activity, go to page 216.

Which goals can you check off? Go back to page 85.

 Go to the CD-ROM for more practice.

Review & Expand

Show what you know!

1 REVIEW

For your grammar review, go to page 229.

- Say: *Today we're going to review the skills that we have practiced in this unit and apply them to a problem. What are some of the skills we have practiced?* (identifying factors that influence job promotion, understanding and discussing performance reviews, responding to constructive criticism, writing a self-evaluation, identifying job-training opportunities, reading a course schedule)

- Ask students to complete the grammar review exercise for Unit 5 on page 229.

2 ACT IT OUT

PAIRS. You are discussing...

- Ask students to read the directions. Explain that they will help each other review the skills they practiced in this unit. Say: *Student A will look back at Lessons 1 and 4 and explain five factors that influence job promotions. Student B will look back at Lessons 2 and 4 and describe the purpose and content of a performance review.*

- *Optional:* Write prompts on the board to help students get started. (For example, *Promotion depends on . . . Another factor influencing promotion is . . . The purpose of a performance review is to . . . It also allows . . . A performance review includes . . .*)

- Have students complete the exercise.

3 READ AND REACT

STEP 1. Read about Diem.

- Say: *Now we're going to apply our knowledge from this unit to a problem involving a character, Diem. Let's read about Diem.*

- Have students read the story.

- Clarify unfamiliar vocabulary as needed.

STEP 2. GROUPS. What is Diem's problem?...

- Ask students to form small groups. Say: *In your group, you will discuss what Diem's problem is and what she can do.*

- Remind students that Lesson 3 discusses ways to respond to constructive criticism. Tell students that they may want to refer to Lesson 3 as they discuss possible solutions for Diem.

- Give each group a sheet of flipchart paper and markers, or ask them to make notes on a sheet of paper. Tell them that they will write a brief description of Diem's problem and suggest at least three possible solutions.

- Ask groups to choose a representative to present the group's ideas to the class.

- Have students discuss the questions. Then ask a representative from each group present the group's ideas.

- After each presentation, encourage feedback or comments from the class.

Possible answers: *Problem:* Diem is upset about her performance review. *Solution:* She should try to view her manager's criticisms positively. She can express her surprise and ask questions about how she might improve in areas in which he thinks she is deficient.

Teaching Tip

Write sample feedback prompts on the board:

I really like the idea of . . .

I disagree with the idea for Diem to . . .

Instead, I think she should . . .

I like the idea for Diem to . . . , but it might not work because . . . What about trying . . . ?

---

4 CONNECT

Turn to page 216 for your Study Skills Activity. See page Txii for general teaching notes for Study Skills activities.

Progress Check

Which goals can you check off? Go back to page 85.

Ask students to turn to page 85 and check off any remaining goals they have reached. Call on them to say which goals they will practice outside of class.

CD-ROM Practice

 Go to the CD-ROM for more practice.

If your students need more practice with the vocabulary, grammar, and competencies in Unit 5, encourage them to review the activities on the CD-ROM.

Unit Overview

Goals

- See the list of goals on the facing page.

Grammar

- Embedded *Wh-* questions and embedded *Yes/No* questions

Listening and Speaking

- Describe medical problems
- Discuss diabetes
- *Communication Skill:* Giving Advice

Reading

- Read an article about making the most of your appointments with your doctor
- Read an article about first aid
- *Reading Skill:* Visualizing
- Read a message board about interpreting casual questions about health
- Read an article about preventive health screenings
- *Reading Skill:* Recognizing Cause and Effect

Writing

- Write a persuasive essay for or against smoking bans
- *Writing Tip:* Introductory paragraphs

Life Skills

- Identify how to take medication properly

Preview

- Welcome students and have them look at page 105.
- Say: *Look at the picture. Where are the people? What's happening?* (Possible answers: The people are in a doctor's office or clinic; the doctor is treating the patient; the little girl has hurt her arm.)
- Say: *In this unit, we'll talk about health issues, including what to say and do when you visit the doctor. But first, I want to know how many of you have ever been to a doctor's office or clinic in this country.* Have students raise their hands.
- Ask: *How did you find a doctor?* Elicit responses from students (for example, referrals from friends, list of providers from insurance company, walked into clinic).
- Ask the second Preview question: *How do you feel about visiting doctors?* Offer prompts as needed to elicit discussion. (For example, *Do you feel frustrated when you try to communicate with the doctor? Are you happy with the medical care available in this country?*)
- Say: *In this unit, you'll learn more about medical problems. You'll practice communicating with medical professionals and identifying medication uses and side effects. You'll also learn about first aid and preventive health screenings.*

Unit Goals

- Ask students to read the Unit Goals.
- Explain unfamiliar vocabulary as needed. (Examples: *first aid*—helping victims of health emergencies such as burns, cuts, or falls until a doctor arrives to provide treatment; *health screenings*—routine medical tests to check for health conditions such as diabetes, breast cancer, and high cholesterol)
- Tell students to circle the goal that is the most important to them.
- Say: *As we complete this unit, we will look back at this page and reread the goals. We will check each goal as we complete it.*

Health

Preview

What is happening to the child? How do you feel about visiting doctors?

UNIT GOALS

- [ ] Describe medical problems
- [ ] Identify how to take medication properly
- [ ] Learn about first aid
- [ ] Ask and answer questions about health
- [ ] Learn about health screenings

Reading

GROUPS. Discuss the questions.

1. Do you prepare before you go to the doctor? What do you do?

2. How do you feel about talking to doctors and other health care professionals? Explain.

3. What kinds of questions do you ask?

CD2 T9

 A Skim the article and check (✓) the main idea on page 107. Then listen and read.

MAKE THE MOST OF YOUR APPOINTMENTS WITH YOUR DOCTOR

Before you go to the doctor, prepare. First, ask questions when you make your appointment. If you have **health insurance**, find out if your visit is covered by your insurance company. Find out if you should have other doctors send any **records**. Second, prepare a **medical history**. Include a list of medical problems and **diseases** you have had, a list of medical problems and diseases that run in your family, and a list of any **symptoms** you have. Also list any medications you take, including OTC (over-the-counter) drugs, **prescription medicines**, and **supplements**. Note **allergies** to any medications. Also write a list of symptoms if you are going because of a problem rather than for a checkup. Third, arrange for someone to go with you if you would like to have another person there to help ask questions or remember answers.

During your appointment, ask questions. Clearly state your main concerns. Describe symptoms in detail. Answer all of your doctor's questions, even if they seem personal or embarrassing. Ask questions. Take notes. Don't be afraid to ask your doctor to repeat or write information, or to draw a picture. For example you can ask, "Can I check that I understand your instructions?" or say, "Let me make sure I understand." Then repeat what the doctor said. If you have doubts about the **treatment** your doctor suggests, say so. Ask if there are other possible treatments or if you might get better without treatment. If you need more time than your doctor can provide, ask if you can speak with a nurse or a **physician's assistant**, or if you can call later to speak with someone.

After you get home, continue to be an active patient. If you don't get better or if you have trouble with medicine, call the office. If there is anything you forgot to ask your doctor or if you have new questions, call. If you had tests but do not hear from your doctor, call to ask for the results. If your doctor suggests that you have tests or wants you to see a **specialist**, be sure to make an appointment.

Learn about being an active patient

Getting Started   10 minutes

- Say: *In this lesson, we will be talking and reading about health care—an important topic for all of us. Specifically, we will be talking about why and how to be an active and informed patient.*

- Ask: *Can anyone give an example or definition of an* active patient? (For example, *Being an active patient means preparing for your appointment by writing questions and asking for clarification during the appointment.*)

- Say: *During this lesson, we'll use several medical words; if you don't understand any of these words, ask for clarification. This will be good practice for talking to the doctor.*

Presentation   15 minutes

 1 BEFORE YOU READ

GROUPS. Discuss the questions.

- If needed, give an example for each question. Examples:

    1. Say: *How do you get ready for a doctor's appointment? Do you think about what you want to say to the doctor? Do you practice English medical words? What else?*

    2. Say: *Do you feel comfortable talking with doctors and other health care professionals?*

    3. Say: *Do you ask the doctor questions or do you mostly listen? Do you practice your questions before the appointment?*

- Set up groups of three. *Note:* Because health issues are personal, make sure to set up compatible groups. For example, you may want to group by age or gender so that you don't embarrass students by grouping a 50-year-old woman with 19-year-old men.

- Say: *In your groups, each person will read one question and lead the discussion about it.*

Community Building

Even in compatible groups, students might find it hard to discuss these or other personal questions. If students look uncomfortable make the activity a class discussion. Use yourself as a model; answer each question. Write appropriate short answers on the board so that students can write them down if they wish.

Tell students it's OK if they don't answer specifically about themselves but say something like "A person should . . ." or "Sometimes people feel nervous and are afraid they don't know the correct words." Elicit additional suggestions from students.

Controlled Practice   25 minutes

2 READ

A **Skim the article and check...**

- Ask students to read the directions. Say: *After you skim the article, put a checkmark next to the main idea.*

- Remind students to look at the title, the first sentence of each paragraph, and boldfaced words to help them understand the text. Confirm that students see the Main Idea exercise on page 107.

- Point out that the words and phrases in boldface (*health insurance, records, medical history, diseases, symptoms, prescription medicines, supplements, allergies, treatment, physician's assistant, specialist*) appear in the glossary on page 245. Encourage students to read the entire article first, before going to the glossary.

- Play CD 2, Track 9, as students listen and read.

- After students listen and read, ask if they have any questions about the content, vocabulary, or pronunciation. Encourage student volunteers to answer students' questions. Then answer any that they cannot.

Expansion: Vocabulary Practice for 2A

- Divide the class into small groups.

- Ask students to make a list of the boldfaced words in the article and to discuss the meaning of each one. Encourage students to guess the meaning if they are not sure.

- Tell students to look for the words in the glossary and to compare the definitions there with what they discussed.

B **Read the article again...**

- Tell students to read the article again so that they understand and can write about both the main idea and the details that support it.

Expansion: Vocabulary Practice for 2B

- Brainstorm with students the type of health and medical vocabulary they want to know more about (such as terms related to a specific disease or reproductive/childbirth terms). Write the list on the board.
- If the list is large, either prioritize what to study by asking for a show of hands and then work on the vocabulary as a class, or break up into interest groups, such as a group for cancer vocabulary and a group for childbirth terms.

3   CHECK YOUR UNDERSTANDING

Write the answers to the questions.

- Say: *Now write the answers to these six questions in your notebook. Don't worry about writing perfectly—just get down the main point of each of the paragraphs in your own words. Then find the answers to the rest of the questions.* Check for understanding.
- Walk around as students write; provide assistance as needed.
- Read each question and elicit responses. Accept reasonably accurate responses.

Answers:

1a. Prepare information and questions before the appointment. 1b. During the appointment, ask questions and ask for clarification. 1c. After the appointment, follow up with the doctor as needed.

2. personal medical history, family medical history, list of medications noting allergies to medicines, list of symptoms

3. to help ask questions or remember answers

4. Ask the doctor to repeat instructions, write information, or draw a picture. Repeat what the doctor says.

5. Ask to speak with a nurse or a physician's assistant, or if you can call later, to speak with someone.

6. if you don't get better, if you have trouble with the medicine, if there is anything you forgot to ask, if you have new questions, or if you need test results but the doctor's office doesn't call back with them

Communicative Practice   10 minutes

4   WORD WORK

GROUPS. Choose three words...

- Set up groups, and ask students to read the directions.
- Say: *Remember when you write in your vocabulary logs, you can always write more than three words or phrases. You can also use the vocabulary log for words you read or hear outside of class.*

5   MAKE IT PERSONAL

GROUPS. Discuss the questions.

- Ask for a volunteer to read each discussion question.
- Acknowledge that even though these are important questions, some students may not want to share personal information. Tell students: *Instead of answering "Did you do any of the things suggested in the article?" you could say what people you know do to prepare or what you think people should do.*
- Walk around the room as students talk, and assist as needed.

Networking

- Invite a health care worker to talk to the class about being an active patient before, during, and after visits, as outlined in the article.
- As part of the preparation for the visit, find out about local free and reduced-cost clinics in your community. Find out how and where students can obtain free screenings. If you have parents in your class, find out where they can go for information about children's health insurance in your community.

MAIN IDEA

☐ 1. Good communication is the responsibility of the patient as well as the doctor.

☐ 2. You can make your doctor's appointments more successful by preparing lists of information and questions to take with you before you go.

☑ 3. You can make your doctor's appointments more successful by being active and taking responsibility before, during, and after your visits.

B Read the article again more carefully.

3 CHECK YOUR UNDERSTANDING

Write the answers to the questions.

1. In your own words, what is the main idea of:

   a. the first paragraph?   b. the second paragraph?   c. the third paragraph?

2. What four lists should you write and take to your appointment?

3. Why might you want another person to go to your appointment with you?

4. What can you do if you aren't sure you understand the doctor's instructions?

5. What can you do if you need more time than the doctor has for your appointment?

6. What are some reasons you might call your doctor after your appointment?

4 WORD WORK

✏ GROUPS. **Choose three words or phrases in the article that you would like to remember. Discuss the words and their meanings. Then record the words and information about them in your vocabulary log.**

5 MAKE IT PERSONAL

GROUPS. **Discuss the questions.**

1. Think about the last time you went to the doctor. How active a patient were you? Did you do any of the things suggested in the article? If so, which ones?

2. Are there things mentioned in the article that you wish you had done? If so, which ones?

3. Choose a suggestion from the article that you think you might like to try on your next visit to the doctor. Explain why.

Listening and Speaking

1 BEFORE YOU LISTEN

PAIRS. Often a general doctor, or general practitioner, will recommend that you see a specialist to help you with a medical problem. Read the chart. Discuss. What other medical specialists do you know of? What conditions do they treat?

Specialists	Conditions They Treat
allergists	allergic reactions and conditions such as rashes, hay fever, and asthma
cardiologists	heart diseases, such as strokes or heart attacks
dermatologists	skin, hair, and nail ailments, such as eczema and nail fungus
neurologists	diseases of the nervous system, such as epilepsy
oncologists	cancer or precancerous conditions
ophthalmologists	conditions and diseases that affect the eyes
orthopedists	bone injuries and diseases, such as fractures, arthritis, and osteoporosis
psychiatrists	mental illnesses, such as depression
surgeons	medical conditions that require operations

2 LISTEN

CD2 T10

Carmen and Bianca are good friends, but they haven't seen each other for a few weeks. Listen to their conversation and discuss the questions.

1. What symptoms has Bianca been having?
2. What did she find?
3. What did she do about it?
4. What kind of specialist does her doctor want her to see? Why?
5. When is her appointment?
6. What does Carmen offer?

Getting Started   10 minutes

- Say: *In the last lesson, we talked and read about how to prepare for a medical appointment, how to talk to the doctor during the appointment, and when and how to follow up. Now we are going learn more about medical specialists. We are also going to listen and talk more in depth about how to describe medical conditions.*

- Assure students that they can ask questions whenever they need to about medical terminology. Say: *Health issues are important to all of us. If you have questions about health vocabulary or medical traditions in the U.S., please ask any time— including before or after class.*

- Ask students whether any of them are health care workers now or were in their home countries. If so, say: *Maybe you will be able help us with this lesson.*

Presentation   15 minutes

  BEFORE YOU LISTEN

PAIRS. Often a general doctor,...

- Say: *Sometimes we call a general practitioner a GP or a family practitioner or family doctor. These doctors often refer people with specific conditions to other doctors who are experts in a certain area. The chart on page 108 lists some specialists and the conditions they treat.*

- Ask pairs to read the chart together and share experiences they may have had with these health care professionals. Then pronounce the term for each specialist and read the words for the conditions they treat. As needed, ask students if they understand. (For example, say: *Do you know what eczema is? Do you know what epilepsy is?*)

- Repeat the directions. Ask: *What other medical specialists do you know of?* (Possible answers: *obstetricians, pediatricians*) *What conditions do they treat?* Students may not understand what *treat* means in this context. Say: *Treat means take care of. What conditions do they take care of?*

Expansion: Reading Practice for 1

If you have access to computers, organize students into small groups or pairs to investigate other specialists. Encourage them to find specialists in your area.

Culture Connection

Some students may be in need of mental health services because of emotional distress. Students may have had trauma in the past, or may have difficult living conditions, financial problems, or homesickness. Substance abuse or physical abuse at home may also be common. Many students may be extremely uncomfortable talking about such issues, so avoid asking personal questions or engaging the class in discussion of such matters. However, you can help students by making information available anonymously. Create flyers with phone numbers of relevant sources of help, such as local mental health clinics, abuse hotlines, and so on. Hand them out to the class and tell students that these are additional sources of health providers they may contact if they wish to.

2 **LISTEN**

  Carmen and Bianca are good friends,...

- Play CD 2, Track 10.
- After students listen, ask: *How was that listening?* If it was too difficult, add more support before the listening.
- Have students discuss the questions. Ask: *What other specialists might Bianca have to go to?* (a surgeon, a chemotherapist)

Answers: 1. strange symptoms; 2. a lump under her arm; 3. she went to the doctor yesterday; 4. oncologist, to rule out the possibility of cancer; 5. Thursday at 4:00; 6. give Bianca a ride and anything else she can do to help

Controlled Practice   15 minutes

3 PRACTICE

A PAIRS. Match the symptoms...

- Ask students to read the directions. Do the example with the class.
- Point out that there may be more than one cause for a symptom. Say: *For example, shortness of breath might be caused by heart disease or asthma.*
- Walk around the room and help as needed.
- Go through each item, calling on each pair in turn. Say, for example: *What is the answer for item 2?* Let students explain variations in answers. For example, a sharp chest pain could be caused by *a, b, c,* or *e.*
- Check for any comprehension or vocabulary issues you noticed while you were listening to the pairs.

B GROUPS. Bianca's doctor recommended...

- Ask students to read the directions. Review the oncologist example to make sure students understand the task.
- Say: *Talk with two or three people sitting near you. Look back at the list of symptoms in Exercise 3A and decide which specialist or specialists might treat each of the symptoms.*
- Walk around the room and assist as needed, particularly in assuring students that more than one answer may be appropriate. For example, loss of appetite could be an important symptom for either a psychiatrist or an oncologist.

Possible answers:
1. blurry vision: opthamologist; 2. painful rash: allergist;
3. loss of appetite: psychiatrist, oncologist; 4. a lump: oncologist, surgeon; 5. a sharp chest pain: cardiologist;
6. shortness of breath: allergist, cardiologist

Communicative Practice   20 minutes

4 MAKE IT PERSONAL

STEP 1. Think of someone you know...

- Make it clear that if students don't know someone who has seen a specialist or don't have enough information, they can use information from the newspaper, radio, or another source, or they can imagine it.

- Say: *The purpose of this activity is to connect a symptom of illness, a specialist who might see someone with that type of symptom, what condition the symptom indicated, and what happened.*
- Say: *In your group, talk about these four elements: symptom, specialist, condition, and outcome—what happened or what might be likely to happen.*
- Walk around as students talk; offer assistance. (For example, give names of types of specialists.) If any new vocabulary words come up during the discussion, write them on the board and briefly review them with the class.

STEP 2. PAIRS. Complete the chart...

- Ask students to read the directions and fill out the chart (at least one whole row).
- Model a dialogue with an above-level volunteer. Take the part of Student A. Example:

  A: *My cousin Reynaldo was sleeping 12 hours a day. He never wanted to get out of bed. The doctor at the clinic said he should see a psychiatrist. My cousin went to a psychiatrist, and she said my cousin was depressed. The psychiatrist helped him find a therapist to talk to—I guess Reynaldo was homesick for Peru. What about you? What did you write on the chart?*

  B: *I don't know anyone who has seen a specialist, but I saw an ER show in which an elderly man was always falling down.*

STEP 3. PAIRS. Think about symptoms...

- Say: *Talk with your partner about various symptoms a person should see the doctor about. This doesn't have to be about you, just people in general. For example, I know someone at work who says she takes six aspirins every day for pain in her back. What do you think she should do?* Ask a volunteer to answer.

Extra Practice

Interactive Practice

3 PRACTICE

A **PAIRS.** Match the symptoms on the left with possible causes on the right. There may be more than one possible cause for a symptom.

Symptoms	Possible Causes
_d_ 1. blurry vision	a. heart disease
_f_ 2. a painful rash	b. cancer
_c_ 3. loss of appetite	c. depression
_b_ 4. a lump	d. farsightedness/nearsightedness
_a_ 5. a sharp chest pain	e. asthma
_e_ 6. shortness of breath	f. eczema

B **GROUPS.** Bianca's doctor recommended that she see an oncologist. Look at the chart on page 108. Discuss. Which specialist would you go to for each of the symptoms in Exercise 3A? You may want to consult more than one specialist.

4 MAKE IT PERSONAL

STEP 1. Think of someone you know well who had to see a specialist.

STEP 2. PAIRS. Complete the chart. Compare your information.

Symptom	Specialist seen	Condition	What happened?

STEP 3. PAIRS. Think about symptoms you might see a doctor about. Describe the symptoms, and offer each other suggestions about what to do.

Life Skills

1 UNDERSTAND TIPS FOR TAKING MEDICINE

A **CLASS.** A side effect is an effect that medicine has on your body in addition to the intended effect. Discuss. Have you or has anyone you know ever had a side effect or allergic reaction from taking medicine?

B **PAIRS.** Read the handout from the U.S. Food and Drug Administration about taking medicine safely. What are some of the risks of taking medicine?

U.S. Food and Drug Administration's TIPS FOR TAKING MEDICINES:

How to Get the Most Benefits with the Fewest Risks

Both prescription and over-the-counter (OTC) medicines can have risks. Medicines may cause side effects or allergic reactions, and they may be affected by interactions with foods, drinks, or other drugs.

For prescription drugs, a patient should ask the doctor questions with each new prescription. For example:

- What is the medicine's name, and what is it supposed to do?
- How and when do I take it, and for how long?
- While I'm taking this medicine, should I avoid:
  - Certain foods or supplements?
  - Caffeine or alcohol?
  - Other medicines, prescription and OTC?

- Will this new medicine work safely with the prescription and OTC medicines I'm already taking?
- Are there side effects, and what do I do if they occur?
- Will the medicine affect my sleep or activity level?
- What should I do if I miss a dose?
- Is there written information available about the medicine? (At the very least, ask the doctor or pharmacist to write out complicated directions and medicine names.)

Source: © 1995, 1997, 2001 U.S. Food and Drug Administration

C Read the sentences. Which questions in the handout do they answer? Write the questions.

1. It might cause headaches or drowsiness; this is normal, so continue the medication.
   Are there side effects, and what do I do if they occur?

2. Don't drink alcohol while you're taking this medicine.
   While I'm taking this medicine, should I avoid caffeine or alcohol?

3. Take it twice a day on an empty stomach for seven days.
   How and when do I take it, and for how long?

4. You may feel weak and sleepy, so don't drive or operate any machinery.
   Are there side effects, and what do I do if they occur?

5. Do not take an additional capsule. Take the next dose at the normal time and in the normal amount.
   What should I do if I miss a dose?

Getting Started   5 minutes

 UNDERSTAND TIPS FOR TAKING MEDICINE

A **CLASS.** A side effect is an...

- Say: *In the last lesson, we talked about medical problems and specialists who can help with them. What are some medical specialists that we identified?* Elicit answers from students. (Possible answers: cardiologist, dermatologist, neurologist, oncologist, orthopedist, psychiatrist, surgeon) Offer prompts as needed. (For example: *Who would I see for heart problems?*)

- Say: *Today we're going to talk about medicine and how to take it properly.*

- Read the first sentence in the directions. Ask: *What are some side effects of medicine?* Elicit answers from students, noting them on the board. (Possible answers: drowsiness or insomnia, nausea or upset stomach, loss of appetite, dry mouth, itchiness, dizziness)

- Say: *Sometimes a medicine can cause an allergic reaction. What is that?* (a reaction caused by an allergy to medicine or one of the ingredients in medicine; it can be a minor reaction, such as a rash, or a serious and possibly life-threatening reaction such as a seizure)

- Read the discussion question and elicit examples from students.

Presentation   10 minutes

B **PAIRS.** Read the handout...

- Say: *Now we're going to learn about how to take medicine safely. The Food and Drug Administration—called the FDA for short—is a federal agency responsible for verifying the safety of all food and medicine sold in the U.S. Let's look at an FDA handout, noting as we read it some of the risks of taking medicine that it describes.*

- Direct students' attention to the handout.

- Clarify unfamiliar terms as needed. (Examples: *benefits*—positive effects; *risks*—potential hazards; *interactions*—when two or more substances are put together and produce an effect; *avoid*—stay away from, not do, or not take; *dose*—amount needed)

- Note as needed that medicines may cause side effects or allergic reactions even when they are taken alone, but they may also be affected by interactions with food, drinks, and other drugs.

Controlled Practice   10 minutes

C Read the sentences. Which questions...

- Read the directions aloud. Confirm that students understand that they are supposed to match the statements or answers with specific questions in the handout.

- Model how to answer Item 1. Say: *First, I read the sentence. It explains certain side effects and what to do about them. Then I skim the handout to find a question about side effects. I find the question Are there any side effects, and what do I do if they occur? which Item 1 answers.*

- Ask students to look for the question for Item 2. If students ask *Caffeine or alcohol?* remind them that they need a complete question. (*While I'm taking this medicine, should I avoid caffeine or alcohol?*)

- Have students complete the exercise. Walk around, offering prompts as needed. (*If the answer emphasizes* empty stomach, *look for a question about food*)

- Call on students to give the questions.

Controlled Practice
15 minutes

2 CONVERSATION

PAIRS. Practice the conversation.

- Say: *Look at the picture. What do you see?* (a pharmacist reading a medicine label to a customer)

- Say: *When you fill a prescription, it's a good idea to read the directions on the label and ask the pharmacist if you have any questions. Let's practice asking a pharmacist questions about a medication.*

- Ask students to close their books and listen while you read the conversation aloud. Then have students follow the conversation in the book as you model it with an above-level student.

- Clarify unfamiliar terms as needed. (Examples: *nausea*—feeling sickness in one's stomach and an urge to vomit; *dizziness*—lightheadedness, sometimes accompanied by a feeling of spinning; *mild*—not very strong)

- Ask a few questions to check students' comprehension. Examples:

    1. What are some possible side effects of this particular medication? (nausea or dizziness)

    2. What should the customer do if she experiences mild side effects to a medication? (call her doctor if they bother her)

- Walk around and help as needed.

- Call on volunteers to present their conversations to the class.

Communicative Practice
20 minutes

3 PRACTICE

 Read and take the medicine safety...

- Say: *Now you're going to take a quiz to see if you know how to use medicine safely.*

- Have students complete the quiz. Check their work.

Expansion: Reading Practice for 3A

Ask students to bring in medicine labels and inserts from over-the-counter medications. Have them look at the labels and inserts in small groups and discuss these questions: *How often should the medicine be taken? What are the possible side effects? Who should not take the medicine? Is it necessary to finish the entire prescription?*

B GROUPS. Score your quizzes:...

- Ask students to score their quizzes.

- Have students form small groups and compare their scores. Model the activity by asking an above-level student: *What was your score? How many did you check* no *for?*

- Have students complete the exercise.

- Ask students to share what they learned from this exercise. Offer prompts and explanations as necessary. For example: *Do you know why it's important to finish your prescription unless the doctor says not to?* (Some medications such as antibiotics are not effective unless you take the entire prescribed dose.)

Teaching Tip

Explain that some companies offer health insurance to employees but may ask them to pay a portion of the monthly cost (known as a *premium*). Many health care companies also sell individual health insurance policies with fixed premiums. In some areas, clinics provide medical services at little or no cost, but these may be limited to those who make under a certain income. If students use the hospital for emergency medical care and do not have health insurance, they can ask for a payment plan allowing them to pay a portion of the bill each month for a fixed period of time.

Progress Check

Can you . . . identify how to take medication properly?

- Say: *We have practiced identifying how to take medication properly. Can you do this? If so, check the box.*

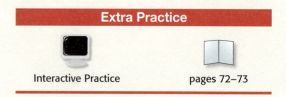

Interactive Practice   pages 72–73

2 CONVERSATION

PAIRS. Practice the conversation.

Patient: Does this medication cause any side effects?

Pharmacist: Sometimes. Some people experience a little nausea or dizziness.

Patient: What should I do if I experience these side effects?

Pharmacist: Any side effects are usually mild, and they're usually nothing to worry about. They'll stop when you quit taking the medication. But call your doctor if they bother you.

Patient: And I should take this medicine twice a day, right?

Pharmacist: That's right. With breakfast and dinner. But be sure not to take it with milk or other dairy products.

Patient: Thank you. You've been very helpful.

3 PRACTICE

A Read and take the medicine safety quiz. Check (✓) *Yes* or *No* to answer each question.

MEDICINE SAFETY QUIZ	Yes	No
1. Do you throw outdated medicine away?		
2. Do you keep all medicines out of children's sight and reach?		
3. Do you finish your prescription unless your doctor says not to?		
4. Do you try to use the same pharmacy to fill all prescriptions?		
5. Do you ask for written information about your medicine?		
6. Do you read the written instructions and the instructions on the label?		
7. Do you use only medicine prescribed for you?		
8. Do you keep medicines in their original, labeled packaging?		
9. Do you make sure there is light to see your medicine when you take it?		
10. Do you store medicine away from dampness or direct sunlight?		

B **GROUPS.** Score your quizzes: 10 *yes* answers = *very safe*, 8 *yes* answers = *not very safe*, 7 or fewer *yes* answers = *extremely unsafe*. Compare your scores.

Can you...identify how to take medication properly? ☐

Reading

A **CLASS.** Why do you think first aid is called "first aid"? What kinds of accidents or emergencies might require first aid?

B **GROUPS.** Discuss the questions.

1. Have you ever received first aid? If so, for what?
2. Have you ever given first aid? If so, for what?
3. Have you ever had any first aid training? If so, tell about it.

> **Reading Skill:**
> Visualizing
>
> It is helpful to visualize, or form mental pictures, as you read. Use descriptive details in a text to picture the things, actions, or events you are reading about. This will help you to understand and remember information.

2 READ

CD2 T11

Listen to and read the article about first aid. Visualize the actions you should take for each emergency. Imagine yourself going through the correct steps.

FIRST AID

First aid is what you do to help someone while you are waiting for **professional** help—it's the first help given in an emergency. And sometimes the first things that are done in an emergency can be the most important things.

BAD BURNS

Before medical help arrives, remove any clothing around the burn, unless the clothing sticks to the burned area. **Immerse** the burn in cool water or run cool water over it for at least ten minutes. A shower is good for this. If it's not possible to run water over the burn, place clean, cool, **moist** towels on the burn—but keep them cool and moist. Don't put anything else on the burn. Don't break blisters. Gently remove items such as rings or belts from the areas around the burn. Later, these areas may swell, and the items may be difficult to remove. It may be necessary to treat a burn **victim** for shock.

SHOCK

A person who has a severe **injury** or emotional **upset** may go into shock. Signs include cold and clammy skin, a colorless or gray face, chills, confusion, weakness, anxiety, **nausea**, fast **pulse**, and weak breathing. The eyes may seem to stare. Until emergency help arrives, have the person lie down with the feet higher than the head, unless this position would cause pain or injury. (Don't move a person who may have a head, neck, or back injury.) Loosen belts and tight clothing, and cover the person with a blanket.

POISON

Call 911 if the person has **collapsed** or stopped breathing. Otherwise, for someone who took the wrong medicine, or too much medicine, call the Poison Control Center (1-800-222-1222 in the U.S.) for instructions. For someone who swallows a household **chemical**, read the poison warning and instructions on the label. Follow the instructions, then call the Center. If a person **inhales** a poison, get the person into fresh air before calling the Poison Control Center. If a person is poisoned through the skin—for example by contact with a chemical—remove any clothing the poison has touched and **rinse** the skin with water for 15–20 minutes, then call the Center. For poison in an eye, rinse the eye with cool water for 15–20 minutes. Adults can stand in the shower to do this. Have a child lie in the bathtub, or support the child over a sink, and pour cool water on the forehead above the eye. If poison has gotten into both eyes, pour the water on the **bridge** of the nose. Don't pour water directly on the open eye. Don't hold the eye open. Call the Poison Control Center.

Learn about first aid

Getting Started   10 minutes

- Say: *So far in this unit, we've talked about how to be an active patient, how to describe symptoms, and how to take medication properly. We've learned or reviewed medical vocabulary, especially related to symptoms, diseases, and types of doctors. Now we are going to read about a practical part of health care: first aid.*

1   BEFORE YOU READ

Ⓐ CLASS. Why do you think first aid...

- Elicit that *first aid* means exactly what it says: It is the first thing you do to help someone who is hurt or sick. Ask students to provide examples of first aid and provide one of your own. Say, for example: *I remember when my son fell off his bike and got a very deep cut on his forehead. Until the ambulance came, I pressed a rolled-up T-shirt on the cut to stop the bleeding.*
- Let students talk generally about first aid and emergencies until most have had a chance to share.
- Ask students to read the directions and discuss the questions. Accept student responses. Give positive feedback for reasonable answers; for less accurate answers, gently correct, for example: *That's an interesting idea. I hadn't thought of that, but . . .*

Presentation   15 minutes

Ⓑ GROUPS. Discuss the questions.

- Read the questions aloud.
- Set up groups of three. Say: *Break up into groups of the three at your table or with people sitting near you. Each group member, please ask one of the questions. Then discuss them together.*
- Ask each group to report one or two interesting items from the discussion.

Teaching Tip

Sometimes groups should be mixed ability so that more proficient students can help less proficient ones. However, proficiency varies with different skills—a strong reader or writer may not be a strong speaker or confident listener. With a task like the above, where everyone is just sharing general experience, you can quickly put together informal groups.

Reading Skill: Visualizing

- Direct students to the Reading Skill box.
- Ask a student to read the text.
- Say: *This reading skill—visualizing or picturing in your mind—helps you consciously start trying to "see" what you are reading. This can help you remember information you read.* Give an example of visualizing. Say, for example: *When I read driving directions, I try to see each right turn, left turn, and traffic light in my mind so that I get a picture in my mind of where I'm going and won't get lost when I start driving.*

2   READ

 Listen to and read the article...

- Ask students to read the directions.
- Reiterate that students should try to visualize what they should do. Say: *Picture yourself going through each step.*
- Point out that the words and phrases in boldface (*professional, immerse, moist, victim, injury, upset, nausea, pulse, collapsed, chemical, inhales, rinse, bridge*) appear in the glossary on page 245. Encourage students to read the entire article first, before going to the glossary.
- Play CD 2, Track 11 as students listen and read.
- Ask: *Were you able to visualize what to do and what not to do?* Accept all student responses.
- After students listen and read, ask if they have any other questions about the content, vocabulary, or pronunciation; answer questions.

Expansion: Vocabulary Practice for 2

- Set up small groups.
- Ask students to make a list of the boldfaced words in the reading and to discuss the meaning of each. Encourage students to guess the meaning if they are not sure.
- Tell students to look for the words in the glossary and to compare the definitions there with what they discussed.

Controlled Practice 20 minutes

3 CHECK YOUR UNDERSTANDING

A GROUPS. Reread the article on page 112.

- Ask students to read the directions. Have them reread the article before they break up into groups.
- Ask: *Do you have one action visualized in your mind?* If most nod or say *yes*, continue; if some shake their heads or say *no*, explain again what it means to visualize and reassure them that this is not as difficult as it sounds.
- Model how students should "talk through" their visualizations. Say, for example: *I saw a bad car accident. I saw that the driver looked like he was going into shock because he was cold and was shivering. I helped the man lie down with his feet up.*
- Ask a confident, above-level student (preferably one with EMT or medical training, or one with small children) to visualize and describe another action.
- Set up groups.
- Say: *In your groups, you will take turns visualizing and describing a first aid action. It's OK if someone else in your group describes a similar action.*

B Write the answers to the questions.

- Point out the example and tell students they don't have to write full sentences but that getting the correct information is very important. Say: *Go back to the article to make sure you have the correct answers.*
- After students have written the answers, ask for volunteers to give answers. Gently correct any incorrect or incomplete (as to content) responses.
- Say: *Now that we all have the right answers, you may wish to copy them and put the information by your telephone at home in case of an emergency.*

Answers: 2. Don't put anything on a burn but clean, cool, moist towels and don't break blisters. 3. Later those areas may swell and items may be difficult to remove. 4. a severe injury or emotional upset; 5. Possible answers: cold and clammy skin, a colorless or gray face, chills, confusion, weakness, anxiety, nausea, fast pulse, weak breathing, eyes may seem to stare; 6. 1-800-222-1222. 7. Get the person into fresh air before calling the Poison Control Center. 8. 15–20 minutes

4 WORD WORK

GROUPS. Choose three words...

- Keep the same groups.
- Confirm that students understand that they discuss first and then write in their vocabulary logs.
- Walk around; intervene only if you hear a question that students can't answer in the group.
- Say: *Remember when you write in your vocabulary logs, you can always write more than three words or phrases. You can also use the vocabulary log for words you read or hear outside of class.*

Communicative Practice 15 minutes

5 MAKE IT PERSONAL

STEP 1. GROUPS. Have you ever been involved...

- Keep the same groups.
- Ask students to read the directions.
- Make sure students know that they do not have to tell a personal story here. Tell them they could also talk about an emergency they read about or saw on TV or use their imaginations to make up an emergency situation.
- Encourage students to use descriptive details so that groups members can visualize the emergency.

STEP 2. PAIRS. After reading the advice...

- Have students read and respond to the question.
- Remind them to give examples and explanations to support their answers.

Teaching Tip

If you think that talking about an emergency might cause stress for any students suffering from post-traumatic stress disorder (PTSD), assign only the question in Step 2.

Extra Practice

Interactive Practice

pages 74–75

3 CHECK YOUR UNDERSTANDING

Ⓐ GROUPS. Reread the article on page 112. Choose one action that you should perform to help a person suffering from burns, shock, or poisoning. Visualize yourself performing the action. Describe the action to the group.

Ⓑ Write the answers to the questions.

1. What should you do if clothing sticks to a burn?
   Leave it.

2. What is something you *shouldn't* do to a burn?

3. Why should you remove rings and belts from the area of a burn?

4. What can cause shock?

5. What are four possible signs of shock?

6. What's the number for the Poison Control Center in the U.S.?

7. What should you do if a person inhales poison?

8. How long should an eye be rinsed if poison gets into it?

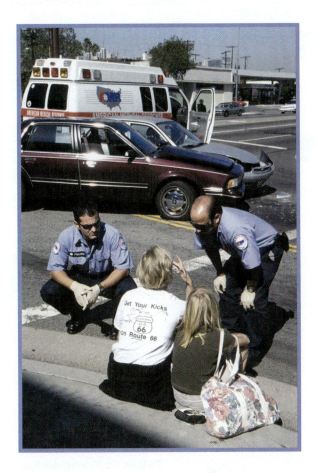

4 WORD WORK

📝 **GROUPS.** Choose three words or phrases in the article that you would like to remember. Discuss the words and their meanings. Then record the words and information about them in your vocabulary log.

5 MAKE IT PERSONAL

STEP 1. GROUPS. Have you ever been involved in an emergency related to burns, shock, or poison? If so, describe what happened. If not, imagine what you would do in one of these emergencies.

STEP 2. PAIRS. After reading the advice in the article, are you better prepared for an emergency? Explain.

Reading

1 BEFORE YOU READ

CLASS. Do you have native-born American co-workers or neighbors?
If so, what greetings do you use with them?

2 READ

CD2 T12

  Listen to and read the message board posts. What are the people discussing?

Message: What does "How are you?" really mean?	
↓ Posted - 10/9 11:02 A.M.	
● **Elsa** From Poland Posts: 4	I'm confused. I work in a big hotel, and there are a lot of employees there. Sometimes, one of the other employees I only **know by sight** will say, "Hi! How are you?" when we pass in the hall, but the person doesn't want me to answer. He'll just keep walking. Why does he ask, "How are you?" Can anyone tell me what he expects me to say?
↓ Posted - 10/09 11:15 A.M.	
○ **Kamila** From Czechoslovakia Posts: 10	Hi, Elsa. I don't know what this guy's problem is, and I'm not sure whether this will help, but that's **normal behavior** for Americans! When people don't know each other well—like co-workers or neighbors—and they greet each other, they often say "Hi! How are you?" but no one expects an answer! You can say, "Fine, thanks. How are you?" Then the other person says, "Fine" and just keeps on going.
↓ Posted - 10/09 11:32 A.M.	
○ **Tuan** From Japan Posts: 24	This **took me by surprise**, too, when I first came to the U.S. One time, someone said, "Hi. How are you?" and I actually answered! I said, "Oh, I don't feel well. I have a bad cold and a sore throat. Thank you for asking." The person looked at me as if I was crazy! I thought the person was angry with me for going out with a cold. I don't know if you know this, but in my country, we wear masks over our nose and mouth when we go out if we have a cold or the flu. The next day, I told the story to my friend, and she told me what I had done wrong. I was really **embarrassed**!
↓ Posted - 10/09 11:59 A.M.	
● **Elsa** From Poland Posts: 5	Could you explain why Americans ask the question if they don't want to know the answer? It seems rude.
↓ Posted - 10/09 12:06 P.M.	
● **Kamila** From Czechoslovakia Posts: 11	I don't know whether it's rude in your home country, but in the U.S. it's not rude. You just have to get used to it.
↓ Posted - 10/09 12:18 P.M.	
● **Tuan** From Japan Posts: 25	I heard two of my American co-workers joking around once. One of them said, "Hi. How are you?" and the other one said, "Do you have an hour?" They both laughed and kept going. I think Americans just don't have time to listen to a lot of details about how you're feeling if they don't know you well. Next time a co-worker or neighbor asks, "How are you?" just think of it as another way of saying, "Hi."

《 previous page   **1** | 2 | 3   next page 》   Reply

Getting Started   10 minutes

- Say: *We having been working on serious health topics such as symptoms and causes, first aid, and emergencies. In this lesson, we are going to examine American culture and language related to talking about health.*
- Say: *First of all, what are some examples of greetings?* Accept all responses and model with examples. (*Good morning. Hello. Hi.*)

1 BEFORE YOU READ

CLASS. Do you have native-born American...

- Have students read the directions.
- Ask students to share their experiences greeting co-workers or people in their neighborhoods. Accept all responses.
- Write some of the responses on the board, an overhead, or a flipchart.
- Say: *Let's keep this list of greetings and add to it as we come up with more examples.*

Presentation   20 minutes

2 READ

Listen to and read the message...

- Ask students to read the directions. Clarify what a message board is. (a web-based message center where users can send, read, and reply to other users' posts)
- Point out that the words and phrases in boldface (*know by sight, normal behavior, took me by surprise, embarrassed*) appear in the glossary on page 245. Encourage students to read the entire article first, before going to the glossary.
- Play CD 2, Track 12, as students listen and read.
- Ask: *What were the people talking about on the message board? Have you heard comments like this?* Accept all student responses.
- After students listen and read, ask if they have any other questions about the content, vocabulary, or pronunciation; answer questions.
- Ask students to give their opinions about the reading. Let students discuss the message board format, the topic, and other related cultural issues for as long as they are engaged.

Expansion: Vocabulary Practice for 2

- Set up small groups.
- Ask students to make a list of the boldfaced words in the reading and to discuss the meaning of each. Encourage students to guess the meaning if they are not sure.
- Tell students to look for the words in the glossary on page 245 and to compare the definitions there with what they discussed.

Teaching Tip

- In activities related to culture, encourage students to compare as objectively as possible their native cultures and American culture. Sometimes students make over-generalizations about the U.S. or their own cultures.
- Ask students to use examples to back up their statements. For example, if a student says that Americans are too informal, ask the student to give an example to back up that assertion. (For example, *Americans go to nice restaurants wearing T-shirts, shorts, and flip-flops.*)
- Explain that looking at two sides of an issue and being able to give examples for a person's ideas are important in speaking and writing and are expected in the workplace, schools, and other sectors of American society.

Expansion: Vocabulary Practice for 2

- Tell students: *This message board includes some idioms such as* took me by surprise. *Let's learn some more idioms related to health.*
- On the board write these idioms:

  be in bad shape
  feel blue
  have a clean bill of health
  be or get back on one's feet
  pull through an illness
  take a turn for the worse
  touch and go
  be under the weather

- Set up groups. Assign at least one or two of the idioms to each group and have them look them up in the dictionary. Then ask them to write one (or two) sentence(s) with their assigned idioms.
- Ask a volunteer from each group to explain the meaning of their idiom to the class and to write their sentence on the board. Correct any sentences with the class if necessary.

Lesson 5 Interpret casual questions about health

Controlled Practice   10 minutes

3 CHECK YOUR UNDERSTANDING

Write the answers to the questions.

- Ask students to read the questions and complete the exercise.

Answers:

1. A co-worker asked *How are you?* but didn't wait for an answer. Elsa doesn't know what she is supposed to say.
2. No one expects a real answer to *How are you?*—just *Fine, thanks.*
3. It seems rude to her. Answers will vary to the second and third questions.
4. In Tuan's home country, people seem to actually answer *How are you?*. People wear masks when they go out with the flu or a cold, which is not typical in the U.S.

4 WORD WORK

GROUPS. Choose three words...

- Set up groups, and ask students to read the directions.
- Say: *Remember when you write in your vocabulary logs, you can always write more than three words or phrases. You can also use the vocabulary log for words you read or hear outside of class. Today you might want to add some of the greetings we discussed to your vocabulary log.*

Communicative Practice   20 minutes

Show what you know!

GROUPS. How do people respond...

- Ask students to read the directions.
- Set up groups so that, if possible, people from different countries are working together.
- Say: *In your group, describe the typical response to* How are you? *in your home country or native culture. Compare the responses with typical American responses.*
- Model the activity with a student. Ask: *How do people respond to the question* How are you? *in your home country?* After the student responds, ask: *Is that different from the way people respond in the U.S.? If so, how?* Have the student respond.

- Answer questions or assist as needed.
- Check with students to find out whether the responses from other countries are generally similar to or different from typical U.S. responses.

PAIRS. Complete the chart. Discuss...

- Ask students to read the directions and look at the chart.
- Explain that languages and cultures have more formal and less formal language that is used in different situations. (For example, we might say *Hello, I'm pleased to see you* at a formal gathering, but *How's it going?* is more appropriate in an informal setting.)
- Ask one or two students to give examples of formal and informal speech in English.
- Say: *Work with a partner to fill in the chart with formal and informal ways to respond to the question* How are you? *in the U.S. and in your home countries.*
- Set up informal pairs. Say: *Work with a person sitting near you—if possible, someone from another country.*

Expansion: Writing Practice

- Ask students to write a descriptive paragraph about how people greet and respond to each other in their home countries. This could be done as homework.
- Encourage students to have a clear topic sentence, give specific examples limited only to the defined topic, and follow punctuation rules for quotation marks. Review punctuation rules. (For example, if a question is in quotation marks, the question mark should be placed inside the quotation marks.)

Teaching Tip

You may want to collect student papers and provide feedback. Use the scoring rubric for writing on page Txv to evaluate vocabulary, grammar, mechanics and how well students complete the task. You may want to review the completed rubric with students.

CHECK YOUR UNDERSTANDING

Write the answers to the questions.

1. What happened to Elsa? Why was she confused?
2. What did she learn about how Americans greet one another?
3. What does Elsa think about the American style of greeting? Do you agree with her? Why or why not?
4. What difference does Tuan describe between practices in his home country and practices in the U.S.?

4 **WORD WORK**

✏ **GROUPS.** Choose three words or phrases in the message board posts that you would like to remember. Discuss the words and their meanings. Then record the words and information about them in your vocabulary log.

Show what you know! Interpret casual questions about health

GROUPS. How do people respond to the question, "How are you?" in your home country? Is it different from how they respond in the U.S.? If so, explain how.

PAIRS. Complete the chart. Discuss similarities and differences.

Responses in the United States	Responses in Your Home Country
Formal:	Formal:
Informal:	Informal:

Grammar

Embedded *Wh-* Questions

Direct Question	Embedded Question
What does he expect me to say?	Can anyone tell me **what he expects me to say**?
Why do Americans ask the question?	Could you explain **why Americans ask the question**?
What is this guy's problem?	I don't know **what this guy's problem is**.

Embedded *Yes/No* Questions

Direct Question	Embedded Question		
Will this help?	I'm not sure	**if**	**this will help**.
		whether	
Do you know this?	I don't know	**if**	**you know this**.
		whether	

Grammar Watch

- An embedded question is a type of question that is included inside another sentence. Use embedded questions to ask for information politely or to express information you don't know.
- Put embedded questions inside questions like *Do you know…?* or *Can you tell me…?* Use a question mark at the end of these sentences.
- Put embedded questions inside statements like *I don't know…* or *I wonder…* Use a period at the end of these sentences.

1 PRACTICE

Change each direct question about health to an embedded question. Answers will vary but may include:

1. When did you start having headaches?

   Can you tell me when you started having headaches?

2. What medications do you take every day?

   Can you tell me what medications you take every day?

3. How tall are you, and how much do you weigh?

   Can you tell me how tall you are and how much you weigh?

4. What can I do to lower my blood pressure?

   I don't know what I can do to lower my blood pressure.

5. Will this medication cause side effects?

   I'm not sure whether this medication causes side effects.

Getting Started 5 minutes

- Say: *In earlier lessons, we practiced describing health conditions and identifying side effects of medications. What are some questions that you might ask your doctor?* Elicit answers from students, offering prompts as needed. (For example, *What can you ask your doctor about a medication? Its side effects? The need to see a specialist?*)

- Say: *Today we're going to practice asking and answering questions about health. To do so, we'll use the grammatical structure of embedded questions.*

Language Note

- Explain that *embedded* means enclosed within something, such as diamonds embedded in rocks.

Presentation 15 minutes

Embedded *Wh-* questions

- Copy the top grammar chart onto the board.

- Ask students to read the Grammar Watch. Reiterate that embedded questions are used to make polite requests for information or to express unknown information. Say: *They are also called* indirect questions *because they do not ask a question directly. Often we use embedded, or indirect, questions to ask or say something politely.*

- Point to the grammar chart and read the first example. Ask: *How is the direct question changed to an embedded one?* (by adding *Can anyone tell me* and changing *What does he expect* to *what he expects*)

- Say: *An embedded question takes a question and places it inside of another question or statement. When this happens, the question words—do or does—are not used.*

- Say: *Let's look at another example.* Point to the chart and read the second example.

- Ask: *What phrase introduces the embedded question?* (Could you explain) *How is the embedded question phrased?* (why Americans ask the question) Reiterate that when the question is embedded, *do* is not included. (Do not say *Could you explain why **do** Americans ask the question?*)

- Say: *Sometimes a question is embedded inside of another question. Other times, it is embedded inside a statement.*

- Point to the grammar chart and read the third example. Ask: *What is the original question? (What is this guy's problem?) What introduces the embedded question? (I don't know) How is the direct question changed when it is introduced by* I don't know? (The word order changes from *What is this guy's problem* to *what this guy's problem **is**.*)

Teaching Tip

To help students comprehend how to change direct questions to embedded ones, write the following on the board:

	What time is it?
Could you tell me	what time it is?
	Why is this taking so long?
I don't know	why this is taking so long.

Draw arrows to show how the question order is reversed in the embedded question. For example, in the first question, draw an arrow from *is* to *is* and from *it* to *it*.

Embedded *Yes/No* Questions

- Copy the bottom grammar chart onto the board. Say: *Now let's see how to embed questions that ask for* yes *or* no *answers.*

- Point to the grammar chart and read the examples. Ask: *What phrases introduce the embedded questions? (I'm not sure/I don't know) What words are added to the embedded questions? (if/whether)*

Controlled Practice 15 minutes

 PRACTICE

Change each direct question...

- Ask students to read the directions. Reiterate that different phrases may be used to introduce embedded questions. (*Can you tell me, Could you explain, I don't know if*)

- Ask: *What words are included with an indirect embedded question?* (*if* or *whether*)

- Read the first example together, noting that the past-tense question *did you start* changed to *you started* (past tense) in the embedded question.

- Have students complete the exercise.

Controlled Practice   15 minutes

2 PRACTICE

A Unscramble the words and phrases...

- Read the directions and the example. Note that students will change the order of the phrases in each item as they rewrite them.
- Have students complete the exercise.
- Call on students to read sentences and say answers.

B Use the phrases below to form...

- Ask students to imagine that they are talking to a health care professional or friend about their health. Emphasize that they may make up questions about their health.
- Have students read the directions and first example.
- Have students complete the exercise. Help students as they work, offering prompts as needed. (For example, *Does an embedded question take* do *or* does?)
- Call on volunteers to share their questions.

Answers will vary; just check that word order is correct.

Communicative Practice   10 minutes

Show what you know!

STEP 1. GROUPS. Discuss. Why is it...

- Ask students to read the directions. Have them form small groups and discuss the questions.
- Have students complete the exercise. Monitor conversations, offering prompts as needed. (For example, *When you have a checkup, should you ask the doctor questions about other family members?*)

STEP 2. Prepare a list of general questions...

- Ask students to read the directions. Say: *With your group, you will now make a list of questions to ask the doctor. You might ask about general health concerns, such as what to do about allergies, or you might ask specific questions about medications. Encourage students to use embedded questions.*

- *Optional:* Give each group a sheet of flipchart paper to use in recording questions to ask the doctor and in presenting the group's list to the class.
- Have students complete the exercise.
- Ask for a representative from each group to present its list to the class. Encourage students to offer feedback and additional questions.

Culture Connection

Explain that Americans call a simple solution to a temporary, nonserious ailment a *home remedy*. For instance, a home remedy for a stomachache might be to drink ginger ale and eat crackers. Say: *However, if you have a nonserious ailment that persists, be sure to see a doctor.*

Community Building

- Ask students to brainstorm common ailments, noting them on the board as students say them. (Examples: a sore throat, headache, stomachache, backache, "tennis elbow," post-holiday holiday weight gain, hangover)
- Write the following prompt on the board: *Do you know what the best home remedy is for a . . . ?*
- Ask students to interview one another about the best home remedy for the ailments. (*Note:* Make sure that they ask with an embedded question such as the prompt on the board.) Encourage them to cite examples of home remedies commonly used in their home countries. Make a list together on the board of suggested home remedies.

Progress Check

Can you . . . ask and answer questions about health?

- Say: *We have practiced asking and answering questions about health. Can you do this? If so, check the box.*

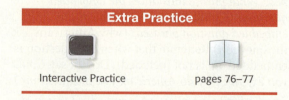

Extra Practice

Interactive Practice   pages 76–77

A Unscramble the words and phrases to create an embedded question.

1. what is causing / my shortness of breath / I'm not sure

   I'm not sure what is causing my shortness of breath.

2. had the same illness / if anyone / I don't know / in my family

   I don't know if anyone in my family had the same illness.

3. make my appointment / I don't know / on Friday / whether I can

   I don't know whether I can make my appointment on Friday.

4. why I need / can you explain / this medication / to take

   Can you explain why I need to take this medication?

5. whether / I wonder / vitamin C / I should take

   I wonder whether I should take vitamin C.

B Use the phrases below to form questions and statements about your own health. Answers will vary.

1. Do you know if *there is a more effective treatment for my headaches?*

2. I wonder whether _____

3. Can you tell me when _____

4. Can you explain why _____

5. Can you tell me if _____

6. I'm not sure how _____

7. I don't know where _____

Show what you know! Ask and answer questions about health

STEP 1. GROUPS. Discuss. Why is it a good idea to prepare a list of questions before you have a medical exam? What kinds of questions should you ask a doctor when you have a regular checkup? Talk about the kinds of questions you should ask. Compare your experiences.

STEP 2. Prepare a list of general questions that patients might ask their doctors during a routine exam. Share your list with the class.

Can you... ask and answer questions about health? ☐

Reading

1   BEFORE YOU READ

CLASS. **Check (✓) the statement that is true for you. Then discuss your answers and the reasons for them.**

☐ I never go to the doctor.

☐ I go to the doctor only when I am very ill.

☐ I go to the doctor whenever I think something may be physically wrong with me.

☐ I go to the doctor for preventive screenings every year, even if I feel fine.

> **Reading Skill:**
> Recognizing Cause and Effect
>
> To understand explanations in texts, look for causes and effects. An effect is "what happened." A cause is "why it happened." Certain words signal causes and effects, including *so, because, because of, therefore, lead to, result,* and *as a result.*

2   READ

CD2 T13

 Skim the article. Then listen to and read it carefully. Identify causes and effects.

PREVENTIVE HEALTH SCREENINGS

Early **detection** of certain illnesses and medical conditions is very important. If left untreated, many problems get worse until they are very serious. Regular **screenings** can catch a problem early enough to **eliminate** it completely or to control it.

■ WHY SCREEN FOR DIABETES?

In the U.S., 20.8 million people have **diabetes**. Almost one-third are unaware that they have the disease. People with diabetes can't produce or properly use **insulin**, a **hormone** needed to change sugar into energy. When this happens, sugar and starches build up in the blood instead of going into **cells**. Untreated, diabetes can lead to blindness, heart disease, kidney failure, and even to conditions requiring **amputations**. The most common form of diabetes, called "type 2 diabetes," can occur at any time. Symptoms of diabetes in its early stages may be mild and are often not recognized or are mistaken for symptoms of minor conditions and illnesses.

■ WHY SCREEN FOR HIGH BLOOD PRESSURE?

Blood pressure is the force with which blood moves through your body. Almost one in three adults in the U.S. has high blood pressure. But because there are often no symptoms, many people live with high blood pressure for years without knowing it. Uncontrolled high blood pressure can lead to stroke, heart attack, heart failure, or kidney failure. The only way to tell if you have high blood pressure is to have your blood pressure checked.

Getting Started · 10 minutes

- Say: *We talked earlier about how to be an active patient and about symptoms and causes of disease. An important part of being an active patient is getting preventive health screenings.*
- Ask students if they know what the title means. Discuss the meaning of *preventive* and what base verb it comes from (prevent). Ask someone to explain or give an example of *screenings*. Help out by relating the word to TV screens, X-ray screens, etc.
- Say: *Many people do not like to go through medical procedures, but preventive health screenings can help people avoid serious illnesses. We will read about three screenings that can help keep people healthy.*

1 BEFORE YOU READ

CLASS. Check (✓) the statement...

- Ask students to read the directions.
- Explain that students should read the list of statements and check the statement that best reflects how often they go to the doctor.
- Discuss briefly. Ask whether some students want to share what statements they marked and why. Do not press anyone to answer orally.

Teaching Tip

- Students can practice their English without having to share more information than they want to. In the discussion above, for example, a student can participate without divulging what statement he or she marked.

Presentation · 15 minutes

Reading Skill: **Recognizing Cause and Effect**

- Direct students to the Reading Skill box.
- Ask a student to read the text aloud.
- Repeat the cause and effect words listed in the box.
- On the board, write two headings: *cause* and *effect*. Ask students to categorize the words in the box as either cause or effect words. Encourage students to explain why they think a specific word belongs in either category. Let students disagree; step in only to help lead students to an appropriate answer.

- Ask students to volunteer other cause and effect words; put them in the appropriate lists. (For example, *since* and *on account of* for cause and *consequently* and *for this reason* for effect.) If suggested words are not appropriate as cause or effect markers, explain why.

2 READ

 Skim the article. Then listen...

- Ask students to read the directions.
- Say: *First, briefly skim the article for the main idea. Remember to look at the title, headings, and photograph and illustration, as well as the introduction, to help you figure out the main idea.*
- Point out that the words and phrases in boldface (*detection, screenings, eliminate, diabetes, insulin, hormone, cells, amputations, cholesterol, arteries*) appear in the glossary on page 245. Encourage students to read the entire article first, before going to the glossary.
- Say: *Now, read the article carefully and to try to identify causes and effects related to health screenings.*
- Play CD 2, Track 13, as students listen and read.
- Ask: *What specific information did you learn about diabetes? High blood pressure? High cholesterol? What was the main idea of this article?* Accept all student responses.
- After students listen and read, ask if they have any other questions about the content, vocabulary, or pronunciation; answer questions. *Note:* Because the article has medical terminology, you may need to spend extra time clarifying the vocabulary.

Expansion: Vocabulary Practice for 2

- Set up small groups. Ask students to make a list of the boldfaced words in the reading and to discuss the meaning of each. Encourage students to guess the meaning if they are not sure.
- Tell students to look for the words in the glossary and to compare the definitions there with what they discussed.
- Assign one or two words or phrases to each group and ask them to write one (or two) sentence(s) with their assigned word(s) or phrase(s).
- Ask groups to read their sentences to the class.
- After each group reads the sentence, ask if anyone has any questions about the word or phrase.

Controlled Practice   20 minutes

3 CHECK YOUR UNDERSTANDING

Write the answers to the questions.

- Ask students to read the directions. After they have written answers in their notebooks, tell them to talk with one or two people sitting near them about the answers. Say: *If you have any answers you don't agree on, we'll talk about the answers as a class.*

- Allow enough time for writing answers and sharing with other students.

- If time permits, ask for student volunteers to read each question and its answer.

Answers: 1. a hormone needed to change sugar into energy; sugar and starches build up in the blood instead of going into cells; 2. blindness, heart disease, kidney failure, and amputations; 3. stroke, heart attack, heart or kidney failure; 4. it builds up on the wall of arteries, so they become clogged and blood flow to the heart is slowed down or blocked; 5. when completely blocked, a heart attack; 6. Check the websites for the U.S. Department of Health and Human Services, the Centers for Disease Control, the American Medical Association, the American Cancer Society, the American Heart Association, the Department of Health and Human Services for your state, and (if you have it) your health insurance website.

Teaching Tip

- Encourage students to find free health information online through the U.S. National Institutes of Health. Write this website on the board: http://medlineplus.gov.

- Tell students they can find information on health topics and medications on this site. They can also look up the definitions of medical words. Say: *This site is also searchable by topic. If you search under the term* diabetes, *for example, you will come to a page with a lot of information and links on diabetes.*

4 WORD WORK

GROUPS. Choose three words...

- Set up groups, and ask students to read the directions.

- Say: *Remember when you write in your vocabulary logs, you can always write more than three words or phrases. You can also use the vocabulary log for words you read or hear outside of class.*

- Say: *Remember to take a paper and pencil with you to a medical screening or a doctor's appointment so that you can ask about any medical words you don't understand and then write down the answers. When you get home, make sure you understand the answers, or call the doctor's office for more information. Then add these medical terms to your vocabulary log so that you remember what they mean.*

Communicative Practice   15 minutes

5 MAKE IT PERSONAL

GROUPS. Discuss the questions.

- Ask students to read the questions and think of answers. Give them a time limit for this.

- Before breaking up into groups, ask if there are any questions about the content of the questions. Confirm that people don't need to give personal examples; the exercise is to practice agreeing and disagreeing, providing explanations, and sharing important local information (such as which drugstores give free blood pressure checks).

- Set up groups of four. Say: *Because there are four questions, we'll have four people in the groups. Each person in the group should ask one question to the others.*

- Direct students to count by 1-2-3-4 and say: *Make your own groups, but make sure each group has a 1, a 2, a 3, and a 4 in it. If there is an extra person, place that person in a group and say, for example: This group will have two 4s.*

- Answer questions and assist as needed.

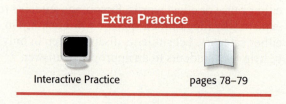

Extra Practice

Interactive Practice   pages 78–79

WHY SCREEN FOR HIGH CHOLESTEROL?

When there is too much **cholesterol** in your blood, it builds up in the walls of your **arteries**. As a result, they become narrow, or clogged, and blood flow to the heart is slowed down or blocked. Blood carries oxygen to the heart, and if not enough blood and oxygen reach your heart, you may suffer chest pain. When the blood supply to a part of the heart is blocked completely, the result is a heart attack. Many people who have high cholesterol are unaware of it; for some, the first symptom is a heart attack.

To find out about other preventive screenings, check the websites for the U.S. Department of Health and Human Services, the Centers for Disease Control and Prevention, the American Medical Association, the American Cancer Society, and the American Heart Association. You can also check the Department of Health and Human Services for your state. If you have insurance, call or check the company website to find out about recommended screenings covered by your insurance.

Artery narrowed by atherosclerosis

Plaque

Source: http:www.cdc.gov/cholesterol/index.htm

3 CHECK YOUR UNDERSTANDING

Write the answers to the questions.

1. What is insulin? What happens when the body doesn't produce or use it properly?
2. What are some possible results of leaving diabetes untreated?
3. What effects can uncontrolled high blood pressure have on the body?
4. What happens when there is too much cholesterol in your blood?
5. When the blood supply to a part of the heart is blocked completely, what is the result?
6. Where can you find more information about preventive health screenings?

4 WORD WORK

GROUPS. **Choose three words or phrases in the article that you would like to remember. Discuss the words and their meanings. Then record the words and information about them in your vocabulary log.**

5 MAKE IT PERSONAL

GROUPS. **Discuss the questions.**

1. Do you agree that it's important to have health screenings? Why or why not?
2. Does anyone you know have diabetes, high blood pressure, or high cholesterol? If so, what do they do about it?
3. Some drugstores and discount stores offer free blood pressure checks at certain times. Do you know of any place that does this in your area?
4. Do you know about any free diabetes or cholesterol screenings in your area? If not, whom could you contact to get this information?

Listening and Speaking

1 BEFORE YOU LISTEN

CLASS. Think about the conditions discussed in the article on pages 118–119. Risk factors are things that make you more likely to get an illness or disease. Discuss. What do you know about risk factors for diabetes, high blood pressure, and high cholesterol? What are some suggestions for prevention or improvement of each condition?

2 LISTEN

CD2 T14

A Listen to three students give a presentation about type 2 diabetes. Take notes in the outline.

In the introduction, the speaker presents the topic and explains what will be discussed in the body of the presentation. ("Pierre will talk about risk factors for type 2 diabetes, and Min-Ji will give suggestions for reducing risk and living with the disease.")

I. INTRODUCTION (Marisa)

II. BODY

  A. Risk factors (Pierre)

  1.
  2.
  3.
  4.

  B. Suggestions for reducing risk (Min-Ji)

  1.
  2.
  3.

III. CONCLUSION (Marisa)

For each subtopic in the body of the presentation, the presenter should identify exactly what he or she will discuss. (Pierre: "There are many different risk factors for type 2 diabetes, but I'm going to focus on four of them." Min-Ji: "I'm going to discuss things people can do to reduce the risk of becoming diabetic or to help control diabetes.")

In the conclusion, the speaker should summarize the main ideas and ask if there are any questions.

Getting Started 15 minutes

- Say: *In the last lesson, we read about preventive health screenings for diabetes, high blood pressure, and high cholesterol. In this lesson, we are going to talk specifically about risk factors for diabetes.*

- Ask: *What do you think* risk factor *means? First, what does* risk *mean? Can someone explain what* risk *means?* (chance of a bad result) Accept correct responses; explain if necessary.

- Say: Factor *means one of several things that influence or cause a situation.* Risk factors *are several things that increase your chances of something bad happening.*

- Say: *Now that we understand risk factors, we will be listening to a conversation about risk factors and diabetes.*

1 BEFORE YOU LISTEN

CLASS. Think about the conditions...

- Ask students to read the directions. Have them turn back to page 118 and review what the article said about the diseases.

- Ask students if they know any risk factors for diabetes, for high blood pressure, and for high cholesterol.

- Accept all comments from students, but—unless a statement is clearly incorrect (for example: *People get diabetes from touching cats.*)—don't say whether it is correct or not. The audio will provide more information about type 2 diabetes.

Presentation 15 minutes

- Direct students to the notes that explain the structure of the presentation.

- Ask a confident, above-level student to read each of the three notes. Answer any questions about format.

2 LISTEN

Ⓐ **Listen to three students...**

- Ask students to read the directions.

- Say: *When you listen to the audio, use the outline to take notes and help you organize the information.*

- Play CD 2, Track 14.

- Ask: *Was the presentation easy to follow? How did the outline help?*

▮ Expansion: Writing Practice for 2A

- Ask students how they take notes. Find out whether they use a formal outline, such as the example in the text, or whether they have their own styles.

- Emphasize that taking good notes is essential if students are thinking of attending post-secondary education in the U.S. Say: *Even those of you who have attended a university in your home country might find it more challenging here when lectures are in English, so a good note-taking form is crucial.*

- Tell students that you are going to give a short speech on a health topic (for example, about health facilities in the community or general information about health insurance). You can adapt your speech from health pamphlets found in a doctor's office, clinic, or hospital; or from a respected community website.

- Ask students to take notes in their usual style. When the lecture is finished, have students compare their notes with at least four other students to compare various formats.

- Say: *As you can see, there are many ways to write notes. It's important to get all the information you need and to be able to read your notes.*

Teaching Tip

- If you observe a student having trouble listening and writing notes at the same time, try to see whether the student is just having trouble doing two things at once (listening and writing) or whether he or she actually has difficulty in either understanding the audio or writing.

- If a student seems to have difficulty with listening and writing (or reading) over time, find a time when you can talk to the student to find out what the challenge is. If the student suggests that he or she sit at a quieter table or closer to the board, try to accommodate him or her.

Controlled Practice 15 minutes

B 💿 **Listen to the presentation again....**

- Ask students to read the directions.
- Tell students that as they listen again, they should answer the questions. Assure them that writing short answers is OK.
- Play Track 14 again.
- After students have listened and answered the questions, ask for volunteers to read each question aloud and give the answer. Let students discuss any differences in answers; intervene only if the class doesn't come up with the correct answer.

Answers:

1. Your body turns sugar into glucose, which gives energy to cells in your body.
2. Insulin takes glucose from the blood into the cells.
3. Cells may not get enough energy; over time, high glucose levels may hurt the eyes, kidneys, nerves, or heart.
4. If a family member has diabetes, a person is more at risk of developing diabetes.
5. People who have unhealthy eating habits are more likely to be overweight, which is one reason they may be more likely to become diabetic.
6. Regular exercise and a healthy diet can help prevent or help control diabetes.
7. Consuming less alcohol and salt will help lower blood pressure and prevent or control diabetes.

3 **PRACTICE**

A **CLASS. Discuss. Are diabetes, high blood...**

- Ask students to read the directions. Confirm that students understand each question, including the meaning of the word *common*, which in this instance means *frequent*. Explain that even if they do not know the answers to these questions, they should try to contribute to the discussion.

B **GROUPS. Diabetes, high blood pressure,...**

- Ask students to read the directions and question. Say: *The question is meant to help us think about health in the U.S. and in the world. There is evidence that Americans have many risk factors, such as not getting enough exercise and eating too much junk food, but we need to be careful not to stereotype people in either the U.S. or other countries. Also, some countries are changing rapidly to include more fast food and less traditional food, so comparisons between countries can change over time.*

- Have the class brainstorm a list of risk factors that can apply all over the world (for example: not enough exercise, living in a polluted area, limited access to health care). Write the list on the board or a flipchart.

***Communication Skill:* Giving Advice**

- Direct students to the Communication Skill box.
- Ask a student to read the text.
- Reiterate the two forms *should* and *ought to*, and emphasize that when people offer advice, they need to use polite words like *maybe*.
- Note that giving advice—especially related to health—is important but it has to be done carefully. Say: *Why is it important to give advice tactfully, especially, in terms of health? What are some examples of delicate situations in which it is hard to give health-related advice?* Give some examples, if necessary. (For example, when someone is very ill but doesn't want to go to the hospital; when someone doesn't want to give up something that is making him or her sick)

Communicative Practice 15 minutes

4 **MAKE IT PERSONAL**

GROUPS. Discuss. Do you know...

- Ask students to read the directions and questions.
- Set up groups.
- Have students review the Communication Skill box before they begin to discuss how to offer advice to someone with diabetes.
- When they finish this part of the exercise, say: *Now discuss how to offer advice to someone who has high blood pressure and high cholesterol.*
- When each group finishes, have them share examples of tactful health advice.
- *Optional:* Have volunteers improvise a role play in front of the class in which one student offers another health advice about diabetes, high blood pressure, or high cholesterol.

Extra Practice

Interactive Practice

CD2 T14

B 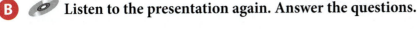 Listen to the presentation again. Answer the questions.

1. What is glucose?
2. What does insulin do with glucose?
3. What two problems can occur if there is too much glucose in the blood?
4. What does family history have to do with diabetes?
5. How can a poor diet lead to diabetes?
6. What can regular exercise and a good diet do for people who have or might get diabetes?
7. Why should people with high blood pressure consume less alcohol and salt?

3 PRACTICE

A CLASS. Discuss. Are diabetes, high blood pressure, and high cholesterol common in your home country? Are other medical problems more common there? What do you know about risk factors and treatment for the problems?

B GROUPS. Diabetes, high blood pressure, and high cholesterol are common in the U.S. In Asia and other parts of the world, these problems have been less common but are now occurring more and more often. Discuss. Why do you think this is true?

Communication Skill: Giving Advice

To give someone advice orally, use *should* or *ought to* followed by the base form of a verb. Start your sentences with polite words and phrases, such as *I think, Maybe,* or *Perhaps.*

> **I think** you **should check** with your doctor before starting an exercise program.
>
> **Maybe** you **ought to go** to a nutritionist to discuss a balanced diet.

---

4 MAKE IT PERSONAL

GROUPS. Discuss. Do you know anyone who has diabetes? If so, how is the person being treated? Is he or she being careful about diet and exercise? If not, what advice would you give him or her? Discuss high blood pressure and high cholesterol in the same way.

Writing

1 BEFORE YOU WRITE

A You are going to write a persuasive essay, or argument, for or against smoking bans in public places. Read about persuasive essays. Then read the writing tip.

> **FYI**   ABOUT PERSUASIVE ESSAYS
>
> Like an opinion piece, a persuasive essay tries to get readers to agree with your point of view, or argument. A good persuasive essay begins with a paragraph that introduces the topic. The opening paragraph presents the argument. The rest of the essay supports the argument with solid reasons, details, and examples.
>
> **Writing Tip: Introductory paragraphs**
>
> An introductory paragraph should attract the reader's attention, give general background information on the topic, and present the main idea of the essay. The main idea should narrow the topic to a specific point or argument that will be supported by solid evidence in the rest of the essay.

B Brainstorm about the writing topic.

STEP 1. Ask yourself these questions.

1. Should the government be allowed to ban smoking in public places, such as restaurants, bars, hotels, banks, bowling alleys, parks, and beaches?

2. Do people have a right to smoke in some or all of these places?

Write down all of your thoughts about this topic—including arguments for and against smoking bans.

STEP 2. PAIRS. Discuss your opinions about smoking bans. Add your partner's arguments and your own to your notes.

C Read the writing model of a persuasive essay on page 208. It is about a related subject. What do you think of Zlatan's argument?

2 ANALYZE THE WRITING MODEL

PAIRS. Discuss the questions.

1. What argument does Zlatan present in his opening paragraph?

2. What reasons does he use to support his argument?

3. What statistic does Zlatan provide to back up his argument?

Getting Started   5 minutes

- Say: *We have been talking about health. We have practiced vocabulary and grammatical structures to discuss health problems and recognize the cause and effect of various health conditions. Today we are going to apply all of this knowledge as we write about whether to prohibit smoking in public places.*

Presentation   5 minutes

 1   BEFORE YOU WRITE

A You are going to write...

- Read the directions. Ask: *What does the word* persuasive *mean?* (able to convince other people to believe or do something) Elicit that a persuasive essay is a piece of writing that argues for or against something.
- Say: *Today, we're going to write a persuasive essay.* Ask students to read the FYI note and Writing Tip. Ask if there are any questions.
- Ask: *What does the opening paragraph of a persuasive essay do?* (It introduces the topic and presents the main idea—in this case, an argument.)

Language Note

Because students will be writing about causes and effects—such as the health effects of smoking or the economic effects of banning it in public places—encourage them to review the Lesson 7 Reading Skill box on page 118 about words that signal these concepts, including *so, because, because of, therefore, lead to, result,* and *as a result.*

Controlled Practice   15 minutes

B Brainstorm about the writing topic.

STEP 1. Ask yourself these questions.

- Say: *Today you are going to write about whether the government should or shouldn't ban smoking in public places. What does* ban *mean?* (prohibit, or officially not allow you to do something)
- Ask students to read the directions.

- Say: *Now you will freewrite about the question in Step 1. Write down everything you can think of related to the question. Don't worry about grammar or organization right now; just get as many ideas and details on paper as you can.*
- Have students complete the exercise. Check their work.

STEP 2. PAIRS. Discuss your opinions...

- Say: *Now you'll discuss your opinions about smoking bans with a partner. Hearing your partner's arguments for or against smoking may give you more ideas for things to include in your essay, so add your partner's points to your own freewrites. For instance, if your partner has ideas that you don't agree with, include them in your essay and explain why you don't agree with them.*
- Have students form pairs, read the directions, and complete the exercise.
- Offer prompts to help students add supporting examples and details. (For example, *What about discussing the economic effects of your argument?*)

C Read the writing model of...

- Tell students that they will now read a persuasive essay that a student wrote about whether companies should hire smokers.
- Ask students to read the directions. Then ask them to turn to page 208 and read the essay.
- Ask: *What do you think of the writer's argument?*
Answers will vary, but some students may say that Zlatan's argument violates smokers' civil rights.

2   ANALYZE THE WRITING MODEL

PAIRS. Discuss the questions.

- Say: *Now read the essay a second time, and discuss the questions.* Explain that question 3 asks for a statistic; explain as needed that a statistic is a mathematical figure, or percentage, of how often something occurs.
- Have students form pairs and complete the exercise.
Answers: 1. Companies shouldn't hire smokers.
2. Smokers hurt the company and other employees.
3. Health care costs are 40 percent higher for smokers than for nonsmokers.

Argue for or against smoking bans

Communicative Practice   35 minutes

3   THINK ON PAPER

A **Before Zlatan wrote...**

- Read the directions. Ask students to look at Zlatan's organizational chart.
- Ask the question in the directions. Note as needed that the author presented a main argument and then provided two reasons, with details and examples, to support that argument.

B **Look at the notes you made...**

- Say: *Now you are going to use the notes that you made in Exercise 1B to make a chart that organizes your argument for or against a smoking ban in public places.*
- *Optional:* On the board, write a blank version of the chart on page 123 for students to use.
- Have students complete the exercise. Walk around and check students' work, offering prompts as needed. (For example: *Can you give me an example of a disease caused by smoking?*)

Teaching Tip

- If students are on computers, have them create a two-column table to organize their argument.
- *Optional:* Show them how to use the Split Cells table function to make the first row span two columns.
- Remind them to copy and paste their notes from Exercise 1B.

4   WRITE

Write a persuasive essay...

- Read the directions, emphasizing that students must clearly state their argument in the introductory paragraph. Then have students write the first draft of a persuasive essay.
- Remind students that each supporting paragraph should be introduced by a topic sentence, include related details or examples, and finish with a concluding sentence.

5   CHECK YOUR WRITING

A **STEP 1. Revise your work.**

- Say: *Read over your persuasive essay a first time and answer the questions in Step 1. If any answers are* no, *revise your work.*
- *Optional:* Have students form pairs, exchange essays, and give each other feedback, noting whether the introductory paragraph is clear and engaging and whether the argument is supported by solid reasons, details, and examples.

B **STEP 2. Edit and proofread.**

- Say: *Read over your essay a second time and edit and proofread your work.* Direct students to check their papers for grammar, spelling, punctuation, and typos.
- As students edit and proofread, walk around and check and/or correct their work, answering questions as needed.
- *Optional:* Have students complete a "clean" second draft of their essay at home, incorporating revisions and corrections from the revision and editing steps.

Teaching Tip

You may want to collect student papers and provide feedback. Use the scoring rubric for writing on page Txv to evaluate vocabulary, grammar, mechanics, and how well students complete the task. You may want to review the completed rubric with students.

MULTILEVEL INSTRUCTION for 5A and 5B

Above-level Have students who finish writing and self-editing read and edit a peer's paper using the criteria in Exercises 5A and 5B. Then have them discuss their feedback with the writer.

Pre-level Have students complete a checklist with the revising and editing criteria from Exercises 5A and 5B, checking off a box for each question and making the necessary changes.

Extra Practice

Interactive Practice

page 80

3 THINK ON PAPER

A Before Zlatan wrote his persuasive essay, he used a chart to brainstorm and organize his argument. Do you think that he organized his argument in a logical way?

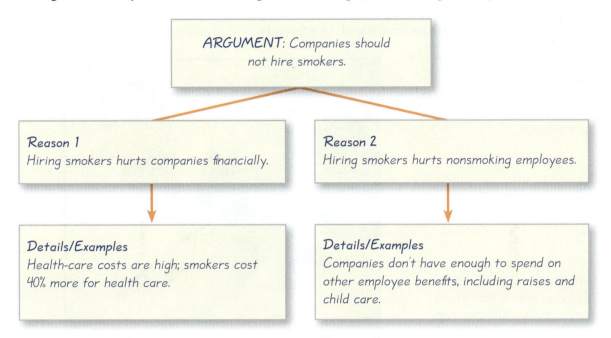

ARGUMENT: Companies should not hire smokers.

Reason 1
Hiring smokers hurts companies financially.

Reason 2
Hiring smokers hurts nonsmoking employees.

Details/Examples
Health-care costs are high; smokers cost 40% more for health care.

Details/Examples
Companies don't have enough to spend on other employee benefits, including raises and child care.

B Look at the notes you made about smoking bans in Exercise 1B. Then use a chart like Zlatan's to organize your argument for or against smoking bans.

4 WRITE

Write a persuasive essay about whether the government should or should not have the right to ban smoking in public places. Be sure to use your opening paragraph to state your argument.

5 CHECK YOUR WRITING

A STEP 1. Revise your work.

1. Have you presented your topic and argument in the introductory paragraph?
2. Does your introduction attract, or "grab," the reader's attention?
3. Do you give solid reasons, details, and examples to back up your argument?

B STEP 2. Edit and proofread.

1. Have you checked your spelling, grammar, and punctuation?
2. Have you proofread for typing errors?

1 REVIEW   For your grammar review, go to page 229.

2 ACT IT OUT   What do you say?

GROUPS. You are discussing health with two friends.

Student A: Review Lesson 1. Give your friends advice about how to prepare for a doctor's appointment.

Student B: Review Lesson 3. Give your friends at least five tips for taking medication properly.

Student C: Review Lesson 7. Tell your friends why health screenings for diabetes, high blood pressure, and high cholesterol are important.

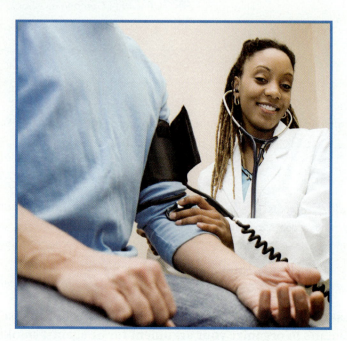

3 READ AND REACT   Problem-solving

STEP 1. Read about Zofia.

Zofia is worried about her ten-year-old son, Oskar, because he is overweight for his age and diabetes runs in the family. Oskar enjoys eating fried foods and drinking soda. He is shy and avoids sports. Zofia wants to do all she can to help her son control his diabetes, but it's hard to change his habits.

STEP 2. GROUPS. What is Zofia's problem? What can she do?

4 CONNECT   For your Study Skills Activity, go to page 217.

Which goals can you check off? Go back to page 105.

 Go to the CD-ROM for more practice.

Show what you know!

1 REVIEW

For your grammar review, go to page 229.

- Say: *Today we're going to review the skills that we have practiced in this unit and apply them to a problem. What are some of the skills we have practiced?* Elicit answers and write them on the board. (For example: describing medical problems, identifying how to take medication properly, understanding first aid, asking and answering questions related to health and medicine, discussing the benefits of preventive health screenings, and so on.)

- Ask students to complete the grammar review exercise on page 229.

2 ACT IT OUT

GROUPS. You are discussing health...

- Ask students to read the directions. Explain that they will work in groups of three, helping each other review the skills they practiced in this unit.

- Say: *Student A will look back at Lesson 1 and give advice about how to prepare for a doctor's appointment. Student B will review Lesson 3 and explain at least five tips for taking medication properly. Student C will review Lesson 7 and describe why health screenings for diabetes, high blood pressure, and high cholesterol are important.*

- Have students complete the exercise.

3 READ AND REACT

STEP 1. Read about Zofia.

- Say: *Now we're going to apply our knowledge from this unit to a problem involving a character, Zofia. Let's read about Zofia.*

- Have students read the story.

- Clarify unfamiliar vocabulary as needed. (Examples: *overweight*—when one's body weight exceeds the recommended amount; *runs in the family*—when a condition or genetic trait is shared by many family members, often over several generations)

STEP 2. GROUPS. What is Zofia's problem?

- Ask students to form small groups.

- Say: *In your group, you will discuss what Zofia's problem is and what she can do about it.*

- Remind students that the Lesson 7 article discusses the causes and effects of diabetes, and Lesson 8 presents risk factors for diabetes and suggestions for reducing them. Tell students that they may want to refer to these lessons as they discuss possible solutions for Zofia and her son.

- Give each group a sheet of flipchart paper and markers, or ask them to make notes on a sheet of paper. Tell them that they will write a brief description of Zofia's problem and a list of at least three possible solutions.

- Ask groups to choose a representative to present the group's ideas to the class.

- Elicit from students language to use for making suggestions. (*First, she should . . . She could also . . .*)

- Have students discuss the questions.

- Ask a representative from each group to present the group's ideas. After each presentation, encourage feedback.

Possible answers: *Problem:* Zofia's son has risk factors for diabetes. *Solution:* She could encourage him to do some kind of noncompetitive sport, such as running and help him find healthy substitutes for the junk food he eats.

4 CONNECT

Turn to page 217 for the Study Skills activity. See page Txii for general teaching notes for Study Skills activities.

Progress Check

Which goals can you check off? Go back to page 105.

Ask students to turn to page 105 and check off any remaining goals they have reached. Call on them to say which goals they will practice outside of class.

CD-ROM Practice

 Go to the CD-ROM for more practice.

If your students need more practice with the vocabulary, grammar, and competencies in Unit 6, encourage them to review the activities on the CD-ROM.

7 Citizenship

Unit Overview

Goals

- See the list of goals on the facing page.

Grammar

- Past perfect
- Passive with *get*

Listening and Speaking

- Discuss how a bill becomes a law
- Discuss becoming a U.S. citizen
- *Communication Skill:* Exchanging Opinions

Reading

- Read a text about the beginnings of the U.S.
- Read an article about the U.S. Constitution
- Read an article about the Bill of Rights
- *Reading Skill:* Using a T-chart to Take Notes
- Read an article about the benefits of citizenship
- *Reading Skill:* Using Text Structure and Formatting

Writing

- Write a formal e-mail to an elected official
- *Writing Tip:* Using a problem/solution structure

Life Skills

- Interpret historical maps of the U.S.

Preview

- Welcome students and have them look at page 125.
- Say: *Look at the picture. Where are the people? What's happening?* (Possible answers: The people are at a ceremony to become U.S. citizens. The woman is promising to obey the laws of the U.S.)
- Ask: *How many of you are U.S. citizens?* Have students raise their hands.
- Say: *If you were not born in this country, you can become a naturalized citizen by living in the U.S. for a certain amount of time and passing a citizenship exam, in addition to fulfilling some other requirements. Are any of you naturalized U.S. citizens?* Have students raise their hands.
- Say: *In the U.S., a special ceremony is held when people become citizens. We say that they are* sworn in; *they raise their right hand and swear to obey the laws of the U.S. Constitution.*
- Say: *In this unit, you'll learn requirements and procedures for becoming a U.S. citizen. You'll learn some U.S. history and how the U.S. government works. You'll also talk about how a bill becomes a law.*

Unit Goals

- Ask students to read the Unit Goals.
- Explain unfamiliar vocabulary as needed. Clarify that a *bill* can mean different things but here it means a law that has been proposed and must be approved by a vote of the U.S. Congress.
- Tell students to check the goal that is the most important to them.
- Take a poll by reading the goals aloud, with students raising their hand for the goal they checked. Write the goal on the board that the most students checked.
- Say: *As we complete this unit, we will look back at this page and reread the goals. We will check each goal as we complete it.*

Citizenship

Preview

What are the people doing? Do ceremonies like this happen in your home country?

UNIT GOALS

- ☐ Discuss the early history of the U.S.

- ☐ Show how the U.S. government works

- ☐ Recognize individual rights in the Constitution

- ☐ Discuss how a bill becomes a law

- ☐ Discuss becoming a U.S. citizen

Reading

1   BEFORE YOU READ

PAIRS. Discuss. What do you already know about these people and events?

> Boston Tea Party   George Washington   Pilgrims   Revolutionary War

2   READ

CD2 T15

Listen to and read the text about the thirteen colonies that became the United States. Were your ideas in Exercise 1 correct?

THE BEGINNINGS OF THE UNITED STATES

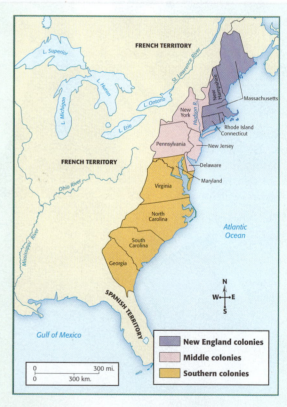

In the early 1600s, settlers began arriving in North America from Great Britain. The London Company **founded** the first **permanent** English **colony** at Jamestown, Virginia, in 1607. The colonists at Jamestown grew tobacco to be sold in Europe. The second permanent English colony was founded by the Pilgrims, who left Britain because they were not allowed to practice their religion there. They arrived in 1620 and founded a colony in Plymouth, Massachusetts.

Other colonies were soon **established** along the eastern coast of North America. By 1750, more than 1 million settlers had made the colonies their new homes. There were thirteen colonies, all ruled by the British government: Connecticut, Delaware, Georgia, Maryland, Massachusetts, New Hampshire, New Jersey, New York, North Carolina, Pennsylvania, Rhode Island, South Carolina, and Virginia.

In Britain, voters elected people to **represent** them in the government. But the British government had not given settlers in the thirteen colonies the right to vote. The colonists had to pay taxes to the British government, but since they had no representation, they felt they were being taxed unfairly. In addition, the colonists wanted to trade with other countries. The British government allowed them to trade only with Britain.

In 1773, Britain placed a very high tax on tea coming into the colonies. In response, the colonists **protested**. They disguised themselves as Native Americans, boarded a ship that was loaded with tea from Britain—and threw the tea into the water. The event became known as the Boston Tea Party.

Learn about the beginnings of the U.S.

Getting Started   10 minutes

- Say: *In this unit, we will be listening, speaking, reading, and writing about American history and government. In the first several lessons, we will be talking about early history, including the early settlers and the War for Independence from Britain, also known as the Revolutionary War. We will also talk about the Constitution, the Bill of Rights, and the structure of the government. Toward the end of the unit, we will focus on how people become U.S. citizens. Right now, let's start by learning about the beginnings of this country.*
- Ask students if any of them have studied U.S. history in their home countries.

1   BEFORE YOU READ

PAIRS. Discuss. What do you already know...

- Ask students to read the directions.
- Set up pairs. Say: *Share what you already know about these people and events.* Read the word box aloud.
- Ask each pair to share what they talked about. Write each new comment on the board, a transparency, or a flipchart. Every time a pair mentions information already on the list, put a checkmark next to the word or phrase.
- Ask students to share other information they know about the beginnings of the U.S. (such as that the French, Dutch, and Spanish were early explorers and settlers in North America). Write down this information.
- Give students time to write notes in their notebooks and new vocabulary in their vocabulary logs.
- Say: *Now we will listen and read a short article about the beginnings of the U.S.*

Presentation   15 minutes

2   READ

 Listen to and read the text about...

- Ask students to read the directions.
- Say: *This article gives a brief overview of some important events and people that helped develop the U.S.*

- Point out that the words and phrases in boldface (*founded, permanent, colony, established, represent, protested, goods, unjust*) appear in the glossary on page 245. Encourage students to read the entire article first, before going to the glossary.
- Play CD 2, Track 15, as students listen and read.
- After students listen and read, ask if they have any other questions about the content, vocabulary, or pronunciation; answer questions.

Expansion: Vocabulary Practice for 2

- Divide the class into small groups.
- Ask students to make a list of the boldfaced words in the reading and to discuss the meaning of each. Encourage students to guess the meaning if they are not sure. Tell students that they have only a few minutes for this.
- Tell students to look for the words in the glossary and to compare the definitions there with what they discussed.
- Assign one or two words to each group and ask them to write one (or two) sentence(s) with their assigned word(s) or phrase(s).
- Ask groups to read their sentences to the class.
- After each group reads a sentence, ask if anyone has any questions about the word.

Expansion: Reading Practice for 2

- Write or adapt paragraphs on other aspects of early U.S. history, such as Native Americans before the Europeans, French (or Dutch or Spanish) settlers, Roger Williams, William Penn, or women's lives in the New England, Middle, and Southern colonies. There is a wealth of information at the U.S. government's official web portal: www.usa.gov/.
- Write or adapt the paragraphs for different reading levels—from slightly below level to advanced—but each with the same number of details.
- Assign the paragraphs to like-ability groups. Every person in a group reads the same paragraph.
- Tell the groups to read and talk about the paragraphs. Say: *I'll be walking around to answer any questions you have about historical events, vocabulary, or pronunciation.*
- Allow students as long as it takes for each of the groups to read and understand their paragraphs.
- Walk around as groups share the information; assist as needed.

Controlled Practice   20 minutes

3 CHECK YOUR UNDERSTANDING

A GROUPS. Write the answers...

- Ask students to read the directions.
- Set up groups of five: have students count off 1-2-3-4-5. Say: *Make your own groups—each group should have a number 1, 2,* etc. *Person 1, you read the first question and direct the conversation on it. Person 2, you read the second question, and so on. Once you all agree on the answer to a question, write the short answer next to the question in the book* (or in notebooks, if students don't own their own books). *Do you have any questions?* Answer any questions.
- Walk around as groups form and students work on the answers; assist as needed.
- Discuss as a whole class only any answers that groups were not sure about.

Answers: 1. Plymouth was founded primarily for religious reasons and Jamestown primarily for economic reasons. 2. Colonies were not represented in the government (Parliament), and so they thought they were being taxed unfairly. They were only allowed to trade with Britain. 3. the Boston Tea Party; 4. the Declaration of Independence; 5. the Constitution, which led to one national government

Teaching Tip

- Setting up groups and pairs can—at least initially—make some students nervous. However, finding their own groups and pairs gives students practice negotiating and problem solving in English. Watch closely and be ready to help organize if needed.

B Complete the timeline...

- Ask students to read the directions.
- Confirm that students understand what a timeline is. Say: *Putting information in a time sequence is a useful strategy for remembering details and also for helping you get an idea of the big picture.*
- Let students work in their same groups or alone, as they choose.
- Draw a long horizontal line on the board; at one end write *1607* and at the far end *1787*. Then write the other dates in order.

- Ask students to give the answers for each date and write short answers.
- Call on students and complete the timeline on the board. Write their answers. Ask students if they have other questions or comments about the article.

4 WORD WORK

GROUPS. Choose three words...

- Set up groups.
- Ask students to read the directions.
- Confirm that students understand that they discuss first, then write in vocabulary logs.
- Walk around; intervene only if you hear a question that students can't answer in the group.
- Say: *Remember when you write in your vocabulary logs, you can always write more than three words or phrases. You can also use the vocabulary log for words you read or hear outside of class.*

Communicative Practice   15 minutes

5 MAKE IT PERSONAL

GROUPS. Discuss. How is the early history...

- Ask students to read the question.
- Tell students to remain in the same groups.
- Say: *There are probably similarities and differences between the early histories of your home countries and the U.S. Take a few minutes and share your thoughts.*
- Write a T-chart on the board, an overhead, or a flipchart; on one side write *similarities* and on the other side write *differences*. Ask groups to share the similarities and differences they came up with.

At a meeting in Philadelphia in 1774, the colonists decided to stop buying all British **goods**. The British had already lost a lot of money because the colonists refused to buy tea. The colonists also wrote to the king of England to complain about the **unjust** British laws. But the British response was not favorable, and the colonists prepared for war. The Revolutionary War began in 1775, with General George Washington leading the Continental Army.

On July 4, 1776, representatives of the thirteen colonies adopted the Declaration of Independence. The thirteen colonies had become the thirteen American states. The war lasted until 1783, when Great Britain recognized the thirteen colonies as free and independent states. In 1787, representatives from the thirteen states met in Philadelphia and wrote the Constitution, establishing one national government with representation from all states.

3 CHECK YOUR UNDERSTANDING

A GROUPS. **Write the answers to the questions.**

1. How did the reasons for establishing the Plymouth and Jamestown colonies differ?
2. What complaints did the colonists have against the English government?
3. What event was meant to protest a tax on tea?
4. What document was written soon after the Revolutionary War began?
5. What document was written after the war ended? What did it lead to?

B **Complete the timeline with the events from the article.** Answers will vary but should include:

1. 1607 _Jamestown colony founded_
2. 1620 _Pilgrims arrive in Plymouth_
3. 1750 _more than 1 million settlers in colonies_
4. 1773 _Britain places high tax on tea_
5. 1774 _colonists decide to stop buying British goods_
6. 1775 _Revolutionary War begins_
7. 1776 _Declaration of Independence is adopted_
8. 1783 _Great Britain recognizes 13 colonies as free states_
9. 1787 _Constitution is written_

4 WORD WORK

GROUPS. **Choose three words or phrases in the text that you would like to remember. Discuss the words and their meanings. Then record the words and information about them in your vocabulary log.**

5 MAKE IT PERSONAL

GROUPS. **Discuss. How is the early history of the U.S. similar to or different from the history of your home country?**

Grammar

The Past Perfect

By 1750, more than 1 million settlers **had made** the colonies their new homes.

The British **had already lost** a lot of money.

The thirteen colonies **had become** the thirteen American states.

By the time the Pilgrims arrived, immigrants to Jamestown **had already established** a successful colony.

When Jamestown was established, the Pilgrims **had not yet come** to North America.

Representatives from the thirteen colonies **had just adopted** the Declaration of Independence **when copies of the document were printed**.

Grammar Watch

Use the past perfect:
- To indicate that something happened before a specific time, event, or action in the past
- With *already, yet,* and *just* to emphasize which event came first
- With *by* + a certain time to indicate the order in which two events happened
- With past time clauses beginning with *by the time, before,* and *when*

1 PRACTICE

Read the sentences. Underline the first event and circle the second event.

1. By the time the first European settlers arrived on the East Coast, the Spanish had already explored the area.

2. Because the British had imposed a heavy tax on tea, the colonists threw a shipload of British tea into Boston Harbor.

3. When representatives from the colonies met to write the Constitution, the Declaration of Independence had already been written.

4. Prior to the Revolutionary War, each of the thirteen colonies had had an independent government. In 1787, the Constitution outlined one common federal government but left some power to individual states.

5. Before he became president of the United States, George Washington had commanded the Continental Army.

Lesson 2 Discuss the early history of the U.S.

Getting Started 5 minutes

- Say: *In the last lesson, we talked about the early history of the U.S. What were some of the early U.S. colonies, and why were they founded?* (Jamestown, founded to grow tobacco; Plymouth, founded to practice religion that was outlawed in Britain) Ask: *Why did the U.S. colonies want independence from Britain?* Elicit answers from students, offering prompts as needed (*Did they pay taxes to the British government? Were they allowed to vote?*).
- Say: *Today we're going to talk more about the beginnings of the U.S. To do so, we'll practice the grammatical structure of the past perfect.*

Presentation 15 minutes

The Past Perfect

- Say: *Use the past perfect to talk about something that happened, or was true, before another action or specific time in the past.*
- Ask students to read the Grammar Watch. Copy the first sentence from the grammar chart onto the board.
- Ask: *How is the past perfect formed?* (had + past participle) Write this on the board.
- Point to the grammar chart and read the first sentence. Ask: *What specific time is given in this sentence?* (1750) Ask: *What happened before 1750?* (More than 1 million settlers had made the colonies their new homes.) Circle *had made* on the board.
- Say: *Use the past perfect in this sentence to show that before 1750, another action had occurred—the settlers had made the colonies their new homes.*
- Read the second Grammar Watch item aloud. Ask students to read the second and third sentences from the grammar chart. Ask: *What other things had happened by 1750?* (The British had already lost a lot of money. The thirteen colonies had become the thirteen American states.)
- Read the third Grammar Watch item aloud. Then read the fourth grammar chart sentence aloud. Ask: *What two actions happened in this sentence?* Write the following on the board:

  Pilgrims arrive

  Immigrants to Jamestown establish successful colony

- Ask: *Which action happened first?* (Immigrants to Jamestown establish a successful colony.) Write *1* next to this sentence on the board. Ask: *What happened next?* (The Pilgrims arrived.) Write a *2* next to the sentence on the board.
- Say: *Use the past perfect for the action that happened first and the simple past for the action that happened next.* Change the sentences on the board as follows:

  *2—Pilgrims arrive**d***

  *1—Immigrants to Jamestown **had already** establis**h**ed successful colony*

- Write the fifth and sixth sentences from the grammar chart on the board. Ask students which event happened first in each sentence. Number the events.

Controlled Practice 15 minutes

 PRACTICE

Read the sentences. Underline...

- Say: *Let's look at some more examples of the past perfect.* Ask students to read the directions. Write the first item on the board. Ask: *What grammatical structure is used with the first event?* (the past perfect) *The second event?* (the simple past)
- Have students complete the exercise. Walk around and check students' work.
- Call on students to say the answers. For item 4, clarify that *had had* is the past perfect form of *have*; it describes that the colonies had separate governments for each colony before the Constitution created one federal government.

MULTILEVEL INSTRUCTION for 1

Pre-level Sit with students in a group and offer prompts to help them get started with the exercise. (For example, *Let's look for the past perfect. Do you see a past participle and* had?)

Above-level After they finish the exercise, have students reread the article on page 126 and underline phrases in the past perfect.

Controlled Practice   10 minutes

2   PRACTICE

> **Language Note**
>
> *Already*, *yet*, and *just* are often used with the past or present perfect. *Already* emphasizes that something has been completed. *Yet* draws attention to the fact that something is expected to happen but has not, prior to this time. *Just* shows that something happened very recently.

GROUPS. Read the timeline about...

- Read the directions aloud.
- Have groups complete the exercise.
- Walk around and help students as they work, referring them to the lists of irregular past participles as needed (on page 225).
- If necessary, point out that in most cases in this exercise, the verb students need to use in the answer is in the timeline (*begins → had just begun*) but that in item 6 they will need to use a different verb (*publishes → had not heard about*)
- Call on students to read sentences and say answers.

▬ MULTILEVEL INSTRUCTION for 2

Pre-level Sit with students in a group and help them with the exercise. Ask them to find the event that each item mentions in the timeline and circle it. Then have them consider whether the event took place before or after the time mentioned in the item.

Above-level After they finish the exercise, have students reread the article on page 126. Have students work in pairs. Ask them to look at the past perfect phrases, underline them if they are not underlined already, and identify the specific time, event, or action that happened first.

Communicative Practice   15 minutes

● Show what you know!

STEP 1. PAIRS. Reread "The Beginnings...

- Ask students to read the directions, form pairs, and complete the exercise.

STEP 2. GROUPS. Discuss. What events...

- Have students read the directions and form groups.
- Say: *Talk about events that had already happened before Paul Revere made his ride in 1775. Use the past perfect and* already *or* just. Emphasize that students should not write anything; they should practice speaking with the past perfect.
- Write a sample prompt on the board:

  By the time Paul Revere made his famous ride, _____ had already _____.

- Have groups complete the exercise.
- Have groups share with the whole class examples of events that had already happened by the time of Revere's ride.

> **Community Building**
>
> For more practice with the past perfect, have students create a personal time line—that is, a list of milestones in their life (for example, when they finished school, when they learned to drive, when they came to the U.S., when they got married, when they got their first job). Have them exchange timelines with a partner. The partner should present the student to the class and say a few sentences in the past perfect about him or her. Example:
>
> *By 2002, Iliana had finished high school. By 2003, she had gotten her first job. . . .*

Progress Check

Can you . . . discuss the early history of the U.S.?

- Say: *We have practiced discussing the early history of the U.S. Can you do this? If so, check the box.*

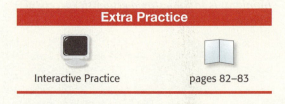

Extra Practice	
Interactive Practice	pages 82–83

GROUPS. Read the timeline about Paul Revere, a hero of the American Revolution. Then complete the sentences below. Use the past perfect, with *already, yet,* or *just* if necessary, to show the order of events.

Answers will vary but could include:

1734 born in Boston, Massachusetts

1754 father dies, begins to work in father's silver shop

1760s becomes famous silversmith, supports colonists seeking independence

1770 after British kill five colonists during the Boston Massacre, makes political engraving, or picture, of the scene

1773 plays active role in revolutionary group, the Sons of Liberty

1775 on April 18, rides from Boston to Lexington to warn patriots that the British are marching toward Lexington; next day, first battles of Revolutionary War begin

1788 opens iron and brass foundry in Boston after war ends

1801 opens first copper mill in North America

1818 dies at age of 83, his ride for freedom mostly forgotten

1861 becomes American hero when Henry Wadsworth Longfellow publishes his famous poem "Paul Revere's Ride"

Paul Revere's engraving of the Boston Massacre

1. It was 1755. Paul Revere <u>had just begun</u> to work as a silversmith in his father's shop.

2. By the end of the 1760s, Revere <u>had already become</u> a famous silversmith and a political activist.

3. Revere <u>had already played</u> an active role in the Sons of Liberty before the British marched toward Lexington in 1775.

4. The Revolutionary War <u>had not yet begun</u> when Revere rode from Boston to Lexington to warn patriots that the British were marching toward Lexington.

5. By 1802, Revere <u>had just opened</u> the first copper mill in North America.

6. Most Americans <u>had not yet heard</u> about Revere when Longfellow's famous poem was published in 1861.

Show what you know! Discuss the early history of the U.S.

STEP 1. PAIRS. Reread "The Beginnings of the United States" on pages 126–127 and the timeline about Paul Revere. List three or four important events that occurred before 1775.

STEP 2. GROUPS. Discuss. What events had already happened in the thirteen colonies before Paul Revere made his famous ride?

Can you... discuss the early history of the U.S.? ☐

Reading

1 BEFORE YOU READ

CLASS. The Declaration of Independence says that "all men are created equal" and that all people are entitled to "life, liberty, and the pursuit of happiness." Discuss. What do you think these ideas mean?

2 READ

CD2 T16

Listen to and read the article about the organization of the U.S. government. What does the Constitution describe?

The U.S. Constitution

When the Revolutionary War ended, the new nation needed to establish a government. This became the task of the Founding Fathers—the men who had been responsible for governing the colonies and winning the war. Using the ideas from the Declaration of Independence, in 1787 in Philadelphia they drafted the U.S. Constitution, which formed the basis of the U.S. government.

The Constitution describes the organization of the **federal** government into three **branches**: the legislative, the executive, and the judicial branches:

- The **legislative branch** is the Congress, which is made up of the Senate and the House of Representatives. The legislative branch makes the laws. Each state has two senators. The number of representatives from each state depends on the size of the state's population. The bigger the state's **population**, the more representatives it has.
- The **executive branch** is led by the president. The president applies and enforces the laws. The president is also in charge of the military during wartime and controls the country's **foreign policy**. In addition to the president, the executive branch includes the vice president and the cabinet. The cabinet is made up of advisers to the president, such as the secretary of state, the secretary of the treasury, and the secretary of defense.
- The **judicial branch** is headed by the Supreme Court. The judicial branch interprets the laws and makes sure that all laws that Congress passes follow the **principles** of the Constitution. Other courts—federal, state, and local—are also part of the judicial branch.

The Founding Fathers wanted to ensure that no single branch of government would have too much power, so the U.S. Constitution describes a system of "checks and balances." Each branch "checks," or "balances," the others. This way, no single branch can become too powerful.

Getting Started   10 minutes

- Say: *In the first two lessons, we studied the early history of the U.S. In this lesson, we are going to talk about one of the most famous documents in the world: the Declaration of Independence. Then we will listen to, read, and talk about another of the world's most famous documents: the U.S. Constitution.*

- Ask students to discuss what they know about the Declaration of Independence and the Constitution.

1 BEFORE YOU READ

CLASS. The Declaration of Independence...

- Have students read the directions.

- Ask students what they think the phrase "all men are created equal" means. Ask questions as needed to start the discussion. (For example: *What does equality mean when we are talking about people? Does this mean that we are all the same? Why do you think the statement says "men," not "men and women?"*)

- Ask: *Do you agree with the idea that all people are "created equal"?* Remind students to explain their opinions.

- Confirm that students understand what *entitled* means. (have the right to have or do something)

- Ask students to give their ideas about what the phrase "life, liberty, and the pursuit of happiness" means. Let students continue the discussion as long as they are engaged.

- Write any new vocabulary words that come up on the board and explain them.

- Say: *Now we will listen to and read a short article about the organization of the U.S. government, which is based on the Constitution.*

Presentation   15 minutes

2 READ

 Listen to and read the article...

- Ask students to read the directions.

- Say: *This short article explains one of the fundamental ideas—the separation of powers—which organizes the federal government. The Constitution is the oldest federal constitution still in existence.*

- Point out that the words and phrases in boldface are in the glossary on page 245. Encourage students to read the entire article first, before going to the glossary.

- Play CD 2, Track 16, as students listen and read.

- After students listen and read, ask if they have any other questions about the content, vocabulary, or pronunciation; answer questions.

> **Teaching Tip**
> - You may want to share and discuss with students a facsimile and transcript of the U.S. Constitution. The Constitution and information about it is available at www.archives.gov under "American Historical Documents."
> - Read the Preamble aloud, and help students understand its meaning. Explain difficult terms, such as *tranquility* (peacefulness), *posterity* (those who will live when you are dead), and *ordain* (make the decision that something will happen).

Expansion: Vocabulary Practice for 2

- Divide the class into small groups.

- Ask students to make a list of the boldfaced words in the reading and to discuss the meaning of each. Encourage students to guess the meaning if they are not sure.

- Tell students to look for the words in the glossary and to compare the definitions there with what they discussed.

- Ask the students to circle any other difficult or new vocabulary words and to discuss their meanings as a group.

Expansion: Reading Practice for 2

- Set up groups.

- Have students read the article again.

- After they finish reading each paragraph, have students discuss the main idea or ideas of that paragraph as a group.

Controlled Practice   20 minutes

3 CHECK YOUR UNDERSTANDING

Ⓐ Write the missing parts...

- Ask students to read the directions.
- Confirm that students understand that a graphic organizer can be any kind of form that helps organize material visually (T-chart, pie chart, etc.).
- Allow enough time for the task.
- Go over the chart with the class; answer questions.

Ⓑ Reread the article. Write...

- Have students read the directions.
- Ask students to check their answers with other students.
- Ask for volunteers to read each question and answer. Tell students that there is more than one way to word the answers.

Answers: 1. the men who were responsible for governing the colonies and winning the war; 2. the Declaration of Independence (some students may also have learned about the Articles of Confederation; accept this as well); 3. makes the laws; 4. applies and enforces the laws; 5. interprets the laws and makes sure that all the laws follow the principles of the Constitution; 6. to make sure that no single branch could become too powerful

4 WORD WORK

GROUPS. Choose three words...

- Set up groups.
- Ask students to read the directions.
- Confirm that students understand that they discuss first, then write in vocabulary logs.
- Walk around; intervene only if you hear a question that students can't answer in the group.
- Say: *Remember when you write in your vocabulary logs, you can always write more than three words or phrases. You can also use the vocabulary logs for words you read or hear outside of class.*

Communicative Practice   15 minutes

Show what you know!

STEP 1. PAIRS. Use the graphic organizer...

- Set up informal pairs.
- Ask students to read the directions.
- Walk around and assist as needed.

STEP 2. GROUPS. The Founding Fathers wanted...

- Ask students to read the directions.
- Tell pairs to join with another pair to make a group.
- Say: *The three branches have different special powers. For example, Congress controls taxes and spending. Congress also has the power to declare war, not the president. The president controls the military but can't declare war. The judicial branch listens to law cases and makes sure that the laws follow the Constitution. But the judicial branch doesn't make the laws. What would happen if one branch had too much power?*
- Have one person in each group take notes.
- Discuss the question with the whole class. Call on the note-taker from each group to summarize the group's opinion.

Networking

- Invite a member of the League of Women Voters or another nonpartisan organization to give a short—but more in-depth—talk about the principles of the U.S. government in relation to the Constitution.
- Send topics or questions to the speaker in advance. For more in-depth directions on preparing for a guest speaker, see page T57.

Progress Check

Can you . . . show how the U.S. government works?

- Say: *We have talked about how the U.S. government works. Now look at the question at the bottom of the page. Can you show how the U.S. government works? If so, check the box.*

3 CHECK YOUR UNDERSTANDING

A Write the missing parts of government in the graphic organizer.

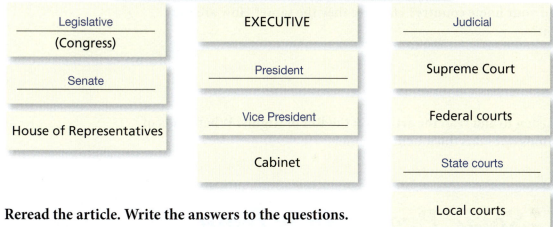

The Three Branches of the U.S. Government

Legislative (Congress)	EXECUTIVE	Judicial
Senate	President	Supreme Court
House of Representatives	Vice President	Federal courts
	Cabinet	State courts
		Local courts

B Reread the article. Write the answers to the questions.

1. Who were the Founding Fathers?
2. What earlier document did they use when they drafted the U.S. Constitution?
3. What is the job of the legislative branch?
4. What does the executive branch do with the laws?
5. What is the judicial branch's responsibility concerning laws?
6. Why did the Founding Fathers build "checks and balances" into the Constitution?

4 WORD WORK

GROUPS. Choose three words or phrases in the article that you would like to remember. Discuss the words and their meanings. Then record the words and information about them in your vocabulary log.

Show what you know! Show how the U.S. government works

STEP 1. PAIRS. Use the graphic organizer to explain how each branch of the government works. Also explain the meaning and importance of the phrase *checks and balances.*

STEP 2. GROUPS. The Founding Fathers wanted to be sure that no single branch of government would have too much power. What problems could occur if one branch had too much power?

Can you... show how the U.S. government works? ☐

Reading

1 BEFORE YOU READ

CLASS. Discuss. What do you know about human rights in the U.S. and your home country? How are they the same? How are they different?

2 READ

CD2 T17

Listen to and read the article on the Bill of Rights. What kinds of protections does this document provide?

Some Protections from the Bill of Rights

The first ten amendments to the Constitution, added in 1791, are called the Bill of Rights. The Bill of Rights guarantees the rights of U.S. citizens, non-citizen residents, and visitors.

The First Amendment guarantees the rights to freedom of religion, freedom of speech, freedom of the press, freedom to peacefully **assemble** (in order to discuss or protest something), and freedom to **petition** the government (to formally ask for a change). The Second Amendment guarantees the right of people to **bear arms**, or carry guns.

The Third and Fourth Amendments limit physical **intrusion** by the government. The Fourth Amendment states that the police must have a **warrant** before they can enter a person's home or take a person's property.

Several amendments protect the rights of people who are accused of a crime. The Fifth Amendment says that a person has the right not to **testify** against him- or herself. He or she can refuse to answer questions. The Sixth Amendment guarantees that in criminal court cases, the accused person has a right to an attorney and a speedy and public trial by an **impartial** jury. The same is true in most civil court cases (non-criminal cases involving business or property); the Seventh Amendment guarantees that the accused person be given a trial by an unbiased jury.

The Eighth Amendment makes sure that a person accused of a crime doesn't have to pay extremely high **bail** or fines, or receive cruel and unusual punishment. The Ninth Amendment says that the people have other rights even if these rights are not stated directly in the Constitution.

Finally, the Tenth Amendment grants the people or the states any power not given to the federal government by the Constitution.

Getting Started   10 minutes

Teaching Tip

Students in your class may have opposite religious beliefs as well as dissimilar cultural and social values. In addition, some students may have experienced oppression or persecution in their home country. For these reasons, limit or control class discussion on controversial topics such as human rights and abuses in the world. Such topics may generate arguments or ill-feeling, or may make students feel uncomfortable.

- Say: *We've talked about the early history of the U.S. and the development of its system of government, which is based on the Constitution. One main reason the colonists broke away from Britain was because they felt they did not have individual rights. When the Constitution was written in 1787, some people were not satisfied with it because they thought it had failed to guarantee individual rights. The first ten amendments to the Constitution, known as the* Bill of Rights, *were added as protections for individual rights. As we learned in the previous lesson, the Supreme Court interprets questions about the Constitution and the Bill of Rights.*
- Ask students to share what they know about the Bill of Rights. Write students' ideas on the board, a transparency, or a flipchart.
- Say: *Now let's talk about human rights here and in your home countries. Then we will listen to and read about the Bill of Rights.*

1 BEFORE YOU READ

CLASS. Discuss. What do you know...

- Ask students to read the directions.
- Expand on the first question. Say: *Some countries have a written constitution, or guarantees of human rights, like the U.S. Does your home country have a written constitution that recognizes human rights? Which ones? If not, are there rights that people in your country still expect, even if they are not written in an official document? What are they? Are there rights in your home country that people argue about? Which ones? Give examples if necessary.*

Presentation   15 minutes

2 READ

Listen to and read...

- Ask students to read the directions.
- Say: *Now you are going to read an article that describes some of the human rights protections offered by the Bill of Rights.*
- Point out that the words and phrases in boldface (*assemble, petition, bear arms, intrusion, warrant, testify, impartial, bail*) are in the glossary on page 245. Encourage students to read the entire article first, before going to the glossary.
- Play CD 2, Track 17, as students listen and read.
- After students listen and read, ask if they have any other questions about the content, vocabulary, or pronunciation; answer questions.

Possible answer: The Bill of Rights protects various human rights. For example, it protects freedom of religion and speech; the right to bear arms; the right to a public and speedy trial.

Teaching Tip

- You may want to share and discuss with students a facsimile and transcript of the Bill of Rights, which you can download from the National Archives website: www.archives.gov. (Go to "American Historical Documents.")
- Ask students to work in groups to read one of the original ten amendments. Have them compare the actual amendment to what they learned about it in the article.

Expansion: Vocabulary Practice for 2

- Divide the class into small groups.
- Ask students to make a list of the boldfaced words in the reading and to discuss the meaning of each. Encourage students to guess the meaning if they are not sure.
- Tell students to look for the words in the glossary and to compare the definitions there with what they discussed.
- Assign one or two words or phrases to each group and ask them to write one (or two) sentence(s) with their assigned word(s) or phrase(s).
- Ask groups to read their sentences to the class.

Controlled Practice   15 minutes

Reading Skill: **Using a T-chart to Take Notes**
- Direct students to the Reading Skill box.
- Ask a confident, above-level student to read the text.
- Say: *A T-chart is a basic graphic organizer that can be very effective for note-taking. A T-chart can be especially useful when you need to review specific information, such as in this case, where you want to remember which amendment says what.*

3 CHECK YOUR UNDERSTANDING

A Make a T-chart...
- Ask students to read the directions. Tell them to make a T-chart in their notebook, with room to write notes.
- Point out the examples on the T-chart. Say: *For each amendment, take brief notes on the main points.*
- Allow enough time for students to reread and write. Walk around; answer questions or assist as needed.

B Write the answers to the questions.
- Ask students to read the directions.
- Confirm that students understand that they need to go back to the text to answer the questions. Give students time to complete the task.
- Ask volunteers to read each question and its answer. Join in only if any of the answers are not fully correct.

Answers:
1. U.S. citizens, non-citizen residents, and visitors;
2. freedom of religion, speech, and the press; freedom to peacefully assemble and to petition the government for change; 3. by guaranteeing the right to an attorney and to a speedy and public trial by an impartial jury

4 WORD WORK

GROUPS. Find the boldfaced words...
- Ask students to read the directions.
- Have them complete the matching exercise.
- Walk around; intervene only if you hear a question that students can't answer in the group.
- Check answers with the whole class.

Communicative Practice   20 minutes

Show what you know!

STEP 1. PAIRS. Compare and contrast...
- Ask students to read the directions.
- Set up pairs.
- Say: *Use your T-charts to talk about each of the amendments.*
- Ask if there are any remaining questions about the meaning of specific vocabulary; respond as needed.

STEP 2. GROUPS. Discuss. Which of the first ten...
- Ask students to read the directions and the question.
- Set up informal groups. Say: *Talk with three or four other students; make sure you all get a chance to express your opinion.* Explain which amendment or amendments you think are most important.
- Walk around; intervene only if students have questions.
- Ask each group whether the group members all agreed on the most important amendment. *Note:* If students do not agree on one, tell them that it is not surprising, since all the amendments are important.

Progress Check

Can you . . . recognize individual rights in the Constitution?
- Say: *We have talked about individual rights in the Constitution. Now look at the question at the bottom of the page. Can you recognize individual rights in the Constitution? If so, check the box.*

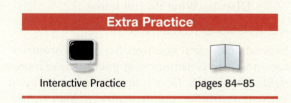

Extra Practice

Interactive Practice   pages 84–85

CHECK YOUR UNDERSTANDING

A Make a T-chart like the one shown here for the ten amendments. Read the article again. Take notes on each amendment.

Amendment	Notes
First Amendment	
Second Amendment	

B Write the answers to the questions.

1. Who is protected by the U.S. Constitution and the Bill of Rights?
2. What freedoms does the First Amendment protect?
3. How does the Sixth Amendment protect someone accused of a crime?

Reading Skill:
Using a T-chart to Take Notes

Taking notes while you read will help you remember information. A T-chart is a simple tool that can help you organize your notes. T-charts have two columns and are very useful when you want to remember information connected with a list of dates or when you want to record definitions or examples for a list of items.

4 **WORD WORK**

GROUPS. Find the boldfaced words in the article. Guess their meaning from context. Then match the words with their definitions. Record the words in your vocabulary log.

<u>d</u> 1. assemble   a. not giving special support or attention to one group; unbiased

<u>e</u> 2. bail   b. make a formal statement of what is true

<u>g</u> 3. bear arms   c. formally ask someone in authority to do something

<u>a</u> 4. impartial   d. come together in the same place

<u>h</u> 5. intrusion   e. money exchanged so that someone can be let out of prison while awaiting trial

<u>c</u> 6. petition   f. official paper that allows the police to do something

<u>b</u> 7. testify   g. carry guns and other weapons for self-defense

<u>f</u> 8. warrant   h. unwanted person or event that interrupts or annoys you

Show what you know!   Recognize individual rights in the Constitution

STEP 1. PAIRS. Compare and contrast your T-charts. Use them to explain the importance of each amendment.

STEP 2. GROUPS. Discuss. Which of the first ten amendments do you think is most important? Why?

Can you...recognize individual rights in the Constitution? ☐

Listening and Speaking

1   BEFORE YOU LISTEN

A   **CLASS.** In recent years, bills regarding immigration, environmental regulations, and health care reform have been proposed in Congress. Discuss. How does an idea become a bill? How does a bill become a law?

B   **GROUPS.** Fill in the blanks with words and phrases from the box.

> abandon   override   speak up   veto   legislation   petition   sponsor

1. The Congress can ____override____ some presidential decisions they disagree with.

2. The senator decided to ____abandon____ her proposal when no one supported it.

3. Citizens should ____speak up____ and express their opinions without fear.

4. Representatives from both parties will ____sponsor____ a bill to improve education.

5. The new ____legislation____ makes it illegal to travel to certain countries.

6. The president opposed the bill, so he chose to ____veto____ it.

7. Thousands of voters signed a ____petition____ that requested lower fuel taxes.

2   LISTEN

CD2 T18

Listen to a segment of *Americans Rising*, a talk radio show, as Professor Klass explains how a bill becomes a law to host Jim Peters. Then read the sentences below and write *T* (*true*) or *F* (*false*).

__F__   1. A private citizen can sponsor a law.

__T__   2. A senator or representative proposes a bill first to his or her own house of Congress.

__T__   3. A committee from the house of Congress where a bill is introduced has to approve the bill before the Senate or House votes on it.

__T__   4. If a bill passes the first house, it goes to the second house for a vote.

__F__   5. After both houses approve a bill, it goes to the Supreme Court.

__F__   6. If the president vetoes a bill, Congress must accept the veto.

Getting Started   10 minutes

- Say: *We've been talking about the history of the U.S. and how the government has been organized and controlled by the Constitution, particularly the ideas of the three branches of government and the principle of the separation of powers. We learned about the first ten amendments to the Constitution—the Bill of Rights—which protect people's civil rights. Now we are going to focus on one branch of the federal government—the legislative branch—and learn how a bill becomes a law.*

- Ask students if they understand what a *bill* is. If needed, explain that a bill is a plan for a new law. Say: *We will listen to a segment from a radio show that will explain how this plan becomes an actual law.*

Expansion: Vocabulary Practice

- Explain that *bill* has at least nine meanings (including idioms) as a noun and two meanings (including an idiom) as a verb—not counting being a nickname for *William*.

- Brainstorm a list of definitions for *bill*. Write the meanings on the board, a transparency, or a flipchart. Unless students come up with all meanings, tell them to find more meanings by going to a dictionary.

- Set up pairs; give each pair an advanced learners' dictionary or, if several computers are available, give pairs the option of looking up the word in an online dictionary.

- Say: *Look up* bill *and read all the entries. Copy any definitions that you don't know—especially the meanings of idioms—into your vocabulary logs.*

- Walk around while pairs work; assist as needed.

- After pairs finish, check for understanding, particularly such idioms as *fit the bill* or *clean bill of health*.

- Encourage students to pay close attention to idioms they hear or read outside of class. Tell students to bring them into class so that you can help explain them. Say: *It's difficult to understand idioms because you can't make sense of them just by looking at the individual words that make them up.* Also encourage students to write down all new words, phrases, and idioms in their vocabulary logs.

1 BEFORE YOU LISTEN

Ⓐ CLASS. **In recent years,...**

- Ask students to read the directions.

- Ask: *Are any of you familiar with how an idea might become a bill or how a bill becomes a law in the U.S.?* If *yes*, let students discuss. If *no*, ask: *Can you talk about how laws are made in your home countries?*

- Let the conversation go on for as long as students are engaged, provided that it is generally related to making laws.

Ⓑ GROUPS. **Fill in the blanks with words...**

- Ask students to read the directions.

- Check answers with the whole class.

Presentation   15 minutes

2 LISTEN

 Listen to a segment...

- Ask students to read the directions.

- Review the directions to make sure everyone understands the true/false process.

- Play CD 2, Track 18.

- Walk around the room as students listen. Observe whether any students are having difficulty listening and answering at the same time.

- Ask for volunteers to read the statements and say whether they are true or false. Let students discuss any disagreements in answers; intervene only if they do not come up with the correct answer.

- Check answers with the whole class. Go over any misunderstandings.

Expansion: Reading Practice for 2

Have students go to this website and read the article: http://bensguide.gpo.gov/6-8/lawmaking/index.html. Explain that this website is intended for middle-school students. However, because law making is very complex, this page is useful to adults because it provides a clear visual overview.

Discuss how a bill becomes a law

Controlled Practice   15 minutes

3   PRACTICE

Grammar Watch: Passive with *get*

- Direct students to the Grammar Watch.
- Ask students to give examples of sentences with active verbs and passive verbs. (For example, *Millions of people <u>voted</u> in the presidential election. The energy bill <u>was passed</u> by the Senate.*) Use as many examples and as much discussion as necessary to make sure that students understand the difference between active and passive sentences.
- Restate the rule. Say: *Sometimes we say* get *instead of* be *in passive sentences. We do this more in speaking than in writing.*
- Ask students to read the two sets of examples and see how a form of *get* can replace a form of *be* in the passive sentences.

Language Note

- Explain that it is usually preferable to write in the active voice because it is direct and more powerful, but some types of government or business texts are typically written in the passive voice.
- Say: *However, it's important for your comprehension and your understanding of English structure to be able to be able to use both active and passive voices.*
- Review active and passive; write several simple active sentences on the board.
- Ask students to change the sentences from active to passive. (*The police arrested the man. → The man was arrested by the police.*)
- Repeat the exercise by writing passive sentences and asking students to convert them into active sentences. (*The car was fixed by Manuel. → Manuel fixed the car.*) Note: This exercise may be easy for many students but will help the pre-level students who may have less grammar background.

Read these statements...

- Ask students to read the directions.
- Review the directions. Tell students to first rewrite the active sentences as passives, using *be*. Then tell them to rewrite the sentences as passives with *get*.
- Say: *This exercise is meant to give you practice understanding the difference between active and passive sentences and to help you to recognize how* get *is often used.*

Communicative Practice   20 minutes

4   MAKE IT PERSONAL

PAIRS. Explain how a bill becomes a law....

- Ask students to read the directions.
- Set up pairs.
- Ask students to take turns describing how a bill becomes a law. Tell students to try to remember the discussion at the beginning of the lesson and to review Exercise 1B and the radio segment.
- Say: *If you have questions about the process, write them down and we'll talk about them in a few minutes.*
- Ask students to share any questions about the process of how a bill becomes a law. Answer the questions and then review the whole process.

Extra Practice

Interactive Practice

Passive with *get*

We can sometimes use *get* to replace *be* in passive sentences. This happens more frequently in conversation than in written language. Look at the examples.

*The people **elected** him because of his position on environmental protection.*
*He **was elected** (by the people) because of his position on environmental protection.*
*He **got elected** (by the people) because of his position on environmental protection.*

*I hope Congress and the president **pass** the bill protecting whales.*
*I hope the bill protecting whales **is passed** (by Congress and the president).*
*I hope the bill protecting whales **gets passed** (by Congress and the president).*

3 PRACTICE

**Read these statements. Rewrite them in the passive voice. Rewrite them
again, changing *be* to *get*.**

1. If enough people sign the petition, it goes to a congressperson.

   Passive: *If the petition is signed by enough people,*

   it goes to a congressperson.

   Passive with *get*: *If the petition gets signed by enough people,*

   it goes to a congressperson.

2. Then a senator or representative sponsors the idea.

   Passive: Then the idea is sponsored by a senator or representative.

   Passive with *get*: Then the idea gets sponsored by a senator or representative.

3. The committee votes on the bill.

   Passive: The bill is voted on by the committee.

   Passive with *get*: The bill gets voted on by the committee.

4. If the president vetoes the bill, Congress has three choices.

   Passive: If the bill is vetoed by the president, Congress has three choices.

   Passive with *get*: If the bill gets vetoed by the president, Congress has
   three choices.

4 MAKE IT PERSONAL

PAIRS. Explain how a bill becomes a law. Use the vocabulary from Exercise 1B
and the information from the listening.

Reading

1 BEFORE YOU READ

CLASS. Discuss. What are your feelings about becoming a U.S. citizen? What advantages do U.S. citizens have that non-citizen residents do not have?

2 READ

CD2 T19

Listen to and read the pamphlet about citizenship. How do the text structure and formatting help you identify the main points?

Reading Skill:
Using Text Structure and Formatting

To better understand what you read, notice a text's structure and formatting. **Boldface type**, bullets (•), and color can help you find the main points. Bullets can also help you identify items in a series.

What Are the Benefits of U.S. Citizenship?

The Constitution and the laws of the United States give many rights to both citizens and non-citizens living in the U.S. However, some rights are only for citizens, such as:

- **Voting.** Only U.S. citizens can vote in federal elections. Most states also **restrict** the right to vote, in most elections, to U.S. citizens.
- **Bringing family members to the United States.** Citizens generally get **priority** when petitioning to bring family members permanently to this country.
- **Obtaining citizenship for children born abroad.** In most cases, a child born abroad to a U.S. citizen is **automatically** a U.S. citizen.
- **Traveling with a U.S. passport.** A U.S. passport allows you to get assistance from the U.S. government when overseas.
- **Becoming eligible for federal jobs.** Most jobs with government agencies require U.S. citizenship.
- **Becoming an elected official.** Many elected offices in this country require U.S. citizenship.
- **Showing your patriotism.** In addition, becoming a U.S. citizen is a way to demonstrate your commitment to your new country.

The above list does not include all the benefits of citizenship, only some of the more important ones.

Source: ©2006, 2008 U.S. Citizenship and Immigration Services

Learn about the benefits of U.S. citizenship

Getting Started   15 minutes

- Say: *We have been learning about early American history and important historical documents—the Declaration of Independence and the Constitution, including the Bill of Rights. We studied how a bill becomes a law in Congress. Now we are going to talk, listen to, and read about becoming a U.S. citizen.*

1   BEFORE YOU READ

CLASS. Discuss. What are...

- Ask students to read the directions.
- Restate, generalize, and expand the questions. Say: *What advantages does becoming a U.S. citizen give you that non-citizen residents do not have? Do you think there are any disadvantages to becoming a U.S. citizen?*
- Accept all responses; allow students to continue the discussion as long as they are engaged.
- Say: *In a few minutes, you will read and listen to a pamphlet that explains the benefits of citizenship.* Ask for a volunteer to explain what a pamphlet is, or explain as needed. (synonyms: *flyer, bulletin*)

Teaching Tip

- Some students in your class may not have legal status to live in the U.S. Because of this, keep the discussion about citizenship at a theoretical, general level. Although many students may offer personal information, do not ask them to give personal responses about citizenship beyond a voluntary show of hands.
- Don't offer any advice to individuals about pursuing permanent residency, asylum, or naturalization, but do provide contact information for the United States Citizenship and Immigration Service (USCIS at http://www.uscis.gov/portal/site/uscis) and local community- and faith-based organizations or ethnic support organizations. Make sure that any organization you give contact information for is a valid, nonprofit, helping organization.

Presentation   15 minutes

Reading Skill: **Using Text Structure and Formatting**

- Direct students to the Reading Skill box.
- Ask a confident, above-level student to read the text.
- Say: *Paying attention to the structure and formatting of a text can help you comprehend the article more easily and better. Boldface, bullets, color, italics, numbered lists—all of these can help you find the main ideas and significant details.*

2   READ

Listen to and read the pamphlet...

- Ask students to read the directions.
- Say: *This short article highlights some of the benefits of citizenship.* If students have already mentioned some of the benefits, note that and ask them to look for other benefits.
- Point out that the words and phrases in boldface (*restrict, priority, automatically*) are in the glossary on page 245. Encourage students to read the entire article first, before going to the glossary.
- Play CD 2, Track 19, as students listen and read.
- After students listen and read, ask if they have any other questions about the content, vocabulary, or pronunciation; answer questions.

Possible answer: Boldface blue type and bullets highlight the main points about the benefits of citizenship. Boldface black type identifies important words that must be understood to comprehend the text.

Expansion: Vocabulary Practice for 2

- Many terms related to citizenship and naturalization may be unfamiliar to students. Write the following words on the board: *naturalization, alien, pending, verify, jurisdiction, waiver (as in filing a waiver), adjust, affidavit, oath, allegiance, obligation.*
- Set up groups. Give each group two words to work on. Have the groups use a dictionary and their prior knowledge to figure out the meanings of each word.
- Ask each group to write a sentence that illustrates the meaning of each word. Then have groups share their words, meanings, and sentences with the class.
- Suggest that students add some or all of these words to their vocabulary logs.

Controlled Practice 15 minutes

3 CHECK YOUR UNDERSTANDING

A Check (✓) the main idea.

- Read the directions aloud.
- Explain to students that they should read the statements and then check the one that best describes the main idea of the pamphlet.
- Tell them to quickly complete the exercise and then share their answers with people sitting near them.

B Check (✓) the most accurate statement.

- Ask students to read the directions. Have them check the statement that is *most* accurate, according to the pamphlet.

C Read the text again. Write...

- Ask students to read the directions.
- Repeat the directions and confirm that students only need to write short answers.
- Ask for volunteers to read each question and its answer.
- Allow students to discuss the content of the article, questions, and answers as long as they are engaged, including their opinions about the laws.

Answers:

1. Only U.S. citizens can vote in federal elections; most (but not all) voting in state elections is restricted to U.S. citizens.
2. Citizens generally have priority when petitioning to bring family members permanently to the U.S.
3. In most cases, a child born to a U.S. citizen is automatically a U.S. citizen, so parents do not usually need to do anything to obtain citizenship for their children.
4. Traveling with a U.S. passport allows a person to get assistance from the U.S. government when overseas.
5. Most federal jobs and many elected offices in the U.S. can only be held by U.S. citizens.
6. You can demonstrate commitment to your new country.

D PAIRS. Discuss. Which two benefits...

- Ask students to read the directions.
- Set up pairs.
- Say: *Take a couple of minutes to look back at the pamphlet. Talk to your partner about which benefits seem most important to you, and explain why.*
- Allow enough time for the discussion.

Teaching Tip

Provide an alternative topic for students who may already be knowledgeable about the subject. Possible topics:

Are there benefits to having dual citizenship? If so, what are they? If not, why not?

Naturalized citizens must take an oath of allegiance, but natural-born U.S. citizens do not have to do this. Should all adult citizens be required to say an oath of allegiance? Why or why not?

4 WORD WORK

GROUPS. Choose three words...

- Set up groups.
- Ask students to read the directions.
- Confirm that students understand that they discuss first, then write in vocabulary logs.
- Walk around; intervene only if you hear a question that students can't answer in the group.

Communicative Practice 15 minutes

Show what you know!

GROUPS. Discuss. What did the pamphlet...

- Ask students to read the directions and questions.
- Tell students that they might want to look back over the text, noting any new information.
- Have students form groups and answer the questions. Walk around and monitor discussions, offering prompts as needed. (For example: *Did you know that you needed U.S. citizenship to be able to apply for many federal jobs? Why is this information helpful?*)
- Ask students which new information was the most helpful. Have groups share their ideas with the class.

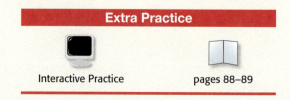

Extra Practice

Interactive Practice   pages 88–89

CHECK YOUR UNDERSTANDING

A Check (✓) the main idea.

- ☐ 1. Non-citizens living in the U.S. have rights.
- ☑ 2. There are certain rights in the U.S. that only U.S. citizens have.
- ☐ 3. Non-citizens cannot travel abroad.
- ☐ 4. Some jobs are open only to citizens.

B Check (✓) the most accurate statement.

- ☑ 1. The main idea of the text is stated in the first paragraph.
- ☐ 2. The main idea of the text is stated in the last bulleted item.
- ☐ 3. The main idea is not directly stated in any single paragraph of the text, but you can identify it based on the title and the bulleted text.

C Read the text again. Write the answers to the questions.

1. How is the right to vote different in federal elections and some non-federal elections?
2. What advantage do citizens have when trying to bring family members to the U.S.?
3. What do citizens have to do to get citizenship for their foreign-born children?
4. How does traveling with a passport help citizens?
5. Do you have to be a citizen to get a federal job and become an elected official?
6. What can you demonstrate by becoming a citizen?

D PAIRS. Discuss. Which two benefits of U.S. citizenship do you think are the most valuable? Why?

4 **WORD WORK**

GROUPS. Choose three words or phrases in the pamphlet that you would like to remember. Discuss the words and their meanings. Then record the words and information about them in your vocabulary log.

Show what you know! Discuss the benefits of citizenship

GROUPS. Discuss. What did the pamphlet explain that you did not already know?

Listening and Speaking

1   BEFORE YOU LISTEN

CLASS. A naturalized citizen is someone who becomes a citizen of a country that he or she was not born in. Discuss. Do you know anyone who has become a naturalized citizen of the U.S.? Do you know anyone who is studying to become a citizen?

ALL OF US WILL LEARN!

2   LISTEN

CD2 T20

A   An instructor is giving a lecture to a new group of students in her citizenship class. She is explaining the requirements for naturalization. Listen to her lecture and take simple notes. Look at the example below.

> REQUIREMENTS FOR CITIZENSHIP
> AGE –
>   18 + yrs.
>
> RESIDENCY –
>   legal perm. resident
>   (has I-551 card) resided continuously past 5 yrs
>   in country at least 30 mo. past 5 yrs
>   not gone for more than yr. past 5 yrs

Make headings stand out by underlining, using capital letters, or by separating them from the details (e.g., writing them on the left, and writing the details under them, to the right).

Don't write full sentences. Write only key words, and use abbreviations.

CD2 T20

B   **PAIRS.** Listen again and check your notes. Then compare them with a partner's. Did you both include the same information? Could you both pass a test on the lecture by studying your notes? Why or why not?

Getting Started   15 minutes

Say: *In the previous lesson, we learned the benefits of becoming a U.S. citizen. In this lesson, we will listen to an instructor in a citizenship class give a lecture about the requirements for becoming a naturalized citizen of the U.S. You will practice taking notes.*

1 BEFORE YOU LISTEN

CLASS. A naturalized citizen...

- Ask students to read the directions.
- Say: *In the last lesson, we discussed people who have become U.S. citizens or who are studying to become citizens. Today we are going to discuss citizenship preparation classes. Do you know anyone who is studying in a citizenship class now?* Allow all student responses.
- Before class, find contact information about well-respected, free or low-cost organizations that provide citizenship preparation classes.
- Ask students if they know where there are citizenship classes (including your program, if appropriate). Write names of programs on the board so that students can copy them down. Add contact information for good programs.
- Say: *Let's listen to an instructor talk about the requirements for naturalization.*

Presentation   15 minutes

TAKING SIMPLE NOTES

- Direct students to the notes about note-taking.
- Ask a confident, above-level student to read the first note. Ask another above-level student to read the second note.
- Ask students if they have any questions or comments about these note-taking strategies.
- Say: *When you take notes, write them so that you can understand what you need to remember and to be able to identify what is important. As the second note says, don't write full sentences—just key words and abbreviations. Be sure that you will be able to remember what your abbreviations stand for.*
- Direct students' attention to the handwritten notes under REQUIREMENTS FOR CITIZENSHIP.

2 LISTEN

A 🔘 **An instructor is giving a lecture to a new...**

- Ask students to read the directions.
- Tell them that as they listen to the lecture, they will take notes in their notebooks.
- Play CD 2, Track 20, as students listen and write notes.
- Walk around the room as students listen. Observe whether any students are having difficulty listening and writing notes at the same time.

B 🔘 **PAIRS. Listen again and check...**

- Ask students to read the directions.
- Tell students to listen again and check their notes, then compare them with a partner's notes and answer the questions together (orally only).
- Set up informal pairs. Say: *Work with someone sitting close to you.*
- Play Track 20 again.
- Ask: *Was this lecture easy, medium, or difficult to follow and to take notes from?* If most of the response is *medium* or *difficult*, ask students what made it so and whether they have questions about the content.

Expansion: Listening Practice for 2A and 2B

- For more listening practice, bring in authentic listenings about topics related to citizenship and immigration. These can be taken from local radio stations, podcasts, or such websites as National Public Radio (http://www.npr.org/) or the Library of Congress American Memory online collection (http://memory.loc.gov/ammem/index.html)
- Ask students to listen and take notes.
- After the first listening, ask if students need to hear the clip again; if the majority do, play it again. Ask whether they have questions about content.

Controlled Practice   15 minutes

3   PRACTICE

A Revise your notes. You can...

- Ask students to read the directions.
- Allow approximately 3–4 minutes for students to revise their notes alone.

B PAIRS. Use your notes to answer...

- Ask students to read the directions.
- Tell students to work with the same partners as in Exercise 2B.
- Allow enough time for pairs to write answers to the questions. Tell students they can work together on one text and that later the other partner can write the answer in his or her notebook (to avoid taking the time to write the answers twice).
- Ask each pair to answer one of the questions.

Communicative Practice   15 minutes

Communication Skill: **Exchanging Opinions**

- Direct students to the Communication Skill box.
- Ask a confident, above-level student to read the text.
- Say: *It's important that you be able to express your opinions. In the U.S., we expect people to say what they think. It's equally important to express your opinions politely and to listen carefully to others' points of view. That's not always easy, but the phrases listed here help.* Repeat each phrase and add the rest of a sentence to give it context. (For example: *How do you feel about the new naturalization exam? In my opinion, the cost for the naturalization process is reasonable.*)

Community Building

- Have students form groups of 4 or 5.
- Say: *We are going to practice exchanging opinions. Please look at the box on page 139. Use the expressions to answer some questions I will write on the board. Do you agree that naturalized citizens should have to pass both the English test and the civics test? Why or why not? How important is it for you to speak English in the U.S.? Should English become the official language of the U.S. or should the U.S. have no official language?*

4   MAKE IT PERSONAL

GROUPS. Discuss the questions.

- Ask students to read the directions and the two questions.
- Set up groups in a different way from usual. For example, pass out colored index cards and have all the reds work together, all the blues work together, and all the greens work together. In this case, if you want to continue the discussion with different groups, you can then ask the groups to re-form, with each new group being composed of one red, one blue, and one green.
- Walk around; listen to the discussions but intervene only if students ask you a question.

Extra Practice

Interactive Practice

PRACTICE

A Revise your notes. You can keep the same organization as in Exercise 2A, or you can put the information into a T-chart like the one used on page 133. Make sure your heads, or main points, and key words are clear. If you used abbreviations, make sure you can remember what they mean.

B PAIRS. Use your notes to answer the questions. Answers will vary but could include:

1. What are some examples of actions that demonstrate lack of good moral character?

   being convicted of a serious crime, being convicted more than once for gambling, involvement with smuggling aliens into the country

2. What document does a person need to show an attachment to?

   the Constitution

3. If an elderly person has lived in the U.S. for a long time, what requirements might he or she be excused from?

   the English language requirement

4. What are the two parts of the civics test?

   U.S. government and U.S. history

5. What is one thing a person promises when he or she takes the Oath of Allegiance?

   to support the Constitution; give up allegiance to another country; join the armed forces

6. Where can you find the complete requirements and documents for U.S. citizenship?

   on the United States Citizenship and Immigration Services website

4 **MAKE IT PERSONAL**

GROUPS. Discuss the questions.

1. Do you think that all of the requirements are reasonable? Why or why not?

2. Do you know whether it is easy or difficult to become a citizen of your home country? If you know, explain the process to your group.

Communication Skill:
Exchanging Opinions

To exchange opinions with others, express yourself clearly and politely, and always listen to others' points of view. You can use the following words and phrases:

How do you feel about...?   *What do you think of...?*
In my opinion,...   *As I see it,...*
I agree with you.   *I think so, too.*
Yes, but...   *I see what you mean, but...*

Life Skills

1 LEARN ABOUT DIFFERENT KINDS OF MAPS

CLASS. Discuss. What kinds of maps have you used? Where and when did you use them? In what ways were they useful to you?

2 INTERPRET A U.S. MAP

A PAIRS. Look at the map of the U.S. Discuss. How can you tell that this is a historical map?

A *political map* shows how governments have divided land into countries, states, provinces, and cities. A *physical map* shows the earth's features, such as mountains, oceans, and deserts. A *historical map* gives information about a particular time and place in the past; it might present political, economic, or cultural information.

Getting Started
10 minutes

1   LEARN ABOUT DIFFERENT KINDS OF MAPS

CLASS. Discuss. What kinds...

- Say: *In this unit, we have talked about the early history of the U.S. One of the tools we used to organize information about historical events was a timeline. Today we're going to explore another tool for organizing historical information: a historical map.*

- Read the discussion questions and elicit answers, offering prompts. (For example: *Have you ever used a map at a shopping mall? Did it help you find the store that you needed?*) List different types of maps on the board as students say them (for example, road maps, bus or subway maps, museum maps, city or country maps, a world map or globe). Ask for a show of hands as to how many students have used each type.

Presentation
20 minutes

2   INTERPRET A U.S. MAP

Ⓐ PAIRS. Look at the map...

- Ask an above-level student to read the note on the right about different types of maps.

- Say: *People use different types of maps for different reasons. What does a political map show?* (how governments have divided land) *A physical map?* (geographical features of the earth) *A historical map?* (information about a time and place in the past)

- Ask how many students have seen each type of map.

- Draw students' attention to the map on page 140. Give them a few minutes to look at it.

- Clarify unfamiliar terms on the map. Examples:

    atlas—a comprehensive book of maps

    territorial—relating to a territory, or piece of land

    acquisitions—things that you acquire, or gain, from another person, company, or country

    cede—to give up something such as a state or territory, sometimes as a consequence of war

    cession—the act of ceding something

    annexation—when one country takes over another country's land and makes it its own

- Tell students to form pairs and take a few minutes to discuss what type of map they think the illustration is—and how they can tell.

- In the full group, elicit an answer to the question in the directions: *How can you tell that this is a historical map?* (It has information about times and places in the past—when different states became part of the country.)

Language Note

The terms *the continental United States* and *the lower 48* are often used to refer to the 48 contiguous (that is, next to each other) states as well as the District of Columbia, which are all south of the northern border with Canada. Although Alaska and Hawaii are also states, they are not considered part of the continental United States.

Expansion: Reading Practice for 2A

Have students find answers to the following questions about the map with a partner or in a small group:

What part of the U.S. was first settled by Europeans? (the East Coast)

When did the Oregon Territory become part of the U.S.? (1846)

What do the states with dots represent? (the states acquired from the Louisiana Purchase)

Which countries ceded land to the U.S.? (Great Britain, Spain, Mexico)

Which countries sold land to the U.S.? (France, Mexico, Russia, Denmark)

Which states were annexed by the U.S.? (Texas and Hawaii)

From which country did the U.S. purchase the Virgin Islands? (Denmark)

When was Hawaii annexed by the U.S.? (1898)

When did the U.S. make the Louisiana Purchase from France? (1803)

From which country did the U.S. purchase Alaska? (Russia)

Controlled Practice   15 minutes

B **Use the map to write answers...**

- Tell students to look at the map on page 140 and to use it to write answers to the questions in Exercise 2B in their notebooks.
- Circulate and help as needed.

Answers: 1. Great Britain, France, Spain, Mexico, Russia (if including Virgin Islands, Denmark); Texas and Hawaii were both "republics," so could be counted as well; 2. 1803; 3. Spain; 4. Russia; 5. Denmark; 6. 1898; 7. Great Britain

3 DISCUSS MAP FEATURES

A **CLASS. Discuss. What are some...**

- Ask students to read the note on page 141.
- Read the directions aloud. Ask students to compare the maps on pages 126 and 140.
- Ask the two discussion questions and elicit answers from students. (*Both maps have a scale and compass rose; the map on page 126 has a key.*)
- Point to the map scales on pages 126 and 140. Say: *The scales on both maps show how many miles and kilometers the units of distance on the maps represent.*
- Point to the compass roses on pages 126 and 140. Say: *The compass rose on each map shows which direction is west, east, north, and south.*
- Point to the map key on page 126. Say: *The map key on page 126 shows the colors used to represent different groups of colonies (New England, Middle, Southern) on the map. There is no map key on page 140.*
- *Optional:* Ask students to look at the map on page 126. Ask: *What do the purple-shaded areas on the map represent?* (the New England colonies)

B **PAIRS. Use the map on page 140...**

- Say: *Now we're going to look at the map on page 140 and find specific information.* Ask students to read the directions and form pairs.
- Have students complete the exercise.
- Call on students to say the answers.

Answers: 1. the map scale; 2. the compass rose; 3. the areas acquired during the Louisiana Purchase

Communicative Practice   15 minutes

4 LISTEN

A **An instructor is giving...**

- Say: *Now, you'll listen to a lecture about the way the U.S. grew, territory by* territory. *But first, let's review the term* territory. *What does this mean?* Explain that it is a piece of land, or geographic region, that is owned or controlled by a particular country.
- Ask students to read the directions. Say: *As you listen to the lecture, take notes. Don't write down everything you hear; you might note dates and a few key words to help you remember what happened on those dates.*
- Play CD 2, Track 21.
- *Optional:* Allow students to hear the lecture again and add information to their notes.

B **Review your notes. Then write...**

- Say: *Now that you've listened to the lecture, look back at your notes and use the information in them to answer a few questions.*
- Ask students to read the directions and complete the exercise.
- Call on volunteers to say the answers.

Answers: 1. Thomas Jefferson; 2. 1848; 3. Spain, Great Britain, Russia, and the United States; 4. They were pleased with the discovery of gold and oil in Alaska.

Community Building

Ask students to locate a historical map of their home country. They may do so alone or in groups with other students from their home country. After they have completed the maps, ask students to present them to the class.

Progress Check

Can you . . . interpret historical maps of the U.S.?

- Say: *We have practiced interpreting historical maps of the U.S. Can you do this? If so, check the box.*

Extra Practice

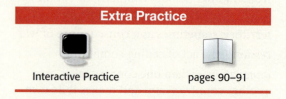

Interactive Practice   pages 90–91

B Use the map to write the answers to the questions.

1. What countries owned parts of the land that later became the U.S?
2. When did the U.S. make the Louisiana Purchase from France?
3. Which country owned Florida before 1819?
4. From which country did the U.S. purchase Alaska?
5. From which country did the U.S. purchase the Virgin Islands?
6. When was Hawaii annexed by the U.S.?
7. Which country once owned parts of North Dakota and Minnesota?

3 DISCUSS MAP FEATURES

A CLASS. Discuss. What are some of the special features of a map? Which special features do the maps on pages 126 and 140 have?

> A *compass rose* shows which way is north, south, east, or west. A *map scale* shows the relationship between the distances on a map and real distances on land. A *map key* is a visual summary of what the colors, patterns, shading, and symbols on a map stand for.

B PAIRS. Use the map on page 140 to discuss the questions.

1. What map feature would you use to figure out the distance from New York to California?
2. What map feature tells you which way is north?
3. If you were creating a map key for this map, what would white with black dots stand for?

4 LISTEN

CD2 T21

A An instructor is giving a lecture on the expansion of the U.S. Listen to the lecture and take simple notes.

B Review your notes. Then write answers to the questions.

1. Who was president when the U.S. made the Louisiana Purchase?
2. When did the U.S. acquire California?
3. Which countries originally claimed the Oregon Territory?
4. Why did the purchase of Alaska become popular with U.S. citizens?

Can you...interpret historical maps of the U.S.? ☐

Writing

1   BEFORE YOU WRITE

A   You are going to write a formal e-mail to an elected official about a problem that concerns you. Read about formal e-mails. Then read the writing tip.

> **FYI**   ABOUT FORMAL E-MAILS
>
> In the U.S., sending formal e-mails or letters to elected officials is an important way to participate in the democratic process. Formal e-mails should be set up like business letters. See the example of a cover letter on page 206. Include the full name, title, business, and e-mail address of the person you are writing to. Provide a short, clear subject line. Use a formal greeting and include the person's title or *Ms., Miss,* or *Mr.* Then write a message that is clear and concise. End your e-mail in a polite, diplomatic way, for example, *Thank you for taking the time to read my e-mail. I look forward to hearing from you.* Then use a formal closing, such as *Sincerely* or *Sincerely yours,* followed by your full name.
>
> **Writing Tip:**   **Using a problem/solution structure**
>
> Stating a problem and suggesting a solution is an easy way to structure an essay, business letter, or formal e-mail. First, explain what the problem is and why it is a problem. Then give one or more suggestions about how to solve the problem. Be sure to explain why your solution(s) will work.

B   List problems in your community that concern you. Write down as many as you can. Select one problem you can write to your local representative about.

C   Read the model of a formal e-mail on page 209. It is to an elected official. What problem does Guillermo present? Is his solution a good one?

2   ANALYZE THE WRITING MODEL

PAIRS.   Discuss the questions.

1. Why is Guillermo e-mailing Representative Garcia?

2. Guillermo presents a problem in his first paragraph. Why is it a problem?

3. What solution does Guillermo suggest in his message? Why does he believe that this solution will work?

Getting Started   5 minutes

Say: *We have been talking about the U.S.—its history and government. We have practiced vocabulary and grammatical structures to discuss how the government works and how to become a U.S. citizen. Today we are going to apply all of this knowledge as we write an e-mail to an elected official about a community concern.*

Presentation   5 minutes

1   BEFORE YOU WRITE

A You are going to write...

- Ask: *When you write an e-mail to your friends, how does it usually sound?* Elicit answers, offering prompts as needed. (*Does the e-mail sound friendly? Casual? Is it like a conversation in writing? Are the grammar and spelling correct?*)

- Ask: *Have you ever written a more formal e-mail, such as a request for information or a response to a job posting?* If students respond affirmatively, ask: *How was the tone different from e-mails that you write to friends?* Elicit answers from students, offering discussion prompts as needed. (For example: *How did you start the e-mail? With Dear Mr. or Dear Ms.? Did you write in complete sentences? Did you sign your full name?*)

- Ask students to read the directions, the FYI note and Writing Tip. Clarify terms or answer questions as needed.

- Say: *You will write a formal e-mail like a business letter, such as the cover letter in Unit 2. Use the same format and a similar greeting and salutation.*

- Ask students to review the format of the model cover letter on page 206.

- Say: *When you write your e-mail, you'll use a problem/solution structure. That is, you'll describe a problem and explain the reasons for it, and then you'll give suggestions for solving it.*

Language Note

Because students will be writing about the causes and effects of a problem, encourage them to review the Unit 6, Lesson 7 Reading Skill box on page 118 about words that signal these concepts, including *so, because, because of, therefore, lead to, result,* and *as a result.*

Controlled Practice   20 minutes

B List problems in your...

- Ask students to read the directions.

- Ask: *What are some concerns that you have about your community?* Elicit ideas from students, noting them on the board.

- Say: *Make a list of the community problems that concern you. Then circle the problems that you could describe to a local official, along with proposed solutions.*

- Have students complete the exercise. Walk around and check students' work.

C Read the model of a formal e-mail...

- Ask students to read the directions and then to turn to page 209 and read the formal e-mail. Clarify vocabulary as needed.

- Ask: *What problem does Guillermo present? Is his idea a good one? Why or why not?* Elicit thoughts from students.

Possible answers: The problem Guillermo presents is that funding for adult literacy has decreased. The solution—to increase funding—is one that many students may agree with.

2   ANALYZE THE WRITING MODEL

PAIRS. Discuss the questions.

- Say: *Now I'd like you to read the e-mail a second time, looking for answers to the questions in Exercise 2.*

- Have students complete the exercise. Walk around and check students' work.

- Call on students to say the answers.

Possible answers:

1. He's worried about decreases in adult literacy funding.

2. Decreased funding for adult literacy programs makes it hard for residents to communicate in the workplace and be productive members of the community.

3. He proposes increased adult literacy funding. This would allow workers to improve their basic skills, enabling them to get and keep jobs that pay well. This would benefit the community at large by creating a strong economy for the city.

Write a formal e-mail to an elected official

Communicative Practice   30 minutes

3   THINK ON PAPER

Ⓐ Before Guillermo wrote...

- Read the directions aloud. Ask students to look at Guillermo's T-chart.
- Ask the question in the directions. If necessary, point out that the author presented two of the three problems from his chart in the first paragraph and the three solutions in the second paragraph of the e-mail.

Ⓑ Think about the problem...

- Say: *Now you are going to use the notes that you made in Exercise 1B to make a problem/solution chart for your e-mail. Pick one community problem that you wrote about and describe its causes and solutions, just as Guillermo did in his T-chart.*
- *Optional:* Write a T-chart on the board for students to use:

Problem	Solution

- Have students complete the exercise. Walk around and check students' work, offering prompts as needed. (For example: *What is another effect of the lack of affordable housing?*)

Teaching Tip

If students are on computers, have them create a two-column table in Microsoft Word™ to organize their list of problems and solutions; remind them to paste their notes from Exercises 1B and 3B.

4   WRITE

Use your T-chart to write...

- Read the directions. Say: *Before we begin to write, let's consider how to identify and contact local elected officials.*

- Ask students to name local government representatives (school board members if elected, board of supervisor or city council members, mayor). Show students how to find contact information for these representatives on your local municipal or state website.
- Have students write the first draft of a formal e-mail.
- Say: *When you finish writing, you're going to read your e-mail and revise it. What does* revise *mean?* (changing your work—adding, deleting, or rewriting details)

5   CHECK YOUR WRITING

Ⓐ STEP 1. Revise your work.

- Say: *You'll read over your e-mail a first time and answer the questions in Step 1; if any answers are no, revise your work.*
- *Optional:* Have students form pairs, exchange e-mails, and give each other feedback and suggestions.

Ⓑ STEP 2. Edit and proofread.

- Say: *Then you'll read over your e-mail a second time and edit and proofread your work.* Direct students to check their papers for grammar, spelling, punctuation, and typos.
- *Optional:* Have students complete a "clean" second draft of their e-mail at home, incorporating revisions and corrections from the revision and editing steps.

Teaching Tip

You may want to collect student papers and provide feedback. Use the scoring rubric for writing on page Txv to evaluate vocabulary, grammar, mechanics and how well students complete the task. You may want to review the completed rubric with students.

Extra Practice

Interactive Practice   page 92

THINK ON PAPER

A Before Guillermo wrote his formal e-mail, he used a T-chart to brainstorm and organize his message. Compare his chart to his final e-mail on page 209. How are they similar?

PROBLEM	SOLUTION
Funding for adult literacy has decreased	Increase city budget for adult literacy
Lack of productivity and satisfaction among workers	Improve basic skills: ability to read, write, speak English well
Workers need to get and keep jobs that pay well, city needs strong economy	Increase literacy rates

B Think about the problem you selected to write about in Exercise 1B. Use a problem/solution chart to plan and organize your formal e-mail.

4 WRITE

Use your T-chart to write a formal e-mail to a local representative. Ask your teacher to help you locate the official's name, street address, and e-mail address. Use Guillermo's e-mail as a guide to the format.

5 CHECK YOUR WRITING

A STEP 1. Revise your work.

1. Have you stated the problem clearly in the opening paragraph?
2. Have you presented a solution and explained why it will work?
3. Does your e-mail contain a formal greeting and closing?
4. Is your wording polite and formal?

B STEP 2. Edit and proofread.

1. Have you checked your spelling, grammar, and punctuation?
2. Have you proofread for typing errors?

1 REVIEW

For your grammar review, go to page 230.

2 ACT IT OUT   What do you say?

GROUPS. You are taking a citizenship class and are in a study group with two other classmates. You are helping one another review.

Student A: Review what you learned in Lesson 3 about the three branches of government. Then explain what the executive, judicial, and legislative branches do. Describe the importance of the checks and balances of power.

Student B: Review the T-chart you wrote for Lesson 4. Then explain to Students A and B why you value three of the ideas expressed in the Bill of Rights.

Student C: Review the notes you took about the requirements of naturalization in Lesson 7. Explain the seven general requirements for U.S. citizenship.

3 READ AND REACT   Problem-solving

STEP 1. Read about Jeffrey.

Jeffrey Yuan lives in a neighborhood where too many new high-rise buildings are being constructed. There have been three construction-related accidents in his community in the past year. One accident injured people in Jeffrey's apartment building. Jeffrey would like to do something to stop the amount of building that is taking place in his community. He is concerned about the safety of the people who live there.

STEP 2. GROUPS. What is Jeffrey's problem? What can he do?

4 CONNECT

For your Study Skills Activity, go to page 218.

Which goals can you check off? Go back to page 125.

 Go to the CD-ROM for more practice.

Show what you know!

1 REVIEW

For your grammar review, go to page 230.

- Say: *Today we're going to review the skills that we have practiced in this unit and apply them to a problem. What are some of the skills we have practiced?* Elicit answers, noting them on the board. (For example: discussing early American history, explaining how the U.S. government works, discussing how a bill becomes a law, analyzing historical maps, explaining the procedures of obtaining U.S. citizenship)
- Ask students to complete the grammar review exercise at the top of page 230.

2 ACT IT OUT

GROUPS. You are taking a...

- Ask students to read the directions.
- Say: *Student A will look back at Lesson 3 and discuss what the three branches of government do and why the checks and balances of power are important. Student B will reread the T-chart made for Lesson 4 and explain why he or she values three of the ideas in the Bill of Rights. Student C will review the notes taken in Lesson 7 and will describe the seven requirements for U.S. citizenship.*
- Have students complete the exercise. Walk around the room and monitor conversations.

3 READ AND REACT

STEP 1. Read about Jeffrey.

- Say: *Now we're going to apply our knowledge from this unit to a problem involving a character, Jeffrey. Let's read about Jeffrey.*
- Have students read the story.

STEP 2. GROUPS. What is Jeffrey's problem?

- Ask students to read the directions and then form small groups.
- Give each group a sheet of flipchart paper and markers, or ask them to make notes on a sheet of paper. Tell them that they will write a brief description of Jeffrey's problem and a list of at least three possible solutions.
- Ask groups to choose a representative to present the group's ideas to the class.
- Elicit from students the language to use for making suggestions. (For example: *First, he should . . . He could also try to . . .*)
- Have students discuss the questions. Walk around the room and monitor conversations.
- A representative from each group presents the group's ideas. After each presentation, prompt students for feedback. (*What do you think of Group 1's suggestions for Jeffrey? Which idea do you like best?*)

Possible answers: *Problem:* Jeffrey's problem is that he would like to stop the amount of building in his community. *Solution:* He could write a letter to his local representative asking for new legislation to control the amount of building.

4 CONNECT

Turn to page 218 for your Study Skills activity. See page Txii for general notes for Study Skills activities.

Progress Check

Which goals can you check off? Go back to page 125.
Ask students to turn to page 125 and check off any remaining goals they have reached. Call on them to say which goals they will practice outside of class.

CD-ROM Practice

 Go to the CD-ROM for more practice.

If your students need more practice with the vocabulary, grammar, and competencies in Unit 7, encourage them to review the activities on the CD-ROM.

8 Knowing the Law

Classroom Materials/Extra Practice

CD 3
Tracks 2–8

Workbook
Unit 8

Interactive Practice
Unit 8

Unit Overview

Goals
- See the list of goals on the facing page.

Grammar
- Future real conditional

Listening and Speaking
- Identify the rights of people accused of crimes
- Discuss types of crimes
- *Communication Skill:* Qualifying Opinions

Reading
- Learn about the right to vote
- *Reading Skill:* Distinguishing Fact from Opinion
- Learn about laws protecting children
- Learn about traffic court
- *Reading Skill:* Making Inferences
- Recognize why fines can be serious

Writing
- Compare and contrast two legal systems
- *Writing Tip:* Showing similarities and differences

Life Skills
- Recognize sexual harassment in the workplace

Preview

- Welcome students and have them look at page 145.
- Say: *Look at the picture. Where is the person? What's happening?* Explain as needed that the man is in court. He is swearing to tell the truth in a trial—that is, a legal case that goes before a judge.
- Ask: *How do you think the man feels?* (Possible answers: nervous, upset, afraid, serious)
- Ask: *How many of you have ever seen something like this on TV? Do you remember why the people were in court? What happened?*
- Ask: *Have you ever known anyone who has been involved in a situation like this?* Elicit answers from students, noting that they may talk about similar experiences in their home countries.
- *Optional:* Poll students as to how many have ever been in an American court of law.
- Say: *In this unit, we'll talk about court trials and the American legal system. You'll explore the rights of people who are accused of a crime, and you'll learn about the right to vote. You'll also learn about sexual harassment in the workplace, different types of crime, and traffic court.*

Unit Goals

- Ask students to read the Unit Goals.
- Explain unfamiliar vocabulary as needed. Examples:

    accused—when someone is suspected of committing a crime, but it has not been proven

    sexual harassment—making unwanted sexual comments, gestures, or advances in the workplace

- Say: *As we complete this unit, we will look back at this page and reread the goals. We will check each goal as we complete it.*

Knowing the Law

Preview

What is happening to this man? Have you ever been involved in a situation like this?

UNIT GOALS

- [ ] Identify the rights of people accused of crimes

- [ ] Learn about the right to vote

- [ ] Recognize sexual harassment in the workplace

- [ ] Learn about traffic court

- [ ] Discuss types of crimes

Listening and Speaking

1 BEFORE YOU LISTEN

A **PAIRS.** Discuss the words and their meanings. If you don't know the meaning of a word, look it up in a dictionary.

> arrest   consult   criminal suspect   custody   interrogate

B **CLASS.** Discuss. What happens when someone is arrested in real life or in the movies? What does the police officer say to the suspect about his or her rights?

2 LISTEN

CD3 T2

A 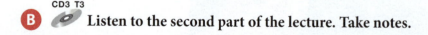 Listen to the first part of the lecture and write *T* (*true*) or *F* (*false*) next to each statement.

___T___ 1. If a suspect answers questions, the suspect's answers can be used as evidence against him or her in court.

___T___ 2. A suspect may remain silent if he or she doesn't want to answer police questions.

___T___ 3. If a suspect wants an attorney but doesn't have money to pay for one, an attorney will be provided.

___F___ 4. If a suspect wants to answer some questions without an attorney present, he or she cannot request an attorney later.

___F___ 5. If a suspect refuses to answer questions, the suspect cannot have an attorney.

CD3 T3

B Listen to the second part of the lecture. Take notes.

3 PRACTICE

PAIRS. Compare and revise your notes. Then use them to discuss the questions.

1. What two Constitutional rights does the *Miranda* decision support?

2. What was the only evidence against Ernesto Miranda at his first trial?

3. Can the police arrest someone without asking the person any questions or giving the person the *Miranda* warning?

4. What can the police ask about without giving a person the *Miranda* warning?

Identify the rights of people accused of crimes

Getting Started   10 minutes

- Say: *Today we are going to learn and talk about rights and civic duties, and to understand the laws that guide society in the U.S.*
- Ask students what words, phrases, or situations come to their minds when they hear the word *law*. (Possible answers: *police, court, arrest, bail*)
- Write responses on the board or a flipchart and keep them visible during this unit. Say: *We'll keep this list up and come back to it later in the unit. In this lesson, we will be learning about the rights of people accused of crimes. These rights go right back to the rights described in the Bill of Rights—the first ten amendments to the U.S. Constitution.*

1   BEFORE YOU LISTEN

A   PAIRS. Discuss the words...

- Set up informal pairs. Have students read the directions. Pass out learners' dictionaries to each pair.
- Walk around. If some pairs finish early, give them other crime and justice words to talk about and define (for example, *bail, convict, acquit*).
- Ask volunteers to define or give examples of the words, including any extra words.
- Explain that while *arrest, criminal suspect,* and *interrogate* are often used to talk about criminal matters, *consult* and *custody* are used in other contexts. (For example, *He consulted his financial advisor. My friend is divorced. She has custody of her three-year-old daughter but the father sees her on weekends.*)

B   CLASS. Discuss. What happens...

- Ask students to read the questions.
- Accept all responses. Allow students to disagree and negotiate; let the discussion continue as long as students are engaged.

Presentation   15 minutes

2   LISTEN

A   Listen to the first part...

- Ask students to read the directions.

- Play CD 3, Track 2.
- Walk around the room as students listen to observe whether any students are having difficulty listening and answering at the same time.
- Ask for volunteers to read the statements and say whether they are true or false. Let students discuss any disagreements in answers; intervene only if they do not come up with the correct answer.

Teaching Tip

Remind students of note-taking strategies. You might first call on students to tell the class what note-taking strategies they use. Then give the class a handout with this information or write it on the board:

- Do not try to write everything you hear. Write down main points or key words.
- Listen for signal words that show time order (*first, second*), examples, (*for example*), and cause and effect (*so, as a result*).
- Write down facts and examples.
- Listen for changes in volume and speed. Important information is often said at a slower pace and louder volume.
- Skip lines when you write. Leave blank spaces so that you can add comments or questions later.

B   Listen to the second part...

- Ask students to take notes and revise them later as necessary.

Controlled Practice   15 minutes

3   PRACTICE

PAIRS. Compare and revise...

- Set up pairs after students listen and revise.
- Ask volunteers to read and answer the questions.

Answers: 1. the right to remain silent and the right to an attorney; 2. Miranda's confession of guilt; 3. yes; 4. such things as a person's name and address

Communicative Practice   20 minutes

4   MAKE IT PERSONAL

A Read the statements,...

- Ask students to read the directions.
- Say: *Ask any questions you have about the sentences before you decide which to check.* Answer any questions.

B GROUPS. Discuss your answers...

- Ask students to read the directions.
- Set up groups.
- Tell students that every student should give his or her choice for item 1 and explain why he or she made that choice. Then have groups do the same for item 2.
- Tell each group to count how many checked *a, b,* or *c.* Compare reasons for the choices.
- Say: *Remember, you are expressing opinions here—there is no right or wrong answer—but it is important to be able to express your opinion and to be able to listen openly to other people's opinions.*
- Walk around; assist as necessary with context, vocabulary, or pronunciation.
- Ask the class whether or not they want to gather a whole-class tally of students' choices. If they indicate *yes* (by a show of hands), ask for each group's numbers, write them on the board, and total them for the whole class.
- Ask students what, if anything, they think the numbers might show. Summarize the results. Say: *These are opinions, not facts, but it looks like the majority of you thought that _____.*

Teaching Tip

- As you walk around the class and monitor group work, listen and watch to make sure that every person in each group has a chance to (and does) speak. If you see some students who routinely do not speak in groups—maybe they are unsure of their speaking skills, they are shy, or someone else in the group is overpowering them—talk to them individually to find out if there is a particular problem (and then help solve the problem); offer encouragement.
- *Note:* Rarely, some students will not feel comfortable in pairs or groups with another particular student—for a personal, social, or cultural reason. If necessary, avoid pairing or grouping those individuals.

C GROUPS. Discuss the questions.

- Ask students to read the questions. Then ask for volunteers to read each question aloud.
- Confirm that everyone understands the issues in each question.
- Tell students to stay in their same groups.
- Explain that while there are no "correct" answers to these and other opinion questions, they are important for at least two reasons: These are very important questions for everyone in a free society to consider, and these discussions give students real-life practice expressing their opinions and explaining ideas, which are necessary skills in American society.
- Say: *As you discuss these questions in your groups, see if you come to a consensus—that is, mostly agree—or not on these three questions. Be prepared to give a brief summary of the discussion; choose one person who will report back to the class.*
- Ask the chosen representative from each group to report on whether the group came to consensus or not and to summarize the discussion.

Extra Practice

Interactive Practice

4 MAKE IT PERSONAL

A Read the statements, and check (✓) the statement in each group that best represents your opinion.

1. ☐ a. If a suspect doesn't want to answer questions, he or she may just be nervous or confused. The police should try to persuade the person to talk.

   ☐ b. If a suspect doesn't want to answer questions, it could mean that he or she is guilty. The police should have methods of persuading people to talk.

   ☐ c. If a suspect doesn't want to answer questions without an attorney present, the police should simply leave the person alone until an attorney is available.

2. ☐ a. If a suspect can't understand the police officer's English, the police should be required to provide the *Miranda* warning in the person's native language.

   ☐ b. If a suspect can't understand the police officer's English but tries to explain or answer questions anyway, this is not the police officer's fault, and it's OK if what the suspect says is used against him or her.

   ☐ c. A police officer shouldn't be required to provide the *Miranda* warning in languages other than English. But the information provided by a poor English speaker without an attorney present should not be used against the person.

B GROUPS. Discuss your answers to Exercise A. For each item, which opinion did most people check?

C GROUPS. Discuss the questions.

1. Do you have laws or protections like the *Miranda* warning in your home country? If so, do you think that such laws are a good thing? If you don't have such laws, should your home country adopt something similar to the *Miranda* warning? Why or why not?

2. Why do you think some innocent people might make inaccurate or false confessions?

3. Why might a suspect want to speak to an attorney before answering a police officer's questions?

Grammar

Future Real Conditional

If you **decide** to answer questions without an attorney present, you **will** still **have** the right to stop answering at any time.

You **will** still **have** the right to stop answering at any time **if** you **decide** to answer questions without an attorney present.

If you **cannot afford** an attorney, one **will be appointed** for you.

An attorney **will be appointed** for you **if** you **cannot afford** one.

Grammar Watch

- A conditional sentence has an *if* clause describing a condition and a result clause describing a result of that condition.
- To form the future real conditional, use the simple present in the *if* clause.
- Use *will* or a modal such as *can, could, may,* or *might* + main verb in the result clause.
- The *if* clause can begin or end a sentence. Use a comma after the *if* clause when it begins the sentence.
- Use the future real conditional to talk about situations that:
  – occur regularly
  – are likely or possible in the future

1   PRACTICE

A **PAIRS. Find the conditional sentences. Underline the *if* clauses. Circle the result clauses.**

If the police stop you for drunk driving, you will be required to take a Blood Alcohol Concentration (BAC) test to determine your blood alcohol level. In most states, if you refuse to take the test, you will be required to pay a fine and you will have your license suspended, in some cases immediately. Also, if you refuse to take the test, you will probably be taken to jail, where you may have to spend the night. If you take the test and your blood alcohol content is over the legal limit, you will probably be taken to jail.

Eventually, you'll go to court. You will probably have to pay a fine if you are found guilty. You may also have to go to jail or go to a driver education program. If it is your first offense, you might just have to do community service. But your insurance payments could go up for even a first offense. If it's not your first offense, your penalties could be severe. Your penalties may also be severe if you are under the legal age to drink alcohol. If you caused injury to another person, your penalties could be extremely severe.

B **Rewrite the sentences with the *if* clause at the beginning.**

1. Your license might be suspended if you refuse a BAC test.

2. Your insurance rates could go up a lot if you are convicted of driving while drunk.

3. Your penalty could be especially severe if you are under the legal drinking age.

4. You will go to jail if the police catch you driving while you are drunk.

Getting Started   5 minutes

- Say: *In the last lesson, we talked about the rights of people accused of crimes. What are some of the rights that you have if you are a suspect?* (the right to remain silent and not answer police questions, the right to have an attorney, the right to receive the *Miranda* warning and be informed of these rights)
- Say: *Today we're going to talk more about the rights of those accused of crimes. To do so, we'll practice the grammatical structure of the future real conditional.*

Presentation   10 minutes

Future Real Conditional

- Ask: *What is the conditional?* Explain that it describes a condition and its consequence or possible consequence. Write two examples on the board:

  (You will pass the test) if you study for it.

  If you don't eat breakfast before the test, (you may not pass it.)

- Say: If *introduces the condition in both sentences.* Will *and* may *in the result clause tell the consequence.*
- Ask: *What is the consequence of the condition of studying for the test?* (you will pass it) *What is the possible consequence of skipping breakfast before the test?* (you may not pass it)
- Say: *Use if clauses with the future real conditional. This grammatical structure describes situations that occur regularly or are likely to happen in the future.*
- Ask students to read the Grammar Watch.
- Read the first two examples in the grammar chart. Point out that when an *if* clause begins a sentence, the clause ends with a comma.
- Read the second two examples in the grammar chart. Ask: *What is the condition in both sentences?* (if you cannot afford an attorney) *What is the consequence of that condition?* (one will be appointed for you)
- Ask students what verb form to use with the *if* clause (the simple present) and the result clause (*will*—or a modal such as *can, could, may,* or *might*—and the main verb).
- Point out that *when, whenever, even if,* and *even though* can replace *if* in one part of the sentence.

Controlled Practice   35 minutes

1 PRACTICE

A PAIRS. Find the conditional sentences....

- Ask students to read the directions. Write the first sentence on the board. Ask: *What is the if clause?* (*If the police stop you for drunk driving*) *What is the result clause?* (*you will be required to take a Blood Alcohol Concentration test . . .*)
- Point out that a comma is used with the *if* clause in the previous example because it occurs at the beginning of the sentence.
- Ask students to read the two paragraphs. Clarify unfamiliar vocabulary as needed. Examples:

  blood alcohol level —the amount of alcohol in your blood; used to determine if you are drunk

  suspended—stopped or prohibited for a certain amount of time (if your driver's license is suspended, you cannot use it)

  community service—actions that benefit the community, such as cleaning up litter

- Have students form pairs and complete the exercise. Walk around and check students' work.
- Call on students to say the answers.

B Rewrite the sentences with...

- Ask students to read the directions. Remind them to use commas at the end of an *if* clause if the *if* clause comes at the beginning of the sentence.
- Have students complete the exercise. Walk around and help, offering prompts as needed. (For example: *Do I say* will might, *or can I use just one of those words?*)
- Call on students to say the answers.

Answers:

1. If you refuse a BAC test, your license might be suspended.
2. If you are convicted of driving while drunk, your insurance rates could go up a lot.
3. If you are under the legal drinking age, your penalty could be especially severe.
4. If the police catch you driving while you are drunk, you will go to jail.

2 PRACTICE

A Use the words and phrases...

- Read the directions and the example together. Note that *not* becomes *won't* in the result clause.
- Have students complete the exercise. Walk around and help students as they write in their notebooks.
- Call on students to read their answers.

Answers:

2. If the police ask for my name and address, I'll give them the information.
3. If I can't afford an attorney, the court will provide one.
4. If I become confused, I won't continue to answer questions.
5. If the police read me my rights, I'll show them a card saying I refuse to talk without my attorney.
6. If you say anything, it will be used against you in court.

B Unscramble the words and phrases...

- Say: *In the previous exercise, we used result clauses with* will *to show a definite outcome of a condition. We can also use result clauses to show possible outcomes. What words introduce a result clause that shows possibility?* (may, might, could)
- Read the directions. Tell students that they will use all of the words in each item to write sentences with *if* and result clauses.
- Have students complete the exercise. Walk around and help students as they work.
- Call on students to read their answers.

Answers:

1. If you jaywalk in New York City, you could receive a $50 fine.
2. If you trespass in Texas, you may receive a maximum fine of $2,000.
3. You might receive a $1,000 fine if you litter in California.
4. You could have to pay between $100 and $500 if you are caught fishing without a license in Mississippi.

Expansion for 2B

- Do a sentence-strip activity to reinforce conditional sentences.
- Make index cards for every word in each of these sentences, and also make a card for each comma:

    If you buy cigarettes in New York, you have to pay a $2.75 cigarette sales tax.
    If you buy gas for your car in New Jersey, you can not pump the gas by yourself.
    If you stand outside a building in Minnesota without a reason, you can be arrested for loitering.
    If you litter in Idaho, you can get a fine of $180.
    If you want to vote in Florida, you have to show a photo ID.

- Clip all the cards needed for each sentence together with a paper or binder clip. Set up groups, and give each group a set of cards for one or two sentences.
- Tell students that they will construct future real conditional sentences, one at a time, by placing the cards in the correct order.
- Have students work in their groups to complete the exercise. Walk around and check sentences.

Communicative Practice   10 minutes

Show what you know!

GROUPS. Discuss the questions.

- Place students in small groups and have them discuss the questions.
- Remind students to use *if* and result clauses to discuss these hypothetical legal situations and what they will do as a result.
- Ask for a representative from each group to present a summary of the group's discussion.
- Ask others in the class if they agree or disagree with the viewpoints presented—and why.

Progress Check

Can you . . . identify the rights of people accused of crimes?

- Say: *We have practiced identifying the rights of people accused of crimes. Can you do this? If so, check the box.*

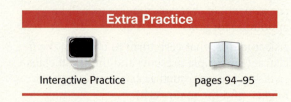

Extra Practice

Interactive Practice   pages 94–95

A Use the words and phrases to write conditional sentences with the *if* clause first and the affirmative or negative of *will* in the result clause.

1. the police / stop me / not answer any questions

   If the police stop me, I won't answer any questions.

2. the police / ask for my name and address / give them the information

3. I / can't afford an attorney / court / provide one

4. I / become confused / not continue to answer questions

5. the police / read me my rights / show them a card saying I refuse to talk without my attorney

6. you / say anything / be used against you in court

B Unscramble the words and phrases to make complete sentences.

1. jaywalk / if / you / you / could / receive / fine / a / New York City / $50 / in

2. you / $2000 / Texas / trespass / if / you / in / receive / may / a maximum fine / of

3. might / fine / you / if / litter / California / in / you / receive / a / $1000

4. if / pay / $100 and $500 / between / fishing / caught / you / are / you / without / a license / in Mississippi / could have to

> **jaywalk:** walk across the street in an area that is not marked for crossing
> **litter:** leave things like pieces of paper on the ground in a public place
> **trespass:** go onto someone's land without permission

Show what you know! Identify the rights of people accused of crimes

GROUPS. Discuss the questions.

1. If the police ever stop you and ask you to take a BAC test, what will you do?

2. If the police ever take you to the police station to question you about a crime, will you talk to them without an attorney present? Why?

3. If you want an attorney but can't afford one, what will you do?

Can you... identify the rights of people accused of crimes? ☐

Reading

1   BEFORE YOU READ

GROUPS. Discuss. How important do you think it is for people to vote?

2   READ

CD3 T4

Listen to and read the article about voting rights in the U.S. Which statements are facts? Which are opinions?

Reading Skill: Distinguishing Fact from Opinion

When you read, look carefully at the information. Is it a fact (something you can prove) or an opinion (a belief or feeling)? Opinions often begin with the words *I think, I believe, I feel, probably, perhaps,* and *maybe.* They may express a judgment about whether something is good or bad, safe or dangerous, fair or unfair.

THE RIGHT TO VOTE

Most Americans probably don't think much about their right to vote. But some of their parents, grandparents, and great-grandparents who lived in the United States were not allowed to vote. In fact, the Constitution had to be **amended** in order to establish or protect the voting rights of certain groups of people.

When the country was founded, only white men who owned land could vote. This meant that poor men didn't have any **official** voice in the government. Later, in the early 1800s, the property requirement was replaced with a poll tax—people had to pay a special **fee** to vote. This also made voting difficult for poor people. Poll taxes were legal until the Twenty-fourth Amendment to the Constitution in 1964.

The Constitution never said that only white people could vote. But it did say that only freemen—people who were not slaves—could vote.

Until after the Civil War, most African-American men were slaves, not freemen. So it was illegal for them to vote. However, after the war, in 1870, the Fifteenth Amendment was added to the Constitution, allowing black men to vote. (No women were allowed to vote yet.) Many states were unhappy with black men having the right to vote. In addition to poll taxes, which most **former** slaves could not pay, these states **imposed** literacy tests. Since many black men coming out of slavery could not read, they were prevented from voting even if they could pay the poll tax. Some southern states added "grandfather clauses" to their **regulations**. These clauses said that if a person's grandfather had voted, the person didn't have to take a literacy test. This helped poor white men, but didn't help black men, whose grandfathers had been slaves. The Voting Rights Act of 1965 removed **restrictions** such as literacy tests.

Women were granted the right to vote by the Nineteenth Amendment to the Constitution in 1920, after many years of struggling to win this right. In 1924, Native Americans were granted the right to vote.

For many years, people had to be 21 years old or older to vote. But during the Vietnam War, many people as young as 18 were **drafted** to fight in Southeast Asia. Many felt that if people were old enough to fight and die for their country, they should be old enough to vote, too. In 1971, the Twenty-sixth Amendment gave people aged 18 and older the right to vote.

There are still people who live permanently in the United States who can't vote. Non-citizens cannot vote, even if they are permanent legal residents. Convicted felons (people who have committed serious crimes) cannot vote in most states.

Getting Started 10 minutes

- Say: *We've been talking about knowing the law in the U.S. Now we are going to study some more about a right we've talked before about—the right to vote. You will listen and read an article about the history of voting rights, and we'll also work on the important skill of distinguishing fact from opinion.*

- Ask a volunteer to explain or give an example of what *distinguish* means as a verb. Explain, if necessary, that it means to recognize or understand the difference between two similar things, people, etc.

- Say: *Now let's think and talk about voting.*

1 BEFORE YOU READ

GROUPS. Discuss. How important...

- Ask students to read the directions.

- Set up informal groups. Say: *Work with the people sitting close to you.* Take turns having each person answer *"How important do you think it is for people to vote?"* Tell students: *Remember to explain why you believe this. Think about voting in your home country, other countries, and here in the U.S.*

- Set up groups, and have students discuss the question.

- Walk around; don't intervene unless someone asks a question.

- Ask whether groups have any questions or comments they want to share with the class.

Presentation 15 minutes

Reading Skill: Distinguishing Fact from Opinion

- Direct students to the Reading Skill box.

- Ask an above-level student to read the text.

- Reiterate that a fact is something can be proven to most people's satisfaction. (Say, for example: *The Civil War began in 1861—there are newspapers, letters, and journals to prove that.*)

- Reiterate that an opinion is the expression of a belief or feeling. (Say, for example: *I think that seat belt laws are unnecessary.*)

2 READ

Listen to and read the article....

- Ask students to read the directions.

- Say: *As you read the article, try to distinguish which statements are facts and which are opinions.*

- Point out that the words in boldface (*amended, official, fee, former, imposed, regulations, restrictions, drafted*) are in the glossary on page 245. Encourage students to read the entire article first, before going to the glossary.

- Play CD 3, Track 4, as students listen and read.

- After students listen and read, ask if they have any other questions about the content, vocabulary, or pronunciation; answer questions.

Answers will vary but should include the one opinion: *Most Americans probably don't think much about their right to vote; or some of the many facts about the history of voting rights. For example: when the country was founded, only white men who owned land could vote; poll taxes were legal until the Twenty-fourth Amendment to the Constitution in 1964; women were granted the right to vote in 1920.*

Expansion: Vocabulary Practice for 2

- Set up small groups.

- Ask students to make a list of the boldfaced words in the reading and to discuss the meaning of each. Encourage students to guess the meaning if they are not sure.

- Tell students to look for the words in the glossary and to compare the definitions there with what they discussed.

- Assign one or two words or phrases to each group and ask them to write one (or two) sentence(s) with their assigned word(s) or phrase(s).

- Ask groups to read their sentences to the class.

- After each group reads the sentence, ask if anyone has any questions about the word or phrase.

Expansion: Reading Practice for 2

- Write or adapt paragraphs on other aspects of the history of voting rights in the U.S. such as the history of Native American and Chinese voting rights.

- Assign the paragraphs to like-ability groups. Have every person in this group read the same paragraph and discuss it.

- Walk around as groups share the information; assist as needed.

Controlled Practice — 10 minutes

3 CHECK YOUR UNDERSTANDING

A PAIRS. Read the statements....

- Ask students to read the directions.
- Set up informal pairs.
- Say: *This time, we are not looking for whether a statement is true or false, but whether it is a fact or an opinion. If you think the statement is a fact, write F in the space. If you think the statement is an opinion, write O in the space.*
- Ask volunteers to read their answers. Intervene only if students do not come up with the correct answers.

Communicative Practice — 25 minutes

B GROUPS. Discuss the questions.

- Ask students to read the directions.
- Set up groups of three. Say: *Write the answers to the questions in your notebooks. Then one person will read and answer each question and the other members of your group will agree or disagree and add other comments.*
- Walk around; assist as necessary. Check for understanding. Answer only questions that students do not understand or that they disagree about.

Answers:
1. Grandfather clauses said that if a person's grandfather had voted, the person didn't have to take a literacy test. This was not fair to black men because their grandfathers were probably slaves and wouldn't have been able to vote, so the black men would have to take the literacy test.
2. Women received the right to vote 50 years after black men (but many African Americans were not able to actually vote until the 1960s).
3. During the Vietnam War, many people felt that if people were old enough to fight or die for their country (men could be drafted into the military), they should be able to vote.

4 WORD WORK

GROUPS. Choose three words...

- Confirm that students understand that they discuss first and then write in their vocabulary logs.
- Have students remain in the same groups. Ask students to read the directions.
- Walk around; intervene only if you hear a question that students can't answer in the group.

5 MAKE IT PERSONAL

GROUPS. Discuss the questions.

- Ask students to read the questions.
- Tell students to work with the same groups they worked with earlier.
- Say: *These are all important questions. If you get involved discussing one or two questions, just continue with it; don't worry if you don't get to every question.*

Expansion: Writing Practice for 5

- Ask students to choose one of the Exercise 5 questions and write a paragraph that expresses their opinions on the topic.
- Encourage students to write a clear topic sentence, give specific examples limited to the defined topic, and follow and double-check punctuation rules for quotation marks. If necessary, review punctuation rules with students.

Teaching Tip

You may want to collect student papers and provide feedback. Use the scoring rubric for writing on page Txv to evaluate vocabulary, grammar, mechanics and how well students complete the task. You may want to review the completed rubric with students.

Extra Practice

Interactive Practice

pages 96–97

3 CHECK YOUR UNDERSTANDING

A **PAIRS.** Read the statements. Write *F* next to the *facts* and *O* next to the *opinions*.

O 1. Most Americans probably don't think much about their right to vote.

F 2. In 1870, no women were allowed to vote yet.

F 3. In 1924, Native Americans were granted the right to vote.

F 4. The Voting Rights Act of 1965 removed restrictions such as literacy tests.

O 5. I believe that convicted felons should not have the right to vote.

B **GROUPS.** Discuss the questions.

1. What was the grandfather clause mentioned in the article? Why wasn't it fair to black men?
2. How many years after black men received the right to vote did women receive the same right?
3. Why was the voting age lowered in 1971?

4 WORD WORK

GROUPS. Choose three words or phrases in the article that you would like to remember. Discuss the words and their meanings. Then record the words and information about them in your vocabulary log.

5 MAKE IT PERSONAL

GROUPS. Discuss the questions.

1. Is 18 a good minimum voting age? Why or why not?
2. What arguments might people have used in favor of literacy tests?
3. Should convicted felons have the right to vote again when they get out of jail? Why or why not?
4. Should permanent residents who are not citizens but who pay taxes and contribute to their communities have the right to vote? Why or why not?

Life Skills

1 UNDERSTAND SEXUAL HARASSMENT

A **CLASS.** What is sexual harassment? Does your company or school have a sexual harassment policy? If so, describe it. If not, should it have one? Why or why not?

B Read the web page on page 153. Check (✓) the types of conduct that are *not* examples of sexual harassment.

- ✓ 1. Welcome conduct of a sexual nature
- ☐ 2. Repeatedly telling sexual jokes
- ✓ 3. Asking a person out one time
- ☐ 4. Treating someone badly if he or she refuses to go out on a date
- ✓ 5. Conduct that has no impact on the workplace
- ☐ 6. Displaying sexual screensavers
- ☐ 7. Sending e-mails that contain sexual language
- ✓ 8. Friendly conversations between professors and students
- ☐ 9. Telling rumors about a co-worker's personal life
- ☐ 10. Looking a co-worker up and down in an overly friendly way

2 PRACTICE

A **GROUPS.** Look again at the key features of the web definition of *sexual harassment*. Discuss. Are they reasonable? Why or why not?

- *unwelcome*
- *conduct of a sexual nature*
- *severe or pervasive*
- *affects working conditions or creates a hostile work environment*

B **GROUPS.** Discuss. Do any of the examples of sexual harassment in the web page *not* make sense to you? If so, which one(s)? Explain.

*Can you…*recognize sexual harassment in the workplace?   ☐

Getting Started   5 minutes

- Say: *We have learned about U.S. citizens' right to vote in this country. Let's talk about another right—the right to a safe workplace. We have already learned that employees have the right to safe working conditions. This includes protection from sexual harassment.*

Language Note

Explain that *harass* means to bother someone with unwanted behavior or constant demands. *Harassment* is usually persistent and continues for a long period of time.

Presentation   10 minutes

1 UNDERSTAND SEXUAL HARASSMENT

A CLASS. **Discuss. What is sexual harassment?...**

- Ask the questions. Explain that sexual harassment involves making unwanted sexual comments, gestures, or advances at work—and it is against the law.
- Say: *Today we'll talk more about sexual harassment. We'll explore what it is and learn how to recognize it in the workplace.*

Controlled Practice   25 minutes

B **Read the web page on page 153....**

- Ask students to read the directions and the web page excerpt.
- Clarify unfamiliar terms as needed. Examples:
    conduct—behavior
    hostile—extremely unfriendly; aggressive
    rumors—false stories about a person or situation
    gestures—physical movements that indicate how you feel
    screensavers—images displayed on a computer screen when it is not in use
    pressure—trying to make somebody do something
    suffer—to become worse in quality
    deny—to refuse to give somebody something

- Tell students that they will read the web page excerpt again and check the types of conduct that are *not* sexual harassment.
- Have students complete the exercise. Walk around and check their work.
- Before you go over the answers with students, say: *The web page gives four criteria to define sexual harassment. What four things define sexual harassment?* Point out the four subheads of the web page.
- Elicit definitions of *severe* (very serious) and *pervasive* (something that happens repeatedly).
- Ask students which items they checked in Exercise 1B that were *not* examples of sexual harassment (items 1, 3, 5, 8).

Communicative Practice   20 minutes

2 PRACTICE

A GROUPS. **Look again at the key...**

- Say: *Now we're going to review the key features of sexual harassment.* Ask students to read the directions.
- Elicit a definition of *reasonable* (fair and sensible). Tell students that they will form small groups and discuss whether they feel the features of the definition of sexual harassment are reasonable.
- Have students complete the exercise. Walk around and monitor conversations, offering prompts as needed.
- Call on a representative from each group to summarize its discussion for the class.

B GROUPS. **Discuss. Do any of the examples...**

- Ask students to read the directions.
- Have students complete the exercise. Walk around and monitor conversations. Clarify any information that is unclear or foreign to students (for example, any example of harassment that is culturally foreign to them).
- If any instances of sexual harassment on the web page remain unclear, go over these examples with the whole class.

NOTES ON THE WEB PAGE

Culture Connection

- Say: *In the U.S., sexual harassment is illegal and it is treated very seriously. Therefore, many workplaces have rules against employee dating. Sometimes these rules prohibit co-workers from dating each other; sometimes they prohibit a supervisor from dating an employee that he or she manages. Many schools and universities also have rules against professors dating students for ethical and legal reasons.*

Expansion: Speaking Practice for 2A and 2B

- Set up groups of four.
- Write these questions on the board:

  1. What is the best way to stop harassment in workplaces? (Possible responses: *Require all workers to watch a video on sexual harassment, survey workers, etc.*)

  2. What should the consequences be for employees who sexually harass other employees? A warning? Suspended pay? Job loss?

- Have the groups discuss the questions and report their opinions to the class.

Teaching Tip

- Sexual harassment in the workplace or schools is handled differently around the world. Be aware that in your students' home countries, there may be different laws, or no laws, to protect people from sexual harassment.
- If your students want to talk about the situation in their home countries, encourage them to share how sexual harassment is viewed there. Be mindful that this is a sensitive topic and that not all students may want to participate. However, if students seem open to the discussion, you may want to prompt them with questions. For example, you can ask: *Do you know if there are any laws to protect people from sexual harassment? If so, what are they? Do you think they are effective? How could they be more effective? If there aren't any, should there be? What sorts of laws would work to protect people from sexual harassment in your country? Do you think this is the responsibility of the government, companies, or individuals?*

Extra Practice

Interactive Practice

pages 98–99

Equal Rights Under the Law

Home | Need Advice? | Legal Assistance

What You Need to Know About Sexual Harassment

Sexual harassment can be defined as "unwelcome verbal, visual, or physical conduct of a sexual nature that is severe or pervasive and affects working conditions or creates a hostile work environment." Let's look at what this means.

- **Unwelcome.** In other words, no behavior is sexual harassment if it is welcome. For this reason, it is important that if someone's behavior is making you uncomfortable, you clearly communicate that the person should stop. You can tell the person to stop and you can communicate your message in writing and by your actions.
- **Conduct of a sexual nature.** Some of the behaviors that can be described as conduct of a sexual nature include comments about a person's body, body language, or clothing; sexual jokes; repeatedly asking a person out; asking a person for sex; or telling rumors about a person's personal or sexual life. Inappropriate touching of a person is conduct of a sexual nature. This includes kissing, hugging—any touching that the person indicates is unwelcome. Looking up and down a person's body or making sexual gestures is an example of conduct of a sexual nature. Following or blocking a person is also an example of conduct of a sexual nature (for example, standing in front of someone who is trying to pass through a doorway). Displaying sexual posters, drawings, pictures, or screensavers is behavior that is sexual in nature. So is sending e-mails with sexual content.
- **Severe or pervasive.** *Severe* means serious, and *pervasive* means the behavior happens repeatedly. A single incident is probably not sexual harassment unless it is severe. For example, a man's asking a woman out on a date, once, and having her refuse is not sexual harassment. Continuing to pressure her after she has clearly said she isn't interested, or treating her badly after she refuses, could well be sexual harassment.
- **Affects working conditions or creates a hostile work environment.** If repeated sexual comments make you so uncomfortable at work that your performance suffers, the sexual comments do affect your working conditions. If you are threatened with being fired, denied a promotion, given a poor performance evaluation, or asked to do less desirable work because you refuse sexual interaction with a supervisor, that is almost certainly sexual harassment: The supervisor's reaction to your refusal clearly creates a hostile work environment.

There are federal and state laws to protect people from sexual harassment. Some of these laws only apply to businesses with fifteen or more employees. Employers are usually required by law to prevent and stop sexual harassment. Sexual harassment laws protect students as well. A professor cannot sexually harass a student. Both men and women can be victims of sexual harassment, and both men and women can be guilty of sexual harassment. Sexual harassment can occur between members of the same sex. For more information, check the laws in your state or contact your Human Resources (HR) Department or your Office of Student Affairs.

Source: Adapted from "Know Your Rights: Sexual Harassment at Work" ©2008 Equal Rights Advocates, Inc.

Reading

1 BEFORE YOU READ

CLASS. Discuss the questions.

1. What is the difference between child discipline and child abuse?

2. Are there any cultural differences regarding child abuse? Explain.

3. Do you know how to report suspected child abuse? If so, how?

2 READ

CD3 T5

Listen to and read the article. What kinds of child abuse does it discuss?

Child Abuse

For many of us, it's unbelievable that an adult would ever seriously hurt a child. Unfortunately, every year, many adults are guilty of physical abuse, emotional abuse, or **neglect** of one or more children. Child abuse is a shame, but it's more than that—it's against the law.

Federal law basically says that an act, or failure to act, is child abuse if it results in death, serious physical or emotional harm, or neglect. States determine their own definitions of physical or emotional harm and neglect. But the following are some possible examples:

Physical abuse: When a parent or guardian injures a child (causing any harm from minor **bruises** to death), this is physical abuse. Beating, kicking, shaking, throwing, choking, and hitting a child are all types of physical abuse. Even if the abuser did not intend, or mean, to harm the child, what matters is whether the child has been injured.

Emotional abuse: When a parent or guardian constantly criticizes a child, this is emotional abuse. Other types of emotional abuse include threats, **rejection**, and failure to give love, support, or **guidance**. Emotional abuse is often hard to prove, and officials may not be able to take any action, unless there is real evidence of harm. However, emotional abuse often occurs alongside physical abuse.

Neglect: When a parent or guardian fails to give a child necessary food or shelter, this is neglect. Other kinds of neglect include denying a child medical or mental health treatment, failing to educate a child, and ignoring a child's emotional needs, including permitting a child to use alcohol or drugs. Emotional neglect is hard to prove.

In some states, anyone who suspects child abuse is required to report it. In other states, only people in certain positions are required to report child abuse. These people include doctors and other medical personnel, teachers and other school employees, social workers, day-care workers, and others who are in frequent contact with children. When these people have a reason to **suspect** abuse, they are required by law to report it.

Usually reports are made to CPS (Child Protective Services). CPS decides whether there is reason to investigate. Investigations may result in criminal charges, but sometimes even if abuse is confirmed, the abuser will not go to jail but instead must attend a special program to learn to stop the abuse. If the CPS workers decide that it's necessary for the safety of a child, the child may be temporarily removed from the home. In such cases, children are often placed in **foster care** while one or both parents get help. For more information, contact your state's Child Welfare Program.

Source: ©2008 Child Welfare Information Gateway

Learn about laws protecting children

Getting Started — 15 minutes

- Say: *We've been talking about the different aspects of knowing the law. In this lesson, we will focus on a crucial legal topic: protecting the rights of children. Even if you don't have children or your children are not living in the U.S. now, protecting children is everyone's business.*

1 BEFORE YOU READ

CLASS. Discuss the questions.

- Ask students to read the three questions.
- To get the discussion started, say: *This reading identifies different kinds of child abuse. When you differentiate (or compare differences) between child abuse and child discipline, you need to look carefully at the situation. Think about the severity of the punishment and also how often it happens. Consider, for example, some questions:*

  If a parent spanked a child once or twice when the child did something bad, do you think this is abuse?

  What if a parent repeatedly hits his or her children with a belt or a shoe and causes injuries?

  Is there a recognizable difference between the two?

- Have students discuss their responses to the examples.
- Say: *Let talk for a minute about teenagers. What do you think about this situation?*

  A parent slaps a teenager because the teenager cursed out the parent with foul language. Was this acceptable or not?

- Now that students have thought about these situations, elicit responses from students for the first question on page 154. Answers will vary about the distinction between discipline and abuse. Accept all responses.
- Say: *Now let's talk about the second question on page 154. Are there ever times when a physical punishment is acceptable discipline in your home country? What kind of punishment? What is considered discipline in your home country and what is considered abuse?*
- Elicit responses for the second question. Answers will vary depending on your students' cultural backgrounds. If students are hesitant about answering, keep the discussion general and impersonal.

- Rephrase the third question aloud: *Do you know how to report child abuse in this country?* Ask for volunteers to answer. Accept all responses, but explain local school and government rules if necessary.
- Tell students about national organizations that help stop child abuse, such as ChildHelp at www.childhelp.org/get_help or the National Child Abuse Hotline at 1-800-252-2873, 1-800-25ABUSE.

Presentation — 15 minutes

Teaching Tip

- Although students need to know the laws and cultural expectations related to child discipline and child abuse, this topic can cause distress among students.
- If you suspect that some of your students may have been physically and/or sexually abused in their home countries or in refugee camps, consider changing the focus of the lesson. Before you begin the lesson, ask students if they want to discuss this topic or if it will be too painful. If the majority of students seem uncomfortable, consider changing the lesson.
- Provide information from the local school system and human services department about child discipline, child abuse, and child welfare.

2 READ

 Listen to and read the article...

- Ask students to read the directions.
- Say: *Now we are going to listen to and read a short article about child abuse.*
- Point out that the words and phrases in black boldface (*neglect, bruises, rejection, guidance, suspect, foster care*) are in the glossary on page 245. Encourage students to read the entire article first, before going to the glossary.
- Play CD 3, Track 5, as students listen and read.
- After students listen and read, ask if they have any other questions about the content, vocabulary, or pronunciation; answer questions.

Answer: The article discusses physical abuse, emotional abuse, and neglect.

Learn about laws protecting children

Controlled Practice   15 minutes

3   CHECK YOUR UNDERSTANDING

Write the answers to the questions.

- Ask students to read the directions and answer the questions.
- Tell students that it is OK if they just write short answers.
- Tell students to share their answers with other students. Intervene only if there is a question or an unresolved disagreement.

Communicative Practice   15 minutes

4   WORD WORK

GROUPS. Find the boldfaced words...

- Ask students to read the directions.
- Set up informal groups. Say: *Work with people sitting close to you. First, match the words and definitions on your own. Then check your answers with your group after you have finished.*

 Expansion: Vocabulary Practice for 4

- Keep the same groups.
- Pass out three topic-related words or phrases to each group such as *cope, battery, shelter, assault, isolation*.
- Pass out advanced learners' dictionaries to each group.
- Tell students that if they already know one of their own words, to write down their own definition and use the word or phrase in a sentence before they double-check in the dictionary. If students don't know the words or phrases, tell them to look them up in the dictionary and write down the definitions and use them in sentences.

- After all groups are finished, tell each group to share their words, definitions, and sentences with all the other groups. Tell students they only need to write down (in their vocabulary logs) the definitions and sentences they don't already know.
- Walk around; assist as needed with context, vocabulary, pronunciation, and writing sample sentences.

■ MULTILEVEL INSTRUCTION for 4

Cross-ability Place at least one above-level student (who has strong vocabulary, is comfortable with an advanced dictionary, and can lead the group in writing sentences) in each group.

5   MAKE IT PERSONAL

GROUPS. Discuss the questions.

- Tell students to stay in the same groups.
- Ask students to read the questions.
- Say: *Discuss these questions carefully and be respectful of others' ideas.*
- Tell each group to write a list of possible solutions to item 3.
- Walk around; intervene only if students are not talking carefully, openly, and respectfully to each other.

3 CHECK YOUR UNDERSTANDING

Write the answers to the questions. Answers will vary but could include the following:

1. What is an example of physical abuse?

   beating, kicking, shaking, throwing, choking, or hitting a child

2. What is an example of neglect?

   failure to give a child food, shelter, medical or mental health treatment, or an education

3. What are some things that might happen if suspected child abuse is reported?
   The parent may face criminal charges, and the child may be removed from the home and
   placed in foster care.

4 WORD WORK

✒ **GROUPS. Find the boldfaced words in the article. Guess their meanings from context. Then match the words with their definitions. Record the words and information about them in your vocabulary log.**

c	1. bruises	a. situation in which a non-relative cares for a child without becoming a legal parent
a	2. foster care	b. lack of care and attention
d	3. guidance	c. injuries caused by a blow or pressure on the skin
b	4. neglect (n)	d. helpful advice about work, education, and so on
f	5. rejection	e. to think that someone may be guilty of a crime
e	6. suspect (v)	f. the act of refusing to give love or attention to someone else

5 MAKE IT PERSONAL

GROUPS. Discuss the questions.

1. Do you believe children should be physically punished? If you do, what do you see as the difference between physical punishment and abuse?

2. How would you feel about having a job that required you to report suspected child abuse?

3. How can child abuse be prevented?

Reading

1 BEFORE YOU READ

A **CLASS.** Have you ever received a traffic ticket? If so, what happened after you got it?

B **PAIRS.** Discuss the words and their meanings.

issue (*v*)	to officially make a statement or give a warning
penalty	a punishment for not obeying a law, rule, or legal agreement
procedure	a way of doing something, especially the correct way
sentence (*v*)	to legally punish someone who has been found guilty of a crime
suspend	to officially stop someone from working, driving, or going to school for a fixed period, because he or she has broken the rules
violation	an action that breaks a law, rule, or agreement

2 READ

CD3 T6

 Listen to and read the handout about traffic tickets. What are the two kinds of traffic cases? What are some examples of each?

Your Traffic Ticket

So you have received a traffic ticket. What do you do now? In our county, there are very clear **procedures** to follow. Read both sides of your ticket carefully. It will tell you what **violation** you are charged with, how you can respond, whether you have to go to court, and what your rights are. The steps you must follow and the **penalties** you may receive depend on whether your case is a civil or criminal traffic case.

Civil traffic cases include violations such as driving without wearing a seat belt, failure to use a child restraint, or speeding. The penalty for a civil traffic violation is usually a fine and/or required attendance at driving school. You may not have to go to court if you agree that you are guilty and send payment for your fine. If you do not think you are guilty, you may request a trial. You can't be **sentenced** to jail for civil violations. However, in addition to a fine, you may get "points" against your license. If you get several points within a certain period of time, your insurance rates will increase.

Criminal traffic cases are more serious than civil cases. DUI (driving while under the influence of alcohol) and driving while your license is **suspended** are examples of criminal traffic violations. These cases require a court hearing. Although most sentences involve payment of a fine and points against your license, jail or prison time is also possible. In a criminal case, you have the right to request a jury trial.

Failure to appear in court is a serious crime. If your ticket says that you have to appear in court and you don't appear, you are in trouble. Whether your case is a civil case or a criminal case, a "bench warrant" could be **issued** for your arrest. This means that if a police officer stops you and checks your records, you can be arrested and taken to jail. Bench warrants can also be issued for failure to pay fines. So if you receive a traffic ticket, don't try to avoid dealing with it.

Learn about traffic court

Getting Started   15 minutes

- Say: *In this unit, we've talked about many aspects of law—the* Miranda *warning, voting rights, sexual harassment in the workplace, and child abuse. Now we're going to explore a very common problem— traffic violations. We are going to learn about traffic court.*

1 BEFORE YOU READ

A **CLASS. Have you ever...**

- Ask students to read the directions.
- Ask: *Would anyone like to talk about your experience getting a traffic ticket?* Accept all responses. If no one responds, give a personal example. (For example: *I remember the one time I was in an extra hurry to get home because there was a problem with my teenager. I didn't come to a full stop at a stop sign and a police officer stopped me. I got a ticket, and I was able to pay it by mail.*)

B **PAIRS. Discuss the words...**

- Ask students to read the directions.
- Set up informal pairs. Say: *Talk about these words and their meanings with someone sitting near you.*
- Walk around; assist as needed with context, grammar, and pronunciation.
- Pronounce each of the vocabulary words. If you have Spanish speakers in the class, confirm that they know how to pronounce *violation* in English.
- Ask volunteers to make up sentences for each word. If necessary, give examples. (For example: *When I didn't stop at the stop light, I was issued a ticket by the police officer.*)

Presentation   15 minutes

2 READ

  Listen to and read the handout...

- Ask students to read the directions.
- Rephrase the questions. Say: *When you listen and read, look for two types of traffic cases and examples of each.*
- Confirm that students understand what a *case* is in this context. (a question or problem that will be dealt with by a court of law)

- Point out that the words and phrases in boldface (*procedures, violation, penalties, sentenced, suspended, issued*) are in the glossary on page 245. Encourage students to read the entire article first, before going to the glossary.
- Play CD 3, Track 6, as students listen and read.
- After students listen and read, ask if they have any other questions about the content, vocabulary, or pronunciation; answer questions.

Answers: The two types of traffic cases are *civil* (for example, speeding, driving without a seat belt) and *criminal* (for example, driving while under the influence of alcohol or driving with a suspended license).

Expansion: Reading Practice for 2

- Help students to access and navigate the traffic court process online. If computers and the Internet are not available for students, pass out handouts downloaded from your local or state traffic court website. Have students read the handouts and follow the same process as below.
- Many states and localities support traffic court websites that explain laws and requirements as well as online payment. Send students to specific traffic court websites.
- Set up groups of three for working at a computer. Give students the local/state traffic court URL, or web address.
- Tell groups to work together to try to decipher the basic meaning of the page they are on. Say: *I don't expect you to understand everything on the page—the vocabulary and sentence structure can be confusing, even for native speakers of English. Try to figure out the main points by talking together. Write down the words and phrases you don't understand. We'll work on those later.*
- Walk around; assist as necessary with content, context, and vocabulary.

Teaching Tip

Outside of class, students need to interact with text and vocabulary that may be very challenging (for example, the traffic court website). Students need to become familiar with difficult official text and how to navigate the websites, texts, and vocabulary. Working through above-level texts with the support of the teacher and fellow students helps students become more able to handle such texts in their own lives.

Controlled Practice   15 minutes

3   CHECK YOUR UNDERSTANDING

A **Reread the handout. Then...**

- Ask students to read the directions.
- Ask students to write short answers to the questions in their notebooks.
- Ask volunteers to read and answer the questions.
- Confirm that students understand the content of the text; answer any related questions, and allow students to talk about the topic as long as they are engaged.

Answers:

1. You can find what violation the person is charged with, how the person can respond, whether the person has to go to court, and what the person's rights are.
2. A person may request a trial.
3. A person's car insurance rates will increase; in most states, a person who gets too many points may lose his or her license or have to go to driving school.
4. A bench warrant could be issued, which means that if a police office stops the person and checks his or her records, that person could be arrested and taken to jail.

Reading Skill: **Making Inferences**

- Direct students to the Reading Skill box.
- Ask a confident, above-level student to read the text.
- Say: *Making an inference is making a logical guess. An inference needs to be supported by facts or other information. For example, if the temperature is below 32°F, and there are low, dark clouds in the sky, you could reasonably infer that it will snow. However, if the weather is 70°F and it is sunny, you can't reasonably infer that it will snow.*

B **GROUPS. Read the sentences...**

- Ask students to read the directions.
- Discuss answers. Talk about making inferences. If necessary, give more examples until you can confirm that most students understand the skill.

Answers: 1. *a*, not *b*, because *b* is explicit in the handout and because the handout says "in our county," which suggests that procedures may be different in other counties; 2. *a*, not *b*, because the text says that civil cases are less serious than criminal cases; it also says that you have a right to request a trial, but no mention is made of a jury trial in civil cases. Therefore, it is logical to infer that people don't have a right to request a jury trial for civil traffic cases. Also *b* is just an opinion, not an inference based on clues in the text.

Communicative Practice   15 minutes

4   WORD WORK

GROUPS. Choose three words...

- Set up groups.
- Ask students to read the directions.
- Confirm that students understand that they discuss first, then write in vocabulary logs.
- Walk around; intervene only if you hear a question that students can't answer in the group.

5   MAKE IT PERSONAL

GROUPS. Read the paragraph. Discuss...

- Tell students to stay in the same groups.
- Ask students to read the paragraph and then discuss the questions. Say: *After you read and think for a minute, share your opinion with the other members of your group. If you don't think the system for paying fines is fair, explain what improvements you might suggest.*
- Walk around; assist as needed with content and context.

Teaching Tip

If students do not seem enthusiastic about the topic of a particular discussion, change the lesson. Consider bringing in an authentic audio or video clip related to the topic. Play the clip, and ask students to summarize the content orally or in writing.

Extra Practice

Interactive Practice   pages 100–101

CHECK YOUR UNDERSTANDING

A **Reread the handout. Then write the answers to the questions.**

1. What is some information you can find on a traffic ticket?
2. If you do not believe that you are guilty of a civil violation, what can you do?
3. What can happen if you get too many points against your license in a certain period of time?
4. What could happen if you don't appear in court when you are required to?

B **GROUPS.** **Read the sentences below. Check (✓) the sentence in each item that is an inference based on the reading. Discuss why it is an inference and the other sentence is not.**

> **Reading Skill:** Making Inferences
>
> When you make an inference, you make a logical guess about something that is not directly stated in the text, based on other information that is provided. In other words, you "fill in" information.

1. ☑ a. Different counties may have different procedures for responding to a traffic ticket.

   ☐ b. There is information on both the back and the front of a ticket.

2. ☑ a. In a civil case, you don't have the right to request a jury trial.

   ☐ b. Bench warrants are unfair.

4 **WORD WORK**

GROUPS. **Choose three words or phrases in the handout that you would like to remember. Discuss the words and their meanings. Then record the words and information about them in your vocabulary log.**

5 **MAKE IT PERSONAL**

GROUPS. **Read the paragraph. Discuss. Do you think the system for paying fines is fair? If not, what improvements would you suggest?**

Sometimes, without the money to pay a fine, poor people fail to go to court when they are required to. Other times, they just don't pay their fine in time. A warrant is issued for their arrest, and, in the end, they go to jail. Keeping people in jail costs taxpayers a lot of money. Some people think this is not a good system. However, other people think it would be unfair to fine different people differently. They believe that the law is the law and that the penalty should be the same for anyone who breaks it.

Listening and Speaking

1 BEFORE YOU LISTEN

A **CLASS.** The box below contains a list of crimes in the U.S. Discuss the words in the box and their meanings. If you don't know the meaning of a word, look it up in a dictionary.

arson	murder	shoplifting
burglary	rape	trespassing
illegal drug use	robbery	vandalism

B **CLASS.** In your home country, what happens to people who are guilty of the crimes above?

C **GROUPS.** Now try to put the words from Exercise A into the correct categories in the chart. You can check your chart when you listen in Exercises 2A and 2B.

Misdemeanors (less serious)		Felonies (more serious)	
trespassing		arson	murder
vandalism		burglary	rape
shoplifting		illegal drug use	robbery

2 LISTEN

A CD3 T7 Listen to the lecture about types of crimes. Check your answers in Exercise 1C.

B CD3 T7 Listen again. Then write the answers to the questions.

1. What are two examples of infractions?
    traffic violations, littering

2. What is the longest prison sentence that can be given for a misdemeanor?

3. What are some other penalties for misdemeanors?

4. What if someone doesn't have money to pay a fine?

5. How long can a person be sentenced to prison for a felony?

6. What is another sentence that is possible for some types of felonies in some states?

Lesson 7 Discuss types of crimes

Getting Started — 15 minutes

- Say: *In this unit, we have been studying different aspects of American law. Now we are going to listen to and talk about different types of crimes in the U.S.—what they are called and how to avoid becoming a victim. This will be a general discussion only; you do not need to share any personal experiences.*
- Ask students if they feel the level of crime in the U.S. is high or not. Encourage them to describe what their perception of crime is based on (things they have seen, heard, experienced). Remind them that crime on TV or in the movies is often sensational (intended to shock people), so it does not necessarily reflect reality.

Teaching Tip
- Be aware that students may feel uncomfortable using some of the words for crimes in a discussion.
- Women may feel uncomfortable talking about rape in front of male classmates. Consider asking a human services worker or a female police officer to talk in a comfortable and safe environment about gender-based crimes to the women in your class, explaining their rights and possible dangers.

1 BEFORE YOU LISTEN

A CLASS. The box below contains...
- Ask students to read the directions. Pass out dictionaries.
- Ask volunteers to explain and/or give examples of the words. Clarify and expand on their answers as needed so that everyone understands each word. Give examples if necessary. (*Arson is when a person burns down a building intentionally. Sometimes a building owner might do that secretly to try to collect insurance on the building, or sometimes a mentally ill person might set a building on fire.*)
- Explain to students that there are many other kinds of crime (for example, kidnapping, blackmail).
- Ask students if they have any other questions at this time.

B CLASS. In your home country,...
- Ask students to read the question and try their best to answer.
- Don't pressure students if they are uncomfortable talking about particular crimes and punishments.

C GROUPS. Now try to put the words...
- Ask students to read the directions.
- Set up groups. Have students complete the exercise.
- Tell students that they will be able to check their choices as they listen to the lecture on crimes.

Presentation — 15 minutes

2 LISTEN

A 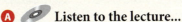 Listen to the lecture...
- Ask students to read the directions.
- Review the directions to make sure everyone understands that they should check their answers for Exercise 1C.
- Play CD 3, Track 7.
- Walk around the room as students listen to observe whether any students are having difficulty.
- Ask students to make any changes necessary to Exercise 1C.

B Listen again. Then write...
- Ask students to read the directions. Say: *You can write as you listen to the lecture or wait until the lecture is over and then answer the questions.*
- Play Track 7 again.
Answers: 2. up to one year; 3. a fine, probation, or community service; 4. The court can set up a payment program. 5. from one year to life; 6. the death penalty

Controlled Practice 15 minutes

3 PRACTICE

Complete the paragraph...

- Ask students to read the directions.
- Rephrase the directions. Say: *Use the words from the box to fill in the appropriate blanks in the paragraph.* Point out the example. Say: *It is a good habit to cross out a word once you've used it, so you know what words you still have to work with.*
- Ask volunteers to read the sentences in the paragraph. Allow students to disagree with word choices; intervene only if students do not arrive at the correct answers.

Communicative Practice 15 minutes

Communication Skill: **Qualifying Opinions**

- Direct the students to the Communication Skill box.
- Ask a confident, above-level student to read the text.
- Explain that qualifying opinions is an important skill. Say: *Using qualifying language like* unless, if, *or* it depends *on makes it seem more reasonable to listeners. Americans have an idiom: "Things are not just black or white." In other words, there is not always an absolute truth about a topic and only one way of looking at it. People will pay more attention to your views if you recognize this.*

4 CONVERSATION

GROUPS. Practice the conversation...

- Ask students to read the directions.
- Set up groups of three.
- Say: *This conversation practices using qualifying language when expressing opinions.*
- Tell groups to decide among themselves who will be Students A, B, and C.
- Walk around, listen, but intervene only if someone asks a question.

5 MAKE IT PERSONAL

GROUPS. Discuss. What do you think...

- Tell students to stay in the same groups.
- Ask students to read the question.
- Remind students to take turns, but tell them that it might be possible for someone not to have formed an opinion yet on appropriate fines or sentences for the various crimes mentioned in Exercise 1A.
- Suggest appropriate language for not wanting to express an opinion. (For example: *I don't feel qualified to express an opinion on that topic. I don't know enough about the topic to feel as if I can answer. I don't feel comfortable expressing my opinion until I know more about the topic.*)
- Remind students to use qualifying language when they do express an opinion.
- Walk around and listen, but intervene only if someone asks a question.

Teaching Tip

- When you give directions (or other information), monitor whether students understand. One technique is to routinely rephrase directions and to give examples.
- Observe body language; if you see that one or more students are not comfortable with your directions or explanations, rephrase, use the board or a flipchart to put up related information.
- If one or two students routinely have difficulty understanding the directions, talk to them privately to find out the possible cause of the problem (for example, difficulty in hearing, needing glasses, being in too advanced a class).

Extra Practice

Interactive Practice

3 PRACTICE

Complete the paragraph with the words from the box.

> crimes   infractions   penalty   sentences
> death   misdemeanor   prison   serious

Our state divides ___crimes___ into three categories: infractions, misdemeanors, and felonies. ___Infractions___ are the least serious crimes. Felonies are the most ___serious___. The ___penalty___ for an infraction is just a fine. No jail or ___prison___ time is involved. For a ___misdemeanor___, a jail sentence of up to one year is possible, along with a fine. For most felonies, people receive prison ___sentences___. In this state, we don't have a ___death___ penalty. The most severe penalty is life in prison.

4 CONVERSATION

GROUPS. Practice the conversation. Notice the boldfaced phrases used to qualify opinions.

A: Do you think a person should go to jail for shoplifting?

B: Not **unless** they've shoplifted before. **If** it's a first offense, I think the penalty should just be a small fine.

C: Well, **it depends**. **If** someone steals something small, maybe a small fine is OK. **If** someone steals something very valuable, I don't think the fine should be small.

B: Well, **it** also **depends on** the reason for shoplifting. I don't think the penalty should be severe **if** a hungry person steals food or **if** someone with mental problems steals something small. But I think the fine could be bigger **if** someone steals something like makeup or a CD or DVD.

A: I agree. And **it** also **depends on whether** the person is a child or an adult. For children or teenagers, I think that community service or counseling would be the best response.

> **Communication Skill:**
> **Qualifying Opinions**
>
> Sometimes when we give an opinion, we want to leave room for exceptions, or we want to indicate that we would need more information before committing to a strong opinion. We want to make it clear that in some cases our opinion might be different. We can do this by using *unless, if,* or *it depends (on)/(whether)*.

5 MAKE IT PERSONAL

GROUPS. Discuss. What do you think would be an appropriate fine or sentence for committing each crime in Exercise 1A? Use the Communication Skill box to help present your opinion.

Reading

1 BEFORE YOU READ

CLASS. Discuss. Have you ever paid a fine for overdue or lost library materials? If so, how much was the fine? What happens if you return the materials but you don't pay the fine when you return them?

2 READ

CD3 T8

Listen to and read the newspaper article. How did Keely Givhan end up in jail for failing to pay a library fine?

Ju$t Fine

Keely Givhan was **pulled over** by a police officer because the lightbulb above her license plate was out. When the officer checked her name in the computer system, he found a warrant for her arrest. She was taken straight to Rock County Jail.

Why was there a warrant out for Givhan, a mother and a student at Blackhawk Technical College? It started with late fines on library books. The Beloit Public Library sends three **overdue notices**: the first when materials are two weeks late, the second when they are four weeks late, and the third when they are six weeks late. After the

third notice, a citation (a notice to appear in court) is sent. And failure to appear in court can lead to a warrant for a person's arrest.

Givhan said that she didn't know there was a warrant out for her arrest and that she never received the overdue notices. "I was moving, so I returned some of the things late," said Givhan. "Because I was moving, I didn't receive the notices. I had a fine and didn't know."

At the time she was taken to jail, Givhan owed $172 in court fees as well as $152 in fines from the library. Unable to pay this amount, Givhan spent six days in the county jail.

One of Givhan's professors, Linda Griesman Christopherson, thought her punishment was a bit **harsh**. "This young woman is working really hard to better her life. She has a little boy, and it'd be nice if he could have a good feeling about the library," she said. "Sure, they send letters, but I think they should make a phone call, too."

But Beloit Police Captain Bill Tyler said a fine is a fine. "If someone has a fine they don't pay—let's say I have a traffic ticket for speeding, and you don't pay that—a warrant can be issued for your arrest."

Library director Dan Zach offered his opinion, too, about not returning library books. "It's no different from walking into a retail store and walking out with the **merchandise**." He said that 75 percent of late **materials** are usually returned after the first notice is sent out and that the second and third notices usually bring back the rest of the materials. "This is a free public library," he said. "All the people have this whole building full of wonderful materials they can check out. They get a card at no cost. It's like a credit card for the library. People can check out thousands of dollars of materials every year. All we ask is that they bring everything back."

Source: http://www.4to40.com/newsat4/index.asp?id=1466

Recognize why fines can be serious

Getting Started 15 minutes

- Say: *In this unit, we have been studying different aspects of American law. We've studied the Miranda warning, the rights of people accused of crime, the history of voting rights, child abuse, sexual harassment in the workplace, traffic court, and different types of crime. Now we're going to read about fines at public libraries for overdue or lost books.*

- Confirm that students understand what *overdue* means related to library materials. Explain that books are *checked out* to library users—or *patrons*—for free for a certain amount of time. Explain that, for example, a book or CD could be checked out for three weeks. Three weeks from the check-out date is the *due date*. Public libraries usually assess a fine for each day (such as $.25 per day). A book or CD that is not returned on time is late, or *overdue*.

- Ask for a show of hands about how many people have library cards for the local public library system. If less than half of the students raise their hands, ask: *How many of you would like to get a library card?* Explain that in most places, it is very easy to get a card; people need only show some proof of their address.

1 BEFORE YOU READ

CLASS. Discuss. Have you ever...

- Ask students to read the questions. Say, for example: *Because not all of you have library cards, I'm asking those of you who do have cards to answer these questions.*

- Ask: *Are any of you willing to talk about fines you've paid for overdue or lost library materials?* If there are no respondents, give a personal example. (For example: *My family used to run up huge library fines. That's because I used to work at the library, and there were no overdue fines for library employees. When I stopped working at the library, my husband and I continued to keep books too long, so we used to spend over a $100 per year in fines.*)

- Rephrase the last question. Ask: *Does anyone know what usually happens at our local library if a person returns materials late but doesn't pay the fine?* Accept all responses, but highlight the correct response. Say, for example: *That's right—what happens is the library blocks your card and you can't check out or renew any more materials until you pay the fine.*

Teaching Tip

It is possible that no student in your class will have a library card. If that is the case, you may wish to consider adjusting the focus of the lesson to talk about a related topic—parking tickets—which can have dire consequences if they go unpaid.

Presentation 15 minutes

2 READ

 Listen to and read...

- Ask students to read the directions.

- Say: *This is an article about a very unusual case— a woman, Keely Givhan, went to jail because she didn't pay a library fine.*

- Point out that the words and phrases in boldface (*pulled over, overdue notices, harsh, merchandise, materials*) are in the glossary on page 245. Encourage students to read the entire article first, before going to the glossary.

- Play CD 3, Track 8, as students listen and read.

- After students listen and read, ask if they have any other questions about the content, vocabulary, or pronunciation; answer questions.

Answer: Keely Givhan was stopped by the police for a traffic violation; the police discovered that there was a warrant out for her arrest because she hadn't shown up in court to pay overdue library fines.

Controlled Practice   15 minutes

 CHECK YOUR UNDERSTANDING

Circle the letter of the sentence...

- Ask students to read the directions.
- Say: *You will probably need to reread or at least skim the article again to decide which of the sentences are accurate.*
- Ask for volunteers to answer and indicate in the text where they found their answers.

Communicative Practice   15 minutes

4 **WORD WORK**

GROUPS. Choose three words...

- Set up groups of four. Say: *We are going to work in groups to talk about vocabulary and about the issue of the library fines in this reading.*
- Ask students to read the directions. Tell students that they can also use the other new words and phrases from the group work, or other new words and phrases they have encountered outside of class.
- Confirm that students understand that they discuss first, and then write in their vocabulary logs.
- Walk around; intervene only if you hear a question that students can't answer in the group.
- Say: *Remember when you write in your vocabulary logs, you can always write more than just a set number of words or phrases. You can also use the vocabulary log for words you read or hear outside of class.*

5 **MAKE IT PERSONAL**

GROUPS. Discuss the questions.

- Ask students to read the questions.
- Tell students to stay in the same groups.
- Say: *The story of Keely Givhan seems amazing— going to jail because of an overdue book fine and missing overdue notices. What do you think about it?*

- Ask each student in the group to read one question, share his or her ideas, and ask the other group members for their opinions. Encourage students to use qualifying language when appropriate (*unless, it depends on, if,* etc.).
- Walk around and listen, but intervene only if someone asks you a question or your opinion.

Community Building

- If many of the students do not have library cards (and if schedules, logistics, and transportation are feasible), take a class trip to the local library so that students can get library cards, see the resources, and check out materials.
- Call up or check the library's website to learn rules and procedures for getting library cards. For example, some libraries prefer to prepare student library cards in advance. If this is true of your local library, have students who want cards print their names and addresses on a list and give the list to the library a week in advance. Then students will show their IDs and sign their cards when you go to the library.
- Many libraries will give tours to adult ESL classes—explain the rules, show them the collections, and explain the many programs that most libraries offer.
- If the class cannot go as a group, develop a checklist of what a student should look for and do at the library (pick up and sign the card at the circulation desk, find out where the restrooms are, pick up a flyer about the library schedule and rules).

3 CHECK YOUR UNDERSTANDING

Circle the letter of the sentence in each pair that is most accurate.

1. a. The police officer stopped Keely Givhan because there was a warrant for her arrest.
   b. The police officer stopped Keely Givhan for a traffic violation.
2. a. Keely Givhan was arrested because she didn't return library books.
   b. Keely Givhan was arrested because she did not make required appearances in court.
3. a. Keely Givhan said that she didn't receive the notices because she was moving when they were sent.
   b. Keely Givhan said that she received the notices but she didn't have time to pay the fines because she was moving.
4. a. Professor Christopherson and Police Captain Tyler thought the punishment was a bit harsh.
   b. Police Captain Tyler and Library director Dan Zach thought the punishment was justified.

4 WORD WORK

GROUPS. Choose three words or phrases in the article that you would like to remember. Discuss the words and their meanings. Then record the words and information about them in your vocabulary log.

5 MAKE IT PERSONAL

GROUPS. Discuss the questions.

1. Do you think the library had a responsibility to try to phone Keely?
2. It takes taxpayers' money to question someone at the police station and to hold them in jail for six days—much more money than the cost of the library materials. If you were a taxpayer in this county and city, would you agree that keeping Keely in jail was a good use of your money? Explain.
3. Do you agree with the library director that not returning library books is the same as stealing something from a retail store? Why or why not?
4. Do you think that putting Keely in jail will help prevent people in her community from returning books late or failing to pay fines? Explain.

Writing

1   BEFORE YOU WRITE

A   You are going to compare and contrast the legal systems in your home country and the U.S. Read about essays that compare and contrast. Then read the writing tip.

> **FYI**   ABOUT ESSAYS THAT COMPARE AND CONTRAST
>
> You will often be asked to compare and contrast two people, places, or things. When you compare, you show how two items are similar; when you contrast, you show how they are different. To write an essay that compares and contrasts choose two topics that have points of similarity and difference. Structure the essay in a simple and logical way. One easy way is to discuss all the similarities in one paragraph and all of the differences in another paragraph.
>
> **Writing Tip: Showing similarities and differences**
>
> Certain words let readers know that you are comparing or contrasting. Use the words *alike, too, both, also, the same,* and *similarly* to show similarities. Use the words *but, yet, in contrast, on the contrary,* and *however* to show differences.

B   Brainstorm about the writing topic. Ask yourself: How are the legal systems in my home country and the U.S. similar? How are they different? Think of specific points of comparison and contrast. Then list them.

C   Read the writing model on page 209. What does Anand compare and contrast?

2   ANALYZE THE WRITING MODEL

PAIRS.   Discuss the questions.

1. What similarities does Anand identify between the legal systems of his home country and the U.S.?

2. What main difference does he present?

3. Which words does Anand use to show readers that he is making comparisons and contrasts?

Compare and contrast two legal systems

Getting Started — 5 minutes

Say: *We have been talking about the American legal system. Today we are going to apply our knowledge as we write an essay to compare and contrast the U.S. legal system with that of your home country.*

Presentation — 5 minutes

1 BEFORE YOU WRITE

A You are going to compare...

- Read the directions. Ask: *What is an essay?* Remind students that an essay is a short composition that explains, describes, or presents something or someone.

- Say: *Today we're going to write an essay that describes the ways in which two legal systems are similar to and different from each other; it's called a compare-and-contrast essay.*

- Ask students to read the FYI note and Writing Tip. Check comprehension by asking a few general questions. For example, ask:

  What do you do when you compare? (show how two items are similar)

  What words let readers know that you are making a comparison? (alike, too, both, also, the same, similarly)

  What do you do when you contrast? (show how two items are different)

  What words let readers know that you are making a contrast? (but, yet, in contrast, on the contrary, however)

  What is a logical way to organize a compare-and-contrast essay? (discuss the similarities in one paragraph and the differences in another)

Controlled Practice — 15 minutes

B Brainstorm about the writing topic...

- Ask students to read the directions and the questions.

- *Optional:* To help students generate ideas for topics, suggest that they spend a few minutes reviewing aspects of the U.S. legal system in Lessons 1, 3, 5, 6, and 7.

- Say: *Make a list of the ways that the legal systems in your home country and in the U.S. are similar and different. Don't worry about grammar or organization right now; just get as many ideas on paper as you can.*

- Have students complete the exercise. Walk around and check their work.

C Read the writing model on page 209...

- Ask students to read the directions and then read the essay on page 209.

- Confirm students' comprehension of the new vocabulary by asking:

  What are common laws? (laws created by the courts, not the government)

  What is an independent judiciary? (a legal system that is separate from other branches of government)

Answer: Anand compares and contrasts the legal systems in India and the U.S.

2 ANALYZE THE WRITING MODEL

PAIRS. Discuss the questions.

- Say: *Now I'd like you to read the essay a second time and answer the questions.*

- Have students complete the exercise. Walk around and check students' work.

- Elicit answers from students and write them on the board.

Answers: 1. Both countries have common laws and an independent judiciary. 2. Although both countries have judges who preside over trials, the U.S. also uses a jury of peers to decide guilt or innocence. 3. comparisons—*both*, *similarities*, *also*; contrasts—*difference*, *in contrast*

Communicative Practice   35 minutes

3   THINK ON PAPER

Ⓐ Before Anand wrote...

- Ask students if they have ever seen a Venn diagram; if so, ask how it looks and what it is used for.
- Read the directions and elicit an answer to the question *Where has he placed the similarities?* Explain as needed that Anand put the features of each system in a circle; the features shared by both systems appear in an overlapping area in the middle of the two circles.

Ⓑ Reread the notes you made...

- Say: *Now you are going to use the notes that you made earlier to create a Venn diagram for your essay. Let's review. Where in the diagram do you show the similarities between the legal systems of the U.S. and your home country?* (in an overlapping area between the two circles)
- *Optional:* Draw a blank Venn diagram on the board, similar to the one in the book but with no text. Invite students to copy it and use it to organize their own ideas.
- Have students complete the exercise. Walk around and check their work.

> **Teaching Tip**
>
> - If students are on computers, have them create Venn diagrams in Microsoft PowerPoint.® (To do so, click the "Insert" menu and select "Diagram"; when the "Select Diagram Type" box pops up, select the picture of the three circles for the Venn diagram.) Encourage students to paste in the notes they have made.

Ⓒ PAIRS. Share your Venn diagrams...

- Ask students to read the directions. Say: *You're going to help your partner with the organization of the essay. If your partner has too many ideas for a short essay, help to select the ones that are the strongest, and cross out the others.*
- Have students form pairs and complete the exercise. Walk around and monitor conversations; ask students their reasons for omitting any ideas from the diagram.

4   WRITE

Use your Venn diagram to write...

- Read the directions, emphasizing that students should structure their essay in a logical way and use the signal words in the Writing Tip to show comparison and contrast.
- Have students write the first draft of a compare-and-contrast essay.
- Say: *When you finish writing, you're going to read your paper and revise it. What does revise mean?* (changing your work—adding, deleting, or rewriting details)

5   CHECK YOUR WRITING

Ⓐ STEP 1. Revise your work.

- Say: *Read over your essay a first time and answer the questions in Step 1. If any answers are* no, *revise your work.*
- *Optional:* Have students form pairs, exchange essays, and give each other feedback and suggestions.

Ⓑ STEP 2. Edit and proofread.

- Say: *Now you'll read over your essay a second time and edit and proofread your work.* Direct students to check their papers for grammar, spelling, punctuation, and typos.
- *Optional:* Have students complete a "clean" second draft of their essay at home, incorporating revisions and corrections from the revision and editing steps.

> **Teaching Tip**
>
> You may want to collect student papers and provide feedback. Use the scoring rubric for writing on page Txv to evaluate vocabulary, grammar, mechanics and how well students complete the task. You may want to review the completed rubric with students.

Extra Practice

Interactive Practice

page 104

A Before Anand wrote his essay, he used a Venn diagram to organize his points of comparison and contrast. Study the diagram. Where has he placed the similarities?

India's Legal System **U.S. Legal System**

Judge decides verdict in trials

Common laws
Independent Judiciary

Juries decide verdicts in most trials

B Reread the notes you made about legal systems in your home country and the U.S. in Exercise 1B. Use them to create a Venn diagram like Anand's for your essay.

C PAIRS. Share your Venn diagrams and give each other feedback. For a short essay, you may need to narrow your topic. If so, cross out any ideas you decide not to use. Discuss your reasons.

Use your Venn diagram to write an essay that compares and contrasts the legal systems in your home country and the U.S.

A STEP 1. Revise your work.

1. Does your essay present points of similarity and difference?
2. Is your essay structured in a logical way?
3. Have you included words that show readers that you are comparing and contrasting?

B STEP 2. Edit and proofread.

1. Have you checked your spelling, grammar, and punctuation?
2. Have you proofread for typing errors?

1 REVIEW   For your grammar review, go to page 230.

2 ACT IT OUT   What do you say?

GROUPS. You are telling two newcomers from your home country about the rights people have in the U.S.

Student A: Review Lesson 1. Tell the newcomers about the importance of the *Miranda* warning and the rights of people accused of crimes.

Student B: Review Lesson 3. Explain about the history of the right to vote in the U.S., including when and how blacks, Native Americans, and women got the right to vote.

Student C: Review Lesson 4. Tell the newcomers how federal and state laws define sexual harassment in the workplace.

3 READ AND REACT   Problem-solving

STEP 1. Read about Arturo.

Arturo is afraid that the couple that lives next door may be abusing their two-year-old son physically and emotionally. Arturo often hears the parents screaming at their child, and the boy sometimes has bruises on his arms and legs. Arturo hasn't actually observed the parents hitting the child, but he has noticed how they ignore him much of the time. One day they left the boy alone in the front yard. He ran out into the street, and Arturo had to catch him. The couple joked about what had happened, but they didn't seem very concerned.

STEP 2. GROUPS. What is Arturo's problem? What can he do?

4 CONNECT   For your Study Skills Activity, go to page 219.

Which goals can you check off? Go back to page 145.

 Go to the CD-ROM for more practice.

Show what you know!

1 REVIEW

For your grammar review, go to page 230.

- Say: *Today we're going to review the skills that we have practiced in this unit and apply them to a problem. What are some of the skills we have practiced?* Elicit answers, noting them on the board. (identifying the rights of people accused of crimes, learning about the right to vote, recognizing sexual harassment in the workplace, learning about traffic court, discussing types of crimes)
- Ask students to complete the grammar review exercise at the bottom of page 230.

2 ACT IT OUT

GROUPS. You are telling...

- Ask students to read the directions. Explain that they will imagine that they are telling two newcomers from their home country about the rights people have in the U.S. Working in groups of three, they will review and summarize different lessons.
- Say: *Student A will look back at Lesson 1 and discuss the importance of the* Miranda *warning and the rights of those accused of crimes. Student B will reread Lesson 3 and explain why the right to vote is so important—and when and how different minority groups gained this right. Student C will review Lesson 4 and will describe how federal and state laws define sexual harassment in the workplace.*
- Have students complete the exercise. Walk around the room and monitor conversations.

3 READ AND REACT

STEP 1. Read about Arturo.

- Say: *Now we're going to apply our knowledge from this unit to a problem involving a character, Arturo. Let's read about Arturo.*
- Have students read the story.

STEP 2. GROUPS. What is Arturo's problem?

- Ask students to read the directions and form small groups.
- Give each group a sheet of flipchart paper and markers, or ask them to make notes on a sheet of paper. Tell them that they will write a brief description of Arturo's problem and a list of at least three possible solutions.
- Say: *Before you discuss Arturo's options, you may want to review the Lesson 5 article on page 154 for some background information about laws protecting children.*
- Ask students to review the Communication Skill box on page 159 about qualifying opinions.
- Ask groups to choose a representative to present the group's ideas to the class.
- Have students discuss the questions. Walk around the room and monitor conversations.
- Ask a representative from each group to present the group's ideas. After each presentation, prompt students for feedback. (For example: *What do you think of Group 1's suggestions for Arturo? Which idea do you like best?*)

Possible answers: *Problem:* Arturo is worried about the welfare of his neighbor's son. *Solution:* Arturo can call Child Protective Services in his city or town and report what he has observed.

4 CONNECT

Turn to page 219 for your Study Skills activity. See page Txii for general notes for Study Skills activities.

Progress Check

Which goals can you check off? Go back to page 145.

Ask students to turn to page 145 and check off any remaining goals they have reached. Call on them to say which goals they will practice outside of class.

CD-ROM Practice

 Go to the CD-ROM for more practice.

If your students need more practice with the vocabulary, grammar, and competencies in Unit 8, encourage them to review the activities on the CD-ROM.

9 Saving the Planet

Classroom Materials/Extra Practice

CD 3
Tracks 9–14

Workbook
Unit 9

Interactive Practice
Unit 9

Unit Overview

Goals
- See the list of goals on the facing page.

Grammar
- The past subjunctive with *wish*
- The past unreal conditional

Listening and Speaking
- Discuss carpooling
- Talk about doing your share for the environment
- *Communication Skill:* Expressing Comparison and Contrast

Reading
- Read an article about how to protect the environment and save money
- Read a cross-cultural blog about recycling
- *Reading Skill:* Understanding the Style and Structure of Blogs (Web logs)
- Read an article about causes and effects of environmental problems
- Read about how to green a community
- *Reading Skill:* Using Visuals

Writing
- Write a personal narrative about the environment
- *Writing Tip:* Using time order

Life Skills
- Discuss recycling rules

Preview

- Welcome students and have them look at page 165.
- Say: *Look at the picture. What are the father and daughter doing?* (Possible answers: The girl and her father are taking out plastic bottles to the recycling bin or center. They are recycling.)
- Ask: *How do you think the girl feels?* (Possible answer: She is happy and proud to be recycling.)
- Elicit a definition of *recycle*. (to reuse something instead of throwing it away) Ask students what types of things they can recycle. (newspapers, glass bottles, plastic containers, paper bags, paper rolls for toilet tissue and paper towels)
- Ask the second Preview question: *Do people do this in your home country?*
- Say: *In this unit, we'll talk about recycling and other ways to help the environment. But first, I want to know how many of you recycle.* Have students raise their hands.
- Ask: *For those of you who answered* yes *to the last question, how do you recycle? Do you take out your recyclables once a week for pickup? Or do you take them to a recycling center?*
- Say: *In this unit, you'll learn more about recycling and other ways to protect the environment. You'll also learn about the causes and effects of environmental problems.*

Unit Goals

- Ask students to read the Unit Goals.
- Explain unfamiliar vocabulary as needed. (For example: *carpooling*—sharing a ride somewhere, such as work; *environmental*—relating to the environment, or the natural world and its elements)
- Tell students to circle the goal that is the most important to them.
- Say: *As we complete this unit, we will look back at this page and reread the goals. We will check each goal as we complete it.*

Saving the Planet

Preview

What are the father and daughter doing? Do people do this in your home country?

- ☐ Discuss recycling rules
- ☐ Discuss carpooling
- ☐ Note causes and effects of environmental problems
- ☐ Identify ways to protect the environment

Reading

1 BEFORE YOU READ

CLASS. A *carbon footprint* is the amount of carbon dioxide (CO_2) put into the atmosphere by a country, organization, or individual. Discuss. What do you know about reducing your carbon footprint?

2 READ

CD3 T9

Listen to and read the article about ways to protect the environment—and save money. What is the green route?

Taking the Green Route

In the past, our ancestors lived without having much of an **impact** on the planet. Today, however, we're not only using up our **natural resources**, we're also **polluting** our planet. What can we do to save the world for future **generations**? Can we work to reduce our carbon footprints—and our spending, too? Here are four tips designed to help us live—and save—green!

LOOK AT YOUR LIGHTING!

The best rule in using lights (and any **electrical appliance**) is to turn them off when they're not in use. But there's more: Although **energy-efficient** lightbulbs cost more, they make it up by having a longer life and using less energy. Besides, these bulbs are tough and they don't **emit** the dangerous heat that the traditional lightbulbs do. All in all, energy-efficient lightbulbs can assist your pocketbook as well as **the environment**!

MIND THE DRIPS!

Make sure you repair dripping **faucets**. Would you believe that a slow, steady drip of water (100 drops per minute) wastes 330 gallons of water in a month? That adds up to wasting nearly 4,000 gallons per year! Keeping an eye on your faucets will not only help **conserve** nature's precious resource but will also save you money on your water bill. When you do your laundry, make sure you only run the machine when it's full. And though many of us love relaxing baths, they often use much more water—and energy to heat this water—than a shower does. You can also save by not letting the water run while doing dishes or brushing your teeth.

SAVE A TREE!

Another money and environment saver is online bill paying. If you pay your bills online—which is now both convenient and safe—you eliminate the cost of stamps and a lot of paper. Furthermore, with online bill paying, companies tell you when it's time to pay your bills so that you can avoid charges for late payments. More paper can be saved by checking bank and credit card balances online and never printing these out.

Getting Started　　　　10 minutes

- Say: *In this unit, we are going focus on saving the planet.* Saving the planet *means trying to lessen pollution, maintain biodiversity, and save endangered species, among other things. The good news is that there is some evidence that we can work on environmental problems and save or make money at the same time.*

Language Note

- Ask if anyone can explain or give an example of a *pun*, or *a play on words.* Accept all responses. Explain, if necessary, that a pun is an amusing use of a word or phrase that has two meanings or of words with the same sound but different meanings. Write the word and the definition on the board for students to copy into their notebooks.
- Give an example of a pun: *What's black and white and read all over?* (a newspaper)
- Explain that in this unit, *green* is sometimes being used as a pun because *green* signifies being related to nature and environmental concerns, but it is also commonly refers to money (for example, *I need some of that folding green*)—the dual topics of the unit.

1　BEFORE YOU READ

CLASS. A *carbon footprint* is the...

- Ask students to read the directions. Rephrase the first sentence. Say: *A carbon footprint is the total amount of carbon dioxide (CO_2) that a country, an industry, or an individual produces and releases into the environment.*
- Explain to students that the term *carbon footprint* is being used often now because carbon emissions are a growing problem. Explain that *atmosphere* generally means the air that surrounds the earth.
- Confirm that students know that carbon dioxide is the gas produced when animals and people breathe out, when carbon is burned in the air, or when animals or vegetables decay.
- Ask if any students have scientific backgrounds and might be able to give a more in-depth explanation about how too much carbon adversely affects the atmosphere.

Presentation　　　　15 minutes

2　READ

 Listen to and read the article....

- Ask students to read the directions.
- Say: *As you read the article, think about what the green route means.*
- Tell students that r-o-u-t-e is pronounced differently in different parts of the country: to rhyme with either *boot* or *out.*
- Point out that the words and phrases in boldface (*impact, natural resources, polluting, generations, electrical appliance, energy-efficient, emit, the environment, faucets, conserve, public transportation*) are in the glossary on page 245. Encourage students to read the entire article first, before going to the glossary.
- Play CD 3, Track 9, as students listen and read.
- After students listen and read, ask if they have any other questions about the content, vocabulary, or pronunciation; answer questions if any.

Answers will vary, but students should understand that the green route is a way of protecting our natural resources and reducing our carbon footprint.

Expansion: Vocabulary Practice for 2

- Divide the class into small groups.
- Ask students to make a list of the boldfaced words in the reading and to discuss the meaning of each. Encourage students to guess the meaning if they are not sure.
- Tell students to look for the words in the glossary and to compare the definitions there with what they discussed.
- Assign one or two words or phrases to each group and ask them to write one (or two) sentence(s) with their assigned word(s) or phrase(s).
- Ask groups to read their sentences to the class.
- After each group reads the sentence, ask if anyone has any questions about the word or phrase.

Controlled Practice 10 minutes

 CHECK YOUR UNDERSTANDING

Write the answers to the questions.

- Ask students to read the directions.
- Tell students to review the article if necessary to find the answers. Assure students that they only need to write short answers.
- Ask volunteers to read each sentence and answer.

Answers: 1. replace standard lightbulbs with energy-efficient lightbulbs; 2. 330 gallons a month, 4,000 gallons per year; 3. pay bills online; 4. find people to carpool with or use public transportation; 5. walk or ride a bike, organize your schedule so that you can combine trips (such as going to the store on the way home from work or school), take public transportation

 WORD WORK

GROUPS. Choose three words...

- Ask students to read the directions. Set up groups.
- Say: *Remember when you write in your vocabulary logs, you can always write more than three words or phrases. You can also use the vocabulary log for words you read or hear outside of class.*

Communicative Practice 25 minutes

Show what you know!

Teaching Tip

Avoid making assumptions about students—their lives, experiences, and knowledge. For example, some students might have training and experience as environmental scientists while others might be too burdened with their daily lives to worry about the environment.

STEP 1. PAIRS. Take turns asking and...

- Ask students to read the directions.
- Rephrase and expand the questions: Say:

  1. *Do you practice any of the tips we read about? If so, which ones, why, and how?*

  2. *Are there any tips that you might be able to adopt or begin to use? If so, which ones, why, and how might you adopt (and adapt) it as part of your daily life?*

  3. *Of the tips we've read and talked about, which ones might be the most difficult for you to do? Why?*

- Set up informal pairs. Say: *Talk with someone sitting near you; take turns asking and answering the questions. Remember there are no "right" or "wrong" answers—you are just sharing ideas.*
- Assist as needed with content, context, and language.

STEP 2. GROUPS. Brainstorm: Add two or...

- Set up groups by telling two pairs (from the previous exercise) to form a group.
- Ask students to read the directions.
- Reiterate that the task is to think about other environmentally friendly suggestions for using electricity, saving water, eliminating paper waste as well as saving trees, and lowering transportation fuel costs.
- Pass out flipchart paper and markers to each group. Say: *Discuss other possible suggestions in these four areas and write the suggestions on the flipchart paper.*

TAKE A HIKE—OR YOUR BIKE!

Walking—or biking—is better than driving your car for both you and the environment. In addition to saving big dollars on gasoline, you'll get the exercise you need. If your job is far from home, try to find people to carpool with or use **public transportation**. If you do have to drive your car to work or school, organize your schedule so that you can pick up items you need—like groceries—on the way home, instead of making another trip. Remember that energy-efficient transportation always includes options such as buses and subways.

3 CHECK YOUR UNDERSTANDING

Write the answers to the questions.

1. What can you replace in your home to save money and electricity?
2. How much water can a dripping faucet waste per month? Per year?
3. How can you save money, time, and paper when it comes to paying bills?
4. If your job is far from your home, what are tips for getting there in a way that will save money and protect the environment?
5. How else can you save money on gasoline and help to preserve the environment?

4 WORD WORK

📝 **GROUPS.** Choose three words or phrases in the article that you would like to remember. Discuss the words and their meanings. Then record the words and information about them in your vocabulary log.

Show what you know! Protect the environment—and save money

STEP 1. PAIRS. Take turns asking and answering the questions.

1. Which of the tips in the reading do you currently practice?
2. Which ones could you easily adopt?
3. Of the tips mentioned, which one is the most difficult for you to do? Explain.

STEP 2. GROUPS. Brainstorm: Add two or three additional suggestions for each category discussed in the article.

Life Skills

1 INTERPRET A RECYCLING CALENDAR

A **CLASS.** Discuss recycling (reusing certain types of garbage). What, if anything, is recycled in your community? Some communities have calendars with information about what, when, and how to recycle. Do you have a recycling calendar? If so, how easy or hard is it to follow?

B **PAIRS.** Read the following calendar, key, and list of recyclable items. Discuss. What kinds of information do the calendar and key contain? What does the list of recyclable items explain?

April 2010

Sunday	Monday	Tuesday	Wednesday	Thursday	Friday	Saturday
				1 GN	2 GS	3 Community Computer & Electronics Recycling Event
4 GN	5 GN	6 GS	7 Recycling—P	8 GN	9 GS	10 City Household Hazardous Waste Drop-Off
11 GN	12 GN	13 GS	14 Recycling—C	15 GN	16 GS	17 Citizen Scrap Tire Drop-Off Day
18 GN	19 GN	20 GS	21 Recycling—P	22 GN	23 GS	24
25 GN	26 GN	27 GS	28 Recycling—C	29 GN	30 GS	

GN—Garbage and trash, North End Zone   **P**—Paper
GS—Garbage and trash, South End Zone   **C**—Commingled (= mixed)

Getting Started   5 minutes

- Say: *In the last lesson, we talked about ways to reduce our carbon footprint.* Remind the class what a carbon footprint is. (the amount of carbon dioxide that you emit into the air)
- Say: *We have talked about ways to reduce our carbon footprint and save the environment. Today we're going to focus on one of them—recycling.*

Presentation   15 minutes

1   INTERPRET A RECYCLING CALENDAR

A   CLASS. Discuss recycling...

- Say: *Let's talk about recycling. What is recycling?* (collecting, sorting, and processing of used or waste materials into new or useful products)
- Discuss the first question, offering prompts as needed to elicit answers. (For example: *Can you recycle plastic in your neighborhood? What about aluminum cans?*)
- Say: *Today we're going to look at a recycling calendar. Some communities have calendars with information about what, when, and how to recycle. Do you have a recycling calendar where you live?*
- Discuss the second question, offering prompts as needed to elicit answers. (For example: *Do you have a schedule for when recyclable items are picked up in front of your building, or for times when there is a special recycling pickup?*)

Controlled Practice   20 minutes

B   PAIRS. Read the following calendar, key,...

- Ask students to read the directions and look at the calendar. Pair students.
- Read the first question aloud. (*What kinds of information do the calendar and key contain?*) Ask students to discuss the questions in pairs.
- Elicit answers from students about the kinds of information that the calendar includes. Explain as needed that the calendar presents the recycling schedule—that is, which days that different types of recyclables are picked up. It also lists the different items that may be recycled as well as the key to the abbreviations.

- Point to each abbreviation and ask: *What does this stand for?* Refer students to the key at the bottom of the calendar for the answers.
- Go through the abbreviations together, clarifying what *commingled* means. (putting different types of items together, such as plastics, metals, and glass)
- Call attention to the Saturday events on the calendar. Ask: *What do you think a computer and electronics recycling event is?* (when you bring old computers, computer parts, or electronic equipment such as TVs, printers, and video cameras and recycle them)
- Ask students to look at the second Saturday event. Elicit a definition of *hazardous waste* (trash that can be harmful to the environment). Ask: *What are some things you might have in your house that would be hazardous waste?* (leftover paint, certain types of cleaning solutions such as drain cleaner, battery acid, antifreeze, motor oil, fluorescent lightbulbs, gardening pesticides) *What do you think a hazardous waste drop-off is?* (a special time at a specific location when you may bring your hazardous waste items for disposal)
- Ask students what is happening on April 17. (a scrap tire drop-off day) Ask: *What do you think this is?* (a day when you may bring your scrap— or used—tires to a specific location for recycling)
- Draw students' attention to the list of recyclable items on page 169. Clarify unfamiliar vocabulary as needed. (For example: *junk mail*—catalogs, circular advertisements, and other mass mailings; *flattened*—to make something flat; *bin*—a large container used for storing items or trash; *trays*— something used to hold or carry food or plates; *tins*—small metal boxes.)
- Have pairs discuss the second question. Offer prompts as needed. (For example: *What does the list tell you about paper products?*)
- Elicit answers. Explain as needed that the list explains categories of recyclable items and tells you what types of items may be mixed together. (Metal, plastic, and glass may be commingled.)

Communicative Practice   20 minutes

Teaching Tip

- Bring in different types of recyclables (a can, a bottle, a milk jug, an old newspaper, a plastic container). Hold them up one by one and ask students what type each one is (paper, metal, plastic, or glass). Point out the number 1 or 2 on the bottom of a plastic container and explain this means it is a recyclable plastic item. Then mix the recyclables with other common items that are not recyclable.
- Have students take turns picking an item, showing it to the class, and saying whether or not it is recyclable.

Community Building

- We use the expression *going green* to refer to changing lifestyle practices to help protect the environment and conserve natural resources. In the U.S., many communities have initiatives and events to help make residents more aware of how they may *go green*. For instance, some municipalities have a Bike to Work day, encouraging residents to ride a bicycle to work instead of driving. Neighborhoods may have an annual clean-up day, when residents gather together to clear trash from a stream or park. Many places also have celebrations and community events to observe Earth Day (April 22 in the U.S.), which is designed to raise awareness of environmental problems and protection.
- Have students write a personal plan for going green. It should include the following: *Ways I can save fuel or water, Ways I can reduce trash or waste, Ways I can keep my community clean.*
- Tell students to form small groups and share their ideas.
- Have a representative from each group present the group's ideas to the class.

2   PRACTICE

PAIRS. Use the calendar, key, and list...

- Set up pairs.
- Have students complete the exercise. Walk around and check their work, directing students as needed to the explanations in the key.

■ MULTILEVEL INSTRUCTION for 2

Above-level Have students who finish the exercise while others are still working write a paragraph about the items they recycled in their home country (using the past tense); things they recycle now (using the present tense); and things that they would like to recycle in the future (using the conditional).

Teaching Tip

If your students have access to computers, have them locate the web page for their municipality. Tell them to work in pairs or groups, and have them locate the recycling information for their community and make a list of the recycling rules and practices as well as any related special events.

■ Expansion: Speaking Practice for 2

- Set up pairs and have students ask one another questions about the recyclable items described in the calendar. For example, *Can you recycle plastic soda bottles?* (Yes, but you should put the caps in the trash.) *What do I need to do before I recycle boxes?* (fold and flatten them) *Can I recycle containers with a number 3 on the bottom?* (no, just those with numbers 1 and 2)

Progress Check

Can you . . . discuss recycling rules?

- Say: *We have practiced discussing recycling rules. Can you do this? If so, check the box.*

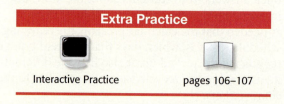

Extra Practice

Interactive Practice   pages 106–107

RECYCLABLE ITEMS

Paper

- Newspaper
- Magazines
- Phone books
- Catalogs
- Junk mail
- Office paper
- Boxes—folded and flattened (one box inside the other or tied)

- Place untied in bin (no larger than 33 gallons) or boxes

Commingled

Metal:

- Drink containers
- Food and soup cans
- Pet food cans

- Food trays and tins
- Clean aluminum foil

Plastic:

- Number 1 or 2 on bottom of container
- Shampoo containers
- Milk and juice containers

- Laundry detergent containers
- Soda, water containers (put caps in trash)

Glass:

- Brown, green, and clean containers (any size)

PRACTICE

PAIRS. Use the calendar, key, and list of recyclable items to answer the questions.
Answers will vary but should include:

1. What days should people who live in the North End Zone leave their garbage out for collection? What about people from the South End Zone?

   North End: Sunday, Monday, and Thursday; South End: Tuesday and Friday

2. What are commingled items?

   mixed metal, plastic, and glass containers

3. On which dates are commingled items recyclable?

   April 14 and 28, or the second and fourth Wednesdays of the month

4. When can residents recycle paper?

   April 7 and 21, or the first and third Wednesdays of the month

5. How should paper be prepared for recycling?

   placed untied in bin (no larger than 33 gallons) or boxes

6. When can computers and other electronic items be recycled?

   April 3, or the first Saturday of the month

7. On what date can residents recycle scrap tires?

   April 17, or the third Saturday of the month

Can you... discuss recycling rules? ☐

Listening and Speaking

1 | BEFORE YOU LISTEN

A CLASS. "Greening" refers to efforts to save resources and protect the environment. Do you know of any efforts to "green" your community? If so, describe them. If not, can you suggest any?

B CLASS. Discuss. Have you ever heard of carpooling? What does it mean?

C PAIRS. Discuss the advantages and disadvantages of carpooling. Use your conversation to complete the chart.

Example:
A: *Carpooling is definitely cheaper.*
B: *Sure, but on the other hand, you might not be able to leave home when you want to!*

Advantages	Disadvantages
It's much cheaper.	You might not be able to leave (home or work) when you want to.

D CLASS. Compare your ideas with the rest of the class.

2 | LISTEN

CD3 T10

A Listen to a talk show host interviewing a city council member about a carpooling program. Write the answers to the questions.

1. According to Councilwoman Frank, how many gallons of gas could be saved each day in the U.S. by carpooling?

2. If people used carpools, how much less carbon dioxide would be emitted each day?

Getting Started   10 minutes

- Say: *We've already discussed several ways each of us can help preserve our environment, from stopping leaky faucets to recycling. Now we are going to listen to and talk about an important energy and money saver—carpooling.*
- Ask a volunteer to explain or give an example of carpooling.
- Ask: *How many of you drive to work?* After students respond, say: *How many of you carpool as drivers? As passengers?*
- Ask: *How many of you walk, ride bikes, or take the bus* (or *subway*, if applicable) *to work or school?*

Teaching Tip

You may adapt the lesson according to the situation in your community and to the experiences and needs of your students. For example, if you teach in a large metropolitan area where most students take the subway or buses, discuss the pros and cons of taking subways vs. taking buses. (For example: *The bus stop is closer to my home, but it only comes every half hour. I can catch the subway any time I want.*)

1   BEFORE YOU LISTEN

A CLASS. "Greening" refers to...

- Ask students to read the directions.
- Explain to students that *greening* is an informal term for *becoming more aware of environmental issues and acting to help protect the local and global environment.*
- Rephrase the first question. Ask: *Do you know of any environmental activities or programs in [your community]?* If *yes*, ask students to tell the class about them. Give examples if necessary (recycling program, turning leaves into mulch, proper disposal of hazardous waste, etc.).
- Rephrase the second question. Ask: *Do you have ideas about other environmental programs that would be good to set up in your community?*

Presentation   15 minutes

B CLASS. Discuss. Have you...

- Ask students to read the directions.
- Ask: *Are any of you familiar with the carpooling programs or rules in your area?* (For example: High Occupancy Vehicle lanes during rush hour on freeways, initiatives to organize carpooling)
- Accept all responses related to carpooling, traffic, the cost of gasoline, etc. Allow the discussion to continue for as long as students are engaged.

C PAIRS. Discuss the advantages...

- Ask students to read the directions.
- Set up pairs. Say: *Talk about the advantages and disadvantages of carpooling. Also discuss carpooling from different perspectives—for example, how drivers, passengers, traffic police, gas station owners, and other groups might feel about carpooling.*

D CLASS. Compare your ideas...

- Restate the directions. Say: *Now let's compare your ideas with those of other pairs.*
- Ask a representative from each pair to read the advantages and disadvantages they discussed. Discuss the different points of view.

2   LISTEN

A   Listen to a talk show host...

- Ask students to read the directions.
- Play CD 3, Track 10.
- Have students answer the questions as they listen.
- Ask volunteers to read the questions and their answers.
Answers: 1. 600,000 gallons; 2. 12 million pounds

Controlled Practice   15 minutes

 B Listen again and take notes...

- Ask students to read the directions. Tell them to take notes as they listen to the interview again. Say: *As you listen, fill in the chart. Don't worry about writing down what you hear word for word—just use key words and phrases.*
- Play Track 10 again.
- Make a copy of the chart on the board or a flipchart. Ask volunteers to go to the board and write their answers (each fills in one space).

Language Note

- Encourage students to take an interest in specific words—their origins and evolution. Use *green* as an example.
- Say: *Language is always changing. Think about how* green *is used today to talk about environmentally friendly things. This is a new usage.*
- Write these sentences on the board:
  I am greening my home.
- Elicit or give more examples of sentences using *green* in this new context. If possible, elicit or give other words with new meanings (for example, the word *text* used as a verb; *wallpaper*, a term referring to the background on your computer screen).

Communicative Practice   20 minutes

3   PRACTICE

CLASS. Imagine that you...

- Ask students to read the directions.
- Say: *As you read the four tips in this article, think about how they apply to our community. Also think of other ways to help provide a healthier environment and save money at the same time.*
- Ask students to comment on the four tips. Ask leading questions, if necessary. For example: *Do you think these suggestions are realistic and practical? Which ones aren't? Explain your answers.*

- Ask students for other suggestions for greening their communities.
- Write the suggestions on the board and keep them there for the duration of the unit.

Teaching Tip

- Writing important information and discussion notes on flipcharts and posting them around the classroom can be useful in helping students (and you) keep focused on key information about the lesson. For example, you could create the charts complete with students' answers on flipchart paper and you could post them around the classroom for the duration of the unit. Keeping the results of students' discussions on flipcharts conveys to students that their input during class, group, and pair discussions is valued.
- The flipchart sheets provide an effective way for pairs and groups to write their own notes and post them when they are finished for you and other pairs or groups to read.

4   MAKE IT PERSONAL

A PAIRS. **Pick one particular way...**

- Ask students to read the directions, and set up pairs.
- Tell pairs to think of a way they might improve the school or community. Say: *Once you have an idea you agree on, figure out how you or the class could let the community know about your idea and start things moving.*
- Pass out flipchart paper and markers. Ask pairs to write their ideas and possible steps on the paper.

B GROUPS. **Meet with another pair...**

- Ask students to read and follow the directions. Tell them to use their flipcharts and refer to them when they talk to the other pair.
- Keep the flipcharts posted throughout the unit.

Extra Practice

Interactive Practice

B Listen again and take notes. Complete the chart. Answers will vary but should include:

How Councilwoman Frank Is Greening Her City
First step: *educate people about the consequences of not doing certain things.*
An example of her efforts: a city-wide ride-sharing program (carpooling)
How people participate online: register and enter a starting point and destination
How people participate by phone: call the carpool hotline; find a specific meeting place
A third option: "vanpooling;" share the cost of renting a van (plus gas and related expenses)
Where people can get more information: www.councilwomanfrank.com

3 PRACTICE

CLASS. Imagine that you want to start greening your own community. Read the four tips. Discuss. What suggestions can you add to these tips?

Tips for Greening Your Community

• **Connect with your community**

To help green your community, you have to be a part of it! Talk to your neighbors, find out what's going on around you, and get involved. Then create a community action plan in order to make some changes.

• **Buy locally**

If you shop locally, you reduce food miles (the food doesn't need to travel so far) and it keeps resources in the community. Plus, it's a great way to get to know your neighbors. When did you last chat with the person who grew your tomatoes?

• **Buy (and sell) used items**

Help save natural resources by taking items and clothes that are no longer needed to a second-hand store. (A second-hand store is a place where people can buy donated items at a cheaper price than if they were to buy them brand new.)

• **Organize a community clean-up day**

Work with your friends and neighbors to clean up an area of your community—like one of the parks, or even a section of your city.

Source: ©2008 Planet Green, www.PlanetGreen.com

4 MAKE IT PERSONAL

A PAIRS. Pick one particular way that you would like to improve your school and/or community. Then talk about what to do in order to tell people about it and make some changes happen.

B GROUPS. Meet with another pair and take turns presenting the ideas you came up with and the steps needed to make them happen.

Reading

1   BEFORE YOU READ

CLASS. Discuss. When have you read or written a blog? What are some topics people write about in their blogs?

2   READ

CD3 T11

Listen to and read the blog entry about recycling. What does Todd learn while in Sweden?

Reading Skill:
Understanding the Style and Structure of Blogs (Web logs)

Blogs are like journals or diaries; they usually contain personal reactions or comments. Most blogs are written in an informal, conversational style and are organized in reverse chronological order (from last to first), that is, the most recent item is posted first. Many blogs have a comments section where readers can submit their reactions to the "blogger," or writer.

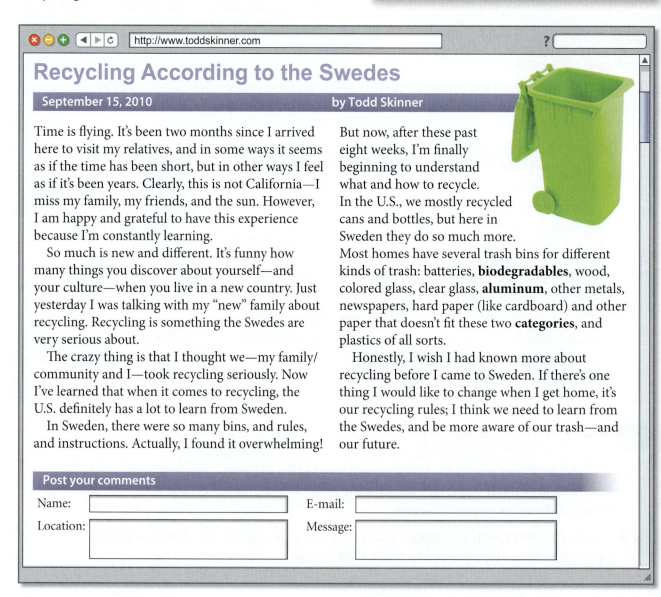

http://www.toddskinner.com

Recycling According to the Swedes

September 15, 2010   by Todd Skinner

Time is flying. It's been two months since I arrived here to visit my relatives, and in some ways it seems as if the time has been short, but in other ways I feel as if it's been years. Clearly, this is not California—I miss my family, my friends, and the sun. However, I am happy and grateful to have this experience because I'm constantly learning.

So much is new and different. It's funny how many things you discover about yourself—and your culture—when you live in a new country. Just yesterday I was talking with my "new" family about recycling. Recycling is something the Swedes are very serious about.

The crazy thing is that I thought we—my family/ community and I—took recycling seriously. Now I've learned that when it comes to recycling, the U.S. definitely has a lot to learn from Sweden.

In Sweden, there were so many bins, and rules, and instructions. Actually, I found it overwhelming!

But now, after these past eight weeks, I'm finally beginning to understand what and how to recycle. In the U.S., we mostly recycled cans and bottles, but here in Sweden they do so much more. Most homes have several trash bins for different kinds of trash: batteries, **biodegradables**, wood, colored glass, clear glass, **aluminum**, other metals, newspapers, hard paper (like cardboard) and other paper that doesn't fit these two **categories**, and plastics of all sorts.

Honestly, I wish I had known more about recycling before I came to Sweden. If there's one thing I would like to change when I get home, it's our recycling rules; I think we need to learn from the Swedes, and be more aware of our trash—and our future.

Post your comments

Name: _____   E-mail: _____

Location: _____   Message: _____

Getting Started
10 minutes

- Say: *We've been talking about environmental topics—tips on protecting the environment and saving money, rules about recycling, as well as the pros and cons of carpooling. Now we will be reading a blog that compares recycling in Sweden and in the U.S.*
- Ask a volunteer to explain or give an example of what a blog is. If necessary, explain that *blog* is a contraction of the term *web log* and is a type of website, usually maintained by an individual with regular entries of commentary, descriptions of events, and graphics or video.

1 BEFORE YOU READ

CLASS. Discuss. When have you...

- Ask students to read the directions.
- Restate and expand the questions. Say: *Do you read blogs? If so, what kinds of blogs do you read?*
- Say: *There are blogs on every topic imaginable. Some seem more like newspaper articles, and some seem more like personal journals.*
- Ask: *Have any of you written a blog? If so, can you talk about why you wrote it, what the topic is or was, and what audience you were or are writing for? Call on volunteers to talk about their blogs. If you yourself have written a blog, tell the class about it.*

Reading Skill: Understanding the Style and Structure of Blogs (Web logs)

- Direct students to the Reading Skill box. Ask a student to read the text.
- Discuss why blogs are written in a conversational style and are arranged in reverse time order.
- Point out that readers can post their comments or reactions to the blog.

Presentation
15 minutes

2 READ

 Listen to and read . . .

- Ask students to read the directions. Say: *As you read the blog, think about what the writer, Todd Skinner, learned while in Sweden.*
- Point out that the words and phrases in boldface (*biodegradables, aluminum, categories*) are in the glossary on page 245. Encourage students to read the entire article first, before going to the glossary.
- Play CD 3, Track 11, as students listen and read.
- After students listen and read, ask if they have any other questions about the content, vocabulary, or pronunciation. Answer any questions.

Answers will vary, but students should mention that Todd learns about and comes to respect the comprehensive recycling practices in Sweden.

Expansion: Vocabulary Practice for 2

- Set up small groups.
- Ask students to make a list of the boldfaced words in the reading and to discuss the meaning of each.
- Tell students to look for the words in the glossary and to compare the definitions there with what they discussed.
- Pass out learners' dictionaries to each group. Give each group two or three (different) computer- or Internet-related words or phrases on index cards (for example, *browser, hyperlink, bookmark, toolbar, URL, subject line, SPAM, search engine, .pdf, download, crash*).
- Have each group look up the new words and phrases, discuss their meanings, and write sentences using the new words and phrases.
- Have a student from each group write the sentences on the board or on flipchart paper.
- Clarify any questions about the vocabulary. Have students write the new words and sentences in their vocabulary logs.

MULTILEVEL INSTRUCTION for 2

Cross-ability. Set up groups so that each group has an above-level student who has strong vocabulary knowledge, grammar, and dictionary skills.

Lesson 4 Read a cross-cultural blog about recycling

Controlled Practice   15 minutes

3   CHECK YOUR UNDERSTANDING

Write the answers to the questions.

- Ask students to read the directions and complete the exercise.
- Explain that students will probably need to reread (or at least skim) the blog to find the answers to the questions.
- Ask volunteers to read aloud the questions and their answer to each question. Allow students to disagree and negotiate; intervene only if students don't arrive at the correct answers.

4   WORD WORK

GROUPS. Choose three words...

- Keep the same groups.
- Ask students to read the directions.
- Say: *Remember, when you write in your vocabulary logs, you can always write more than three words or phrases. You can also use the vocabulary log for words you read or hear outside of class.*

Communicative Practice   20 minutes

5   MAKE IT PERSONAL

GROUPS. Discuss the questions.

- Keep the same groups.
- Ask students to read the questions.
- Say: *These are all important questions. Choose one or two questions for your group to discuss. Alternatively, assign one question to each group.*

Culture Connections

- Students are usually very interested in comparing and contrasting their home countries and the U.S. and/or other students' home countries.
- Set up clear boundaries for cross-cultural activities of any kind. Let students know that these activities are a "two-way street" (that is, each side has information, skills, and knowledge worth sharing, and each side should be willing to learn from the other side).

Expansion: Writing Practice for 5

- Ask students to take the idea from question 5 and write a blog-style informal essay about their cross-cultural experiences.
- Brainstorm a list of possible cross-cultural topics, but tell students they can write about any related topic they wish as long as it is specific and focused.
- Reassure the students. Say: *Writing is a good way to organize your thoughts about a particular topic.*
- Have students read their essays aloud either at the end of this class or at the beginning of the next class. Give one overall positive comment. If possible, also give one substantive comment on structure and one comment on usage or mechanics.

Teaching Tip

You may want to collect student papers and provide feedback. Use the scoring rubric for writing on page Txv to evaluate vocabulary, grammer, mechanics, and how well students complete the task. You may want to review the completed rubric with students.

Extra Practice

Interactive Practice

pages 108–109

CHECK YOUR UNDERSTANDING

Write the answers to the questions. Answers will vary but could include:

1. Where is this blogger from? How long has he been way from home?

   California; two months

2. What is a benefit of living in another country, according to Todd?

   You discover new things about yourself and your culture.

3. How is recycling different in the U.S. than it is in Sweden?

   In the U.S., mostly cans and bottles are recycled. In Sweden, many more materials are recycled.

4. What was hard for Todd to understand at first?

   what and how to recycle

5. What would Todd like to change about his hometown?

   the recycling rules in his hometown or community

4 **WORD WORK**

✎ **GROUPS. Choose three words or phrases in the blog entry that you would like to remember. Discuss the words and their meanings. Then record the words and information about them in your vocabulary log.**

5 **MAKE IT PERSONAL**

GROUPS. Discuss the questions.

1. What are some of the recycling rules in your home country? Are there any that you follow here? If so, what are they?
2. Do you think that everyone should recycle their trash? Why or why not?
3. Is there anything that would help the environment—like recycling—that you would like to "bring" to your home country?
4. Is there anything that you wish you had known about recycling before coming to the U.S.?
5. If you were going to write a blog about your cross-cultural experiences, what would you would write about?

Reading

1 BEFORE YOU READ

CLASS. Discuss. How is our environment being affected by things we do on a daily basis?

2 READ

CD3 T12

Listen to and read the article. How is our environment changing?

How Daily Life Is Changing Our World

Have you noticed that the weather seems crazy lately? Do you feel as if it's getting warmer every year? Scientists who study these things believe that many of the environmental changes that are happening now have speeded up because of human activities. Here are five aspects of our lives that are causing problems.

ELECTRICITY
Most of the electricity we use comes from **power plants** that run on **fossil fuels** (especially coal) and are responsible for emitting huge amounts of **greenhouse gases** and other pollutants.

WASTE
We produce large quantities of waste, and a lot of this is in the form of plastics that remain in the environment forever. Since 1960, the amount of waste produced in America has nearly tripled. In fact, Americans produce 251.3 million tons of garbage per year, much of which contributes to land and water pollution.

FORESTS AND TREES
We use a huge amount of paper made from wood, which is also used in large quantities for building houses. This means that large areas of forest have to be cut down. Trees that are cut down can no longer **absorb** carbon dioxide (CO_2) from the **atmosphere**, and as they

decay, they add new CO_2 to the air.

TRANSPORTATION
Most types of transportation that are used to move people and goods from one place to another run on fossil fuels, such as oil and gas. This type of fuel is responsible for a great deal of our **current** air pollution.

AGRICULTURE
Because the land that we can use for **agriculture** is limited (and getting smaller because of population growth), new varieties of **crops** are being grown to increase agricultural production. However, these crops require large quantities of **fertilizers**, and more fertilizer means more emissions of nitrous oxide, which is a greenhouse gas that contributes to **global warming**. Also, the fertilizer sometimes gets into our water systems and causes more pollution.

Note causes and effects of environmental problems

Getting Started   10 minutes

- Say: *We've been talking about a variety of topics related to the environment. So far, we've focused on personal and local environmental issues. In this lesson, we will be reading about environmental issues on the global level.*
- Ask: *Before we go further, what do you think are the biggest environmental issues facing our world? Who or what do you think is responsible for these problems?*
- Accept all responses; write the environmental issues and possible causes on the board or a flipchart. Keep the list posted for the rest of the unit, if possible.

1 BEFORE YOU READ

CLASS. Discuss. How is our environment...

- Ask a student to read the question. Say: *We just identified some environmental concerns, but this question connects the global concerns with our daily lives. Ask: Can you give specific examples of how our daily activities affect the world's environment?* Accept all student responses.

Teaching Tip

- Repeating and rephrasing language helps students understand the topic at hand.
- Repeating content—in a natural manner, not just saying the same thing over and over—allows students in a diverse class to become comfortable with the content and language at their own pace. For example, a topic (and related language and issues) can be introduced in the Getting Started segment of the lesson and then repeated when reading the direction line for Exercise 2. Less proficient listeners then have two chances to be introduced to the topic before the listening and reading activities. Higher-proficiency students, who already understand the content and vocabulary, can benefit from hearing the variations in language patterns involved in rephrasing the content and questions.

Presentation   15 minutes

2 READ

Listen to and read the article...

- Ask students to read the directions. Say: *As you read, think about your own observations and experiences—here and in your home country or other places you've lived in—about changes in the environment.*
- Point out that the words and phrases in boldface (*power plants, fossil fuels, greenhouse gases, absorb, atmosphere, decay, current, agriculture, crops, fertilizers, global warming*) are in the glossary on page 245. Encourage students to read the entire article first, before going to the glossary.
- Play CD 3, Track 12, as students listen and read.
- After students listen and read, ask if they have any other questions about the content, vocabulary, or pronunciation. Answer any questions.

Answers will vary, but students should say that the following five human activities are changing our environment for the worse: (1) heavy reliance on electricity, which produces greenhouse gases; (2) excessive waste that pollutes land and water; (3) destruction of forests that used to remove CO_2 from the air; (4) transporting people and goods via cars and other vehicles that cause air pollution; and (5) use of fertilizers in agricultural production, which contributes to pollution and global warming.

Expansion: Vocabulary Practice for 2

- Set up small groups.
- Ask students to make a list of the boldfaced words in the reading and to discuss the meaning of each. Encourage them to guess the meaning if they are not sure.
- Tell students to look for the words in the glossary and to compare the definitions there with what they discussed.
- Assign one or two words or phrases to each group and ask them to write one or two sentences with their assigned words or phrases.
- Ask groups to read their sentences to the class.
- After each group reads the sentence, ask if anyone has any questions about the word or phrase.

Lesson 5   Note causes and effects of environmental problems

Controlled Practice   15 minutes

3   CHECK YOUR UNDERSTANDING

A **PAIRS. Write the answers to the questions...**

- Ask students to read the directions and to write the answers in their notebooks. Say: *You will probably have to reread or skim the article to answer the questions.*
- Set up pairs. Say: *After you answer the questions, work with someone sitting next to you and compare your answers.*
- Explain further only if pairs have any questions or unresolved disagreements.

Answers: 1. electricity from power plants; 2. They emit huge amounts of greenhouse gases and other pollutants. 3. 251.3 million tons of garbage per year; 4. via types of transportation that run on fossil fuels; 5. There will be less land available for agriculture.

B **Use the information in the article...**

- Ask students to read the directions and look at the chart.
- Review the categories *Causes* and *Effects*. Say: *Causes are why something happens. Effects are what happen as a result. When you review the article, you will be looking for the causes of environmental problems and the effects.*
- Model the first answer. Say: *Our use of electrical power causes an environmental problem. It results in the release of greenhouse gases into the atmosphere.*

C **GROUPS. Compare your charts...**

- Ask students to read the questions. Set up groups.
- Reread the questions aloud. Say: *Discuss the questions. Give reasons for your opinions.*

4   WORD WORK

GROUPS. Choose three words...

- Keep the same groups. Ask students to read the directions.
- Say: *Remember, when you write in your vocabulary logs, you can always write more than three words or phrases. You can also use the vocabulary log for words you read or hear outside of class.*

Communicative Practice   20 minutes

Show what you know!

GROUPS. Talk about specific environmental...

- Ask students to keep the same groups.
- Pass out flipchart paper and markers to each group.
- Say: *We've been talking about global environmental issues. Now let's bring the discussion back down to our local community. Talk about specific problems here in _____. It's easy to talk about problems, but it's more difficult to talk about realistic solutions. So discuss problems and realistic solutions. Use the flipchart paper to write down local environmental issues and possible solutions. Make a chart with two columns, using these as heads:* Problems *and* Solutions.
- Tell students to post the flipchart paper when the groups are finished talking and writing. Say: *I'll ask someone from each group to explain the problems you identified and possible solutions.*
- Ask a representative from each group to explain (using the flipchart as a reference) what the group discussed. Keep the flipchart sheets posted for the rest of the unit, if possible.

Progress Check

Can you . . . note causes and effects of environmental problems?

- Say: *We have noted causes and effects of environmental problems. Now look at the question at the bottom of the page. Can you note causes and effects of environmental problems? If so, check the box.*

T-175   UNIT 9

A PAIRS. Write the answers to the questions. Then compare your answers.

1. What is the main source of power in most urban areas?

2. Why are fossil fuels a problem?

3. How much garbage do Americans produce annually?

4. How are most goods and people moved from one place to another?

5. What is one of the consequences of an increasing population?

B Use the information in the article to complete the chart.

Causes	Effects
use of power (electricity)	*greenhouse gases in atmosphere*
producing large amounts of waste	land and water pollution
cutting down forests	adds carbon dioxide to the air
using oil and gas	air pollution
using large amounts of fertilizer	contributes to global warming and causes water pollution

C GROUPS. Compare your charts. Discuss. Do you think that rules or laws can solve the problems listed in the article? Why or why not? What are some other ways that we can work to preserve our planet?

4 WORD WORK

📝 GROUPS. Choose three words or phrases in the article that you would like to remember. Discuss the words and their meanings. Then record the words and information about them in your vocabulary log.

Show what you know!   Note causes and effects of environmental problems

GROUPS. Talk about specific environmental problems in your community and changes that could improve them.

Can you... note causes and effects of environmental problems? ☐

Listening and Speaking

1 BEFORE YOU LISTEN

A **CLASS.** Discuss. Does this picture look familiar to you? Do you or your neighbors have bins like these?

B What do you do in these situations? Write the answers to the questions.

1. You've just finished drinking a can of soda in the park.

   You put it in the recycling bin.

2. You have just received a lot of junk mail (advertisements and useless information).

3. You've finished making a salad and have lots of vegetable peelings.

4. You have children's clothing that no longer fits.

C **GROUPS.** Discuss. Compare your answers. Which answers are best for the environment? Why?

2 LISTEN

CD3 T13

Listen to a conversation between two neighbors talking about recycling and answer the questions.

1. Does Joseph think that it's important to recycle?

2. What's Hector's tip for figuring out which items are recycled on which days?

3. Were the regulations the same for recycling where Joseph used to live?

4. What does Joseph wish about the rules in his former town?

5. What does Hector wish he had done differently?

6. Who is Joseph's big helper? How does he help?

7. Who taught Hector about the three Rs?

8. What does Joseph say about his parents and recycling?

Getting Started   10 minutes

- Say: Doing your share *is a common phrase and sentiment. For example, parents might explain to their children that they are required to wash the dishes, clean their bedrooms, and empty the garbage* to *do their share as part of a family. Donating blood, donating money for cancer research or to support a children's hospital are other examples of doing your share for the community.*

- Explain that many individuals and local, state, national, and international organizations work to alleviate—to lessen or to fix—environmental problems, but many more people are needed to do their share to fight global warming, save the oceans and forests, and work on other environmental problems.

- Say: *In this lesson, we will be listening to and talking about how people can do their share on the local level.*

1 BEFORE YOU LISTEN

A CLASS. Discuss. Does this picture...

- Ask students to read the directions and to look at the picture. Read the questions aloud.
- Ask: *Do you think local recycling can help lessen global warming and the pollution of air, land, and water?* Encourage students to come up with their own questions about doing their share, recycling, and working locally to help solve global environmental problems.

Culture Connection

- If possible, go to the Wikipedia website (http://en.wikipedia.org) and search under the keywords *Walt Kelly 1971 Earth Day Poster.* Then locate and print out the famous poster and comic strip by cartoonist Walt Kelly in which the cartoon character Pogo, looking at a scene of environmental degradation in his home (the Okefenokee Swamp in Georgia), says, "We have met the enemy and he is us."
- Ask students what they think the statement means and if they agree with it.

Presentation   10 minutes

B What do you do in these situations?

- Ask students to read the directions and skim the questions.
- Ask them to write what they would do in each situation.

C GROUPS. Discuss. Compare your answers...

- Set up groups, and have students compare all their answers.
- Restate the question. Say: *Which answers do you think are best for the environment? Why?*

Teaching Tip

Be sensitive to possible situations in which students may not be able to do their share even though they know what is "right." For example, some students may have limited autonomy within their families and cultural groups and are constrained to do what their families or their cultures require. Be careful not to make assumptions about what students can do or inadvertently make them feel guilty about what they cannot do.

Controlled Practice   10 minutes

2 LISTEN

 Listen to a conversation...

- Have students read the directions and write the answers to the questions in their notebooks as they listen.
- Play CD 3, Track 13.

Answers:
1. Yes, he does. 2. "Always look in front of Tony's house," because he is always the first one to put out the recycling. 3. No they weren't. 4. Joseph wishes that they had the same type of regulations as in his current community because in the former place "so much garbage was thrown away without being recycled." 5. He wishes they had started recycling earlier because they used to throw away a lot of junk without sorting. 6. His 13-year-old son, who makes sure that the family keeps the trash sorted. 7. His daughter did. 8. If his parents had been aware of the damage they were doing, they would have done things differently.

Controlled Practice   15 minutes

 3   PRACTICE

GROUPS. Hector mentions...

- *Note:* Before class make sure you know the local or state return policy on cans and bottles. Research other local policies, such as which grocery stores give cash back when customers use their own bags, so you can explain them to students.
- Ask students to read the directions.
- Go over the examples to make sure that everyone understands the three Rs and types of examples.
- Set up groups. Say: *Work together to think about ways people can reduce, reuse, and recycle, which will help the environment and probably save money.* List examples for each category.
- Post flipchart paper: Label one sheet *reduce*, one sheet *reuse*, and one sheet *recycle*. As groups finish working on their lists, ask them to post their ideas for each category on the chart paper. Tell groups that if another group has already listed one of its ideas, to mark a large checkmark (✓) next to it.
- Ask volunteers to read the lists on the flipcharts. Ask other volunteers to summarize how they can reduce, reuse, and recycle. Keep the lists posted for the rest of the unit.

Communicative Practice   15 minutes

Communication Skill: **Expressing Comparison and Contrast**

- Direct students to the Communication Skill box, and ask a student to read the text.
- Say: *Comparing and contrasting is probably something we do naturally, almost subconsciously. However, when you are writing or speaking—or even thinking to yourself—it's important to know the proper words to use.*
- Discuss the words and phrases for comparing and contrasting mentioned in the box, and encourage students to mention others.
- Say: *When you listen and read outside of class, record other compare and contrast words that you come across.*

- Say: *In Exercise 4, you will be comparing and contrasting the ways in which people in this country and your home countries deal with environmental issues. Please try to be aware of the words you use, and try out some of the new compare and contrast words.*

4   MAKE IT PERSONAL

GROUPS. Do any of the suggestions about...

- Keep the same groups as in Exercise 3.
- Ask students to read the directions.
- Reread each question aloud.
- Recognize that sometimes it might seem difficult to talk about a particular issue in one's home country. A student may not have been in his or her home country for many years. He or she may have been a child when he or she was in his or her home country. Or, a student might have been more focused on other life issues when he or she lived in the home country. So offer help and prompts when needed.
- Give a time limit for the discussion.

Teaching Tip

Make sure that the classroom is a comfortable and safe place where students feel they can discuss possibly controversial topics. For example, in this unit, students should feel free to express an opinion. If a student expresses a controversial opinion, don't respond to it yourself; instead, make it an opportunity for a small-group or whole-class discussion, which will give more opportunities for students to express opinions and compare and contrast.

Extra Practice

Interactive Practice

3 PRACTICE

GROUPS. Hector mentions the three Rs (reduce, reuse, and recycle). These are ways that you can help the environment and also save money. What are some examples of each? Write your ideas and share them.

Examples:

Reduce (use less of): Use lunch boxes (again and again) instead of buying brown bags.

Reuse (use again): Use heavy boxes from the store for storage instead of buying boxes.

Recycle: Return cans and get cash back.

Reduce

_____

_____

_____

Reuse

_____

_____

_____

Recycle

_____

_____

_____

4 MAKE IT PERSONAL

GROUPS. Do any of the suggestions about how to improve the environment differ from what you heard in your home country? Compare and contrast some ways people deal with environmental issues here and in your home country.

Communication Skill:

Expressing Comparison and Contrast

Here are some expressions you can use to compare and contrast.

Words for comparing: *also, similarly, in the same way, like, still, at the same time*

Words for contrasting: *instead, however, on the other hand, on/to the contrary, yet, but, in contrast*

Grammar

The Past Subjunctive with *Wish*

Actual Situation (the Facts)	Expressing Regret
They didn't start recycling years ago.	I **wish** (that) we **had started** recycling years ago.
When he lived in his old town, they had different recycling rules.	I just **wish** (that) we **had had** these types of recycling rules back in my old town.
They weren't as educated then about waste as they are now.	I **wish** (that) we **had been** more educated about the amount of waste we generated.

The Past Unreal Conditional

Actual Situation	Conditional	
	If Clause	Result Clause
Our parents **weren't aware** of the damage they were doing, so they **didn't do** things differently.	If our parents **had been aware** of the damage they were doing,	they **would have done** things differently.
I **didn't know** that before, so I **had** trouble.	If I **had known** that before,	I **wouldn't have had** trouble.

Grammar Watch

- To form the past subjunctive with *wish*, use *wish* + *had* + past participle.
- Use the past subjunctive with *wish* to talk about a past situation you regret (feel bad or are sad about).
- After *wish*, *that* is optional (and is usually omitted when speaking).

For a list of past participles for irregular verbs, see page 225.

Grammar Watch

- A conditional sentence has an *if* clause describing a condition and a result clause describing a result of that condition.
- To form the past unreal conditional, use the past perfect in the *if* clause and *could*, *might*, or *would* + *have* + past participle in the result clause.
- Use the past unreal conditional:
  - to talk about unreal situations in the past.
  - to describe what you would have done differently or how something could have happened differently.

1 PRACTICE

Read the dialogue. Underline sentences that contain examples of the past subjunctive with *wish*. Double underline sentences that contain examples of the past unreal conditional.

Ilya: Did you hear about the government's plan for getting rid of nuclear waste?

Rosa: Yeah. They're going to bury it under a mountain in Nevada. There are earthquakes in those Nevada mountains! I wish they had thought of a better solution.

Ilya: You know, I wish they had never built those plants in the first place. I'll bet if they had known what we know now, they wouldn't have built them.

Rosa: Maybe you're right, but if they hadn't built nuclear plants, they would have built more plants that use coal, and they're big polluters.

Ilya: What a mess! I wish we didn't need so much electricity!

Rosa: Really? Just try doing without it for a few days!

Identify ways to protect the environment

Getting Started   5 minutes

- Say: *Today we're going to talk more about ways to protect the environment. To do so, we'll practice the past subjunctive and the past unreal conditional.*

Presentation   15 minutes

The Past Subjunctive with *Wish*

- Ask students to read the first Grammar Watch.
- Say: *When we make statements, ask questions, or talk about facts, we use the indicative mood, for example,* I have a dog. *When we talk about actions or conditions that are not facts but rather things that we wish for, we use the subjunctive, for example,* I wish I had a dog. *Write the sentence on the board and ask: Does* had *express a past action in this sentence?* (No, it means contrary to fact or not true.) Elicit or give an example of the subjunctive. (For example, *I wish you were feeling better. I hope you pass the test.*)
- Explain that the subjunctive can be used to talk about a past situation—something that you regret or something that you wanted to happen but didn't.
- Say: *Let's look at some examples of past situations that contain wishes for things to have happened differently.* Read the examples in the first grammar chart.
- Ask: *In the first example, what was the actual situation?* (They didn't start recycling years ago.) *What is the author's regret?* (He or she wishes that they had started recycling years ago.)
- Direct students to the second example. Ask how the past subjunctive is formed in that sentence. (*I . . . wish we had had.*) Ask: *Why is* had *used twice?* (The first time, it is used with *wish* to form the past subjunctive; the second time, it is used to form the past participle.)

The Past Unreal Conditional

- Say: *To talk about regrets—or things that you wish had happened differently—use the past subjunctive. To talk about something you would have done differently in the past—or something that was possible in the past but didn't happen—use the past unreal conditional.*
- Ask students to read the second Grammar Watch.
- Ask: *What are the two parts of a conditional sentence?* (An *if* clause describing a condition and a result clause describing the consequence)

- Say: *In the last chapter, we used future unreal conditionals to talk about something that could possibly happen in the future. Today we'll use past unreal conditionals to talk about something that could have happened in the past—but didn't.*
- Explain that the past unreal conditional has an *if* clause and a result clause. The *if* clause describes something that was not true in the past. It uses *had* and the past participle. (*If I had known . . .*) The result clause describes what would have happened if that condition were true in the past. It uses *could have, might have,* or *would have* plus the past participle. (*I would have . . .*)
- Say: *Let's look at some examples of the past unreal conditional.* Read aloud the examples in the bottom grammar chart.
- Have students complete the exercise.
- Have students turn to page 225 of the Grammar Reference for the list of irregular past participles.

Controlled Practice   25 minutes

1 PRACTICE

Read the dialogue. Underline sentences...

- Ask students to read the directions. Clarify any difficulties about the activity.
- Have students complete the exercise.
- Call on students to say the answers.

MULTILEVEL INSTRUCTION for 1

Pre-level Offer prompts to help students start the exercise. (For example: *Let's look for phrases introduced by* wish. *Is* wish *followed by* had *and the past participle? Underline these sentences. Next, let's look for* if *clauses* with *the past perfect. Are they followed by* result clauses *with* would *or* wouldn't have? *Double underline these sentences.*)

Above-level After they finish the exercise, have students list the actual facts next to the examples of the past subjunctive and unreal conditional. Then have them share these with pre-level students to help them understand both verb forms.

2 PRACTICE

A Read the sentences about actual...

- Read the directions and the example.
- Remind students that they will use the past subjunctive to talk about the **opposite** of the actual fact—that is, Lupita threw away the containers but wishes she hadn't.
- Tell students that for the purposes of this exercise, they may change the verb, as in the example, or use the same verb to express regret.
- Have students complete the exercise. If students need help, refer them to the lists of past participles on page 225.
- Note that in forming the third-person past perfect, one may say *he/she had* or *he'd/she'd*.

B Complete the sentences using...

- Tell students that they will now practice using the past unreal conditional.
- Read the directions, noting that the *if* clause may be placed at the beginning or in the middle of the sentence.
- Have students complete the exercise.

Community Building

- For an entertaining way to practice the grammar point, have students do a creative group activity. Tell them to imagine that they are hosting a dinner party. Make a list of the following prompts, one per index card: *you were a vegetarian; you loved chocolate; you were married; you were allergic to peanuts; you played the accordion; you won an Olympic gold medal.*
- Each small group gets a set of index cards, one per group member. A student makes an *if* statement with the past perfect, based on the card's prompt, and points at another student to complete the sentence. That student says *I would have* or *I wouldn't have* and finishes the sentence with a verb in the past participle. Example:

    A: *If I had known that you were married . . .*
    B: *I wouldn't have invited your ex-girlfriend.*

Communicative Practice   15 minutes

Show what you know!

STEP 1. Based on what you have learned...

- Read the directions. Tell students to write in their notebooks anything they remember from previous lessons about ways to improve the environment. (For example: carpooling, composting, recycling, using alternative sources of energy.)
- Have students complete the exercise.
- Ask volunteers to share ideas with the class.

STEP 2. Take notes about how...

- Say: *Now that you've thought of ways to improve the environment, think about what you might have done differently if you had known these tips before.*
- Ask students to read the directions. Tell them that they may use the past subjunctive with *wish* or the past unreal conditional with *if*.
- Elicit an example, such as *I wish I had known about composting when I was growing up.*
- Have students complete the exercise.

STEP 3. GROUPS. Use your notes...

- Ask students to read the directions. Say: *Now you'll talk about the ideas that you wrote in the last step and respond to other group members' ideas.*
- Note ways to give feedback on the board. For example: *I agree with you. I also wish I had known about . . . I feel the same way. If I had . . . I see your point, but I think it depends on whether . . .*
- Set up groups and have students do the exercise.
- Ask for volunteers to share ideas with the full class.

Progress Check

Can you . . . identify ways to protect the environment?

- Say: *We have practiced identifying ways to protect the environment. Can you do this? If so, check the box.*

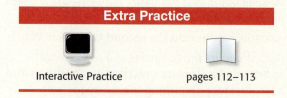

Extra Practice

Interactive Practice   pages 112–113

2 PRACTICE

A Read the sentences about actual situations. Use *wish* + the past subjunctive to explain that the people regret those situations. Answers will vary but could include:

1. Lupita threw away a lot of plastic containers.

   Lupita wishes she had recycled the containers instead.

2. Andrei didn't reuse any of the boxes from the supermarket.

   Andrei wishes he had reused (or recycled) the boxes from the supermarket.

3. Maria didn't return any of the cans.

   Maria wishes she had returned some of the cans.

4. Nicholas put his batteries in the trash.

   Nicholas wishes he had recycled his batteries.

B Complete the sentences using the past unreal conditional.

1. Many families would have used less electricity if they _____had known_____
   (know)

   how much pollution power plants caused.

2. They would have been better informed about recycling if someone

   _____had taught_____ them when they were in school.
   (teach)

3. She would have carpooled to work if there _____had been_____ other people
   (be)

   in her neighborhood who worked at her company.

4. If we had known about the causes of climate change 100 years ago, we

   _____would have changed_____ many of the ways we do things.
   (change)

Show what you know!   Identify ways to protect the environment

STEP 1. Based on what you have learned, make a list of ways to improve the environment.

STEP 2. Take notes about how you might have done something differently had you known before what you know now.

STEP 3. GROUPS. Use your notes from Step 2 to discuss what you might have done differently.

Can you...identify ways to protect the environment? ☐

Reading

1 BEFORE YOU READ

CLASS. Imagine that you are designing and building an entirely "green" community. Discuss. What would the houses and streets look like?

2 READ

CD3 T14

Listen to and read the article. What happened in Greensburg? What is occurring as a result?

Reading Skill:
Using Visuals

Using visuals—such as photographs and drawings—will help you better understand what you read. Notice what the visual shows. Read any labels or captions carefully. Sometimes a visual will give information that is not in the text.

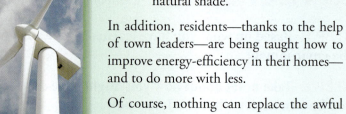

The Greening of Greensburg, Kansas

Greensburg was not always a green city. In fact, most of the town contained **traditional** houses and public buildings, like many other villages in the central U.S. However, on May 4, 2007, Greensburg was nearly destroyed by a tornado. On that day, a **twister** struck the town of about 1,500, killing nine **residents** and destroying most of Greensburg's homes and businesses.

Today, Greensburg is being rebuilt. Only this time, it will go green. **Civic leaders** and environmentalists are **reconstructing** the town with features that will make it a model environmentally friendly community. Wind **turbines,** tinted windows, and water-saving toilets are just a few of the elements the new buildings will have. The Leadership in Energy and Environmental Design (LEED) Green Building Rating System is a program that sets construction standards for environmentally friendly buildings. The town has decided to follow the very strict LEED **standards** for energy-efficient design, which is expensive but will bring about a 30 to 50 percent savings on energy bills.

Greensburg before

Greensburg after

Here are some of the other changes that are being made as Greensburg is reconstructed:

- Homeowners and businesses are being encouraged to think about energy-saving lights and rainwater-collection systems.
  - Nearly forty families were advised to rebuild with extra **insulation,** double-pane windows, and high-efficiency compact fluorescent lights.
  - Homes will use **solar energy** for heat and light.
  - Builders are being encouraged to use local recycled building materials.
  - Residents are being encouraged to use native plants that don't need so much watering and that give natural shade.

In addition, residents—thanks to the help of town leaders—are being taught how to improve energy-efficiency in their homes—and to do more with less.

Of course, nothing can replace the awful loss caused by such a disaster, but it certainly seems that Greensburg is coming back with great promise for the future.

Getting Started
10 minutes

- Say: *We've been talking about a variety of topics related to the environment—conserving energy while saving money, rules for recycling, comparing recycling in the U.S. and Sweden, carpooling, learning about environmental problems and possible solutions on global and local levels, and doing our share to protect the environment. In this lesson, we are going to read and talk about one city that became green.*

Reading Skill: Using Visuals

- Direct students to the Reading Skill box, and ask a student to read the text.
- Explain that while we naturally turn toward photos or drawings to help with comprehension, we should also carefully read any captions or labels because they sometimes contain important information that is either not in the text or is not obvious from the visuals.
- Ask: *Have any of you heard the saying "A picture is worth a thousand words?" or do you have a similar saying in your native language?* Accept all comments. Ask students whether they agree or disagree with the statement and to explain why.

Expansion: Speaking Practice

- Bring in copies of several famous evocative photographs or drawings—enough to distribute one to each group. Set up informal groups.
- Say: *Here are some famous visuals—photographs or drawings. Look at the visual and share your ideas and feelings about it with the members of your group. For example, think about who the people, places, or things might be in the picture or drawing; what's going on in the picture; what the story behind it is; and how looking at it makes you feel.*
- Assure students that there are no right or wrong responses and that this is an informal opportunity to share ideas and feelings.
- *Note:* Possible choices for visuals include photographs from the Library of Congress's American Memory website, or photos from news magazines or *National Geographic*.

Presentation
15 minutes

1 BEFORE YOU READ

CLASS. Imagine that you are...

- Ask students to read the directions.
- Rephrase and extend the question. Say: *We have talked about ideas for greening our communities and the whole world to make it environmentally friendly and sustainable. If you didn't have to worry about money or laws, what kind of a green community would you design? For example, what would the houses and streets look like, what would the transportation system be like, what kind of clothes would we wear, and what would we eat?*
- Encourage all or most of the students to respond.
- If students seem especially interested in this topic, pass out blank paper, colored pencils, or thin markers. Give students the option of either drawing and labeling the imaginary green community or writing a detailed description of it.
- Post the drawings and descriptions on a bulletin board or wall (if possible).

2 READ

 Listen to and read...

- Ask students to read the directions. Say: *As you read, think about what happened in Greensburg, Kansas, and what the result has been.*
- Show Kansas on a map of the U.S., and if possible show Greensburg.
- Point out that the words and phrases in boldface (*traditional, twister, residents, civic leaders, reconstructing, turbines, standards, insulation, solar energy*) are in the glossary on page 245. Encourage students to read the entire article first, before going to the glossary.
- Play CD 3, Track 14, as students listen and read.
- After students listen and read, ask if they have any other questions about the content, vocabulary, or pronunciation; answer questions.

Answers will vary, but students should mention that the town of Greensburg was nearly destroyed by a tornado; as a result, civic leaders, environmental activists, and residents decided to rebuild the city according to strict energy-efficient, environmentally friendly principles.

Controlled Practice · 20 minutes

3 CHECK YOUR UNDERSTANDING

Ⓐ Write the answers to the questions.

- Ask students to read the directions.
- Tell students to review the article if necessary to write the answers.
- Ask volunteers to read each sentence and its answer. Allow students to disagree and negotiate about answers; intervene only if they don't arrive at the correct answers. Encourage students to continue to talk about the article or questions as long as they are engaged.

Answers: 1. tornado/twister; 2. Nine residents were killed and most of the town's homes and businesses were destroyed. 3. about 30 to 50 percent savings on energy bills; 4. to think about energy-saving lights and rainwater-collection systems; 5. local recycled materials; 6. native plants that don't need so much watering and that give natural shade; 7. how to improve the energy efficiency of their homes and to do more with less

Ⓑ PAIRS. Write the answers...

- Ask students to read the directions.
- Say: *You will probably need to reread or skim the article to answer the questions.* Assure students that short answers are OK.
- Set up informal pairs. Say: *After you answer the questions, compare them with someone sitting near you.*

Answers: 1. May 4, 2007; 2. about 1,500; 3. water-saving toilets; 4. tinted windows

Ⓒ GROUPS. The people of Greensburg...

- Ask students to read the directions and think about another difficult situation that had a positive result.
- Set up groups.
- Say: *In your group, take turns giving examples of a bad situation that turned out well. If you can't think of an example at first, listen to the other members of the group, and maybe their examples will help you think of one of your own.*
- Ask each group to share one example with the class.

4 WORD WORK

GROUPS. Choose three words...

- Keep the same groups as above. Ask students to read the directions and complete the exercise.

Community Building

- Take a tour of the school building and grounds. Ask students to take notes about what is eco-friendly and what isn't.
- Explain that adult education programs are usually on tight budgets but that there might be some simple and inexpensive ways to make the school environment more eco-friendly, pleasant, and safe—for example, planting trees and native plants, if possible; reusing paper in class when possible; and organizing a campaign to stop littering.
- After the tour, ask students to share their ideas of what the class might do to help make a more healthy, eco-friendly, and beautiful school and also save money. Ask students to vote on their favorite idea and, if feasible, develop a project in which students can improve their environment as they work together and continue to learn more English.

Communicative Practice · 15 minutes

Show what you know!

GROUPS. Discuss what you...

- Keep the same groups as in Exercise 3.
- Ask students to read the directions and questions.
- Clarify any questions about the activity.
- Tell students to also discuss any eco-friendly initiatives they know about in the local community, region, or state and whether or not they seem effective.

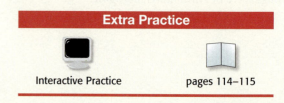

Extra Practice	
Interactive Practice	pages 114–115

3 CHECK YOUR UNDERSTANDING

A Write the answers to the questions.

1. What was the event that so greatly changed Greensburg?
2. What were the consequences of that event?
3. How much can Greensburg save on energy bills because of strict LEED building standards?
4. What are Greensburg's homeowners and businesses being encouraged to do?
5. What materials are the builders being encouraged to use?
6. What kinds of plants are Greensburg's residents being encouraged to grow?
7. What else are the residents being taught?

B PAIRS. Write the answers to the questions. Compare your answers.

1. When did the disaster in Greensburg take place?
2. What was the population of Greensburg before the disaster struck?
3. What kinds of toilets are being included in many of the new buildings?
4. What kind of windows were some families advised to use in rebuilding?

C GROUPS. The people of Greensburg are making the best of a difficult situation and using it as an opportunity to make positive changes. Discuss a similar example of a positive—or good—result that has come out of a negative—or bad—event.

4 WORD WORK

GROUPS. Choose three words or phrases in the article that you would like to remember. Discuss the words and their meanings. Then record the words and information about them in your vocabulary log.

Show what you know! Discuss how to green a community

GROUPS. Discuss what you have learned about greening a community. Which methods do you think are most useful and which are least useful? Why? Are such methods being used in your community? If so, are they working? If not, should they be used?

Writing

1 BEFORE YOU WRITE

A You are going to write a personal narrative, or story, about how you have tried to help the environment. Read about personal narratives. Then read the writing tip.

> **FYI** ABOUT PERSONAL NARRATIVES
>
> Personal narratives are a type of essay that tells a story. They have a relaxed tone and style, and usually reveal the personality of the writer. You can write a personal narrative about almost any topic, from your experiences in an English class to a visit with a relative. The narrative can be about a person, place, event, or issue. It can include memories, ideas, and details that appeal to the five senses (sight, hearing, taste, touch, and smell).
>
> **Writing Tip:** Using time order
>
> One way to structure a personal narrative is to use chronological order, or time order. To let readers know the order in which events occurred, you can use these words and phrases: *for a long time, before, a month ago, later, soon, as soon as, afterwards, ever since,* and *since then.*

B Brainstorm about the writing topic. Ask yourself: Have I planted trees, grown my own vegetables, or ridden a bicycle instead of driving a car? Do I follow local recycling rules and reuse plastic containers? Think about ways that you have tried to avoid waste and have had a positive effect on the environment. List them.

C Read the writing model of a personal narrative on page 210. How is Anka's narrative structured?

2 ANALYZE THE WRITING MODEL

PAIRS. Discuss the questions.

1. What is this personal narrative about?

2. What are some of the steps Anka has taken to help the environment?

3. What words has she used to let readers know the sequence in which events occurred? Give three or four examples.

Write a personal narrative about the environment

Getting Started   5 minutes

- Say: *We have been talking in depth about the environment. We have practiced vocabulary and grammatical structures while identifying ways to protect the environment and green a community. Today you are going to apply all of this knowledge as you write a personal narrative about how you have tried to help the environment.*

Presentation   5 minutes

1 BEFORE YOU WRITE

A You are going to write...

- Read the directions aloud. Ask: *What is a personal narrative?* (an essay that tells a story about yourself or your experiences) Say: *Let's read some tips about writing a personal narrative.*
- Ask students to read the FYI note and Writing Tip aloud.
- Say: *One way to organize your personal narrative is to put events in chronological order. What words can you use to signal the order in which events occur?* Elicit time order words and phrases from students. (For example: *for a long time, before, a month ago, later, soon, as soon as, afterwards, ever since, since then*)

Controlled Practice   10 minutes

B Brainstorm about the writing topic...

- Ask students to read the directions. Say: *Think about some things that you have done to help the environment. You might want to consider some of the topics we talked about in this unit, such as carpooling, recycling, and cleaning up your neighborhood. Make a list of these things. Don't worry about grammar or organization right now; just get as many ideas on paper as you can.*
- Have students complete the exercise. Offer prompts as needed. (For example: *Let's think about nonrenewable resources such as gas and electricity. Have you made any changes to your lifestyle to use less gas and electricity?*)
- *Optional:* Have students form pairs, discuss their lists, and give each other feedback.

C Read the writing model of a...

- Tell students that they will now read a personal narrative that a student wrote about reducing her carbon footprint. Have students turn to page 210 and read the essay.
- Clarify unfamiliar vocabulary as needed.
- Ask: *How is Anka's narrative structured?*
Answer: in time order, or the order in which events occurred

2 ANALYZE THE WRITING MODEL

PAIRS. Discuss the questions.

- Say: *Now I'd like you to read the narrative a second time and find answers to the questions in pairs.*
- Have students form pairs and discuss the questions and answers.
Answers:
1. The narrative is about the changes that the author's children convinced her to make in order to help reduce her carbon footprint.
2. using cloth bags and a reusable coffee cup instead of plastic bags and cups; recycling paper products and using rechargeable batteries; maintaining her car and using less fuel and air conditioning
3. Answers will vary but should include *ever since, a few months ago, at first, after awhile, as soon as, before, soon, still.*

Language Note

- Ask students to reread the first paragraph of the essay. Say: *The author talks about two things that started in the past and have continued to the present. What verb forms does she use?* (the present perfect continuous and the present perfect) Write the phrases with these verb forms on the board:

    Ever since . . . they've been trying to convince me to change my ways.
    My kids have convinced me to make a few changes . . .

- Remind students that specific actions that started and were completed in the past take the simple past. However, ongoing conditions or actions that began in the past take the present perfect or the present perfect continuous.

Communicative Practice   40 minutes

3   THINK ON PAPER

A Before Anka wrote her...

- Ask students to look at the sequence-of-events chart and read the directions.
- Say: *Something happened to make Anka want to learn about the environment. What happened?* (Her kids began learning about the environment.)
- Point out that each box in the chart describes a change that she made and that the changes are listed in chronological order, with time signal words (*a few months ago, soon, finally*).

B Use the notes you made...

- On the board, draw a diagram similar to Anka's— but leave the boxes blank.
- Say: *Now you are going to use the notes that you made earlier to organize ideas for an essay that describes what you have done to help the environment. You can use a chart like Anka's, with each box describing one step that you took, or some other graphic organizer.*
- Remind students to use time signal words.
- Have students complete the exercise.

Language Note

Reiterate that a personal narrative should include memories and details that help the writer's personality to come through. Ask students to look back at the model essay for details that help readers to imagine what the author is like as a person. Elicit examples from students and list them on the board. Examples:

She describes her life as hectic and admits that she often forgot to bring bags with her, so we know that she is busy and forgetful.

She writes that she drives a "big old car," so we know she is unpretentious and down-to-earth.

She uses informal phrases like "I can't believe how much stuff I was throwing away," so we know she is friendly and relaxed.

4   WRITE

Use your graphic organizer to write...

- Read the directions, emphasizing that students should use words to signal the sequence in which events occurred.
- Have students write the first draft of a personal narrative.
- Remind students to include details to help the reader imagine the writer's personality.
- Say: *When you finish writing, you're going to read your paper and revise it. What does* revise *mean?* (changing your work by adding, deleting, or rewriting details)

5   CHECK YOUR WRITING

A STEP 1. **Revise your work.**

- Say: *Read over your personal narrative a first time and answer the questions in Step 1. If any answers are* no, *revise your work.*
- *Optional:* Have students form pairs, exchange narratives, and give each other feedback.

B STEP 2. **Edit and proofread.**

- Say: *Then you'll read over your personal narrative a second time and edit and proofread your work.* Direct students to check their personal narratives for grammar, spelling, punctuation, and typos.
- *Optional:* Have students complete a "clean" second draft of their personal narratives at home, incorporating revisions and corrections from the revision and editing steps.

Teaching Tip

You may want to collect student papers and provide feedback. Use the scoring rubric for writing on page Txv to evaluate vocabulary, grammar, mechanics, and how well students complete the task. You may want to review the completed rubric with students.

Extra Practice

Interactive Practice

page 116

A Before Anka wrote her personal narrative, she used a chart to arrange the events. Notice how Anka puts events in a logical order.

My kids started learning about the environment. Got me interested, too.

↓

I began to make changes to reduce my carbon footprint.

↓

A few months ago, my son suggested that I use cloth bags for groceries.

↓

Soon, I began to recycle as much as possible.

↓

Finally, I decided to drive more slowly and use the car air conditioner sparingly so I would save money and gas.

B Use the notes you made in Exercise 1B about how you have helped protect the environment. Use them to make a chart for your personal narrative. You can use a chart like Anka's or some other graphic organizer.

4 WRITE

Use your graphic organizer to write a personal narrative about how you have helped the environment. Be sure to use words to show readers the sequence in which events happened.

5 CHECK YOUR WRITING

A STEP 1. Revise your work.

1. Is your narrative in a logical order?
2. Does it have a casual tone and style that expresses your personality?
3. Is the sequence of events clear?

B STEP 2. Edit and proofread.

1. Have you checked your spelling, grammar, and punctuation?
2. Have you proofread for typing errors?

1 REVIEW

For your grammar review, go to page 231.

2 ACT IT OUT   What do you say?

GROUPS. You are part of a panel discussion about ways to improve your community's environment. Present information and discuss your opinions about the issue.

Student A: Review Lessons 1 and 5. Tell the rest of the panel about the causes and effects of common environmental problems. Explain what *carbon footprint* means. Describe simple ways that people can reduce their carbon footprint.

Student B: Review Lessons 3 and 6. Add to what Student A has said by explaining some tips for greening a community, including carpooling.

Student C: Review Lessons 2 and 4. Add to the discussion by talking about the importance of recycling. Before you begin, write a comment about Todd Skinner's blog entry. Read it aloud and discuss your ideas with Students A and B.

3 READ AND REACT   Problem-solving

STEP 1. Read about Francesca.

Francesca has just been promoted to office manager at a small newspaper in a suburban town. Most of the employees live close by, but they drive to work. She has been asked to make the office more green and energy-efficient. Although she doesn't have a lot of money to spend on changing the physical office space, she must reduce the money and energy the company uses for lighting, water, paper, and transportation. She also has to improve the company's recycling practices.

STEP 2. GROUPS. What is Francesca's problem? What can she do?

4 CONNECT   For your Study Skills Activity, go to page 220.

Which goals can you check off? Go back to page 165.

 Go to the CD-ROM for more practice.

Review & Expand

Show what you know!

1 REVIEW

For your grammar review, go to page 231.

- Say: *Today we're going to review the skills that we have practiced in this unit and apply them to a problem. What are some of the skills we have practiced?* Elicit answers, noting them on the board. (For example: reading about recycling rules, discussing carpooling, identifying causes and effects of environmental problems, analyzing ways to protect the environment.)
- Ask students to complete the grammar review exercise at the top of page 231.

2 ACT IT OUT

GROUPS. You are part of a panel discussion...

- Ask students to read the directions. Explain that they will imagine that they are part of a panel discussion about ways to improve their community's environment. Working in groups, they will review and summarize different lessons.
- Say: *Student A will look back at Lessons 1 and 5 and discuss the causes and effects of common environmental problems, as well as the meaning of* carbon footprint *and ways to reduce this. Student B will reread Lessons 3 and 6 and present some tips for greening a community, such as carpooling. Student C will review Lessons 2 and 4, talk about the importance of recycling, and write a comment about Todd Skinner's blog entry and share it.*
- Have students complete the exercise.
- Have volunteers share their opinions with the class.

3 READ AND REACT

STEP 1. Read about Francesca.

- Say: *Now we're going to apply our knowledge from this unit to a problem involving a character, Francesca. Let's read about Francesca.*
- Have students read the story.

STEP 2. GROUPS. What is Francesca's problem?

- Ask students to form small groups.
- Say: *In your group, you will discuss Francesca's problem and what she can do.*

- Give each group a sheet of flipchart paper and markers, or ask them to make notes on a sheet of paper. Tell them that they will write a brief description of Francesca's problem and list at least three possible solutions.
- Ask students to review the Communication Skill box on page 177 about expressing comparison and contrast. Elicit things to say to introduce a similar or related idea (*similarly, in the same way, like, still, at the same time*) and to present a contrast (*instead, however, on the other hand, on/to the contrary, but, in contrast*). Encourage students to introduce similar or different ideas with these structures.
- Ask groups to choose a representative to present the group's ideas to the class.
- Have students discuss the questions.
- Have a representative from each group present the group's ideas.
- After each presentation, encourage feedback, prompting students as needed. (For example: *What do you think about Group 1's suggestions for Francesca? Which idea do you like best?*)

Possible answers: *Problem:* Francesca's problem is how to make her office more green and energy efficient. *Solution:* She could start a rideshare program, install energy-efficient lightbulbs and recycling bins, and fix any leaky faucets.

4 CONNECT

Turn to page 220 for your Study Skills Activity. See page Txii for general notes about teaching Study Skills activities.

Progress Check

Which goals can you check off? Go back to page 165.

Ask students to turn to page 165 and check off any remaining goals they have reached. Call on them to say which goals they will practice outside of class.

CD-ROM Practice

 Go to the CD-ROM for more practice.

If your students need more practice with the vocabulary, grammar, and competencies in Unit 9, encourage them to review the activities on the CD-ROM.

Technology

Classroom Materials/Extra Practice

CD 3
Tracks 15–20

Workbook
Unit 10

Interactive Practice
Unit 10

Unit Overview

Goals

- See the list of goals on the facing page.

Grammar

- Adjective clauses

Listening and Speaking

- Talk about the growth of the Internet
- Discuss the pros and cons of the Internet
- *Communication Skill:* Expressing Agreement and Disagreement
- Identify how technology affects our everyday lives

Reading

- Read an article about virtual driving
- *Reading Skill:* Identifying an Author's Purpose
- Identify events in the history of the Internet
- *Reading Skill:* Using a Timeline
- Learn about computer training

Writing

- Write an autobiographical essay about a challenge
- *Writing Tip:* Using concrete examples and sensory details

Life Skills

- Understand how to use an instruction manual

Preview

- Welcome students and have them look at page 185.
- Say: *In this unit, we'll talk about the growth of computers and about other forms of technology.*
- Ask the Preview question, offering prompts as needed to elicit answers. (For example: *Is it easier to stay in touch with your friends? Get directions to places you don't know?*)
- Say: *As we begin this unit, I'd like to know how many of you own computers.* Ask for a show of hands.
- *Optional:* Ask: *What do you use computers for?* Offer prompts to elicit discussion as needed. (For example: *Do you use them to buy things on the Internet? Write papers for class? Keep track of your finances? Chat with friends online?*)
- Say: *In this unit, you'll learn more about technology. You'll learn how to use an instruction manual. You'll also learn about virtual training, the positive and negative effects of the Internet, and ways that technology affects our daily lives.*

Unit Goals

- Ask students to read the Unit Goals.
- Explain unfamiliar vocabulary as needed. Example:

    instruction manual—a book that gives you directions for setting up or using electronic equipment

    virtual reality—an environment produced by a computer that looks and seems real to the person experiencing it

- Tell students to circle the goal that is the most important to them.
- Take a poll by reading the goals aloud, with students raising their hands for the goal they checked.
- Record on the board the goal that the most students checked.
- Say: *As we complete this unit, we will look back at this page and reread the goals. We will check each goal as we complete it.*

Technology

Preview

How has the Internet changed how we connect with one another? What happens when you turn on a computer or send a text message or an e-mail?

UNIT GOALS

- ☐ Understand how to use an instruction manual
- ☐ Discuss the pros and cons of the Internet
- ☐ Discuss virtual training
- ☐ Identify how technology affects our daily lives

Listening and Speaking

1 BEFORE YOU LISTEN

A **CLASS.** Discuss. Do you use the Internet? If so, what do you use it for? How often do you use it?

B **PAIRS.** Discuss the meanings of the words in the box. If you don't know the meaning of a word, look it up in a dictionary.

analyze	data	psychologist	vision
calculator	network	store (*v*)	

2 LISTEN

CD3 T15

A An instructor at a community college is giving a lecture on the history of the Internet to the students in her Technology and Society class. As you listen to her lecture, take notes. Use the example notes below as a guide.

> I. Internet grew out of Licklider's unique idea/vision of the future
>
>   A. In 1940s, J. C. R. Licklider—experimental psychologist—had different view of computers
>
>   B. He collected and analyzed data with computers; thought computers were more than fancy calculators
>
>   C. He wanted to use computers as a communications tool, one that would allow computers and humans to work together
>
>   D. He envisioned "thinking centers" for storing and finding information; something like libraries, but larger and connected to one another and to individual people in a network
>
> II. Today's Internet is very similar to Licklider's ideas

CD3 T15

B **PAIRS.** Listen again and check your notes. Then compare them with a partner's. Did you both include the same information? Could you both pass a test on the lecture by studying your notes? Why or why not?

Getting Started 10 minutes

- Say: *In this unit, we will be investigating several aspects of technology, including the pros and cons of the Internet. In this first lesson, we are going to listen and talk about the growth of the Internet.*
- Explain that while many people typically use the word *Internet*, others may say *online*, *the Web*, or just *the Net*.

1 BEFORE YOU LISTEN

A **CLASS. Discuss. Do you use...**

- Ask students to read the directions.
- Repeat the questions. Also ask: *Where do you use the Internet—at home, at work, at the library?*
- Encourage responses from all (or almost all) of the students. Ask students whether they enjoy using the Internet and feel comfortable with it.
- Summarize the general conclusions of the class. (For example: *Most of us use the Internet several times a week, although a few of you are using it every day and a few don't use it except in class.*)

B **PAIRS. Discuss the meanings of...**

- Ask students to read the directions.
- Say: *Before we listen to a lecture on the history of the Internet, I'd like you to talk with a partner about some of the words that will come up in the lecture.*
- Set up pairs. Say: *Work with someone sitting near you. Go through the list of words and share your definitions and ideas about the words.*
- Note that *store* is being used as a verb.
- Walk around; assist as needed with context, pronunciation, and sentence formation.
- Ask volunteers to give the part of speech of each word (for example, *analyze is a verb, calculator is a noun*).
- Ask volunteers to define and use the words in appropriate sentences. If a definition or sentence is not correct, model it correctly. Write a short definition of each word on the board or a flipchart. Continue until all students understand all the words. Allow time for students to write some or all of the new words in their vocabulary logs.

Language Note

- Several words on the list can easily be changed to another part of speech [for example, *analyze* (v) to *analysis* (n) or *analyst* (n)]. Use this list of words to review the parts of speech.
- Explain the example of *analyze*. Then ask pairs (from the previous exercise) to see what other parts of speech they come up with for *calculator*, *network*, *psychologist*, *store*, and *vision*.
- Ask for volunteers to share their results and go through each example with the class.
- Explain that a good way to learn new words is to understand root words and their affixes (prefixes and suffixes, or a group of letters added to the beginning or end of a word to change its meaning, such as *un-* or *mis-*, or its part of speech, such as *-ness* or *-ly*).
- Refer students to a good learners' dictionary. Say: *Dictionaries contain a great deal of information about parts of speech, root words, prefixes, suffixes, and other basic elements of American English grammar.*

Presentation 15 minutes

2 LISTEN

A **An instructor at a community...**

- Ask students to read the directions.
- Ask students to take notes as they listen, following the model of the example notes.
- Play CD 3, Track 15. Walk around and monitor as students work to be sure they understand the task.

B **PAIRS. Listen again and...**

- Ask students to read the directions.
- Say: *Now please listen again and check your notes. Fill in any missing information and correct any errors in your notes.*
- Play Track 15 again.
- Set up pairs. Say: *Compare your notes with your partner's. Check to see whether you both included the same information in your notes.*
- Ask students whether, using their notes, they could do well on a test or quiz on the lecture.

Controlled Practice   15 minutes

3   PRACTICE

A Review your notes...

- Ask students to read the directions.
- Say: *Look over your notes one more time and use them to answer the questions.* Assure students that short answers are OK.
- Ask volunteers to read and answer the questions. Allow students to disagree and negotiate; intervene only if they don't arrive at the correct answers.

Answers: 1. engineer; 2. not much more than very powerful calculators; 3. experimental psychologist; 4. to collect and analyze data; 5. to work together; 6. they each had different strengths; 7. "thinking centers"

Communicative Practice   20 minutes

B PAIRS. Discuss. What surprised you...

- Keep the same partners.
- Rephrase and expand the question. Say: *Did anything surprise you about the lecture? If so, what? Did you find it interesting? Why or why not? What else would you like to learn about the history of the Internet?*
- Say: *Talk with your partner about some of these questions. Or, if you know more about the history of the Internet, share that information with your partner.*
- Allow pairs to talk as long as most of the class is engaged.

4   MAKE IT PERSONAL

GROUPS. Read these quotes...

- Ask students to read the directions and the quotes silently.
- Set up groups of three. Say: *Each of you reads one of the quotes and its discussion question, and leads the discussion about it. Make sure that each group member participates.*
- Walk around; assist as needed with vocabulary, content, context, and pronunciation.
- Ask a representative from each group to share an interesting point or idea they talked about in the group.

MULTILEVEL INSTRUCTION for 4

Cross-ability Set up groups of three so that a confident and above-level student is in each group. This student should also be able help explain the meanings of the quotations.

Teaching Tip

Some students are more comfortable getting help with language and content from a fellow student, and others are more comfortable getting help from you (or finding out what they need later after class). Monitor students' preferences and try to honor them as often as you can.

Extra Practice

Interactive Practice

3 PRACTICE

A **Review your notes and write the answers to the questions.**

1. What was the profession of most people working on early computers?
2. What did they see computers as?
3. What was Licklider's profession?
4. What did he want to use computers for?
5. What did Licklider want to find a better way for humans and computers to do?
6. Why did he think that humans and computers could do more working together than either could do alone?
7. What did Licklider call his early version of networks?

Early computers were usually just powerful calculating machines.

B **PAIRS. Discuss. What surprised you about the lecture?**

4 MAKE IT PERSONAL

GROUPS. Read these quotes taken from some of Licklider's writings. Discuss the questions that follow each quote.

J.C.R. Licklider

1. *Computing machines can do readily, rapidly, and well many things that are difficult or impossible for man, and men can do readily and well, though not rapidly, many things that are difficult or impossible for computers.*

   What can computers do that are difficult or impossible for people to do? What can people do that are difficult or impossible for computers?

2. *In a few years, men will be able to communicate more effectively through a machine than face-to-face.*

   This quote comes from a paper written in 1968. What do you think it means to *communicate through a machine*? Give some examples.

3. *Take any problem… and you find only a few people who can contribute effectively to its solution. Those people must be brought into close intellectual partnership so that their ideas can come into contact with one another. But bring these people together physically in one place to form a team, and you have trouble, for the most creative people are often not the best team players, and there are not enough top positions in a single organization to keep them all happy.*

   This quote gives one of the reasons that in some cases it might be better to communicate online than face to face. Do you agree with this opinion? Explain.

Life Skills

1 USING NEW ELECTRONIC DEVICES

PAIRS.   Discuss. When you get a new electronic device, such as a DVD player, how do you usually set it up and learn how to use it? Do you find such tasks easy or hard to do? Why?

2 READ INSTRUCTIONS AND DIAGRAMS

Read the excerpt from an instruction manual for setting up a remote control for a DVD player. Look at the diagram as you read.

Electronic devices such as cell phones and televisions come with instruction manuals. Often the manuals contain diagrams explaining how to use the device. To understand how to set up and use a machine, read the diagram and instructions carefully. Follow the steps in order. Be sure you understand what the terms in the manual mean.

Programming the TV remote control to operate your DVD player

1 Find the three-digit code for your brand of DVD player.

2 Press the FUNCTION button several times until the DVD button lights up.

3 Press SELECT for five seconds or until the DVD button flashes.

4 While the DVD button is flashing, enter the three-digit code (Step 1) on the remote control's number pad.

5 Press ENTER once.

6 Aim the TV's remote control at the DVD player and press SELECT. When the DVD player turns on, you're done.

Codes for Different Brands	
DVD Players	
Sovy	571
Parasovic	673
Peer	275

Understand how to use an instruction manual

Getting Started 5 minutes

- Ask: *What are some electronic devices that have changed the way we work or spend our free time?* Elicit answers from students, offering prompts as needed. (*What electronic devices enable us to communicate with our friends when we're away from home?*)

Community Building

Have students walk around and ask each other which three electronic devices (for example, computer, cell phone, MP3 player, GPS) they use the most every day. Write the chart that follows on the board and have students copy it and use it to ask each other questions. Then tally the results and see which three devices are used the most. Ask students if the results surprised them, and if so, why.

Name	Electronic Device 1	Electronic Device 2	Electronic Device 3

Presentation 15 minutes

1 USING NEW ELECTRONIC DEVICES

PAIRS. Discuss. When you get...

- Have students read the instructions.
- Ask students to form pairs and discuss the questions. Walk around and listen to conversations, offering prompts as needed. (*Do you read the directions in the instruction manual, or do you follow the pictures and diagrams?*)
- In the full group, ask students to summarize their conversations.
- *Optional:* Take a survey of how students set up and learn to use electronic devices. On the board, list methods mentioned by students (*read the instructions, follow the pictures in the instruction manual, try to make it work myself, ask a friend to help me*). Ask students to raise their hands to indicate the method that they use the most. Then ask students to vote on whether it is easy or hard to set up and use an electronic device. Tally the results on the board.

Controlled Practice 40 minutes

Teaching Tip

For the following exercise, bring in an instruction manual that has a diagram. A manual for a kitchen appliance such as a food processor with different attachments would be fine. Show this to students to help them understand the note.

2 READ INSTRUCTIONS AND DIAGRAMS

Read the excerpt from...

- Say: *We're going to read directions from an instructional manual that explain how to set up and use electronic equipment.*
- Ask students to read the note on electronic devices. Ask if they have ever seen a diagram in an instruction manual and, if so, whether the illustration made it easier to understand the directions.
- Read the directions. Have students look at the title of the excerpt. Ask: *What do the instructions in this excerpt tell us how to do?* (program the TV remote control so that it operates a DVD player)
- Clarify as needed that *programming* means setting up something so that it does what you want it to do.
- Remind students to look at the diagram as they read the instructions.
- Have students read the excerpt. Clarify unfamiliar terms as needed. Examples:

   code—a set of numbers or letters that you use to access electronic equipment or services; *icon*—a symbol that denotes a function (such as an envelope icon to denote e-mail); *number pad*—a small keyboard with numbered buttons that you punch; *aim*—point at something.

- Ask a few questions to check comprehension:

   Which manufacturers make DVD players compatible with the remote control? (Sovy, Parasovic, Peer)

   How do you know if you have programmed the remote control correctly? (You point the remote control at the DVD player, press the SELECT button, and see it turn on.)

Lesson 2   Understand how to use an instruction manual

3   PRACTICE

A You need to understand...

- Say: *Now we're going to look back at the instructions and guess the meaning of some words used.*
- Have students complete the exercise. Walk around and check their work.
- Call on students to give answers. As they do so, note the following:

    Question 3—Explain that you need to point the remote control at an electronic device in order to activate it. (Illustrate this by using a remote control to turn on something in your classroom, such as a TV or DVD player.)

    Question 4—Illustrate the concept of flashing by turning the light switch in your classroom on and off several times.

B Read the sentences and number...

- Ask students to read the directions. Emphasize that students should try to remember what they read and should **not** look back at the instructions.
- Have students complete the exercise.

C PAIRS. Check and compare your answers.

- Say: *Now you're going to compare your answers to a partner's and see if you remembered the order of the directions correctly.*
- Ask students to form pairs and complete the exercise. Tell students to look at page 188 when they are finished comparing answers to see if they remembered the order correctly.
- *Optional:* Ask for a show of hands as to how many students were able to remember the steps in the correct order.
- Point out that students can often save time by referring to the diagram and the captions that go with it.

Expansion: Reading and Writing Practice for 3B and 3C

- Bring in instruction manuals for different electronic devices.
- Ask students to form groups of three. Have each group look at the instruction manual and write three to five questions about the directions or diagrams for another group to answer. (For example: *How do you set the alarm on the digital clock?*) Ask students to write answers to the questions on a separate sheet of paper.
- Have each group trade questions and instruction manuals with another group's. Have the group use the instruction manual to answer the questions.
- Have each group submit its answers to the group that wrote the questions. This group uses this answer sheet to correct its answers.
- *Optional:* Have each group repeat the exercise with a different group.

Progress Check

Can you . . . understand how to use an instruction manual?

- Say: *We have practiced understanding how to use an instruction manual. Can you do this? If so, check the box.*

Extra Practice

Interactive Practice   pages 118–119

A You need to understand how words are used in instruction manuals in order to follow each step correctly. Complete the sentences based on the way each word is used in the manual on page 188. Circle the letter of the correct answer.

1. A **digit** is _____.
   a. an amount
   (b.) a single number

2. The **code** for a brand of machine is _____.
   (a.) a series of numbers and/or letters
   b. a system of laws and regulations

3. When you **aim** something, you _____.
   (a.) point it carefully at something
   b. try to achieve something

4. When a light **flashes**, it _____.
   a. goes on once and then goes off
   (b.) goes on and off quickly several times

5. When you **program** a machine, you, _____.
   a. arrange instructions in order
   (b.) set the machine to operate in a certain way

6. The **number pad** on a remote control is for _____.
   a. writing notes
   (b.) entering numbers

7. A **brand** of DVD player is _____.
   (a.) the name of the company that makes it
   b. a special mark on the player

B Read the sentences and number the steps in order.

__4__ 1. As soon as the DVD button flashes, type the 3-digit code of your brand.

__6__ 2. Aim the remote control at the DVD player and press SELECT.

__2__ 3. Press the FUNCTION button several times or until the DVD button lights up.

__3__ 4. Press SELECT for five seconds or until the DVD button flashes.

__5__ 5. Press ENTER once.

__1__ 6. Find the code for your brand of DVD player

C PAIRS. Check and compare your answers.

Can you...understand how to use an instruction manual? ☐

Listening and Speaking

1 BEFORE YOU LISTEN

CLASS. **Discuss the questions.**

1. How does the Internet help people communicate?

2. How might the Internet harm communication?

3. Do you know anyone who spends too much time on the Internet? How much time does he or she spend? Are there any negative effects?

2 LISTEN

CD3 T16

 A Listen to part of a radio talk show. Psychiatrist Dr. Albert Knowles and host Michelle Allen discuss how the Internet is affecting communication. As you listen, take notes. Answers will vary but could include:

Positive Effects	Negative Effects
easier to stay in touch	some people use online communication to replace or avoid actual human contact
isolated people and people with disabilities can communicate with others	shy people might not develop social skills
scientists can share information instantaneously	online communication can't provide physical contact or true emotional contact

CD3 T16

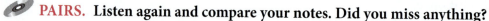 **B** PAIRS. **Listen again and compare your notes. Did you miss anything?**

C **Write the answers to the questions.**

1. For which two groups of people has the Internet improved communication?

2. What is one of the most important uses of the Internet today?

3. Does Dr. Knowles believe that the Internet has done more harm or more good?

4. When is using the Internet a problem for young people?

5. What will happen to a naturally shy person who spends too much time online?

6. What part of communication does not exist online?

Getting Started · 10 minutes

- Say: *In this lesson, we are going to listen to part of a radio show and talk about the positive and negative effects of the Internet.*
- Ask: *Before we go any further, what do you think are some of the positive and negative aspects of the Internet—the pros and cons?* Draw a T-chart on the board, write *Internet* above the chart and label the left half *Positive* and the right half *Negative*. Write all responses on the chart.
- Say: *We'll keep this list posted and look at it later on in this discussion.*

Teaching Tip

- Make sure to follow up on activities. Students closely monitor teacher behavior, and if they see that you don't follow up on activities, they may conclude that the activities or their own participation in class is not important. If this happens, students may lose their enthusiasm for participating in class.
- If you forget something (such as going back to an earlier discussion or referring to a posted list) or you run out of time, acknowledge it and say that, if possible, you will get to it during the next class.

1 BEFORE YOU LISTEN

CLASS. Discuss the questions.

- Ask students to read the directions and the questions.
- Rephrase and extend the questions and give students time to respond after each question. Say:

    Do you think the Internet helps people communicate? If so, in what ways?

    Do you think the Internet might be harmful to communication? If yes, why? If no, why not?

    Do you know anyone who you think spends too much time on the Internet? How do you know it is too much? That is, how much is <u>too</u> much?

    How much time does this person spend on the Internet? What negative effects do you see?

- Accept all responses and allow the discussion to continue as long as students are engaged. Write issues, questions, possible answers, and other student comments on the board so students can refer to them throughout the lesson.

Presentation · 15 minutes

2 LISTEN

A 🔘 **Listen to part of a radio...**

- Ask students to read the directions.
- Ask students to take notes as they listen.
- Play CD 3, Track 16.
- Walk around the room as students listen to observe whether any students are having difficulty listening and taking notes at the same time.

B 🔘 **PAIRS. Listen again and compare...**

- Ask students to read the directions.
- Say: *Now let's listen to the conversation again while you review and add to your notes.*
- Play Track 16 again.
- Set up pairs. Say: *Work with someone sitting near you. Compare your notes with your partner's notes. Do you agree with Dr. Knowles about which effects are positive and which ones are negative? Did you miss anything? Take a few minutes to check, and then we will talk about the pros and cons together.*
- Ask students to compare the notes they took from the lecture and the chart the class worked on earlier (in Getting Started). Say whatever is evident from comparing the two lists.

Controlled Practice · 15 minutes

C **Write the answers to the questions.**

- Ask students to read the directions.
- Ask students to write the answers to the questions; tell them that short answers are OK.
- Ask volunteers to read the questions and their answers. Allow students to disagree and negotiate; intervene only if they don't arrive at the correct answers.

Answers: 1. people who live in isolated areas and people with disabilities; 2. sharing scientific ideas; 3. more good; 4. when they use online communication to replace or avoid face-to-face interaction; 5. he or she won't develop the social skills needed to feel comfortable communicating in person; 6. physical contact (or interaction)

Communication Skill: *Expressing Agreement and Disagreement*

- Direct students to the Communication Skill box.
- Ask a confident, above-level student to read the first paragraph.
- Ask other volunteers to read each category.
- Say: *In American culture people are supposed to express opinions and to agree or disagree with others' opinions, but they are expected to be able to do this politely and respectfully.*
- Say: *Choose a new expression from each of the four categories and write the category and the expression in your vocabulary logs. If you are familiar with all the expressions, write a sample sentence for one expression from each category.*

Communicative Practice   20 minutes

3   CONVERSATION

A GROUPS. Discuss the questions....

- Ask students to read the directions and questions.
- Set up groups.
- Say: *Take turns agreeing, disagreeing, or expressing no opinion about each question. Use the expressions in the box and explain. Make sure that everyone in the group talks. If you haven't formed an opinion about the pros and cons of the Internet, you can practice expressing no opinion.*
- Tell students to add at least two positive and two negative effects to the chart they worked on in Exercise 2A. Remind students that they can refer to the T-chart that the class worked on at the beginning of class.
- Tell groups that you will ask a representative from each group to share what the group added to the chart and why. Say: *Each group needs to choose someone to write down the pros and cons it added to the chart and another to report back to the whole class.*
- Walk around; assist as needed with content, context, vocabulary, pronunciation, and intonation.

Teaching Tip

It's important to help students focus on the "why" part of questions and answers. Students need to know that they are not only expected to have opinions but also to be able to support what they say with logic and information.

B GROUPS. Tell the class...

- Ask students to read the directions.
- Ask a representative from each group to tell what his or her group added to the chart. Remind students to explain, as best as they can, why the group added these positives and negatives.
- Ask the rest of the class to respond to each group's presentation using the expressions from the box.
- Refer to the T-chart from Getting Started. Ask students if they want to make changes to the chart. Make any changes the majority of the class agrees on. Keep the chart posted for the rest of the unit, if possible.

4   MAKE IT PERSONAL

GROUPS. Discuss the questions.

- Ask students to read the directions and the questions.
- Keep the same groups.
- Walk around and listen. Do not intervene unless someone asks you a question.

Expansion: Speaking Practice for 4

- Set up pairs.
- Ask one person in the pair to role-play a concerned friend or family member and the other to role-play a person who is spending over twenty hours a week on the Internet. Have each student take a few minutes to write notes about his or her character and then work on the dialogue with his or her partner.
- Have pairs practice the role play.

Communication Skill: Expressing Agreement and Disagreement

When you discuss your opinions, it is important to make clear whether you agree, disagree, or have not yet formed an opinion. It is also important to express your opinions in a polite way. Here are some expressions you can use.

Giving your opinion
From my point of view…
I believe that…
In my opinion…

Agreeing
I couldn't agree more! (= I completely agree with you.)
I agree.
I feel the same way.
That's a really good point.

Disagreeing
I see your point, but…
You've got a good point, but…
That's one way of looking at it, but…
I see things a little differently.

Expressing no opinion
I really haven't thought about it much.
I see both sides.
I'm not sure how I feel about…
On the one hand…on the other hand…

3 CONVERSATION

A GROUPS. **Discuss the questions. Use the expressions in the Communication Skill box to express your opinions.**

1. Do you agree with Dr. Knowles? Which points do you agree with? Which points do you disagree with? Why?

2. What effects has the Internet or other types of technology had on human relationships and communication? Add at least two positive effects and two negative effects to the chart in Exercise 2A.

B GROUPS. **Tell the class what your group added to the chart and why. Express your opinions about other people's views. Use the language in the Communication Skill box.**

4 MAKE IT PERSONAL

GROUPS. **Discuss the questions.**

1. Do people in your home country worry much about the negative effects of using the Internet? If so, what specific problems concern them?

2. Do you think people in the U.S. worry too much about the harmful effects of the Internet and other forms of communication technology? Explain.

3. If a friend or family member was experiencing harmful effects from overuse of the Internet, what would you do?

Reading

1 BEFORE YOU READ

CLASS. Are you familiar with virtual reality (VR) computer games? Have you ever played such games? How might VR be used to train people to perform certain tasks?

Virtual reality (VR) refers to an environment produced by a computer; the environment seems real to the person who experiences it and things happen in real time.

2 READ

CD3 T17

Listen to and read the article about virtual training. How is VR being used to teach driving?

Virtual Driving

Virtual reality, or VR, is an environment that is produced by a computer. However, it looks and seems real to the person who experiences it. VR is used in two main areas: for training and education, and in computer games. VR was first used as a training tool for pilots. Today, with teenage drivers responsible for more fatal car crashes than drivers in any other age group, some communities are investing in VR programs to train drivers. The idea is to give new drivers the practice that they need in front of a **computer screen** rather than on a busy highway.

At about $20,000 each, VR driving **simulators** are not cheap. However, they can also be **leased**. In 2007 there were about 200 simulators leased to driver's education programs in the U.S., and the number is growing. In some cases, the parents of teens who have died in accidents raise money for simulators for the schools in their communities.

One such program, *Virtual Driver Interactive (VDI)*, is made by the same company that makes virtual reality programs to train soldiers. *VDI* takes about five and a half hours to complete. The simulation is very realistic. Students can look in the virtual rear-view or side mirrors and see traffic behind them, just as in real life. If they hit something, they feel and see the results immediately.

During the simulation, drivers are **continuously** evaluated on eighty-five different **criteria**. Mistakes that they make affect their scores. Some violations, such as not wearing a seatbelt or following too closely behind another car, result in a lower final score. More serious violations result in failure.

There are also virtual reality games for **novice** drivers. Chrysler Corporation has developed an online game, which promotes its cars and provides virtual driver training at the same time. The game, *StreetWise*, can be downloaded for free from Chrysler's website. According to the description on the website:

*The game includes five missions which cover the three levels of **learning permits** recognized by the driver education programs of most states. Making the right decisions and mastering basic and advanced driving skills will allow the player to progress through the game. Each level gives the player new liberties and new responsibilities.* *

Will driving simulations be as successful at training drivers as flight simulators have been at training pilots? No one knows. However, with the number of teenagers involved in accidents every year, many agree that it is worth trying.

Learn about virtual training

Getting Started   10 minutes

- Say: *In this lesson, we are going to read about virtual training.*
- Review with students what they know about virtual training. Accept all responses and write them on the board to refer to later.
- Ask an above-level student to read the note.
- Say, for example: *This is a general definition of virtual reality, but it may not be specific enough for those of us who don't play computer games to understand. Let's talk about virtual reality and see if some people can explain VR and give examples.*

1   BEFORE YOU READ

CLASS. Are you familiar...

- Ask students to read the directions.
- Let students discuss the questions as long as they are engaged. Accept all comments.
- Prompt students who are knowledgeable about VR computer games to give examples of how the computer environment "seems real to the person who experiences it."
- Rephrase the final question. Say: *How do you think virtual reality might be used for training?*
- Accept all responses. Tell students that they will now listen to and read an article about using virtual reality for training.

Presentation   15 minutes

2   READ

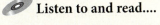 **Listen to and read....**

- Ask students to read the directions.
- Say: *As you read the article, think about how virtual reality is being used to teach people to drive.*
- Point out that the words in boldface are in the glossary on page 245. Encourage students to read the entire article, before going to the glossary.
- Play CD 3, Track 17, as students listen and read.
- Refer back to the list of ideas about virtual reality from Getting Started. Ask students whether they now have a different concept of VR.

Answer: VR simulators are being used in driver's education programs in the U.S.

Expansion: Vocabulary Practice for 2

- Divide the class into small groups.
- Ask students to make a list of the boldfaced words in the reading and to discuss the meaning of each. Encourage students to guess the meaning if they are not sure.
- Tell students to look for the words in the glossary and to compare the definitions there with the meanings they discussed.
- Assign one or two words to each group and give them 1 minute to write one (or two) sentence(s) with their assigned word(s).
- Ask groups to read their sentences to the class.
- After each group reads its sentence, ask if anyone has any questions about the word or phrase.

Teaching Tip

- Taking a break from your routine can give students more opportunities to bond with each other and give them more (and different) opportunities to use their English. Below are some suggestions for stimulating activities on topics that students have studied in Units 7–10.
- Go on a relevant field trip (for example, visit the local courthouse while reading the units on legal issues and citizenship; visit a recycling facility while studying the unit on the environment; learn about technology-related careers by setting up a tour of a local high-tech firm).
- Invite an information technology specialist to speak to the class about advances in computer technology, including how to perform special functions on your cell phone or laptop.
- Set up a social hour with another class so that students can practice expressing opinions, giving advice, and performing other language functions with different people.
- Watch a classic movie with appropriate language and a relevant theme (such as *The Long Walk Home* during African-American History Month). Provide a list of questions for students to answer as they watch. Have them list unfamiliar vocabulary as they watch. After the movie, lead a discussion in which you encourage students to express their opinions about the movie.

Controlled Practice   10 minutes

3   CHECK YOUR UNDERSTANDING

A **Write the answers to the questions.**

- Ask students to read the directions.
- Tell students to check back in the article if necessary to write the answers in their notebooks.
- Ask volunteers to read each question and its answer. Allow students to disagree about and negotiate answers; intervene only if they don't arrive at the correct answers. Encourage students to talk about the article as long as they are engaged.

Answers: 1. as a training tool for pilots; 2. VR programs used to train drivers, to give new drivers the practice they need in front of a computer rather than on a busy highway; 3. because they are very expensive to buy ($20,000); 4. in some cases, parents of teens who have died in car accidents; 5. Virtual Driver Interactive; a realistic simulation of driving that also scores the simulated driver's performance; 6. Chrysler Corporation

Reading Skill: **Identifying an Author's Purpose**

- Ask a confident, above-level student to read the text.
- Say: *Writers always have one or more purposes for writing. Understanding the writer's purpose may help you understand the text. So when you read something, try to figure out whether the author wants to inform, entertain, persuade, or do a combination of the three.*
- Say, for example: *In his novel, A Christmas Carol, the famous British author Charles Dickens was able to do all three at once. He informs the reader about difficult conditions in England; he entertains with his amusing or unusual characters—think about Scrooge and Tiny Tim—and he persuades by making his selfish character become generous and caring.*

Communicative Practice   25 minutes

B **GROUPS. Discuss. What is...**

- Ask students to read the directions.
- Set up groups. Say: *Talk with people sitting nearby. Talk about what you think the author's purpose was in writing the article. Try to back up what you say, but remember that an author can have more than one purpose for writing an article.*

Answer: to inform and persuade

4   WORD WORK

GROUPS. Choose three words...

- Have students stay in the same groups.
- Ask students to read the directions.
- Confirm that students understand that they should discuss first, and then write in their vocabulary logs.

5   MAKE IT PERSONAL

A **GROUPS. Discuss the questions.**

- Have students stay in the same groups.
- Ask students to read and think about the questions.
- Say: *Talk together about these three questions. There are no right or wrong answers, but it is important to support your opinions with facts and logic.*
- Walk around and listen; intervene only if someone asks you a question.

Expansion: Writing Practice for 5A

- Ask students to choose one of the questions and write a paragraph that expresses their opinions on the topic.
- Encourage students to have a clear topic sentence, to give specific examples, and to follow the rules for spelling, grammar, and punctuation.
- *Optional:* Collect the paragraphs. Read them and give one overall positive comment, one substantive comment on structure, one comment on usage, and one comment on mechanics.

B **Look at the chart. Check...**

- Ask students to read the directions.
- Say: *Think about people you know—your friends, co-workers, family—and yourself. What do you think about their driving?*
- Have students form pairs or small groups. Ask them to explain and discuss their responses.

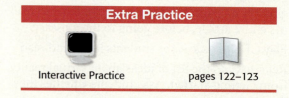

Extra Practice

Interactive Practice   pages 122–123

3 CHECK YOUR UNDERSTANDING

A Write the answers to the questions.

1. What was VR first used for?
2. What are driving simulators? What are they used for?
3. Why do many driver's education programs lease VR simulators?
4. Who raises money to pay for some of the simulators?
5. What is *VDI*? How does it work?
6. What corporation has developed VR games for novice drivers?

B GROUPS. Discuss. What is the author's purpose for writing "Virtual Driving"? Explain.

4 WORD WORK

GROUPS. Choose three words or phrases in the article that you would like to remember. Discuss the words and their meanings. Then record the words and information about them in your vocabulary log.

5 MAKE IT PERSONAL

A GROUPS. Discuss the questions.

1. Do you think that the use of VR driving simulators and games will reduce the number of accidents caused by teen drivers? Why or why not?
2. At what age should people be allowed to get a driver's license?
3. Do you think that the government should set an age at which older people should stop driving? Why or why not?

B Look at the chart. Check (✓) the groups you think are the safest drivers. Explain and compare your responses.

Age Group	Male	Female
20–39		
40–54		
55 and up		

Grammar

Adjective Clauses

Main Clause		Adjective Clause	
	Noun/Pronoun	Relative Pronoun	
It seems real to	the person	**who**	**experiences it**.
Virtual reality is	an environment	**that**	**is produced by a computer**.
The game includes	five missions	**which**	**cover the three levels of learning permits**.

⋮

Grammar Watch

Adjective clauses:

• are dependent clauses that modify nouns.

• identify, define, or give further information about nouns.

• begin with a relative pronoun. Use *who* or *that* for people and *that* or *which* for things.

1 PRACTICE

A Look at the article on page 192. Underline the adjective clauses.

B Complete the sentences with *that*, *which*, or *who*. More than one answer is possible for each item.

1. Rescue personnel ___that/who___ respond to terrorist attacks can train using VR.

2. The simulated program ___that/which___ is used is called *BioSimMER*.

3. A company in Santa Clara, California, has developed simulators ___that/which___ teach people to use electric shovels and other machines in mines.

4. Truck drivers ___that/who___ must learn to handle icy roads and other hazards can use VR for training.

5. In the field of sports, there is a golf simulator ___that/which___ promises to improve your game.

6. Cadets at the U.S. military academy ___that/who___ may become tank commanders train with a tank simulation game called *Steel Beasts*.

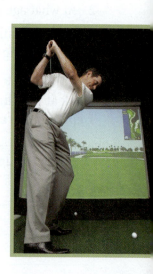

Discuss virtual training

Getting Started   5 minutes

- Say: *In the last lesson, we talked about virtual reality and ways in which it is used. What are some examples?* Elicit answers from students, offering prompts as needed. (For example: *Does anyone remember how the Chrysler Corporation used virtual reality to help new drivers?*)
- Say: *Today we're going to talk about using virtual reality to train people in the workplace. We'll also practice using a grammatical structure called an adjective clause.*

Presentation   10 minutes

Adjective Clauses

- Copy the grammar chart onto the board.
- Review the definition of an adjective: a word that describes a person, place, or thing.
- Say: *An adjective clause is a group of words that, together, distinguish one person or thing from another.*
- Ask students to read the Grammar Watch. Clarify that *modify* means to give information about something.
- Ask: *Which relative pronoun do you use for people?* (*who* or *that*) *Which one do you use for things?* (*that* or *which*)
- Point to the grammar chart and read the first example. Ask: *What is the adjective clause describing?* (a person) *Which person?* (the person who experiences it)
- Read the second example. Ask: *Does the adjective clause describe a person or a thing?* (a thing—the environment) *How is this environment different from other environments?* (It is produced by a computer.)
- Read the third example. Ask: *What noun does the adjective clause modify?* (*five missions*) *What relative pronoun introduces it?* (*which*) *What does the adjective clause tell us about the five missions?* (that they cover the three levels of learning permits)

Controlled Practice   35 minutes

1   PRACTICE

A   Look at the article...

- Say: *Let's look at the article on page 192. Underline the adjective clauses and circle the relative pronouns.*
- Write the first sentence from the article on the board. Ask: *What is the adjective clause?* (*that is produced by a computer*) Underline this on the board. Ask: *What is the relative pronoun that introduces it?* (*that*) Circle this on the board.
- Have students complete the exercise. Walk around and check students' work, offering prompts as needed.
- Call on students to read sentences and say answers.

B   Complete the sentences...

- Read the directions. To review, ask: *Which relative pronouns do you use to talk about a person?* (*that* or *who*) *Which pronouns do you use to talk about a thing?* (*that* or *which*)
- Read the example together. Ask: *Why are there two possible answers?* If necessary, remind students that *who* or *that* can be used to talk about people.
- Have students complete the exercise.
- Walk around and check students' work, offering prompts as needed.
- Call on students to read sentences and say answers.

2 PRACTICE

A Complete the sentences...

- Read the directions and the example. Tell students to match the sentence endings on the right with the sentence beginnings on the left.
- Look at question 2. Ask: *Which noun does the adjective clause modify?* (*rail employees*)
- Ask: *Which relative pronouns can we use for persons?* (*who, that*)
- Ask: *Which clauses in the chart start with* who *or* that? (*b, c, d, e, g, h, i*).
- Ask: *Which of those answers make sense with question 2?* (*g*)
- Have students complete the exercise.
- Call on students to read sentences and say answers.

B Combine the two sentences...

- Read the directions and do the first example.
- Have students complete the exercise.
- Call on students to read their sentences.

Answers: 2. A novice driver is a person who/that hasn't been driving for very long. 3. Driving simulators are virtual reality programs that/which are used by novice drivers to learn how to drive. 4. Virtual Driving Interactive (VDI) is a driving simulator that/which is being used in some communities. 5. VDI is a realistic simulation that/which takes about five and a half hours to complete.

Teaching Tip

Modify Exercise 2B so that it appeals to those with a kinesthetic learning style.

Step 1: Write each sentence on a large strip of paper; write relative pronouns (*that, which, who*) on individual index cards.

Step 2: Place students in small groups.

Step 3: Give each group the sentence strips, connector cards, and scissors.

Step 4: Say: *Combine the two sentences for each item. Cut off the words you don't need—like he or she—when you put sentences together and add the connector cards with relative pronouns.*

Step 5: Have groups complete the exercise and display their combined sentences.

Step 6: Encourage groups that finish early to try to form additional sentences.

Communicative Practice   10 minutes

Show what you know!

GROUPS. Suggest new fields...

- Read the directions and write the example on the board.
- Explain that *Why not* + base form of verb is used to make a suggestion.
- Elicit a few examples from the full group. (*Why not use haircut simulators that show stylists how a haircut would look?*)

Expansion: Show What You Know!

- To help students formulate ideas, write three prompts on the board:

  Why not use _____ simulators that/which _____?

  Employees who _____ could use simulators that/which _____.

- Have students form groups of three.
- Tell groups to brainstorm as many examples as possible, noting them on a sheet of paper.
- Walk around and offer suggestions.
- Have one representative from each group present the sentences.
- Encourage students to react to the ideas with some of the Communication Skill vocabulary they learned on page 191. (*That's a really good idea. I see your point, but . . .*)

Expansion: Show What You Know!

- Turn this activity into a class competition: The group with the most sentences gets a prize, or students can vote on the VR training idea they like the most (and the group with that idea wins).

Progress Check

Can you . . . discuss virtual training?

- Say: *We have practiced discussing virtual training. Can you do this? If so, check the box.*

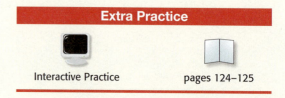

Extra Practice
Interactive Practice   pages 124–125

PRACTICE

A Complete the sentences. Write the letter of correct clause. Be careful. There are three extra clauses.

1. Medical students and nurses practice opening veins to draw blood with a VR program __e__.

2. A classroom VR program teaches groups of rail employees __g__.

3. Even medical students __c__ can learn using VR.

4. Experienced surgeons __i__ also use VR.

5. Drivers of police cars, fire trucks, and ambulances can use simulators __a__.

6. Some psychiatrists are using virtual reality to learn more about the strange worlds __b__.

a. which help them to learn how to travel safely at high speeds

b. that exist inside their patients' minds

c. that hope to become surgeons

d. that teach them how to write speeding tickets

e. ~~that allows them to train without touching living patients~~

f. which they may find when traveling abroad

g. who learn how to evacuate underground stations

h. who want to get easy grades

i. who want to learn and to practice complex techniques for operating on the heart and the brain

B Combine the two sentences using adjective clauses. Write the sentences.

1. Virtual reality is a training tool. It is being used more and more often.

   Virtual reality is a training tool that/which is being used more and more often.

2. A novice driver is a person. He or she hasn't been driving for very long.

3. Driving simulators are virtual reality programs. They are used by novice drivers to learn how to drive.

4. *Virtual Driving Interactive (VDI)* is a driving simulator. It is being used in some communities.

5. *VDI* is a realistic simulation. It takes about five and a half hours to complete.

Show what you know! Discuss virtual training

GROUPS. Suggest new fields for VR training. Use adjective clauses.

Why not use simulators to train people who want to become ships' captains?

Can you... discuss virtual training? ☐

Listening and Speaking

1 BEFORE YOU LISTEN

CLASS. Can you read the message? What does it say? Do you use text messaging or e-mail? If so, do you use any abbreviations or shorthand? If you do, which abbreviations or shorthand do you use? What do they mean?

2 LISTEN

CD3 T18

A  A radio commentator is talking to his daughter about the language of text messaging. Listen and complete the notes with either the shorthand or the meaning of the shorthand.

SHORTHAND	MEANING
ASAP	As Soon As Possible
FYI	for your information
NMU	Not much. How about you?
AAS	Alive and smiling
BFF	best friends forever
WTG!	Way to go!
P911	Parent alert
H&K	hugs and kisses
K	OK
CP	sleepy
DNBL8	Do not be late.
gratz	Congratulations!
XLNT	excellent
ADBB	All done, bye bye!

CD3 T18

B PAIRS. Listen again and check your notes. Make sure that you have the same answers.

Getting Started 10 minutes

- Say: *In this unit, we've been talking about several aspects of technology. Now we are going to work on identifying how technology affects our everyday lives. For example, we will spend some time talking about text messaging and e-mail.*
- Ask: *How many of you use e-mail on a regular basis? How many of you use text messaging regularly?*

▨ Expansion: Vocabulary Practice

- Write *Identify how technology affects our everyday lives* on the board. Beneath this, write *effect* and *affect* on the board. Say: *The title of this lesson is* Identify how technology affects our everyday lives. *Does anyone know the difference between* affect *and* effect?
- Say: *Usually,* **affect** *is the verb and* **effect** *is the noun.*
- Give brief definitions: Affect *means to do something that produces a change in someone or something.* Effect *means the way in which an event, action, or person changes someone or something.*
- Give several examples for each word. Examples:

    Damp weather **affects** *my sinuses, but dry weather has no* **effect** *on them.*

    Do you think the downturn in the economy will **affect** *your ability to pay for a house? The economy will have an* **effect** *on many people's plans, and fewer people will buy houses next year.*

- Ask students to write two sentences for *affect* and two sentences for *effect.*
- Walk around and assist as necessary.
- Give students time to write the rules and their sample sentences in their vocabulary logs.

1 BEFORE YOU LISTEN

CLASS. Can you read...

- Ask students to read the directions.
- Ask a volunteer to read the message in the picture; assist if necessary.
- Ask for volunteers to write answers on the board or flipchart and explain these abbreviations to the class. Keep the abbreviations on view for the entire lesson.
- Say: *Now let's listen to a radio commentator talk about the language of text messaging.*

Presentation 15 minutes

2 LISTEN

Ⓐ **A radio commentator...**

- Ask students to read the directions.
- Ask students to fill in the missing blanks while they listen by using either the shorthand notes or the meaning of the shorthand.
- Play CD 3, Track 18.
- Walk around the room as students listen to observe whether any students are having difficulty.

Controlled Practice 15 minutes

Ⓑ ⊙ **PAIRS. Listen again and check...**

- Ask students to read the directions.
- Say: *Now please listen again and check your notes.*
- Play Track 18 again.
- Set up pairs. Say: *Work with someone sitting near you. Compare your notes and adjust them if you need to.*
- Walk around and listen, but do not intervene unless someone asks you a question.
- When pairs are done, draw the chart in the text on the board. When pairs are finished working, ask volunteers to fill in the blanks. Make sure the answers are correct; ask students to correct any errors.

Communicative Practice   20 minutes

3   PRACTICE

A **PAIRS. Study your notes...**

- Tell students to stay in the same pairs.
- Ask pairs to read the directions, review their notes, and take turns quizzing each other.

B **GROUPS. Play this game...**

- Ask students to read the directions.
- Explain that playing games is one way to learn a language. Say: *There are many ways to learn more about a language. Playing games can be a useful change from typical reading, writing, and speaking activities.*
- Set up groups. Ask two pairs to form groups of four.
- Point out the example. Say: *Work with the members of your group to try to figure out what these shorthand text messaging phrases mean. It's OK if you can't figure out all the meanings. The main idea is for you to practice your conversation skills. Then we will see what each group has come up with.*
- Write the chart on the board. Ask a person from each group to write his or her group's answers/guesses on the chart. As a class, decide which answers are correct.

Teaching Tip

- Before (or after) students complete Exercises 3A and B, ask them to give their opinions about whether learning specialized language (such as text messaging abbreviations) helps them meet their language learning goals. Many classes will probably find the text messaging language activities engaging and useful. Others may be frustrated because they want to focus on acquiring more standard English language.
- Explain that students should focus first on mastering standard English but that computer technology has introduced many new terms into the language. Assure the class that many native speakers do not know the shorthand phrases of texting; they too, have trouble keeping up with the flood of new words, expressions, and abbreviations. Still, it's helpful to know something about the more commonly used terms.

Expansion: Vocabulary Practice for 3A and 3B

- Give students time to research idioms and idiomatic expressions online. If computers with Internet access are not available, bring in several ESL idioms texts and advanced learners' dictionaries.
- Let students work alone, in pairs, or in groups, and let them choose the idioms they want to copy into their vocabulary logs. Give them a minimum number of idioms to find (such as five).
- If students search for idioms on the Internet, have them type "online list of idioms" into the search box of a search engine.
- Walk around as students search for idioms; assist as needed with content, pronunciation, intonation, and usage.
- *Note:* Students may be interested in specific categories, such as workplace idioms. If so, help them to find what they need.

4   MAKE IT PERSONAL

GROUPS. Discuss the questions.

- Ask students to read the directions and the questions.
- Keep the same groups.
- Walk around; assist as needed with context, vocabulary (such as *emoticon*), and pronunciation.

Extra Practice

Interactive Practice

---

3 PRACTICE

A **PAIRS.** Study your notes from Exercises 2A and 2B. Then take turns quizzing each other. Cover the left column of the chart in Exercise 2A and give the shorthand. Then cover the right column and give the meaning.

B **GROUPS.** Play this game. Talk in your group about what each of the following abbreviations means. (These are often used in e-mails, as well as in text messages.) Complete the chart. The group with the greatest number of correct answers is the winner.

Shorthand Phrase	Meaning
2moro	tomorrow
AAMF	as a matter of fact
B/C	because
CM	call me
EZ	easy
GTG	good to go
JAM	just a minute
NRN	not right now
OTP	on the phone
TBH	to be honest
TC	take care

4 MAKE IT PERSONAL

GROUPS. Discuss the questions.

1. What is your opinion of text messaging as a way of communicating? What are the advantages and disadvantages of writing this way?

2. Some people worry that the shorthand young people use for text messaging is having a negative effect on their writing skills. Do you agree? Why or why not?

3. An emoticon is a symbol that people use in e-mail or text messages to show their feelings. For example, :-) is an emoticon that means *I'm happy* or *I'm smiling*. What other emoticons do you know? Draw them and discuss their meanings.

Reading

1 BEFORE YOU READ

CLASS. Discuss. What do you know about the history of the Internet? When did it appear? What events led to its existence?

2 READ

CD3 T19

Listen to and read the web page carefully. As you read, circle the important dates and events.

---

http://www.evolutionofinternet.com

History of the Internet

Question: Who invented the Internet?
Answer: The Internet was not invented; it **evolved**. The evolution involved many inventions and **innovations** as well as a large number of people. Many of the people involved in the early days were graduate students at universities. Some of them are big names in technology today. (For a list, click here).
Question: How did the Internet evolve?
Answer: The story begins after World War II, in the 1950s. At that time, the U.S. and the **former** Soviet Union (U.S.S.R.) were in what was called the Cold War. It was not an actual war, because there was no fighting. However, both governments were very worried that the other side would attack their country. When the U.S.S.R. sent the world's first artificial satellite, Sputnik I, into space in 1957, the Americans became convinced that the Soviet Union had gained a dangerous advantage over them. For that reason, in 1957 the U.S. government created the Advanced Research Projects Agency, or ARPA. The agency's goal was to regain a military advantage over the Soviet Union.

To achieve that goal, ARPA needed the best scientists and **engineers** to work closely together. They needed to share ideas, large amounts of **data**, and the computer programs and power to analyze all that data, and they needed to do it fast. However, there was a problem. Computers at that time were not advanced enough for such work. So in 1962, ARPA created the Information Process Techniques Office (IPTO). Its job was to improve computer technology as quickly as possible.

Just seven years later, in 1969, computers at four universities were connected to create the world's first wide area computer network, ARPANET.

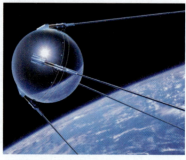

A model of Sputnik I

Question: When did the **general public** start to use the Internet?
Answer: Many improvements were made to ARPANET in the 1970s and 1980s, but most of the users still worked for **research institutions** or the government. In 1983, a common language was established as the official language of what was now called the Internet. At that point, networks all over the world could communicate with each other. In 1981, another important year, the first **personal computers** (PCs) became available. However, it wasn't until 1989 that those first PC owners really discovered the Internet. That was when businesses introduced the first **commercial** e-mail systems. It was also when the first commercial dial-up Internet service provider became available to the public. Suddenly, anyone with a computer and the money to pay the connection fee could go online. In 1991, the U.S. government removed all limitations on commercial use of the Internet. Since then, the number of users has grown at an amazing rate. Today, there are more than 1 billion Internet users worldwide.

Identify key events in the history of the Internet

Getting Started   10 minutes

- Say: *We've just finished talking about some current applications of the Internet and related technologies. In this lesson, we are going read more about the history of the Internet.*

1 BEFORE YOU READ

CLASS. Discuss. What do you know...

- Ask students to read the directions.
- Extend the questions. Say: *Do any of you know about the history of the Internet—maybe by studying about it in a class or reading about it online?*
- Give a personal account to model responses. Say, for example: *I grew up when computers were just beginning to be used, but I was not particularly aware of the Internet until sometime in the 1980s. I didn't start using it until sometime in the mid-1990s, and I still don't know much about the history of it.*
- Remind students that they learned a little about the history of the Internet in Lesson 1. If you wish, have students look back at page 186 and talk about some of the main points from the lecture.
- Assure students that you don't necessarily expect them to know about the history of the Internet. Some students may know about its history, especially if they are computer buffs, work in the field of technology, or worked in science, engineering, or defense in their home countries. If you have such students, encourage them to become "teachers" to the rest of the class.
- Accept all responses and let the discussion continue as long as students are engaged.

Presentation   15 minutes

2 READ

Listen to and read...

- Ask students to read the directions.
- Say: *As you read the web page, circle important dates and events.*

- Point out that the words and phrases in black boldface (*evolved, innovations, former, engineers, data, general public, research institutions, personal computers, commercial*) appear in the glossary on page 245. Encourage students to read the entire article first, before going to the glossary.
- Play CD 3, Track 19 as students listen and read along.
- After students listen and read, ask if they have any other questions about the content, vocabulary, or pronunciation; answer questions.

Teaching Tip

- Say: *When you use the Internet, it is important to verify information and find reliable sources.* Explain that "you can't believe everything you read." Also talk about the importance of **reading critically** (that is, thinking about what you read before automatically accepting that the information or ideas are valid).
- Tell students that one way to judge a text is to consider the source. For example, educational institutions and government agencies usually give reliable data.

Culture Connection

- Make sure students understand what plagiarism is. Say: *We're going to talk for a minute about plagiarism, what it is and why it is a problem. In this country, plagiarism means using someone else's words, ideas, or work and pretending they are your own. Sometimes students plagiarize without meaning to and get into trouble. Therefore, you must understand how to properly use and cite sources (give credit to other people's ideas). Teachers consider any material taken directly or directly paraphrased (review paraphrasing, if necessary) from the Internet or another source to be plagiarism. Plagiarism is considered a serious offense in American schools and colleges. In some universities, students are expelled for copying ideas and not citing the source.*

Controlled Practice 20 minutes

3 CHECK YOUR UNDERSTANDING

A **Write the answers to the questions.**

- Ask students to read the directions.
- Tell students to look back at the web page before doing the exercise.
- Ask volunteers to read their answers aloud.
- Encourage students to continue to talk about the article or questions as long as they are engaged.

Answers:

1. It was not invented; it evolved. 2. The U.S. was afraid that the U.S.S.R. had a dangerous advantage because it had produced the first artificial satellite. This fear led the U.S. to establish ARPA, an agency whose scientists and engineers shared ideas, data, and computer programs. 3. ARPA's goal was to regain a military advantage over the Soviet Union. 4. 1989; 5. more than 1 billion

Reading Skill: Using a Timeline

- Direct students to the Reading Skill box.
- Ask a confident, above-level student to read the text.
- Say: *Using a timeline—either reading one or constructing one yourself—is a good way to organize, retain, and review specific information. Separating information into specific time periods is an efficient way to think about events.*

B **Use the information...**

- Ask students to read the directions.
- Say: *You will probably need to reread or skim the web page to be able to fill in the rest of the timeline.*
- Walk around; assist as needed.

Expansion: Writing and Speaking Practice for 3B

- Have students make timelines of their own lives. Ask them to develop their own timelines based on education or work experiences or both (rather than strictly personal or family history). It's important to stress the past, present, and future aspect of a personal timeline so that learners can focus at least as much on their short- and long-term goals as they do on other elements. Students can construct pared-down timelines following the model and use them to present a 2- or 3-minute talk in front of the whole class.

4 WORD WORK

GROUPS. Choose three words...

- Have students stay in the same groups.
- Ask them to read the directions.
- Confirm that students understand that they should discuss first, and then write in their vocabulary logs.
- Walk around; intervene only if you hear a question that students can't answer.

Communicative Practice 15 minutes

Show what you know!

GROUPS. Look at your timelines...

- Ask students to read the directions.
- Rephrase and expand the directions. Say: *The idea here is to use the timeline as your notes about the evolution of the Internet.*
- Keep the same groups. Say: *Work with the group you are in now. Take turns explaining the history of the Internet. For example, starting on the left side of the timeline, one member of your group describes what happened in the 1950s, then someone else describes what happened in the 1960s, and so on until you've gotten to the present time.* Confirm that students understand the process.
- Walk around; listen but do not intervene unless someone asks you a question.

Extra Practice

Interactive Practice   pages 126–127

CHECK YOUR UNDERSTANDING

A Write the answers to the questions.

1. Who invented the Internet?
2. What role did the Cold War play in its development?
3. What was ARPA's goal?
4. When did ordinary people begin to use the Internet?
5. How many people use the Internet today?

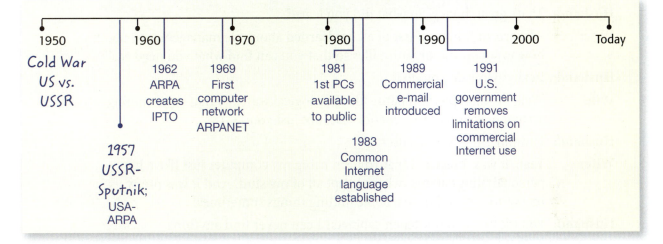

Reading Skill:
Using a Timeline

When you are reading about a historical event, it is often helpful to use a timeline. Timelines are usually divided into specific time periods, such as decades (10-year periods) or centuries. Events from long ago are placed on the left; more recent events go on the right. Use your timelines to review what you have read.

B Use the information in the web page to complete the timeline. Answers will vary but could include:

1950	1960	1970	1980	1990	2000	Today

Cold War
US vs.
USSR

1962
ARPA
creates
IPTO

1969
First
computer
network
ARPANET

1981
1st PCs
available
to public

1989
Commercial
e-mail
introduced

1991
U.S.
government
removes
limitations on
commercial
Internet use

1957
USSR–
Sputnik;
USA–
ARPA

1983
Common
Internet
language
established

4 WORD WORK

✎ **GROUPS.** Choose three words or phrases in the web page that you would like to remember. Discuss the words and their meanings. Then record the words and information about them in your vocabulary log.

Show what you know! Identify key events in the history of the Internet

GROUPS. Look at your timelines and describe the evolution of the Internet. One student says a few sentences. Then another student continues, and so on until you finish. Do not look back at the web page.

Reading

1 BEFORE YOU READ

CLASS. Discuss. Do you know how to use a computer?
If so, how did you learn?

2 READ

CD3 T20

Listen to and read the dialogue about computer training.

Husband: Hey, honey, how was your day? How did the computer training go?

Wife: It was really exhausting, but exciting too. The best part is that when I finish the course, I'll be able to apply for that job in the accounting department.

Husband: That's great, honey. So what did you learn?

Wife: All sorts of things…First of all, we learned about file management—about how to set up and organize files so that you can find what you need easily.

Husband: Really? How do you do that?

Wife Well, for example, you name files in a logical way…so that your naming system make sense to someone else, not just you.

Husband: Hmmm…that sounds useful.

Wife: Yeah, it was. I realized that I'd been using my computer just like a big personal filing cabinet, where I kept all of my stuff. And it was pretty messy, too. Even I have trouble finding things sometimes!

Husband: You mean like our kitchen cabinets? I can never find anything in there.

Wife: Exactly! Anyway, they helped us reorganize all of our computer files. Then they had us **switch** computers and see how long it took us to find a document we might need if that person was out sick, for example.

Husband: And did it work?

Wife: It was amazing! Everything was so organized and easy to understand. It only took me a few seconds to find what I was looking for. I can already see how this is going to save all of us a lot of time.

Husband: That's great, honey. So what's tomorrow's topic?

Wife: Hakim from Accounting is going to teach us how to use a **spreadsheet**. You know, where you enter lots of numbers or other information in columns, and then you tell the computer what **calculations** to do?

Husband: Fantastic! Well, I know what we're doing this weekend.

Wife: Really? What's that?

Husband: You're going to be teaching me everything you've learned!

Getting Started 10 minutes

- Say: *In this lesson, we are going to listen to and read a dialogue about basic computer training.*

1 BEFORE YOU READ

CLASS. Discuss. Do you know how...

- Ask students to read the directions.
- If most or all of your students know how to use a computer, rephrase and extend the question. Say, for example: *I know that many of you use computers frequently and most of you use computers at least occasionally. What can you do on the computer and what would you still like to learn more about?*
- Rephrase and extend the second question. Say: *Where and how did you learn to use computers? What more would you like to learn about computers and the Internet?*
- Accept all responses and allow the discussion to continue as long as students are engaged.

Presentation 15 minutes

2 READ

 Listen to and read...

- Ask students to read the directions.
- Say: *While you listen and read, focus on what the woman in the dialogue is learning about in her computer training.*
- Point out that the words and phrases in boldface (*switch, spreadsheet, calculations*) are in the glossary on page 245. Encourage students to read the entire dialogue first, before going to the glossary.
- Play CD 3, Track 20, as students listen and read along.
- After students listen and read, ask if they have any other questions about the content, vocabulary, or pronunciation; answer questions.

Expansion: Vocabulary Practice for 2

- Set up small groups.
- Ask students to make a list of the boldfaced words in the reading and to discuss the meaning of each. Encourage students to guess the meaning if they are not sure.
- Tell students to look for the words in the glossary and to compare the definitions there with the meanings they discussed.
- Pass out learners' dictionaries to each group. Give each group two or three (different) computer- or training-related words or phrases on index cards (for example, *HTML, HTTP, USB drive [flash drive], Intranet, cookie, maximize and minimize [referring to Microsoft Windows programs], WYSIWYG, firewall, function key*). Adapt the new list of words to students' interests. For example, if students are interested in learning more about computers for word processing, choose additional vocabulary related to that topic. Or, if students seem more interested in the Internet, use additional vocabulary related to that subject.
- Alternatively, you could use the words in the vocabulary box in Exercise 4B on page 201 as the additional vocabulary words, so that students would be able to discuss these words when they do the exercise.
- Give groups several minutes to look up the new words, acronyms, and phrases and to talk about how the words are related to computers and computer training. Ask groups to write computer-related sentences with their new words or phrases.
- Walk around; assist as necessary to provide context and advice on writing appropriate sentences.
- Ask a representative of each group to write each group's sentences on the board. Ask another member of each group to read the group's sentences.
- Ask if anyone has any questions.
- Give students time to write the new vocabulary and sentences in their vocabulary logs.

MULTILEVEL INSTRUCTION for Expansion

Cross-ability Set up groups so that there is a student who has strong vocabulary and grammar knowledge and dictionary and computer skills in each group. This student will be able to help less proficient students complete the dictionary and sentence-writing tasks.

Controlled Practice   20 minutes

3   CHECK YOUR UNDERSTANDING

A Read the dialogue...

- Ask students to read the directions and skim the topics.
- Say: *Reread the dialogue and look for what the woman is learning.*
- Ask volunteers to provide the answers.

B Mark the statements...

- Ask students to read the directions and the statements.
- Say: *Reread the dialogue. Decide whether the statements are true or false.*
- Have students read and complete the exercise.
- Walk around; assist as needed.
- Ask volunteers to provide the answers.

4   WORD WORK

A GROUPS. Choose three words...

- Ask students to read the directions.
- Set up groups of three or four.
- Confirm that students understand that they discuss first, and then write in vocabulary logs.
- Say: *Remember when you write in your vocabulary logs, you can always write more than three words or phrases. You can also use the vocabulary log for words you read or hear outside of class.*

B CLASS. Discuss. What does each...

- Ask students to read the directions and the words in the vocabulary box.
- Ask for volunteers to explain or give examples of the words.
- *Note:* If you used this set of words in the Vocabulary Expansion for Exercise 2, students should already know what the words mean. In this case, ask them to share any further questions about these or other computer-related vocabulary.

Communicative Practice   15 minutes

5   MAKE IT PERSONAL

GROUPS. Discuss the questions.

- Keep the same groups as in Exercise 4A.
- Ask students to read the directions and the questions.
- Ask groups to share with the whole class any community resources that offer computer training courses. Have them write the resources on the board.
- Walk around; assist as needed.
- *Note:* Before the discussion, identify local free and low-cost computer training opportunities. Bring in contact information and flyers (if available). Add the contact information to the list groups are writing on the board.

Teaching Tip

- It's important to regularly ask for students' input on the class and its activities. This helps you plan effective lessons, it allows adult students to have a voice in their own education, and it gives them practice in speaking or writing about their personal goals, ideas, and opinions.
- Write on the board: *Was this unit on technology useful for my personal goals for learning English? Why or why not? To what extent?*

  extremely useful
  somewhat useful
  not useful

- Say: *I am asking this question because I want to make sure that the class focuses on what you need and want to learn, so I need you to express your opinions to me. Thanks.*
- Alternatively, pass out copies of this question and have students write their answers. In this case, tell students they may put their names on the form or not, as they choose.

3

CHECK YOUR UNDERSTANDING

A Read the dialogue again. What is the woman learning how to do? Check (✓) the topics.

☐ 1. apply for a job online   ✓ 3. use a spreadsheet

✓ 2. manage computer files   ☐ 4. prepare her taxes

B Mark the statements *T* (*true*) or *F* (*false*).

__T__ 1. The woman wants to change jobs.

__F__ 2. She is studying computer science at a university.

__T__ 3. She is taking a computer course at work.

__F__ 4. The woman doesn't know how to use a computer.

__F__ 5. In today's class, she learned about spreadsheets.

__T__ 6. Her husband knows less about computers than she does.

__F__ 7. Her husband thinks she should study on the weekend.

__F__ 8. The woman is going to go to class this weekend.

4 **WORD WORK**

A GROUPS. Choose three words or phrases in the dialogue that you would like to remember. Discuss the words and their meanings. Then record the words and information about them in your vocabulary log.

B CLASS. Discuss. What does each of the computer terms in the box stand for? Share what you know.

browser	document	file	keyboard	monitor	PowerPoint®
desktop	Excel®	folder	mouse	Outlook®	spreadsheet

5 **MAKE IT PERSONAL**

GROUPS. Discuss the questions.

1. What do you know how to do on a computer?

2. Talk about the things you are interested or not interested in learning how to do on a computer. Explain your reasons.

3. If you want to get computer training, what can you do? Talk about any community resources you know of that offer computer training courses.

Writing

1 BEFORE YOU WRITE

A You are going to write an autobiographical essay about a challenge you faced. Read about autobiography. Then read the writing tip.

> **FYI**   ABOUT AUTOBIOGRAPHY
>
> Current technology has made it possible for many people who are not professional writers to publish autobiographical essays online. In an autobiographical essay, you describe important people, events, and places in your life. Every person has a life history that's worth telling. You look back and recall, in words, those experiences that have made you who you are.
>
> **Writing Tip:** **Using concrete examples and sensory details**
>
> Vivid examples and concrete details are what make your life story come alive. When you describe an important moment or person, try to create a picture in the reader's mind. Use sensory details that will help readers see, hear, and touch what you are describing. Be specific about when and where an event occurred. Avoid general phrases such as "a good time" or "a nice person." Show *why* the time was good or *what* the person did that was nice.

B Begin thinking about your life story. Ask yourself: What difficult situations have I faced in my life? What were some key moments during these periods? How did I overcome the challenges? Who helped me? Take notes.

C Free-write about your topic for ten minutes. Write down everything you remember. Get all of your memories and thoughts down on paper.

D Read the writing model on page 211. What is Alexandra's essay about?

2 ANALYZE THE WRITING MODEL

PAIRS. Discuss the questions.

1. What challenge did Alexandra face when she came to the U.S.?
2. What steps did she take to overcome her difficulties?
3. What people and events helped her succeed?

Getting Started   5 minutes

- Say: *We have been talking about technology and the growth of the Internet. We have practiced vocabulary and grammatical structures to discuss virtual training. Today we are going to apply all of this knowledge as we write an autobiographical essay about a challenge that we faced.*
- Write the terms *biography* and *autobiography* on the board.
- Say: *A biography is a story that someone writes about someone else. An autobiography is a story that someone writes about his or her own life.*
- Ask: *What types of people write autobiographies? Why do you think that people write them?*

Presentation   5 minutes

Teaching Tip

For the exercise that follows, direct students to an Internet blog, preferably an autobiographical one. Ask: *Why do you think that this person wrote the blog?*

1 BEFORE YOU WRITE

A You are going to write...

- Have an above-level student read the FYI note aloud.
- Say: *One way to write and publish a story about yourself online is to have a blog.* Review what a blog is.
- Remind students that a blog is a personal website that many people use to write about their lives or recount a personal experience.
- Have students look back at Todd Skinner's blog on page 172. Ask: *What did Todd write about?*
- Direct students' attention to the Writing Tip and read it aloud.
- Explain that a *concrete detail* is something that is described in such a realistic way that you can easily imagine it.
- Emphasize that when students write, they will want to use concrete examples and sensory details to help readers visualize their story.

Language Note

- Explain that concrete examples and sensory details help readers to imagine a scene. Read the following sentences aloud:

My grandmother's kitchen was tiny but inviting: There were bright white countertops, yellow flowered wallpaper, and a tiny linoleum table with two padded yellow chairs. Afternoon talk shows played from a portable television balanced on top of the refrigerator. The smell of garlic and tomatoes hung in the air. Whenever I entered the room, I felt calm.

- Ask: *What details do you remember about the passage that I just read? What can the reader see, hear, touch, and smell?*

Controlled Practice   10 minutes

B Begin thinking about your...

- Ask students to read the directions.
- Have students complete the exercise.

C Freewrite about your topic...

- Ask students to read the directions. Tell them to write down everything they can about their topic.

D Read the writing model on page 211....

- Have students read the autobiographical essay on page 211, and clarify unfamiliar vocabulary.
- Ask students what the author's essay is about.

Answer: Alexandra's essay is about her life story—how she came to the U.S., found work, learned English, and became successful.

2 ANALYZE THE WRITING MODEL

PAIRS. Discuss the questions.

- Say: *Now, read the essay a second time. Then discuss your answers to the questions.*
- Elicit answers and write them on the board.

Answers: 1. Since she didn't know enough English to communicate well, she couldn't find a well-paying job.

2. She worked as a babysitter and studied English.

3. Her English teacher encouraged her to work on her English all the time. She got a job at a nonprofit organization. Her English improved and she was promoted.

Communicative Practice 40 minutes

3 THINK ON PAPER

A Before Alexandra wrote...

- Read the first sentence of the directions for the problem/solution chart. Have a volunteer read the text in the chart.
- Say: *What is an* outcome? (a result or consequence)
- Read the rest of the directions, and ask students to complete the exercise.
- Elicit answers to the questions. (Possible answers: Both the essay and the chart present the author's problem, solutions, and outcomes. However, the problem/solution chart summarizes these points; the essay adds details about the author's personal life and jobs and about her teacher's methods.)

B Look at the notes you made...

- Have students read the directions.
- Tell students to make problem/solution charts. Monitor students' work, helping as needed. (For example: *Is that a solution or an outcome?*)

4 WRITE

Use your problem/solution chart...

- Read the directions, emphasizing that students should include concrete examples and sensory details to help readers visualize their life story.
- Have students write the first draft of an autobiographical essay.
- Say: *When you finish writing, you're going to read your autobiographical essay and revise it. What does* revise *mean?* (change your work—add, delete, or rewrite details)

5 CHECK YOUR WRITING

A STEP 1. Revise your work.

- Read the directions. Say: *Read over your autobiographical essay a first time and answer the questions in Step 1; if any answers are* no, *revise your work.*

- *Optional:* Have students form pairs, exchange papers, and give each other feedback. Tell them to note whether the essay described a personal challenge, used concrete examples and sensory details to help readers picture the story, and was structured in a logical way that readers could follow.

B STEP 2. Edit and proofread.

- Say: *Read over your essay a second time and edit and proofread your work.* Read the directions and direct students to check their essays for grammar, spelling, punctuation, and typos.
- As students edit and proofread, walk around and check their work, answering questions as needed.
- *Optional:* Have student complete a "clean" second draft of their essay at home, incorporating revisions and corrections from the revision and editing steps.

Teaching Tip

You may want to collect student papers and provide feedback. Use the scoring rubric for writing on page Txv to evaluate vocabulary, grammar, mechanics and how well students complete the task. You may want to review the completed rubric with students.

MULTILEVEL INSTRUCTION for 5A and 5B

Pre-level Have students complete a checklist with the revising and editing criteria from Exercises 5A and 5B, checking off a box for each question and making any changes.

Above-level Have students who finish writing and self-editing read and edit a peer's essay using the criteria in Exercises 5A and 5B. Then have them discuss the essay with the writer.

Extra Practice

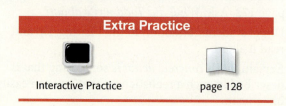

Interactive Practice   page 128

THINK ON PAPER

A Before Alexandra wrote her essay, she used a problem/solution/outcome chart to structure her memories. Compare the chart to her essay on page 211. How are they similar? How are they different? For example, what details does the essay provide that are missing from the chart?

> PROBLEM: Came to Los Angeles without enough English or education to get a good job

> SOLUTIONS: Took English class at the high school; had a great teacher (Mr. Stevens) who helped me learn; studied hard and used all kinds of methods

> OUTCOME: English improved; got a better job; learned more English on the job—even slang; moved up within the company; got GED; went on to college

B Look at the notes you made of challenges you faced in Exercises 1B and 1C. Select a topic. Use your notes to create a problem/solution/outcome chart for an autobiographical essay.

4 **WRITE**

Use your problem/solution/outcome chart and your notes to write an autobiographical essay about how you overcame a challenge. You may want to include your future goals the way Alexandra did.

5 **CHECK YOUR WRITING**

A STEP 1. Revise your work.

1. Does your essay describe a challenge you faced?
2. Have you used concrete examples and sensory details to help readers picture this period in your life?
3. Is your essay structured in a logical way that readers can follow?

B STEP 2. Edit and proofread.

1. Have you checked your spelling, grammar, and punctuation?
2. Have you proofread for typing errors?

1　REVIEW

For your grammar review, go to page 231.

2　ACT IT OUT　What do you say?

PAIRS. You are debating the pros and cons of the Internet in our daily lives. Review Lessons 1, 3, 6, 7, and 8.

Student A: Argue in favor of the Internet. Tell Student B how the Internet has improved our lives at home and at work. Include some information about the history of the Internet.

Student B: Take a stand against the Internet. Tell Student A how the Internet and e-mail have had negative effects on our lives at home and at work. Include some information about texting.

3　READ AND REACT　Problem-solving

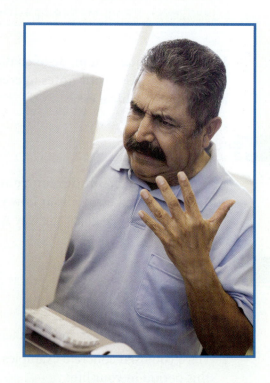

STEP 1. Read about Edwin.

Edwin has just started a new office job. It is a step up for him, but he is having trouble learning the technology used at the new company. He's had problems with his computer. He can't figure out how to change his computer password, and his mouse isn't working properly. In addition, he never had to prepare Excel® spreadsheets or PowerPoint® presentations before. His new boss expects him to learn these skills quickly. Edwin is feeling very nervous about his skills. He's even having trouble with some of the abbreviations his boss uses in e-mails.

STEP 2. GROUPS. What is Edwin's problem? What can he do?

4　CONNECT

For your Goal-Setting Activity, go to page 221.

Which goals can you check off? Go back to page 185.

 Go to the CD-ROM for more practice.

1 REVIEW

For your grammar review, go...

- Say: *Today we're going to review the skills that we have practiced in this unit and apply them to a problem. What are some of the skills we have practiced?* Elicit answers, noting them on the board. (For example: understand how to use an instruction manual, discuss the positive and negative effects of the Internet, discuss virtual training, identify how technology affects our daily lives)
- Have students complete the grammar review exercise on page 231.

2 ACT IT OUT

PAIRS. **You are debating...**

- Say: *Earlier in this unit, we explored the birth of the Internet. Today we'll debate the pros and cons of the Internet in our daily lives.*
- Ask students to read the directions. Set up pairs.
- Clarify that *take a stand against* means to argue against something.
- Say: *Student A will argue in favor of the Internet, explaining how the Internet has improved our lives at home and at work and citing information about the history of the Internet, such as what it was originally created to do.*
- Say: *Student B will argue against the Internet, explaining how the Internet has negatively affected our lives at home and at work and using the example of texting to support his or her arguments.*
- Ask students if they remember ways to express agreement and disagreement. Write the following functions on the board and elicit ways to state them: *Giving your opinion; Expressing no opinion; Agreeing; Disagreeing.*
- As needed, refer students to the Communication Skill box on page 191, which presents ways to politely express agreement and disagreement. Give students a few minutes to review the box.
- Have students complete the exercise.
- Have volunteers share their opinions with the class.

3 READ AND REACT

STEP 1. **Read about Edwin.**

- Say: *Now we're going to apply our knowledge from this unit to a problem involving a character, Edwin. Let's read about Edwin.*
- Have students read the story.
- Clarify unfamiliar vocabulary as needed. (Examples: *a step up*—a promotion or move to a higher level; *figure out*—understand)

STEP 2. GROUPS. **What is Edwin's problem?**

- Ask students to form small groups.
- Say: *In your group, you will discuss what Edwin's problem is and what he can do about it.*
- Ask each group to make notes on a sheet of paper. Tell them that they will write a brief description of Edwin's problem and a list of solutions.
- Elicit language to use for making suggestions. (*First, he should. . . . He could also try to . . .*)
- Have students discuss the questions.
- Have a representative from each group present the group's ideas.

Possible answers: *Problem:* Edwin needs to improve his technical skills. *Solution:* He can ask someone in IT for help or ask his boss to let him take a training course.

4 CONNECT

Turn to page 221 for your Goal-Setting Activity. See page Txii for general notes about teaching Goal-Setting activities.

Progress Check

Which goals can you check off? Go back to page 185.

Ask students to turn to page 185 and check off any goals they have reached. Call on them to say which goals they will practice outside of class.

CD-ROM Practice

 Go to the CD-ROM for more practice.

If students need more practice with the vocabulary, grammar, and competencies in Unit 10, encourage them to review the activities on the CD-ROM.

Unit 1   Descriptive Essay

My Interests, Skills, and Goals

I have a wide variety of interests, but my main interests are science and nature. Even as a child, I always loved spending time outdoors. I enjoy gardening, and I'm interested in organic gardening methods. I grow vegetables, herbs, and flowers in the community garden in my neighborhood.

I have many skills. I'm good at math, and working with computers has always been easy for me. I keep up with new computer programs, and I do a lot of things online. I think my interpersonal skills are good, too. I'm outgoing and patient. I often help my friends with their computer problems.

I want to work at something that combines my interests and skills. My career goal is to work as a landscape architect for the City Parks and Recreation Department. Right now I'm taking ESL classes at the community college. After I finish my ESL classes, I want to enroll as a credit student and study landscape architecture. While I'm taking classes, I hope to work as a tree climber and pruner in the city parks.

Andrea Fernández

Unit 2   Job Ad

Megametro Media

Growing media firm seeks an entry-level accountant. The qualified candidate will have a degree or certificate in accounting and will have knowledge of Microsoft Office®, QuickBooks®, and other accounting software. Related experience a plus. Team environment. Excellent problem-solving and communication skills required. Only honest, dependable, hardworking candidates need apply.

Unit 2   Cover Letter for a Résumé

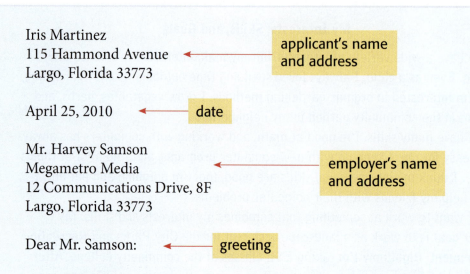

Iris Martinez
115 Hammond Avenue   ← applicant's name and address
Largo, Florida 33773

April 25, 2010   ← date

Mr. Harvey Samson
Megametro Media   ← employer's name and address
12 Communications Drive, 8F
Largo, Florida 33773

Dear Mr. Samson: ← greeting

    I am writing in response to your ad for an entry-level accountant in the *Largo Gazette*. My education and qualifications are a great match for this position.

    As you can see in my attached résumé, I am completing a program in accounting at Hillsborough Community College. I will have my AA degree in one month. I can use all Microsoft Office programs, as well as QuickBooks. In addition to attending classes, I have been working as an Assistant Manager at Robertson's Supermarket, and this job has given me an opportunity to perform some basic bookkeeping and accounting duties.

    Megametro Media is a well-known and respected company. I believe that it is the kind of company where I will be able to make valuable contributions as I grow and learn. I'm dependable, hardworking, and responsible. I'm a team player. And I have excellent problem-solving and communication skills.

    Thank you for considering my application. I look forward to meeting you and discussing the opportunity to work for Megametro Media.

← thank you and indication of eagerness for further contact

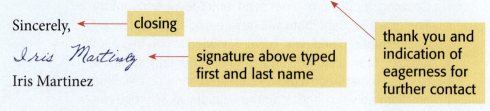

Sincerely,   ← closing

Iris Martinez   ← signature above typed first and last name
Iris Martinez

Unit 3   Letter to the Editor

Letters to the Editor
November 24, 2010
Re: Eating While Driving

Eating while driving is dangerous, and it definitely should be banned. People should eat before they get into the car so that they can focus on the very important job of driving. This would be safer for drivers, passengers, and everyone around them.

One of the reasons eating while driving is so dangerous is because it forces the driver to take a hand off the steering wheel. Even though eating doesn't require brainpower, it does require coordination. Unwrapping a burger or picking out a French fry involves taking a hand—or sometimes two—from the steering wheel. If something suddenly happens, which is always a possibility while driving, without having both hands on the wheel, the driver will not have complete control.

Another reason eating while driving is dangerous is that the food can spill or drop on the driver or critical parts of the car. For example, if someone is driving to work and eating a breakfast sandwich that starts to leak sauce, the driver is going to be more worried about ruining clothing than watching the road. Or imagine that part of the sandwich slips out and onto the brake or gas pedal. A simple attempt to brush it away with a foot could cause an accident. If the food a driver is eating is greasy, it could get onto the steering wheel and cause loss of control. If it is hot, the driver could get burned, causing him or her to make a sudden move and be distracted from the most important task: driving.

Though our lives are all very busy, we should be able to find the time to have a bite before getting behind the wheel. Eating is one of the most distracting and dangerous activities to do while driving. Taking an extra ten minutes to eat something at home could save lives.

Fazil Shankar
San Francisco, California

Unit 4   Safety Instructions

How to Prevent Falls at Home

Falling at home is a serious problem. The good news is that one-third of all falls in the home could be prevented if people followed a few simple steps.

To prevent falls in your home, first, identify potential hazards. Be sure that all areas of your house are well lit. If not, put in brighter light bulbs where needed, and install night-lights in areas you walk through at night. Remove loose objects from the floor and stairs, and keep electrical cords away from walkways. Make sure that handrails and steps are secure and in good condition. Tape down or eliminate area rugs that could cause someone to trip, slip, or fall. Close cabinet doors and drawers—including doors to the dishwasher and clothes dryer. Use rubber mats to prevent slipping in the bathtub.

Next, look at the kind of shoes you typically wear. Wear sturdy shoes, even at home. Walking around in socks or slippers can cause a fall, especially when going up and down stairs. Always be sure that your shoelaces are tied, and avoid high heels or unstable sandals.

Then consider some form of exercise to improve your balance, flexibility, and coordination. Studies show that certain types of exercise, such as yoga and tai chi, can improve balance and prevent falls among people of all ages. The better shape you are in, the less likely you are to fall.

Finally, investigate the side effects of any medications you take. Some drugs can cause fatigue, lack of coordination, or dizziness. If you are taking such a medication, take extra care because you have a higher risk of falling.

Eva Tran

Unit 5   Self-evaluation

Self-evaluation

Since last year, I have been working as a Certified Nurse's Assistant (CNA), taking care of elderly patients. My strengths as a CNA are my compassion and my attention to detail.

I have had a number of successes that show my strengths. For example, I was named "CNA of the Month" in October because of the many positive reports from patients' relatives about the care I gave their loved ones. In addition, I was praised by the lead nurses during my three-month review for the accuracy of my patient records. These achievements, along with my record of never missing a shift, are why I choose to give myself a "superior" rating.

Even though I believe the "superior" rating is well deserved, I know there are still areas in which I could improve. First, I would like to learn more about some of the medical equipment used in our workplace. At times, I have had to depend on more experienced CNAs to help with complicated types of medical equipment. In the future, I would like to be the CNA that others come to for help. Second, I would like to learn more about the unique medical problems that affect our elderly patient population. I get a lot of satisfaction out of helping older people stay healthy. For this reason, I would like to receive more training in elder care.

This year has been a challenging and productive one for me, and I'm looking forward to next year. My future goals are to take a series of workshops to learn more about medical equipment, as well as a special nursing course to learn more about typical medical problems the elderly face. I know these courses will make me a better CNA and will help my long-term career goal of becoming a Registered Geriatric Nurse. Finally, I plan to make next year as successful as this one.

Pham Tuyen, Certified Nurse's Assistant

Unit 6   Persuasive Essay

Why Companies Should Not Hire Smokers

Today, more and more companies who pay employee health care costs prefer not to hire smokers. I think that this policy is a good one because hiring smokers hurts a company as well as its nonsmoking employees.

Hiring smokers hurts a company financially. Smoking causes serious health problems. It increases a person's chances of getting heart disease, emphysema, lung cancer, and many other serious diseases. All of these illnesses require expensive long-term medical care. In fact, according to *The New England Journal of Medicine*, health care costs for smokers can be as much as forty percent higher than those for nonsmokers.

If companies hire smokers, they are also hurting nonsmoking employees. When companies pay too much for health care, they have less money in the budget for other employee benefits. For example, they can't hire additional staff, provide child care, or give raises. Companies and nonsmoking employees should not have to pay the price for people who continue to smoke. This is why I believe that companies should not hire smokers.

Zlatan Ramic

Unit 7   Formal E-mail

From: Camacho, Guillermo <gcamacho@coldmail.com>
Date: 10/9/2010 10:52:47
To: Edwin.Garcia@assembly.state.fl.us
Subject: Funding for Adult Literacy

Representative Edwin Garcia
55 Colonial Drive
Orlando, Florida 32804

Dear Representative Garcia,

I am very worried about what is happening to the adult literacy programs in our community. In the past five years, city funding for these programs has decreased. As a result, local residents are not getting the help they need in order to be productive and happy members of the community. This is a serious problem, one that we need to work to solve.

To solve this problem, I urge you to increase the city budget for adult literacy. Making adult literacy a top concern in our city will help our residents and our economy. In order to be successful in the workplace, our residents must possess good basic skills. Employers want to hire workers who can communicate well in English. Workers need to know how to read, write, and speak English well. We need to increase literacy rates so that our workers can get and keep jobs that pay well. This would improve the economy and well-being of our community.

Funding adult literacy is an investment in the financial success of our residents and our city. The more literate our city is, the stronger our workforce and economy will be. If you work to increase the city budget for adult literacy, you will help all of our residents, our local workforce, and our economy.

Thank you for your attention to this problem. I look forward to hearing from you.

Sincerely,
Guillermo Camacho

Unit 8   Essay That Compares and Contrasts

Legal Systems in India vs. the United States

To many people, my home country of India seems very different from the United States. However, when you look at the legal systems of the two countries, you will find some surprising similarities as well as differences.

Both India and the United States are former colonies of England, which is why their legal systems have similarities. Both countries have *common laws*—laws created by the courts, not the government. Both nations also have what is called an *independent judiciary*. This means that the legal system is separate from other branches of government, such as the executive branch and Congress.

The main difference between the legal systems of the two nations is the way in which trials are conducted. In India, a judge determines the verdict in almost all trials. A single person determines a defendant's guilt or innocence. In contrast, the legal system in the United States puts legal power in the hands of a group of ordinary citizens. Anyone accused of commiting a serious crime has a right to a trial by a jury of his or her peers. The jury is usually is made up of twelve citizens. They hear all the evidence in the case and decide whether the person is guilty or innocent.

Anand Ramesh

Reducing My Carbon Footprint

Ever since my kids started learning about the environment at school, they've been trying to convince me to change my ways. Well, if you're a parent, you understand that sometimes things get so hectic it's hard to focus on anything—especially, the environment. However, despite my busy schedule, my kids have convinced me to make a few changes to reduce my carbon footprint.

A few months ago, my seven-year-old son suggested that I use cloth bags instead of plastic ones to carry groceries and other products. At first, it was difficult because I kept forgetting to bring the bags with me. After awhile, though, it became a habit. As soon as I use the bags, I return them to the car. This way I always have them with me. So far, this is working out very well.

Soon, I found myself paying more attention to recycling, too. I decided to buy rechargeable batteries and recycle all my newspapers, magazines, paper bags, and cardboard boxes. My daughter bought me a reusable coffee cup for my birthday. I take it almost everywhere I go. My garbage has been reduced by fifty percent. I can't believe how much stuff I was throwing away before!

Although I'm still driving my big old car, I'm trying to maintain it better. I only use the air conditioning on extremely hot days. I also drive more slowly in order to save gas. These were the tips my kids gave me, and I have to say that they were right. I may not get somewhere as fast as I used to, but I'm saving some gas and money. It amazes me that a little effort can have a big effect on helping the environment.

Anka Sawicki

Unit 10 Autobiographical Essay

http://www.homedeliverytoelders.org/blog

Home Delivery.com

Search

HOME | DELIVERIES | **EMPLOYEE BLOG** | ABOUT US

Home Delivery: Employee Success Stories

November 25, 2010 | Posted by: Alexandra Zambrano

Nothing Can Stop Me Now

I remember when my husband and I first came to the United States to work. I was twenty-two years old. We had borrowed several thousand dollars, and had come to California to start a new life. I didn't know much English—in Ecuador, I had had to quit school in the sixth grade to help raise my brothers and sisters. Now that we were living in Los Angeles, I needed to get a job right away to pay the rent. I didn't have much work experience, but I knew how to care for children, so I spent my first six months babysitting for a neighbor for very little money.

Without enough English to communicate well, I couldn't find a better paying job. So I signed up for an English class at the local high school. The class met three evenings a week. The teacher, Mr. Stevens, was a tall, thin man in his fifties. He had spent years helping students like me learn—and actually love—English. He was a wonderful teacher, who gave me puzzles, games, and exercises to expand my vocabulary. He encouraged me to work on my English all the time. He told me to listen to the radio, read newspapers, and watch TV and movies in English. He even suggested that I get an English pen pal online. Mr. Stevens told jokes in class and made learning English fun.

As my English got better, I decided to apply for a cooking job at a nonprofit organization called *Home Delivery*. This organization prepares and delivers meals to the elderly. I thought, "Great! My English doesn't have to be perfect to cook!" But, as it turned out, I did need English to communicate with my co-workers. Soon I was speaking English in the kitchen and learning a lot of American slang. When supervisors at *Home Delivery* recognized how much better my English was, they offered me a job in the food inventory department. Mr. Stevens was proud of my success and encouraged me to take a GED class. After studying hard, I took and passed the GED exam. Soon I was promoted at work to office assistant. Three years later, I was managing the office.

After five years at *Home Delivery*, I realized that I had a solid nonprofit résumé, so I decided to get a college degree in nonprofit management. I found a local college that offered classes at night. When I think of how I felt when I came to New York seven years ago, I'm amazed at how my life has changed. Today, I am in college and have a full-time job at a nonprofit organization. I plan to finish my degree in four or five years and start my own organization some day. My goal is to start a nonprofit organization to help new immigrants. I still have a long way to go, but I have come so far. Nothing can stop me now.

Alexandra Zambrano

Sign in to comment on this post | 3 Comments

Unit 1   Exploring Your Expectations

Expectations are the things that you think will occur or will happen in a new situation, based on the information and experiences you have had in the past. For example, when you start a new English class, you may have expectations about how the teacher will behave, the kind of work that you will do, or what you will learn.

A Think about the expectations you had when you started this English class. Look at the situations in column 1. Write your response to each expectation in column 2. If you had additional expectations, write them at the bottom of column 2.

Situation	Your Expectation
Amount of work/homework for the class	
Attendance	
English-speaking ability of other students	
Tests	
Amount of reading and writing	
Amount of listening and speaking	
Teacher	
Other:	

B PAIRS. Talk about your expectations. Where did your expectations come from? Have your expectations been met in the class so far? What could be changed in class to meet your expectations? If they have not been met in certain areas, make suggestions.

C GROUPS. Discuss your expectations with another pair. Discuss: For any expectations that have not been met, how could the class be changed to help you learn English better?

Unit 2 Speaking English Well

We all want to become better English speakers. Sometimes, when you are learning something, it helps to think of and imitate role models—people who do that thing well. Who do you know who speaks English well?

A GROUPS. **Think about people you know who speak English well. They can be people you know personally or people you have seen on TV or heard on the radio. Discuss the questions.**

1. In what ways do these people speak English well? Give examples.
2. Do they have a large vocabulary?
3. Do they speak quickly or slowly?
4. Do they have a formal or informal style of speaking?
5. Do they use body language?
6. Do they use a lot of idioms or slang?
7. Do they use *um* and *ah* often when they are speaking?

B **Use the word web below to list the most important characteristics of a good English speaker.**

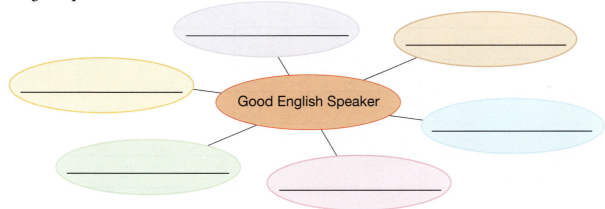

C CLASS. **Share your group's list with the class. Discuss your individual lists and create a class list of the main characteristics of a good English speaker.**

D CLASS. **Look at the class list of characteristics of a good English speaker. Which characteristics do you already have? Which ones do you want to develop? Choose at least one characteristic that you want to work on throughout this class.**

Unit 3   The Importance of Reading

Reading is an important language skill. When you read, you are exposed to many new words, grammar structures, and idioms. You see models of good English, both formal and informal. You use strategies to comprehend what you read, and you use the information you learn for many purposes. So it is important to read regularly and to read different types of texts: novels, magazine articles, labels, forms, street signs, textbooks, notes, work manuals, the newspaper, and so on. Each type of text challenges you to learn more and improve your English skills in different ways.

A Think about a typical week in your life. What do you read? Complete the chart. If you need more space, draw the chart on a piece of paper and make it bigger.

What I read	How often I read it	Why I read it

B **PAIRS.** Talk about the information in your charts. What do you read in your daily life? How does it help you improve your English? Can you recommend a reading material that your partner might benefit from? Why do you think your partner would learn something from reading it?

C Make a list of at least three types of texts that you don't read now but would like to read in the future. Check back in a month and make a chart like the one above. Are you reading any new types of texts? If so, how are they helping you?

Unit 4 Sharing Strengths and Challenges

We all have different strengths and challenges when learning a language such as English. It is good to share our strengths with others and help them with their challenges. It is also helpful to know people who can help us practice and improve our skills.

A Think about what you do well in English. Use the categories in the chart to help you brainstorm. If some of your ideas don't fit the categories on the chart, add your own categories.

In English:	What I do well
Reading	
Writing	
Listening	
Speaking	
Grammar	
Culture	
Other:	

B PAIRS. Share your charts. Talk about what you can do well in English and what you can help others practice and learn. Find out who might need your help. Find out who can help you.

Unit 5   Building Your Vocabulary All the Time

It is important to continue building your vocabulary in English.

A Think about how you learn English vocabulary. What are your vocabulary learning strategies?

B GROUPS.   Discuss. Which of the strategies listed below do you and your classmates use? Are there other strategies that you use? What advice can you give about the strategies you use? Make notes on the chart.

Vocabulary learning strategy	Person who uses this strategy	Advice/Notes
Visualize (make a picture of the word in your mind)		
Say or write new words ___ number of times		
Translate words into your native language		
Keep a vocabulary log or notebook		
Make and use vocabulary cards		
Consult a dictionary or thesaurus		
Use the keyword method		
Other:		

C PAIRS.   Discuss the questions.

1. What vocabulary do you have difficulty learning? Individual words? Idioms? Slang or colloquial expressions?

2. Why do you think it is hard for you to learn these types of words?

3. Do you think any of the strategies above might help you learn and remember these words more easily? Which strategies?

> colloquial expression: an informal expression used in everyday conversation but not usually used in written communication, for example, *keep your shirt on*, which means *be patient*.

Unit 6   Studying in the U.S.

A Think about what it is like to study in your home country and what it is like to study in the U.S. Then complete the chart.

	In your home country	In the U.S.
What you study		
Where you study		
When you study		
How you study		
Relationship between teacher and student		

B GROUPS. Talk about the information in your charts. Discuss the questions.

1. How is studying in the U.S. similar to studying in your home countries?

2. How is it different?

3. What surprised you about education in the U.S.? What changes did you have to adapt to?

C GROUPS. Make a group list of the things that are different about studying in the U.S.

D Write a short letter to a student who is coming from a foreign country to study in the U.S. What advice do you have for the student? How should the student prepare? What will that student need to do to be a successful student in a U.S. classroom?

Unit 7   Writing Strategies

Writing can be challenging for anyone, but it is especially challenging when you are writing in a foreign language such as English. It is a good idea to have a collection of strategies and skills that you know work for you: a "toolbox" that you can use to work on any writing task.

A **Review the writing lessons in this book and the tools they provide.**

1. Before starting each writing assignment, an FYI box helps you understand the genre, or type of writing you are being asked to do.

2. Then a Writing Tip helps you develop, structure, or format your writing.

3. Throughout the lesson, brainstorming activities, models, questions, graphic organizers, and editing and proofreading checklists help you succeed in every part of the writing process—before writing, while you are writing, and after you have written.

B PAIRS. **Look back at the writing you did. Discuss the questions.**

1. Which writing tools helped you the most? Why?

2. Were particular tools helpful for specific kinds of writing? Which ones?

3. Which writing tools have you used in other writing tasks outside of class?

C **Complete the chart.**

My Writing Toolbox		
	Purpose	**Writing tips or strategies that worked for me**
Before writing	To help you plan and generate ideas	
During writing	To help you develop and organize information	
After writing	To help you revise, edit, and proofread your writing	

D PAIRS. **Share and discuss your Writing Toolboxes. Explain why certain tools are helpful when you are writing in English, both in and outside of class. Consider using some of your partner's tools. Do you think they would help you? Do you want to add them to your toolbox?**

Unit 8   Reading Skills/Strategies

Most of the readings in this textbook are accompanied by a Reading Skills box. For example, on page 13, a Reading Skills box explains the importance of highlighting or underlining key information as you read. All twenty reading skills in this textbook help you use and develop skills to improve your reading comprehension.

A There are two Reading Skills boxes in each unit of this textbook. Review them all. In the chart below, list the reading skills that helped you the most. You can also add any other reading skills and strategies that you use on your own.

My Reading Skills/Strategies	
Reading skills/strategies I use	**Other resources and materials I use**

B What other resources help you when you read? Do you use a dictionary, thesaurus, or grammar reference book? Write these down too. All of these skills, strategies, and resources are tools that can help you read and comprehend different kinds of texts.

C PAIRS. Share your reading skills/strategies. Explain how they help you when you are reading in English. Does your partner use different skills, strategies, and resources? Do you think they would help you? Add them to your chart and give them a try!

Unit 9   Becoming a Lifelong Learner

Lifelong learning means focusing on what you need and want to learn throughout your life. You might need to learn a new computer software application to help you in your job. You might want to learn yoga in order to stay fit, improve your balance, or relax and focus your thoughts. In both cases, learning is important to you and to your life.

A Think about the subjects and skills that you have learned in the past. What did you need to learn in order to do your job, raise a family, or contribute to your community? What did you want to learn to make you feel happy or fulfilled? What steps did you take to learn all these things? Complete the chart.

What I learned	Why I learned it	Steps I took

B Think about your life right now. What do you need to learn in order to improve your situation or to be more fulfilled? What steps will you take to learn more in these areas? Complete the chart.

What I will learn	Why I will learn it	Steps I will take

C **PAIRS.** Compare your charts. Discuss. What are the challenges of being a lifelong learner? What are the benefits of always learning new things? How do you find time to learn and grow? What steps can you take to keep on learning? How do you balance what you need to learn with what you want to learn for self-fulfillment?

Unit 10 Moving Forward

In the first unit of this textbook, you talked a lot about your goals and dreams for the future: what you want to be, what you want to have, and what you want to do. You also wrote at least one long-term SMART goal and a flowchart to illustrate your move toward that goal.

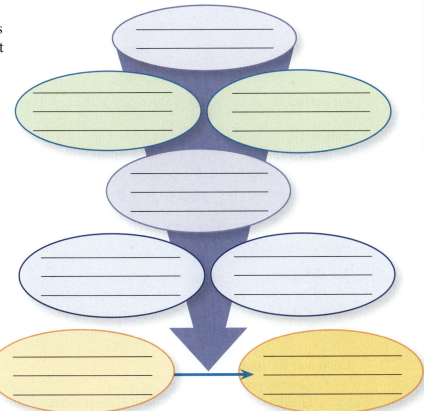

A Review what you wrote in Unit 1, particularly your SMART goal and your flowchart. Then think about this class, the activities you did, and the skills and information you learned. Use the graphic organizer on the right. Write some of the ways this class has helped you move toward your SMART goal.

B PAIRS. Share your organizers and talk about your SMART goal and flowchart from Unit 1. Discuss the questions.

1. How has this class helped you move toward your goals?

2. Can your partner think of any other things that you did or learned in class that might help you? Add them to your flowchart.

C Ask yourself the questions below. Then add them to your flowchart. Make an action plan for yourself for the next week or two so that you can continue working toward your goals after this class ends!

1. What plans do you need to make now that this class is finished?

2. Do you need to take another English class or a different kind of English class? (For example, you might need to take one that focuses on pronunciation.)

3. Do you need to find a class that teaches skills for the job you want?

4. Are there any steps you need to add to your flowchart or other goals you want to pursue?

Nina Sanchez
235 Balboa Street
Markleeville, CA 96120
nina.sanchez@fastmail.com
(915) 555-7686

Objective: To use my practical experience with animal care in a position as a veterinary assistant.

Summary
- Strong career interest in veterinary medicine and care.
- Educational background in science: biology major, with courses in chemistry and physics.
- Extensive experience caring for pets: grooming, feeding, walking, training, showing affection.
- Excellent people skills; good at dealing with customers over the phone and in person.

Professional Achievements

Animal Care
- Provided expert care to dogs and cats of many sizes, ages, breeds, and temperaments.
- Exhibited exceptional ability to work with troubled—fearful or aggressive—pets.
- Learned about grooming and health issues associated with specific breeds.

Customer Relations
- Greeted pet owners.
- Handled phone calls and e-mail correspondence with customers.
- Helped store owners display pet products and services in store windows.

Work History

2006–present:	Assistant and Receptionist, Jill's Pet Grooming and Care, Woodfords, CA
2005–2006:	Independent Dog Walker, Markleeville, CA
2003–2005:	Waitress, Flannigan's Restaurant, Markleeville, CA
2000–2002:	Cashier, Dog-gone Discounts Pet Supply Store, San Francisco, CA

Education

2003–present:	Western Nevada College, Carson City, NV BS in Biology Expected 2010
1999–2003:	Lowell High School, San Francisco, CA High School Diploma Received

Community Service

2006–2009:	Volunteer, Dogs for Seniors—a group that brings dogs to nursing homes, Gardnerville, NV
2005–2006:	Volunteer, Pet Rescue, Gardnerville, NV

References/Transcripts Provided on request.

Grammar Reference

UNIT 1, Lesson 2, page 8

Verbs Followed by the Gerund (Base Form of Verb + -ing)

acknowledge	enjoy	prevent
admit	escape	prohibit
advise	feel like	quit
appreciate	finish	recall
avoid	forgive	recommend
can't help	give up (*stop*)	regret
can't stand	imagine	report
celebrate	justify	resent
consider	keep (*continue*)	resist
delay	mention	risk
deny	mind (*object to*)	suggest
discontinue	miss	support
discuss	postpone	tolerate
dislike	practice	understand
endure		

Verbs Followed by the Infinitive (*to* + Base Form of Verb)

agree	help	prepare
appear	hesitate	pretend
arrange	hope	promise
ask	hurry	refuse
attempt	intend	request
can't afford	learn	rush
can't wait	manage	seem
choose	mean (*intend*)	volunteer
consent	need	wait
decide	neglect	want
deserve	offer	wish
expect	pay	would like
fail	plan	

Verbs Followed by the Gerund or the Infinitive

attempt	hate	regret
begin	like	remember
can't stand	love	start
continue	prefer	stop
forget	propose	try

Phrasal Verbs

Separable Phrasal Verbs sb = somebody sth = something		Inseparable Phrasal Verbs	
Phrasal verb	**Meaning**	**Phrasal verb**	**Meaning**
add sth **up**	calculate the total	**break down**	stop working properly
call sb **back**	return a phone call	**break into**	enter something illegally
call sb **up**	telephone a person	**call on**	ask someone to speak
clean sth **out**	(1) get rid of dirt;	**come across**	unexpectedly find something
	(2) remove contents or occupants	**come in**	enter
clean sth **up**	clean or wash something completely	**come on**	turn on (for example, *My engine light*
close sth **down**	stop operating		***came on.***)
do sth **over**	do something again	**count on**	depend on someone
drop sth **off**	leave or deliver someone or something	**do without**	manage without having something
	somewhere	**drop in**	visit by surprise
figure sth **out**	think about until you understand or find	**drop out of**	quit, especially school
	the answer	**get ahead**	(1) make progress;
fill sth **out**	complete a form with information		(2) succeed
fix sth **up**	make a place look attractive by doing small	**get into**	(1) be allowed in;
	repairs or by decorating		(2) be interested in something
flag sth **down**	make the driver of a vehicle stop by waving	**get together**	meet
give sth **back**	return	**get off**	leave a bus, train, boat, etc.
hold sth/sb **up**	delay something or someone	**get out of**	(1) leave;
leave sth **out**	omit		(2) avoid doing something
look sth/sb **up**	(1) try to find information;	**get through**	finish
	(2) visit someone you know	**look after**	take care of
make sth **up**	invent	**look into**	try to find out the truth
start sth **over**	start again	**pull over**	drive to the side of the road and stop the car
take sth **off**	remove clothing	**run into**	(1) meet someone by chance;
think sth **over**	think about something carefully		(2) accidentally hit a part of your body on
try sth **on**	put clothing on to see how it fits or looks		something
turn sth **down**	(1) refuse;	**run out of**	not have enough
turn sth **off**	(2) lower the heat or volume	**sign up**	register
turn sth **on**	stop a machine or light	**slow down**	make someone or something slower
turn sth **up**	start a machine or light	**take off**	depart (a plane)
work sth **out**	make louder (a TV/radio)	**watch out**	be careful
	find a solution		

Irregular verbs

Base form	Simple past	Past participle	Base form	Simple past	Past participle
awake	awoke	awoken	keep	kept	kept
be	was/were	been	know	knew	known
beat	beat	beaten	lead	led	led
become	became	become	leave	left	left
begin	began	begun	lend	lent	lent
bite	bit	bitten	let	let	let
blow	blew	blown	lose	lost	lost
break	broke	broken	make	made	made
build	built	built	mean	meant	meant
buy	bought	bought	meet	met	met
catch	caught	caught	pay	paid	paid
choose	chose	chosen	put	put	put
come	came	come	quit	quit	quit
cost	cost	cost	read	read	read
cut	cut	cut	ride	rode	ridden
dig	dug	dug	ring	rang	rung
do	did	done	run	ran	run
draw	drew	drawn	say	said	said
drink	drank	drunk	see	saw	seen
drive	drove	driven	sell	sold	sold
eat	ate	eaten	send	sent	sent
fall	fell	fallen	shake	shook	shaken
feed	fed	fed	sing	sang	sung
feel	felt	felt	sit	sat	sat
fight	fought	fought	sleep	slept	slept
find	found	found	speak	spoke	spoken
fly	flew	flown	spend	spent	spent
forget	forgot	forgotten	stand	stood	stood
forgive	forgave	forgiven	steal	stole	stolen
get	got	gotten	swim	wam	swum
give	gave	given	take	took	taken
go	went	gone	teach	taught	taught
grow	grew	grown	think	thought	thought
hang	hung	hung	throw	threw	thrown
have	had	had	understand	understood	understood
hear	heard	heard	upset	upset	upset
hide	hid	hidden	wake	woke	woken
hit	hit	hit	wear	wore	worn
hold	held	held	win	won	won
hurt	hurt	hurt	write	wrote	written

Grammar Review

UNIT 1

A Unscramble the words and phrases to make sentences. Use the simple present with gerunds and infinitives.

1. avoid / Zofia / with computers / work

   Zofia avoids working with computers.

2. enjoy / Mr. Jung / blueprints / read

   Mr. Jung enjoys reading blueprints.

3. take / Dennis and Mark / plan / a computer course

   Dennis and Mark plan to take a computer course.

4. not mind / Angelique / do / the budget

   Angelique does not mind doing the budget.

5. need / improve / his communication skills / Rodrigo

   Rodrigo needs to improve his communication skills.

6. Guo / be / a manager / not want

   Guo does not want to be a manager.

7. hope / Larry and Rita / the problem / solve

   Larry and Rita hope to solve the problem.

B Match the items in Column A with those in Column B to create six logical sentences.

Column A

<u>c</u> 1. Choi is good

<u>f</u> 2. He is interested

<u>a</u> 3. He will begin

<u>e</u> 4. Choi will ask the counselor

<u>b</u> 5. He is also thinking

<u>d</u> 6. He will soon thank her

Column B

a. by talking to a career counselor.

b. of taking more English classes.

c. at solving math problems.

d. for helping him get a great job.

e. about writing résumés and cover letters.

f. in finding a job as a computer programmer.

UNIT 2

A Complete the conversation with the present perfect form of the verbs in parentheses.

Martina: Hi, Serio. When is your interview?

Serio: It's tomorrow. I'm really nervous. I ___have not/haven't slept___ well since Saturday!
(1. not sleep)

Martina: ___Have___ you ___prepared___ for it?
(2. prepare)

Serio: Yes. I ___'ve/have___ already ___written___ my résumé, and
(3. write)
my mom ___has helped___ me by doing a practice interview with me.
(4. help)

Martina: That's good. ___Have___ you ___researched___ the company?
(5. research)

Serio: No, I ___have not/haven't had___ an opportunity to go online. But I will tonight.
(6. not have)

Martina: ___Have___ you ___finished___ all the requirements for
(7. finish)
your degree?

Serio: Yeah. I ___'ve/have completed___ all the basic business courses.
(8. complete)
I ___have not/haven't taken___ many computer courses, but I ___'ve/have used___
(9. not take)   (10. use)
a computer since I was a kid.

Martina: I'm sure you'll do well. Good luck!

B Complete the sentences. Circle the correct form of the verb.

1. Over the past year, I **(have learned)** / have been learning many new skills that I could apply to this job.
2. Omar **(has been driving)** / has driven a taxi since 2001. He enjoys his job and makes a good salary.
3. Hanh **(has been making)** / has made desserts since 2003. She plans to open her own bakery.
4. Francisco and Luz **have been finishing** / **(have finished)** their résumés. Now they need to start their job search.
5. Jonathan **has been working** / **(has worked)** the night shift since June. Now he works days.
6. Aisha **(has been applying)** / has applied to colleges for several weeks. She has three more applications to complete.
7. Naomi and Tamara **have been studying** / **(have studied)** together for four years. Now Naomi plans to return to her home country.
8. We **(have been doing)** / have done a lot of research for this project. How much more do we have to do?

UNIT 3

Unscramble the words and phrases to make sentences. There may be more than one answer.

1. Maria / up / pick / don't forget to

   <u>Don't forget to pick up Maria.</u>

2. broke / car / down / Sofia's / in front of her house

   <u>Sofia's car broke down in front of her house.</u>

3. turns / Mr. Suarez / on / his headlights / always / at night

   <u>Mr. Suarez always turns on his headlights at night.</u>

4. down / flag / anyone / did you / for help

   <u>Did you flag down anyone for help?</u>

5. when you drive / pedestrians / watch / for / out / please

   <u>Please watch out for pedestrians when you drive.</u>

UNIT 4

Complete the sentences using past modals. Write the first sentence in the active voice and the second one in the passive voice.

1. **should / warn**   ACTIVE: The police <u>should have/should've warned</u> us about the storm.

   PASSIVE: We <u>should have/should've been warned</u> about the storm.

2. **might / evacuate**   ACTIVE: The rescue workers <u>might have/might've evacuated</u> the building.

   PASSIVE: Our neighbors <u>might have/might've been evacuated</u> from the building.

3. **could / prepare**   ACTIVE: Chia-Ling <u>could have/could've prepared</u> for the disaster but didn't.

   PASSIVE: An exit plan <u>could have/could've been prepared</u> but it wasn't.

4. **shouldn't / risk**   ACTIVE: You <u>should not/shouldn't have risked</u> your life for your belongings.

   PASSIVE: Their lives <u>should not/shouldn't have been risked</u> when it wasn't necessary.

5. **couldn't / protect**   ACTIVE: Elsa <u>could not/couldn't have protected</u> her car from the tornado.

   PASSIVE: Elsa's car <u>could not/couldn't have been protected</u> from the tornado.

UNIT 5

Complete the conversations with *although* or *unless* and clauses from the box.

1. **A:** Are you going to stay at your job?

   B: Well, I'm not going to stay _____unless I get a promotion_____.

2. **A:** Did you hear about Alex?

   B: No, what happened?

   A: His boss told him he wasn't getting a promotion _____although he had great ratings on his performance review_____.

3. **A:** I didn't get that job _____although I was qualified for it_____.

   B: That's too bad.

4. **A:** _____Although Janice's interpersonal skills are good_____, she doesn't always speak clearly.

   B: Really? I don't have any problem understanding her.

5. **A:** I have so much to do!

   B: You won't be able to finish _____unless I help you_____.

I was qualified for it
I get a promotion
I help you
Janice's interpersonal skills are good
he had great ratings on his performance review

UNIT 6

Rewrite the direct questions as embedded questions. Use the prompts in parentheses.

1. Why isn't Patricio feeling well? (Could you tell me)

   Could you tell me why Patricio isn't feeling well?

2. Does he have a doctor's appointment on Tuesday? (Do you know)

   Do you know if he has a doctor's appointment on Tuesday?

3. When is his doctor's appointment? (I don't know)

   I don't know when his doctor's appointment is.

4. Will he take medicine for his cold? (I wonder if)

   I wonder if he will take medicine for his cold.

5. What are his symptoms? (Can anyone tell me)

   Can anyone tell me what his symptoms are?

UNIT 7

Complete the sentences about early U.S. history and William Penn. Use the past perfect form of the verbs in parentheses.

1. The British _____ had _____ already _____ put _____ a tax on tea before the
   (put)
   colonists held the Boston Tea Party.

2. By 1733, people in North America _____ had established _____ thirteen colonies.
   (establish)

3. William Penn had not/hadn't returned to England yet when he founded Pennsylvania.
   (not return)

4. The colony Pennsylvania _____ had _____ already _____ granted _____ freedom
   (grant)
   of speech before the Constitution was written.

5. Penn _____ had _____ just _____ tried _____ to sell Pennsylvania back to
   (try)
   England when he became sick.

6. By the time he died, Penn _____ had lost _____ all of his money.
   (lose)

UNIT 8

Rewrite the sentences using the correct form of each verb.

1. If you **trespass / might trespass**, you **might trespass / might have** to pay a fine.
   If you trespass, you might have to pay a fine.

2. If Abder **gets / got** another ticket, his license **was / will** be suspended.
   If Abder gets another ticket, his license will be suspended.

3. Yong-Jin's penalties **are / might be** reduced, if he **admits / might admit** he's guilty.
   Yong-Jin's penalties might be reduced if he admits he's guilty.

4. You **go / could go** to jail if you **refuse / will refuse** to take a BAC test.
   You could go to jail if you refuse to take a BAC test.

5. If Pauline **is / may be** arrested, her parents **hire / will hire** a good attorney.
   If Pauline is arrested, her parents will hire a good attorney.

UNIT 9

Complete the conversation using the past subjunctive or the past unreal conditional.

Eva: Did you look at that environmental website Sun Mi told us about?

Thomas: Yes, I did. But I wish ___had not/hadn't seen___ it.
(1. not see)

Eva: Why? If I ___had not/hadn't read___ it, I ___would not/wouldn't have learned___ all those tips on how
(2. not read)   **(3. not learn)**
to protect the environment.

Thomas: I guess you're right. But if I ___'d/had ignored___ them, I ___would not/wouldn't feel___
(4. ignore)   **(5. not feel)**
so bad about throwing out all that paper last week.

Eva: You can make simple changes and still help the environment. For

example, I'm recycling my son's baby food jars now. It's easy, and I wish I

___'d/had started___ sooner.
(6. start)

Thomas: You're right. My parents ___would have/would've done___ more to help the environment if
(7. do)

they ___'d/had known___ about these problems. I'll start by doing something
(8. know)
simple, like turning off unnecessary lights!

UNIT 10

Complete the sentences with *who*, *that*, or *which* and the correct phrases from the box. There may be more than one correct answer.

are in Mr. Costa's class	created a website	don't use the website
improve every day	students do online	

Mr. Costa is the teacher ___who created a website___ to help students with their

English. The website includes games and interactive exercises ___that students do online___.

The students ___who are in Mr. Costa's class___ love the website. Their test results are higher

than those of students ___who don't use the website___. Mr. Costa thinks the scores,

___which improve every day___, will help prove how important it is to motivate students.

Audio Script

Page 10, Listen, Exercises B and C

Counselor: Hello, Ruben. Come on in and have a seat.
Ruben: Thank you.
Counselor: So, you want to explore some career options—is that right?
Ruben: Yes. I haven't decided on a career yet. I've been thinking about going to school to become a chef.
Counselor: So, you enjoy cooking.
Ruben: No, not really. But right now I work in a hotel restaurant as a waiter. I'm friends with the chef. I found out that he makes a lot more money than I do, and that chefs at top restaurants make a lot of money. And I thought learning to cook might be easy.
Counselor: But you're not good at cooking now. . .
Ruben: My sandwiches are OK. But no, not really.
Counselor: Well, what *are* you good at?
Ruben: I guess I'm good at math. I'm good at working with all kinds of co-workers, and I'm good at dealing with customers. I think I have good interpersonal skills. . .

Page 11, Practice, Exercise B

Counselor: Well, I think there might be jobs that are a better match for you than a job as a chef. Tell me more about yourself.
Ruben: Well, I'm a student, Colombian, single. . .
Counselor: OK. But what are some of your personality traits? What are some *adjectives* you'd use to describe yourself?
Ruben: Oh. Well, I'm honest. For example, sometimes customers leave things in the restaurant—like purses or wallets or cell phones. I always try to find the owner. And I'm cooperative. If another waiter is busy and I'm not, I pour water and coffee for his customers.
Counselor: Your bosses and colleagues must like you.
Ruben: I hope so. . . I like to have good relationships at work. I'm always friendly with new staff; I try to teach them everything they need to know. And I make people laugh—I tell jokes when things get too serious.
Counselor: Um-hmm. So you're extroverted.
Ruben: Yes, I guess you could say that.
Counselor: You said earlier that you have good interpersonal skills . . . What other things do people like about you?
Ruben: I'm optimistic. I don't know what career I want, but I believe it's waiting for me. And I believe I'll find it. I guess I believe in luck. I'm intuitive. When I find the job that's right for me, I'll just *know*. I trust my feelings when I make decisions.
Counselor: Well, you'll make some decisions soon enough. Let's schedule some tests for next week. Talk to Linda, my secretary. She'll set up the times.
Ruben: OK. Thank you.

Page 18, Listen, Exercise A

Counselor: Hi, Ruben. How has everything been going?
Ruben: Great. Thanks.
Counselor: So tell me what you've done since I saw you last.

Ruben: Well, first I looked online for descriptions of jobs in the hotel industry. Second, I met with my manager to talk about careers with our hotel. Then I had an informational interview with the catering manager in my hotel. It was really helpful. Hotel catering didn't really sound that interesting or challenging—and I don't think hotel—catered food is so good. During the informational interview, I asked our catering manager if he'd ever thought about starting his own business. He said no, but he offered to contact someone with a catering business in another city to see if she might talk with me. Oh—and I also went to the library and got the names of places to contact about starting a small business.
Counselor: That's incredible, Ruben. . . . It sounds like you have an idea for a new career.
Ruben: Yes, I think I've made a decision. I want to own a successful catering business someday.

Page 18, Listen Exercise B

Counselor: Well, Ruben, I don't want to discourage you, but starting and running a business could be very difficult. You'll have to spend some time preparing.
Ruben: I know. It may take several years.
Counselor: It's important for you to plan a very clear career path—steps that will move you toward your long-term goal.
Ruben: Well, first I need to pass my last ESL class.
Counselor: What's step two?
Ruben: I'm not sure. I'll probably keep working at the hotel and save money.
Counselor: Well, do you want to stay in your current job at the hotel?
Ruben: No. Maybe, I should switch to the catering department, and change to full-time. I could save more money and take culinary arts classes at night.
Counselor: Well, you would learn cooking techniques in culinary arts classes, so that makes sense. So your second step has two parts: You're going to take a class and you're going to continue working at your hotel, but full-time, and in the catering department.
Ruben: Yes.
Counselor: Well, running a business requires management and accounting skills.
Ruben: I know. Maybe I could get a promotion to supervisor in the catering department. I could learn a lot that way.
Counselor: I suggest talking with the catering manager to find out if that might be possible. Becoming a supervisor might be a good third step.
Ruben: And my fourth step could be to become a manager— either at my hotel or at another hotel. And at the same time, I could collect more information about starting a small business. After getting enough training and saving enough money or getting a loan, my fifth step would be to open my catering business near the campus.
Counselor: Well, plans can change, but this sounds like a good start.
Ruben: Yes. And I'll finish with a successful business here in this city!

UNIT 2

Page 32, Listen, Exercise A

Hello. I'm Dr. Williams from Career Courage—an employment counseling agency. I'm here to talk about do's and don'ts for job interviews.

Answers to interview questions are important, but so are other things. First impressions are very important. So dress appropriately for the job you want. For example, you can wear jeans for a construction job interview, but wear business clothes for an office job. If you're not sure what to wear, be conservative. Always be clean and well-groomed. Don't wear heavy perfume or cologne. Ladies, don't wear too much jewelry.

Body language is important. It should indicate that you are interested, but relaxed. Sit and stand up straight. Use a firm handshake, and smile when you meet your interviewer. Look at your interviewer, make eye contact when he or she speaks, and smile and nod to show that you are listening. Don't make nervous movements, such as tapping your fingers or your feet.

Your voice is important. Speak clearly so that the interviewer can understand you—don't mumble! Your voice should indicate interest. Relax so that you don't sound nervous, and don't speak too quickly or too slowly. Don't use too many sounds like "uh" or "um."

The way you address an interviewer is very important. Always use "Mr." and "Ms.," unless the interviewer indicates another preference. Say "please" and "thank you" if the interviewer offers to do something for you. Show respect by saying "Yes, ma'am," or "Yes, sir" when your interviewer asks questions like "May I call your references?"

So appearance, body language, voice, and the way you address and respond to your interviewer are all important. Just a few other do's and don'ts: Don't bring anything except materials you need for your interview. And always turn off your cell phone before you walk into the building where you will be interviewed. Any questions . . . ?

Page 33, Listen, Exercise D

1. Beatriz

Interviewer: Have a seat, Beatriz.
Beatriz: Thank you.
Interviewer: I see in your résumé that you're getting a certificate in computer repair.
Beatriz: Yes. I'll get my certificate in six weeks.
Interviewer: I'm sorry. I didn't hear that.
Beatriz: I'm sorry. I'm getting my computer repair certificate in six weeks.
Interviewer: I see. And I see that you've been working at Computer Universe.
Beatriz: Yes. I work at the computer service counter three nights a week and on Saturdays.
Interviewer: You know it's a little hard to hear you with that air conditioner on. Did you say you work at the checkout counter?

2. Said

Interviewer: Hello. You must be Said. I'm Dave Mathews.
Said: Hi, Dave! Nice to meet you.
Interviewer: Please have a seat.
Said: Thank you.

3. Bruno

Interviewer: Tell me a little about yourself.
Bruno: Well, um . . . I'm studying to be a medical technician. . . Uh. . . I work part-time at a home improvement store, . . . and, uh . . . I'm dependable and I have good interpersonal skills.

4. Shin-Hae

Interviewer: Please sit down.
Shin-Hae: OK.
Interviewer: I'd like to start by asking you a few questions. I've arranged to show you around the office when we've finished.
Shin-Hae: Cool!

Page 38, Listen, Exercise A

Harvey: Hello. You must be Iris Martinez. I'm Harvey Samson.
Iris: Hello, Mr. Samson. It's nice to meet you.
Harvey: Please come in and have a seat.
Iris: Thank you.
Harvey: Would you like some coffee or tea?
Iris: No, thank you.
Harvey: Tell me a little about yourself.
Iris: Sure. I've been taking courses at Hillsborough Community College, and I'll receive a certificate in accounting next month.
Harvey: And will you be available to start full-time work then?
Iris: Yes. I've been working evenings and weekends as an assistant manager at a supermarket. I'd like to give my supervisor two weeks' notice.
Harvey: How long do you plan to stay here if you're hired?
Iris: I've done a lot of research, and I am very interested in working here. I hope to continue in the job and grow with the company.
Harvey: What do you think is your greatest strength?
Iris: I think my greatest strength is my attention to detail. I keep sight of the big picture, but I focus on every task or problem I encounter, even very small ones. I make sure I don't miss anything. I double- and triple-check my math.
Harvey: And what would you say is your greatest weakness?
Iris: Well, sometimes I become so focused on my work that I might seem shy or unfriendly. But for the last few months, I've been making an effort to greet everyone at the beginning of my shift. And I've been taking a few minutes to help other staff members clean up before I do my bookkeeping and close the store at night.
Harvey: I see. Great. Do you have any questions?
Iris: When will a hiring decision be made?
Harvey: We'll contact you within two weeks. Thank you for coming in.
Iris: Thank you.

Page 38, Listen, Exercise C

Harvey: Hello. You must be Liam. I'm Harvey Samson.

Liam: Hi, Harvey!

Harvey: I'm glad you took a seat. I was caught in a meeting. I'm sorry I'm late.

Liam: No problem.

Harvey: Would you like some coffee or tea?

Liam: Do you have decaf?

Harvey: Certainly. I'll be right back. . . . Here you are. I brought you some sugar and some creamer in case you want it.

Liam: Thank you.

Harvey I see on your résumé that you've been working for Quality Exterior Home Repair for three years. Why do you want to leave your current position?

Liam: Really, I like my position. But I can't stand my new boss. He doesn't know anything about the business, and he's really an obstacle. He has no interpersonal skills whatsoever.

Harvey: It must be hard for you to work there. How do you handle the stress?

Liam: Well, my co-workers and I joke about him a lot. That helps.

Harvey: I see. So obviously, we can't call your supervisor for a reference. Do you have other references we can call if we get to the stage where we'd want to contact someone?

Liam: Uh, . . . a reference? . . . Um . . . I think one of my co-workers would do it. Would that be OK?

Harvey: We accept references from applicants' co-workers. But we only call references after we've made a decision about who we want to hire. I'll be talking with several more applicants, and we won't decide anything for a couple more weeks. If you'd like, you can e-mail or call Human Resources to provide the name of your reference. If you want to come with me, I'll get you the director's card on your way out. Do you have any questions?

Liam: No. Not right now. Maybe later. Do you have any information about the company?

Harvey: I'll get that for you on your way out, too. This way, please.

Page 40, Practice

1. I've been working on my résumé.
2. I've been attending night classes.
3. My friend has proofread my résumé.
4. I've been applying for full-time jobs.
5. Miriam has taken classes in landscape design.
6. Sheena has finished all of her classes for her degree.
7. We've been studying all day for our math exam.
8. She's finally completed her applications for college.

UNIT 3

Page 47, Listen, Exercise A

Conversation 1

A: Person with the Honda Civic?

B: Yes, that's me.

A: Everything looks good. We changed your oil and we checked your other fluids. Your windshield wiper fluid was a little low, so we added a few ounces—just to top it off. We added air to your tires, and we checked your headlights. Your right headlight is out. Would you like us to replace that for you today?

B: How much will it cost?

A: Twenty-two dollars.

B: OK.

A: How are your windshield wipers working?

B: Fine.

A: OK. Well, we'll put that new headlight in. It should just take a few minutes.

Question 1: What is the situation?

a. The woman had a problem with her car and brought it to a mechanic for repairs.

b. The woman brought her car to a shop that does express oil changes and other car maintenance work.

c. The woman is shopping at an auto parts store.

Question 2: What does the woman have changed or replaced?

a. her oil and her headlight

b. her oil and her windshield wipers

c. her headlight and her windshield wipers

Conversation 2

A: Excuse me. Could I borrow your cell phone to make a call? I left mine at home, and my car won't start.

B: Sure. Do you have any idea what the problem is?

A: Well, it might be my battery. It could be dead. Last winter it died when the weather got cold.

B: Do you want me to try to jump-start it for you? I have the equipment in my car.

A: Oh, I do, too, in the trunk. But I don't know how to use it. Do you?

B: Yeah. I had to call a roadside assistance service a couple of times to jump-start my own car. I learned how to do it by watching them.

A: Well, OK. Thanks. I really appreciate it. Do you need me to do anything?

B: Just raise the hood for me, and then turn the key in the ignition when I tell you to. Don't pump the accelerator, though—just step on it once or twice. And if we get the car started, we'll run it for a few minutes. Then you should drive it for at least 20 minutes—out on the highway, if possible. And be sure to get your battery checked as soon as you can.

A: Thanks so much.

Question 1: What seems to be the problem?

a. A woman's car won't start and her cell phone doesn't work.

b. A woman's car has been dead since last winter.

c. A woman's car battery could be dead, but she doesn't know how to jump-start it.

Question 2: If the car is jump-started, how long should it be driven afterward?

a. for a few minutes

b. for at least 20 minutes

c. for as long as possible

Conversation 3

A: I want to take our car in to the garage next week. Can you find a ride to work?

B: Sandra could probably take me. Is something wrong with the car?

A: I'm not sure. I hear a strange noise when it starts sometimes. Haven't you heard it?

B: No.

A: Well, I hope nothing's wrong. But I want to take it in anyway.

B: We shouldn't spend money on that car unless it's necessary. Remember, we want to get a new car next year.

A: I know, but if we keep it in good condition, we'll probably get more money for it when we trade it in. We're overdue for a tune-up, and besides, we're driving to visit your sister at the end of the month.

B: That reminds me. I also want to get a car adaptor for my MP3 player so we can listen to it on the way.

Question 1: What does the man want the woman to do?

a. give him a ride to work
b. find someone to take her to work
c. listen to see if she hears a strange noise when the car starts

Question 2: What does the woman remember?

a. She did hear a noise.
b. There's something wrong with the stereo system.
c. She wants to buy something.

Page 47, Listen, Exercise B

Excerpt 1
Your windshield wiper fluid was a little low, so we added a few ounces—just to top it off.

Excerpt 2
And if we get the car started, we'll run it for a few minutes.

Excerpt 3
. . . if we keep it in good condition, we'll probably get more money for it when we trade it in. We're overdue for a tune-up, and besides, we're driving to visit your sister at the end of the month.

Page 52, Listen, Exercise A and Exercise B (Step 2)

Good morning, everyone. Today I'm going to talk about what to do if you have an accident involving your car and another vehicle. I hope you never have this experience, but you need to be prepared. Basically, there are 10 steps you should follow. Take notes on these steps, because you will be tested on them.

Step number 1. What's the first thing you do if you hit another car or another car hits you? If it's safe and legal, stop your vehicle! Many people don't. But it's illegal to leave the scene of an accident. Stop immediately.

Number 2. Move your vehicle out of traffic. If you can, drive it to the side of the road. But this advice is only for our state. If you are driving in another state, you need to know the laws of that state. In some states, moving your car from the place where it stopped is illegal.

Step number 3. Turn off your ignition. Don't leave your car running. Make sure your car is turned off before you get out. And it's a good idea to take your keys with you.

Step 4. Make necessary phone calls. Check to see if anyone is badly hurt and if they are, call 911. Moving an injured person can be dangerous. Wait for an ambulance, trained personnel, and the police to arrive. If no one is hurt, call the police.

OK. The fifth step is to mark the scene of the accident with reflecting triangles. Do you all know what I'm talking about? Triangles with bright yellow or orange lines on them? Stand these on the road in front and in back of the area of the accident. This will help other drivers see the accident as they approach.

Step number 6 is to collect the names of all the people in the cars and all the people who witnessed the accident. Getting the names and phone numbers of witnesses is important.

Number 7 is a step that many people forget to take. Take notes. Include the date, time, and weather conditions. It's also a good idea to take a picture or draw a diagram of the accident.

Step number 8. Exchange licenses and insurance cards with the other driver. Write down the other driver's name, license number, insurance company, and policy number.

Number 9. This isn't really a step because it's not something you should do. It's something you should NOT do. Don't talk about who caused the accident. It isn't a good idea to talk about whose fault the accident is.

OK. This is the last step. And it's one you do a few days after the accident. A police officer will write a report about the accident. You should get a copy of the report. Call your local police department, and find out if they can send it to you or where you can go to get it.

Page 55, Practice, Exercise A

Rosario: Hi, Hua-Ling. Can I ask you a question?

Hua-Ling: Sure. What's up?

Rosario: You have a car, right?

Hua-Ling: Yes. I share it with my brother. We just bought our car last year.

Rosario: Well, *I'm* going to buy a car . . .

Hua-Ling: That's great!

Rosario: Yes, but now I need to think about car insurance.

Hua-Ling: You sure do! It can be expensive. You know, it depends on the state you're in.

Rosario: Really? What about here in California?

Hua-Ling: Well, here the law requires you to have liability insurance for bodily injury and property damage.

Rosario: Oh, yeah. How much?

Hua-Ling: The minimum coverage you have to have in California is 15/30. That means that for each occupant in a vehicle who gets injured, the insurance will pay up to $15,000 to cover the person's medical expenses. If more than one person is injured, it'll cover up to 30,000 in expenses, total.

Rosario: Is that enough? Medical expenses are so high!

Hua-Ling: I know. I work in a hospital, and the cost of medical care is ridiculous. That's why some drivers get more than the minimum. You may be personally responsible if the insurance doesn't cover everything.

Rosario: Are you serious? That's terrible.

Hua-Ling: I know. But the state only requires 15/30 for bodily injury. So it's up to you to decide if you want more.

Rosario: I see. And what about property damage? What's the minimum coverage for property damage?

Hua-Ling: That's only $5,000.

Rosario: That's so little! So, if you wreck someone else's car, the insurance company pays them only $5,000? Even if it costs them more than that to fix, or even if they can never drive it again?

Hua-Ling: Yup. That's why some drivers buy more than the minimum. You should definitely shop around. Check at least three insurance companies. And go to the California Department of Insurance website. Let me get the website for you . . . oh, here it is . . . it's www.insurance.ca.gov. It has a lot of information.

UNIT 4

Page 66, Listen, and Page 67, Practice

A: I just read this amazing story in the paper.

B: Really?

A: Yeah. You know about the earthquake that happened last week in China?

B: Of course. I heard that about 50,000 people died. It's awful.

A: I know. It was horrible. Well, this story is about one of the survivors. This man, Mr. Liu, was a factory worker in a small town. Apparently, the earthquake struck on a Monday morning after people had gone to work or school.

B: Right. That's what I heard, too.

A: Well, anyway, this man, Mr. Liu, was trapped under the rubble of the factory after the earthquake on Monday, and no one knew if he was alive. But his 23-year-old daughter, Yuan, wouldn't give up hope. On Thursday night, she and some other people in their family were searching the rubble when they heard a muffled cry. She called out to him and he answered back and said he was thirsty.

B: Oh, wow. Thursday? That was the third day after the earthquake! So, did they get him out right away?

A: Well, no. The daughter first had to go for help, and it took the rescuers twelve hours to free him. He was under the rubble for a hundred hours! And the rescue was very dangerous because of the soldiers.

B: The soldiers?

A: Yes, the rescuers were soldiers. So if the soldiers took a wrong step or if they disturbed any piece of rubble in the wrong way, the whole building could have collapsed.

B: It all sounds terrible. I can't imagine what it must have been like.

A: They said that the reason he was rescued was because his daughter wouldn't give up hope. Let that be a lesson for all of us!

Page 70, Listen, Exercise A

On August 29th, 2005, Hurricane Katrina hit New Orleans. Eighty percent of New Orleans was flooded when the levees failed. The government was criticized for its lack of preparation and its failure to respond quickly or effectively. There were no plans to evacuate people without cars, the elderly, or the sick. There were no arrangements for public buses to be used to get people out of the city. And there were no arrangements for bus or taxi drivers to stay and help in an emergency.

Many people without transportation were directed or taken to the Superdome, a football stadium in downtown New Orleans, but there wasn't enough water, food, medical care, or security there. After the hurricane, food, water, and medical supplies were available, but they were not distributed. People were told to leave pets at home. But there were no plans for their rescue after people were evacuated.

Page 70, Listen, Exercise B

More than 1,800 people died, and there was more than $81 billion in damages. What went wrong? Katrina might not have been such a disaster if there had been better planning. For example, there should have been plans to evacuate hospitals and nursing homes. Public buses could have been used to evacuate people without cars. And what about all of those poor people in the Superdome? There should have been police there to keep them safe. And people should not have been told to leave pets at home.

Since Katrina, better preparation, evacuation, and communication systems have been developed in order to provide better responses to events like Hurricane Katrina in the future.

Page 71, Listen, Exercises A and B

Before you are told to evacuate, it's important to be ready. Know where you can stay. It's best to stay with friends or family members outside of the emergency area, or know which hotel or shelter you'll go to.

If you have a family, decide in advance on a safe meeting place. It could be dangerous to come back to your house from work or school. If you have children, contact the school to learn its emergency plans. Learn different routes from your home and workplace to your safe place.

Plan for your pets. Arrange for them to stay with friends or relatives outside the emergency area, if possible. If that's not possible, call your local animal shelter to find out about pet evacuation plans in your area.

Make sure everyone in your family has the name, phone number, and e-mail address of a contact outside your state. You might not be able to make local calls in an emergency, because so many people are trying to call each other. But you can often reach a person in another state.

Prepare an emergency kit, especially if you plan to go to a shelter. FEMA, the Federal Emergency Management Agency, has a website where you can find out what to include in your kit. Basics include a battery-powered radio, a flashlight and batteries, food and medicine, disinfectant wipes to clean yourself, blankets, water, and baby and pet supplies.

If you have a car, try to keep half a tank of gas in it at all times. When your area is under a flood watch, fill your tank. During an evacuation, gas stations will be very crowded.

If you live in a house, protect your property. Bring in any outdoor items. Open your basement windows to let the water come in so that your basement walls don't collapse. Check government websites for more detailed information.

If you are ordered to evacuate, go immediately. Take your emergency kit and important documents, such as your passport and birth certificate, if you have them ready. Unplug electronic equipment and appliances, except your refrigerator and freezer. Shut off your utilities, such as gas and water. Lock your doors. If you have time, leave a note on your property or in your mailbox saying when you left and where you are going. Check TV or radio for the roads you should use to evacuate. Don't take shortcuts. Shortcuts could lead to blocked or flooded areas where you may not be able to get through. Don't drive through water. If your car breaks down in water, get out immediately, and move to higher ground.

For more information, check your federal, state, and local government websites.

Next week, I'll discuss what to do if you are not ordered to evacuate. It's also necessary to be ready to "shelter in place"—to be ready to live for three or four days without help and without leaving your home.

Page 75, Listen, Exercises A and B

Tania: Hi. Nick. How are you doing?

Nick: Oh, I'm fine. What's new with you? I don't see you much anymore.

Tania: Oh, I've been busy. I'm still working at the airport, but my hours changed.

Nick: I hope you don't have to work the night shift.

Tania: No. I work 10 to 6. It's hard, because I don't have mornings, afternoons, or evenings completely free. And I can't be here when Greg gets home from school.

Nick: You mean he's home alone?

Tania: Just for a couple hours. And he's 12 and he's a responsible kid. But I still worry. I mean, what if strangers call? I don't want strangers to know he's here alone.

Nick: Why don't you tell him to say that you're busy? He should say, "I'm sorry. My mom can't come to the phone right now. If you want to leave your number, she'll call you back as soon as she can."

Tania: What if someone comes to the door?

Nick: You already have a peephole and a strong chain lock, right?

Tania: Yeah. I've told him to use the peephole before he opens the door.

Nick: Right. Well, if I were you, I'd tell him not to answer the door unless the person is a neighbor or friend he knows *really* well.

Tania: Sometimes it's friends that I worry about! What if his friends come over? They could get into all kinds of trouble without an adult around.

Nick: Could you make a rule that no friends can come over when you or another adult isn't home?

Tania: Maybe. He's pretty good about following rules.

Nick: He can always call me or come over to my house, you know, if he has any kind of trouble.

Tania: Thanks. Actually, I'd like him to call me if anything happens. But sometimes I can't answer the phone while I'm working. I'd like him to call me when he gets home every day, but sometimes I'm in meetings then.

Nick: Maybe you could have him send you a text message.

Tania: That's a good idea. And for emergencies, I'll give him your number. I worry about kitchen fires if he tries to cook.

Nick: Have you thought about writing a fire safety plan with him?

Tania: Hmmm. We could talk about when and how to get out of the house, the smoke alarm, the fire extinguisher. I could make sure he knows how to call 911.

Nick: That's important. Tell him to give his location first, then his name, then the problem.

Tania: These are all great ideas. You know, I think I'll sit down with Greg and make a list of rules. I'll write contact numbers, and I'll include yours. We'll role-play different situations involving strangers and different emergency phone calls.

Nick: And talk to him about how he feels. He may not tell you if he's afraid or worried or bored or lonely, unless you ask.

Tania: Thanks, Nick. I'll do that. See you later.

Nick: Good talking to you.

Page 77, Listen, Exercises A and B

Conversation 1

A: Did you finish installing it?

B: Yes, I finally got it on. Here . . . try to open it.

A: I can't do it! How does this thing work?

B: You could try reading the instructions.

A: Come on . . . just *show* me! I need some cleanser to clean up that mess.

Conversation 2

A: Are you finding everything you need?

B: I'm not really sure what I'm looking for. My sister and her family are going to visit. They have a son who's one and a half. I'm worried because some of our rooms aren't safe for him. And he could fall down the stairs . . .

A: Well, one thing I would definitely recommend is a safety gate. We have several models.

B: Do they work?

A: Yes! I used them when my own kids were young. Pressure gates aren't as secure as the type that you screw into the wall, but they won't leave holes in the wood of your door frame when you remove them. And you can move them from room to room. We have both kinds.

B: I'm not worried about the wood of my door frame. The safety of my nephew is more important. And I can buy more than one gate. I'd like to see the most secure gates you have.

Conversation 3

A: Here. I brought you something. You told me that Jane hurt her fingers in a door last week. I was out shopping, and I saw these: doorstops and door holders.

B: What a good idea! I never thought of these.

A: I was in the drugstore, and I saw them.

B: How much were they? I'll pay you for them.

A: Oh, don't be silly. They just cost a few dollars.

B: Well, thanks. That was really thoughtful of you.

Conversation 4

A: As you can see, we're very child-friendly and child-safe.

B: Yes, I can see that you take the safety of the children very seriously.

A: We do. You know, there was an article in the paper just last month about a child who almost fell from a window. That simply couldn't happen here. We watch all the children at all times. Also, if you look right here, . . . we have these on all the windows of our building. See?

B: Well, hopefully Pamela will enjoy it here.

A: I'm sure she'll love it.

UNIT 5

Page 90, Listen, Exercises A and B

Elena: Do you have any questions about your ratings?

Eva: Just a few. I don't really understand why I got a 3 in communication. I talk with everyone, and I understand everything you ask me to do. I know my English isn't perfect, but I can do my work.

Elena: Well, although you can do your work, your writing needs improvement. Your reports aren't very clear or thorough. You're a great employee, and you perform most of your duties really well. But I can't give anyone a 2 in communication unless their reports are well written.

Eva: Thanks. I understand. I need to continue to work on my English. Do you have any suggestions for what I can do to improve?

Elena: Actually, yes. I had to give a lot of 3s in communication. So I've decided to start a new "conversation partners" program. Some of the native English speakers on staff will meet once a week with co-workers who are still learning English. I hope you'll participate in this program.

Eva: I will. It sounds great. And I'm going to continue taking English class at night.

Elena: Terrific.

Eva: Was there a reason you didn't give me a 1 in initiative and problem solving?

Elena: Yes. I know that you recognize and solve some kinds of problems on your own. But I've noticed that when groups discuss problems, or team members have to reach an agreement, you're usually quiet. Unless you can offer suggestions in group discussions, I can't say you meet expectations in initiative and problem solving.

Eva: I see. Thanks. I'll work on that.

Elena: And I don't give anyone a 1 in attendance / punctuality. Everyone's expected to be here and on time. There's really no way to exceed that expectation.

Page 91, Practice, Exercises A and B

Conversation 1

A: Joe, your work is good, and I can always count on you to finish on time. But although you're a hard worker, you don't follow safety procedures, and that's a serious issue.

B: Can you give me some examples?

A: Well, for one thing, you run electrical cords across the floor and aisles. The other day, I saw that you had joined three cords together, and you left them on the floor at the end of your shift. Someone could trip on the cords—and joining three together is against our fire code. That's one example. Another is how you handle chemicals. I've seen you carry the cleaning chemicals without tops on the containers, and I've noticed that you don't always wear gloves when you use them.

B: Thanks. You're right. I hadn't thought about the electrical cords. They could cause an accident. I won't leave them out across the floor or aisles again, but what should I do when I don't have a long enough cord?

A: Just ask me for one—we can send someone out to buy one, or I can order it.

Conversation 2

A: You have many strengths, but I can't keep you in the department unless you learn to communicate better on the phone. Customer calls are very important.

B: I didn't realize this was a problem. I'll work on it from now on. What should I do differently in the future?

A: Well, first of all, you need to be clear and professional.

B: Can you give me some examples?

A: Yes. Start with "Hello. Electronic Solutions. How may I assist you today?" instead of "Hi, I need to verify some information." There are scripts for our phone calls in the Procedures file.

B: I see. I didn't realize there were scripts in our files. Of course I should use them, and I will.

A: You went over this in your training during the first weeks you were here.

B: I missed a couple of days of training. But you're right. It was my responsibility to find out what I'd missed. I'm sorry I didn't do that. I'll be sure to do it now.

Page 94, Listen, Exercise A

André: Hi, Claudia. How are you doing?

Claudia: Well, I just had my performance review.

André: Oh! How'd it go?

Claudia: Really well. My supervisor had some great suggestions. . .

André: Who's your supervisor, again?

Claudia: Max.

André: Oh, right. He's a good guy.

Claudia: So we talked a little about promotions.

André: Great! What did he say?

Claudia: I asked him if he thought I was qualified for the administrative assistant position.

André: Good for you!

Claudia: He was very encouraging. He said that I was well organized but that I needed to develop some of my skills. For example, he said that I should try to improve my oral communication skills because the assistants talk with customers and sales reps a lot.

André: So did he give you any ideas about how to do this?

Claudia: Yep. He said I should look into taking a career training course at the community college. Apparently, they have non-credit courses in the evenings and they aren't very expensive.

Page 95, Listen

Mei: Hi, Marco, I was just thinking about you. How are things going?

Marco: Really well. This is a great company to work for. Thanks for helping me get this job.

Mei: You work in Manufacturing, right?

Marco: Yes.

Mei: So you like the job?

Marco: Oh, yes. But I've been thinking. I've always had this knack for fixing things, like office equipment, and I'd really like to develop that skill and use it on the job.

Mei: That's a great idea. This company encourages people to grow and move around. What kinds of equipment would you want to work on?

Marco: Well, maybe copying machines and computer equipment.

Mei: You'd need some training on our equipment.

Marco: How would I get that?

Mei: I think the company offers some on-the-job training for computer repair and maintenance. There may be some training sessions soon. Have you looked in the kitchen on the bulletin board?

Marco: Thanks, I'll do that right away.

Mei: You should also check out the company Intranet site. They're always updating lists of job openings and job-training programs.

Marco: Thanks so much, Mei. Those are great suggestions!

Mei: No problem. I'd really like to know how things go. Keep me posted.

UNIT 6

Page 108, Listen

Carmen: Hi, Bianca. I haven't heard from you lately. How are you?

Bianca: Oh, hi, Carmen. Actually, I've been having some strange symptoms, and I went to the doctor yesterday.

Carmen: Nothing serious, I hope. . .

Bianca: It's probably nothing. I found a lump under my arm, and my doctor wants me to see an oncologist, just to rule out the possibility of cancer.

Carmen: When is your appointment?

Bianca: Thursday at 4:00.

Carmen: Do you have a ride? Is there anything I can do? . . .

Pages 120–121, Listen, Exercises A and B

Marisa: Type 2 diabetes is the most common form of diabetes. In type 2 diabetes, either the body does not produce enough insulin or the cells are unable to use the insulin. What is insulin? Insulin is a hormone. When you eat food, your body changes all of the sugars into glucose, which gives energy to the cells in your body. Insulin takes the glucose from the blood into the cells. When glucose builds up in the blood instead of going into cells, it can cause two problems: First, your cells may not get enough energy. Over time, high blood glucose levels may hurt your eyes, kidneys, nerves, or heart. Type 2 diabetes is a very serious disease, and it is very common in the United States. Pierre will talk about risk factors for type 2 diabetes, and Min-Ji will give suggestions for reducing risk and living with the disease.

Pierre: Thank you, Marisa. There are many different risk factors for type 2 diabetes, but I'm going to focus on four of them. One risk factor that you can't do anything about is a family history of diabetes. If a parent or brother or sister is diabetic, you are at risk. Another risk factor is a lack of exercise. People who are not active are more likely to become diabetic than people who lead physically active lives. A third risk factor is poor diet. People who have unhealthy eating habits are more likely to be overweight, which is one reason they may be more likely to become diabetic. The fourth factor is high blood pressure. It's important for people who have risk factors to take whatever actions they can to reduce their risks. Min-Ji will talk to you about that.

Min-Ji: I'm going to discuss things people can do to reduce the risk of becoming diabetic or to help control diabetes. Pierre mentioned that poor diet and lack of exercise are risk factors for diabetes. The good news is that people can control these things. Regular exercise and a healthy diet can help prevent diabetes. If your blood pressure is too high, reduce your use of salt and alcohol, and take any medications your doctor prescribes to help you lower your blood pressure. Doing these things will help prevent diabetes, and if you already have it, they will help you control the disease.

Marisa: This ends our presentation. Diabetes is a big problem for many people. There is no cure. However, if you know you are at risk, you and your doctor can work together to try to reduce your risk. If you are diabetic, you can do things that can help you live longer and better with diabetes. Are there any questions?

UNIT 7

Page 134, Listen

Jim Peters: Welcome to *America Rising* on KXYZ. Our guest today is Professor Susan Klass from Haymond Community College. Dr. Klass will be talking to us about the process of lawmaking. Welcome, Dr. Klass.

Professor Klass: Thank you, Jim. It's a pleasure.

Jim Peters: And it's a pleasure to have you here. So tell us, how is a federal law made?

Professor Klass: Well, basically a law starts as an idea. Anyone can think of the idea for a new law. Then they get others to sign a petition supporting the idea. If the petition gets signed by enough people, it goes to a congressperson. If the congressperson likes the idea, he or she sponsors it—introduces and supports it in Congress.

Jim Peters: OK, so someone has an idea, finds enough people to support it, and the idea gets sponsored by a senator or representative. Then what?

Professor Klass: Well, the idea is proposed as a bill in the House or Senate. The bill gets sent to the appropriate committee. For example, if the bill is about school reform, it gets sent to the Education Committee.

Jim Peters: Right.

Professor Klass: The bill gets voted on by the committee. If it gets approved, it goes back to the full House or Senate.

Jim Peters: Depending on whether the bill came from a senator or representative.

Professor Klass: Yes. It goes back to the sponsor's part of Congress. If it passes there, it moves to the other part of Congress, which then votes on the bill. The bill either gets approved or rejected, or it goes back to the original committee for revision.

Jim Peters: So, for example, if a bill starts in the House of Representatives, and it passes there, it goes to the Senate, which then votes on it.

Professor Klass: Yes. And if the bill is approved, it goes to the president, who can sign or veto it. If the bill gets vetoed, Congress has three choices. It can make changes to the bill and try again, it can give up on the bill, or vote to override the president's veto.

Jim Peters: You mean the president's decision isn't final.

Professor Klass: Not necessarily. It requires a vote of two-thirds of both houses of Congress to override. That means 67 senators and 290 representatives. If one house or the other doesn't get a two-thirds majority, the president's decision stands and the bill will not become a law. But a two-thirds majority in both houses of Congress is more powerful than the president's veto.

Jim Peters: Well, this is all wonderful information. This is why it's so important to contact our representatives about important legislation.

Professor Klass: Exactly. Our elected officials can't represent us unless we speak up. And they are under constant pressure from big business and from special-interest groups. Individual citizens need to know what bills have been proposed, and we need to let our representatives know how we feel. If we have an idea about a law that we believe should be passed, we should understand that it may remain an idea unless we do something about it.

Jim Peters: Thank you, Professor Klass, for this valuable information. We'd like to take some calls from our listeners now, about bills that are currently being considered in the United States Congress . . .

Page 138, Listen, Exercises A and B

Good morning and welcome to your Citizenship class. I'm Ms. Miller, and I'm looking forward to being your instructor.

As many of you know, to apply for citizenship, you need to fill out documents from United States Citizenship and Immigration Services. After you submit the documents, you have an interview with a USCIS official, who will check the information on your forms, ask you questions, and confirm that you are telling the truth. It's extremely important to tell the truth because if anything is found to be untrue, you will not be admitted as a citizen and will not be able to try again for five years. You will also need to speak and understand English well enough to pass a simple dictation test. You'll also need to pass a civics test, which includes two sections—one on U.S. government and a section on U.S. history. If you make it through all of this, you will take an Oath of Allegiance and be sworn in as a United States citizen.

So . . . let me go through each of the major requirements for citizenship in a little more detail.

First, there's an age requirement. Applicants must be at least 18 years old.

Second, there's a residency requirement. You need to have been lawfully admitted for permanent residence. This means you need to produce an I-551 card—the card that used to be called a green card . . . because it used to be green. You need to have lived in the United States for five years, and you need to have been physically present for thirty months of those five years. You can't have left the country for more than a year at a time.

Requirement number three is one that we will discuss in later classes. Basically, an applicant is required to demonstrate good moral character. This means you are ethical, that you behave morally. The government has identified things that indicate that a person does not have good moral character. Some examples are if you have been convicted of a serious crime, have been convicted more than once for gambling, or have been involved with smuggling aliens into the country. This is just a partial list.

The fourth requirement is that you must show attachment to the Constitution. You must convince government officials that you value the ideas expressed in the United States Constitution and support them.

The fifth requirement is the language requirement. You must speak, read, and write everyday English. There are some exceptions for people over 55 who have lived in the country fifteen years or more, or people who are over 50 who have lived here twenty years or more.

The next requirement, the sixth, is that you demonstrate knowledge of the government and history of the United States. You do this by passing a civics test.

Finally, you have to take the Oath of Allegiance. You promise to support the Constitution, to give up any allegiance to any other country, and to bear arms in the armed forces or perform non–military services for the government, if required.

For most people, these are the seven general requirements, although there are some exceptions, for example, for people who are married to U.S. citizens or people who are in the military. For those of you who have access to a computer, you can read about these requirements and find study materials on the United States Citizenship and Immigration Services website. I'll give you a handout with the URL—the address for the site. You can find the forms you need on the site. In this class, you'll be studying all of the information that you might need to include on your forms. You'll practice listening, speaking, and dictation to make sure you have the English skills needed to pass the test. And you'll spend a lot of time learning about the United States government and history.

Page 141, Listen, Exercise A

Today, we'll be talking about the expansion of the United States—not about states and the dates they became states, but about larger territories, because most of the land was acquired that way.

We still have states today with the names of the original thirteen colonies, but before independence, Britain owned essentially all of the land from the East Coast to the Mississippi River. After Britain lost the Revolutionary War in 1783, all of that territory became the United States of America.

If you look at your map, you'll see a large territory just west of the Mississippi River. This area was the Louisiana Territory, and although it had been claimed at one time by Spain, it was controlled by France in December 1803, when the United States purchased it. Thomas Jefferson, the president at the time, was very happy about this purchase, which almost doubled the size of the United States and guaranteed free movement along the Mississippi River.

East Florida, West Florida, and a small area at the southeast of the Louisiana Territory were all part of Spanish Florida after the Revolutionary War. All of these areas were added to the United States in 1819, by a combination of negotiations and military actions.

Territories including Texas and California became part of the United States after wars with Mexico. The area that was then Texas was acquired in 1845, and a large area including present-day California was acquired in 1848.

Spain, Great Britain, Russia, and the United States had all originally claimed the Oregon Territory, but in the end, the United States acquired it from Britain. The two countries reached agreement in 1846. Alaska was purchased from Russia in 1867. Russia was having financial difficulties, the profit from trade in the Alaskan settlements was low, and it did not want to see Alaska fall under British control. The purchase was unpopular with American citizens at the time, but later the discovery of gold and oil in Alaska would prove that the purchase had been a good one. Although acquired by the United States in 1867, Alaska waited until 1959 to become a state.

Hawaii was annexed to the United States in 1898 and became a territory two years later, but it didn't become a state until 1959.

UNIT 8

Page 146, Listen, Exercise A

Today we're going to discuss one of the most famous Supreme Court cases—*Miranda* v. *Arizona*. Many of you have probably heard the *Miranda* warning on TV—when a police officer reads a suspect his or her rights. This is basically the warning:

"You have the right to remain silent. Anything you say can and will be used against you in a court of law. You have the right to have an attorney present during questioning. If you cannot afford an attorney, one will be appointed for you."

Sound familiar? In some states, police officers are supposed to check to confirm that the person understands. In these states, a longer version is used, such as this one:

"You have the right to remain silent and refuse to answer questions. Do you understand? Anything you say may be used against you in a court of law. Do you understand? You have the right to consult an attorney before speaking to the police and to have an attorney present during questioning now or in the future. Do you understand? If you cannot afford an attorney, one will be appointed for you before any questioning if you wish. Do you understand? If you decide to answer questions now without an attorney present, you will still have the right to stop answering at any time until you talk to an attorney. Do you understand? Knowing and understanding your rights as I have explained them to you, are you willing to answer my questions without an attorney present?"

So that's the *Miranda* warning—the short version and the long version.

Page 146, Listen, Exercise B

OK. Now I'm going to give you a little background . . . tell you a little about the *Miranda* case. And then I'm going to describe a common misunderstanding related to the *Miranda* warning. First the case.

The Constitution gives rights to people suspected of a crime. The people who wrote it knew that governments could be unjust—government authorities could do whatever they wanted to people if they accused the people of being criminals. The Constitution tries to protect people who could be wrongly accused. The right to remain silent and the right to an attorney are two protections.

In 1963, Ernesto Miranda was accused of kidnapping and raping an 18-year-old woman. He was brought to the police department for questioning, and he admitted that he had committed the crime. However, he was not told about his right to remain silent, and he was not told about his right to have an attorney present.

At the trial, his defense attorney tried to get Miranda's confession thrown out. It was the only evidence against Miranda. But the confession was not thrown out, and Miranda was found guilty.

Miranda's attorney took the case to higher courts, and in 1966 the Supreme Court decided that the statements Miranda made to the police could not be used as evidence, since Miranda had not known his rights.

Since then, police have been required to read or tell criminal suspects their rights before interrogating them.

Miranda did not go free. New evidence was found against him. He was found guilty at a second trial, and he went to prison.

TV has helped make the *Miranda* rights well known. But TV has also contributed to some misunderstandings. On TV, you often see police officers stopping someone on the street, and you hear them reading the person his or her rights. Actually, police are required to read these rights only to people they take into custody—people they are going to question at the police station, in the police car, and so on. The police can arrest someone without asking questions, and in this case, the police don't have to read the person any rights. Also, police don't have to read someone his or her rights to ask for personal information such as the person's name and address.

Page 158, Listen, Exercises A and B

Professor: I'm going to be talking briefly about infractions, misdemeanors, and felonies. These are the three types of crimes recognized under our state law. We've already talked about infractions. These are things that don't stay on your criminal record and that don't carry a jail or prison sentence. These are usually civil offenses like minor traffic violations or littering. Today, I want to focus on the two more serious types of crimes—misdemeanors, which are more serious than infractions, and felonies—such as robbery and illegal drug use, which are the most serious. I'll start with misdemeanors. . . Give me some examples of misdemeanors. Yes, Shannon.

Shannon: Trespassing?

Professor: That's right. Trespassing is a misdemeanor. Have you ever seen fences out in the country that have "No hunting or trespassing" signs on them? Well, it's a crime to climb the fence and go onto that property. It's a misdemeanor. Another one. . . Justin?

Justin: Um, vandalism.

Professor: That's right. One more. Emil?

Emil: Is shoplifting a misdemeanor?

Professor: Yep. In this state it is. Good. Now, does anyone know what kind of penalties people can receive for misdemeanors?

Justin: Fines.

Professor: That's right. Often the penalty for a misdemeanor is a fine. There can be jail time, too. Up to one year. But the time would be in a county jail, not a state prison. Or sometimes a person who commits a misdemeanor might get probation—a person on probation does not have to go to jail but must demonstrate good behavior and must report regularly to a probation officer. Another penalty might be community service. This is common for a first offense, especially for young people. Now for a felony, you can receive a large fine, but you can also go to prison. Felony charges carry prison sentences from one year to life. And some states have the death penalty for the very worst crimes. In some states, if you commit first-degree murder or another terrible crime, you will receive the death penalty. A person who is found guilty of a felony can still have to pay a fine, too. Sometimes a very big one. In addition to murder, felonies include arson, burglary, and rape. That's it for today. Any questions?

Shannon: What if someone can't pay a fine?

Professor: Oh, I think the courts often set up payment programs. The person can pay a little each month.

Barbara: How long will a misdemeanor stay on a person's record?

Professor: Forever. So don't do anything stupid. OK. That's it for today.

UNIT 9

Pages 170–171, Listen, Exercises A and B

Ross Simon: Welcome to *Focus on Green*, on KXYZ. Our guest today is Councilwoman Janine Frank, from West Burbank. Councilwoman Frank will be telling us about one particular effort to make her city a greener one, and how each of us can do our share—and make a difference. Good morning, Councilwoman Frank!

Councilwoman: Good morning, Ross! It's so nice to be here.

Ross Simon: I know you're very busy, Councilwoman, so we really appreciate your being here. Now, we're very interested in all of your city wide environmental projects—especially one that relates to carpooling. But first, can you tell us a bit about how you're greening your city?

Councilwoman: First Ross, I have to tell you that none of my work would be possible without the good people of my city, West Burbank. And I also have to say that my hard work is shared by all; this is truly a team effort.

Ross Simon: Well, it seems to be a great team! So tell us about how your program got started.

Councilwoman: Well, the first step, of course, was to educate people about the consequences of not doing certain things. In this case, that means showing them what will happen if we don't start conserving our resources. The next step was to offer solutions. Of course, there's no single solution to every problem, but once we start brainstorming, you'd be amazed at what we can think of.

Ross Simon: Right. Can you give us some examples?

Councilwoman: Let's take carpooling, for example. Everyone knows that we should do it, but how can we implement a successful program? My committee and I proposed a city wide ride sharing program that is a big success. It's also simple to use. People can register online; they just need to enter their starting point and destination, and then they will be put in touch with similar travelers.

Ross Simon: Sounds great, Councilwoman. But what if someone's shy or doesn't feel comfortable doing that online?

Councilwoman: Good point, Ross. Well, we also have "casual carpooling." People can call our carpool hotline or go online to find a specific meeting place. Then they can join others in their commute to work.

Ross Simon: That's great!

Councilwoman: Yes. And there's a third option; other groups—several, in fact—who travel longer distances have joined together to form a "vanpool." They share the cost of renting a van, plus gas and any other related expenses.

Ross Simon: Talk about a team effort!

Councilwoman: Yes, Ross—it's always interesting to me how people can work together to find so many wonderful solutions to a problem.

Ross Simon: That's certainly impressive. And tell us, Councilwoman. What are the consequences of *not* carpooling?

Councilwoman: Well, Ross, I must tell you that I was surprised to learn these facts. Did you know that if every commuter car in the U.S. carried just one more person, we'd save up to 600,000 gallons of gas and 12 million pounds of carbon dioxide every day?

Ross Simon: Wow! That is surprising—and yet now I'm sure my listeners will join me in being excited about the fact that we can do something—like ridesharing—to make a difference. Thank you again, Councilwoman, for joining us, and we wish you all the best!

Councilwoman: Thank you, Ross. And I'd like to invite interested listeners to check out my website, at www.councilwomanfrank.com, to find out how they can start this kind of program—or any of the initiatives we've started—in their own city.

Page 176, Listen

Joseph and his family have recently moved to a new community. Hector is one of his new neighbors.

Hector: Good morning, Joseph! How's it going?

Joseph: Hey, Hector. Great. I'm just trying to get this recycling thing straightened out.

Hector: What? No recycling back in your old town?

Joseph: No, we had recycling. It's just the rules were different! Here it seems a bit more complicated—not that I'm complaining because honestly, I do think it's important!

Hector: I know—it can be confusing! Here's a tip: Look in front of Tony's house; he's always the first one to put out his recycling. You'll always know what day it is if you check in front of his house!

Joseph: Ah! Thanks. If I'd known that before, I wouldn't have had trouble. Between Tony and the calendar, I should get it straight soon! Well, I have to tell you, I just wish we had had these types of regulations where I used to live. So much of our garbage was just thrown away without being recycled.

Hector: That's a shame. I wish we had started recycling years ago. Hmmm. I can't tell you the amount of junk we threw away without sorting!

Joseph: I can imagine. Believe it or not, my thirteen-year-old is great at helping us keep the trash sorted. He's the one who makes sure we have all of our paper, plastics, and metals separated and sorted correctly. He's like the recycling police!

Hector: Yeah, well, they do talk about it in school these days. My daughter taught me the three Rs: reduce, reuse, and recycle. I wish they had taught us about the environment back when we were kids! Actually, I wish we had all been more educated about the amount of waste we produced.

Joseph: Come on, Hector! Back in those days they were just thinking about using, not conserving! I think if our parents had been aware of the damage they were doing, they would have done things differently.

Hector: Well, I guess we're moving in the right direction then! You know, the best thing would be if everyone in the whole country could sort their trash. Maybe if we had more kids around like your son, we wouldn't have a lot of the problems that we currently have!

UNIT 10

Page 186, Listen, Exercises A and B

Our topic this week is the growth of the Internet. Like many important advances in technology, the Internet did not start with an invention. It started with an idea and a vision for the future. And that idea and vision came from a man named J.C.R. Licklider. Today, I will talk about Licklider's vision.

First, you need to understand something about Licklider's background. Unlike others who worked with early computers, Licklider was not an engineer. He started his career in the 1940s as an experimental psychologist. In his work, he used computers to collect and analyze data. Most engineers of the time saw computers as not much more than very powerful calculators. And, in fact, that's what most computers were in those days. But as a psychologist, Licklider saw computers very differently. He was interested in using the computer as a communications tool.

Licklider was frustrated by the slow progress of his research, so he decided to keep a record of how he spent his work time. He discovered that he spent 85 percent of his time putting together the data he needed to make a decision or to learn something that he needed to know—even with the help of computers. In other words, he spent most of his time finding information. But once he had the information, he could often understand what it meant and make a decision very quickly—sometimes in just seconds.

Because of his own experience, Licklider wanted to find a better way for humans and computers to work together.

He thought they should be equal partners because they each had different, but equally important, strengths. By "thinking" together, Licklider believed that both computers and people could do far more than either could do alone. This is how he explained it in an article he wrote in 1960:

"…Human brains and computing machines will be coupled together very tightly, and . . . the resulting partnership will think as no other human brain has ever thought and process data in a way not approached by the information-handling machines we know today."

He also described how in ten to fifteen years computerized "thinking centers" would exist. These "thinking centers" would be used to store and find information, like libraries, but would be much, much larger. And they would be connected to each other and to individual users through a network.

Not new ideas today, of course, but Licklider, who was trained in psychology, not computer science, wrote these words in 1960. Amazingly, he had come very close to describing *today's* Internet.

That's all we have time for today. Next time, we will talk about how Licklider's vision became the reality of today's Internet.

Page 190, Listen, Exercises A and B

Michelle Allen: Good afternoon, Dr. Knowles, and welcome to *Technology Today.*

Dr. Knowles: Thank you, Michelle. It's nice to be here.

Michelle Allen: So, Dr. Knowles, lately we've been hearing a lot, both positive and negative, about the effects that the Internet has had on human communication. Let's start with the positive.

Dr. Knowles: Well, there are many positives. We all know that the Internet has made it incredibly easy for people to stay in touch with family, friends, and business contacts who are far away. With the Internet, we can also reconnect with people from our past. And we're able to make new friends and contacts with people we would never have even met before. For example, the Internet has given people who live in isolated areas the chance to communicate with others who share their interests and concerns. For people with disabilities that prevent them from going out and meeting others face to face, the Internet has opened a whole new world. And, of course, the Internet has made it possible for scientists to share information instantaneously. The sharing of scientific ideas was the original reason for the creation of the Internet. It remains one of its most important uses today.

Michelle Allen: That's a pretty impressive list . . .

Dr. Knowles: Yes, it is . . .

Michelle Allen: Why, then, are there so many warnings about the Internet harming human communication?

Dr. Knowles: First of all, let me say that I strongly believe that the Internet has done more good than harm. However, I do have some concerns about heavy Internet use, especially among young people.

Michelle Allen: Such as?

Dr. Knowles: Well, when young people use online communication to replace or avoid face-to-face interaction, I think that's a problem. For example, a naturally shy person who spends all of his or her time online won't develop the social skills he or she needs to feel comfortable communicating in person. Humans are sociable by nature. We need emotional, intellectual, and physical contact to be truly happy. Although you might be able to get the emotional and intellectual contact you need online, you can't hug a computer or see the effect that your words and actions have by looking into its eyes. Body language and eye contact are a huge part of human communication, but they don't exist in online communication.

Michelle Allen: Well, people do use emoticons, you know, smiling faces, and so on . . . Isn't that a form of body language?

Dr. Knowles: Oh, I don't think you can compare the two. People express hundreds, even thousands of emotions with their eyes and bodies. There are only a handful of emoticons.

Michelle Allen: Very interesting . . . well, let's bring some callers into the conversation . . . Our first caller is Mike from Ontario . . .

Page 196, Listen, Exercises A and B

Nick: I've always thought of myself as an up-to-date kind of guy. And as a writer, I was also pretty certain that I understood the English language. Until yesterday, that is, when my 13-year-old daughter gave me a little language quiz . . . And I failed miserably. As I pointed out to her, however, it wasn't really a fair quiz, since it was in a foreign language—sort of. Foreign, that is, to a middle-aged not-as-up-to-date-as-he-thought-he-was kind of guy. What I'm talking about, if you haven't guessed already, is the language for sending text messages, or "texting," as they call it.

Now, I'm not talking about the shorthand that has been used for years in business—things like ASAP (*as soon as possible*), or FYI (*for your information*). Those abbreviations are still used, and even old guys like me know what they mean. I'm talking about something much newer than that.

To help me here, I've brought along a native speaker, my thirteen-year-old daughter Tiffany. Actually, I should say native *writer*; this language is mostly a written one at the moment, although more and more expressions are making their way into the spoken language.

Nick: Hey, Tiff, 'sup?

Tiffany: NM.U?

Nick: AAS . . . Did you understand that? Well, neither did I yesterday, but as you can see, I'm a fast learner. Tiff, can you translate that for our audience, please?

Tiffany: Sure, Dad. You asked me 'sup', which means "What's up?" Then I answered NMU—which means "Not much. How about you?" And you answered AAS, which means "Alive and smiling."

Nick: Alive and smiling indeed . . . OK, so Tiffany has agreed to give me a second chance on my quiz, and I've been up all night studying. So . . . here goes.

Tiffany: Okay, Dad, the first one is easy: BFF

Nick: No problem! BFF means "best friends forever."

Tiffany: WTG, Dad! Oh, sorry, that means "Way to go!" OK, number 2: P911.

Nick: Parent emergency? Like if your father is having a heart attack or something?

Tiffany: No, Dad. It means "Parent alert," like when your parents come into the room, and you have to stop texting . . . Okay, here's another easy one: H&K.

Nick: Hugs and kisses.

Tiffany: Yes! Now you're going to translate the shorthand, OK?

Nick: K. (That means OK, for anyone over 20 in the audience today.)

Tiffany: How do we write "sleepy"?

Nick: Hmmmm . . . let me think . . . ah . . . S . . . no, no, CP, right?

Tiffany: Yes! Here's one you'll like: How do we write "Do not be late?"

Nick: DNBL8 . . .

Tiffany: I knew you'd remember that one! OK, just one more. What does "gratz" mean?

Nick: Congratulations!

Tiffany: Gratz, Dad. You did XLNT!

Nick: THX, Tiff. For *What's on Your Mind*, I'm Nick Amado . . . ADBB, my friends!

Tiffany: That means "All done, bye-bye!"

Glossary

absorb *v.* take something in through the surface

adapt *v.* change your behavior or ideas in order to fit a new situation

adjust *v.* gradually become familiar with a new situation

agriculture *n.* science or practice of farming

alleged violation *adj.* an action that breaks a law, rule, or agreement, which is believed to have happened but has not been proven

allergy *n.* condition that makes you sick when you swallow, touch, or breathe a particular thing

aluminum *n.* type of metal

ambitious *adj.* having a strong desire to be successful or powerful

amend *v.* make small changes or improvements, especially in the words of a law

amputation *n.* cutting off a part of someone's body for medical reasons

approach *v.* move toward or near someone or something

aptitude test *n.* test used for finding out what someone's best skills are

arrangement *n.* something that has been organized or agreed on

artery *n.* one of the tubes that carries blood from your heart to the rest of your body

assemble *v.* come together in the same place

atmosphere *n.* mixture of gases that surrounds the earth

automatically *adv.* without thinking about what you are doing

bail *n.* money exchanged so that someone can be let out of prison while awaiting trial

bear arms *v.* carry guns and other weapons for self-defense

biodegradables *n.* materials, chemicals, and so on that are changed naturally by bacteria into substances that do not harm the environment

branch *n.* a part of government or other organization that deals with one particular part of its work

break *n.* a period of time in which you stop what you are doing in order to rest, eat, and so forth

bridge *n.* upper part of your nose between the eyes

bruise *n.* mark on the skin of a person or piece of fruit where it has been damaged by a hit or a fall

calculation *n.* act of adding, multiplying, or dividing numbers to find out an amount, price, and so forth

category *n.* group of people or things that are all of the same type

cell *n.* smallest living thing

central *adj.* in the middle of an area or an object

chemical *n.* substance used in chemistry (the science of studying substances and the way they change or combine with each other) or produced by a chemical process

cholesterol *n.* substance in your body which doctors think may cause heart disease

citation *n.* official order for someone to appear in court or pay a fine for doing something illegal

civic leader *n.* authority figure working for the local government

collapse *v.* fall down or inward suddenly

colony *n.* group of people who have left their home country to live in a new place

comfortable *adj.* relaxed or not worried about what someone will do or what will happen

commercial *adj.* relating to business and the buying and selling of things

commitment *n.* promise to do something or to behave in a particular way

comply *v.* do what you are asked to do or what a law or rule tells you to do

computer screen *n.* flat part of a computer on which you see words, images and so on

concentrate *v.* think very carefully about something you are doing

confidential *adj.* secret and not intended to be shown or told to other people

conserve *v.* prevent something from being wasted, damaged, or destroyed

continuously *adv.* without stopping or being interrupted

crash *v.* suddenly stop working

criteria *n.* facts or standards used in order to help you judge or decide something

crop *n.* plant such as corn, wheat, and so on that farmers grow and sell

current *adj.* happening, existing, or being used now

customer *n.* someone who buys things from a store or company

damaged *adj.* physically harmed

data *n.* information or facts

decay *v.* be slowly destroyed by a natural chemical process, or to destroy something in this way

detection *n.* the process of detecting, or the fact of being detected

diabetes *n.* a disease in which there is too much sugar in the blood

discourage *v.* persuade someone not to do something, especially by making it seem difficult or bad

discrimination *n.* the practice of treating one group of people differently from another in an unfair way

disease *n.* illness that affects a person, animal, or plant, with specific symptoms

display *n.* part of a piece of equipment that shows information

distracted *adj.* unable to pay attention to what you are doing

ditch *n.* long, narrow hole in the ground for water to floe through, usually at the side of a field, road, and so on

diverse *adj.* very different from each other

document *n.* piece of paper that has official information written on it

draft *v.* order someone to fight for his or her country during a war

electrical appliance *n.* piece of equipment such as a stove or washing machine, used in people's homes

eliminate *v.* get rid of something completely

embarrassed *adj.* ashamed, nervous, or uncomfortable, especially in front of other people

emergency flashers *n.* hazard warning lights

emit *v.* send out gas, heat, light, sound, and so on

employment agency *n.* business that makes money by finding jobs for people

energy-efficient *adj.* energy-saving

enforce *v.* make people obey a rule or law

engineer *n.* someone whose job is to design, build, and repair roads, bridges, machines, and so forth

environment (the) *n.* land, water, and air in which people, animals, and plants live

equipment *n.* tools, machines, and so forth that you need for a particular activity

establish *v.* start something such as a company, system, situation, and so on, especially one that will exist for a long time

evolve *v.* develop and change gradually over a long period of time

exercise your rights *v.* use your legal freedoms and advantages

factor *n.* one of several things that influence or cause a situation

faucet *n.* thing that you turn on and off to control the flow of water from a pipe

federal *adj.* relating to the central government of a country which consists of several states

fee *n.* an amount of money that you pay to do something

fertilizer *n.* substance that is put on the soil to help plants grow financial security enough money to live on comfortably

flag down *phr v.* make the driver of a vehicle stop by waving at him or her

flexible *adj.* able to change easily

foreign policy *n.* politics, business matters, and so on, that affect or concern the relationship between your country and other countries

former *adj.* having a particular position in the past, but not now

fossil fuel *n.* resource such as gas or oil that has been formed from plants and animals that lived millions of years ago

foster care *n.* supervised care in an institution or temporary home for delinquent or neglected children

found *v.* start an organization, town or institution that is intended to continue for a long time

furnish *v.* supply or provide something

general public *n.* ordinary people in the community

generation *n.* all the people in a society or family who are about the same age

global warming *n.* increase in the world temperatures, caused by an increase of carbon dioxide around the earth

goods *n.* things that are produced in order to be sold

greenhouse gas *n.* a vapor, especially carbon dioxide or methane, that traps heat above the earth and causes a warming effect

guidance *n.* helpful advice about work, education, and so forth

harsh *adj.* unkind, cruel, or strict

hazard *n.* something that may be dangerous or cause accidents, problems, and so on

health insurance *n.* an arrangement in which you pay a certain amount of money each month to a company with the promise that this company will pay a certain amount of money toward your medical bills

highway patrol *n.* police who make sure that people obey the rules on highways in the U.S

hormone *n.* substance produced by your body that influences its growth, development, and so on

Human Resource (HR) department *n.* section or division of a company that deals with employing, training, and helping people

imagination *n.* ability to form pictures or ideas in your mind

immerse *v.* to be or become completely involved in something

impact *n.* effect or result of an event or situation

impact *v.* have an important or noticeable effect on someone or something

impartial *adj.* not giving special support or attention to one group; unbiased

impose *v.* introduce a rule, tax, or punishment, and force people to accept it

impression *n.* the opinion, belief or feeling you have about someone or something because of the way she, he, or it seems

in demand *(adj)* needed or wanted by a lot of people

in exchange *adv.* in return for something; in payment for something

inform *v.* formally tell someone about something

inhale *v.* breathe in air, smoke, or gas

injury *n.* physical harm or damage that is caused by an accident or attack, or a particular example of this

innovation *n.* introduction of new ideas, methods, or inventions, or the idea, method or invention itself

insulation *n.* the material used in order to cover or protect something, especially a building

insulin *n.* a substance produced naturally by your body that allows sugar to be used for energy

interior *n.* inner part or inside of something

interstate *n.* road for fast traffic that goes between states

intrusion *n.* unwanted person or event that interrupts or annoys you

issue *v.* officially make a statement or give a warning

know by sight *v.* recognize by seeing

learning permit *n.* official document that gives you permission to learn to drive

lease *v.* use or let someone use buildings, property, and so forth, when he or she pays rent

martial art *n.* sport such as karate in which you fight with your hands and feet

master *v.* learn something so well that you understand it completely and have no difficulty with it

material *n.* things that are used for making, doing, or learning something, for example, books or school supplies

measurable *adj.* able to be measured in terms of size, length, amount

medical history *n.* your past illnesses, doctor visits, vaccinations, and so on, that have been documented by your doctor

mentor *v.* teach, advise, and encourage people in order to help them succeed at work or in school

merchandise *n.* things that are for sale in stores

mobile home *n.* type of house made of metal, that can be pulled by a large vehicle and moved to another place

moist *adj.* slightly wet, in a pleasant way

natural resources *n.* all the land, minerals, energy, and so on that exist in a country

nausea *n.* feeling you have when you think you are going to vomit

neglect *n.* failure to take care of something or someone well

normal behavior *n.* usual way of acting

notify *v.* tell someone something formally or officially

novice *n.* someone who has just begun learning a skill or activity

numerous *adj.* many

obstacle *n.* something that makes it difficult for you to succeed

occupation *n.* job or profession

official *adj.* approved of or done by someone in authority, especially the government

operate *v.* if a machine operates or you operate it, it works or you make it work

outcome *n.* final result of a meeting, process, and so on

overdue notice *n.* written or printed statement telling you that something that was supposed to be completed or handed in is late

overturn *v.* turn upside down or knock onto its side

penalty *n.* punishment for not obeying a law, rule, or legal agreement

petition *v.* formally ask someone in authority to do something

permanent *adj.* continuing to exist for a long time or for all time

personal computer (PC) *n.* small computer that is used by one person at a time, at work or at home

personnel *n.* people who work in a company or for a particular kind of employer

physician's assistant someone who is trained to give basic medical treatment, in order to help a doctor

pollute *v.* make air, water, soil and so on dangerously dirty

population *n.* the number of people or animals living in a particular area, country, etc.

power line *n.* large wire carrying electricity above or under the ground

power plant *n.* building where electricity is produced to supply a large area

prescription medicine *n.* drug that can be obtained only with a written order from the doctor

principle *n.* moral rule or set of ideas about what is right and wrong, that influences how you behave

priority *n.* right to be given attention first and before other people and things

procedure *n.* way of doing something, especially the correct or normal way

professional *adj.* skilled, trained, or expert at something

promotion *n.* move to a better, more responsible position at work

protest *v.* say or do something publicly to show that you disagree with something or think that it is wrong or unfair

public transportation *n.* buses, trains, and so on that are available for everyone to use

pull over *v.* drive to the side of a road and stop your car, or to make someone do this

pulse *n.* the regular beat that can be felt as your heart pumps blood around your body

racial prejudice *n.* unfair feeling against someone who is of a different race

reconstruct *v.* build again

records *n.* information about something or someone, which is either written on paper or stored on a computer

registration *n.* official piece of paper containing details about a motor vehicle and the name of its owner

regulation *n.* official rule or order

reference letter *n.* letter containing information about you that is written by someone who knows you well, usually to a new employer

referral *n.* act of sending someone or something to another place for help, information, and so on

rejection *n.* situation in which someone stops giving you love or attention

represent *v.* do things or speak officially for someone else, or express his or her views or opinions

research institution *n.* large establishment or organization devoted to the study of a particular subject

resident *n.* someone who lives in a particular place

restrict *v.* limit or control something

restriction *n.* rule or set of laws that limits what you can do or what is allowed to happen

retail *adj.* referring to goods sold in a store for personal use

retaliation *n.* action against someone in order to pay them back for something they have done

rinse *v.* use running water and no soap to remove dirt, soap, and so on

rotating *v.* turning around a fixed point

screening *n.* medical test that is done on a lot of people to make sure that they do not

sentence *v.* legally punish someone who has been found guilty of a crime

share credit *v.* share the approval or praise doing something good

shoulder *n.* area of ground beside a road where drivers can stop their cars if they are having trouble

simulator *n.* machine that is used for training people by letting them feel what real conditions are like

solar energy *n.* power from the sun that is used to produce heat, make machines work, and so on

specialist *n.* doctor who knows more about one particular type of illness or treatment than other doctors

spreadsheet *n.* computer program that can show and calculate financial information, or a printed version of this information

standard *n.* level of quality, skill, or ability that is considered to be acceptable

statistics *n.* numbers which represents facts or measurements

sturdy *adj.* strong and not likely to break or be hurt

substance *n.* a particular type of solid, liquid, or gas

supplement *n.* something added to improve your diet, especially a vitamin

supplies *n.* things necessary for daily life, especially for a group of people over a period of time

suspect *v.* think that something is probably true, especially something bad

suspend *v.* officially stop someone from working, driving, or going to school for a fixed period, because she or he has broken the rules

switch *v.* change from doing or using one thing to doing or using something else

symptom *n.* physical condition that shows when you may have a particular disease

take (someone) by surprise *v.* surprise or shock someone by happening or doing something in a way that is not expected

take the initiative *v.* be the first one to take action to achieve a particular aim or solve a particular problem

team player *n.* someone who works well as a member of a group or team

testify *v.* make a formal statement of what is true

tornado watch *n.* checking an area in order to warn people about the danger of a tornado

tow truck operator *n.* someone who drives a strong vehicle that can pull cars behind it

toxic *adj.* poisonous

traditional *adj.* following ideas, methods, and so on that have existed for a long time

transportation *n.* system for carrying passengers or goods from one place to another

treatment *n.* method that is intended to cure an injury or sickness

turbine *n.* engine that works when the pressure from a liquid or gas moves a special wheel around

twister *n.* a tornado

uniformed *adj.* dressed in a uniform

unjust *adj.* not fair or reasonable

uproot *v.* pull up a plant or tree and its roots out of the ground

upset *n.* unpleasant, disturbing feelings

vehicle *n.* thing such as a car, bus etc. that is used for carrying people or things from one place to another

victim *n.* someone who has been hurt or killed by someone or something, or who has been affected by a bad situation

violation *n.* action that breaks a law, agreement, principle, and so on

violently *adv.* happening in such a way as to be liable to hurt people, destroy property, and so on

warrant *n.* official paper that allows the police to do something

work ethic *n.* idea or belief that hard work and persistence are morally good

working conditions *n.* situations or environments in which someone works

Index

Credits